To Dean.

I HOPE
There are some
useful things here
Happy Birthday
Sham.

TRADING TIME

New Methods in
Technical Analysis

TRADING TIME
New Methods in Technical Analysis

Shaun Downey

Dedication

To my wife Joanne, Daughters Abigail and Kay, not forgetting Grandson Jack.

To my late Father John who would be very proud.

Sister Siobhan, who as a chief librarian has promised that the latest Harry Potter book will be unceremoniously ousted from the front desk and replaced with my one.

Oasis Disclaimer

This publication is designed to provide accurate and authoritative information in regard to the subject matter covered. If professional advice or other expert assistance is required in regard to the subject matter, the services of a competent professional person should be sought, before engaging in any investing or trading.

First published 2007

ISBN 13: 978 0 9554668 0 9

All rights reserved. No part of this book may be reproduced or transmitted in any form or by any means, electronic or mechanical including photocopying or by any information storage and retrieval system without permission from the Publisher in writing.

Published by: Oasis Research Limited
Produced by: Footprint Innovations Limited
Printed in England

Contents

Trading Time — 10

Introductory notes	10
Volatility Time Bands	13
Range Deviation Pivots	44
Volatility Time Average Bands	50
Trade Flow	55

Market Profile® — 72

Introductory notes	72
Market profile philosophies	79
Market profile and Traditional analysis	88
The merging of Time and market profile	92

Concepts of Time — 118

Introcuctory notes	118
Do self fulfilling prophecies provide trading opportunities?	124
OaR Stochastic Steps	127

Relative Strength Index — 149

Introductory notes	149
Rsi Steps as Divergence tool	160

Peak — 166

Introductory notes	166
True measures of Overbought and Oversold	182
Peak patterns and connections With Steps, Profile and Time	187
Peak Range and Peak Volume	227

Appendix — 236

Trade Flow. New theories and aggregation	236
Range Deviation Pivots. Patterns and probability	238
Stochastic Steps Update on existing long term trends	241

Acknowledgements

There is no doubt that without one person, who was prepared to take a gamble on a shy, spotty, 16-year old, none of my subsequent career would have happened. It could all have ended very prematurely as this person then, in the next few years, continued to defend a somewhat psychotic, anarchist teenager, whose idea of office relations was to have something obscene about his attitude to people and work on a badge pinned to his loose-fitting tie. I suppose I must have been doing something right. That person's name was Derek Robshaw. The next key person was Mike Barker, Rudolf Wolff's company secretary, who found me a job at Fulton Prebon after the international tin crisis broke. This proved to be a life- defining move, as I then worked for another understanding boss called David Langton, who not only knew the bond market inside out, but also knew how to enjoy himself whilst recognizing his responsibilities. Finally a chance meeting on a plane led to me going to Australia as a head of trading in equities, and whilst this moving into equities one month before the 1987 crash ruined me financially and professionally in trading, (not to mention the mental scars that took years to heal), as I rebuilt my career, it was invaluable in understanding and appreciating what is needed, not only to succeed, but to be happy. It was also the moment that I finally appreciated and understood the morals and structure to life that my Dad John had tried to instill in me.

In contrast, but probably not surprisingly in a business as singular as trading, over the last fifteen years that I have been advising and consulting in the trading arena, there have been very few people who have ever volunteered any information whatsoever. It has been very much a one-way street in that respect. Also, the few people who have contributed have not necessarily come from the trading environment. Top of the list is Andy Webb, the editor of Automated Trader, who has been invaluable in being able to quickly programme my thoughts and provide insight into what else could be done. All of the Time-based creations in Chapter 1 originally came from Andy, and set off a chain reaction and Pandora's Box of discovery that I still haven't completed. The second person to thank is my partner at Oasis Research, David Knox, who's had the hellish task of being editor-in-chief. He's a pleasure to work with and, in our business relationship, he's been prepared to put his money where his mouth is; he constantly thinks about how we can succeed and grow. The completed book you see today is light years away from my somewhat manic warbling of the original manuscript, which was effectively written in three weeks, as I sat 20 hours a day over the laptop, as it all gushed out. Without him the finished book would be a pale imitation. Neither of us realized what a huge task the whole project involved, as usually books written by novices are closely worked on by the publishers. As the original publisher said, "the manuscript is vibrant and full of enthusiasm, but it's like walking into a city and there's no traffic lights or road signs, I've no idea where you're going". Hopefully, whilst the book is complicated, has no fluff or filler and could have been tinkered with indefinitely, you will be able to find a route through it that's satisfying. That has also been made possible by the guys at Footprint Innovations (who designed, advised and printed) and Frank Beardow (proof read) , who have both taken the extra care and time required to create a physical book that would not have happened with a mass publisher. The next person I'd like to thank is Mark Voller of Mizuho. Whilst there is nothing in this book of the knowledge he gave me, the structure and trading environment he created has been an inspiration. It's no coincidence that the house I bought has a similar place in the garden for a professional trading room. His insight into position sizing was particularly crucial in my developing my own risk and expectations, radically changing my trading- time horizons, and stripping down the components of what works for me within the constrictions of how I can trade and analyze. The fourth person to thank is Paolo Taranta at Banc Intensa in Milan, who inspired part of chapter 5. This was a project in which we attempted to overcome the problem of trailing stops in quiet markets and especially in the Asian time-zone in FX. This later expanded into other methods of linking range with swing patterns and many other aspects of trading that are not relevant to this book. I've also been very fortunate that the mandate for my job at Cqg has allowed me to do what very few in the trading environment ever have. The infrastructure, encouragement and most of all, the time to actually analyze the world of technical analysis and all its meandering roads. The fifth person is Tim McGavin who opened my mind to the importance of mental structure, a lifestyle and philosophy to aspire too. This was invaluable in understanding what was important in my own personal trading and goals. Finally, and most of all, I'd like to thank my wife Joanne, who's had to listen to endless monologues about theory, hopes and worries that must be as interesting to someone who doesn't trade as Vogon poetry. She's been inspirational in displaying the physical and mental courage and strength through all her health problems in recent years, whilst still having the love to coerce and cajole me through my own over-dramatized frailties, including completing this project through the ups and downs of wondering whether I would ever get the book that I wanted. In the end that meant taking the risk and expense of self -publishing, but if the book is not a success and critically panned, there's only one person to blame – me, and just as with trading and life, ultimately success or failure is only down to oneself.

Preface

Who the book is for

This book is written for the professional trader or experienced retail investor with a knowledge of technical analysis. It is important to note that in many ways this book is a complex and in places heavy read, especially when looking at certain subsections that examine a case study in detail. To grasp all of the concepts and methods would take more than one read. In order to make this process easier, where possible, text appearing at the bottom of the right hand page will not refer to a chart on the page overleaf. This means that there are natural blank areas where you can write notes.

How we can help you once you've read the book

Unfortunately books by nature are inanimate objects, but because many of the studies and concepts are predictive in nature, the real power of the analysis comes through when you are viewing markets in real time. Therefore, in order to help you through this process, for those of you who are CQG users the studies are available on trial. When possible, depending on geographical location, I'm more than happy to run seminars and go through the markets in real time, and for those in remote locations on-line tutorials can be given. The commentaries that OaR provide cover some forty markets, and whilst not using every single method that is listed in the book, it contains a large educational element on how the commentaries' conclusions are derived. Therefore, the aim is that you evolve your trading with the book, the commentaries or the studies, or simply take the parts that suit your current trading method.

The contents of the book should appeal to all types of traders, from scalpers all the way up to long-term players. In fact, Chapter 3 deals specifically with how a trade can begin in a timeframe as low as 15 minutes, moving up to a weekly timeframe with a trade length of over 3 years.

The book also provides examples of how the array of principles and rules are applicable to all asset classes covering bonds, FX, stock indices, commodities and single equities. Therefore there is something for all players in the professional arena.

Note: Due to the complexity of some of the concepts, many of the studies can only be reproduced with good technical analysis software.

What the book covers and how the book is structured

Not surprisingly, given the book's title, the concentration of the material is based on Time.

- Timing of entry
- Timing of Exit
- Range and expectation in relationship to time
- Defining the correct timeframe to be trading
- Establishing the dominant timeframe chart

Whilst there are only five chapters in the book, four are of considerable length and cover a wide range of studies and strategies.

Chapter 1 concentrates on risk and expectation depending on the time of day and the timeframe(s)chart(s) the trader is using. The studies are largely built on a bar's opening so have predictive powers and uses for many types of trader. The studies shown are OaR Volatility Time Bands, OaR Range Deviation Pivots, OaR Volatility Time Average Bands, and TradeFlow™ which is a Cqg Chart type

Chapter 2 deals exclusively with Market Profile® and this provides the glue to hold some of the subsequent studies together. Many of the Market Profile®-based rules can be used in isolation, but as the book progresses, it is evident to the reader that layers of analysis can be built, in order to grade and understand the extra power that certain trading scenarios have.

Chapter 3 looks in detail at one of the perennial problems in technical analysis: what is the correct timeframe chart to use? Once this is defined, it then looks at how trends must develop in order to move up to higher timeframes, so that positions can be initiated with low risk on short-term charts and end up with a position that is referencing a weekly chart years later. This is achieved by what is called Stochastic Steps logic.

Chapter 4 provides further detail on the Stochastic Steps concept with the RSI. Elements of how this can be developed into powerful divergence patterns are discussed.

Chapter 5 analyses swing patterns in considerable depth, using the Peak study and its derivatives: Hi Count/Lo Count, Peak Range and Peak Volume. These studies act as a guide to a trend's strength, start and finish, by providing a trailing stop for all asset classes and all timeframes.

In the **Appendix** there is a short section that looks at how some of the various case studies continued to develop after this book was completed. This serves to show how trades can be ridden through time for months and years, from simple beginnings. As this book is self-published, in years to come the appendices will be updated and previous buyers of the book will be able to download the updates from www.oasisresearch.co.uk.

Notes

- All the times in the book are GMT.
- All the charts are supplied by CQG.
- Market Profile® is copyrighted or trademarked by the CBOT, Trade Flow™ by CQG, the Kase© Peak Oscillator by Cynthia Kase and the rest of the studies by OaR.
- The copyrighted studies that relate specifically to time in the first chapter are only available to CQG subscribers. Whilst this may seem unfair, CQG is arguably the best software in the market (I work for CQG), and if you are to treat trading with the seriousness it deserves, then paying for a quality product can only aid your chances of success.
- The book was written in July and December 2005, finally edited in July and October 2006, and the appendix in February 2007
- Many of the examples were written as the position evolved and not from a retrospective standpoint and some of the trades are still valid positions, which highlights how trends can be ridden through time if the correct methods are used.

Supporting web sites
The web sites supporting this book are:

www.oasisresearch.co.uk
www.trading-time.com
www.cqg.com
www.cbot.com
www.ransquawk.com
www.tradertv.tv

1 Trading Time

Trading Time: a double meaning referring to
1. allocating the time to trade, and then
2. understanding the critical information regarding where you are in time when a trade is placed.

This facet of time has many definitions:

- What was the timeframe of the chart used?
- How critical is the price action directly after the trade is placed?
- At what point in time is the trade within the trend or are we at the end of the trend?
- How strong is the trend based on the time it has existed?
- What is the risk in relationship to time?

These are all important questions. But in my experience of visiting many traders over the years, they are questions that are rarely asked.

First question: timeframe

One of the first questions I ask a trader when we first meet is: 'what timeframe charts do you use?' The answer is always a variation on the same theme: 'I use a 30-min, 60-min daily and weekly'. Not one person has ever said: 'I use the timeframe chart that is relevant to my concepts of risk, volatility and range'.

The reality is that most traders have a completely fixed view of what timeframes they use - regardless of risk, volatility and range - and either adjust volume to risk or, more worryingly, will use a tighter stop regardless of whether it is likely to be hit due to the normal variance of range.

A second type of trader changes the timeframe of the chart depending on what their gut feeling is. For the good trader, their success with this somewhat random method is proof enough of their inherent ability! For the not-so-good trader, this is a recipe for disaster as greed and, more damagingly, fear mean that the timeframe is changed until the chart or indicator tells them what they want to know. If you ever find yourself lowering your timeframe chart, you are probably falling into this trap. Of course, fear can also just lead to a position being liquidated without any analysis at all.

Therefore, obtaining a true measure of expectation in any one period of time is critical to improving the chances of success. Fear and greed can then be removed from the equation.

This book

This book looks at the facets of time in detail. Many of the studies are proprietary ones that have been developed over many years and have uses in other areas of analysis, such as divergence and true measures of overbought and oversold. However, as this book is about time, while such topics may be touched upon, they are not examined in depth.

In terms of providing a complete methodology for trading success, therefore, this book is not the answer. Rather, this book concentrates on what I feel is a neglected area of analysis. The advantage of this approach is that the information contained has relevance to whatever markets you trade and whatever your current indicators of choice are.

For purposes of clarity and consistency, I have often used Market Profile® as the glue that holds all the different time-based tools together, but the ideas contained can be applied to other traditional areas of technical analysis.

Optimization

A key point to mention is that none of the proprietary tools referred to in this book has the optimized variables and in some cases they have never had any such tests done at all. This means that it is highly likely that those that wish to examine the methods in more detail will inevitably derive better results than posted here.

Why I have I not optimized?

The first and critical reason is that when most of these studies were initiated there was no optimization software. Despite the fact there is now, the studies' inherent stability over time has bred confidence in the variables used. I feel that optimization is an essential ingredient in technical analysis, but not so essential to find the best variables. This is a recipe for disaster. The reason for optimization is so that a set of variables can be analysed to see what its stability is.

Pure Concepts

The second reason for not optimizing is that, when originally creating ideas, if you significantly change the variables of the study, you might as well call the study by a different name. Two Slow Stochastics put on a chart with different variables are still called 'Slow Stochastics', although they may look and act completely differently. Therefore I have attempted to build a structure around the same variables, checked robustness, by looking at many different markets and timeframes, but avoided simply curve fitting an indicator's variables to a piece of data. One of the benefits of using such an approach is that you are continually brought back to the same pure concepts, which are:

- time
- price patterns
- volume
- standard deviations
- measures of extremes

A third reason is that while optimization plays an integral part in understanding a study's sensitivities and provides clues to the robustness of a trading system and insight into where to look if a system fails to live up to its originally tested performance, it is not necessary for the trader who simply uses technical analysis as a support structure for their trading. Very few traders are completely mechanical and therefore the rules in this book remain open to further interpretation and improvement for those who are prepared to put in the time and effort.

Time and expectations

All trading systems, if they want to withstand the rigours of having money allocated to them, require detailed statistics on VAR (value at risk) among other measures of risk. These aim to quantify how bad any particular position, or combination of positions, could get in any time period (a day, week or month). An example of VAR analysis would look at the last 1000 days and calculate the biggest ranges within 10 of those days.

Whilst these are laudable and necessary measurements, a great deal can happen in a day. Therefore, as for most market participants day trading is their primary focus, having an understanding of daily VAR is largely irrelevant. While this gives extremes of risk, that's exactly what it is: extremes that are only touched one in every hundred trading days. Experienced traders appreciate that there can always be unexpected events that cause sudden jumps in price, this is simply a fact of life. There will be times that stops just don't do the job, when price simply gaps to a new level without trading or a stop suffers from huge slippage.

Therefore, for the day trader, it makes far more sense to concentrate on what extreme behaviour happens over and over again within the trading day. What is needed is the understanding of expectation and risk at each moment in time throughout the day in relationship to the timeframe chart that is being referenced. This is invaluable in building and understanding trading strategies. It is essential that the time of day that any trading system entry point occurs has variable risk and expectation parameters.

Complexity of the markets

When analyzing variations of expectations and extremes throughout the day there are many potential problems:

- For European bond markets the variation in the first 2 hours can largely be dependent on what early statistics are coming out and what their impact will be on the opening of the equity markets. Once the afternoon arrives, the problems can escalate as the huge number of statistics and the different times they arrive mean that range ebbs and flows like an accordion.
- American markets are no different. Bonds are notorious for putting the vast majority of the range in the first hour. The monthly unemployment report can often account for a large percentage of the entire month's range.
- Equity markets are characterized by a wide-ranging first 2 hours, followed by a three-hour lull and then a directional last hour.
- Foreign exchange markets are the worst of all. Overnight in Asia, ranges used to be reasonably consistent, but this has changed especially on Sunday nights and on the opening of Tokyo. During the day the early trading in London can be very volatile before price calms down as the market waits for the afternoon deluge of volatility. Even then, this can change from week to week. Some weeks are reasonably light on news, others are full. The first week of the December 2005 unemployment report saw no fewer than twenty-three American numbers and a prospective ECB rate hike. This is a time when liquidity can be at its lowest point, until the market has digested all the day's news.
- For commodities there are seasonal tendencies, weather-based ballistic years, and years of dormancy due to oversupply.

All these continual changes mean that adjusting timeframes to reflect the trader's comfort zone is simply too complicated, and opens up a Pandora's box of unknowns. Emotion, fear and greed can enter the equation. It makes more sense for the traders to have either a fixed range of timeframes and have a firm understanding of expectation and risk, or more importantly, be able to connect this over different timeframes, whilst having a firm grasp of what the correct focus timeframe is. All of this is covered in later chapters.

TA methods not keeping up with changes in markets

Whilst it is obvious that the increase of statistics and trading hours have changed the trading environment drastically over the last few years, the desire to meet these changes with more dynamic technical methods seems to have been overlooked on many trading desks. Whilst it can make sense for the timeframes of charts to be fixed, why do the variables of momentum-based indicators need to be as well?

If they are fixed, once again, we come back to the inherent ability of the good trader to ride the waves of volatility.

It seems nonsensical to me that a twenty one-period, simple moving average is any more useful than a fourteen-period exponential average. There will be times when they're next to useless in terms of providing any leading indication of price. There is no guarantee that even the most rigorously tested combination of averages or any indicator is going to be successful in the future. A test by a leading bank many years ago computed the optimum average combinations on a variety of markets and they were all different combinations. The changes in the oil market (between 2003 and 2006) is a classic example of how a market can mutate into a completely different animal. In my experience, the only average of consistent worth is the Drummonds Geometry-based 3 periods moved 1 bar forward, and even then its primary value is in managing risk, not predicting price activity.

Problems with the concept of risk/reward

Another area that I believe is a much-abused market mantra is the concept of risk reward. Countless words have been wasted on this subject. They concentrate on the risk/reward ratio and how it must be a certain number before a trade can be entered. Whilst I have no problem, and believe it is essential to quantify risk, who am I to tell the market what my reward will be? Beyond the scope of very short-term scalping methods, which can quantify risk/reward, it's completely unrealistic for me to predict that a market will reach a certain profit (and justify my risk/reward ratio when I place the trade).It is also fanciful that I can have an accurate prediction of the pattern that will be created to get to that point or - just as crucially - how long it will take to get there. All I can do is:

- quantify risk,
- use measurements that understand strength of the trend in relationship to time,
- know what the focus or dominant timeframe is,
- know where trail stops are, and
- consider using partial profit targets that link time in the trade in relationship to typical trend length.
- capture short-term movements to enhance the return, if I wish to trade the position more actively.
- look for extremes and true measures of overbought and oversold,
- look for supports within the trend to provide entry points, and
- identify times when trading one side of the market can be eliminated.

No two trades are ever the same and why should they be? In building a trading system the probability that the sequence of the last hundred trades in the back-test will be exactly replicated in the next hundred is approximately eleven billion to one - and that's without the variances in how the pattern developed to reach the potential of an eleven billion to one sequence. Therefore, the only rule when managing a trade is:

The chart tells you, you don't tell the chart.

This is not to dismiss all established mantras about which studies actually work or can be made to work. As mentioned earlier, I believe that technical analysis is simply a support structure for good traders and an excuse for poor ones. What differs is the relative contribution technical analysis makes to the individual trader's decision-making processes.

Problem of momentum-based indicators

The problem with the established rules of momentum-based indicators is the fixed nature of the variables, which takes no input from the actual time of day that the indicator is referencing.

For example, a 10-period moving average on a 30-minute chart at 7 a.m. London time on a spot FX rate is referencing the 5 hours back to 2 a.m. – a time period over which it is likely that not much has happened. The following 5 hours go to 12 p.m. , during which volatility, range and the likelihood of directional movement are far greater. However, some mornings may be quiet as a market waits for American statistics, whilst other mornings are busy as European statistics dominate and there are no American ones in the afternoon. Therefore the behaviour of the average from one day to the next constantly evolves, making it impossible to have any real feel for what the relevance of the average actually is.

Therefore, if you accept the concepts of continual fluctuation in range, and the occasional longer-term mutation of a market into a different range of volatility, then the answer must be to make that variable of the average continually adjustable, based not only on the range of any particular bar, but also the time of day that that bar was created.

The study is called OaR Volatility Time Average

OaR Volatility Time Average

Definition
The average range for each bar's time of day is computed over a user-defined period. For example, on a 30-minute chart, the 12 p.m. bar has its range calculated over the last n days. Then the highest and lowest value of range for that time of day is computed over a much larger sample of bars. The difference between the current range is recorded against the highest and lowest range, and depending on the difference, an exponential moving average is calculated. This average is given a user-defined minimum and maximum range which in the examples in the chapter are between a three and twenty one-period. The conclusion is that if, range is narrow in relationship to the history of that time of day, the average slows, but if range is large, the average speeds up. Due to the often large differences in range between consecutive intraday bars the differences in the speed of the average from one bar to the next can be considerable.

Comparison with adaptive moving averages
The performance of the average has similar characteristics to an adaptive moving average in that it will speed up when price trends (especially if range expands for the time of day as well) and slows down in sideways action. The adaptive average will often lose all movement in sideways and move horizontally. In a trend they can behave in contrasting fashion. Adaptive averages will simply accelerate with a trend whilst the Volatility Time Average will do likewise in association with the time of day. This means there will be times when it is more sensitive than the Adaptive and others when it is slower.

The other key difference is that because the Volatility Time Average is always looking back to the previous period's time of day the current bar's average is already computed and does not move when we look at the current bar. This means there is always a fixed reference point.

Figure 1:
Adaptive and Time-based averages

Whilst the Volatility Time Average has an evolving dynamic and will maintain its flexibility whatever the market's conditions or mutations, it is a limited tool in terms of understanding risk and expectation within any given time period. This leads us onto a more comprehensive study.

OaR Volatility Time Bands & OaR Range Deviation Bands

Definition
Removing the variable of the average and maintaining the variable that looks at each specific time of day to previous days, and then placing 1,2 and 3 standard deviations around that range maintains flexibility to market changes and crucially provides fixed concepts of what risk and expectation can be.

I call these the OaR *Volatility Time Bands*. Each bar's point in time is referenced to previous bars of the same time through a user-defined period and an average is derived from that range. On daily charts the time element is removed and the study is simply reduced to be a user-defined average of range. These are referred to as Range Deviation Bands. Then 1, 2 and 3 standard deviations are placed around the opening price. Once again, because the opening is used the bands will not change. This is a critical component in fixing risk and expectation.

Be wary of closing prices

The use of the opening has one other crucial component. I have always found it curious that almost every study invariably references the close to calculate the study. The close is subject to manipulation or false skew purely because the close is often distorted by the need for day traders (who account for the overwhelming majority of volume) to exit their positions. Anyone who has ever placed a market on close order in the CBOT grain pit will know just how far away your fill can drift.

Whilst the day trader may remember a false close in the short term, there is no escaping the fact that late movement can totally change the perception and the pattern of the daily bar and create false conclusions especially when we look at reversal patterns.

In FX the problem is prevalent on weekly charts. On Fridays the major spots can move to uncharted territory for the day or week in the last 3 hours when London has closed and New York has very thin volume, meaning the close is near the high or low for the day or week. These distortions can have a major impact on patterns and momentum. However, for the experienced trader, the behaviour on Sunday night's opening or price action in London early Monday morning often reveals whether this late move was real or is signalling an overshoot in the short term.

Later sections in the book shed some light on whether the close was real, but they still only scratch the surface of the subject. What is really needed is the ability to manipulate data that re-defines the true range and an unmanipulated close. This is something Oasis is working on. This would reshape patterns, support and resistance and provide a more accurate momentum calculation. In the meantime, especially as more and more markets become electronic, the only way to avoid distortion is to concentrate on the opening. The matching engine of an exchange cannot distort the opening in the same way as the pit can. This problem is analyzed in later chapters.

OaR Volatility Time Bands are superior to pivots

The use of the opening creates a study with predictive powers

Since the bands' calculation references the current opening they automatically create bands around this level. For the day trader using short-term charts, this means there is an immediate reference, however big an opening gap may be. For the historical trader and the day trader there is a range of extreme and expectation as well. This is an improvement on the traditional pivots that remain so popular today.

Pivots suffer from various flaws. If the previous day's range is narrow, the next day's pivots will contract. They take no consideration of the domination that news flow creates as the time bands do. Conversely, when there is a large range day, the following day's pivots expand. The average of the last few days' ranges can be taken to try and smooth out this problem but it still lacks the dynamic nature of the Volatility Time Bands. Even the problem of the clocks changing can be adjusted in the CQG software, so that the timing of news events has not changed and do not adversely affect the Time-based studies. Another problem with pivots is opening gaps. As the values are based on the previous bar they take no consideration of gaps, meaning that they can be irrelevant from the opening. By using the opening, the volatility time bands and the range deviation bands are still relevant, however big the gap. This is particularly useful for stocks where overnight news sees a dramatic shift in value.

The deviation bands are split into two studies:

1. **Volatility Time Bands:** for intraday charts
2. **Range Deviation Bands:** for historical charts

Looking at the latter study, we can see below that in spite of a huge gap up in Google, price actually reaches and goes beyond its 3rd standard deviation down.

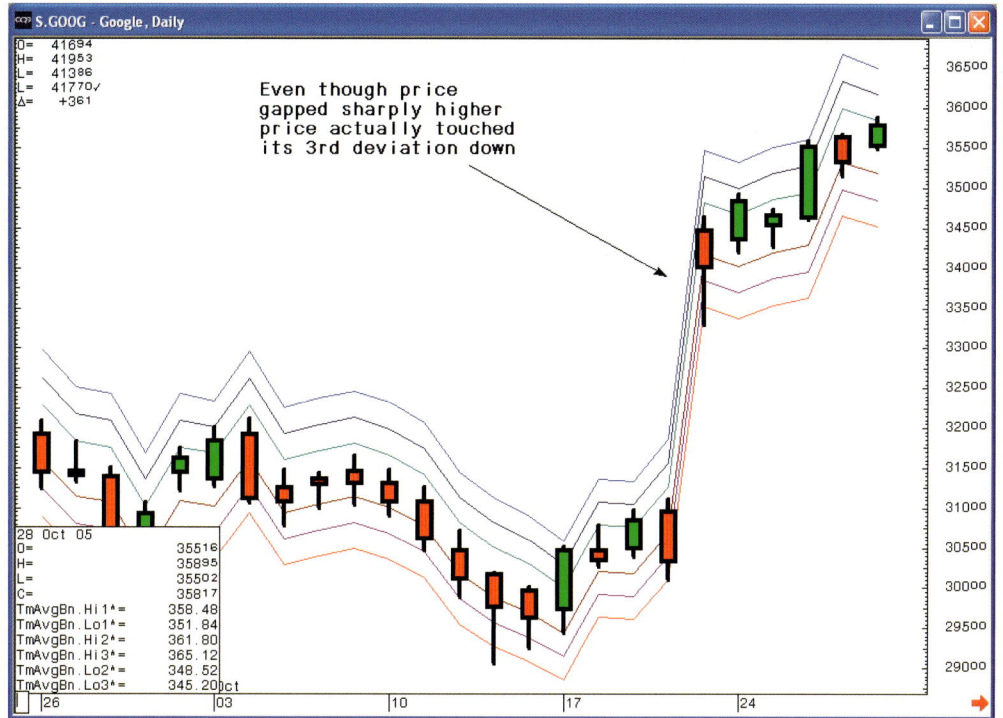

Figure 2:
Basing a study on the opening removes the problem with gaps

OaR Volatility Time Bands

The first consideration is: over how many bars or days should the volatility be calculated?

Logic suggests that the minimum period to calculate is 22 days. This should always cover an entire month's statistics. They will also retain a more dynamic relationship to any changes in range and volatility. With more uniformed markets, such as FX, the range can move up to 100 days. For US stocks, in order to capture the quarterly reports the companies produce, it makes more sense to move higher still to 200, or even 400, days. This is especially relevant if you are looking to build breakout systems. My own personal preference for markets (apart from stocks) is 22 days, as this has the most sensitive dynamic to market changes.

The second consideration is: what timeframe chart should be used?

As it is the time of day that dictates the study's usefulness, the timeframe chart is entirely dependent on the trader's time horizon for how long a typical trade should last and the time of day that positions are being taken. This study has applications for the scalper on a 5 or 10-minute chart, for example on bonds and equity markets. The day trader can utilize 30 or 60-minute bars. The longer term trader has a constant reference point when managing strategic trades. The connection between different timeframes also provides opportunities.

For those who don't know what timeframe chart to use, the later Stochastic Steps chapter provides the focus timeframe when price is trending.

The two charts below highlight how the bands provide an insight into the different types of trader. The time is 1.30 p.m. London time when many American statistics appear. The first uses the 5-minute bars and the second is a 30-minute chart on the 10-year note. The 5-minute chart has a wider outer range than the 30-minute due to greater volatility that happens after economic numbers but the 3 standard deviations of both charts create a range of resistance. The number comes out and, whilst it never reaches the top on the 5-minute chart, it fails directly at the 3rd deviation on the 30-minute. For the scalper, price never reached optimum resistance, but the 30-minute trader sold at the highs.

Figure 3:
OaR Volatility Time Bands

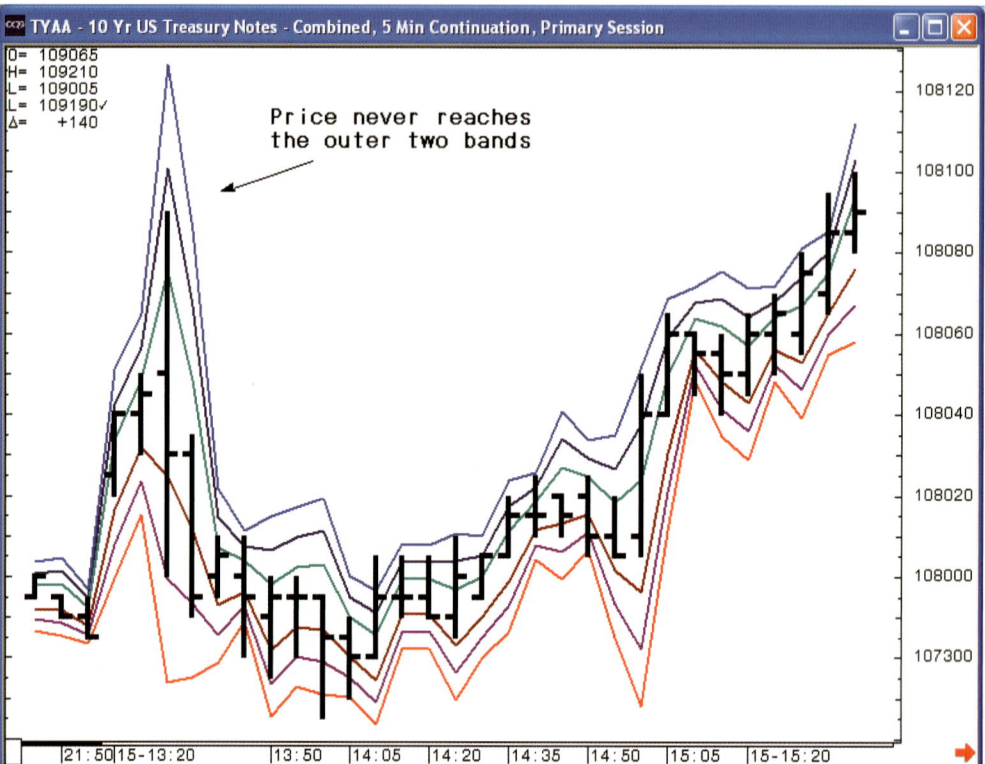

Figure 4:
Combing timeframes creates zones of risk and expectation

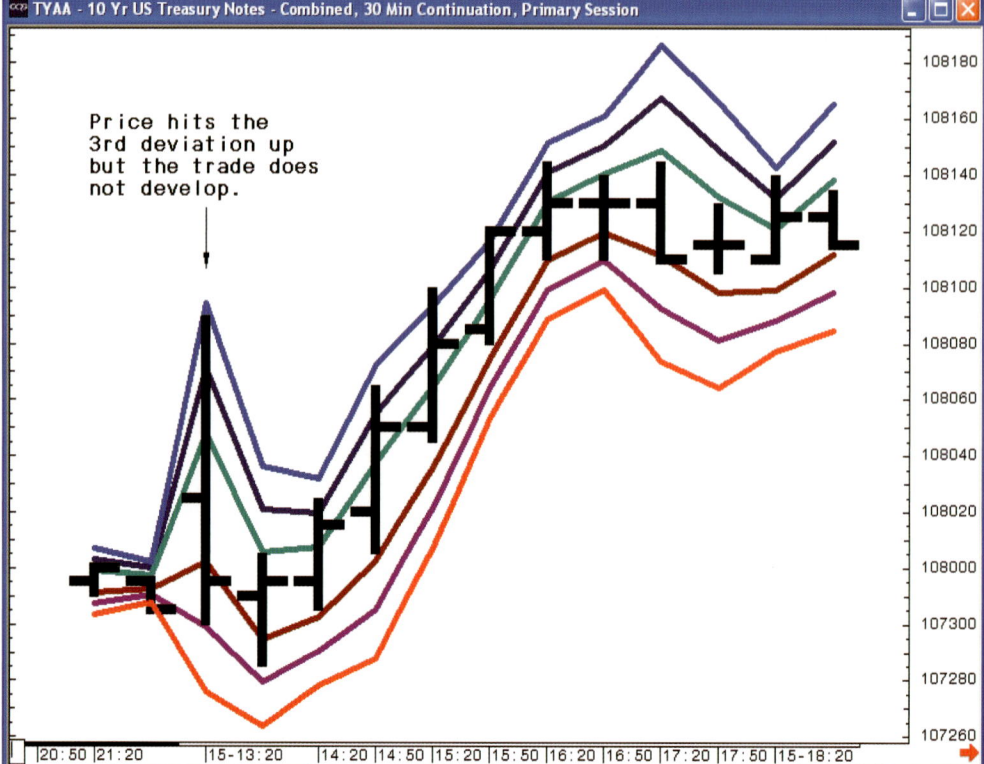

I have purposely picked an example in which the trade did not develop. The bearish initial reaction to the number was subsequently rejected. The economic report would have suggested that the trade was set to be a winner but even though this is not the case, the good entry point means that losses are kept to a minimum. As we will see later on, there were many clues subsequent to the trade to show that it was not developing favourably and for the risk-adverse trader a profit would still have been made.

There are various questions that can be answered by studying the bands:
- What is the trend?
- How strong is the trend?
- Is the trend accelerating?
- Has the trend changed?
- Has the trend reached an extreme?
- Is that extreme likely to mark the end of the trend?
- What are the expectations of a trade depending on the timeframe chart used?
- How can the short-term movement be predicted on a heavy news story day?
- How can different timeframe bands connect to quantify the power of any conclusions made?

There are many ways to ascertain whether price is in a trend, whether it is a moving average, MACD or a trend line. But these indicators simply tell us what the trend has been, and often are a considerable distance away from the current price or would require a large shift in direction to make the indicator of choice suggest that the trend is ending. Another problem, as noted earlier, is that many traders base their momentum studies on the close, meaning that there is no predictive basis of risk on the current bar. With Volatility Time Bands the trend can be defined and risk quantified.

Method 1
If the market is trending higher, then prices must at least reach the 1st standard deviation above, and not close lower than the 1st deviation below. The level acts as a support in an up trend and a stop out point on a close below. This is for the most risk-averse trader.

Method 2
If the market is trending higher, then prices must reach at least the 1st deviation above and never touch the 1st deviation below. This highlights a very strong trend.

To return to the 10-year note, the market reverses from the initial bearish reaction and then begins to hold above or at the 1st deviation low whilst the highs are closing above the 1st deviation higher. The market is now trending up strongly.

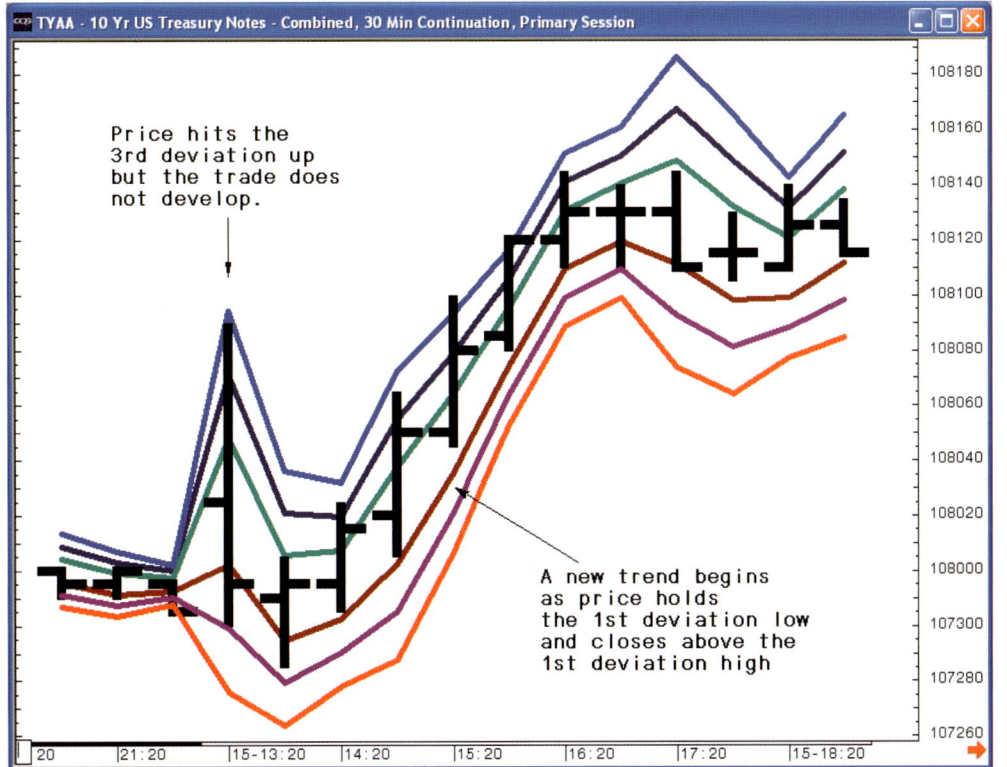

Figure 5:
Tracking the trend

Micro management of a trade to lower risk

The same is true of the 15-minute chart. Once a trend has been identified it is possible to lower timeframes if we wish to control risk and expectation to a more micro level. Once the market reverses upwards there is only one instance when price touches the 1st deviation below before the next rule provides an exit.

Figure 6:
Risk can be tightened to a lower timeframe than the original timeframe of the trade

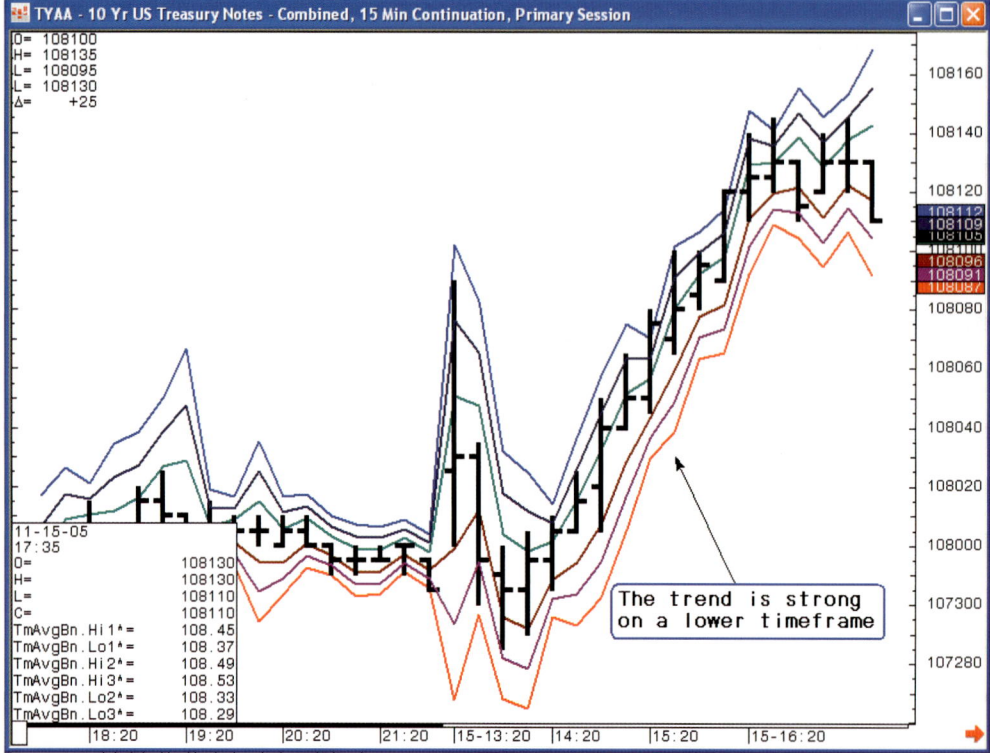

Method 3

If the market has been trending up and then prices do not reach the 1st deviation up, and close below the 2nd deviation down, the trend has ended.

Figure 7:
When has the trend ended?

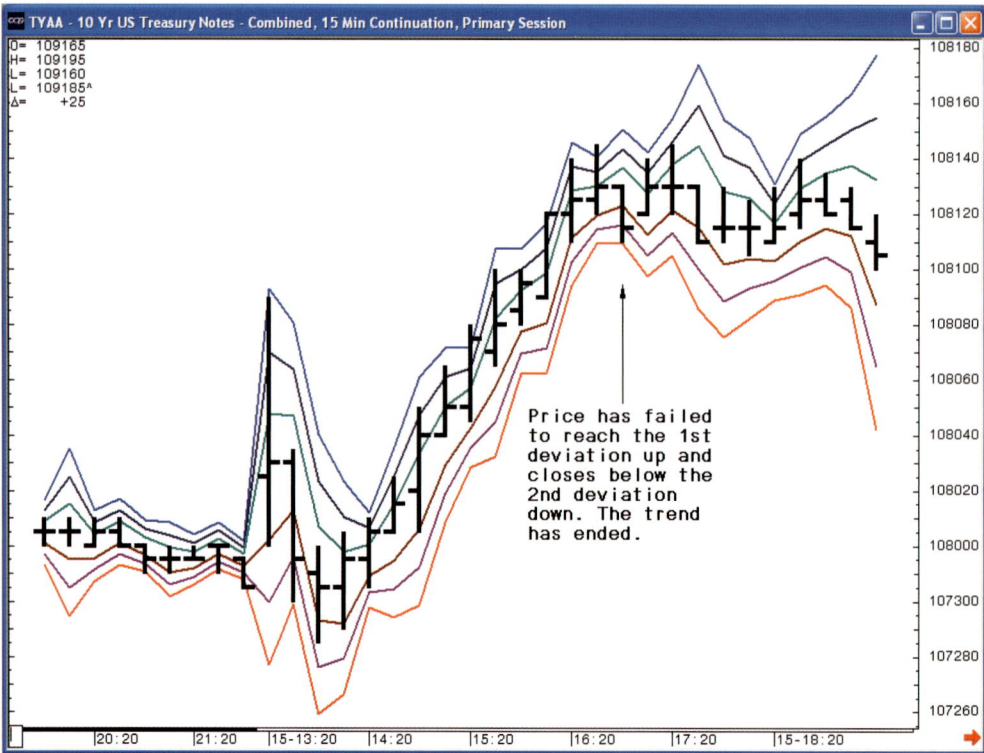

Adjustment for markets that do not open on the half or full hour

Whilst this is a good example of the short-term trend, there is one flaw in the logic of what constitutes the correct timeframe that needs to be monitored and subsequently traded for markets that do not open on the half or full hour. 10-year notes open at 20 past the hour. therefore, on 15-minute charts and above they have a period of inactivity prior to the economic numbers. This is followed by a potentially volatile period post numbers. In order to have a pure reflection of how the fundamental news has affected the price it is necessary to adjust the way the bars are calculated. This means that the first 10 minutes from the opening is a bar and then all other bars are built from 1.30 p.m. This is also useful as the closing minutes often have more volatility and are captured more closely by having a lower timeframe reference. These adjustments can be done within CQG software where the alignment of bars is fixed from the day's close and not the open. Re-analysis of the 10-year note shows how much difference this makes. This time because the range will usually be larger from 1.30 to 2.00 p.m. than it would be from 1.20 to 1.50 p.m. , when the economic number was released, price does not reach the 3rd standard deviation high and prevents a poor trade.

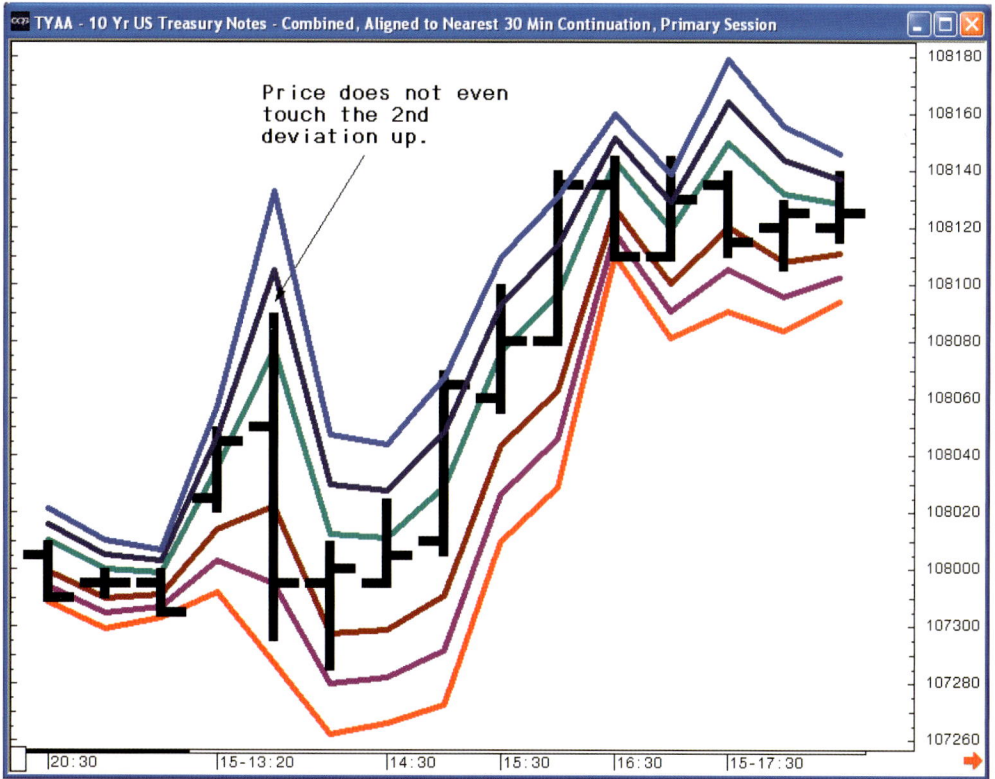

Figure 8:
Make sure you have your chart timings set correctly

FX based systems use ticks instead of percentages.

By nature, FX's 24-hour trading environment means that far more time is spent moving sideways, with trends typically being short-lived within the trading day. Ranges are also more uniform at certain times of the day and have remained very consistent over recent years on historical data.

Extensive testing of exit strategies in trading systems, which revealed that, in contrast to all other markets where profit targets and money management needed to be based on percentages to maintain consistency, in a comparison of risk on foreign exchange this actually made results worse. The difference in daily range when Dollar Swiss was at 1.80 and 1.20, which is equivalent to a 50% difference in price, is not reflected in a corresponding difference in range which averages around 25% more. This means that using percentages when at 1.80 meant money management widened but profit targets were rarely reached compared to when price was at 1.20. Therefore all FX based systems use ticks instead of percentages.

Method 4
Foreign exchange

When we use the bands, one method is to look for small repeatable patterns against the trend when markets are not influenced by economic statistics. This is predominately in the Asian time zone and midmorning London time. The chart shows that there is often volatility when Japan opens, but after that price will rarely move beyond the outer deviations. This means that scalping opportunities are common. After the opening bar at 10 p.m., when range is at its lowest and price hits the 3rd band up, the inner bands act as support and resistance.

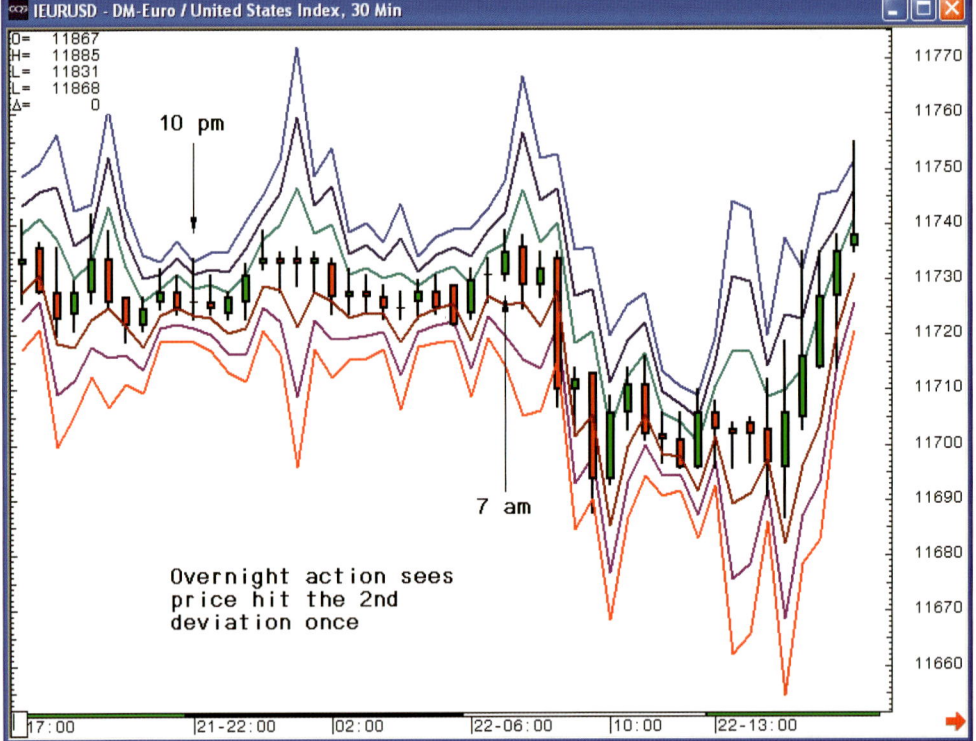

Figure 9: *Track repeatable patterns when the market is not influenced by economic statistics*

In the afternoons trends are more likely and the same principles of trends in bond markets apply. In fig 10 on EurUsd price drops over 100 points before London's close at 5 p.m. This is followed by day traders exiting positions, which causes a close above the 2nd deviation up.

Figure 10: *Trends are more likely in London's afternoon session. Note how low a timeframe chart is being referenced.*

Trading Time

Multiple timeframe confirmation

Combining timeframes adds power to the trade. This reversal coincides with the 120-minute chart hitting 1 deviation up. Note that in this higher timeframe, for the entire London trading hours, price remained below 1 deviation up, thus confirming a firm downtrend.

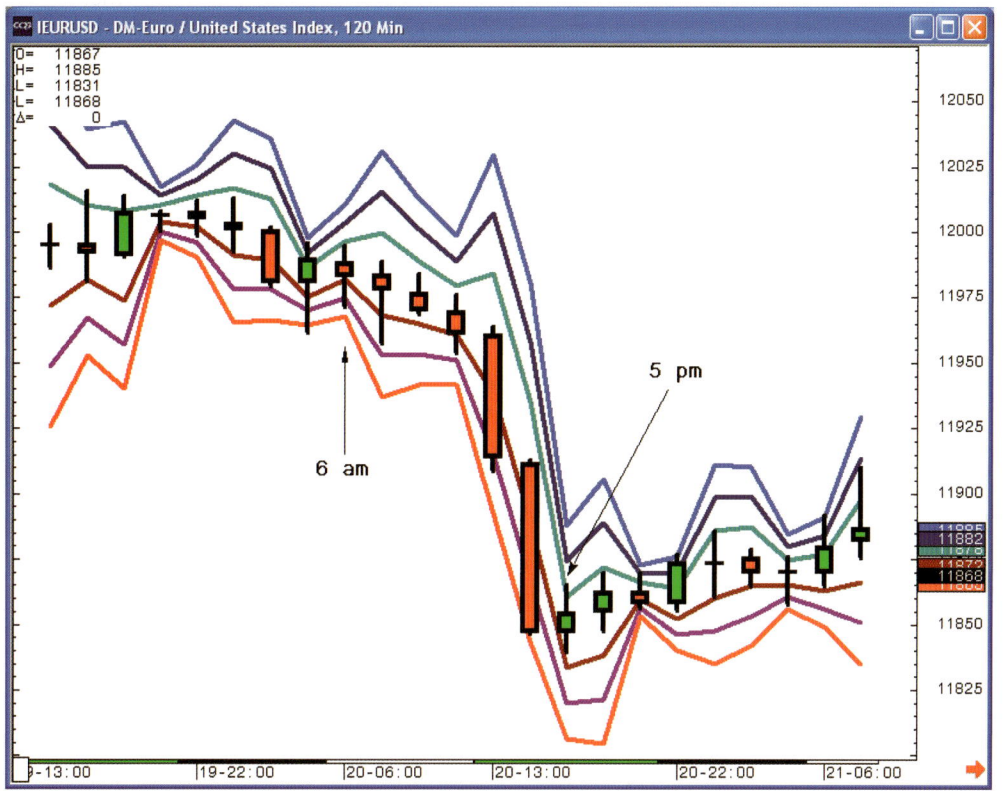

Figure 11:
Combining timeframes adds power to a trade

Stocks and Indices

The principles are true for stock markets as well. Here on the Dax (see fig. 12), price gaps higher and never moves below the 2nd deviation down throughout the whole day. Midmorning is characterised by sideways drift before the trend restarts in the afternoon. On the chart at the midmorning slumber point, there is a period of no activity where price does touch the 2nd deviation down. It is the traders' call whether this reflects a reversal of meaningful magnitude.

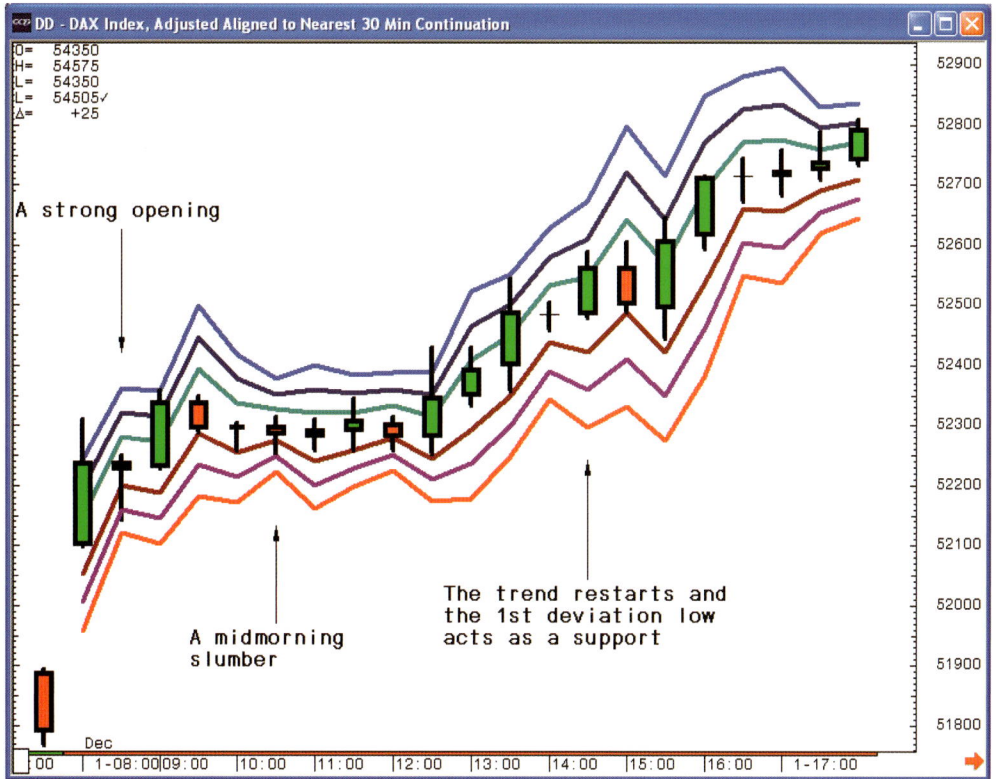

Figure 12:
Price keeps a tight range mid morning

Linking Volatility Time and Range Deviation Bands

Even though the original concept was to quantify risk intraday, switching to historical data can act as a further guide to price action, especially when markets trend or are highly volatile.

Google's volatility is considerable, meaning that structure is critical to success whether in day trading or trading strategically. Day traders begin by using the 30 and 60-minute charts as their primary focus, whilst maintaining reference to the Range Deviation Bands on the daily chart.

Let's begin with the 60-minute chart. The 1st trend higher is marked by prices reversing sharply after coming close to the 3rd standard deviation low. Throughout the subsequent rally the area between the 1st standard deviation low and 2nd deviation low acts as a consistent support until the uptrend is aborted by a close below the 2nd standard deviation low. This chart (fig. 13) also highlights another aspect of the bands.

Figure 13:
The first uptrend never breaks below the 1st deviation low.

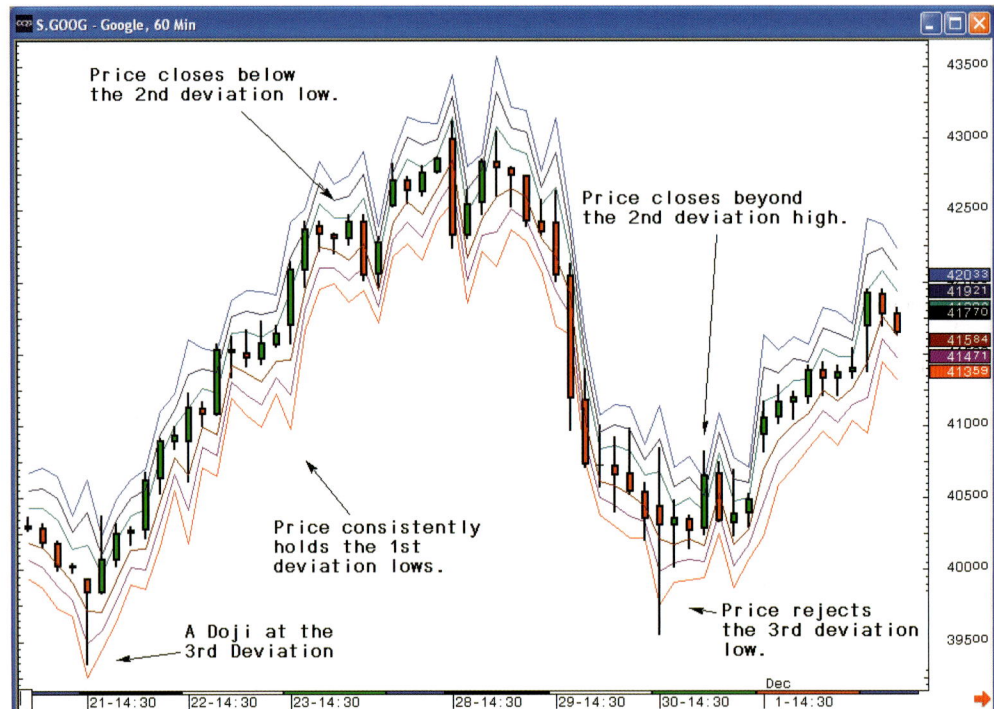

Method 5
Stocks

Closes beyond the 3rd band. Is the trend accelerating?

When price subsequently drops sharply, on the 29 November, the price moves below the 3rd standard deviation low and, more significantly, also closes substantially below. This shows behaviour out of the norm and suggests an acceleration of the trend. Only if this occurs on the closing bar of the day can this assumption be questioned. (This is covered in detail in the Market Profile® section).

Analysis of the daily chart also shows a close significantly below the 3rd band down, which suggests a breakout to the downside as well. Whilst this appears to be a powerful bearish scenario, the mantra that a trade is simply managed according to how it develops within its relationship to your technical structure prevents sentiment entering the equation.

Subsequent to the initial 60-minute breakout bar, price continues to fall, consistently failing at the 2nd deviation up and does not react upwards until a Doji appears at the lows, having first moved below the 3rd standard deviation down. This highlights an example of a forward-looking indicator receiving confirmation from a retrospective pattern.

The prospect of a reversal, or at least a short-term exhaustion point in the downtrend, gets confirmation on the daily chart. The market comes close to the 3rd down band before reversing and creating a Doji on this timeframe as well.

Trading Time

The combination of timeframes provides a powerful signal that price has exhausted itself, at least for today. Shortly after the intraday Doji on the 60-minute chart, price closes above the 2nd standard deviation high and the downtrend is over.

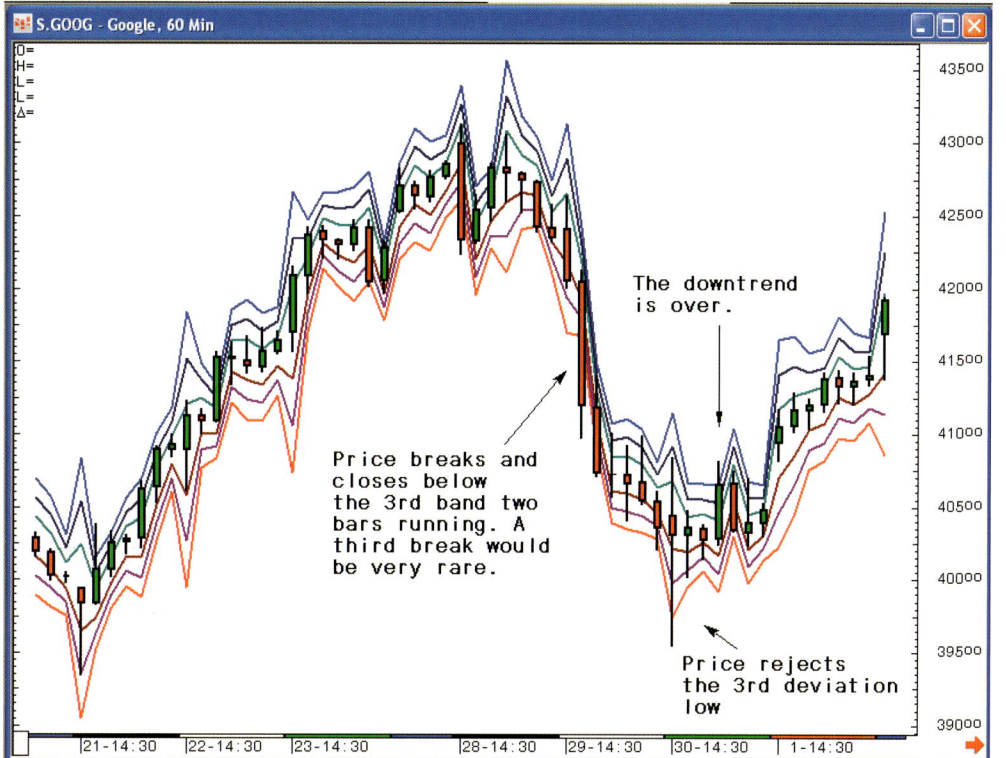

Figure 14:
Tracking a trend in Google

Figure 15:
Linking the time of day with the historical bands creates zones of risk and expectation

TRADING TIME: New Methods in Technical Analysis

Managing in the micro timeframe

Whilst the management of that trade involved beginning with a 60-minute and then referencing a higher timeframe, which is a common method of analysing, the bands can allow for a flexible approach. Once a trend has developed, the trader can decide whether they wish to change timeframes depending on their concept of risk. The risk-averse could move down to the 30-minute chart.

Looking once again at Google we see that in spite of the lower timeframe on the first trend, price consistently holds the 1st standard deviation low and the eventual end of the trend with a close below the 2nd deviation down is at the same time as the 60-minute chart.

Figure 16:
Risk can be tightened by using a tracking timeframe chart lower than the one on which the trade was instigated.

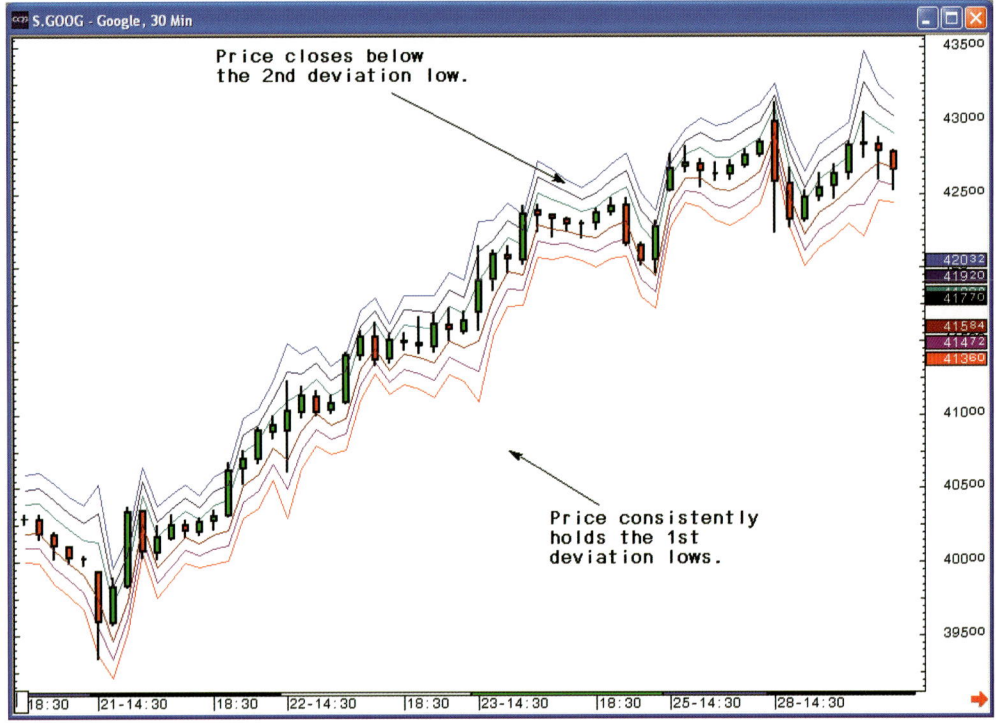

The next trend down shows similar characteristics, but this time the 2nd deviation up caps rallies, before a close above that band, which is also at the same time as the 60-minute flagged a reversal.

Figure 17:
Two timeframes signal the end of the trend at the same time.

24

Trading Time

Method 6:
Trend changes and reversals
Bonds

We know closes beyond the 3rd band can signal acceleration phases but they can also flag the beginning of a new trend or major reversal.

The greater the move beyond the 3rd deviation, the stronger the move and the more significant the breakout, depending on the time of day. This is critical to the trader's decision-making. Breakouts when economic statistics have been released are an example of a valid time. Breakouts that are close to the close of the day can be potentially viewed as invalid. The 10-year note shows a major shift upwards at 3 p.m. when statistics are released. The trend extends through the day and price closes on the highs, although price did hit 3 down at one point.

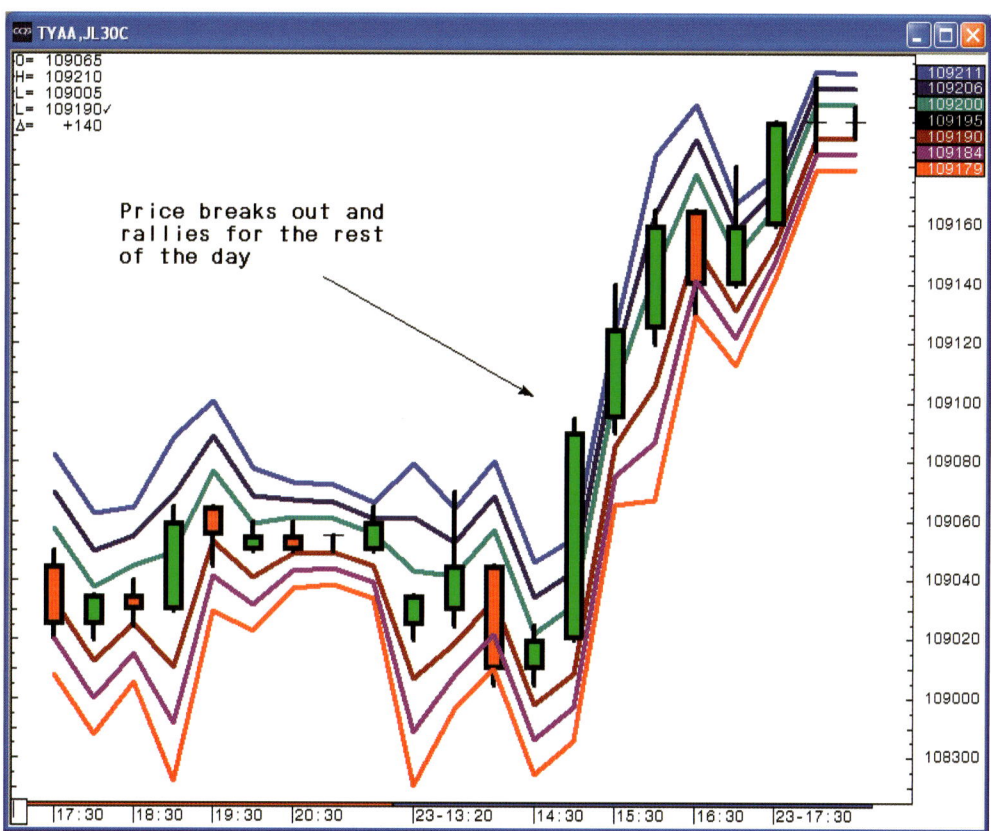

Figure 18:
The time of day of a breakout defines its likelihood of being sustainable

25

TRADING TIME: New Methods in Technical Analysis

Foreign exchange
What time of day is a breakout occurring?
Once again, FX trends are generally short-lived and care must be taken depending on the time of day. A breakout at 4.30 p.m. when London is closing is an obvious point where the move is more likely to be exhaustive as London day traders exit and create a false close for that section of the market.

Figure 19:
The time of day of a breakout defines its likelihood of being sustainable

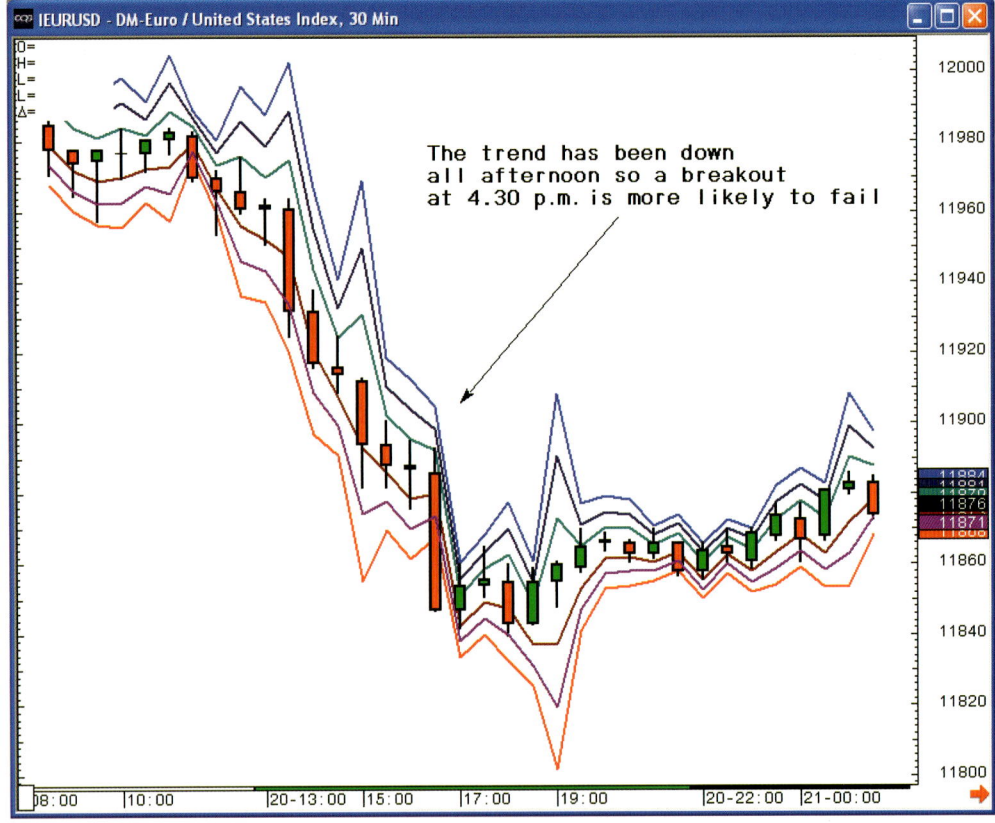

The same applies to breakouts in Asia. In the absence of major news out of Japan, and Sunday nights where directional moves do occasionally occur, any breakouts are more likely to be false. The EurUsd chart shows 5 false closes outside the 3rd band in one night.

Figure 20:
The Asian time zone on FX

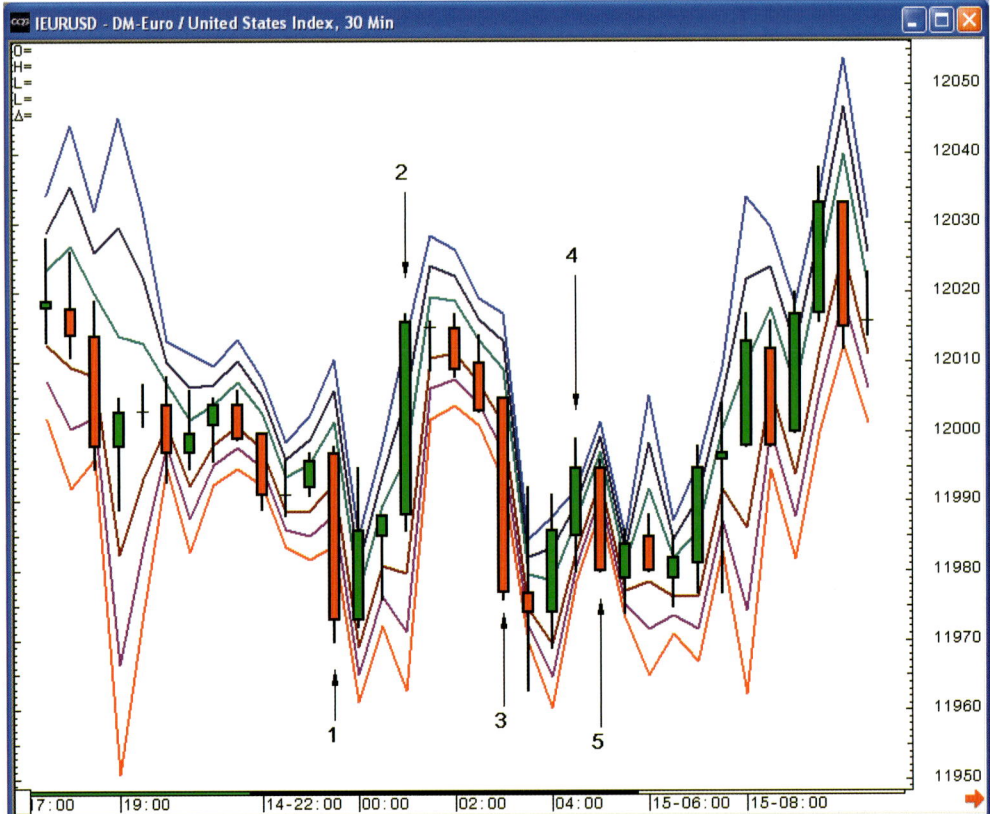

Trading Time

Figure 21:
Breakouts in the American morning are more likely to be sustained

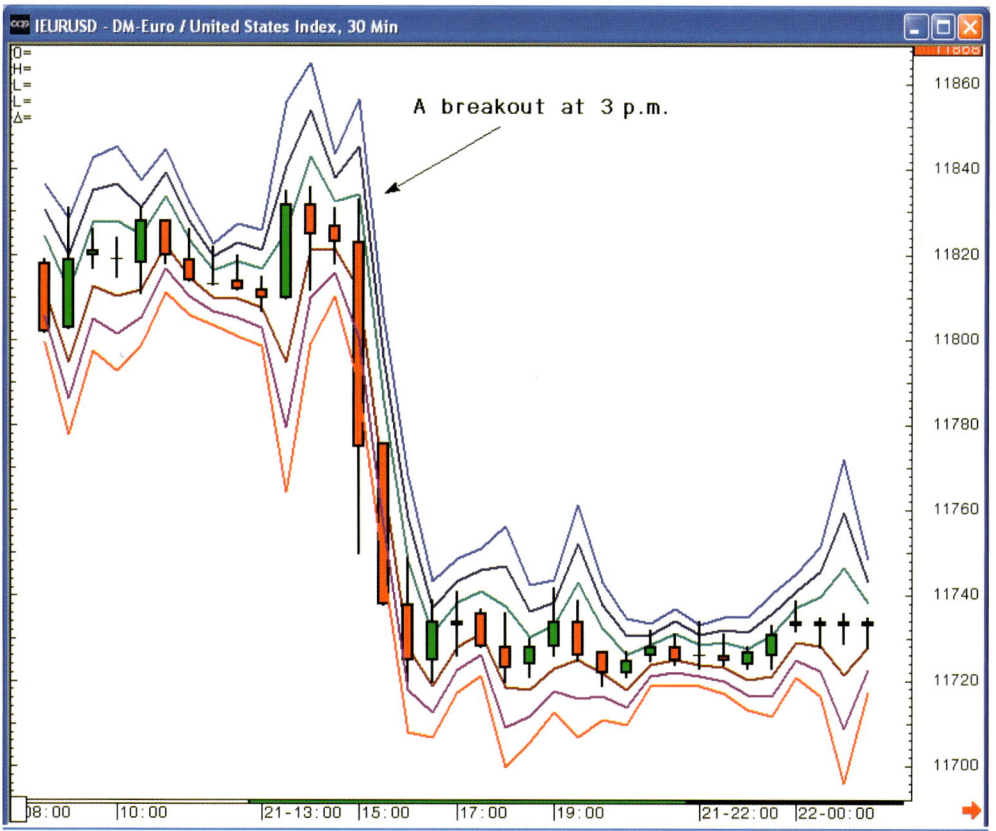

Figure 22:
This is especially true if all the day's statistics have been released

27

Stocks

Breakouts on news stories

These are the most powerful if it is the last news item of the day and price is still distant from the Range Deviation Bands limits

Figure 23:
A breakout takes place at 3 p.m. London time following the release of some economic numbers

Stocks

On stocks where volatility and daily range is high and trends strong, such as on Google, 30 and 60-minute charts can provide opportunities, although for most stocks daily charts can be the focus. Using 400 days as the range means that signals will be rare and truly reflect movement out of the normalized range. This allows for a larger portfolio of stocks to be referenced. Yahoo (see fig. 24) shows how rare signals can be.

Figure 24:
For stocks, settings can be much higher to get fewer breakout signals. The close below the 2nd band down signals an end to the trend

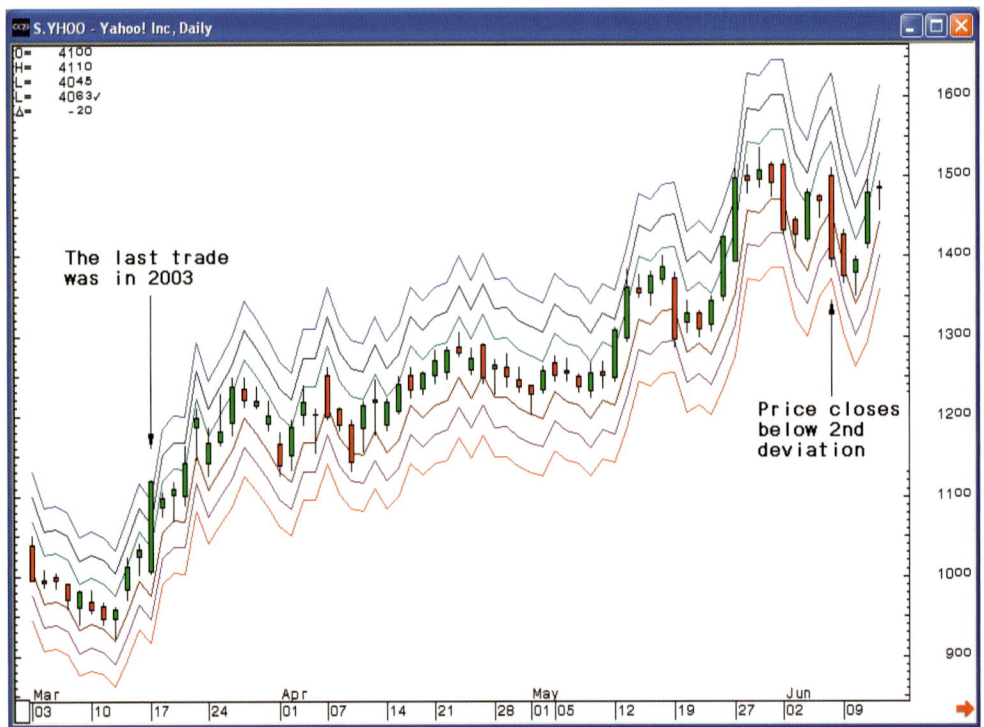

However, setting the bands to reference just 25 bars will obviously produce far more signals. The final signal has a rare double breakout. Triple breakouts are extremely rare and provide a short-term reference.

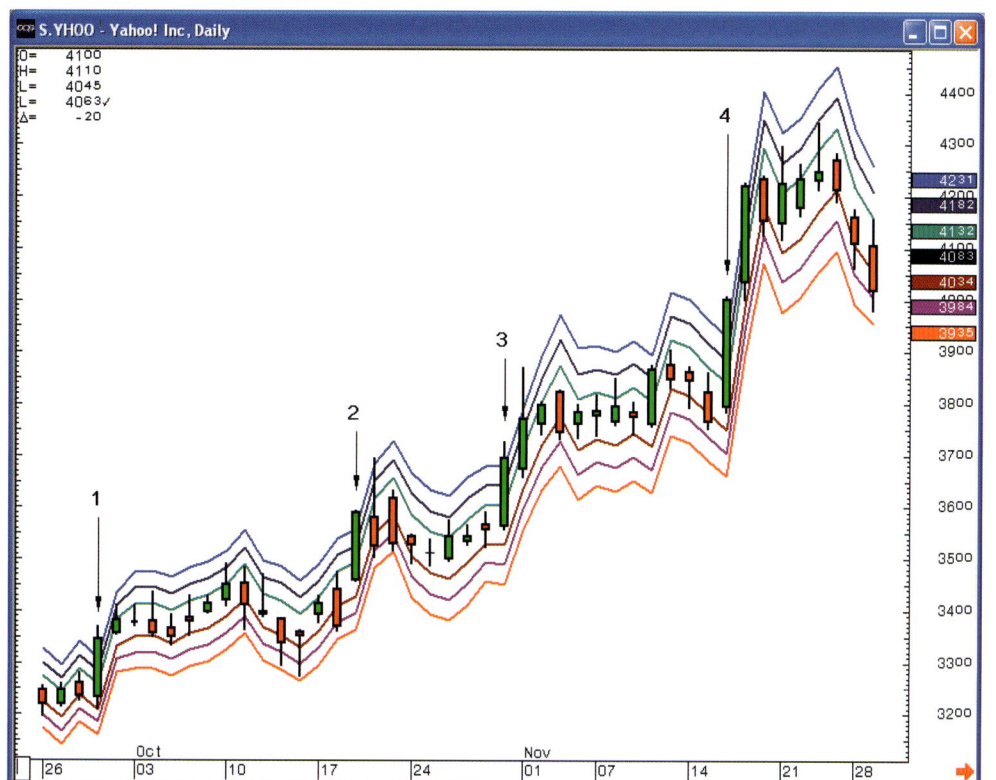

Figure 25:
Yahoo with a lower threshold for breakouts

Method 7
Has the trend reached an exhaustion point?
Whilst a significant close beyond a 3rd deviation marks acceleration, in normal conditions the 3rd deviation marks the limit of fair value. Once again, the time of day can influence when a signal is more likely to work as well as how far the trend has already been in existence. The news flow regarding the day's statistics can also provide insight.

A later chapter on Peak looks at how these can be quantified more accurately but for now, some basic interpretations.

On 10-year notes the later in the day the signal appears, the more likely the signal is to mark a short-term extreme (see fig. 26).

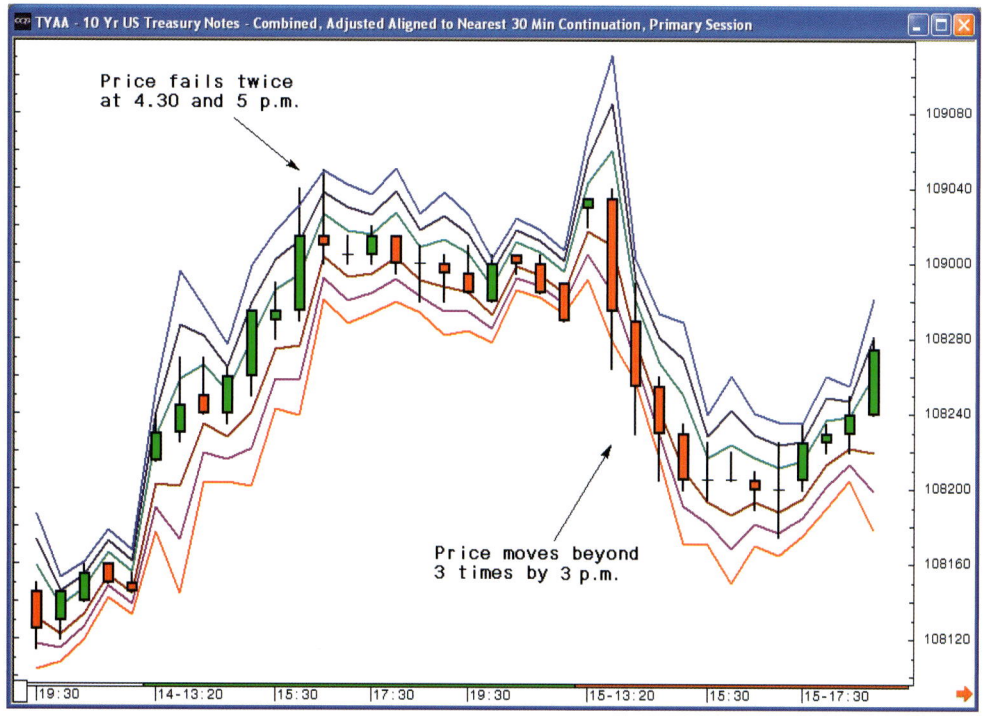

Figure 26:
Breakouts and the time of day give different results

29

TRADING TIME: New Methods in Technical Analysis

With FX, the mornings in London see consistently normalized ranges. The day in question sees five extremes before volatility and range expands in the afternoon.

Figure 27: London's morning has breakouts that are more likely to be false

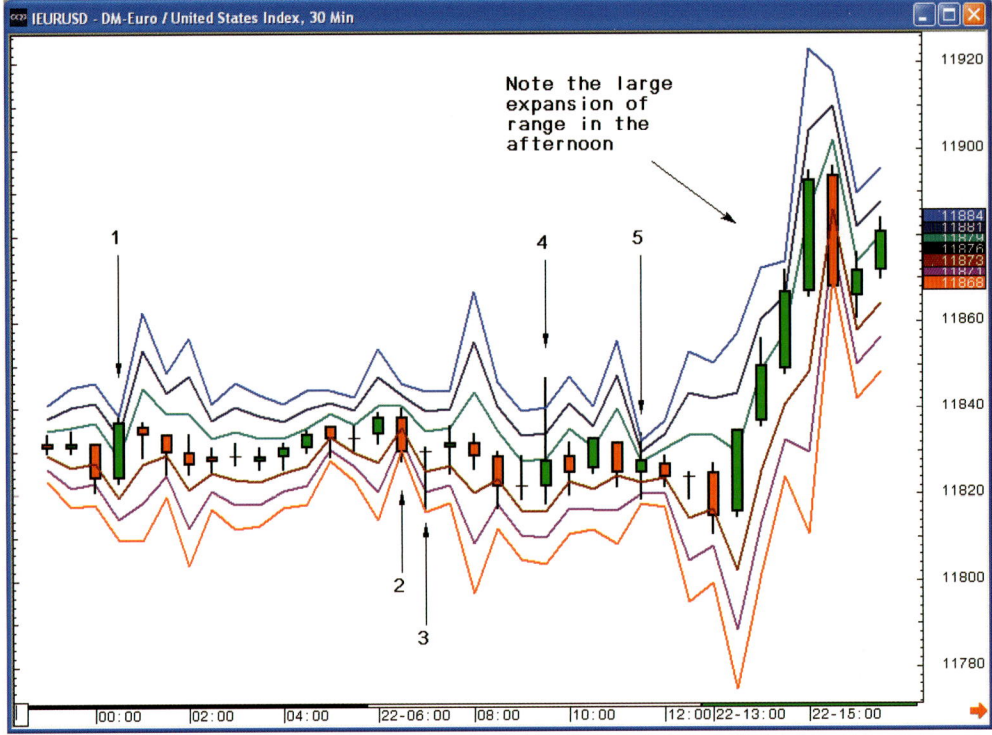

Knowing the news flow provides insight into what sort of day can be expected in terms of volatility.

No news suggests that price will have less volatility.

Figure 28: No news sees a day where bands never reach an extreme and never close outside the 1st deviation.

30

Method 8
Scalping
Bonds

In European bond markets this is even more prevalent when no news is being released, especially midmorning. The huge rise in the number of trading arcades in Europe and the prospect that more will appear worldwide suggest that, in the absence of external events, the huge amount of volume by these scalpers will continue to restrict volatility. Whilst this has destroyed many methods of technical analysis on a day-trading basis, especially for the interest rate markets, the FTSE and Dax, the adaptive qualities of the bands suggest that this study will continue to provide insight whatever happens.

Very few technical indicators have the ability to provide real insight into the short-term movements that the scalper feeds from. The bands' adaptive nature to time means that the deviation levels give the scalper a real sense of what can happen in the next few minutes. Even when price reaches the 3rd standard deviation there is often the opportunity to scratch the trade even if the subsequent bars go against the trade. This is especially powerful in the mornings. The Bund chart shows how seven opportunities in 2 days appeared and even when the market was trending there was always at least a scratch trade.

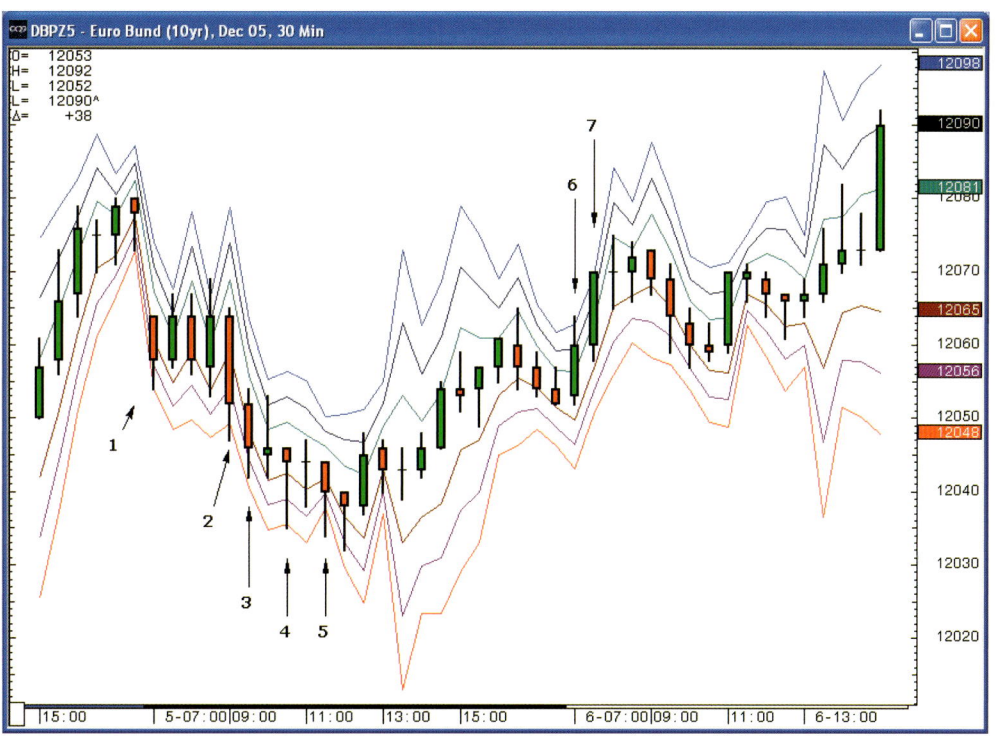

Figure 29: *The 3rd deviation, especially in London's morning, mark short-term scalping extremes*

Insights provided by a basic trading system on 10-minute charts

The creation of a basic trading system provides insight into what can be achieved. The code states that a contra trend entry is made when price moves to the 3rd band and has the added robustness that it must move 1 tick beyond the level so a fill in real time would be achieved. The exits are simply a profit target, stop and withdrawal on the old close at 6 p.m. You could also consider exiting at 5 p.m. London time when the cash market closes. The extension of trading hours sees far less volume and does not reflect true market dynamics as range narrows.

The key point to note is that this system takes no account of the actual time of day the entry signal occurs or whether there was an economic statistic, when an entry was flagged. Therefore it is a somewhat blunt instrument, which a trader should be able to develop further with their insight and experience. Even without these abilities the results are revealing and provide a firm grip on what can be expected in terms of a stop loss and profit point. As stated earlier it is only on very short-term trading methods that the concept of risk reward can be entertained.

Therefore the system test has taken the buy signals on the Bund on a 10-minute chart over the last 10,000 bars.

TRADING TIME: New Methods in Technical Analysis

An optimization needs to be performed in order to understand what the variables' influence on profit are. The complete methods of how optimization should be both performed and interpretated are beyond the scope of this book, but a key element is to make sure that if the variables change slightly, the results do not deteriorate significantly.

First, it's necessary to look at some of the more important statistics.

The best results have a short length of look-back in the number of days to calculate the bands at 15 to 25 days. Money management is quite wide at 7 – 10 ticks, whilst the profit target is low at 2 – 4 ticks. Whilst this seems somewhat illogical, on a 10-minute chart the move beyond 3 deviations is only a short-term extreme so the small profit target makes more sense. The large number of trades means that only those with very low commission rates (that can be found, for example, in arcades) can consider theoretically taking all the signals.

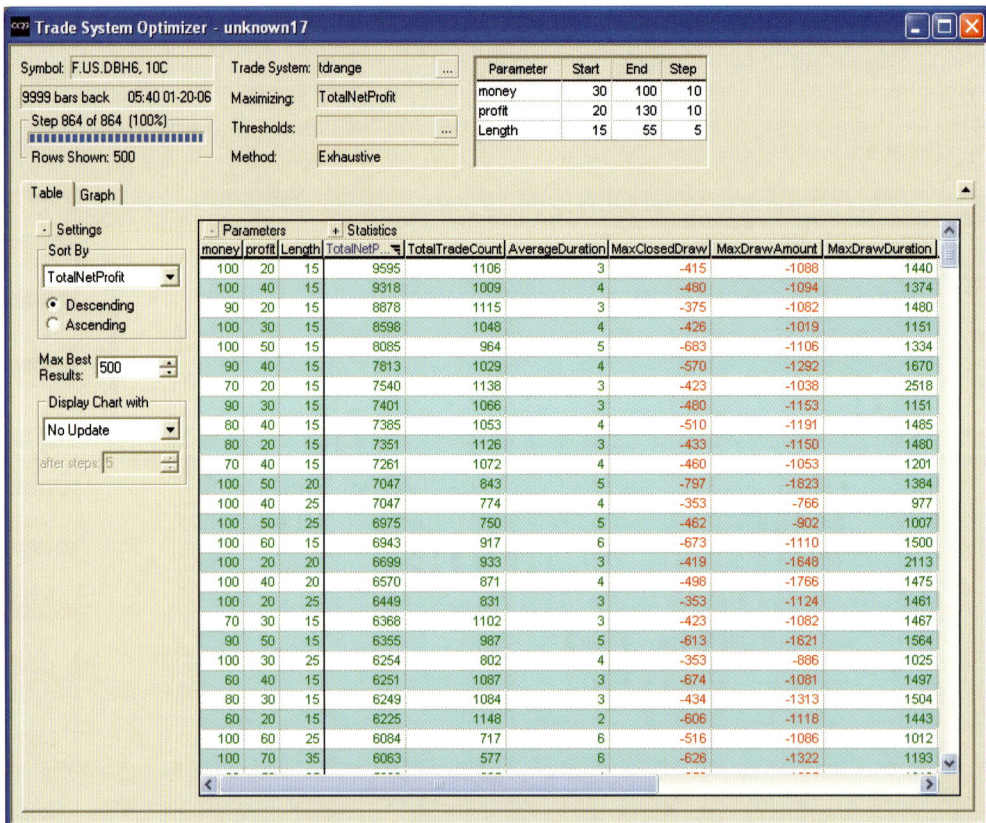

Figure 30: Optimization results. The first three columns show the best combination of variables between the stop, the profit and the number of bars to calculate the bands over.

This next graphic (fig. 31) shows more statistics on the same test. The low profit target in relationship to the stop creates a very large difference between the consecutive wins and losses, which translates into a very high accuracy in the percentage of winners.

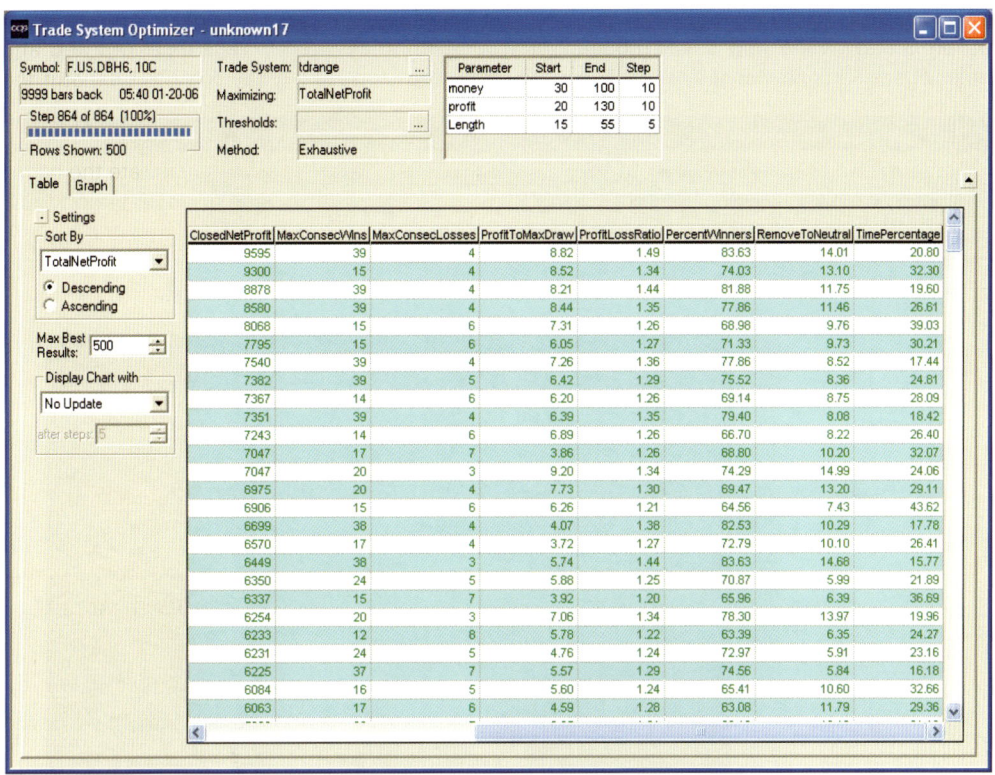

Figure 31:
Optimization results

Robustness

However, those raw statistics only paint a rosy picture and tell us nothing about robustness.

Analysis of a 3D graphic provides a clearer picture (see fig. 32). From left to right the scales show the length of the look-back period of the study in relationship to profit. The money management stop is fixed at 9 ticks. This confirms that if the profit target remains low and the length of the look-back is below 25, the system is reasonably robust. However, it deteriorates significantly if the profit target rises and the length of look-back increases. That the drop off in profit is deeper on the profit-target scale than the length of look-back highlights the fact that the profit target is the real driving force behind this system.

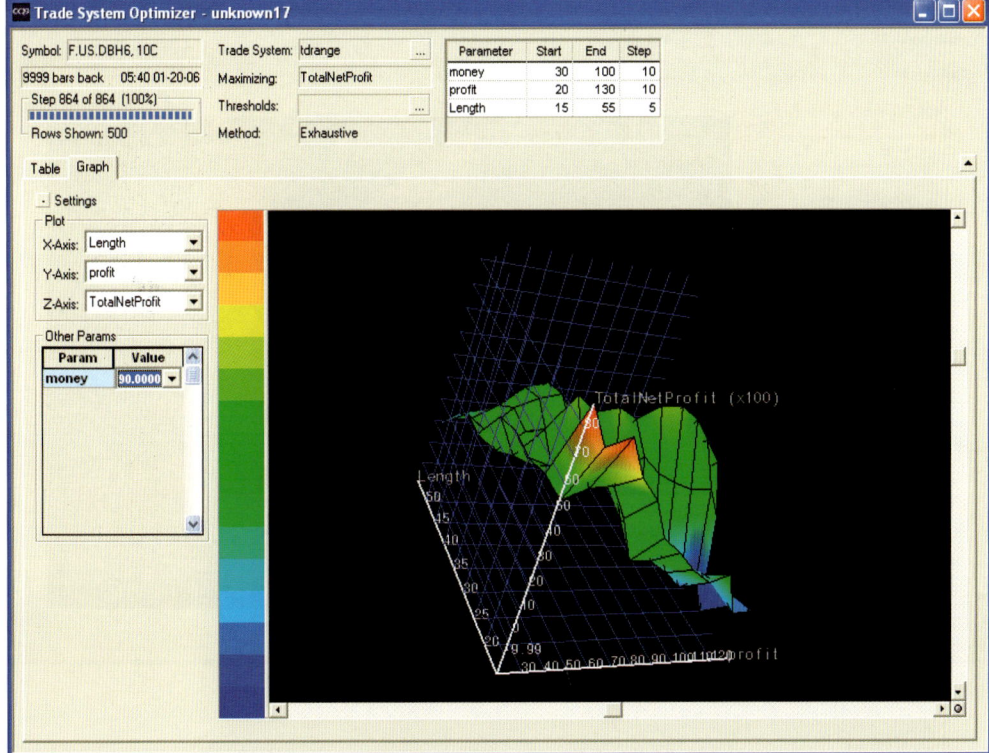

Figure 32:
3D graphics of variables

With the profit target set at 5 ticks, a look at the Money Management stop and the length confirms that a wide stop is also required, otherwise profit falls steeply regardless of the length of look-back. This now confirms that the profit target and stop are the key components.

Figure 33:
3D graphics of risk

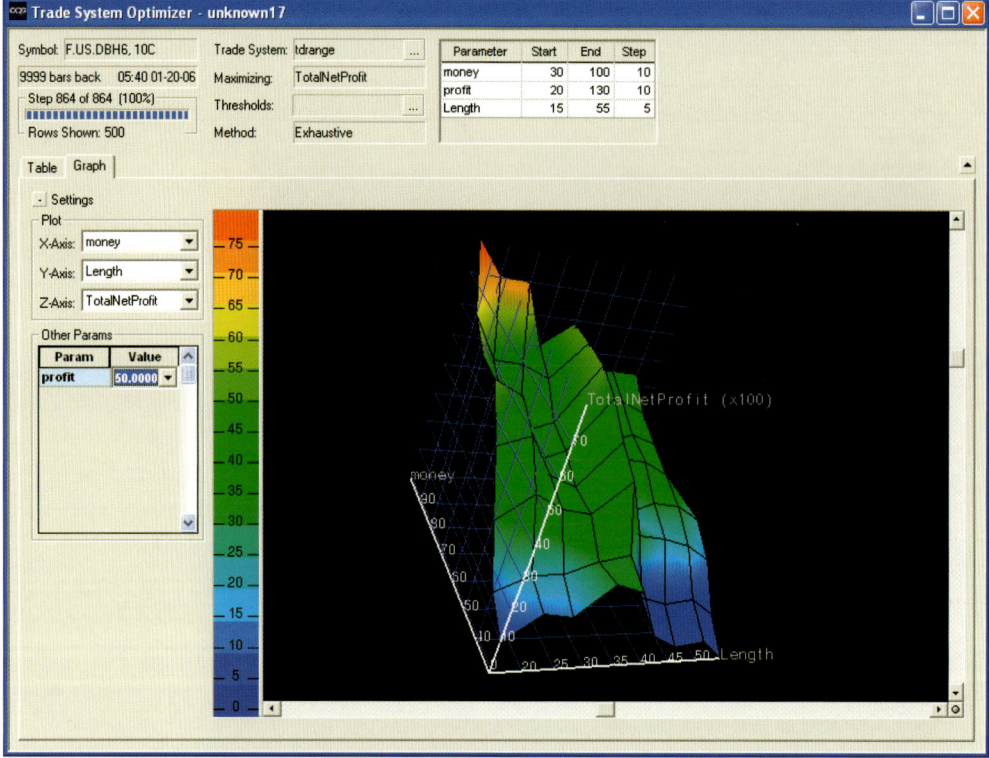

The last graphic (see fig. 33), which analyses the percent winners, confirms the previous two conclusions.

Figure 34:
3D graphics

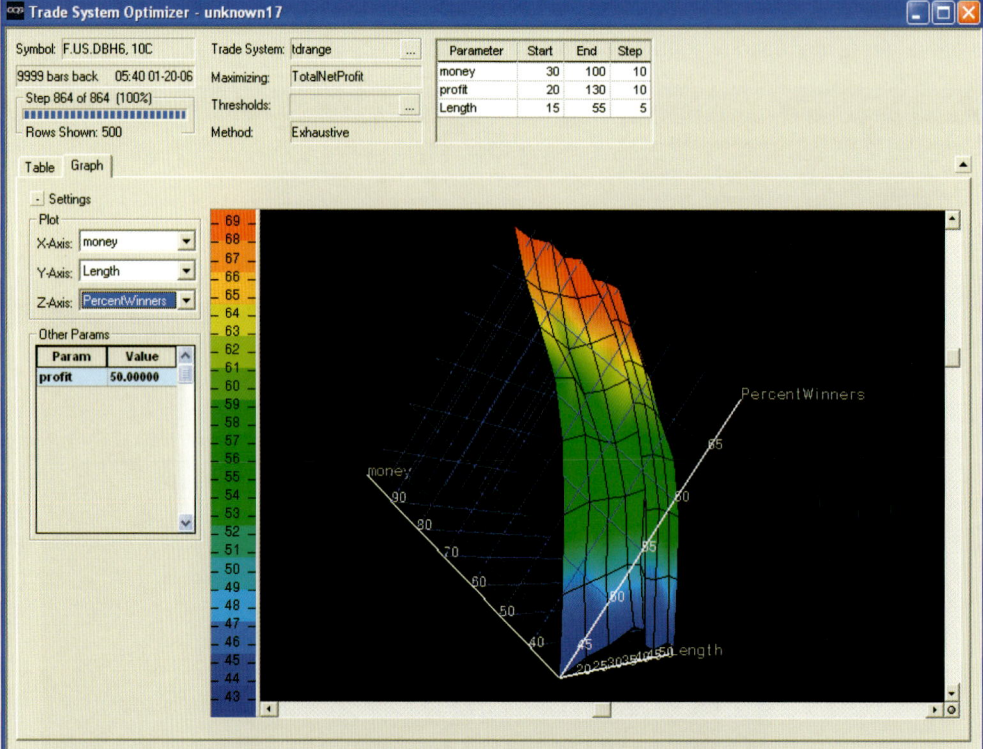

The need for optimization

These tests are not comprehensive enough for automatic trading. However, they do provide the scalper with insight into what they should be concentrating on if they make a judgment call to trade the short-term moves to extremes. This is vital analysis in many ways. Often traders who use technical analysis with certain variables do not carry out any basic tests to see whether there is the possibility they are making a huge mistake in using an indicator with their chosen variables.

Some years ago I built a system that looked at trading a sideways markets via the ADX and Stochastics. The back-test results including out of sample and walk-forward analysis were spectacularly good. But the tester who does not perform comprehensive tests – including optimization - has no clue whether the system will work in the future. I performed an optimization and the 3D result showed that I had purely by chance stumbled upon the perfect combination of variables. However, just changing the ADX by 3 periods from 36 to 33 and lengthening the stochastic from a 5,3,3 to a 7,3,3 saw the profits collapse. The market would only have to display slightly different behaviour in the future before the losses would be considerable.

What is the real influence on your trading strategy?

Another worrying trait is that if traders use a combination of indicators or methods, they have no idea what the real influence on their strategy is. If they do not know what the key components are, they will have no idea where to look in order to adjust the strategy to see whether the market has changed in its behaviour. The simple tests performed here immediately tell the trader that profit target and stop are the driving forces and that the length of look-back is irrelevant in comparison.

Returning to the concept of short-term extremes, we see there was a similar number of signals in the 30-minute Bobl (see fig. 35). Two moves lower to the 3rd band are followed by a brief move beyond the 3rd band above. At point 3, there is another move lower. Then there are three moves up at 4 to 6, which has another move to the 3rd down in between this area.

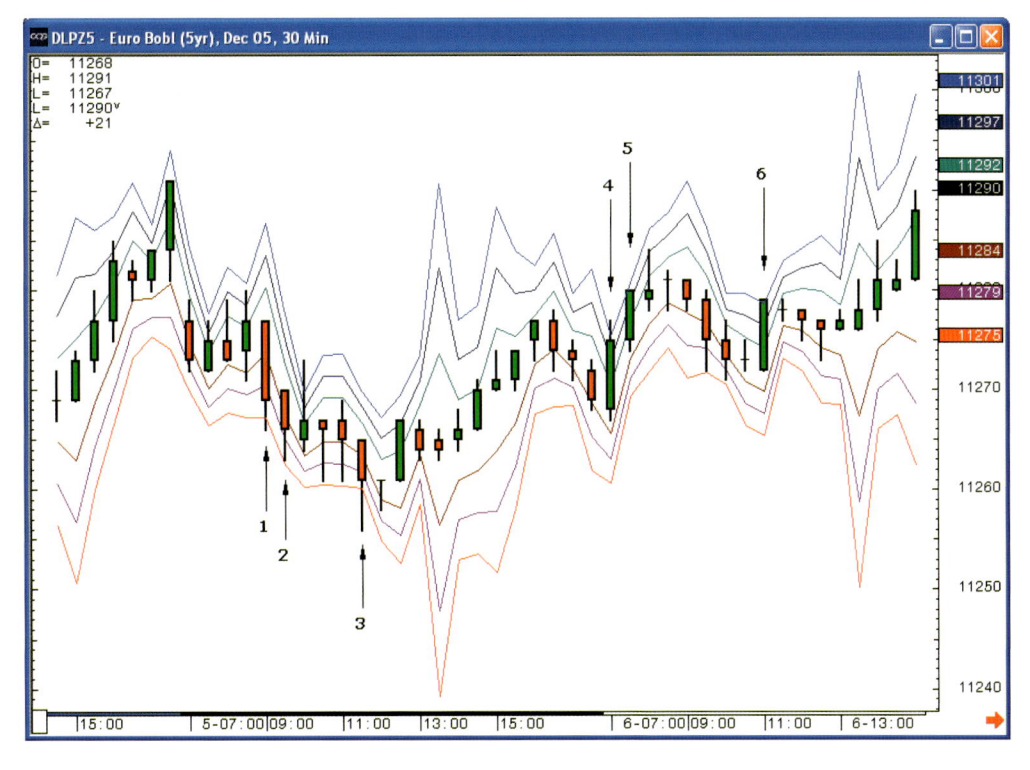

Figure 35:
The Bobl contract and short-term extremes

The dynamic nature of the method is revealed by there being no fewer than 12 opportunities in one day on the 10-minute Bund chart. In all cases price went beyond the 3rd standard deviation band so a fill would have been obtained.

Figure 36:
Scalping on a 10-minute Bund chart

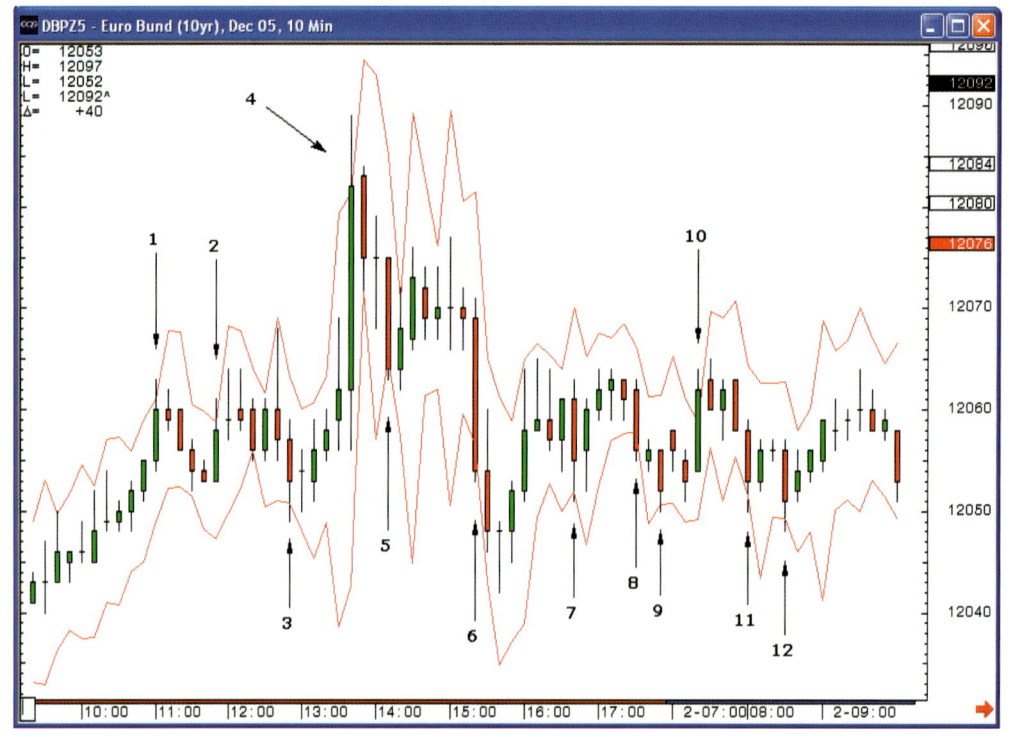

A good trader is better than a good system

If we turn to the 10-year note once again, the obvious problem is the huge jumps that often occur just after the opening when economic numbers are released and then again an hour and a half later when further numbers are released. On the chart in question (fig. 37) the reaction to the economic number at 1.30 p.m. remains within the normal boundaries for that time, but the second number sees price close significantly below the 3rd standard deviation low, which suggests a more powerful bearish dynamic is in force compared to normal behaviour. The automatic trading system would post a loss here, whereas a trader would have been wary of taking the signal as the final statistic of the day had just been released.

Figure 37:
Price waits for the final statistic of the day before breaking out

Trading Time

It is far easier to analyse when the studies' values are fixed on the current bars opening.

Foreign exchange

Not surprisingly, with FX markets the bands automatically converge in Asian time (excluding Tokyo's opening hour) and expand in the early part of American and London time. Whatever the time, the study does not include the data regarding the current bar. Logic suggests that not including the current bar is dangerous. However, many traders will agree that analyzing when a market is closed removes many of the mental problems associated with trading. By removing the current bar from the calculation we can do likewise and coldly compare this bar's performance with the recent history of what that time of day has done in the past.

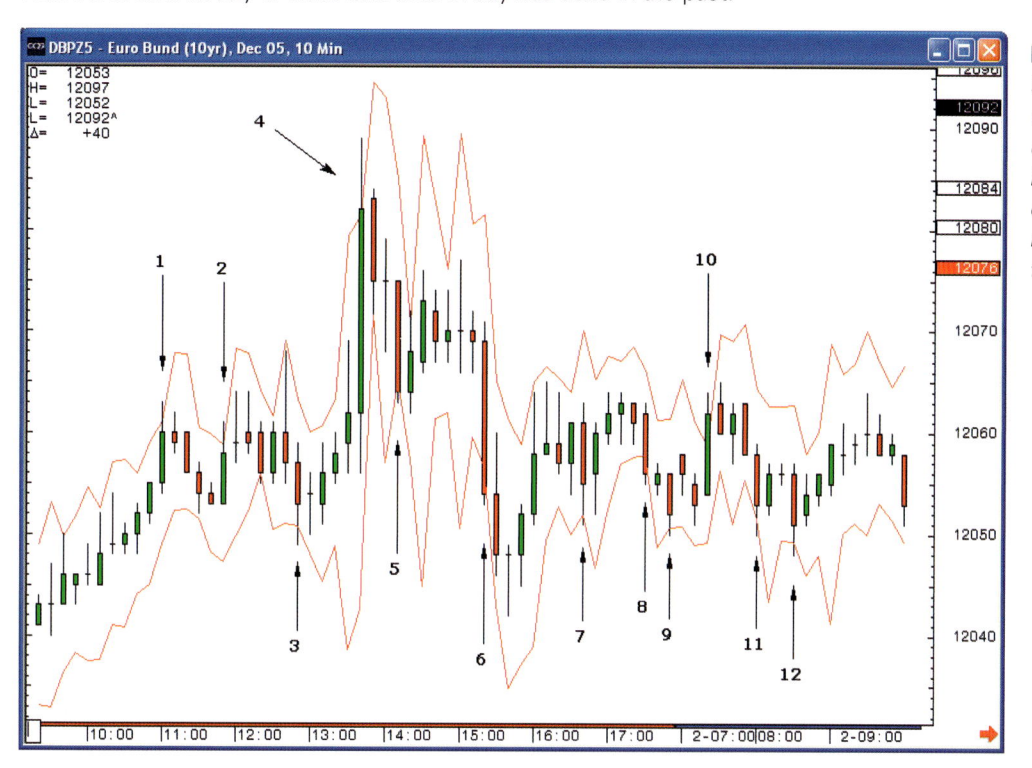

Figure 38: *Studies that work on extremes but are based on the close are not recording the true extreme*

Bars that haven't even been built can have the risk and expectation estimated

Another crucial advantage is the ability to estimate the risk and expectation of a bar that still hasn't opened. This is done by looking at the previous day's time of day bar and seeing what the distance was from the opening to the three bands. This gives an idea of how a trade needs to develop in the immediate future and allows for forward thinking and planning.

EurUsd. A case study

The next chart (see fig. 39) is a 60-minute Euro v Dollar chart from 29 November 2005, which highlights the variety of price action within a day. The first bars around point **A** in Asia show that the bands are very narrow. The real action begins with the bars at 1 a.m. and 2 a.m. London time, which is when Tokyo and Singapore are both open. Short-term directional moves in this period are increasingly prevalent, although the cause is unclear. Price moves lower at 1 a.m. beyond the 3rd standard deviation, highlighting an extreme move **B**. This is unlikely to be sustained at that time and once again creates a short-term exhaustion point. Price then respects the 1st and 2nd standard deviation band **C** all the way until the durable goods numbers that are released in the US at 1.30 GMT. **D**.

This is typical behaviour, as in the absence of news price simply ebbs and flows around one standard deviation and provides scalping opportunities. Crucially for the longer term player - who may hold positions for a number of days – it provides an opportunity to work the position whilst retaining the core view. Even if this is not within their remit, it does mean that they should be able to relax and not get spooked by short-term movements. 1.30 p.m. arrives and the fun begins. Price moves briefly through, but closes close to the 3rd standard deviation point **D**.

The failure to close beyond the level and settling directly on it is one of the hardest points of interpretation. Will the trend continue or reverse? Subsequent bars will tell the story. In this case the subsequent bar above makes a close above the 1st standard deviation band high suggesting an inability to trend. Price then makes a low for the day at the 2nd standard deviation band low on the

3 p.m. bar. For many, this failure to extend the trend lower would be surprising as the economic number showed the highest jump in consumer confidence numbers in three years **E**. This implied that interest rates would need to rise and would be negative for the Euro and positive for the Dollar.

Whilst it appears that there is no way of knowing that price will stop and post the day low at the 2nd standard deviation band, the daily Range Deviation Bands can often mark the extreme point for the day (see fig. 40). A key advantage of such a combination of methods is that it helps you to keep a cool head regardless of the volatility. You simply select the timeframe that reflects your trading style and then cross reference to the daily extremes.

Figure 39:
Eurodollars - a typical trading day

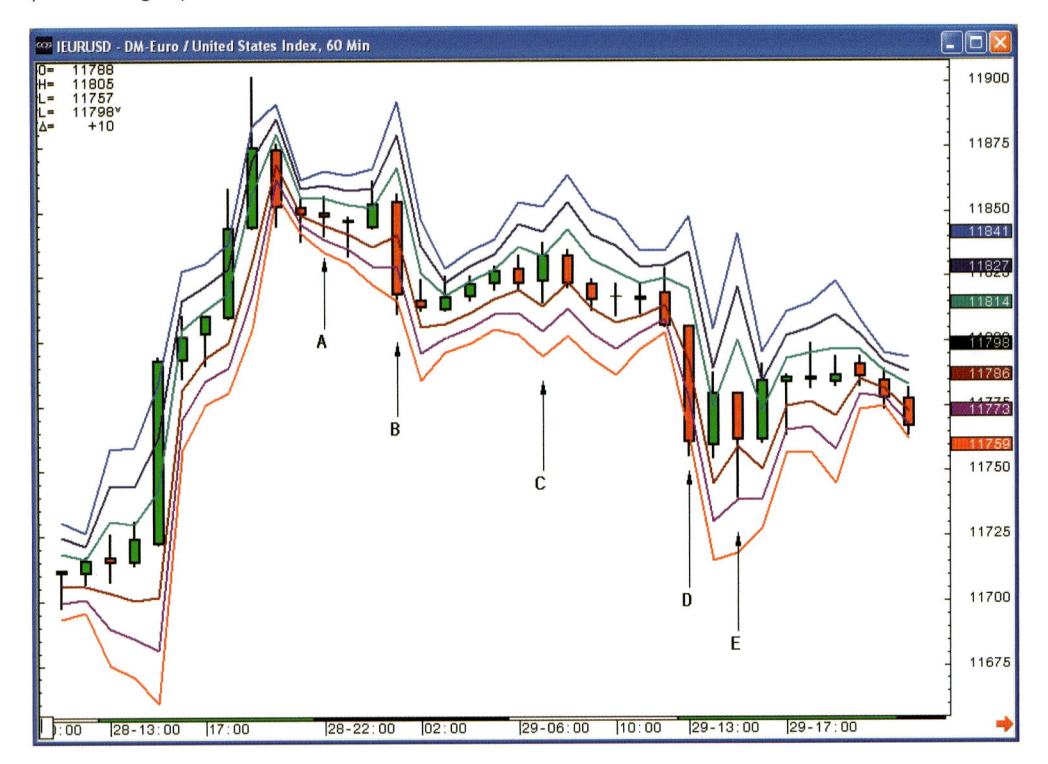

Figure 40:
Linking the time of day with historical extremes can mark the day's highs and lows

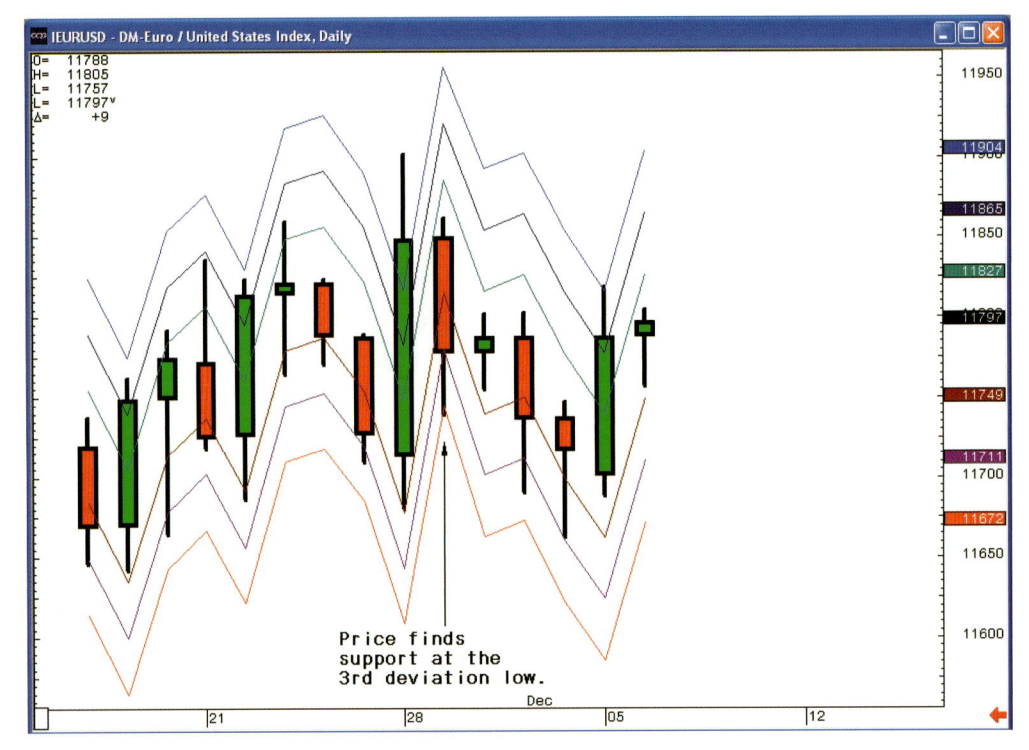

Price finds support at the 3rd deviation low.

38

Bonds - a case study on the same day

As stated previously, Bond markets display similar repeatable patterns. Bunds on the same day highlight this phenomenon and also provide an insight into how, when directional moves begin, the next bar's reactions can provide low-risk entry points. [It is especially prevalent if connected to some of the methods referred to in the Market Profile section.]

29 November 2005 is a day trader's nightmare! There are no fewer than three separate inflation numbers between 7.45 a.m. and 9.00 a.m. At 9.10 a.m. an ECB source says rates may peak at 2.75% by the end of 2006, and to cap it all the OECD produces its monthly report at 10.00 a.m.and states that it sees no reason why rates should go up at all in the immediate future.

Just to compound the confusion, there's a comment in the OECD report that oil price may have overshot in the short term. Well, with price having been at 70 bucks three months ago and now close to lowest point since then at 56, the question is whether they have overshot in the longer term upwards or overshot on the downside in the short term. That's before all the statistics from the US on the afternoon of the same day. On balance, the morning's inflation numbers are tame and the OECD questions the needs for rate rises, which is bullish for Bunds. However, with the key durables goods numbers and consumer confidence coming later, will long-term traders commit themselves? Unlikely.

[The concept that long-term traders dictate price trends is discussed in depth later in the Market Profile® section.]

Analysis of the period till 11.30 a.m. (see fig. 41) sees prices trade to and beyond the 3rd standard deviation five times and then reverse. The bar for the period at 1.30 p.m. has prices moving lower to the 2nd standard deviation **A**, but with another number coming out at 3 p.m. there is a chance of another reaction. Price bounces on the 2 p.m. bar to 1 standard deviation up and on the next bar shows a lack of upward confirmation, as price fails to reach one band up and touches one band down.

This is a key tool for understanding whether price is rejecting the previous trend whilst awaiting the next economic number. The 3 p.m. report is bearish and price then moves directly to and closes beyond the 3rd standard deviation on the downside **B**, which is bearish.

Now the market has received all the information the day has to offer and continues to press lower without any meaningful correction. This is where there is a divergence between the momentum in the Euro v Dollar and the Bund. In the former, price was already close to its daily 3rd band. However, in the Bund there is still room for a trend. Eventually, in a similar vein to the Euro v Dollar, price bottoms out at the daily 3rd deviation point at 5 p.m. an hour before the (old) close. The connection between a daily extreme and the time of day creates the low point in the trend.

Figure 41: At 3 p.m. on a breakout, the Bund has not yet reached a daily extreme. It does by 5 p.m. and marks the low

Figure 42:
The time of day links with the historical extreme at 120.01.

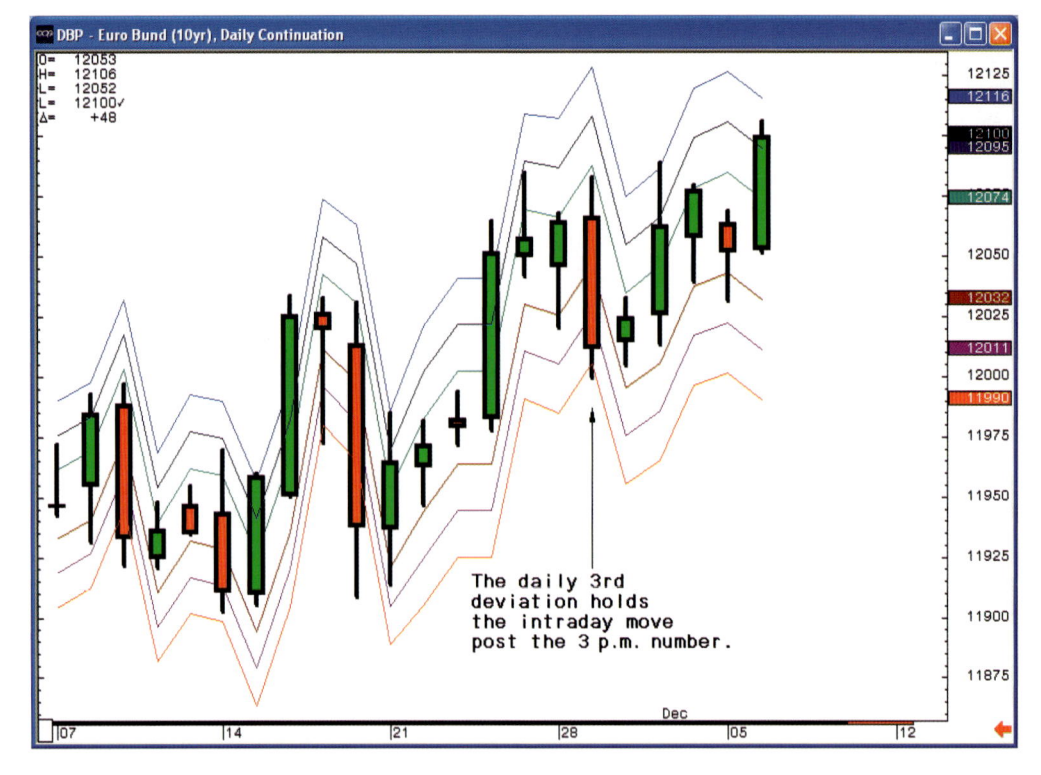

The daily 3rd deviation holds the intraday move post the 3 p.m. number.

Method 9
The use of OaR Range Deviation Bands in isolation
They can provide structure on historical charts in volatile markets.

With the time element removed in the calculation, the study is far more simplistic. However even in isolation they have merits.

One use is for the trader trying to keep a position or for the longer-term trader who can use wide stops and trade strategically. Even then, for the day trader, they provide exact entry points and once the trend is understood they also allow for short-term contra day trades to be executed or provide precise profit taking points.

The 3rd deviation bands as shown earlier on Bunds and the Euro v Dollar indicate how a daily extreme is formed, especially once all the day's fundamental information has been released.

Grains.

A case study in using the daily bands in isolation.
Grains are an area where the huge seasonal changes and different problems with crops in some years mean that range and volatility differs substantially. The fluid nature of the bands means that any new dynamic or increase in range is swiftly reflected in the deviations. The user can decide how sensitive they may be, but all the charts used have a default of 25 days in order to capture the previous monthly USDA report.

Using a number in this area has other benefits (see fig. 43). Analysis of Nov.beans at the beginning of 2005 shows a quiet market with outer deviations at 14 points. The candle at point **B** shows a large expansion of range and price closes beyond the 3rd standard deviation indicating a strong market. Two more candles display similar characteristics at **C** and **D**. By the time price reaches March at point **E** the deviation range has expanded to 32 points thus reflecting the changed dynamic.

Trading Time

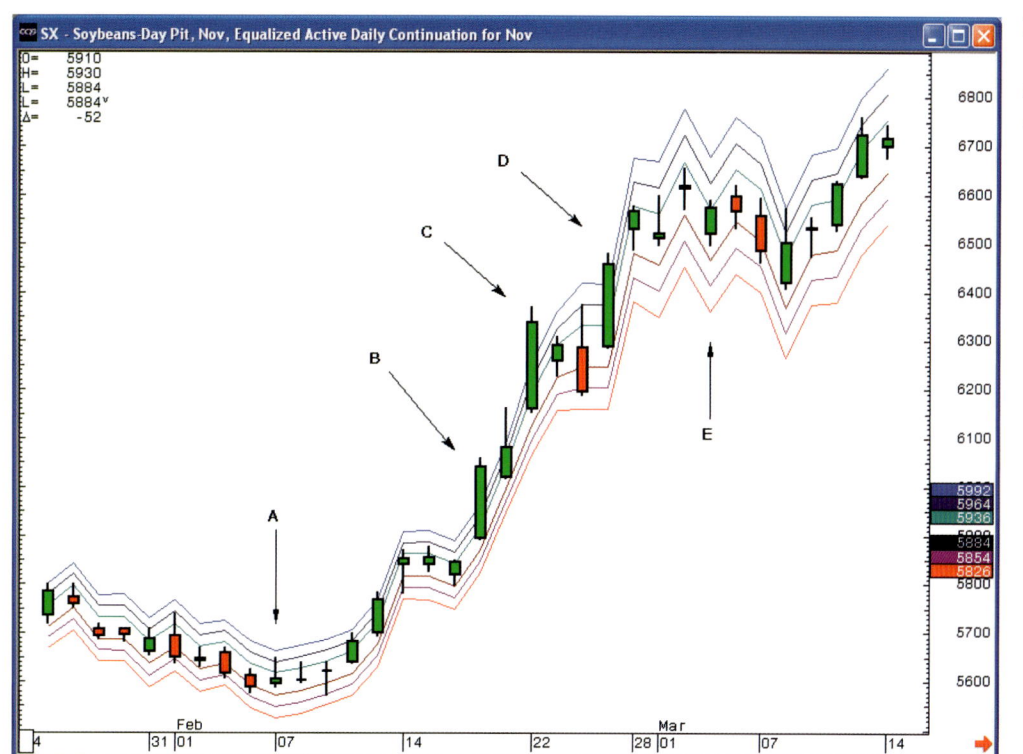

Figure 43:
The 3rd deviation bands mark the reference points

Once grains enter critical phases in the crop cycle, large gaps are common and changes in trend often dramatic. Therefore the need to use the opening for the calculation of the bands is a crucial element, meaning the bands always maintain relevance. This extreme volatility combined with the gaps makes it easy for irrational trading to occur, but with the study, clear analysis can be made, however volatile (see fig. 44). This is where the sole use of the 3rd band for confirmation and end of trend is more suitable and usually means that the trade is held for days and possibly weeks. Therefore only the 3rd deviation bands have been shown.

Figure 44:
The extreme volatility in Natural Gas is quickly captured

TRADING TIME: New Methods in Technical Analysis

The trend begins at **A** with what subsequently is proven to be a false break down as price closes beyond the 3rd deviation down. The following bar sees a swift reversal to the 3rd standard deviation up, which is a strong indication that the previous day's move was suspect and should act as a stop out point for shorts and is really a stop and reverse point. Stop and reverse trades are one of the most difficult to execute due to the emotional impact of shifting from one side to the other. However, structured analysis allows for these trades to be executed. In fact the speed of the change in sentiment is an added confirmation of the bullish breakout.

For the more reticent, further confirmation may be required. At point **B** price closes at the 3rd deviation up but it is at point **C** and **D** that real strength emerges as price closes beyond the 3rd standard deviation up. Point **E** and **F** see price slip below the 3rd standard deviation down but react and close away from those levels, before **G** sees a close below. This indicates at least a temporary turning point in the trend and is an exit point for longs. Price drifts lower before at **H** price closes back above the 3rd standard deviation up, indicating that the trend has restarted. Price just holds the 3rd deviation low on the following day before acceleration comes at **I**. The 5 bars from J highlight a tug of war before the trend switches to down. **J** sees price reject the third band down, the next bar the third up, followed by close on the third down. Two days later price hits 3 up before a decisive break below 3 down signals a new trend

Figure 45:

The 3rd deviation bands mark the points of reference

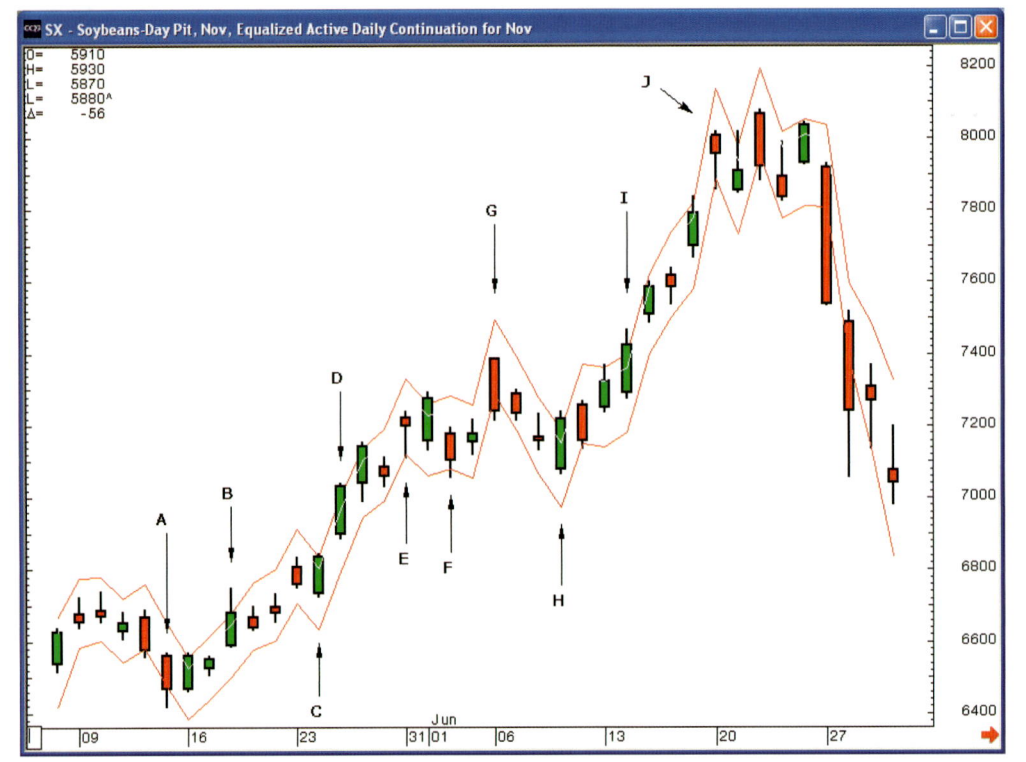

The volatility in silver at the end of 2005 (see fig 46) is another classic example where range expands but the outer bands still provide reference. The rally saw three accelerations with closes above the 3rd deviation high, before a top is signalled with price failing at the upper band and closing below the lower one. The following bar also closes below the 3rd deviation low as longs head for the exit. Price then closes near the low band a few days later but by this time the range is at 70 pts. This is far too wide for most traders if they are trying to manage a position – however, there remains value for those that can.

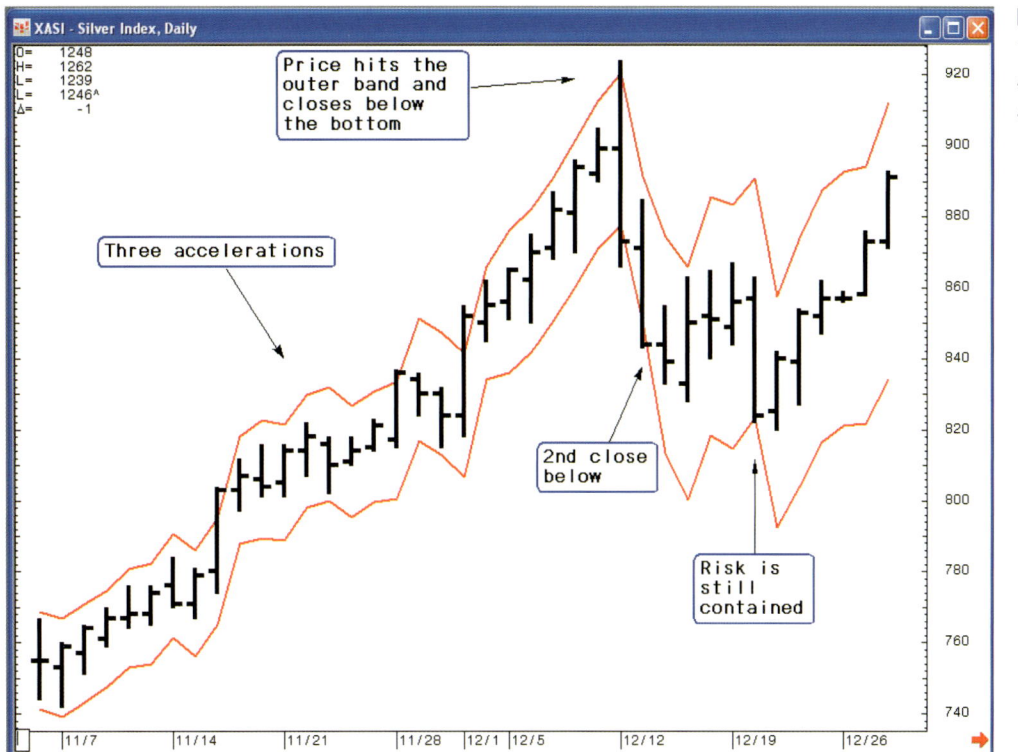

Figure 46:
The volatility in silver uses similar methods

The trader can look to a lower timeframe to reduce the risk. 15 December 2005 sees price hit the 3rd deviation in both the 720 and 360-minute chart and reverse (see fig. 47).

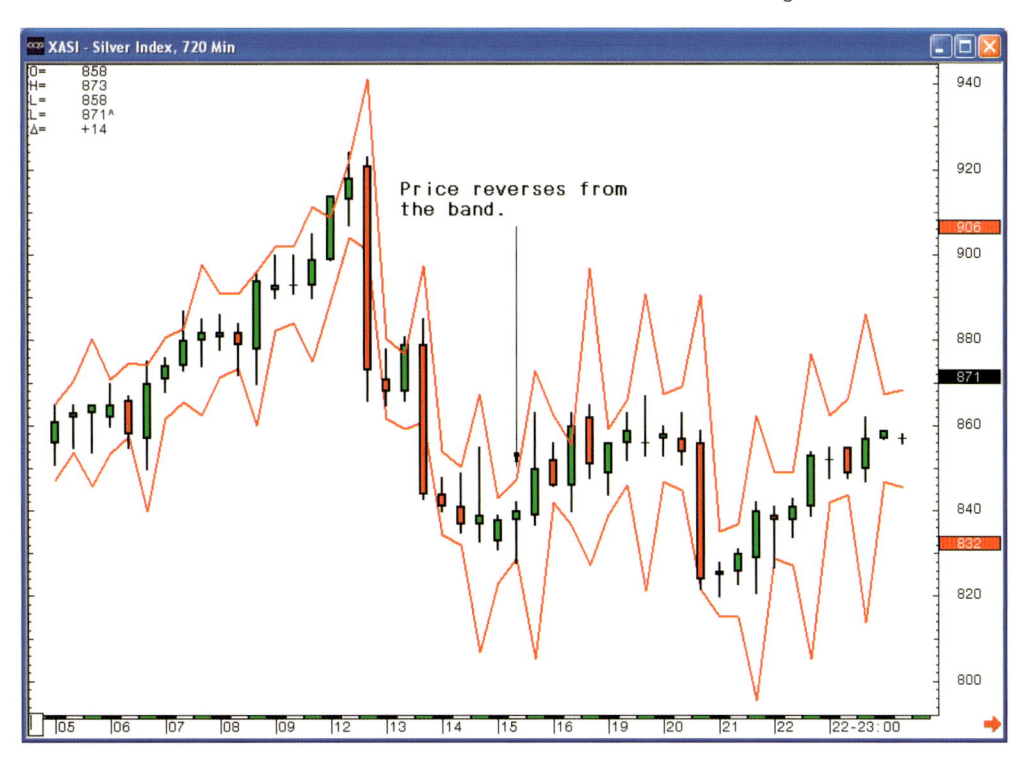

Figure 47:
The half day chart also uses the 3rd deviation

Figure 48:
High volatility means that the quarter day chart is referenced

OaR Range Deviation Pivots

The Volatility Time Bands and Range Deviation Bands, whilst having many applications, do not have any directional bias built into their formation. They simply place deviation around range. Therefore it was necessary to create daily levels that had a bias. These are called *OaR Range Deviation Pivots*. The difference in the calculation is simply that the high bands reference the high of the bar and the low bands the low and then place the three deviations around that calculation. Many times the difference between the high and low bands seems identical to the naked eye but, when a sharp change in trends occurs, it is far more visible. The late 2005 collapse in the Dollar Yen shows how the bands are far wider on the downside than on the upside. The lower the calculation period, the more sensitive to changes in market direction the bands will be and vice versa.

Figure 49:
OaR Range Deviation Pivots have an added variable as they are placed through the high and low

Method 1

The first application is the ability to connect the Time and Range Bands with the Deviation Pivots to create zones of support and resistance. The same Dollar Yen chart shows an example where the 3rd and 2nd levels are almost identical and then a 3rd deviation band halts price.

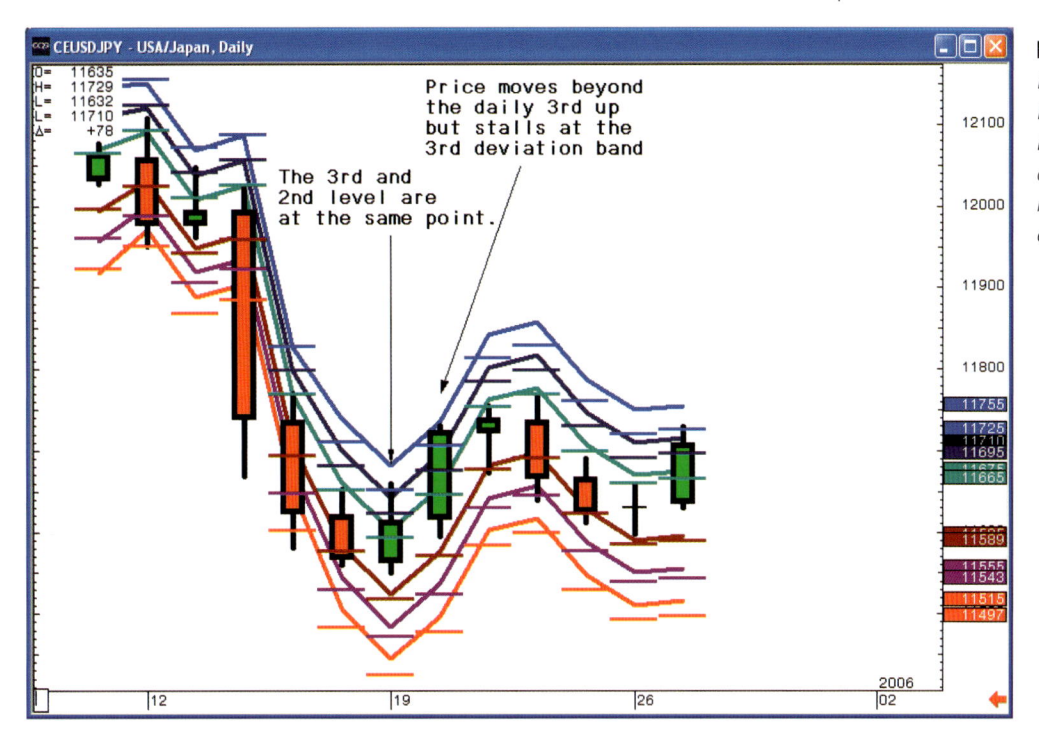

Figure 50:
Linking the Time Bands and Range Deviation Pivots creates zones of risk and expectation

Foreign exchange

Whilst the study has no specific time element, that is not to say that when the Range Deviation Pivots are hit, depending on what time of day this occurs, action cannot be taken.

The first example looks at the Asian time zone on FX markets. With the exception of Sunday night/Monday morning, where occasionally seismic events do occur, the 1st standard deviation level represents a formidable support or resistance, whatever the longer-term dominant trend. If these are in combination with Market-Profile® based supports and resistances and the Time Average Bands, the power increases significantly.

Figure 51:
The Asian time zone provides short term opportunities

Figure 52:
Monday mornings are an exception

[Chart: IEURUSD - DM-Euro / United States Index, 60 Min, with annotation "Mondays are an exception when the Asian opening can have bigger directional moves."]

The following charts (see figs. 53 and 54) show two examples. In the first one price hits the 3rd deviation down on the Volatility Time Bands at 4 a.m. which is also close to the daily 1st deviation down. This provides a low-risk, short-term trade. The second chart (see fig. 54) shows an example where no statistics are coming out that morning and price approaches its 3rd deviation high on the Volatility Time Bands at 9 a.m., which is close to the daily 1st deviation level. This proves to be the high of the day and is a short-term opportunity.

Figure 53:
The Asian time zone

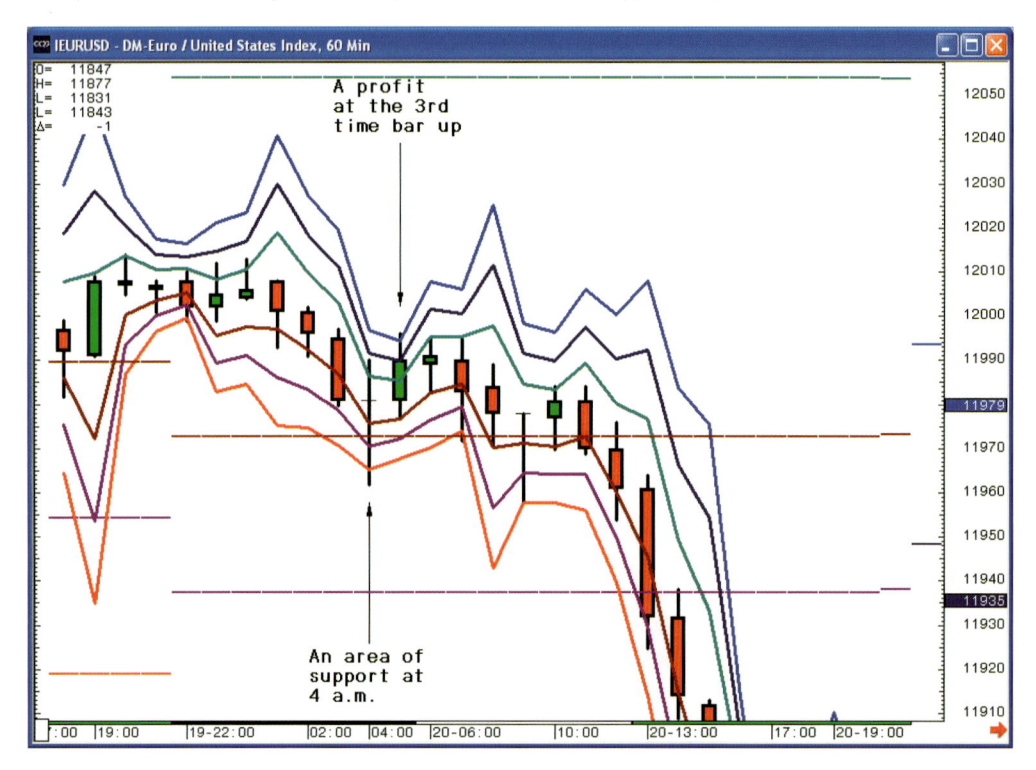

[Chart: IEURUSD - DM-Euro / United States Index, 60 Min, with annotations "A profit at the 3rd time bar up" and "An area of support at 4 a.m."]

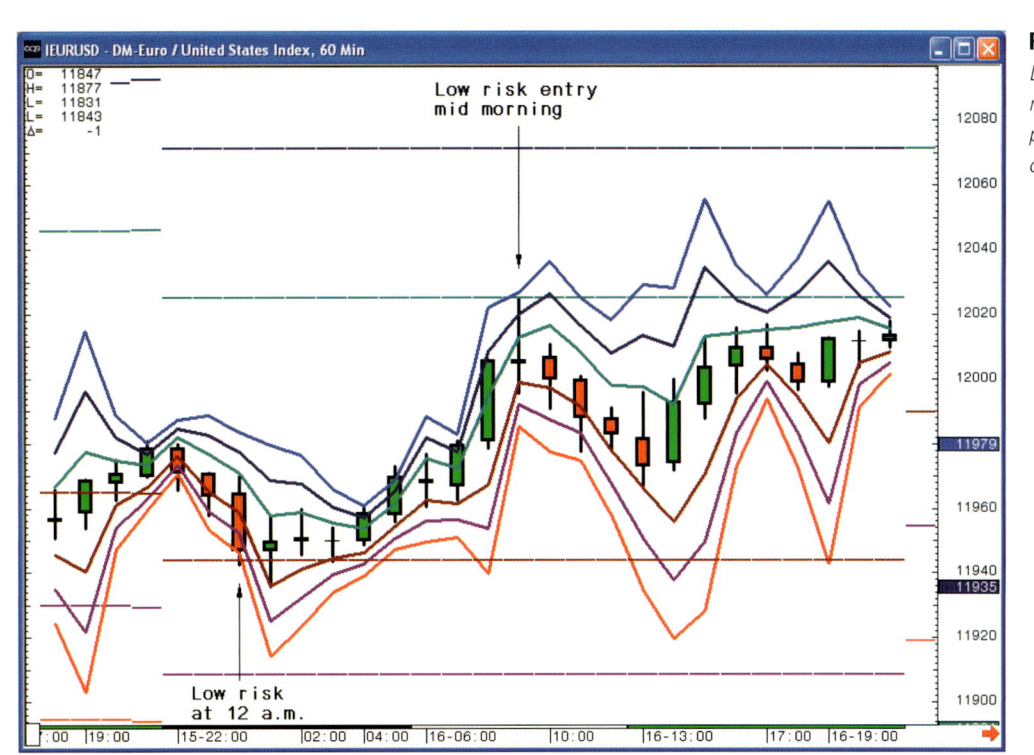

Figure 54:
London's morning also provides opportunities

Stocks

Stocks display different characteristics. While the theory of gaps is the same as for the previous study mentioned, stocks are much more likely to be influenced by news events specific to it. This means that when price goes beyond the 3rd daily band, without there having been a gap, this could be the beginning of a new trend, as mentioned in the examples on the Range Deviation Bands.

The breakout theory is the same but upside breakouts can occur more often, especially if price has been in a strong downtrend, which would mean that the Deviation Pivots that reference the highs would be far narrower than the Range Deviation Bands.

It is also important to consider using a much longer length of range as statements are normally only on a quarterly basis. At least a 200-day range should be used. The examples here use 400 days to cover 8 quarters of events. This is important as in nearly all cases it expands the bands' ranges to take more of the extreme days into account and therefore qualifies genuine breakouts with more authority.

This is highlighted by some basic tests using the CQG Entry Signal Evaluator. This enables traders to take a technical piece of code and analyze its performance up to 60 bars from the entry. Even though there is no facility to put in stops, it does provide insight into the basic power of an entry point. The accuracy at each point in time is the key feature to monitor.

TRADING TIME: New Methods in Technical Analysis

The table below (see fig. 55) shows the raw signals accuracy taking the S&P 500 from 1995 to 2005. There have been some great up trends in that period, so it is questionable whether the results are encouraging.

Figure 55:
Signal Evaluation. Key rows are accuracy % and the sum percentage at the top

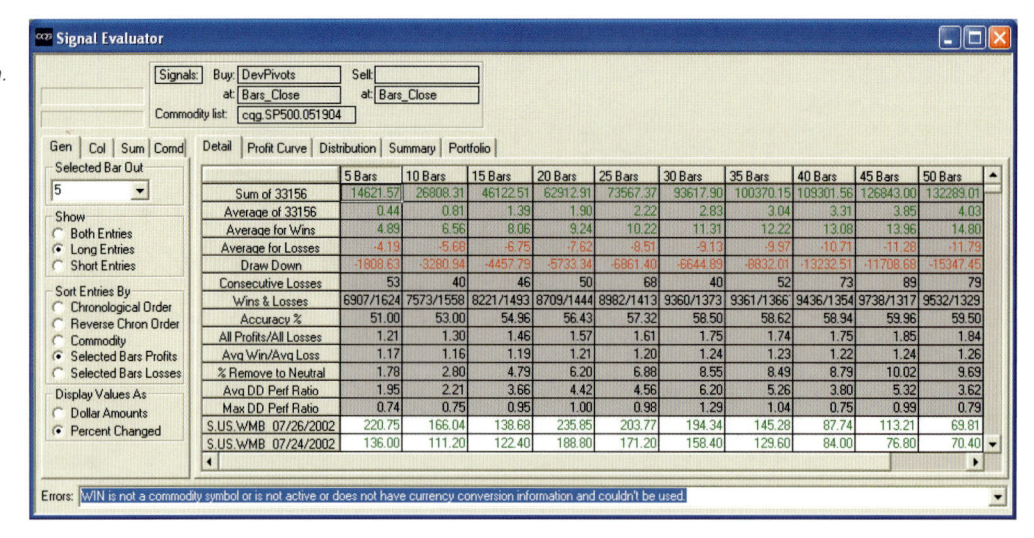

However, the second table (see fig. 56) uses data from 1 January 2000 to 10 October 2001, which includes the events of 11 September 2001 - a vicious bear market. The accuracy is still above 50%, which suggests that it will still recognize strength when the overall market is very weak.

Graphic 56:
Signal evaluation

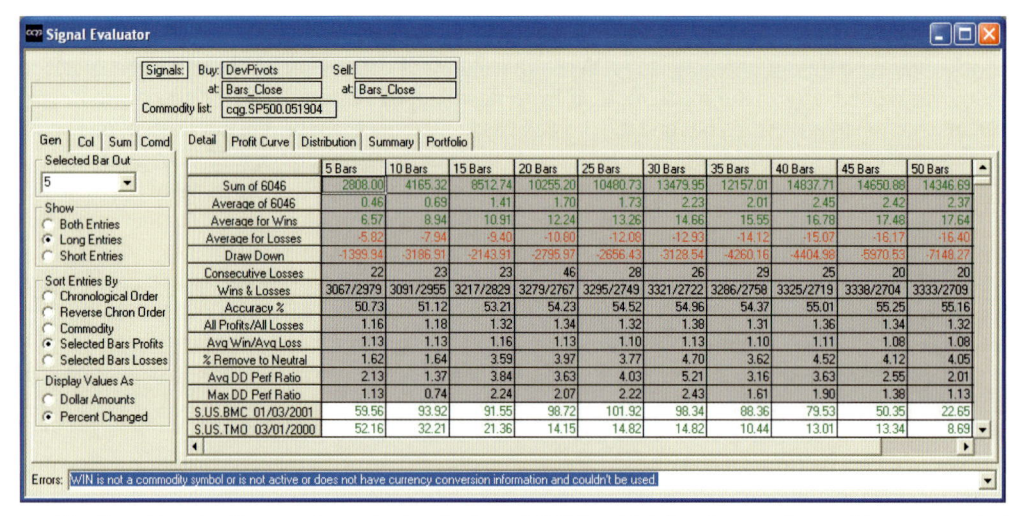

Finally taking the 2 years from the beginning of 2004, which has been a large sideways period with a positive bias, shows the highest accuracy numbers of all (see fig. 57).

Figure 57:
Signal evaluation

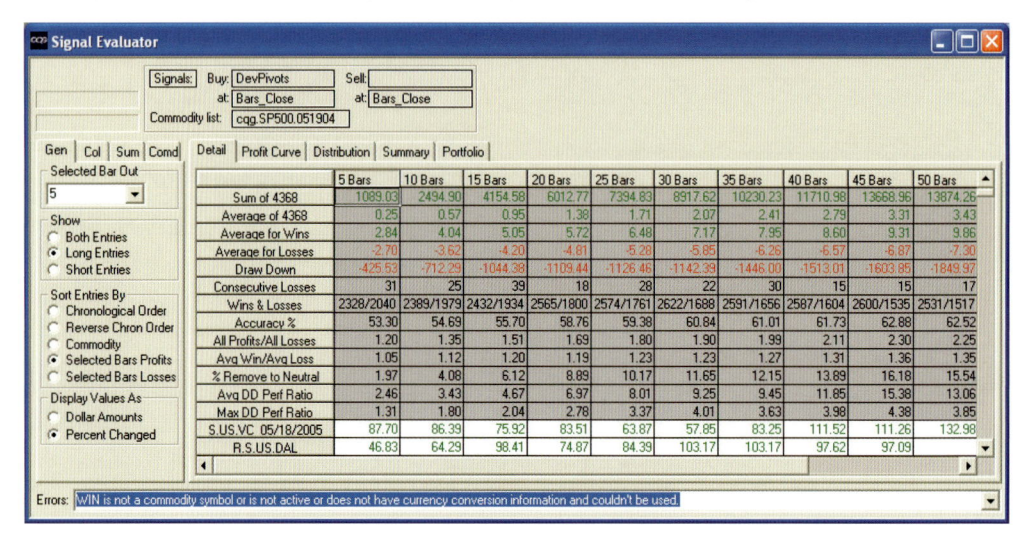

Trading Time

Yahoo shows a typical example (see fig. 58). Price surges for 2 days before the next day when price closes below the 1st deviation and shows the first sign of weakness. A 5% return in 3 days.

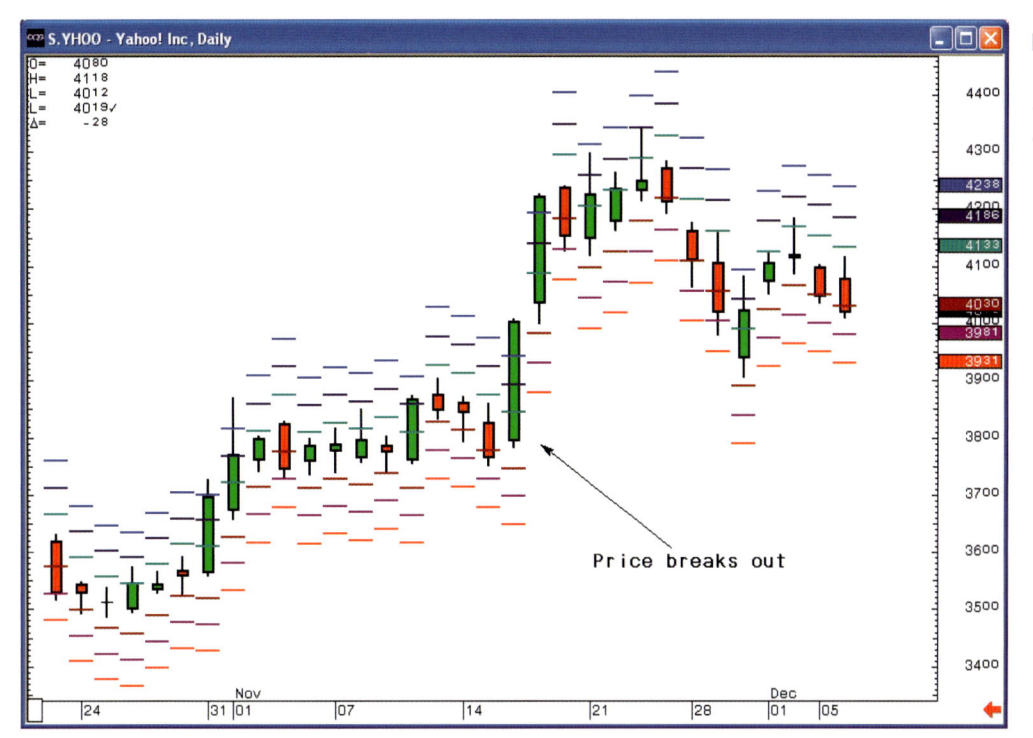

Figure 58:
Stocks - break outs on historical data

Even if the trend does not develop, the power of a one-day move will usually have some follow-through and produce a short-term trading opportunity. Newmont shows 5 trades between mid-September and early-December of varying success, where price closes above the 3rd pivot up (see fig. 59).

Figure 59:
Short term break outs

OaR Volatility Time Average Bands

The first part of this chapter concentrated on the concept of a moving average that adjusted based on the:

- time of the day,
- range,
- comparison between that range and the long-term average of range to create a dynamic average.

However, whilst this is flexible, it does little to help in understanding risk and extremes.

Once again in order to try and understand extremes 1,2 and 3 standard deviations are placed around the variable average, the definition of which is at the beginning of the chapter.

OaR Volatility Time Average Bands versus Bollinger Bands

Given that the moving average changes on every bar and looks at the relationship between range as opposed to the close-to-close, the behaviour of the standard deviations is significantly different from how a traditional Bollinger Band would perform.

The first major difference is that the Volatility Time Average Bands normally do not expand in opposite directions in a strong trend. This is because of the differences in analyzing range instead of the close. This is a far more stable relationship as the differences in range are not as large as the difference between one close and the next. Typically, if the market trends up, this will cause the average to rise and the top bands will expand upwards as well, but the bottom bands will also move higher. The only time that the bands will move in opposite directions is if there is a significant change in range. If the market then pauses and range contracts, it will take a considerable time for the bands to come back together.

Foreign Exchange

The example on the 60-Minute Cable chart shows the basic premise. The bands were close together before the economic number at 3 p.m. The effect of the number causes a huge expansion of range and prices close below the 3rd standard deviation down. The bands expand, indicating a strong breakout. However, subsequent to the initial break the market inevitably calms down and range contracts. From that point onwards the first deviation band down marks short-term exhaustion points and the moving average as a resistance point.

Figure 60:
OaR Volatility Time Average Bands

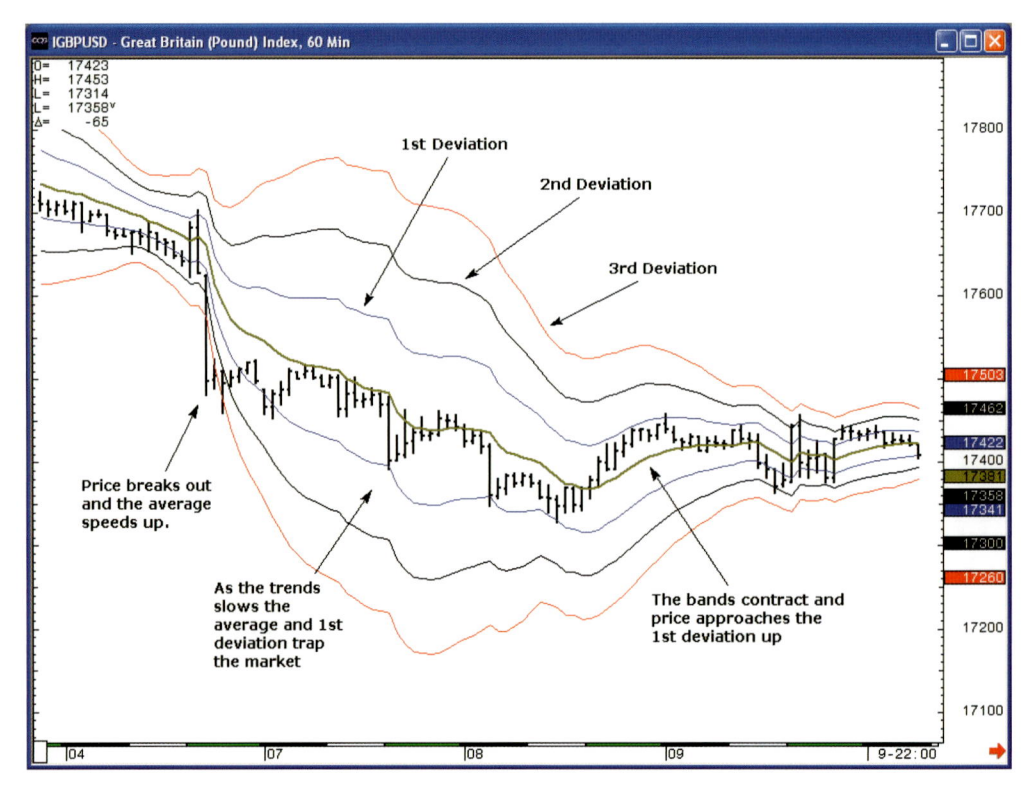

Trading Time

In contrast, whilst the Bollinger Bands flag the initial break, and the average does act as a resistance point, price rarely actually reaches the average. More significantly, after the initial trend move, the Bollinger Bands have two closes outside of the bottom band, which could be interpreted as further breakouts downwards (see fig. 61). However the OaR Volatility Time Average Bands have those lows as supports (see fig. 60). This is where referencing the range rather than the close can prevent trading false breakouts.

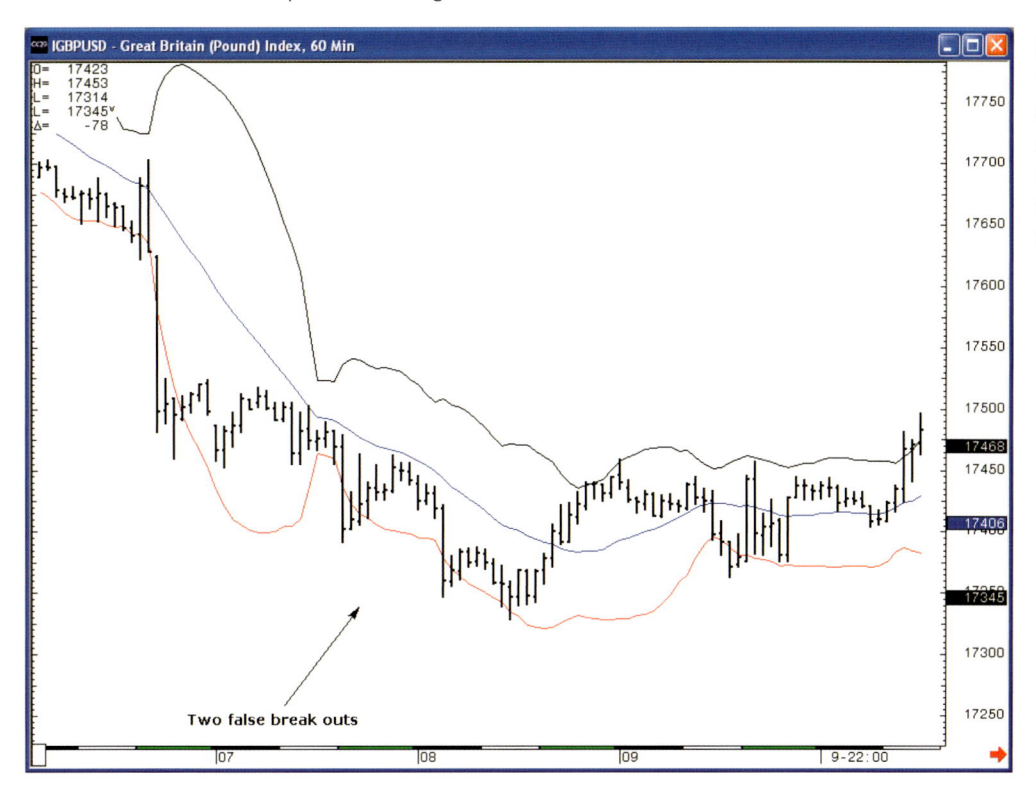

Figure 61:
The difference from Bollinger Bands - the range is a less volatile variable than the close

A breakout is indicated when Volatility Bands condense

In a similar fashion to normal Bollinger Bands, periods when the Volatility Time Average Bands condense indicate that a breakout is due. A key difference is the frequency with which this happens. This is due to the greater length of time that it takes after a trend or an increase in range for a contraction to take place. Bollinger Bands can signal a false breakout as bands expand due to volatility from close-to-close while staying in a broadening sideways pattern. Volatility Time Average Bands typically require direction and expansion of volatility of range, thus adding an extra dimension.

If we return to the Cable chart (see fig. 62), in the subsequent sideways movement at point **A**, both the Bollinger 2nd standard deviation high and the Volatility Time Average Bands have the same resistance points and price holds. However, once again a close outside the Bollinger Band at **B** is still within the Volatility Time Average Bands and therefore prevents a false breakout. In fact price only reaches the 1st deviation down as the mid line is the moving average. This highlights how normal bands suggest a trend breakout whereas the OaR Volatility Time Average bands have those lows as support points.

Figure 62:
OaR Volatility Time Average Bands still qualify breakouts but take longer to contract

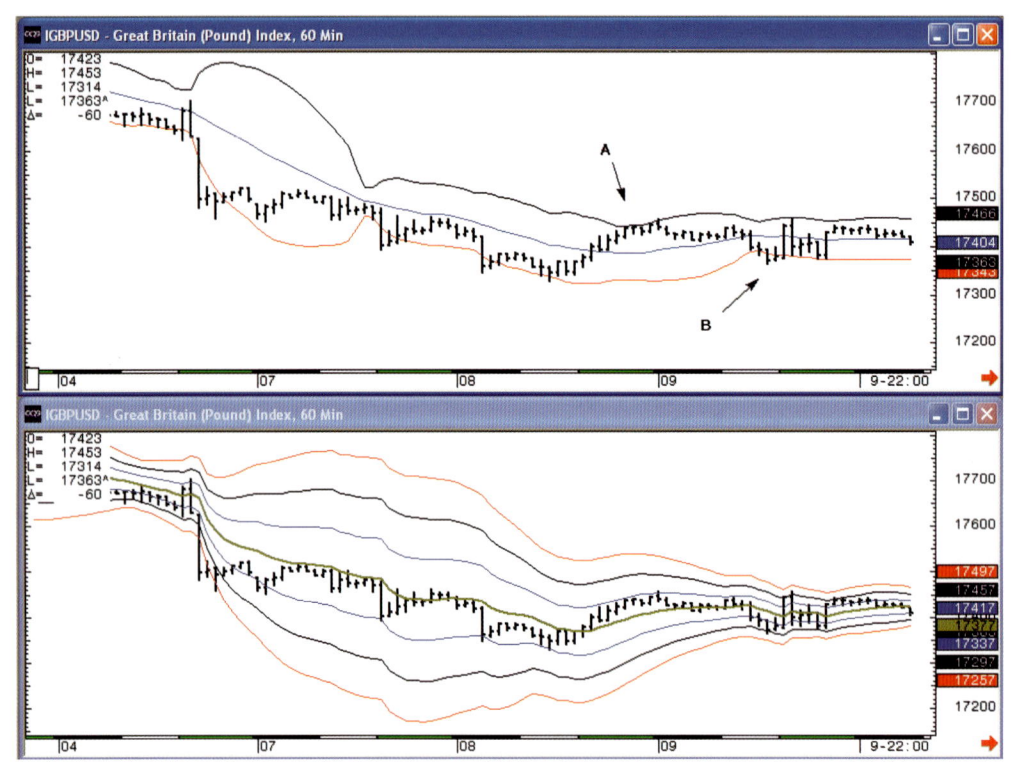

Reference is made to the previous bar. A true visualisation of the bands performance.

Another point to remember in the calculation – as opposed to the current bar – is that by always referencing the previous bar the bands are fixed for the current bar, which removes one of the perennial problems that Bollinger Bands have. They appear to hold price extremes but that extreme is based on the close of the current bar and would have a different value when price was actually at the high or low. OaR Volatility Time Average Bands provide the range as soon as the bar begins and create a true visualization of whether they hold a level or fail.

Linking them with the Range Deviation Pivots or Range Deviation Bands provides such structure.

The Cable chart (see fig. 63) shows that both the bands moving average and the bands themselves provide more sustainable supports and resistances when combined with the Volatility Time Average Bands.

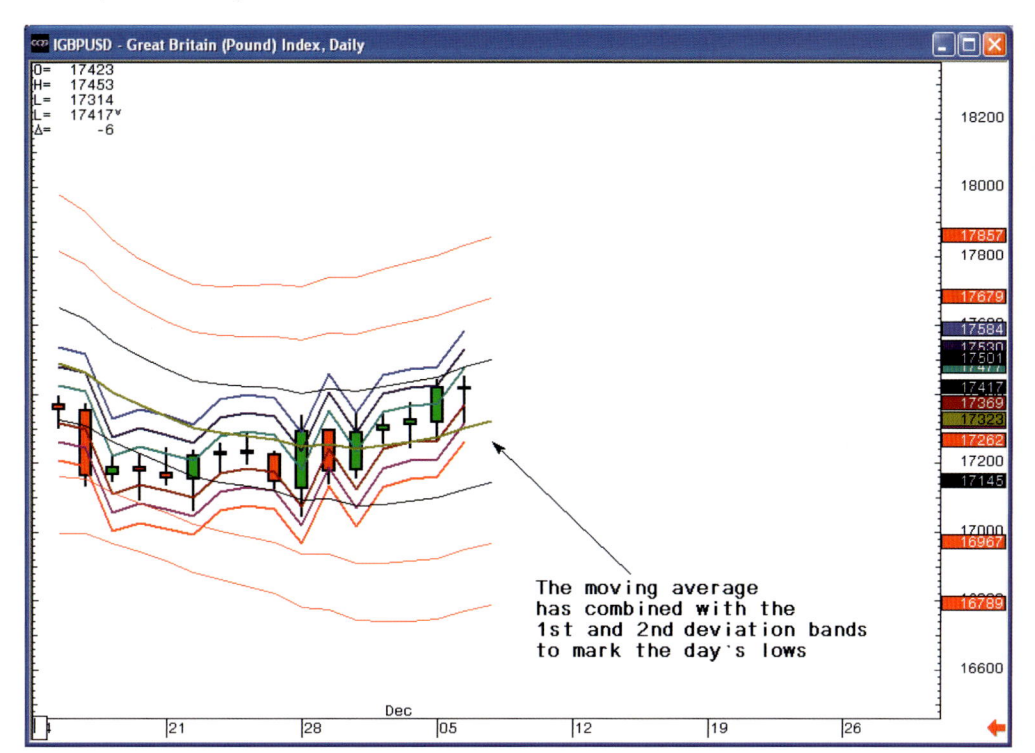

Figure 63:
The Bands in combination with the Range Deviation Pivots

Combination with Range Deviation Pivots

These bands can also be used in conjunction with the Deviation Pivots to monitor the trend and for the risk-conscious the inner Deviation Pivots can be used. If price trends and that trend is strong, we should not see price close beyond 1st standard deviation of the Daily Deviation Levels in the opposite direction. A weaker trend should not touch the 2nd standard deviation in the opposite direction of the trend.

The Aussie Dollar daily (see fig. 64) shows the theory. From the top, prices never touch the 2nd standard deviation up until 15 November. It is time to exit. The strength of the downtrend until the 8 November is highlighted as prices remain beneath the 1st standard deviation above.

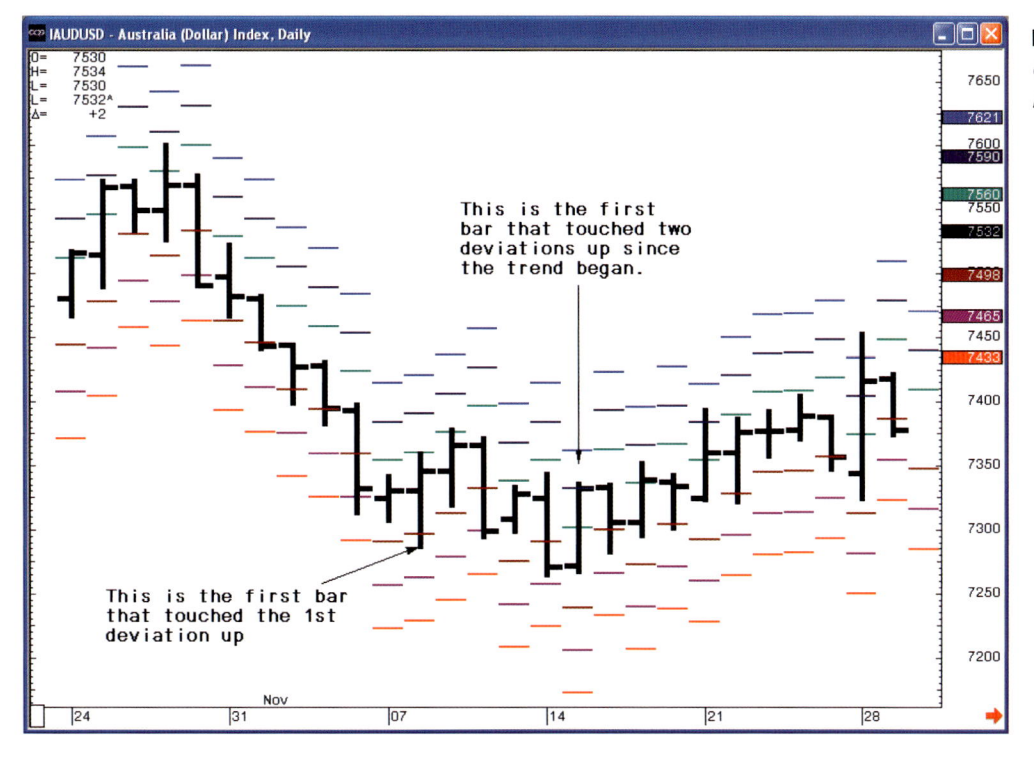

Figure 64:
OaR Range Deviation Pivots

If placed in combination with the Volatility Time Average Bands (see fig. 65) the lows are initially held by the 3rd standard deviation down. As the trend tires, it begins to ebb and flow between the 1st and 2nd bands before the trend finally ends on the bar after the 14 November.

Figure 65:
Connecting the two studies together

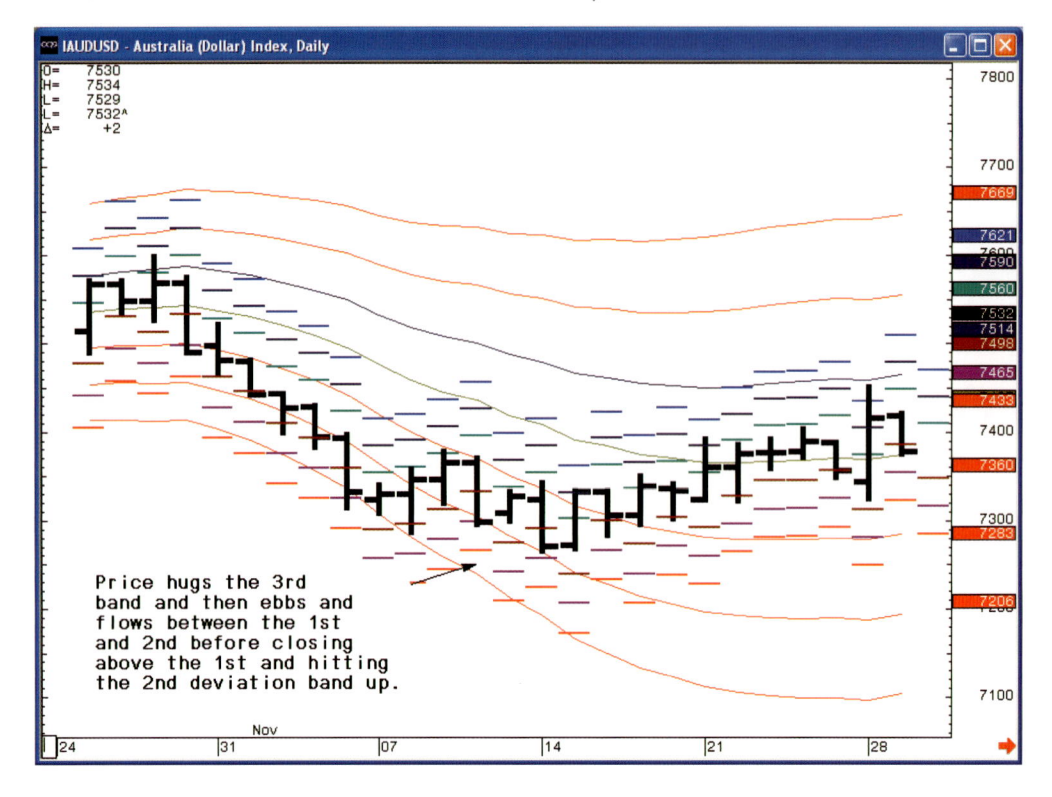

How many Pivots can be touched?

Other relationships are questions to do with how many Deviation Pivots can be touched in any one day. If price has gone to 2 deviations below it is very rare that it will make it to 2 deviations above. Other relationships include how many breakouts beyond 3 bands can occur consecutively. It is very rare even on stocks. How many times can a day hit 2 up and 2 down? This is all important information to day traders and detailed analysis of markets reveals other relationships and patterns

Averaging against the trend based on the time of day

In a similar vein how often will price close significantly beyond 3 standard deviations? Once again it is rare but is often a sign of a very strong trend outside of the potential false moves at the end of the day. Normally averaging against a trend is usually frowned upon, but if a position is at a 3rd deviation extreme, the good trader should be able to make a judgment call on how much more damage can be done, depending on the time of day it is happening. Linking with Market Profile® can assist this process and create powerful short-term supports and resistances

Trading Time

TradeFlow™

Analysing and trading on the micro level.

1. **What is the short-term buying and selling pressure?**
2. **Is volume building for a breakout?**
3. **Connecting the most micro set-up available in the market to scalping methods.**
4. **Using TradeFlow™ to confirm the power of the OaR Volatility Time Bands.**
5. **Creating a confluence of risk and expectation via the various Time-based studies in order to manage strategic positions and identify potential high lows for the day.**
6. **The Appendix has recent examples and more advanced theories as this new Chart type evolves.**

An innovative charting tool has been introduced by CQG called TradeFlow™. TradeFlow™ highlights whether traders are executing trades at the offered price or at the bid on electronically-traded markets. This groundbreaking approach to charting now enables traders to see at an instant the flow of executions.

For example, when the market is in an uptrend, TradeFlow™ bars will indicate that traders are persistently lifting offers, keeping the market moving in the direction of the trend. Many times, just as the market is about to move in the direction of the uptrend, traders step up and show their hand and the TradeFlow™ bars will display this aggressive activity.

During trading ranges, TradeFlow™ analysis will display when traders are selling at resistance and buying support, boxing in the market. The TradeFlow™ bars will show these reversal points.

Finally, when a market hits a key resistance level, you can determine through TradeFlow™ analysis whether the level is attracting sellers and will check the rally, or is likely to fail and the market will head higher. The same can be said for a test of a key level of support.

The Past

Technical analysis in the past has been primarily built around four prices: the open, high, low, and (for the majority of the time) the close. Bar studies, such as the Relative Strength Index, Stochastics and others use the closing price or the relationship of the closing price to other bar values. Candlesticks, bar charts, point & figure and tick charts all use the close or last price for plotting. What is missing, (and as traders we can gain an edge by knowing), is the most important information needed: was the last price a trader hitting the bid or taking the offered price? This is information that could be obtained through the Pits. Following their closure it was lost but TradeFlow™ can assist us once again.

For example, if the market had advanced and moved into a short-term trading range and we could see that traders were continuing to lift offers during the sideways action, we could expect that the steady buying would lead to another up leg in prices.

Or, if the market reached a key resistance level, and we could see that traders were starting to overwhelm the bid with selling, then this should be a point where a low-risk short position could be placed. Never before could we see this action by traders in the market, but now we can with CQG TradeFlow™.

A TradeFlow™ chart

First, the high and low of each TradeFlow™ bar is the best bid and best ask. Time is not a component. New TradeFlow™ bars are created when a bid is reported by the exchange at a price equal to, or greater than the best ask that occurred during that bar or when an ask is reported that has a price equal to, or lower than the best bid that occurred during that bar.

For example, if the E-mini S&P 500 (the reference contract for the following discussion) were bid 1250.25 and offered at 1250.50, the TradeFlow™ bar would show a high of 1250.50 and a low of 1250.25, and a new TradeFlow™ bar would not be plotted until the bid moved to 1250.50 or higher or the offer dropped to 1250.25 or lower. If the bid dropped to 1250.00, then the high of the TradeFlow™ bar would still be 1250.50 and the low would be 1250.00. Whether trades occur at the offer or the bid does not determine the high and low of the TradeFlow™ bar or when a new TradeFlow™ bar is plotted.

However, the width and colouring of the TradeFlow™ does reflect the actions by traders; this feature is the innovative display that gives many traders an edge. First, the width of the TradeFlow™ bars is determined by volume of executed trades during this TradeFlow™ bar; the wider the bar the more executions by traders at the offer or into the bid. Next, the bar is coloured on a percentage basis, reflecting the percentage of contracts bought at the offer or sold into the bid.

For example, if traders paid the offered price of 1250.50 for 400 contracts and sold 100 contracts into the 1250.25 bid, the bar would be 80% green (from the top down) and 20% red (400 over 500 total contracts traded).

Through TradeFlow™, traders can see immediately whether other traders are predominantly lifting offers, which should move the market to higher prices, or are traders hitting bids, which should ultimately move the market lower.

The example below (see fig. 66) is typical TradeFlow™ behaviour. At point **A**, the market has moved to 1269.00 bid, but the TradeFlow™ bars are narrow, indicating that traders are not aggressively hitting bids. The lower prices are not attracting sellers.

Then bar **B** is a much wider bar (increased volume) and the bar is almost entirely green, which indicates that traders are aggressively lifting offers and the market takes off.

Figure 66
TradeFlow Volume study

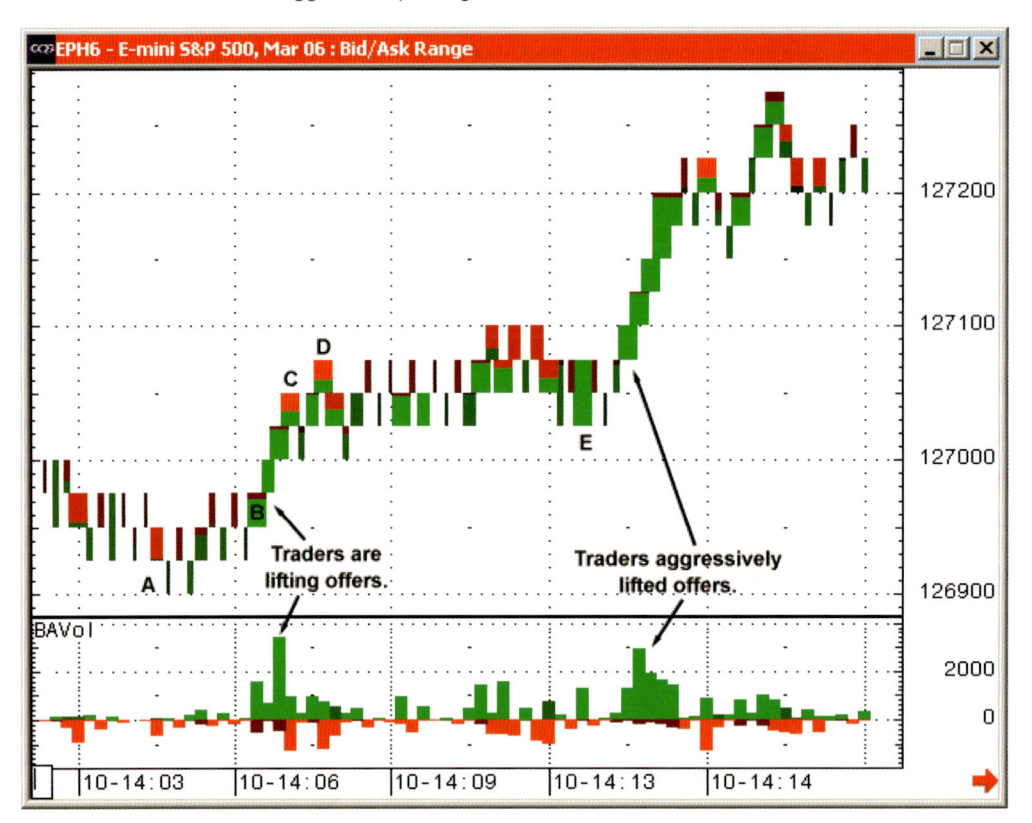

TradeFlow™ bars display on a percentage basis the number of trades executed into the bid (red) or at the offer (green). The TradeFlow™ Volume study shows how many contracts traded at the offer (green histogram bars), or at the bid (red histogram bars).

An additional study is the TradeFlow™ volume histogram, which displays volume of contracts traded at the offer (green histogram bars) versus trades into the bid (red histogram bars).

At bar **B** (see fig. 67), and moving forward, the tall green TradeFlow™ volume bars indicate that traders are lifting offers. This set the market into a solid uptrend, which was capped off by traders hitting bids at bar **C** and **D** (the TradeFlow™ bars are mostly red). At this point, traders hitting bids set the market into a trading range. However, at Bar **E**, the bulls returned and lifted offers creating a wide green bar (high volume signalling good demand) and the market started trending again.

Another example (see fig. 67) shows traders started to hit bids and formed a resistance level. Area A is a point where the market had advanced to 1264.50 offered, and each time the market went 1264.25 bid, 1264.50 offered, traders hit bids (red TradeFlow™ bars and larger red TradeFlow™ Volume histogram bars).

Trading Time

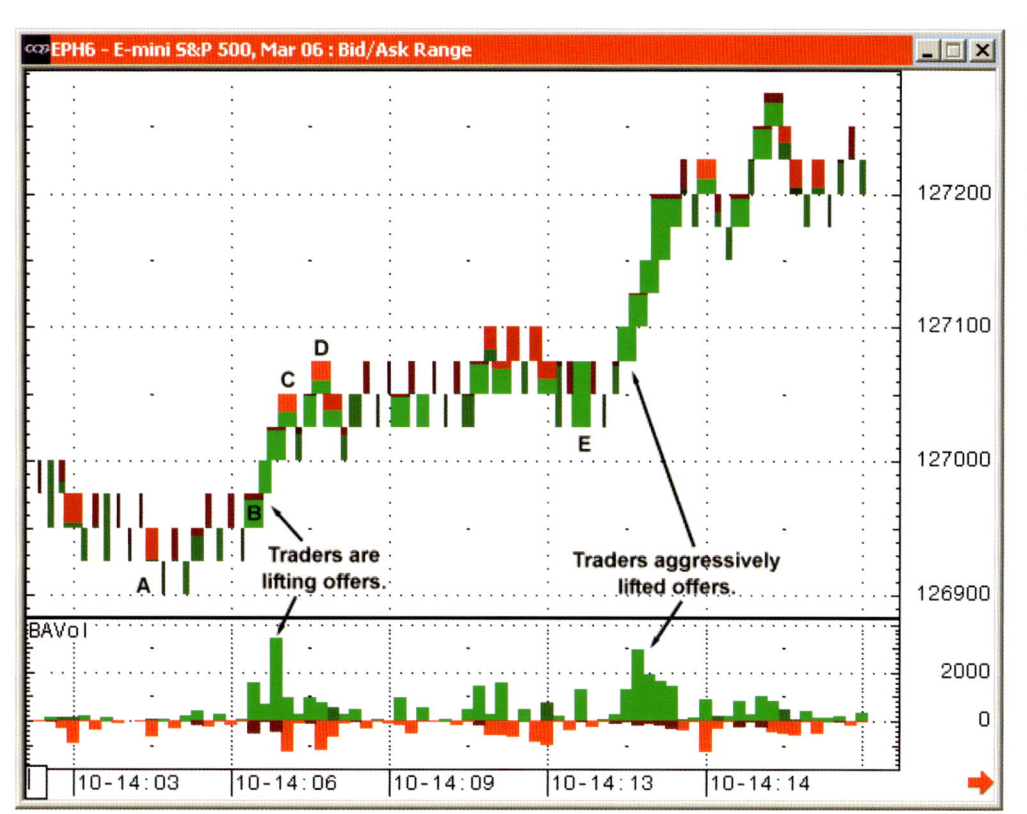

Figure 67:
Trading at the micro level. TradeFlow™ provides information previously lost with the Pit

When the market backed off to 1264.00 bid, 1264.25 offered, trading subsided. In other words, traders didn't hit bids, but they did not step up and lift offers, and then on the final bar for area **A**, traders hit bids and broke the market down to 1261.50 bid, 1261.750 offered. Traders will establish resistance by hitting bids. If traders do not step up and lift offers, the market is likely to move lower. Area **A** is an example of traders selling at resistance. Next, the market moved sideways with very low activity (narrow TradeFlow™ bars) until bar **B** when traders started hitting bids and the market broke through support. This led to cascading selling as shown by the very negative red TradeFlow Volume bars.

TradeFlow™,
Tracking momentum and exit strategies.
Speed of analysis and execution of your plan.

When we watch price action on such a micro level, speed of decision-making has to be at its quickest and execution speed must also be swift. In times of high volume or directional moves just after economic statistics the speed with which bars build can be bewildering. Therefore a firm grasp of strategy is essential. This is where having methods that track momentum quickly, and the predictive nature of the Time-based studies are powerful allies.

Momentum.
Scalping techniques.

The huge number of bars that are being built in any trading day presents both opportunities and problems. The opportunity is the number of data events that can be truly analysed. The problem is the fact that trends in such a micro timeframe are usually very short-lived. Therefore, whilst short-term extremes or breakouts can be predicted, it's essential that if a trend does develop it can be tracked, but at the first sign of any meaningful reaction, the position is liquidated.

Placing a long-period moving average will help stay in any sustained directional move, but as those are rare, it is of little use. Having a short-period moving average runs the risk of being continually whipsawed and giving back any profits in trends.

A 40-period moving average will track a trend, but lose in sideways (see fig. 68). A shorter average such as 14 period will fare even worse (see fig. 69).

Figure 68:
The 40-period average

Figure 69:
The 14 period average is worse

Moving Linear Regression Lines

Moving Linear Regression, also known as the End Point Moving Average, begins by fitting an unseen line to a set of data points. These points are specified by the Price and Period parameters. The process of fitting the line to the data points uses the fewest squares technique. This technique finds the line that minimizes the sum of the squares of the distances between each point and the line.

The value of the fitted line at the last point (end point of the line) for the specified period is plotted on the chart. The set of data points then shifts to the next most recent bar and another line is fitted to these points. The end point of this line and of successive lines is plotted on the chart. The displayed Moving Linear Regression line connects these calculated end points.

Using a Moving Linear Regression line attempts to solve the problem that normal averages suffer from. Since the linear regression attempts to track the best fit within the data, it will track the trend closely as long as it continues. More importantly, it will still have the sensitivity to change direction if the trend dies or reverses. This is essential when scalping. The chart (see fig. 70) shows a Moving Linear Regression line that uses an 80-period average. Note how it still tracks closer and reverses move quickly than a 40-period moving average (see fig. 70).

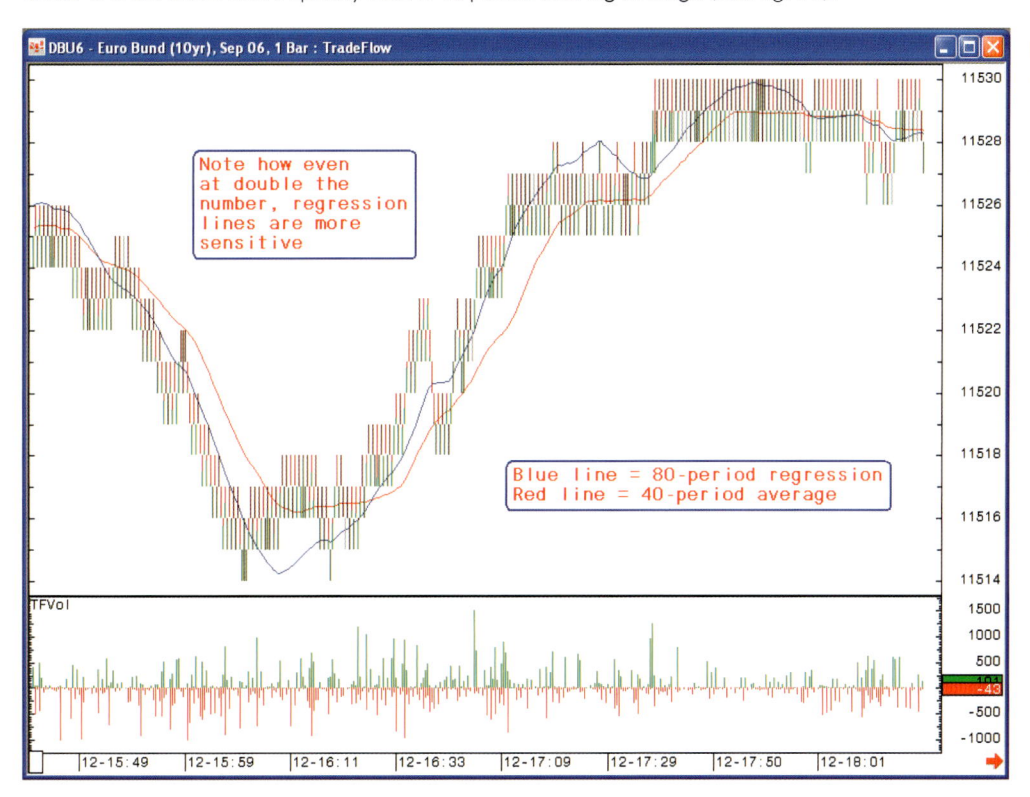

Figure 70:
Regression lines maintain a close relationship to the trend and maintain sensitivity.

TRADING TIME: New Methods in Technical Analysis

A shorter period average compared to linear regression

Note how the regression has a close relationship to a 14-period average in a trend but will take longer to mark the end of the trend. It will also track the trend far better. (see fig. 71)

Figure 71: *tracking the trend*

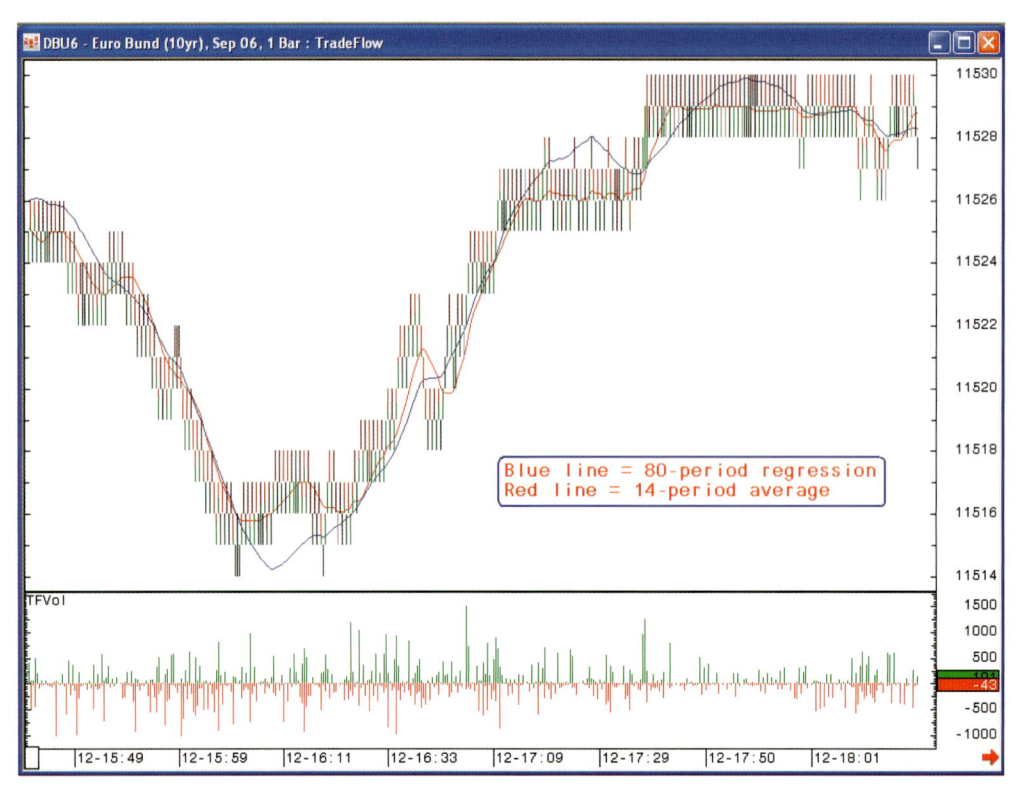

Standard Error bands and Regression lines.
How strong is the trend?

As the regression line tracks any trend to its best fit, the concept of placing standard errors can provide insight into the price action. (see fig. 72). If the TradeFlow™ bar is trending powerfully it should hug the 3rd error band.

Figure 72: *3 standard error bands highlight when price is trending strongly*

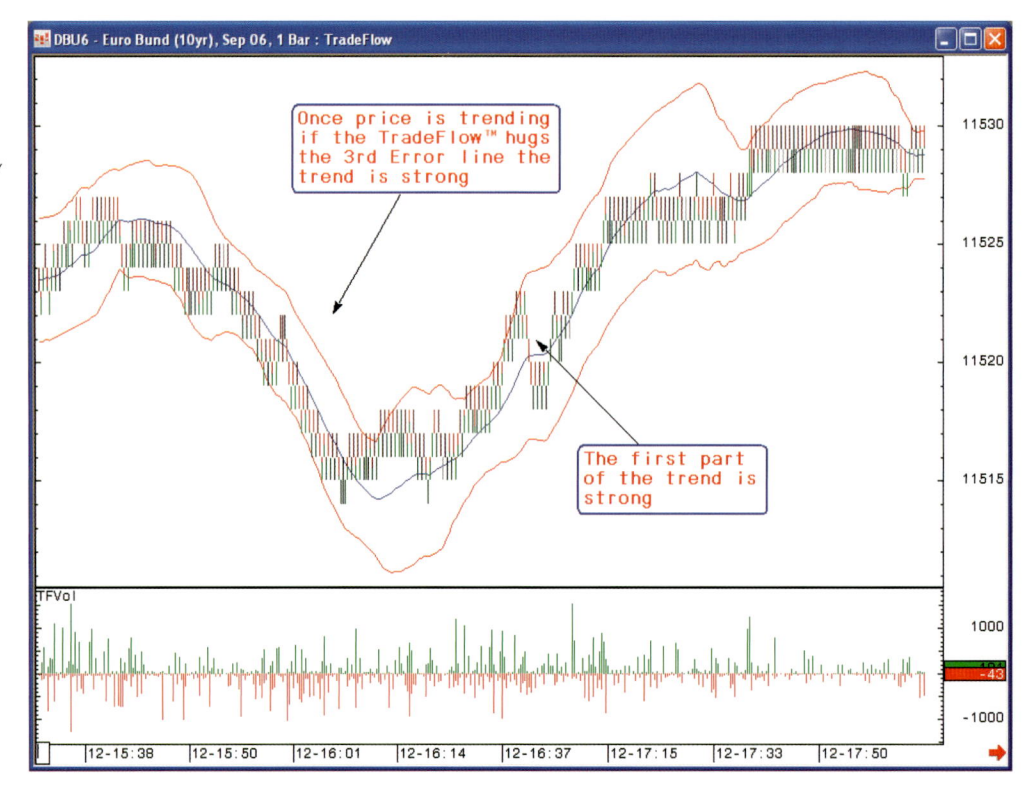

Trading Time

Scalping with the trend with the Error bands

If the trend has been strong and has touched the extreme and if the moving linear regression line is still indicating a trend, any move to the opposite band acts as a support point and short-term opportunity. Signals throughout the day are relatively rare in view of the number of bars produced per session (fig. 73).

Any change in the direction of the Regression line signals the exit.

Figure 73:
Scalping with the trend

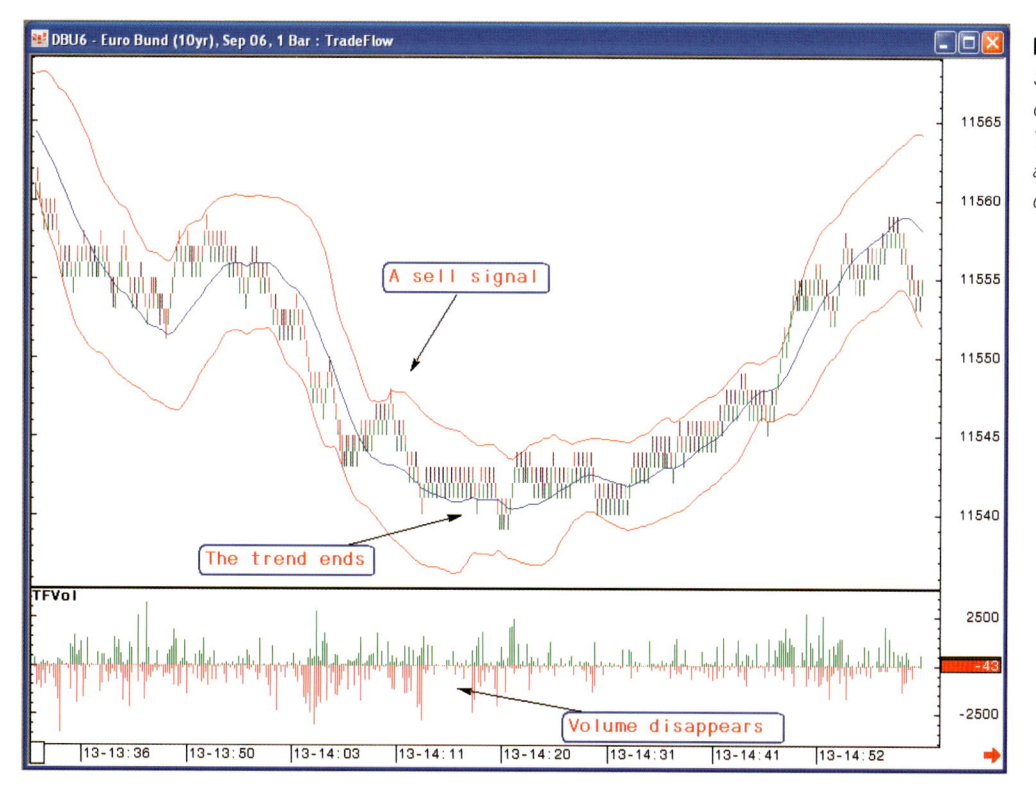

Figure 74:
Scalping with opposite band. The trend ends as volume disappears

61

TRADING TIME: New Methods in Technical Analysis

Volatile Markets

In volatile markets, and especially on Index futures, the speed of movement and sharpness of short-term trends means that traditional timeframe charts, are simply too slow for the trader to exploit the opportunities.

TradeFlow™ charts mimic tick charts but show far more information.

Figure 75:
Volatile Markets

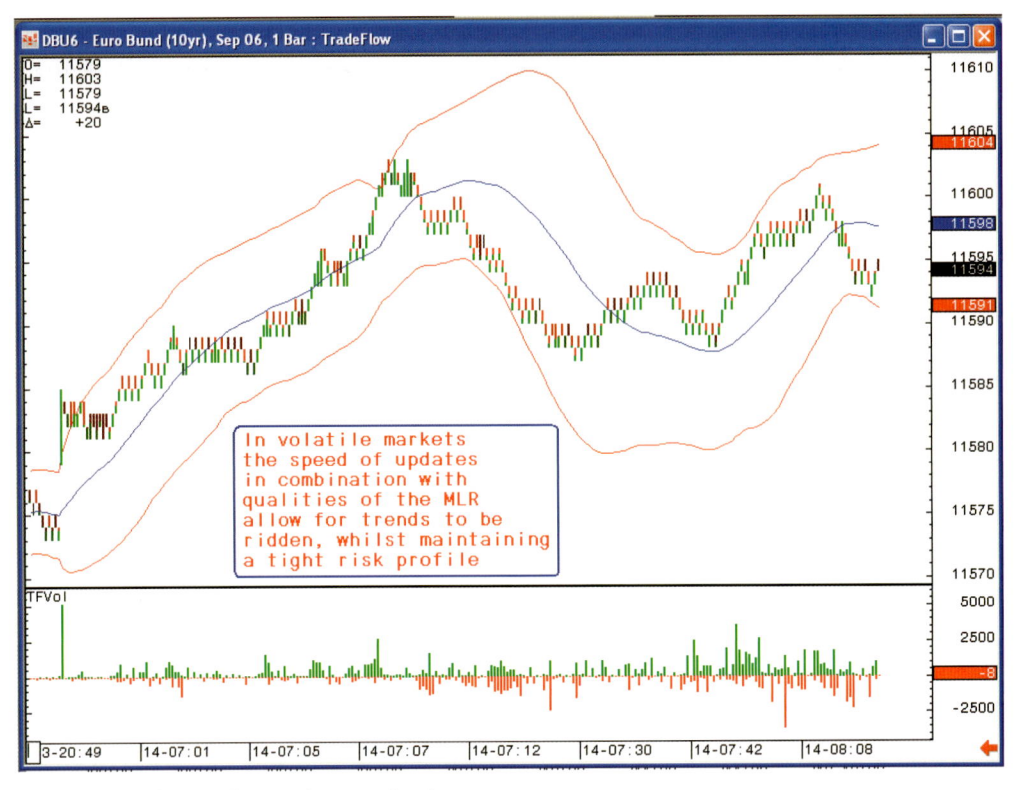

In volatile markets the speed of updates in combination with qualities of the MLR allow for trends to be ridden, whilst maintaining a tight risk profile

Exceptional trends can be tracked

Whilst TradeFlow™ will catch the micro movements, when price trends strongly it can still be tracked. It also has benefits in the immediate movements after economic statistics are released

Figure 76:
A swift trend in the Bund is tracked to its conclusion.

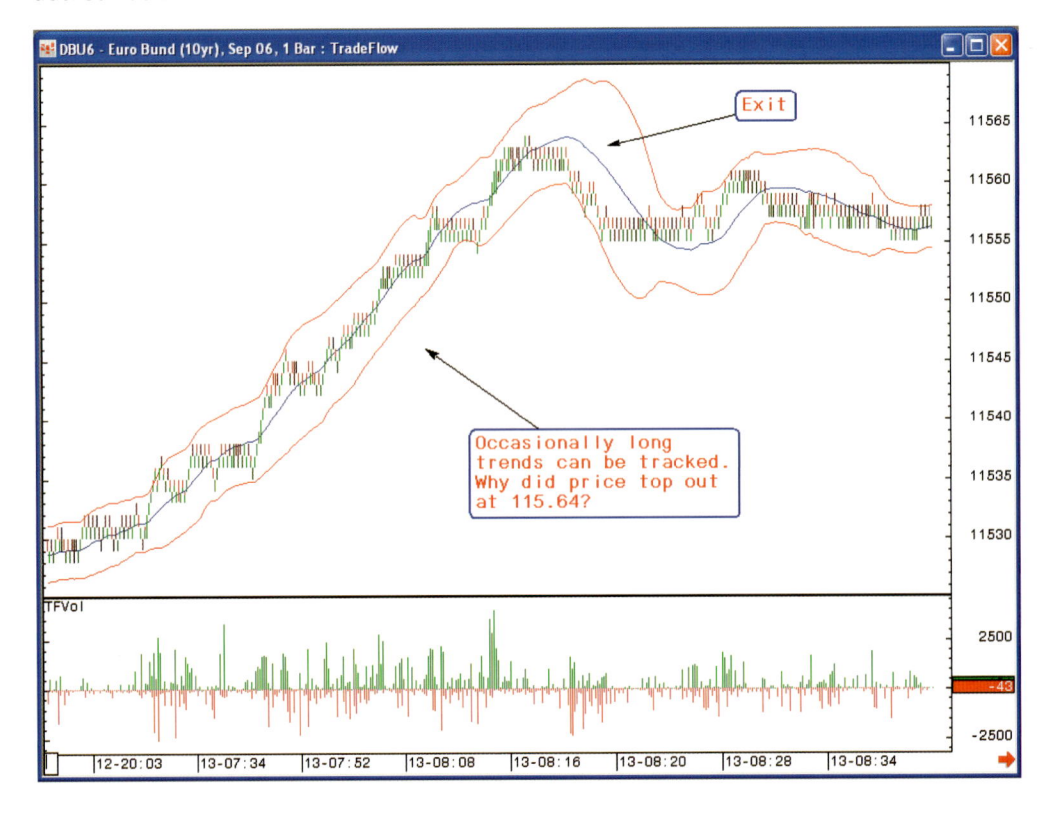

Occasionally long trends can be tracked. Why did price top out at 115.64?

62

Trading Time

TradeFlow™ and the OaR Volatility Time Bands

TradeFlow™ and the Volatility Time Bands can be used in unison in order to determine whether supports and resistances will work. In the example shown (see fig. 77), it appears that the 3rd deviation up on the Time bands is a failed signal. However, the 115.64 level was touched in the first 10 minutes of the hour, meaning there was ample time for price to make at least a temporary reaction.

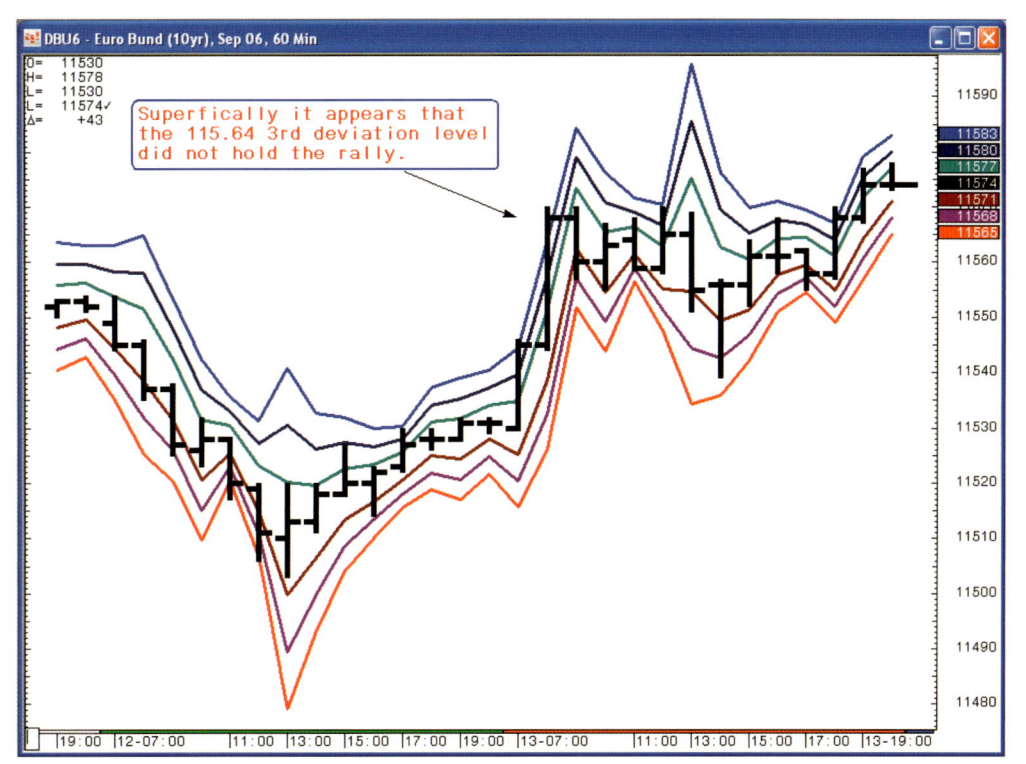

Figure 77:
Connecting the Micro with the Time of day

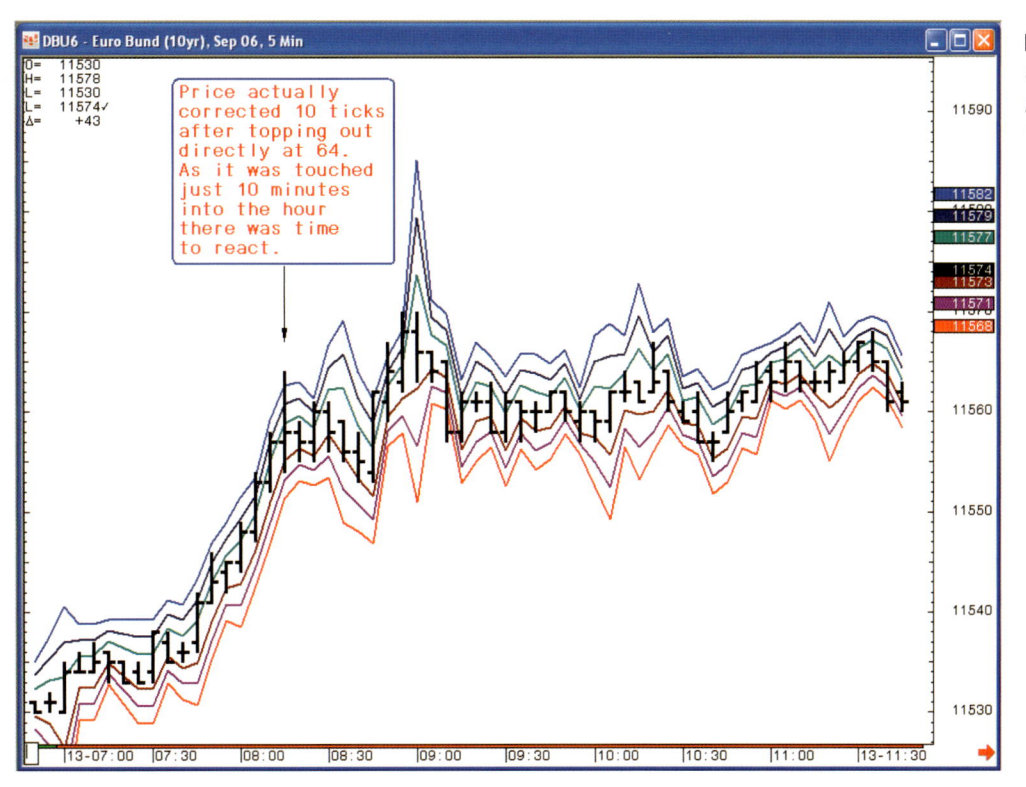

Figure 78:
Connecting the Micro with the Time of day

63

TRADING TIME: New Methods in Technical Analysis

Analysis of the TradeFlow™ bars shows that price has been trending very strongly until hitting the 115.64 point. The sensitivity of the Moving Linear Regression provides a swift exit at a known resistance point. The drop in buy volume then provides an opportunity to trade against the trend for a swift scalping opportunity.

Figure 79:
Scalping opportunities

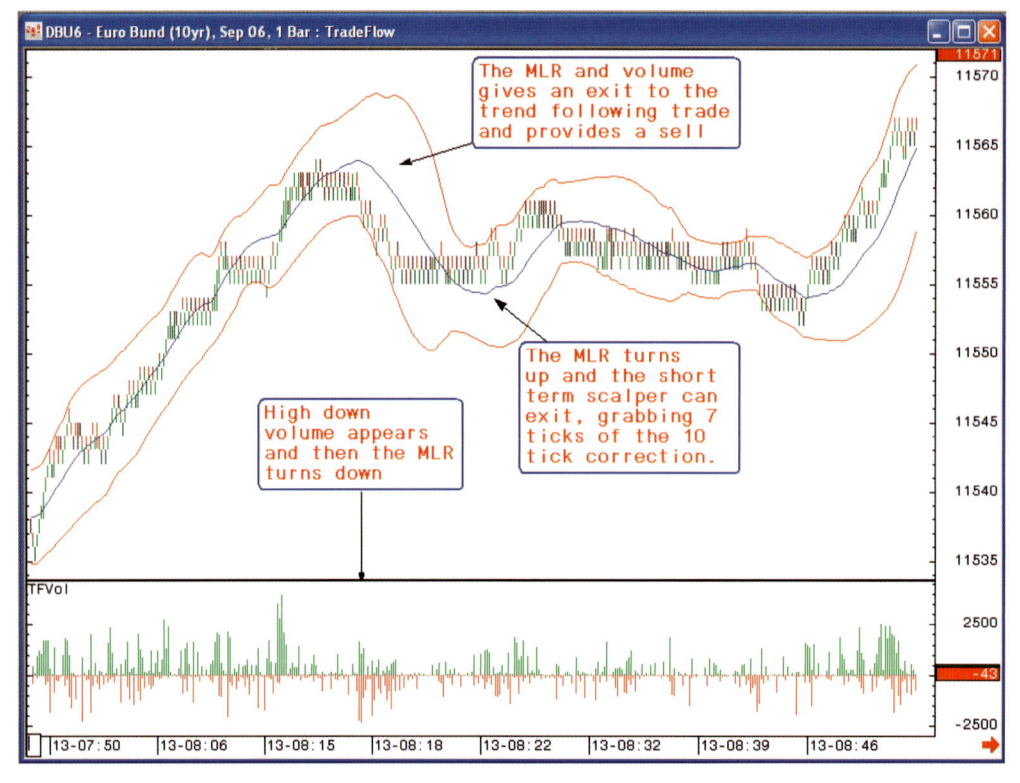

Whilst it is possible to simply use the TradeFlow™ to manage the trade, it is possible to use the Volatility Time Bands if trying to hold a position for a longer period. This is especially true if trying to find low-risk entry points with the trend. (In an uptrend, buying 1st deviation down).

This trade was against the trend, so the trade is likely to be shorter in terms of time. Note (see fig. 80) how the trend died on a very low timeframe when the 5 minute chart closed below the 1st deviation down. In fact, it ended up below the 3rd deviation down for a stronger confirmation that the trend had ended in this timeframe

Figure 80:
Micro management of a trend following trade.

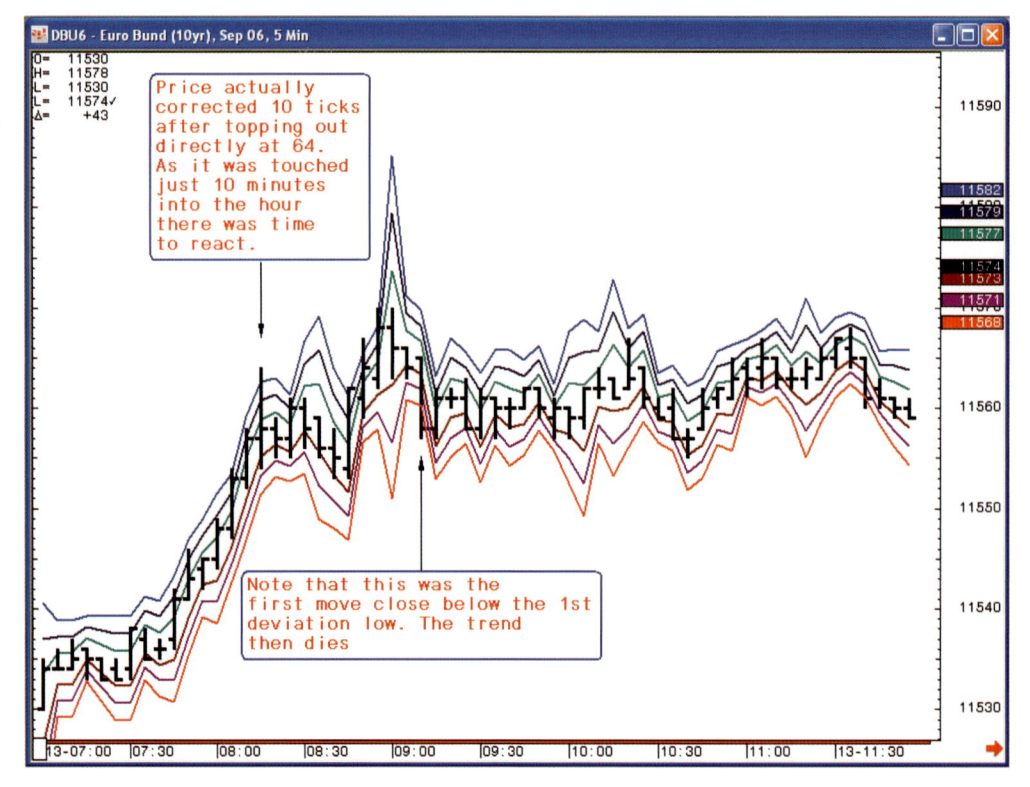

OaR Range Deviation Pivots

Patterns and limits of range for the day trader
There are many patterns and relationships between the Pivot Points and other studies, and there are specific interpretations when connected with the Volatility Time Bands as the time of day and the limit of range within a short timeframe can be quantified. This has particular power to the day trader as extremes can be quantified with high accuracy. In this section we look at a some of the more basic patterns.

Pattern 1
The use of the Signal Evaluator was invaluable in swiftly identifying rare occurrences in any market. The first pattern simply indicated that the market must hit at least the 2nd Range Deviation Pivot down and the 2nd Range Deviation Pivot up.

The first test was taken on 10-bond futures market over a 10-year period. With approximately 250 trading days a year this meant that the test was over 25,000 trading days for the portfolio. I must admit I was staggered when the test revealed that the market only fulfilled pattern on 180 occasions. This is because the Pivots are based on the opening value so are not affected by gaps. Additionally, the in-built skew means that the Pivots are different widths apart depending on the trend and its strength. Therefore, they naturally ebb and flow with the trend and range, which means that moves of high volatility or uncertainty are qualified properly. It does not matter how a market's behaviour changes as the Pivots will usually catch anything out of the ordinary. This was backed up by tests on markets such as Soybeans that have massive changes in range and volatility from season to season. It didn't matter what the range was from year to year. The number of signals per year is similar.

The next tests looked at how many times the 2nd pivot was hit in one direction and then the opposite 1st Pivot. This happened far more often at 1400 times over the same period. Whilst it's impossible to see from looking at historical data what event happened first, this has a huge implication for the day trader. It means that once price has hit the 2nd in one direction and then 1st in the other, there were 1200 times where price never reached the 2nd in the other direction. This creates times when there is a firm grasp of what the limit of range may depend on:

1. the news events of the day and what events are still to come
2. the time of day that this event has occurred
3. the limits of range in the Volatility Time Bands
4. Market Profile®-based supports and resistances

The first 3 connections require input and interpretation from the trader and with the Volatility Time Bands there is a predictive dynamic to what can happen in the next 15, 30 or 60 minutes.

The final connection with Market Profile® is something where the work on support and resistance is done in advance. This means the trader can be prepared and ready to act as soon as the pattern has been completed. This method is one of the key components on the day-trade commentaries that appear under the RanSquawk banner. Please see www.ransquawk.com.

Method 1: Price has hit the 1st Pivot and now is at the 2nd Pivot in the opposite direction.
The Bund shows a typical connection. Price has already made a new high for the trend on the 27 September and so a Market Profile® is merged from that day. The Market Profile® shows that the most amount of the time (control point) is at 118.38. These theories are explained in depth in the next chapter, but the control point is the inflection point between bullishness and bearishness and is always a powerful indicator. Being armed with the knowledge that a powerful resistance is also the 2nd Pivot up makes this a short-term selling point.

TRADING TIME: New Methods in Technical Analysis

Figure 81:
The market is touching the 2nd Pivot up

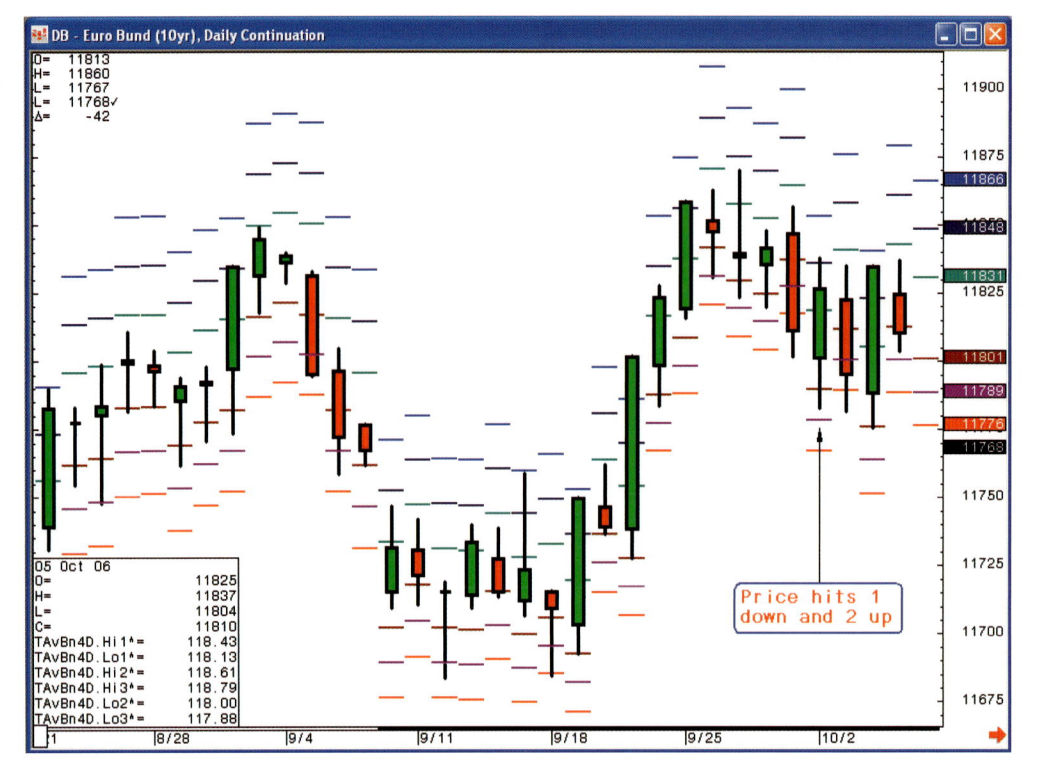

Figure 82: *the control point marks a powerful resistance point as can be seen on the 2 October when prices stall there.*

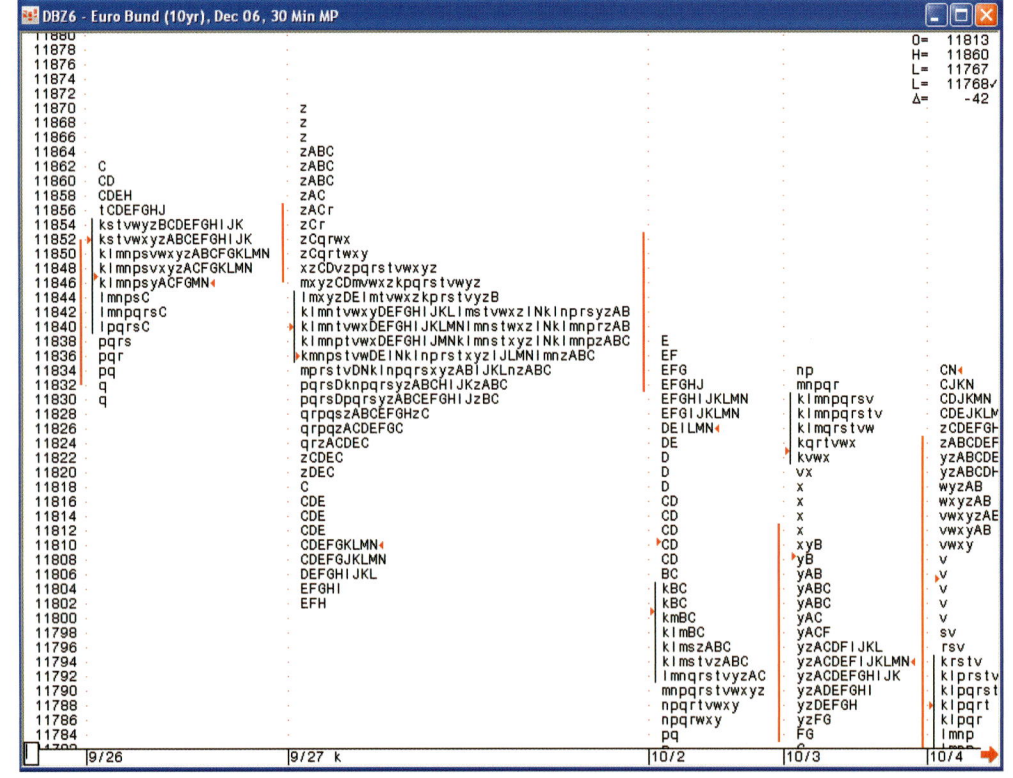

Trading Time

Linking Profile, Range Deviation Pivots and Volatility Time Bands.

Analysis of the Volatility Time Bands creates a limit of movement within the next hour. Multiple timeframe extremes have more power and the bands show that they have an identical extreme at 118.38 on both the 30 and 60-minute. It is also the hour up to 6 p.m. so there is no more news and this time of day is the period where most the day traders exit their final trades. All of this creates a powerful confluence of analysis that the day's limit will be made.

Figure 83:
The limit on the 30-minute.

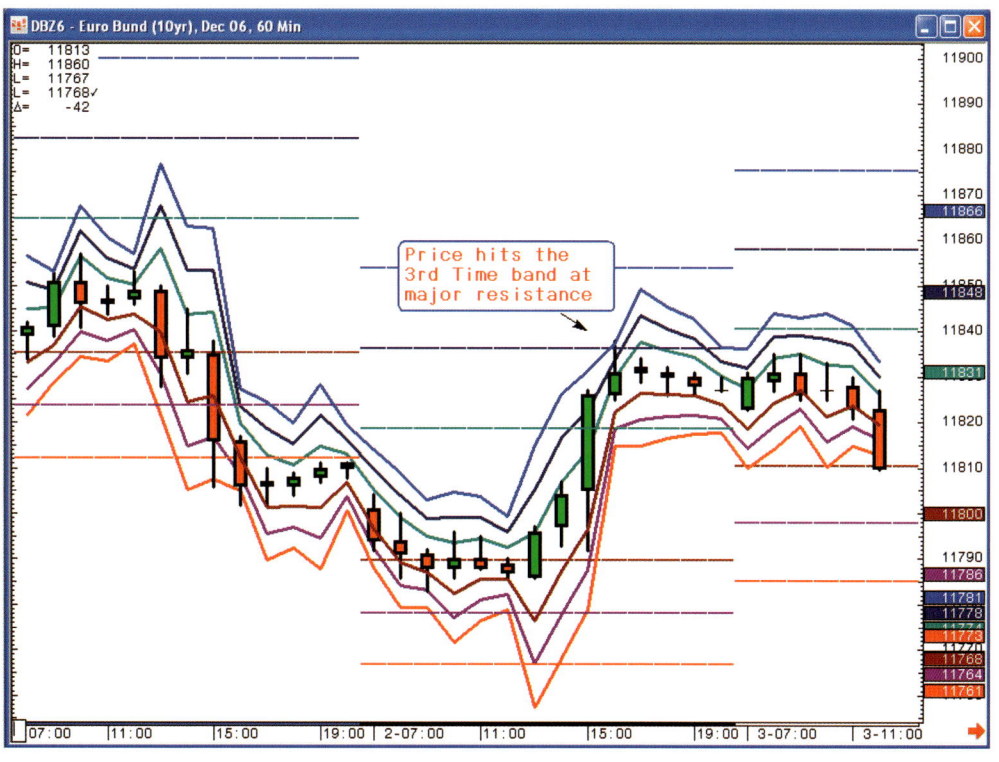

Figure 84:
The 60-minute has the same level

TRADING TIME: New Methods in Technical Analysis

Method 2: Price has hit the 2nd Pivot and is now at the 2nd in the opposite direction.

In this example (see figs. 85/86/87) on the S&P 500 the use of multiple timeframe bands creates the signal. Analysis shows that both the 15 and 30-minute are at 3rd band extreme and at the 2nd daily pivot; the 60-minute is at the 2nd band. With the market in the last hour of trading there will be little time for the market to trend further.

Figure 85:
Linking Bands and Pivots 15-minute

Figure 86:
Linking Bands and Pivots 30-minute

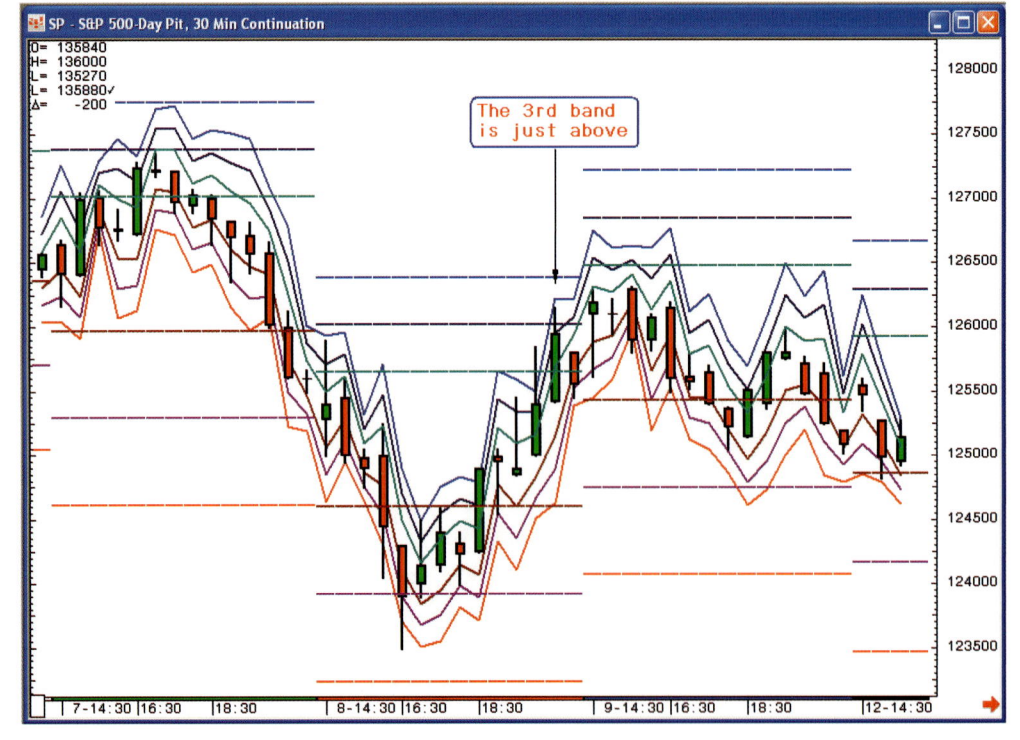

68

Trading Time

Figure 87:
Linking Bands and Pivots 60-minute

What is the extreme of range on big news days?

It is actually extremely rare for price to hit 5 of the 6 pivots which each day creates but the unemployment report is one day where extremes can be hit in both directions as the initial reaction to the number is incorrect. The next chart shows how the dominant trend dictates the width of the Pivots so it may be easy to hit the extreme of the opposite of the trend, but very difficult to hit the extreme in the direction of the trend. Markets that are balanced with no major trend have the most chance of hitting both.

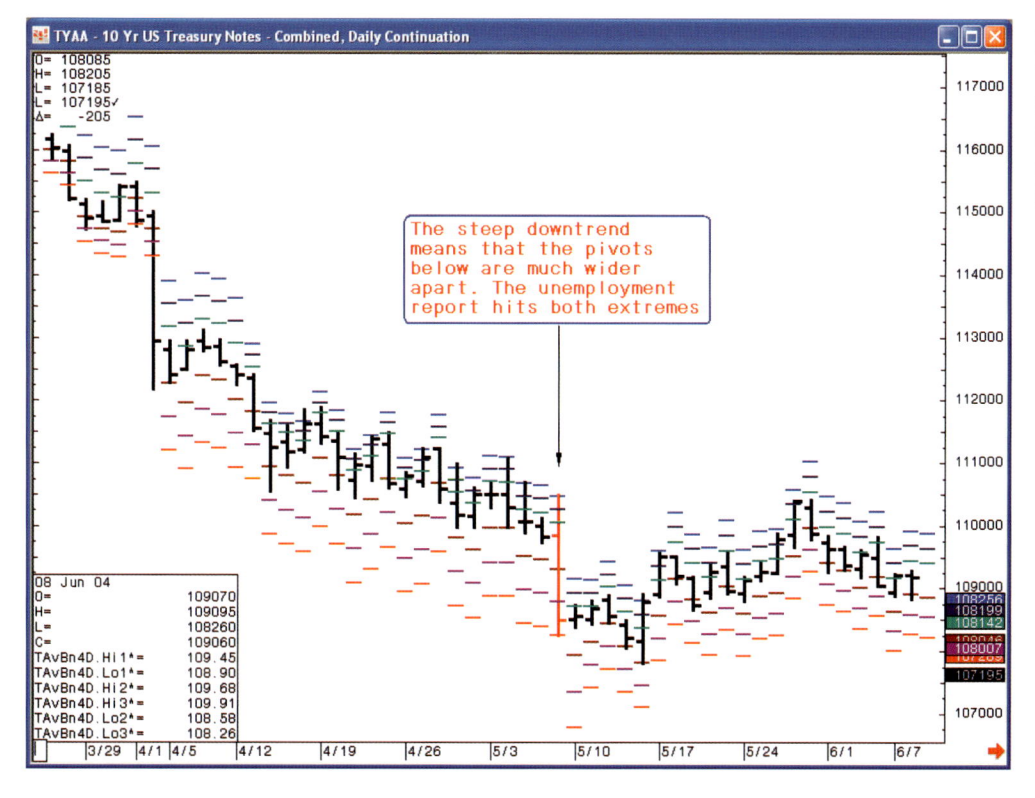

Figure 88:
The 10-year note is one market where both extremes can be hit.

69

Figure 89:
A very unusual signal On Bobl's. Price was just one tick off both extremes.

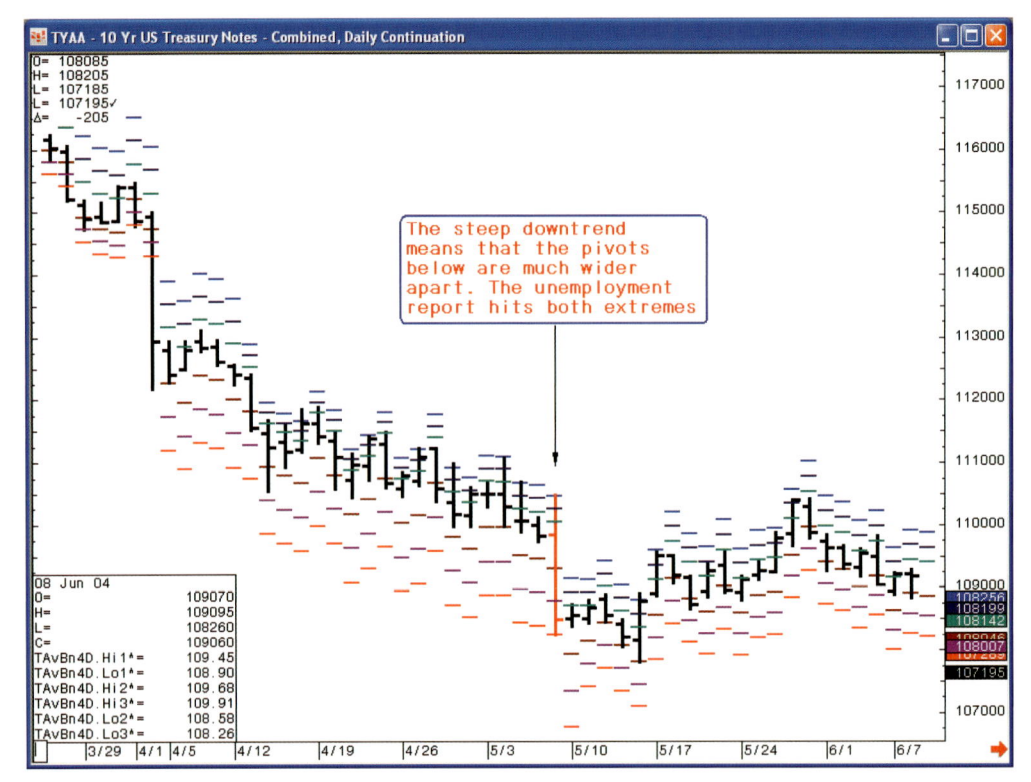

Conclusion

Whilst the various studies, either on their own or in combination, provide many opportunities for different traders, they also can be used with your own indicators of choice including, as we will see, Market Profile® and the other time-based studies that are explained in the rest of the book. The concepts are not just limited to range and time. The principles can be applied to other areas of analysis, and refer to the appendix.

Key points-

- **Indicators based on the opening have predictive powers.**
- **Risk and expectation can be quantified, all the way to the micro level.**
- **Different timeframes can be referenced to create confluences.**
- **TradeFlow™ allows scalping in the most micro level.**
- **Instant decision-making and execution is crucial.**
- **TradeFlow™ functionality and theory continues to evolve and you can contact me for the latest developments.**

2 Market Profile®

What you will learn in this chapter

Scalping

Day trading

Structured plays

Providing targets

Correct placement of stops

The strength of the trend

Optimum points for where corrections should begin
Where long-term trends should end

The timing point for when a trend phase begins

Defining the short-term bias of direction

Pyramiding a core position

Linking with divergence patterns, true measurements of overbought and oversold, and/or the Time-based studies in the previous chapter

The creation of low-risk entries with tight stops

Origins of Market Profile®

This study originated in the grain pits at the CBOT in the early 1980s. Peter Steidlmayer, an exchange local, found that for much of the time price simply ebbed and flowed with the pit traders. He noted that it was orders coming into the pit that dictated when price trended. He came to the conclusion that he needed to find a way to distinguish between the short, medium, and long-term trader, and thus Market Profile® was born.

My own theories came from my time at Fulton Prebon and Dean Witter. I started in commodities and FX at Rudolf Wolff and then found myself trading and broking the alien T Bond contract. The vast majority of the customers were day traders who traded large volume intraday, although they would sometimes take a core strategic position. It was my job to identify the short-term moves, advise clients, and, for some, take proprietary positions on their behalf. Whilst the touch and squawk boxes were valuable tools, any other help would be devoured.

At the time the buzz was going round the bond pits that Market Profile® was fast becoming the greatest day-trading tool. Up to that point, with computers still in the dark ages, daily pivot points were the most commonly used tool. Their dominance in the pit was such that they were successful often because they were the only reference anyone had. Pivot theory remains a common method of obtaining short-term supports and resistances, although the trading structure and implementation are far more sophisticated today. When these levels coincide with Market Profile®-based levels the chance of success is increased.

In the absence of software to record and analyse Market Profile®, the voice broker would give us the range as each 30-minute period completed and I would keep records manually on graph paper. At that time, there was no real theory or literature. It was also not possible to know the values of certain elements such as those associated with volume. Therefore, all the theories and conclusions I came to were my own and were concentrated solely in the area of price action. Volume and time information was noted along with the positioning of the locals.

Manually writing the Market Profile® charts led me to understand how the close of the previous day related to the opening of the current day. In those days there was also a T Bond contract on LIFFE, and theories that developed between the differences in London's morning and Chicago's opening ended up transferring their logic to the current overnight session and the regular trading hours. The conclusions I came to became my road map to short-term movement and this has developed over the years. The study that can now be found on CQG has greatly simplified matters.

Market Profile® remains my first port of call, whatever asset class or instrument I'm trading. The theories now extend to methods of scalping, day trading, structured plays, providing targets, placement of stops, the strength of the trend and optimum points for where corrections should begin and trends should end. Once the structure has been understood, the trader can switch their focus to the other studies used in their technical framework.

It can often be the case that, by the time the main strategic trade concludes, the short-term trades working the core position have made more than if the actual strategic position was simply left alone from entry to eventual exit. Understanding the short-term bias when it's in the opposite direction to the core trade allows the overall entry point to change to a more advantageous position. For the aggressive, it can highlight moments when the existing core trade can be pyramided for a day trade, via Market Profile® techniques, divergence patterns, true measurements of overbought and oversold, and/or the Time-based studies in the previous chapter.

Whilst the ability to shift between short and long-term focus requires practice, discipline and skill, once mastered it provides the structure to actively manage positions. The full range of trading techniques are beyond the scope of this book as the concentration is on time with an emphasis on the short-term movement, although it does touch on the long-term distribution techniques that are a core element in defining major supports and resistances. Even so, the section that follows still provides an in-depth guide to some of the timing techniques. Dedication and effort are required to master the concepts and be able to trade with great confidence. The majority of the theories apply to most markets and asset classes but where there are differences they have been flagged.

Briefly, the connection between long-term profiles and the short-term movements enables low-risk entries with tight stops. The mantra "the chart tells you don't tell the chart" means, however, that the risk/reward ratio cannot be calculated but the exit point is certain.

Linking price, time and volume

Market Profile® has a unique property which helps us to understand price action. It links price, time and volume. No other study does this so concisely and in one picture. The vast majority of existing analysis concentrates on the bar or candle pattern or the level of a momentum indicator based on the closing price. Volume has been the most neglected aspect of all, and attempts to

Market Profile®

create meaningful studies have been thwarted simply because there are so many internal factors that distort the actual volume. Both intraday and historically, the fundamental setup of a market has a huge impact on volume. In bond markets the major numbers such as non farms payroll and the trade deficit see volume reduce in the lead up, whilst in recent years the explosion of statistics at 3 p.m. London time has meant that large long-term traders have little opportunity to assess and trade accordingly within the same session. If they do, they find themselves as big fish in a small pond as the arcades and short-term traders have disappeared by 5 p.m. It is therefore no accident that the often excess movements late in the afternoon provide clues to probable price action the following day, as the long-term trader is forced to take delayed appropriate action. This is why trends still develop throughout London's morning sessions. In addition tops and bottoms are often created within this period.

This applies to FX markets as well, and especially European stock indices which are held to ransom by the Dow and S&P. For Market Profile® users, they would often be better served by trading European indices in the morning and once the American markets open, simply trailing stops or placing profit targets on any remaining positions. The Dow and S&P are often so dominant in dictating the short flows of the European indices that it makes sense to move to trading the primary instrument.

The beauty of Market Profile® is that linking price, time and volume provides a clearer picture of the state of the market. This can then be used to quantify the more traditional methods of patterns and momentum and place them in a context of importance.

The first concept to understand is:

Price + Time = Market Acceptance

Every time a market trades there is a buyer and a seller. They have made a bargain and exchanged contracts. At the time of the trade it is impossible to know the circumstances of the transaction but the aftermath can be analysed and conclusions drawn.

The news and who has been doing what

In the financial industry huge resources, time and print are pumped out to try to analyse who is doing what and why in order to justify the price action. For the most part this is idle speculation. As a trader at Fulton I would be trading intra-day, from a hedge or strategic basis and in addition via spreads or across markets. The Fulton floor staff would execute the vast majority of this but at least 30% would be given to the locals in order to hide the true nature of the trades. With the advent of electronic trading the idea of having a clear idea of who is doing what is even more fanciful. In any case, normally 90% of volume is day trading so while the actual price action is revealing, the minutiae of who did what is irrelevant.

Comments that the funds were big buyers or sellers are difficult to verify. Any big fund will have many prime brokers executing trades for them. The only meaningful measurement of the structure of who has what, is from the 'Commitment of Traders'. This is a report that comes out every Friday and shows the cumulative long and short positions of large traders or funds, commercials and short-term traders based on the close of the previous Tuesday. This can be very revealing in understanding if one type of trader is on the wrong side or is overly exposed to the market moving in one direction. Its drawback is that it is three days late and that the numbers of market participants is increasing, meaning that the old perceived limits of exposure are being re-written. Sugar and crude are two classic examples.

Figure 1:
The rules of participation are being re-written

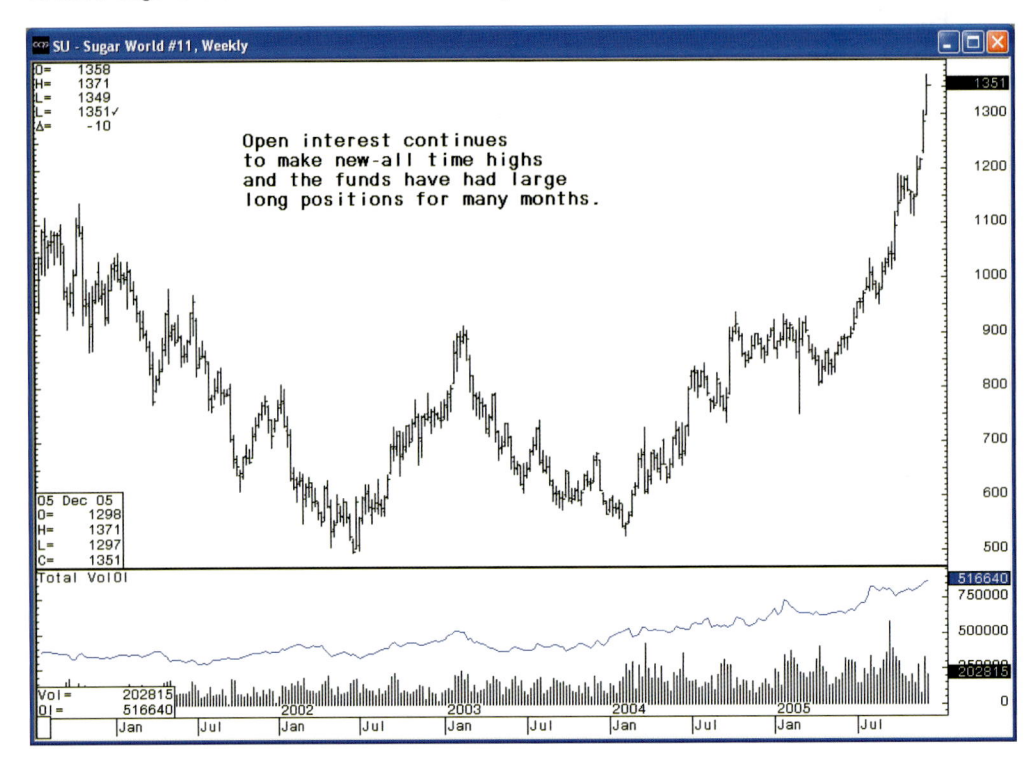

[Chart: SU - Sugar World #11, Weekly. Open interest continues to make new all-time highs and the funds have had large long positions for many months.]

The only other certainty is that a news story about the reason for market movements will always come to a spurious or irrelevant conclusion to justify it. My advice is to ignore it. Interpretation or understanding of fundamentals is fine and definitely helps me on occasion. What doesn't help is some unknown analyst telling me why something happened. All I need to know is what I glean from the charts and, if I wish, I can link that to what the news of the day was.

The link between the news and price action

The most important linking of news to Market Profile® is the connection between what was the estimate of an economic number, what it actually came out at and, critically, what was the price action in reaction to it. The myriad of statistics and more importantly the huge amount of research that goes into working it all out would suggest that the forecasting industry should be accurate. Decades of trading have shown that much of the time the forecasts are inaccurate and I have noticed no discernable improvement. This is no doubt due to the complexities of trying to understand what is going on. In fact, the problem is so mind-boggling to me that it would be a miracle if the market could accurately forecast. To the cynical it is questionable whether there is any intention to be accurate. If the statistics always came out as the market forecast there would be less reaction to it and less opportunity to make money.

For most market participants who wish to reference economics, it makes more sense to look at the big picture statistically and come to some broad-based conclusions about the state of the economy. This may provide a bias to the direction of trend but is of a sufficiently long-term basis that it is relatively easy to avoid getting married to a view.

For example, in July 2005 (when this was written), it could be reasonably forecast that as long as long-term US rates stayed low, the housing boom would continue and this in turn should maintain a robust consumer spending. [Coming back to the book in December revealed that that was the case in spite of Hurricane Katrina.]

Short-term knee-jerk reactions to movements based on a series of statistics appearing in one day are a recipe for disaster unless a true measurement of risk and expectation can be created such as the Time-based studies in Chapter 1. Often important, unrelated statistics can come out at the same time, such as PPI and Industrial Orders. One can be bullish and one bearish - which one will the market focus on? Your guess is as good as mine. If you find yourself switching from bullish to bearish more than once on the basis of news, you are probably falling into a mind trap. This is where the Volatility Time Bands provide a structure to the chaos and when linked to Market Profile® can provide relatively calm, low-risk opportunities.

Market acceptance

We now move onto the next concept.

Price + Time = Market Acceptance

Which leads us to:

Market Acceptance = Volume

Every time there is a trade the volume associated with market acceptance potentially provides clues to future direction, although at the moment that it occurs it often provides little insight. It is only the subsequent price movement that dictates interpretation. That is unless the volume can be linked to other indicators allowing immediate conclusions to be drawn.

This is a key component in analysing the market and is the reason that from a Market Profile® standpoint there is no such thing as overbought or oversold. From a Market Profile® perspective we only know that price displayed that characteristic afterwards. Many mantras regarding overbought and oversold will be called into doubt in later chapters. Those perceived rules are a major factor contributing to exiting a trend prematurely. Therefore it is critical to have a firm grasp of what true measures of overbought and oversold are, which will be touched on later in the Peak chapter. Let's remain with pure Market Profile® theory, with no concept of overbought and oversold; this leads us to the final building block in theory.

Volume = Market (fair) value

Every time price trades it is fair. This is an important psychological aid. A key component to Market Profile® is that it is long-term players who dictate and end trends.
There are two established theories about how the end is formed:

1. When in an uptrend sellers suddenly match buyers in high volume and prevent further progress.
2. There is no volume as there is simply no one left to buy, as the final capitulation of losing shorts has completed its painful exit. At that point the supply side strengthens, demand drops and price reverses swiftly back to a point where buyers and sellers feel value is fair and volume goes back up.

The reality is that from a Market Profile® standpoint both reasons are valid. Therefore, while it's impossible to know whether a high or low is being made at that instant, once a reaction has occurred, any subsequent move back to that area is highly significant. This re-enforces the theory that we have no idea of the importance of any trade at any price unless we can link it to previous price action or the day's extreme deviation points.

Types of activity
If we return to analysing the behaviour of long-term players, we see that this activity is split into two areas:

1. **Initiative activity**
   Long-term players dictate trends and when the volume they wish to trade cannot be satisfied at one price their perception of fair value shifts and price trends.

2. **Responsive activity**
   Long-term traders dictate the end of the trend by withdrawing initiative activity, taking profits or establishing countertrend positions. They also dictate when the reaction to a trend has been completed.

Long-term traders are often identified by single letter prints within a day. These single prints start trends and end them at extremes and at rejections of value.

TRADING TIME: New Methods in Technical Analysis

So how is Market Profile® displayed?

Figure 2: Market Profile®

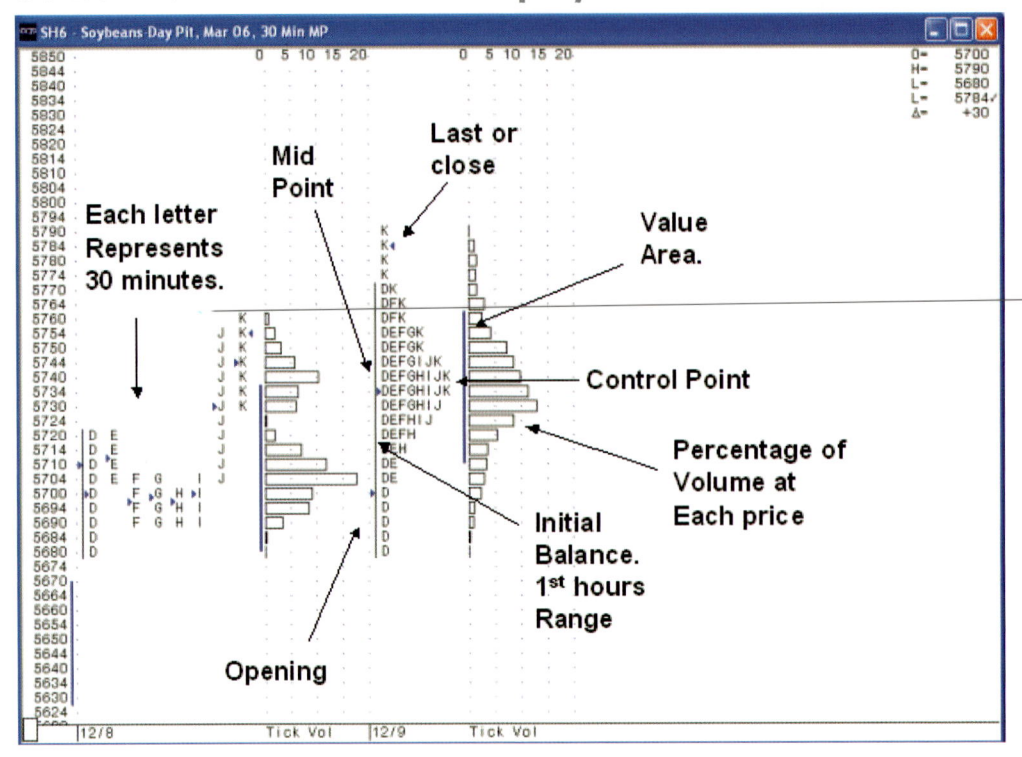

The standard format is that each letter represents the range of a 30-minute period. As the day progresses, each period is overlaid to provide a horizontal format of the day's price action.

Different Timeframes for different markets

Whilst the vast majority of the Market Profile® users never adjust from 30-minutes, volatility, range and standard deviations are methods with which to measure what time frame suits your concept of time and risk. Therefore, short-term scalpers can move down to 5-minute profiles, whilst for FX traders the 24-hour nature of the market means creating profiles of 120 or 240 to provide a clearer picture. Especially in Europe, due to the long trading day, stocks can be used on 60-minute for the day trader or half day for the intermediate trader as they typically hold a position for a longer time

Figure 3: The daily chart gives no real idea of supports in the bottom half of the distribution

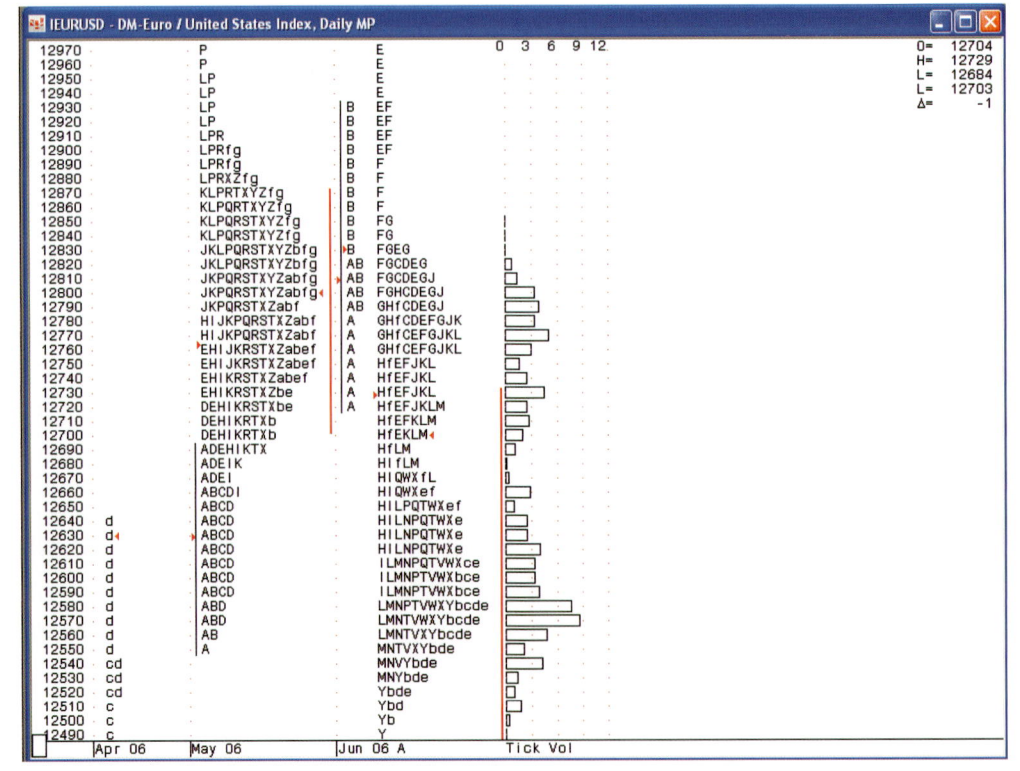

76

Market Profile®

period. The theories extend to the strategic picture where Market Profile's® can be based on dailies or even weekly data sets for the longer-term trader. If using these longer time frames it's important to remember that the levels lose some of their pinpoint accuracy. Therefore the creation of years of data being referenced in, say, a 240-minute timeframe provides the accuracy needed.

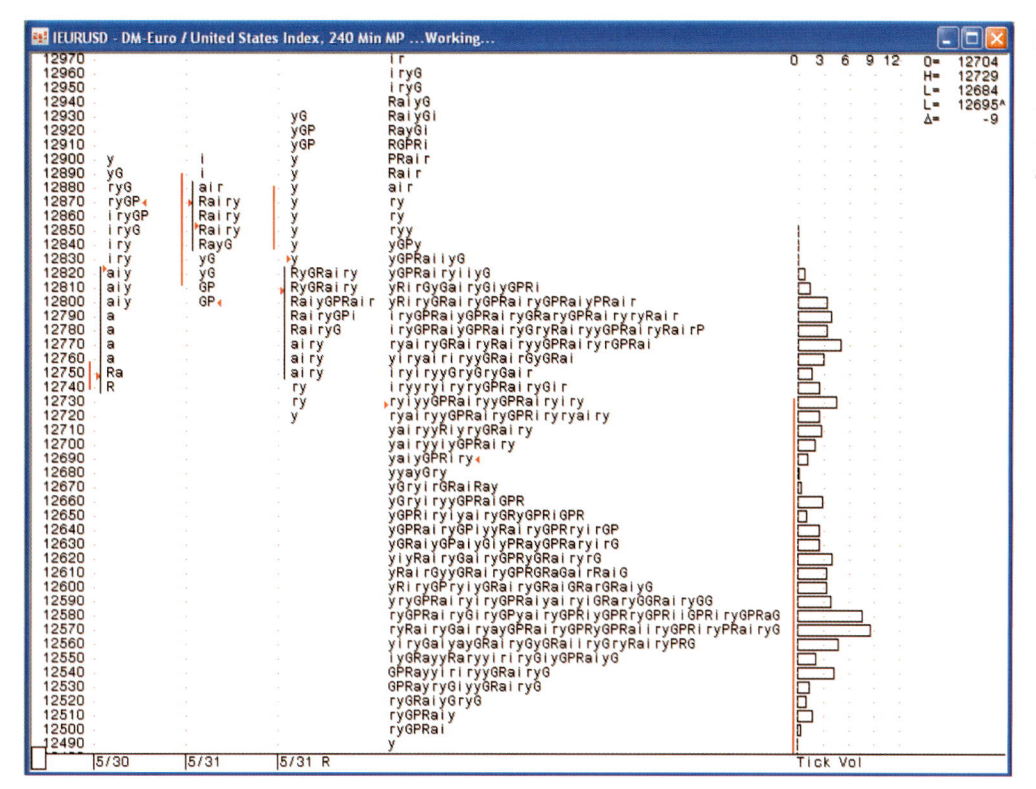

Figure 4: *The 240-minute chart shows a much clearer picture.*

True support and Resistance, the right data is essential!

This brings up another conflict with an established mantra. Commentators and traders alike will often use short-term charts over the last 3 months of the current front month or active contract to identify support and resistance. Subsequently, support and resistances from further back suddenly switch to daily data and simply reference high or low points in that longer timeframe. Whilst this was understandable for many years as more intraday data was not available, there is no excuse in the 21st century. True support and resistance is never at the absolute high or low of a historical bar. There will always have been some rejection of value ahead of that point whether it is Market Profile® or deviation-based. CQG provides up to 5 years of intraday data; this is invaluable in solving this problem, allowing risk and exact support and resistance levels to be quantified with precision.

Initial Balance

This is marked by the black line to the left of the letters and represents the range typical of the first hour's trading. The theory was that in that time the short-term traders or locals would push prices higher and lower until outside orders from the hedge funds and banks etc. arrived and created short-term tops and bottoms. In spite of the removal of the pits, in many cases, the theory still holds true. What has changed is what represents an accurate amount of time for the market to establish its short-term boundaries.

- On a market such as the **Bund**, it is the first major market to open so therefore must wait for its connected markets to establish their own patterns. This usually means the Dax Cash Market, which opens one hour later. Therefore the Initial Balance for the Bund is at least 1½ hours.

- For the **Dax** the Initial Balance can vary wildly. In the huge downtrend of 2000 to 2001 ranges and volatility were so high that the Initial Balance could be as low as 15 minutes. Recently the market has been less volatile and therefore it has generally been 1 hour.
- **Gilts** are typically at 1½ hours especially if statistics are coming out at 9.30 a.m. London time.

- On the American markets the **T Bonds** must wait for the S&P to open so it is 1½ hours as well.

- For those trading **grains** these are dominated by seasonal factors so at times when crop prospects are not weather-critical, the Initial Balance is irrelevant, as the market is open for such a short period of time, and range relatively low. When the volatility increases, typically in July and August, the Initial Balance can be down to 10 minutes.

- The **softs** markets are also open for such a short period that Market Profile®-based day trading and reference to Initial Balances is currently redundant.

- The 24-hour nature of trade in **FX** means that it is difficult to truly understand where the most relevant opening point of the day begins.

- As more and more markets have longer hours or move to almost 24-hour trading this leads to a common crucial question.

Do you use the entire sessions including overnights on Market Profile®?

The answer is no. The lack of volume overnight means that the time-price-volume relationship is distorted. The original pit hours are where the action is. However, I do reference the highs and lows that are made outside the pit session and will often trade specific levels that are either connected to longer-term true measures of support or resistance or alternatively supports and resistances that were created in the recent pit hours. The low volume associated with out-of-hours trading means that if these sessions reach areas of high volume from the pit, positions can be established. Sometimes the subsequent pit session will never return to this area. Deviation levels in out-of-hours trading also have relevance. In summary, analyse the pit sessions but utilize the key levels outside of these hours.

The Control Point (or Longest Line as it is also referred to)

This is the price, or price area, where the most time has been spent and therefore is the point of maximum contentment. The longer the timeframe analysed, the more important this value is as it acts as a flip point between a bullish or bearish outlook. The areas just ahead of control points are often critical supports and resistances.

The percentage of volume at each price

This is shown by the horizontal bars and is referenced by the scale at the top. However, care must be taken. High percentage points must be connected with what the actual volume was on the day so that a consistent relationship can be formed. Therefore, if this is to be used in your armoury, it makes more sense to record either the number of ticks at each price in an absolute terms or the actual volume in absolute terms. Personally, I prefer the former because this is a gauge of activity. The actual volume can be distorted in many ways such as hedging against cash, spreading along the curve or against other markets. Even in stocks the huge increase in pairs trading and buy-sell hedge funds means that it is difficult to know what is purely directional volume. The only way at present I am aware of to record this information is to download it into Excel and build your own charts. This is time-consuming but for the scalper and day trader the additional depth of analysis can provide exact timing and entry points and often reveals levels not visible in the traditional percentage display.

Value Area

This is represented by the blue line to the left of the letters and records the range of 70% of the day's ticks or volume. This is one standard deviation and therefore mathematically is the extreme of normal fair value. It provides one support and one resistance level primarily in a balanced contented market.
Finally, there are three blue arrows. The one to the left of the black line is the opening, the one to the right of the line is the midpoint and the one on the letters is either the last trade or the close.

TPOs – why no mention?

Those who are familiar with Market Profile® will note that I have made no mention of TPOs (time price opportunities). The reasons behind this are first that I was not introduced to the concept for a number of years and was content with my analysis as it stood at that time. Second, having finally tested some of the theories, as well as my own, I came to the conclusion that TPOs - and by definition rotation – overcomplicated the picture and for me had dubious benefits. As we will see, the vast majority of my analysis using Market Profile® concentrates on single letters, the close-to-open relationship and the points where either a small or large amount of time has been spent.

Market Profile® philosophies

It is primarily used as a day trading tool for the vast majority of participants
However, for the experienced user, Market Profile® can be used for all time horizons and has particular use in managing strategic positions and subsequent day trading within that core view.

Often it is possible to eliminate one side of the market
This is a huge plus when day trading as it often dictates which side you can play from and removes one third of the problem. Buy, sell or do nothing. For example, the market has a bullish setup so I can only buy and then sell partial amounts before looking to re-establish the full long position. This enables short-term traders to have the opportunity to ride some more of their position on a trend day.

Analysis goes back 5 days
This is because the short-term trader can't remember more than five days back. In fact, often the long-term trader can't either. Can you remember the open/high/low/close in a market you traded 8 days ago?

Market Profile® often provides very precise support and resistance levels and therefore it highlights correct levels for the placement of stops and profit-taking opportunities

This can be defined by:
- Long-term distribution highs and lows
- The areas between distributions
- The ends of vacuum areas
- Control Points
- Ledges of time
- The point where single letter prints end

What is the true close?
Most traditional analysis of markets, especially momentum-based ones, reference the relationship from close to close. Inspection of this highlights many flaws in this established mantra. As mentioned previously, 90% of the day's volume is concentrated in day trading. The explosion of arcades has increased overall volume but the vast majority of these establishments allow no overnight positions regardless of the experience of the trader. Therefore an overwhelming majority of participants exit the market purely on time. An added complication is that these arcades will not wait for the absolute close but look to finish the day's trading around 5 p.m. London time. The European cash-bond market also finishes at the same time meaning there is less chance of physical-based hedging. The dominance of London in FX markets means this has always been a problem.

Thus volume tails off in the last hour of European futures trading and the period from 5 p.m. to 2 a.m. London time in FX. This leads to the possibility of rogue moves in low volume. On Fridays this problem is even worse as people finish earlier for the weekend, which leads to the possibility of a false weekly close. One reason for this is that traders may have been on the wrong side of a position for most of the week and simply throw in the towel and exit rather than hold a position over the weekend.

TRADING TIME: New Methods in Technical Analysis

This is an area where the OaR Volume Bands provide real insight into confirmation of a directional move, depending on the time of day it occurred.

Figure 5:
Low volume. Eurodollar trading on the EBS platform

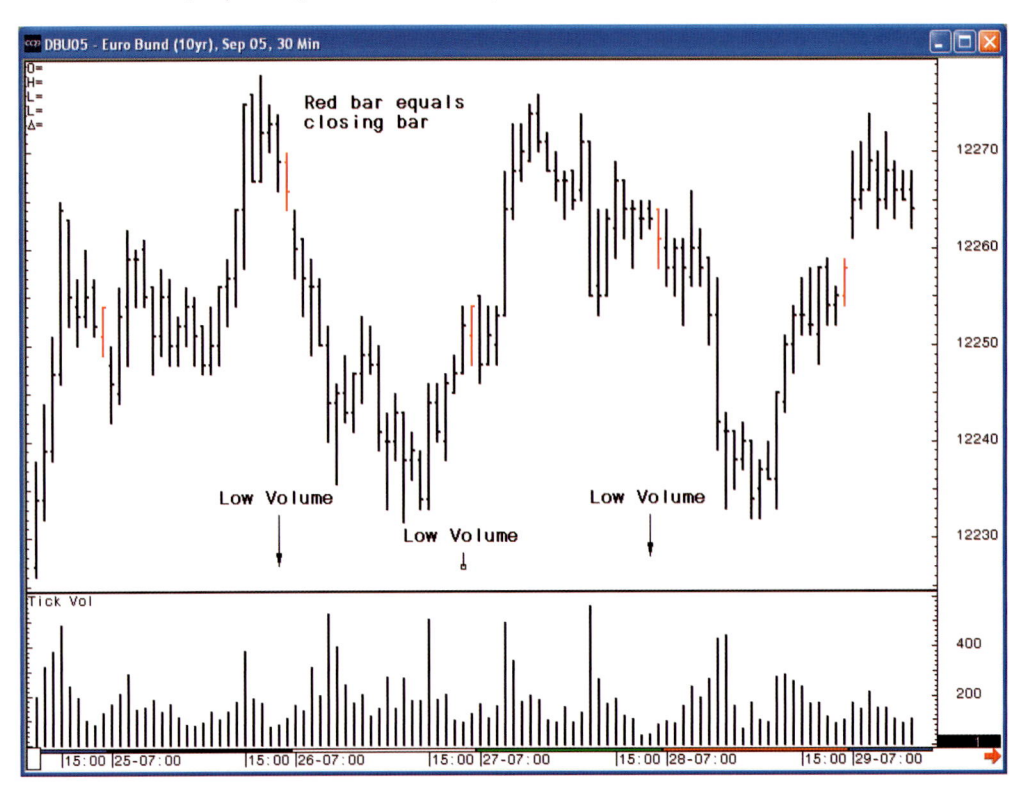

Figure 6:
Low volume

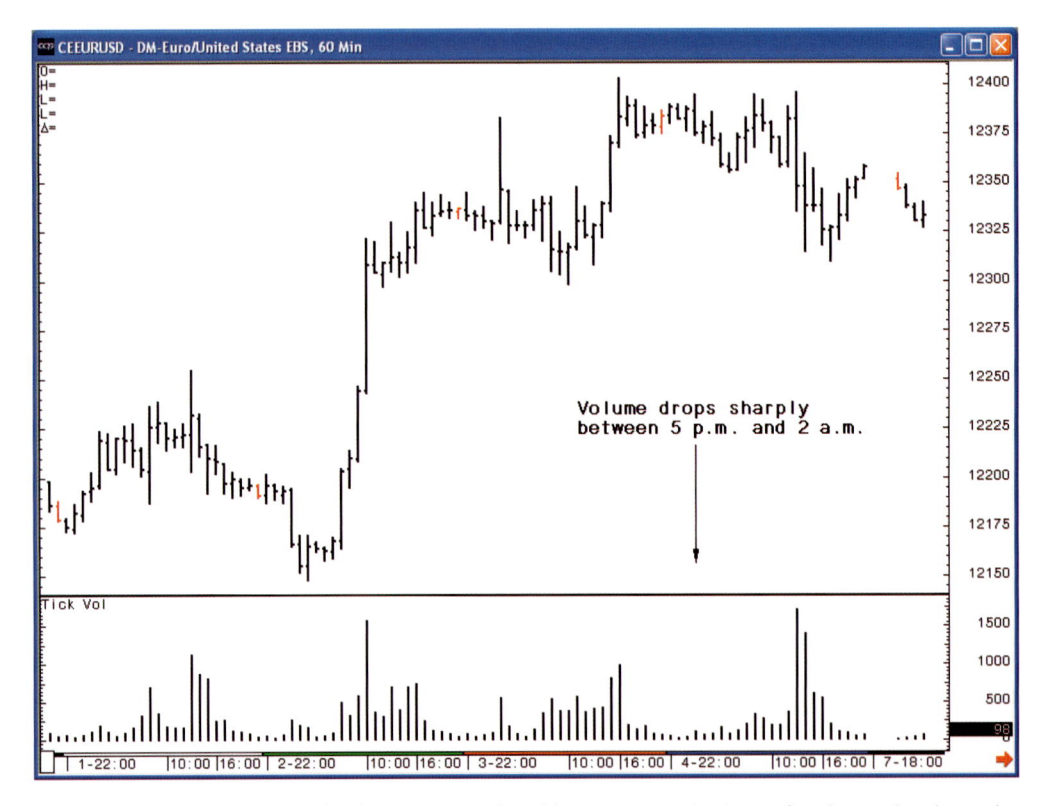

In America, the shorter opening hours mean that this appears to be less of an issue, but here the concentration of time means that day traders are left with a condensed period to make their daily targets. Long-term traders also have limited scope. This can also lead to extreme and late moves in indices and is especially prevalent in the grain and cattle markets.

CQG allows for daily charts to be built based on custom sessions provided that you have the extended intraday data which allows closes to be taken prior to the low volume time. The differences in momentum readings can be significant and illuminating.

Market Profile®

The relationship between yesterday's close and today's opening
The key question for Market Profile® users, especially when price has made a late move to close near the highs or lows, is:

Was the close real and a reflection of long-term players being dictators of trend or short term players being forced out?
To answer this question we look at the relationship between the open and the close of the previous day. From those conclusions we look for single letter prints for confirmation. From this one area various questions and conclusions can be made. The first is the opening call.

Did price exceed, match, or fail to meet the opening call level?
Each day various calls on how the market will open are made before the opening, up to the last 5 minutes. If big stories emerge on commodities, the call is made long before that. On stock indices insight via the spread-betting companies appears on television and even electronic markets have an opening auction where users connected to the exchange itself can see the orders filling before the opening trade occurs.

Whilst the call can change substantially up to the last 5 minutes, it is in that final period of time before the opening that significant information is revealed. What can possibly change the perception of a market to open 10 up and then open 2 up? Obviously the reality is that the actual market is nowhere near as strong as it was perceived to be. Therefore, although the market is still higher, it has disappointed and where it was due to open is now a resistance point. The S&P main contract has a short 15-minute gap before the Dow opens. This is especially true when economic numbers are to be released at 1.30 p.m. (London Time). A substantial change between the call and the opening can be revealing.

A Corn Profile on the day of the monthly crop report in 2004 paints a typical picture. At certain times of the year this has a huge influence on the direction of the market, often lasting all the way to the next report. The market was due to open at 197.0 to 194.0 on 10/12/04 after a highly bearish report. In fact price opens much higher at 199.0, which places the opening call as the first support. Price bottoms out directly at the top of this area at 197.0 and shows responsive behaviour within the Initial Balance period in **D**. The aggressive trader had a low-risk entry point but for others further confirmation is required. This appears with Initiative behaviour in **F**, confirming that the opening represented unfair value and that a trend the other way is beginning. This proved to be the low for the next few weeks.

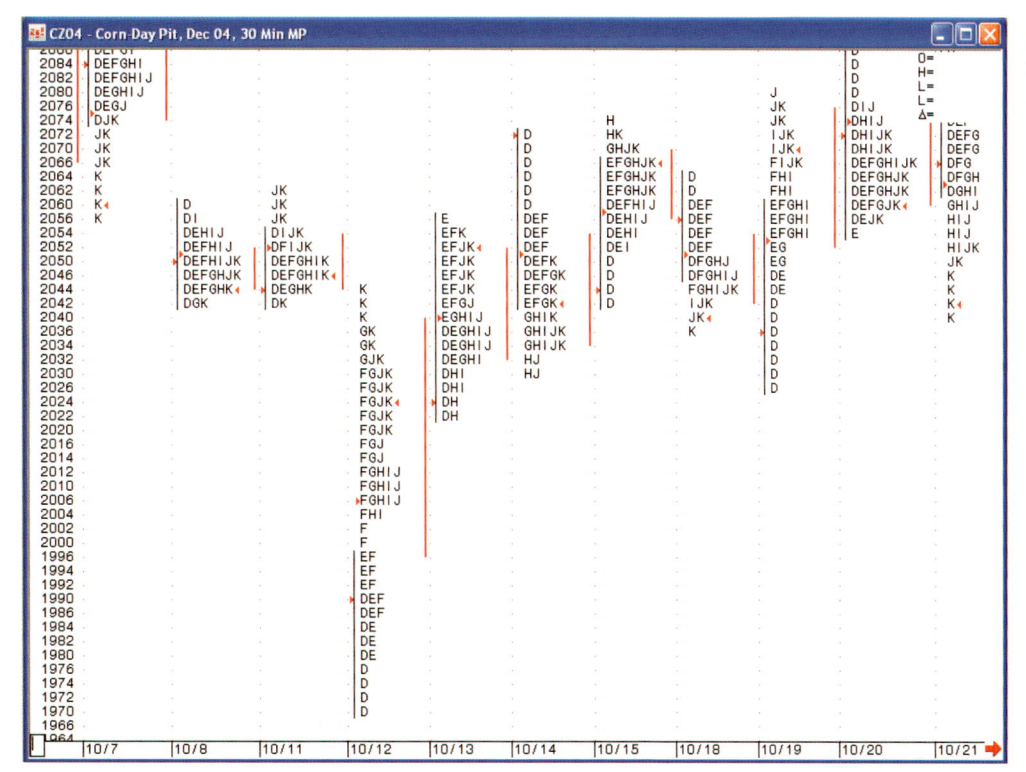

Figure 7: The opening call

Grains and the opening call
For grains, when the weather is dominating, the instances where the opening price does not match the call can be numerous. Normally, news wires will quote an anonymous source from the pit that will state what the call is and what the market is focusing on. Think about this for a moment.

TRADING TIME: New Methods in Technical Analysis

Why would somebody who rides on the back of all the paper that comes into the pit, and has a permanent edge over everybody else, want to help you?
This is especially true in the last few minutes before an opening, as the majority of opening market orders have been passed down to the pit.

A case study: Soya Beans

To provide a background: I'm long and wrong on my Soya bean position from the moment I place the trade on 6 July. It's a strategic trade as a drought intensifies. This is an example where my length of time trading means that for good or bad, fundamentals, especially on commodities, still influence my thinking. Then I use technical analysis to manage the trade and have a healthy skepticism regarding the day-to-day news events. I am also long corn at the same time due to the big gap higher on the previous day along with various Market Profile®-based arguments. With weather the dominant factor, experience tells me I will be in for a wild ride and therefore need wide stops. For corn, July is the critical time, although even with the weather being poor overall stocks are high, so I'm not expecting a massive bull market. The soya bean market is a different story, as August is the key month and the stock situation is more critical. The long-term forecast is for hot and dry weather.

Prices gap lower the following day. However, the gap is filled in the Initial Balance period and responsive behaviour is seen, which is encouraging. The strength disappears 8 July maintaining the pressure on the position. However, suddenly an unexpected weather event emerges to cloud the picture still further. Hurricane Dennis threatens Florida, the Gulf oil platforms and, as is common with hurricanes, its path is difficult to predict. I cannot remember a hurricane ever affecting corn pollination. But lo and behold this is the third earliest hurricane in over a hundred years and one of the most powerful. Speculation on Friday is that the path is through Florida and then up the East coast of America. If this is true it will miss the Mid West and the drought will continue. However, by Sunday evening, I am glued to Fox news.

Figure 8:
Soya Beans

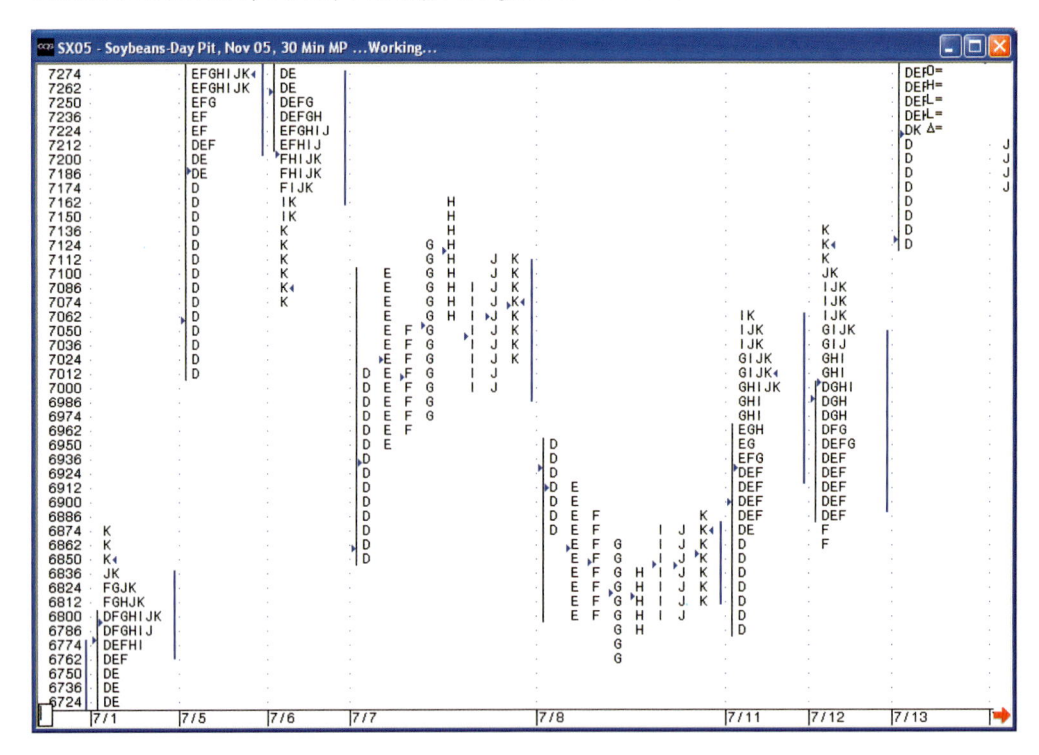

The path has changed and now looks like it will head straight for the midpoint of the Gulf and from there surge straight up the centre of the country, dump a deluge directly on the corn fields by Tuesday and save the crop. As I sit there watching the satellite path, it's clear that my position will probably be similarly dumped on and what has been a bad trade from day 1 is going to get a lot worse.

Now the question of time and structure comes in. As mentioned earlier, I reference the out-of-hours trading, monitoring the action, but only enter positions in those sessions if the pit analysis tells me to. I don't place stops there. Sounds fine until my profit and loss is facing potential major problems. The risk is that by the time the pit opens the following afternoon the markets could be limit down and I will be left with having to buy options when volatility is at its highest to provide any sort of cover. This could get ugly.

Therefore, do I set the alarm for 2 a.m. and watch the initial reaction?
If I don't set the alarm and do not have a structured game plan, am I going to wake up at 1.59 a.m. anyway in that spooky way that when it wants to, your mind can tell the time with the accuracy of

Market Profile®

Mr Spock. Then I'll probably be forced by morbid fascination to go downstairs and just have a peek anyway. Without structure and confidence to manage bad events, the chances are you will do one or the other. For me, I shrug my shoulders, stick by the rules that stops are for the pit only and that looking at the price at 2 a.m. is only going to keep me awake and make me do something emotional.

A sound night's sleep and I look at the price which is already looking a little brighter. The opening overnight is the low and price held above my strategic (long term Market Profile® distribution) pit-based stop at 666 making a low at 668. Analysis of the Volatility Time Average Bands puts the whole price action in perspective. Price has not even reached the 1st deviation band down! What superficially looks like a serious price decline has merely moved towards that day's limit of contentment. Now price is almost unchanged from Friday's close. When the pit opens prices are only slightly lower and then move lower to a powerful support area. This is the control point or price with the most time when taking the distribution from the June highs. This therefore is the point of most contentment within the recent trend and is a formidable point. The market moves down directly to this level and then shows responsive behaviour, finally ending up above Friday's close and at the 3rd deviation up in spite of a hurricane.

Panic over?

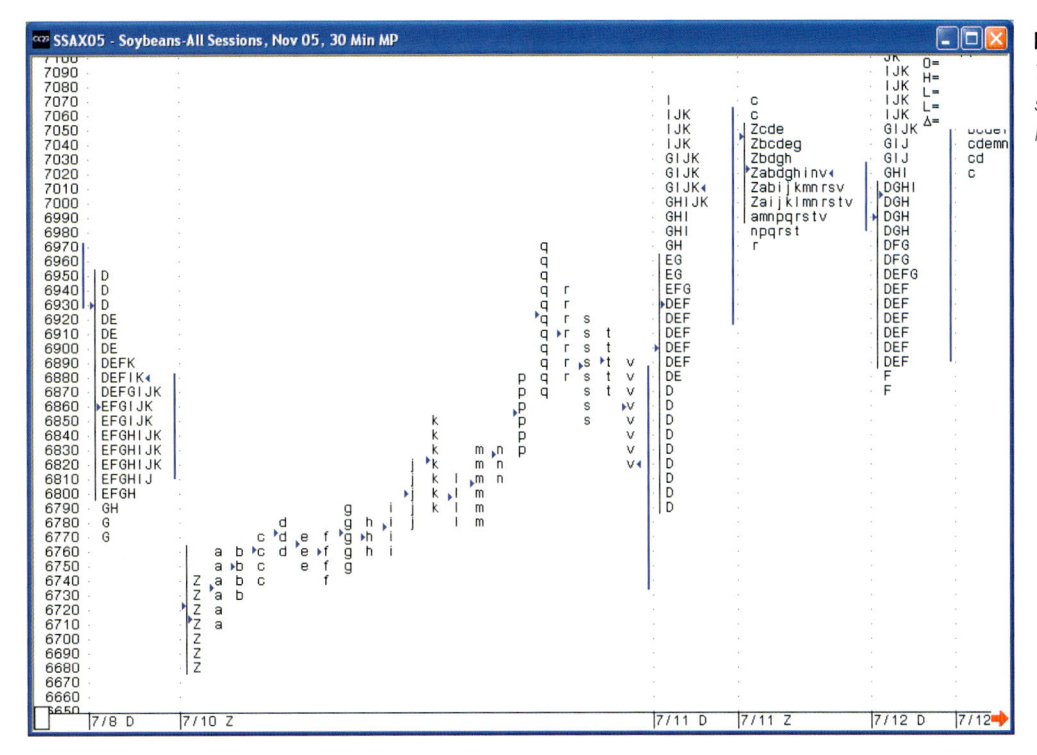

Figure 9:
The overnight session is the low

TRADING TIME: New Methods in Technical Analysis

Figure 10:
The time bands highlight how bullish the price action actually was.

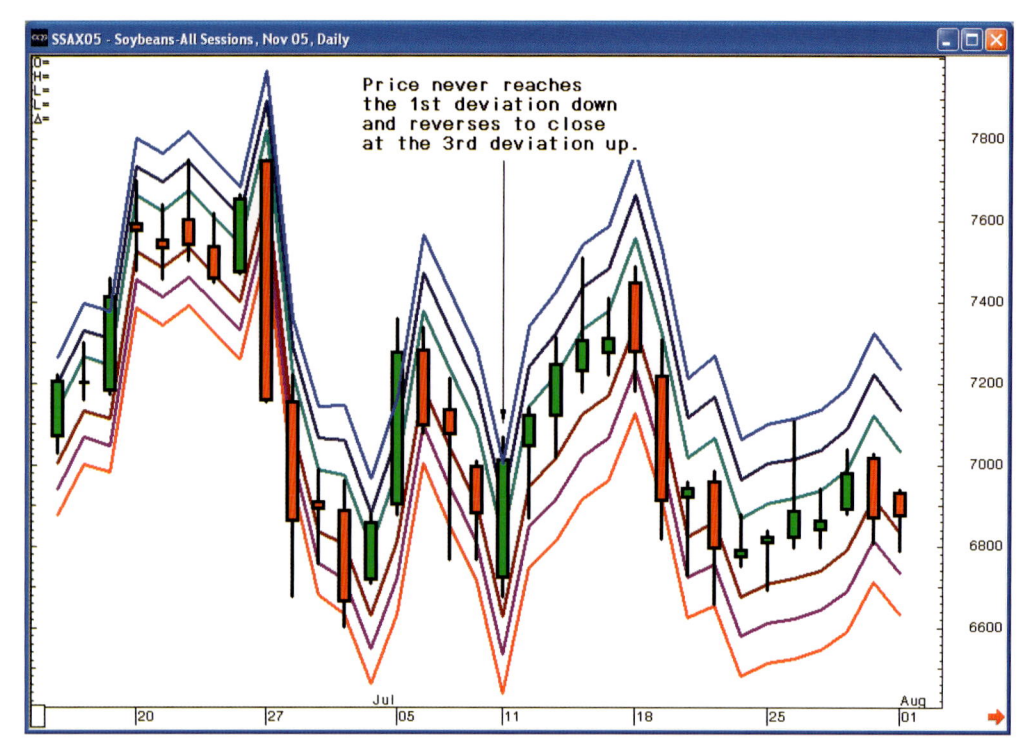

No, as Wednesday's opening call 13 July is 5 to 10 lower due to the amount of rain that has reached the crop. In addition, there are comments that this could see funds exiting. As always I am sceptical of the opening call comment and the opening sees prices unchanged from the previous session. The market surges in the first 5 minutes in initiative behaviour. I may be cynical but obviously the rain didn't hit the right spots. Or was the pit looking for an opportunity to buy from nervous longs exiting their positions?

Whilst that day's opening was instantly bullish, the following day quickly displays the opposite behaviour. Price is called 10 to 15 higher and meets that call. However the Initial Balance in **D** shows responsive behaviour. Price is overbought (on true measures which are covered in later chapters) and when it breaks back below the Initial Balance low it suggests a short-term top is in place. I liquidate the position and wait for another opportunity. Note (see fig. 11) how the next two days post highs that are just below the previous day's control point. Price has reached its optimum point for bears and failed. Remember, the Control Point is the flip point between bullishness and bearishness.

Figure 11:
The gap opening is rejected

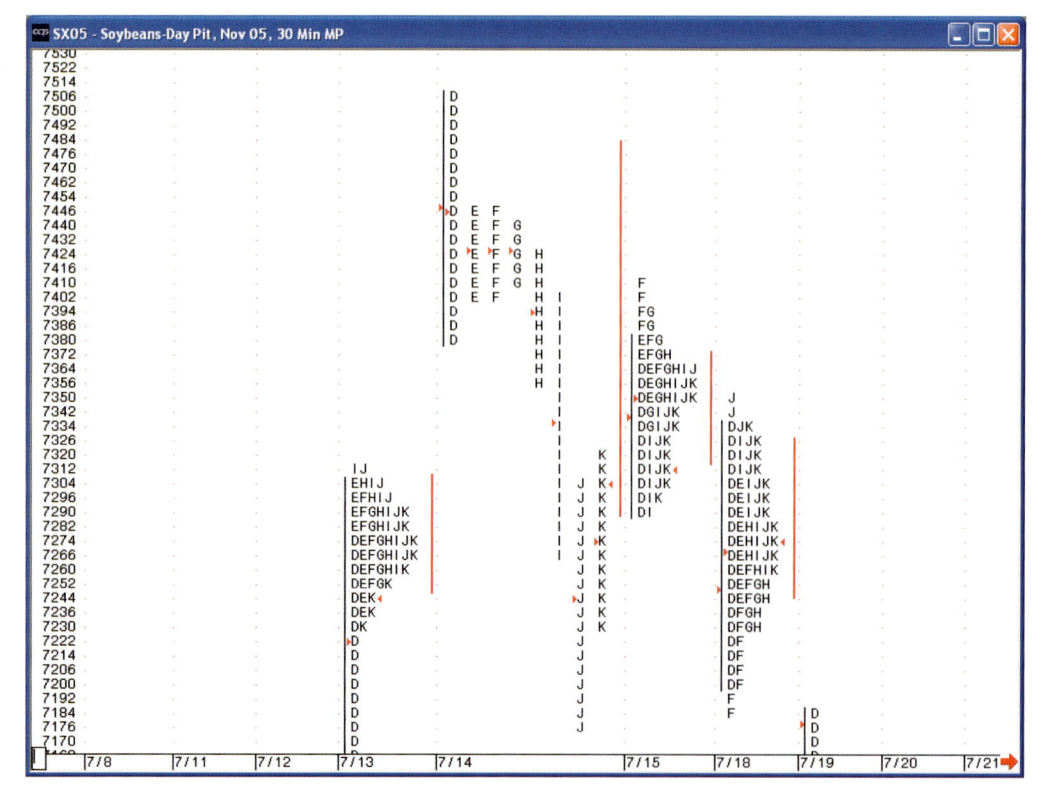

Market Profile®

Is the opening significantly higher or lower than the previous close?

Any large change in this relationship highlights that other markets or news releases have created a change in perception. The Dax chart (see fig. 12) shows how price opens higher and a single print in the Initial Balance is created with initiative behaviour in **l**. Price moves higher and shows more of the same behaviour in **m** and **n**. There have been 4 separate confirmations that this will be a big trend up day. We will look at how a stop can be trailed against the position in the Peak chapter.

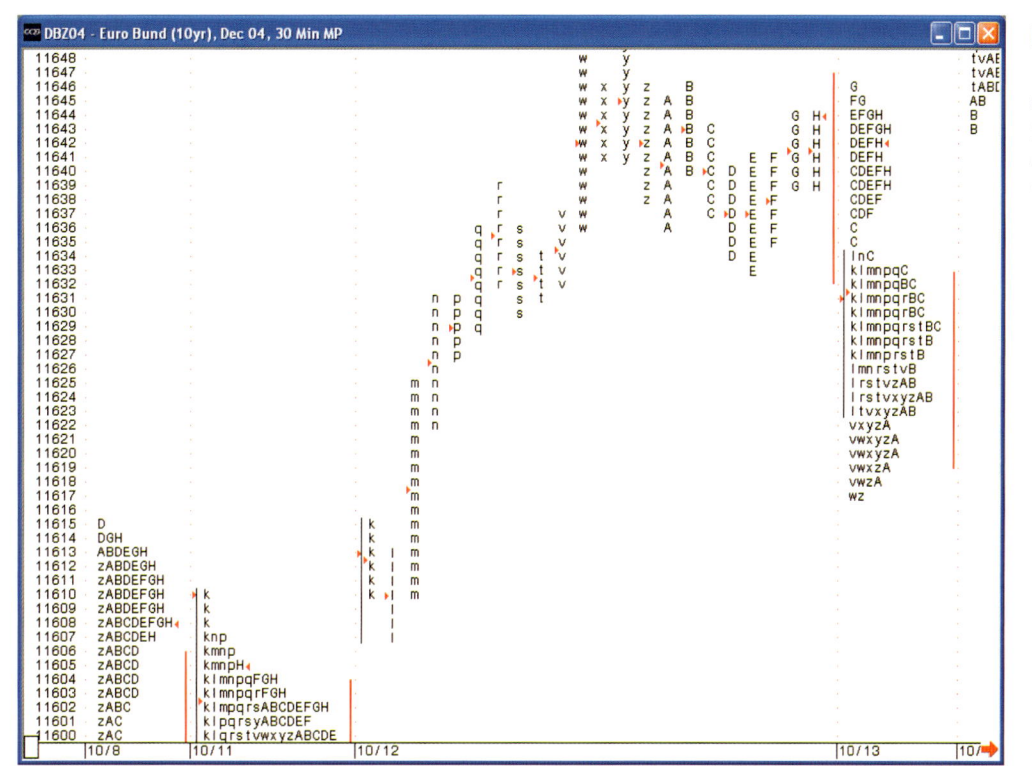

Figure 12:
The relationship between yesterday's close and today's opening

Another example in the same market highlights that a change in sentiment between the open and the close over a weekend has more power. The market has had a longer time to reflect on what the new week will bring and initiative and responsive behaviour in the early part of Monday has more significance. (see fig. 13)

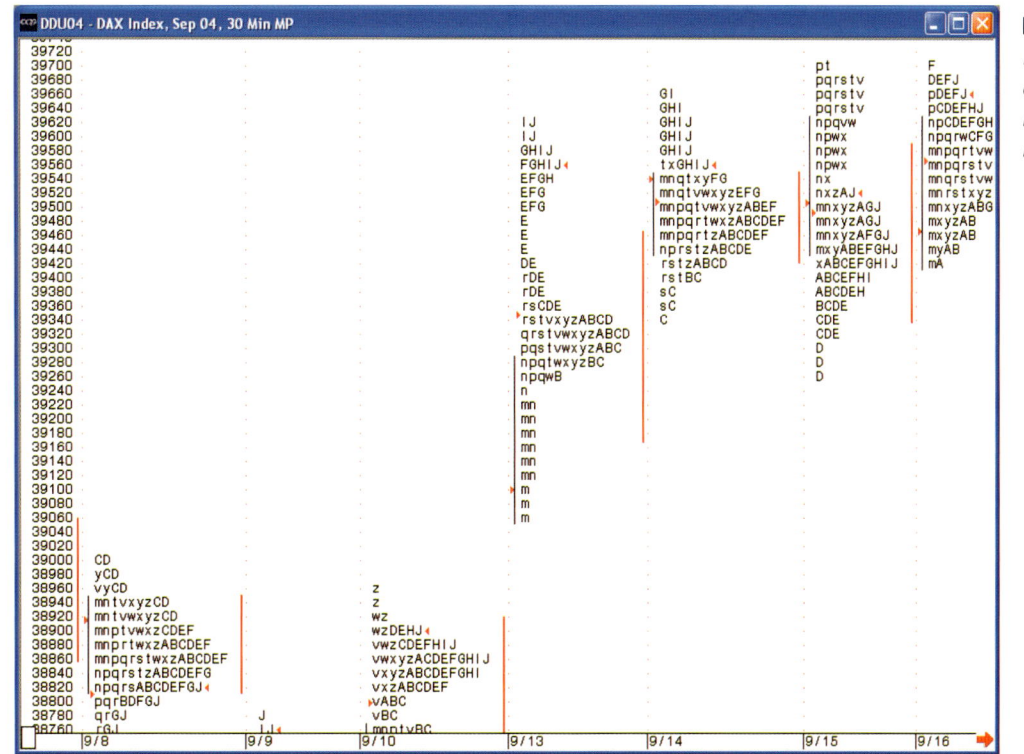

Figure 13:
Price gaps higher on 9/13 and maintains momentum

TRADING TIME: New Methods in Technical Analysis

The same example (see fig. 14) shows an opening on Monday that is above the Value Area for the previous week. The sentiment change is so big that price holds its first support point with initiative behaviour in the first hour and then extends higher.

Figure 14:
Changes on Monday have more power as the move overcomes all of the previous week. Here the opening on 13/09 sets a new tone.

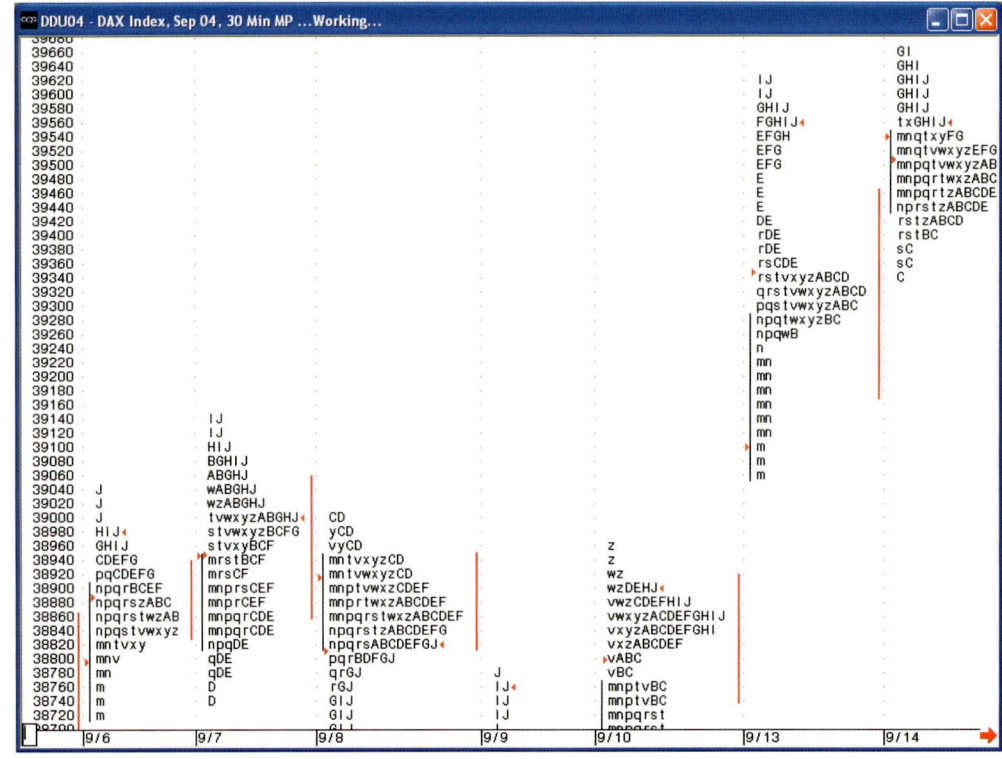

Is the day's close real or false?

This has particular significance when the close is near the high or low of the day. Analysis of historical charts shows that this occurs frequently. This ties in with the fact that the vast majority of players need to be out by the close and are therefore forced by time. When the extreme close has been marked by a trend with just the last one or two letters of the day, this is a clue that short-term traders have been forced out and that it may be a false move.

When an extreme close has been marked by far more letters, this suggests long-term traders are in control and the trend is beginning or continuing to develop. The opening price the following day, any single letter activity is a key indicator to either scenario and dictates that day's first bias. The emergence of responsive or initiative behaviour is also a key barometer.

The next chart (see fig. 15) illustrates that price has been in balance for three days. The weak close (7 May ahead of the three day congestion) and an acceptance of value towards the low of the range suggest longer-term players are involved. The market gaps down on the next day's opening and then fills the gap in the first hour. This is confirmed by responsive behaviour in **y** and provides a low-risk short position. The trend does not develop on the day but is still profitable for the session.

The next day (14 May) the price opens sharply lower. This is also bearish, but the responsive behaviour in **y** within the Initial Balance quickly raises a warning. The rally is of such momentum that the Initial Balance high ends up above the Control Point of the day before. The Control Point represents the flip point between bullishness and bearishness. This is another warning that what was fair value yesterday is no longer true today. The ensuing rally is messy and provides no further initiative behaviour with single letter prints. However, it does hold the Control Point of the previous day on three separate occasions, **C**, **D** and **E**. The high is the top of the fair value from the sideways move from the previous sessions of the last five.

This profile setup highlights the need to be nimble and recognise when the picture is shifting from one bias to another. The clues are often there and provide the structure for the management of risk whatever time or risk horizon you are trading.

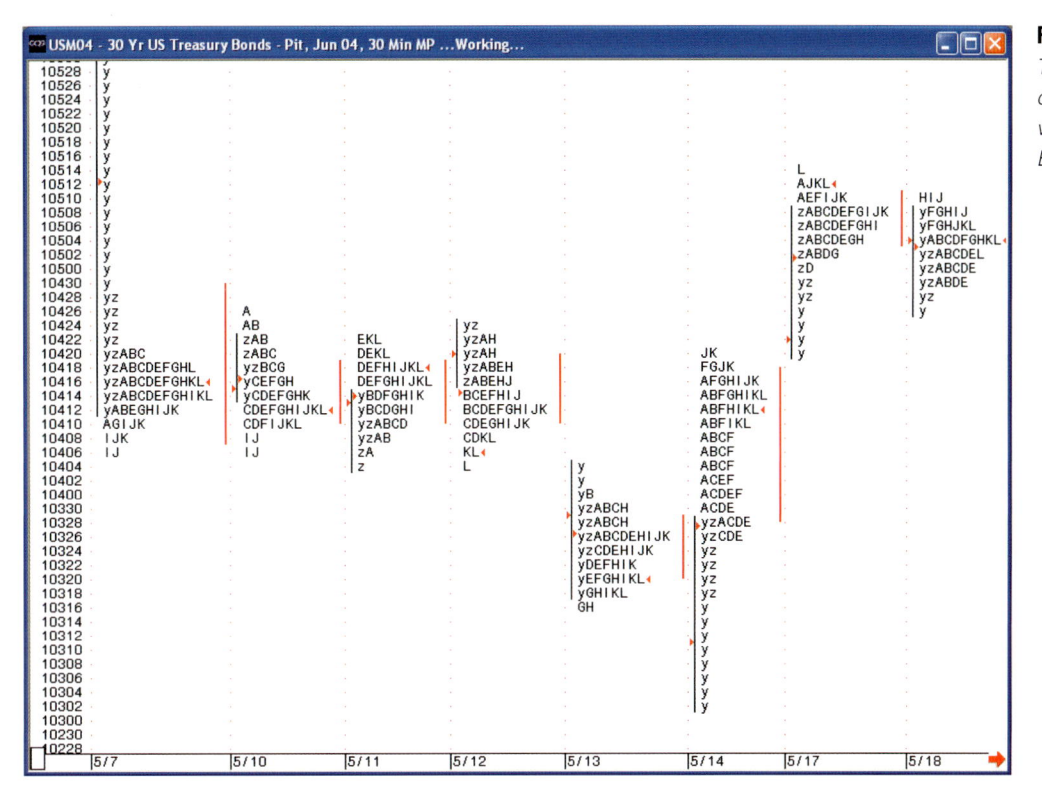

Market Profile®

Figure 15:
The picture can change quickly within the Initial Balance period.

T Bonds

This is highlighted once again in T Bonds. 21 May sees a similar pattern to the previous day as price opens significantly higher and then shows initiative behaviour. However, that is where the similarity ends. Price breaks out of the Initial Balance in **A** but by **D** has reversed this sentiment and has broken down the other way. This can mean two things:

1. price may simply have extended its Initial Balance range and will rotate in a sideways manner, or
2. the break higher was false and the market could slide quickly.

In either scenario the only way to manage risk is to exit when the Initial Balance break has moved in the opposite direction. It is far better to see if price does indeed rotate back up than hope that it does. Trading has no room for hope.

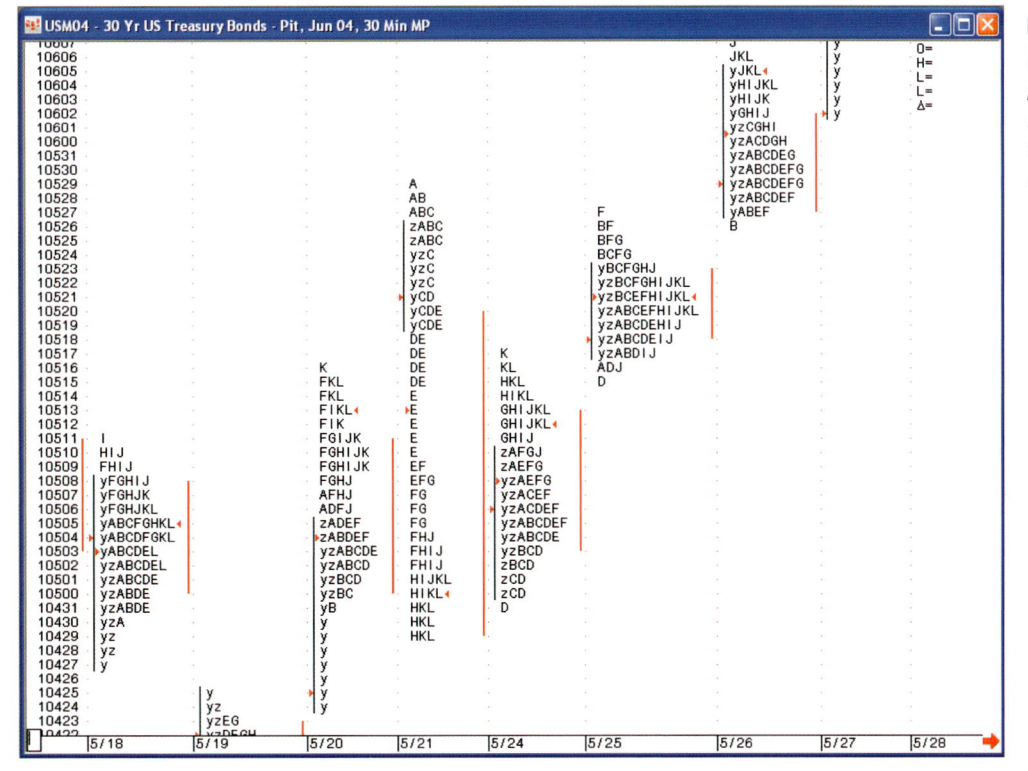

Figure 16:
Single letter prints must be confirmed by the subsequent letter

TRADING TIME: New Methods in Technical Analysis

Market Profile® and Traditional Analysis

This section looks at how Market Profile® can be used to quantify more traditional analysis and help confirm whether areas and levels well known by the market will work or not. As markets remain hard to interpret - let alone trade – on the basis of fundamentals, the importance of understanding the established technically-based mantras becomes a key part of any trader's armoury.

You may not agree that many of the established mantras are false, but even if you don't, you can take advantage of when those mantras fail. The reason I prefer to concentrate on their failure is that the subsequent move or trend should be that much more powerful. Anytime when both short-term traders and a proportion of long-term traders are holding the wrong positions the subsequent move should be swift. Therefore referencing major trend lines, the Fibonacci and Elliot Wave clubs, whilst not forgetting the long-established Stochastic club, is essential.

Trend Line breaks

The daily chart shows a well-defined resistance line on the S&P. It is so obvious that you can be sure that the value of its of consequence to many traders. For me, trend lines represent the point of maximum uncertainty. Waiting for two-day confirmation or weekly confirmation can mean that the move gets away from the trader or widens risk considerably. This opens up the possibility of never getting involved, which can be deeply frustrating if it proves to be a major breakout. For now, the problem is whether the trend line will succeed or fail. The first attempt, two days before the breakout, saw prices stop at the trend line. Now it has closed above it.

Is the breakout for real?

Figure 17:
Has the S&P broken out?

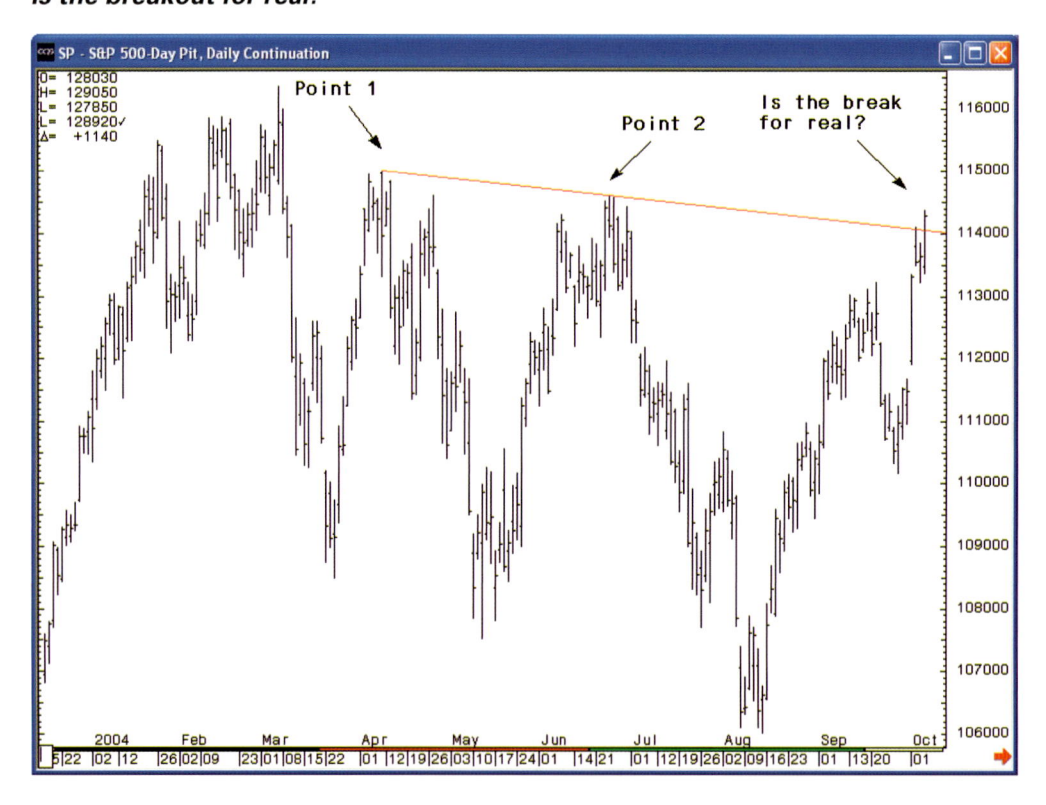

Market Profile®

The first clue that it may be a false move is the timing of the break which is late in the day. This suggests that short-term traders were forced out by time. By the opening of the following day this scenario is confirmed by the weaker opening (see fig. 17a). Initiative selling is evident in **B** and the opening is the high of the day. The market then shows initiative behaviour in **E** and price closes on the lows. Once again the late nature of the move lower suggests that short-term traders may have been active. However, the weak opening the following day confirms that the trend should be down, the original breakout higher was false and subsequently a major top is formed.

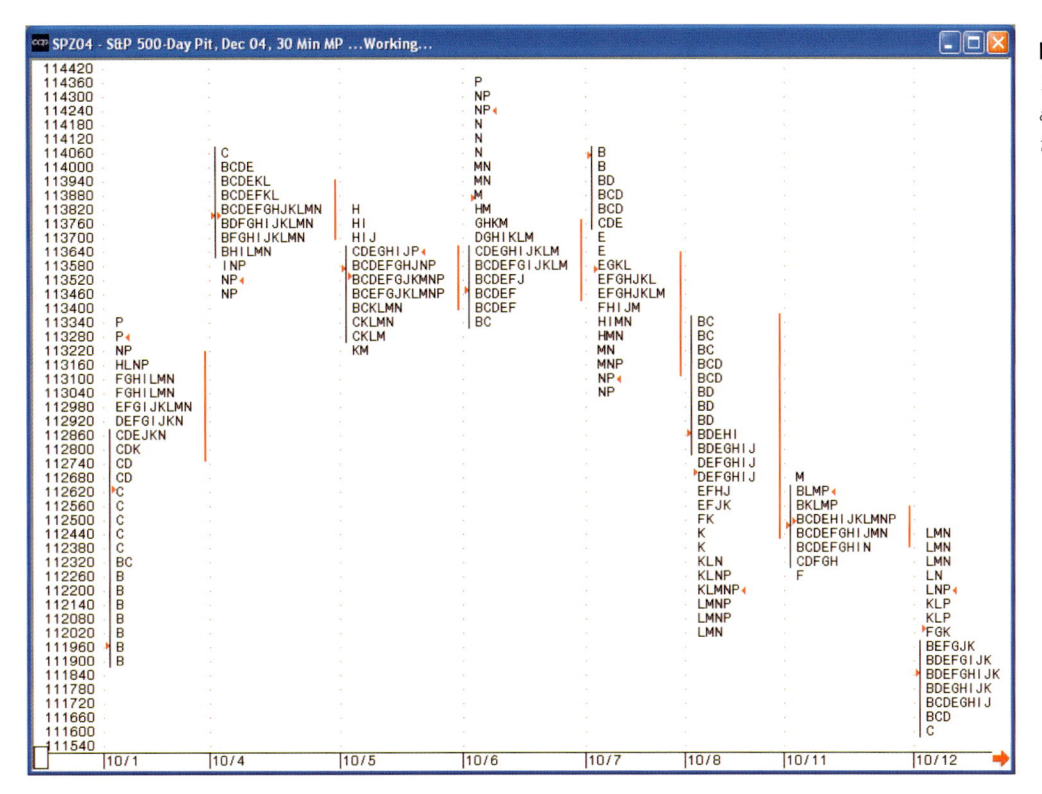

Figure 17a:
7 October shows a rejection of the trend line break

A look at the Fibonacci club

Whilst the retracement is a widely used study, Fibonacci extensions are used less often. However, they remain a key tool for Elliot wave theory and provide targets primarily for trends. Whilst I won't elaborate how these lines are drawn, as there are various interpretations and reference points, I would suggest the following. For beginners it is necessary to take three significant turning points and look for the projection of the 0.618, 1.00 and 1.618 lines.

Whilst not being a fully paid-up member of the Elliot wave club, I think that extensions are a powerful tool when prices reach new ground on an extended move. At such times there is very little an analyst has to study apart from volume and open interest or true measures of overbought and oversold. From a Market Profile® perspective it is necessary in an up trend to wait for the market to form resistance based on its own momentum. In strong trends, until this happens, it can mean that supports are distant, risk-considerable, and therefore traders must use other trailing stop methods (see the Peak chapter).

Bunds. Fibonacci levels that create zones of support/resistance.

Next, we look at a chart (see fig. 18) that shows the Bund at an all-time high. It shows how the connection of a shorter-term extension has merged with a 1.618 extension that is at exactly the same point. Fibonacci zones, (especially when retracements match with extensions) are more powerful but this is a rare setup. What is clear is that there will be plenty of shorts interested at that price point.

Figure 18:
A Fibonacci area of rare power - will it work?

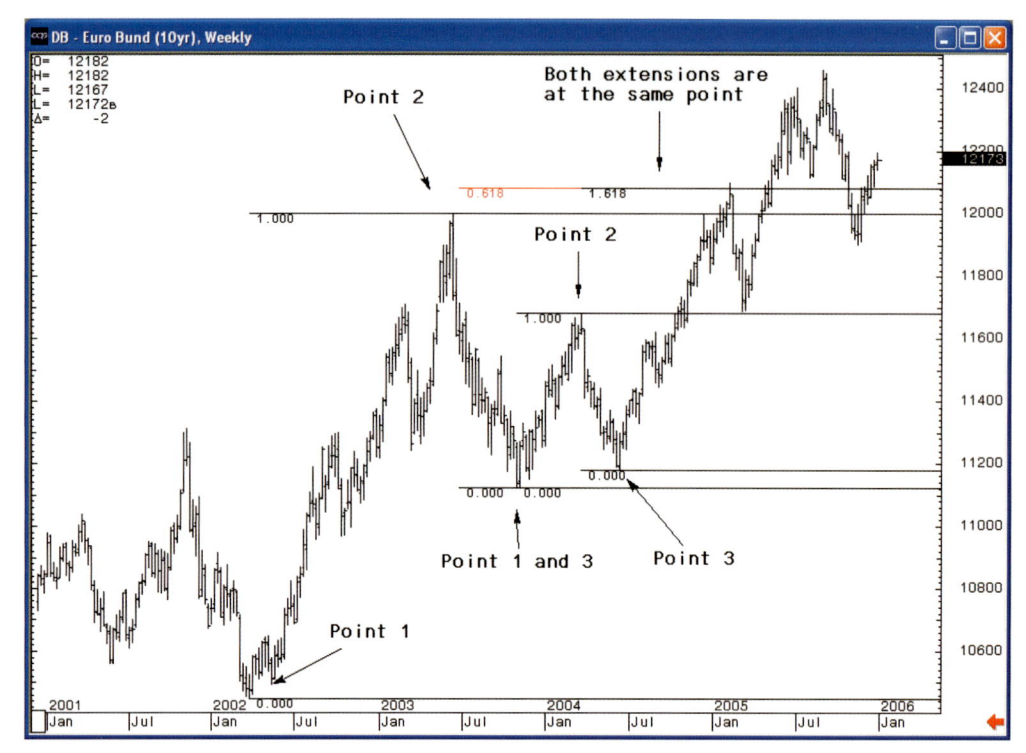

Market Profile®

Figure 19:
The close causes confusion.

A glance at the chart shows that price closed directly (not exactly) at the zone. The opening the following day (see fig. 21) shows a bullish setup as price opens above both the Value Area and the close of the day before. This picture swiftly changes as responsive behaviour within the Initial Balance questions the move. The ensuing few hours sees the tug of war that is occurring.

Eventually this buying power is overcome and the market's close is weak. Whilst it is easy to see with hindsight that a top was formed, which was followed by a 250-point correction, the connection between Market Profile® and a long-term strategic reference point to Elliot wave traders created turmoil in the short term. This is why it is necessary to know what other participants are doing as far as is possible in order to be ready for such events. The key is that when price hits these targets, be prepared for volatility.

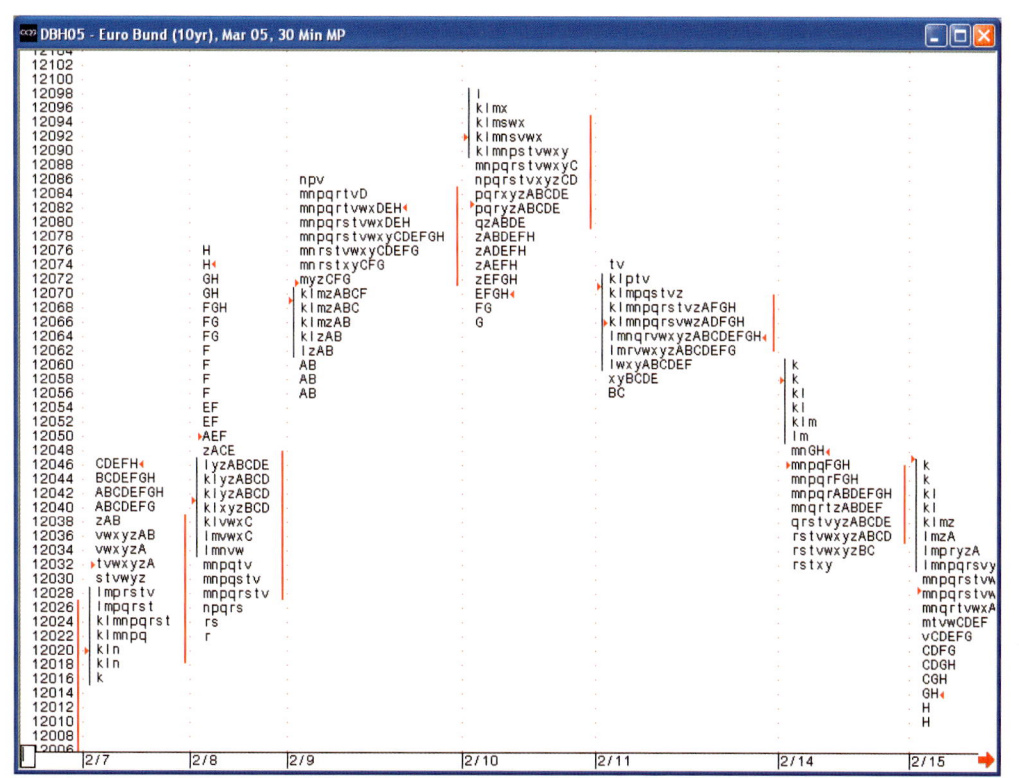

Figure 21:
Intraday volatility marks the top forming day

91

TRADING TIME: New Methods in Technical Analysis

Doing nothing is often the best solution at this time of maximum uncertainty. For those looking to engage, the 2nd standard deviation on a 10-minute chart can provide a useful reference. Aggressive traders can add at the 3rd standard deviation with a close beyond it as a stop

Figure 22:
The OaR Volatility Time Bands still provide structure on wild days

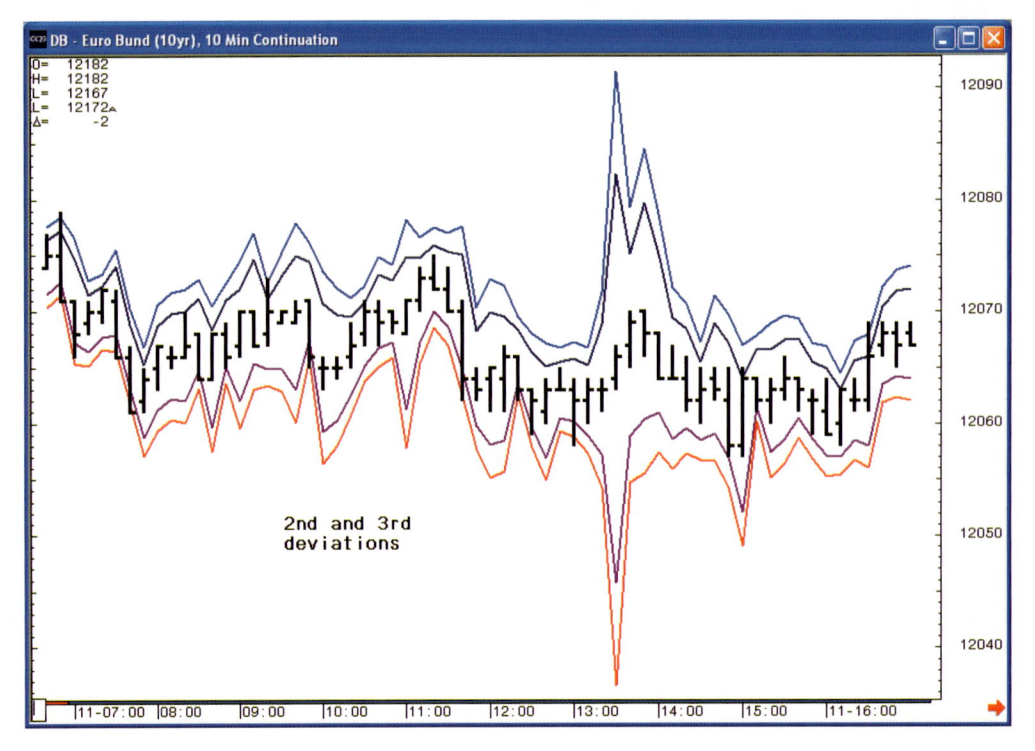

Shifts in time

Key supports and resistances.

The merging of time.

This section looks at ledges of time. These are the points at which there are great differences in the numbers of letters from one price to the next. These are often close to the Control Point and at such times provide low-risk entries against the short-term trend.

Up to this point we have looked at individual Market Profile® days, but for the short-term trader the merging of up to the last 5 days provides a clearer picture. The merging of distributions over longer timeframes is a far more delicate task and it's crucial that the correct rules and methods are followed. If not, the analysis will be fatally flawed. How different length distributions are merged and analysed is beyond the remit of this book, but it is a key tool in the analysis which is undertaken by OaR in identifying highly accurate strategic points of support and resistance.

The next chart (see fig. 23) has moved on from the Fibonacci-based high which was illustrated in fig. 18 and has merged the last 3 days from the high. After the tug of war, the picture is much clearer. The opening 11 February appears to provide little in the way of clues. However, it is below the Control Point, which promotes a negative bias. The break higher in **t** fails directly at the ledge of time shown in the merged Market Profile®. This provides a low-risk opportunity, as price must overcome the Control Point a few ticks higher up to switch the bias to the upside.

Market Profile®

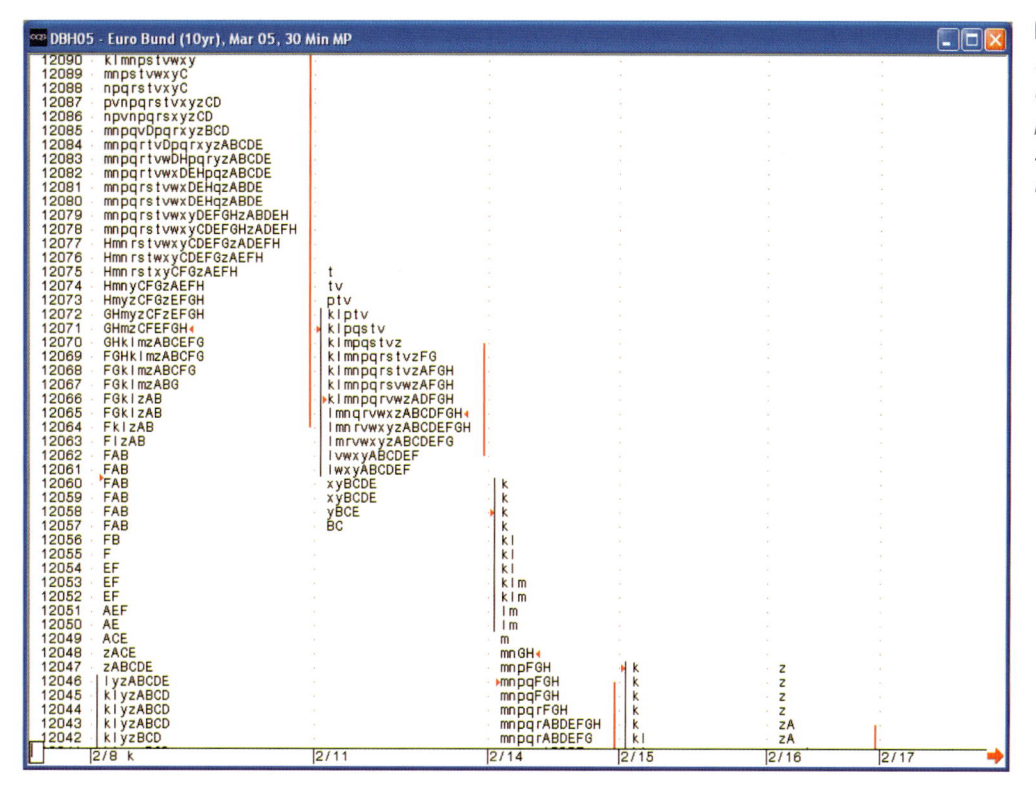

Figure 23:
Merging to create a clearer picture of trend, support and resistance

The next critical question is: what is the risk?

The merged Market Profile® suggests a move above the Control Point at 120.78 would not be ideal, but 87 is a more comfortable stop, as a ledge is evident at 84. When prices in **t** reach the ledge of time at 120.74/75 it can be seen also that this is the 2nd standard deviation point on the Volatility Time Bands (see fig. 24). When the market is waiting for economic numbers this can be a good sell point in the short term. So a sale at 120.73 can be added to by a sale at the 3rd deviation at 120.79 with a stop if price closes above the 3rd deviation on that bar. Price ambles until 1.30 p.m. where risk widens significantly up to 120.95 at the 3rd deviation. As is turns out the number is a damp squib and the short position comfortably remains intact.

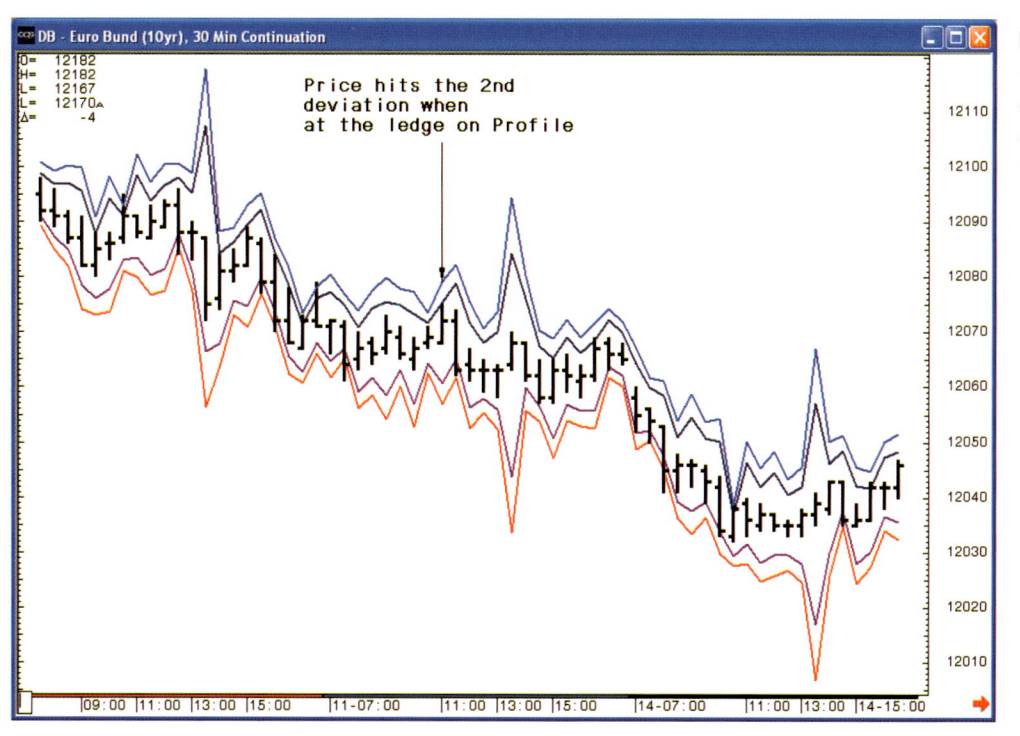

Figure 24:
Connecting supports and resistances with the time of day

TRADING TIME: New Methods in Technical Analysis

Now the Market Profile® has been merged for 4 days (see fig 25).

The Control Point has moved lower to 120.68 which means fair value has done likewise. This is bearish as the market is accepting a lower price. The opening is below both the previous day's close and the Value Area from the day before. The rally from the opening is insipid and fails at its first resistance point, which is the ledge of time. Adding power means that this level coincides with the low of the merged Value Area, which represents the low of the merged profiles' fair value. Initiative behaviour appears in the Initial Balance and is confirmed by more of the same in **m**. A cautionary note – the close in **H** was all the way back towards the highs, which emphasises the need for the short-term trader to trail stops and look to book profits in stages. This once again is where the deviation bars come into play.

Remember: the chart tells you, you don't tell the chart.

Figure 25:
Ledges of time are key points

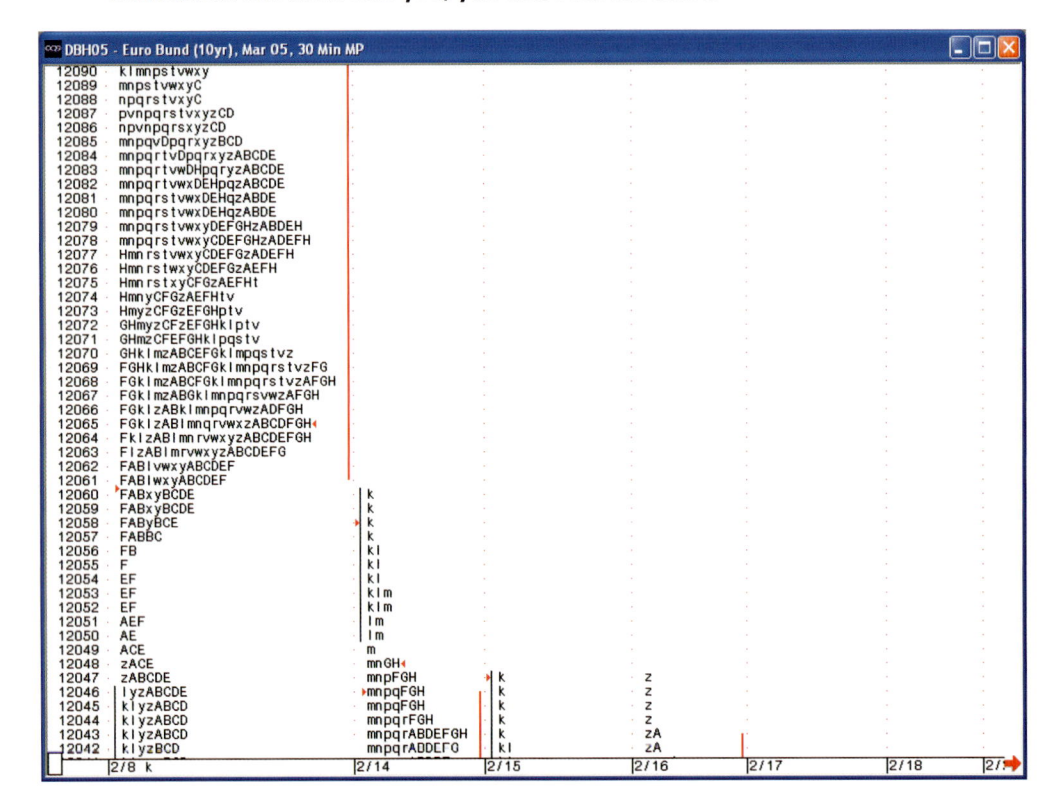

94

Market Profile®

The bands (see fig. 26) highlight the weakness of the early trading. Price remains beneath the 1st standard deviation until 10.30 a.m. and then drops 20 ticks from 120.58 to 120.38 where it reverses and hits the 3rd standard deviation up.

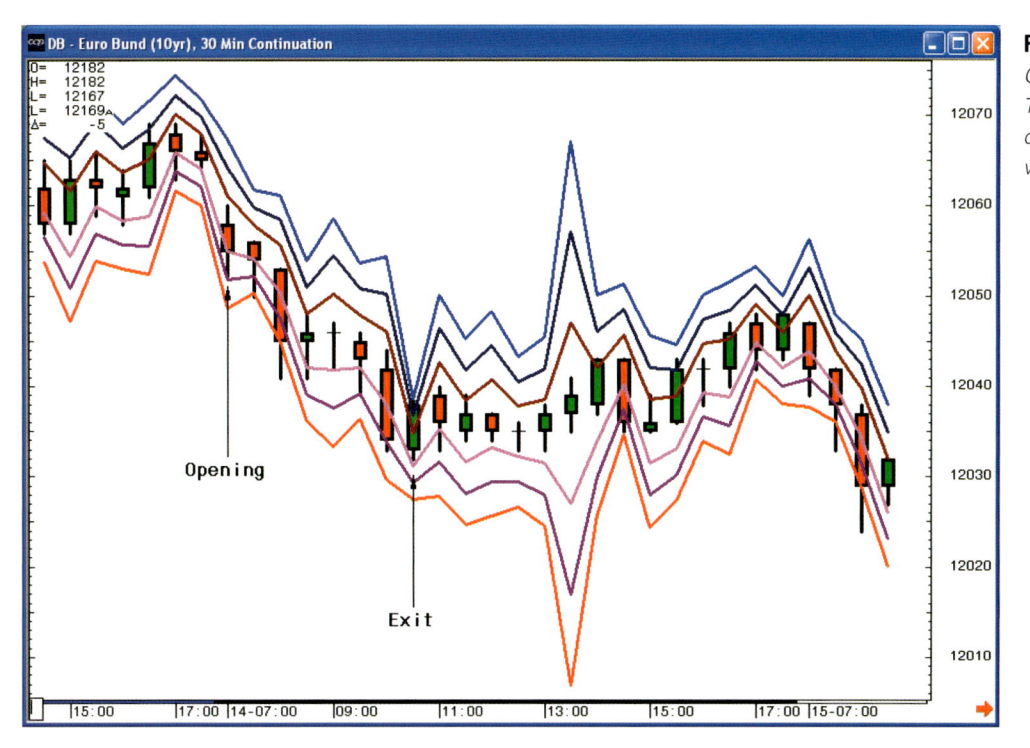

Figure 26:
OaR Volatility Time Bands confirm the early weakness

The chart (see fig. 27) has had 5 days merged. The close on 14 February (see fig. 27), the 5th day, had been strong, considering the previous weakness and the downward initiative behaviour from that day's opening.

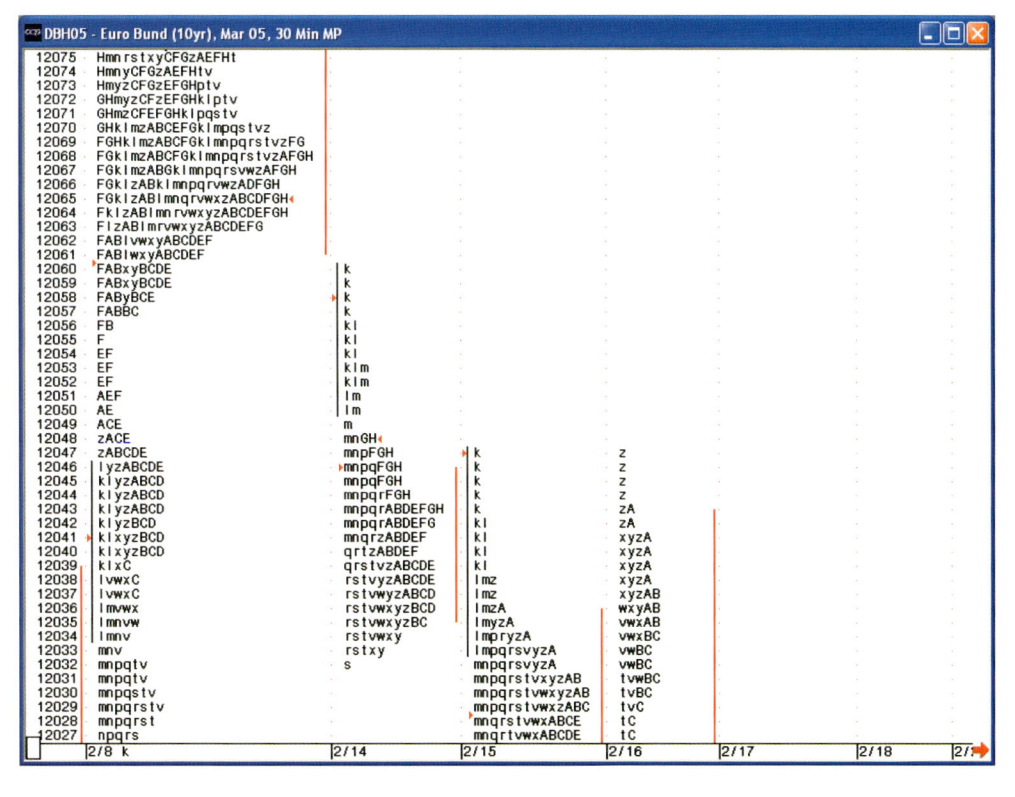

Figure 27:
Merging to understand support and resistance

The next day sees a similar pattern, as the opening is the high. Prices then halt at the first resistance, which is the ledge (see fig. 28) and then display downward initiative behaviour on the opening. In contrast, this time the close is weak, near the lows and the time that has been spent at the lower levels suggests acceptance of a lower value.

Figure 28 :
A lower ledge acts as resistance

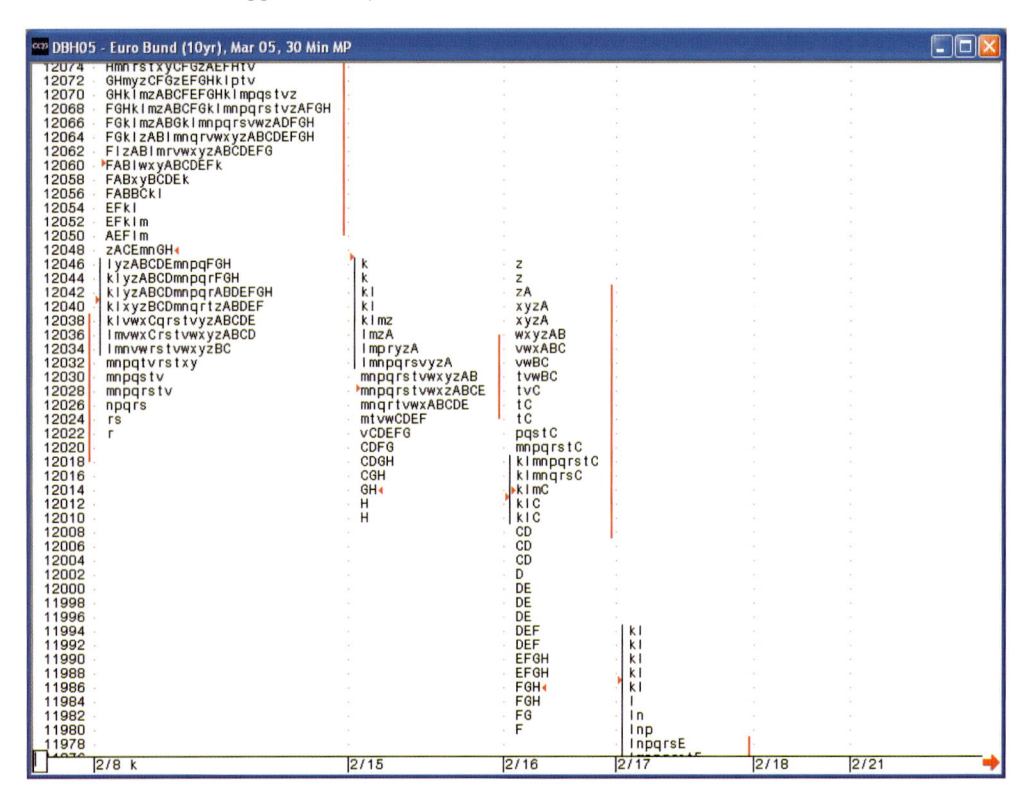

A 15-tick fall from the opening takes place before the 1st standard deviation (see fig. 29) above is touched. The 2nd standard deviation band is only met on 2 occasions.

Figure 29 :
The bands contain any corrective rallies against the dominant trend of the day

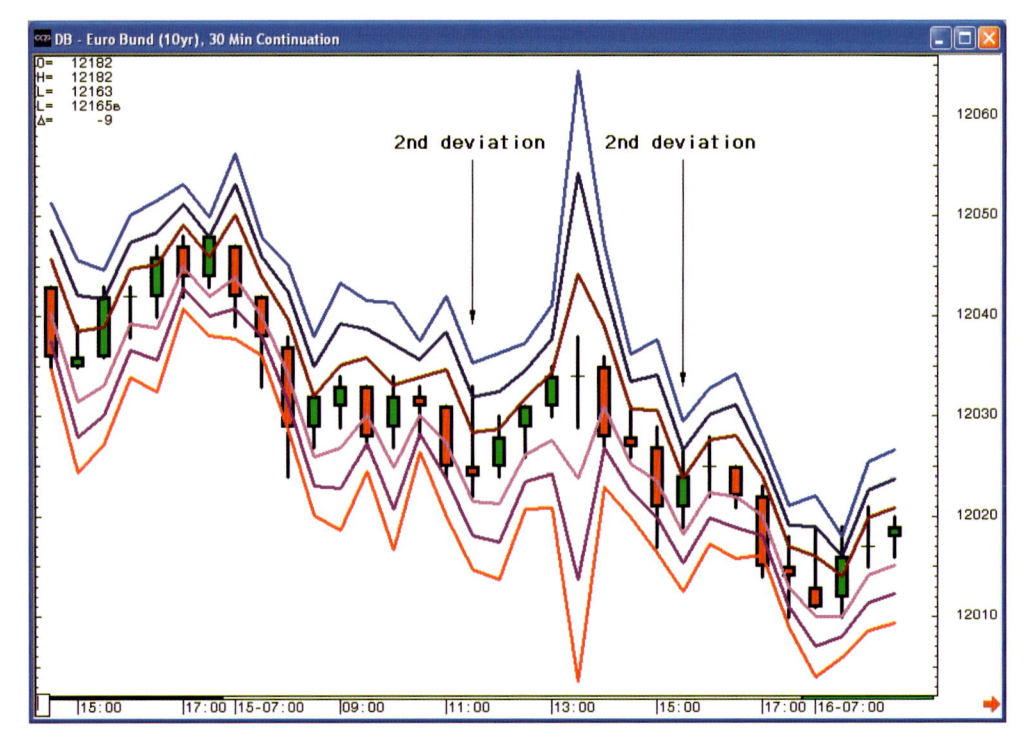

We will return to the next day later in this section.

Market Profile®

Super Tankers

They take a long time to stop and turn around.

Remember, Market Profile® aims to separate the long-term trader from the short-term trader and so we are primarily interested in a relatively small proportion of the total volume traded each day. On bond markets the price action after Non Farm Payroll day is often a clue to the overall trend for the immediate future. Fed interest rate decisions are also pivotal moments. For payroll days the key question is:

Does the Monday and Tuesday confirm the Friday's price action post Non-Farm Payrolls?

The unemployment number is often the key statistic of the month for interest rate markets, as the trade deficit is to the dollar. Long-term traders need at least one day to evaluate their positions and then, if need be, take action. As mentioned earlier, in the hurly burly of the Friday afternoon many wish to wait for price to settle down and see where it closes. The following Monday will see more commentaries reflect on the fundamental impact of the story and for many there will be discussion about what action is to be taken. If they are on the correct side of the move the discussions will relate to where strategic stop and profit levels should be and if the winning formula should be added to. Of more interest, however, is an understanding of what the long-term traders on the wrong side are doing.

I refer to these types of traders as **super tankers**: it takes a long time for them to stop and exit and then turn their position around. Analysis of the 'Commitment of Traders' report, in spite of the delay and more timely information, can still provide insight. For some players the sheer scale of their positions means that they have to take care and work the market. They often employ a number of brokers to manage their trades. Therefore, instead of acting hastily to open new positions or liquidate existing positions, they are more likely to try and finesse their exits. The long-term traders who are looking to open positions or wish to add to an existing one will do likewise. This means that the first two days after the number provide numerous clues as to what the real state of the market is.

The next chart shows (see fig. 30) a bullish payroll reaction (8/10/04) where price moves sharply as is the norm and then holds that value for the rest of the day. Tuesday (there had been a holiday on Monday) sees price gap up and then hold value once again as long-term traders look to buy. The following day shows the true picture as the market gaps back down. This is initially bearish, but price shows responsive behaviour in **z** within the Initial Balance period. Long-term traders regard this move back down to the Value Area low and high volume point of the payroll day as an opportunity to build longs. This provides a low-risk opportunity at the end of **A** for short-term traders, as price should not now break back through the Initial Balance low. However the rally is not particularly dynamic, so partial profits could have been taken in **C**, which is the previous day's Value Area low and high volume point, and at **F** (the Control Point and 2 ticks below the Value Area high), whilst finally leaving the rest of the position for the close, which is near the highs of the day.

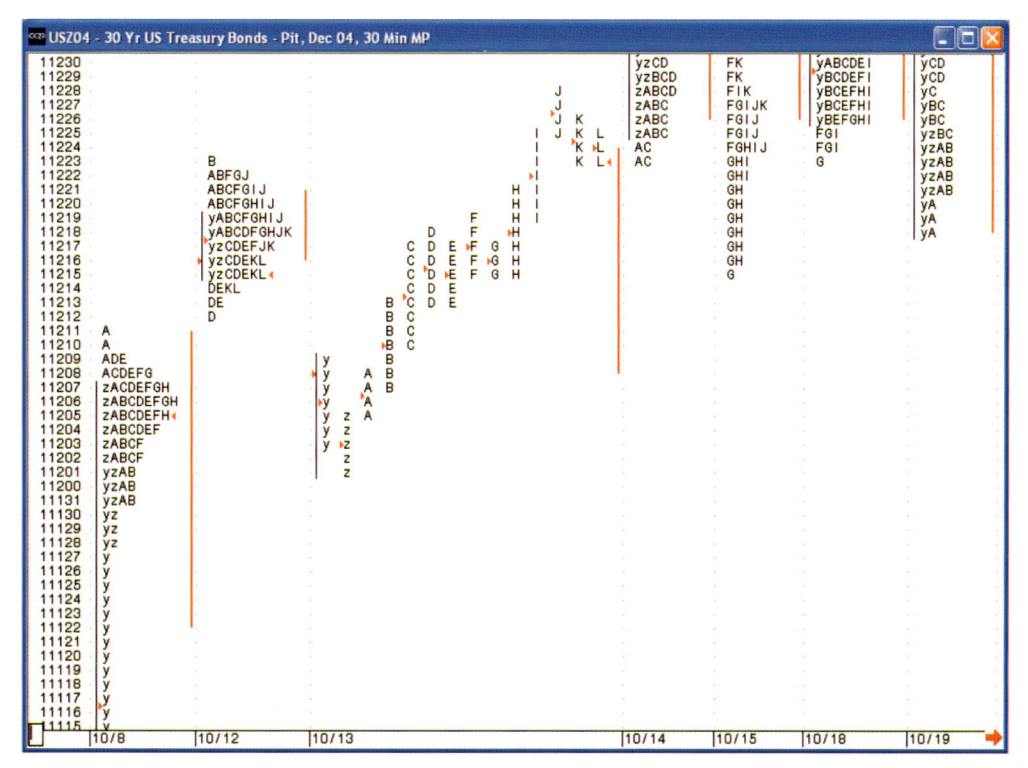

Figure 30: *Non Farm Payroll*

TRADING TIME: New Methods in Technical Analysis

Adjustments for Short-Term Interest Rates

Short-term interest rate contracts present some difficulty for analysis as there is simply not enough movement to provide a clear picture. Therefore in a sideways grind it is necessary to merge the data. The following two pictures (see fig. 31 and fig. 32) show how much clearer the merged picture is. Price has been accepting value at the top end of the range, which is bullish. The Control Point is also skewed upwards. In a highly unusual occurrence in this market the breakout higher is marked by two sets of initiative activity in **l** and **z** and the start of a new trend begins.

Figure 31:
The Short End creates problems of definition

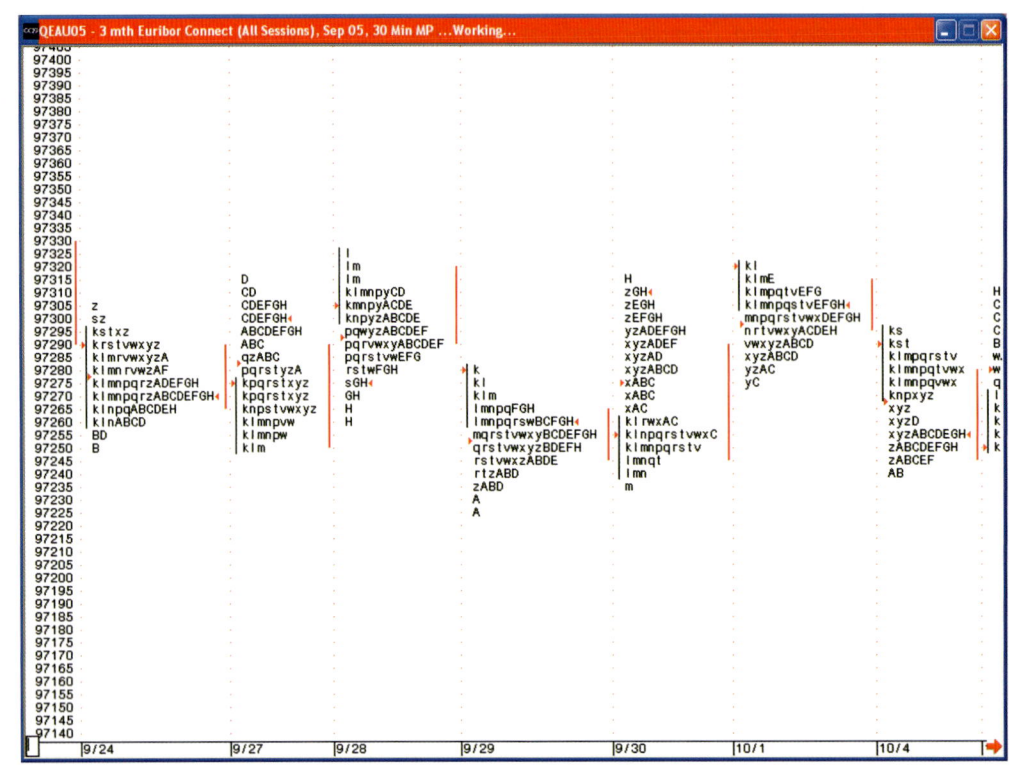

Figure 32:
Merging creates a much clearer picture

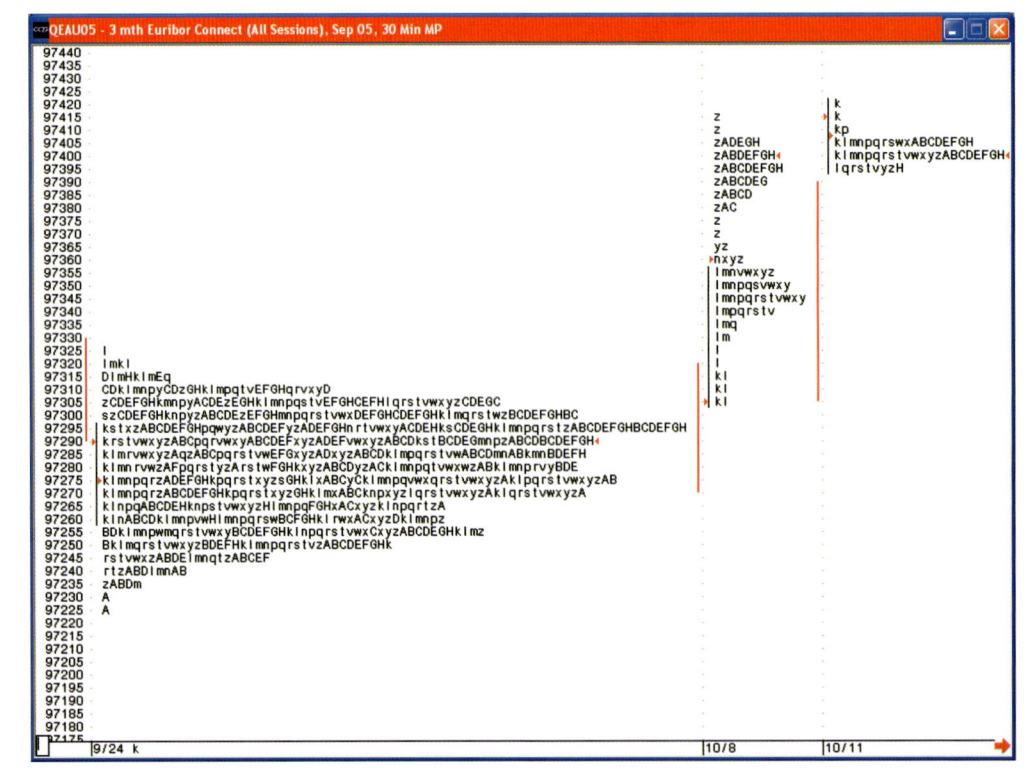

Market Profile®

Volume Peaks
Next we study where the highest level of volume was.

As mentioned earlier, traditional Market Profile® views this as a percentage, so it has some inherent flaws. For those prepared to download data and manipulate it, the use of ticks as an absolute value is far more useful. However, the traditional method can still be used as a reference point, especially if linked to other Market Profile® setups or traditional technical analysis.

The Bund chart (see fig. 33) 27 January shows a typical example. Price makes new highs in the key **z** period after an economic report. It stops directly at the beginning of a high volume area from the day before.

Armed with the knowledge that another number is due at 3 p.m., and it's a Friday, will long-term traders commit themselves?
Unlikely. Analysis of the Volatility Time Bands (see fig. 34) shows that price has hit the 3rd standard deviation up, so providing a low-risk opportunity. However, by the time the 3 p.m. number is released, the positions risk/reward adjusts as the OaR Bands widen in preparation for the expected volatility after the number.

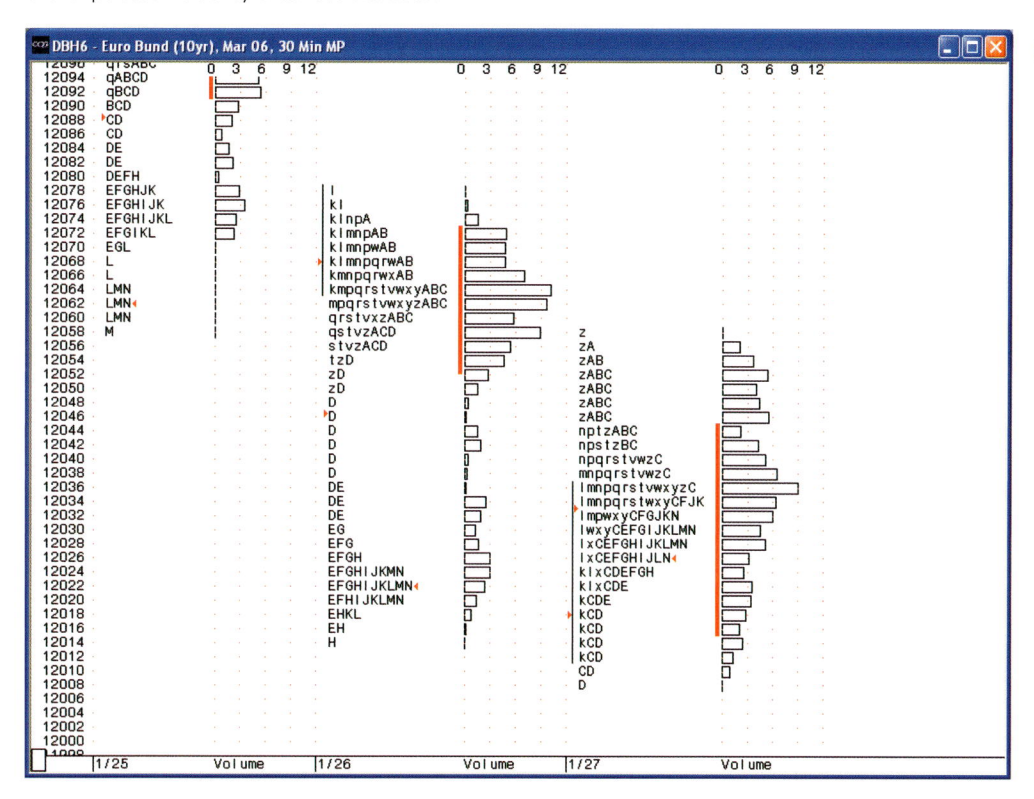

Figure 33:
Volume Peaks

Figure 34:
Time bands qualify and provide a low-risk opportunity.

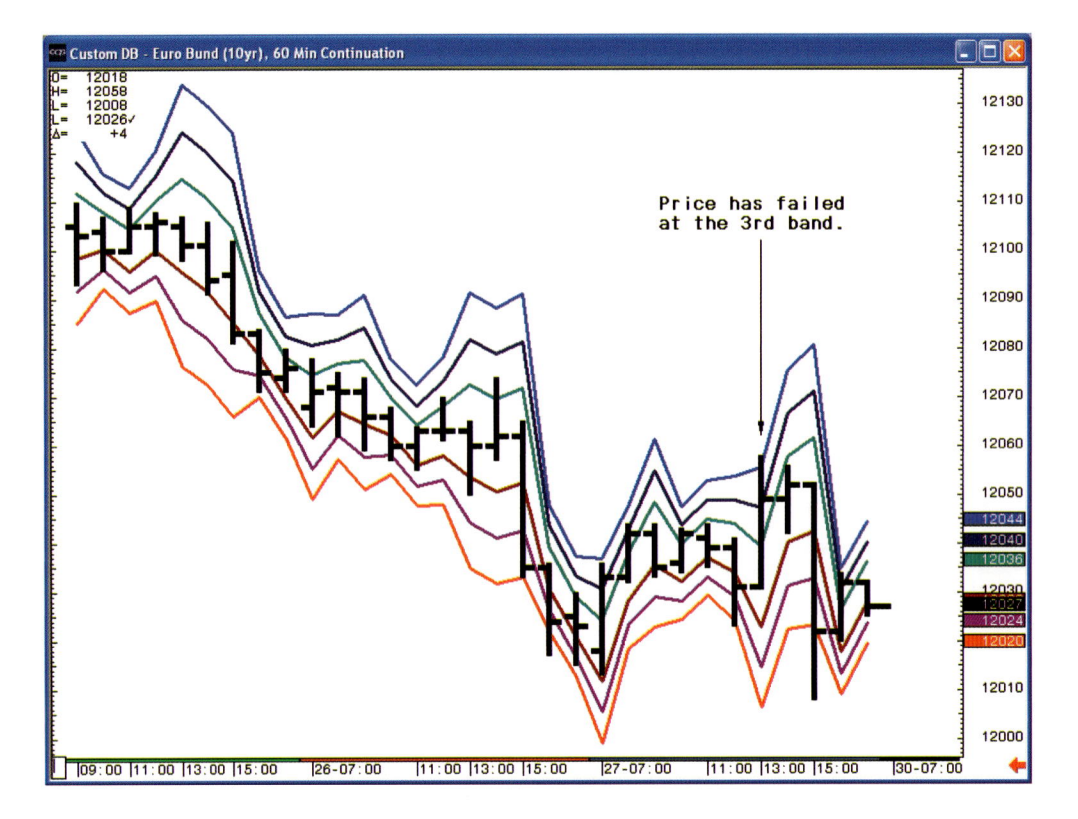

Analysis of the bigger picture (see fig. 35) shows that price has been in a steep downtrend with price consistently failing at or ahead of the 1st standard deviation up until the current bar. There have also been various moves beyond the 3rd deviation down. The daily 3rd standard deviation up is at 120.59. The combination of the 60-minute (see fig. 34) and the daily 3rd standard deviation (see fig. 35) provides a powerful entry zone of 120.56 to 120.59.

Figure 35 :
Historical resistance connects with the time of day.

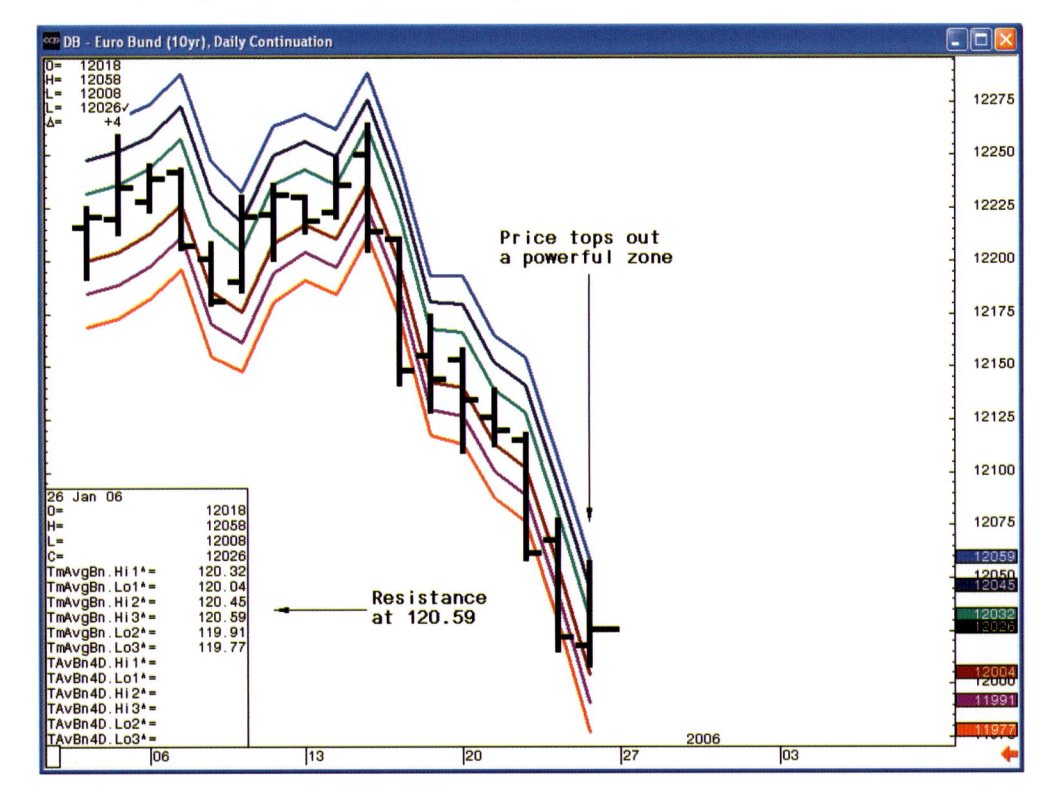

Vacuums

Stop placement and the relevance of the speed of movement within this area.
Vacuums (or prices where little time has been spent at certain prices) often become the inflection or flip points between distributions. These can also be utilised for short-term trading and intelligent stop placements. The theories concerning vacuums are many. Here I list two of the more common patterns.

Fast speed
While high-volume points can create support and resistance levels, especially when linked to time, areas where there is little volume are equally revealing. The chart below (see fig. 36) shows an initiative move 7 June in **C**. Two days later 11 June (see fig. 36) price has displayed responsive behaviour at the lows and breaks up in **C**. This is confirmed in the **D** period 11 June when price enters the beginning of the vacuum at **C** created 7 June. Price then extends all the way through the vacuum to where it stops at 101.04.

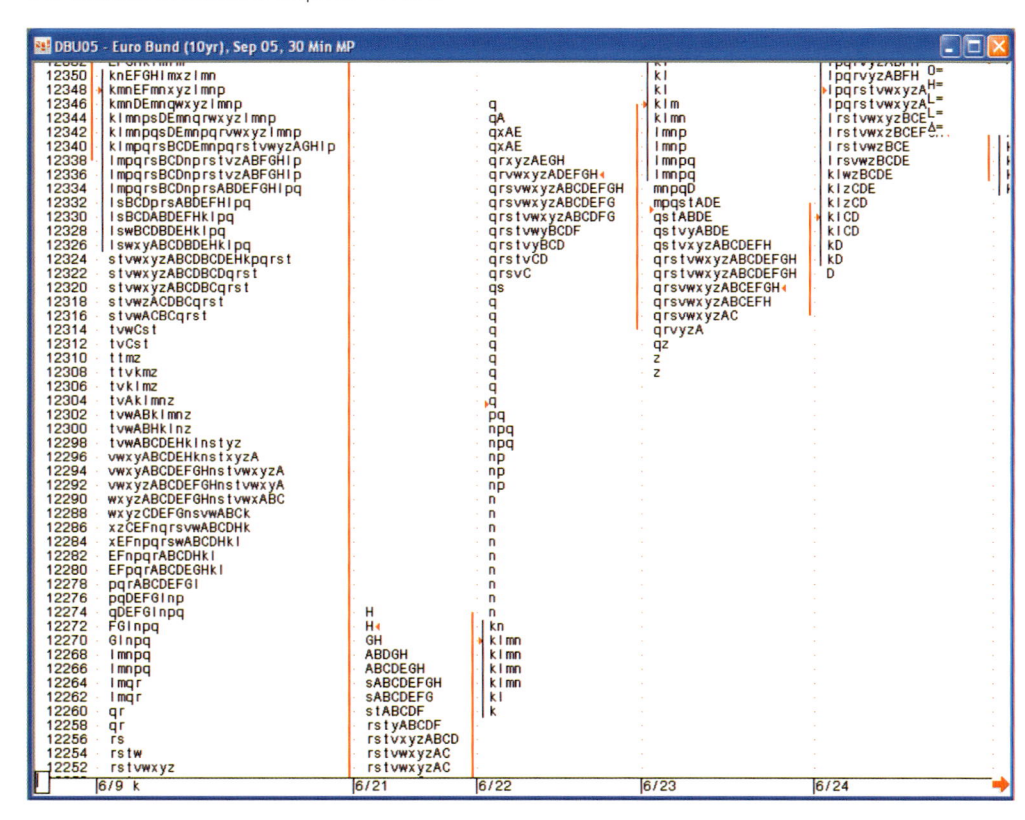

Figure 36.
Vacuums

Therefore, another rule can be introduced:

vacuum up = vacuum down (and vice versa)

Once price enters a vacuum there is little point in placing a stop within the area, as there is nothing in terms of price, time or volume to stop it reaching the other side. This means that the beginnings and endings of vacuums provide precise points at which to enter new positions. In addition, if you are placing stops, they must be at the beginnings of vacuums or beyond the other side of them depending on your risk appetite and trading strategy.

TRADING TIME: New Methods in Technical Analysis

In contrast to many Market Profile® rules, vacuums have a longer reference than the five days, but ideally the quicker the price re-enters a previous vacuum the more significant it is. The FX markets are notorious for producing vacuum reversals within the same day or following day. The Dax (see fig. 37) shows a small vacuum that is created in **w** period 5 July. The following day once price enters the vacuum in **p** it rises quickly to the ledge of time in **q**. The high in **x** is the previous day's control point.

Figure 37:
Price moves swiftly up a vacuum and stalls at the next two resistance points in place for the previous day's price action.

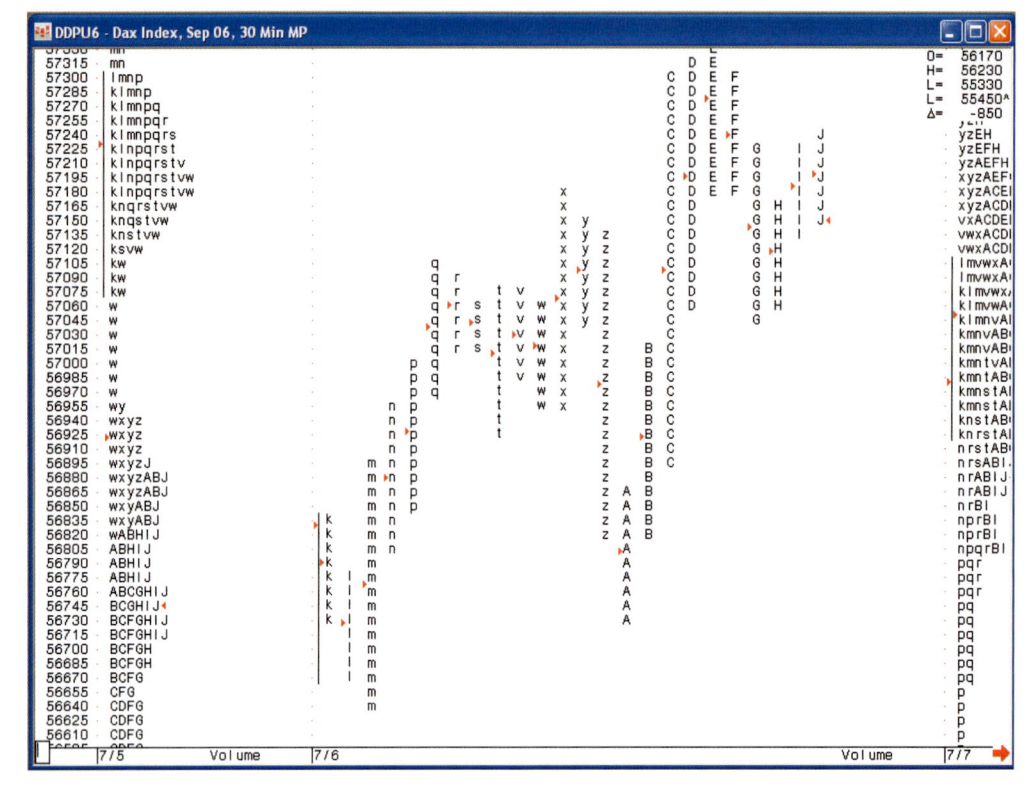

Price enters a vacuum 30 June (see fig. 38) and moves directly to the other side at 115.16 in the **n** period (low 115.15).

Figure 38.
Vacuums

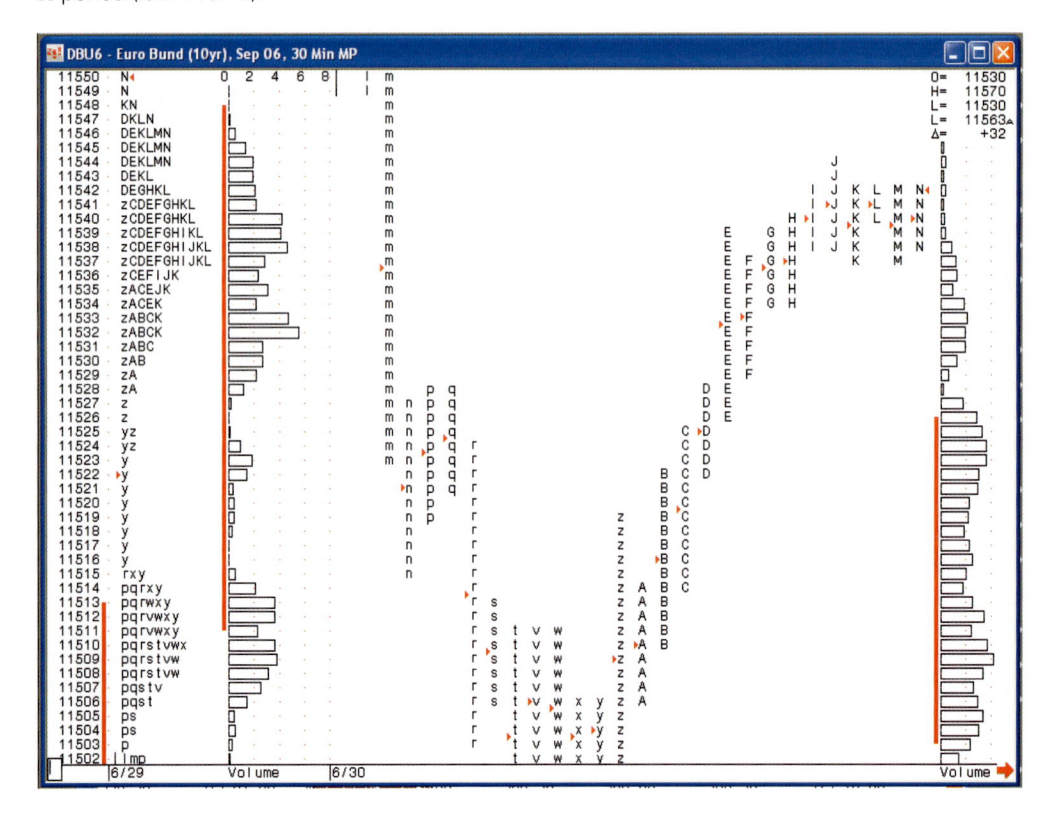

102

Market Profile®

Forex and vacuums

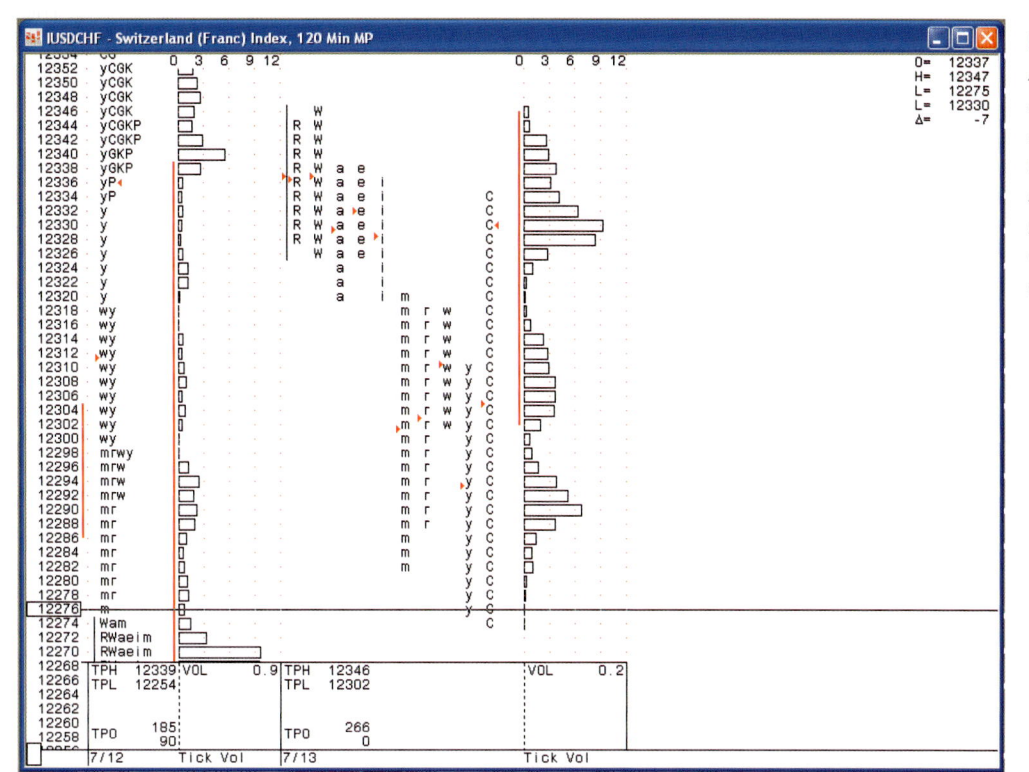

Figure 39.
A typical setup on FX. Price moves directly to the vacuum low and then rallies back up the vacuum in even quicker fashion

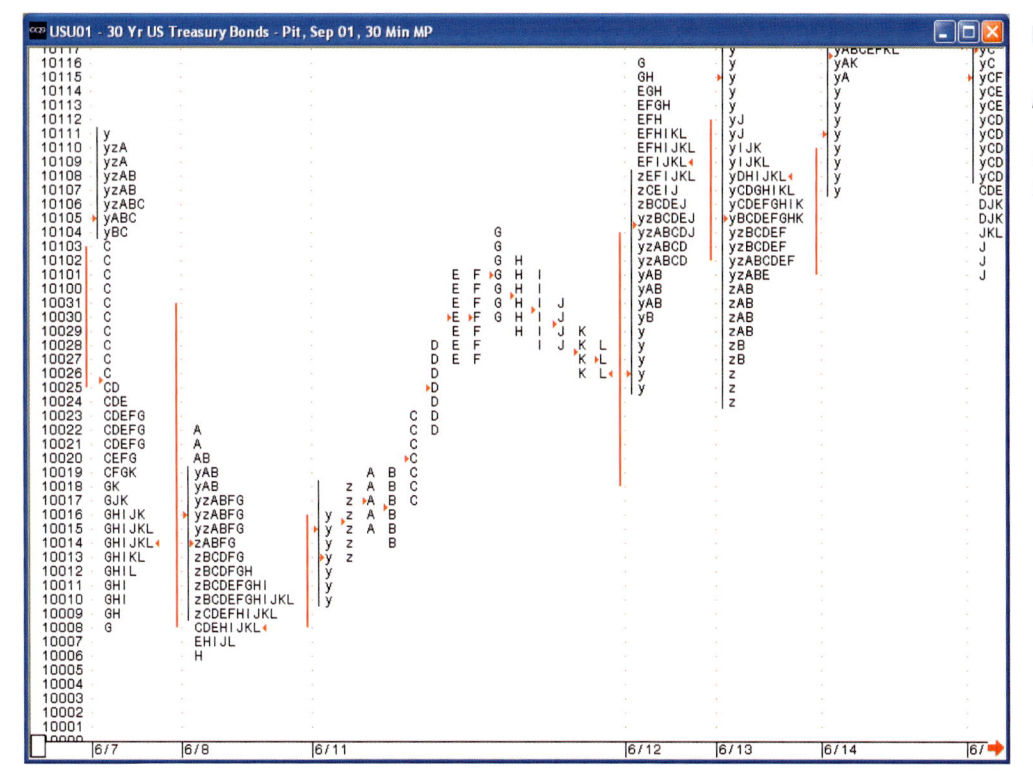

Figure 40:
11 June once price trades at 11026 there is nothing to stop a move to 10104

TRADING TIME: New Methods in Technical Analysis

Slow speed

Slow moves into vacuums that fail to reach the other side are also significant. If price cannot extend through an area where little time or volume has been spent it suggests that the correction has ended and the dominant trend is resuming. Once again this is particularly common in FX markets.

The first example (see fig. 41) shows the last 4 letters on the Dax 29 June (**K**, **L**, **M** and **N**), which with the extended hours has very low volume. The following day sees price enter the vacuum of volume but cannot extend to the other side down at 5631. Price then recovers and the uptrend resumes.

Figure 41:
Slow movement in vacuums shows the dominant trend is resuming.

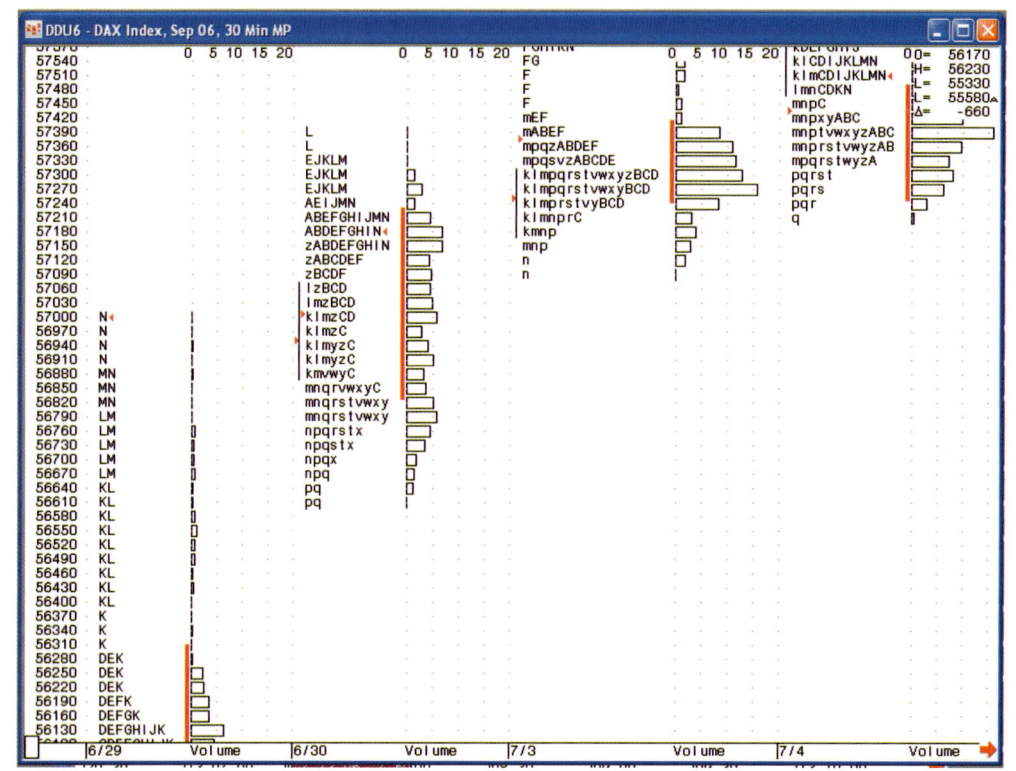

Cross rates on FX often display vacuum characteristics. Fig. 42 shows that price fails to extend fully down the vacuum and ambles within it until it then goes on a sharp short covering rally in **C**.

Figure 42.
Vacuums on FX

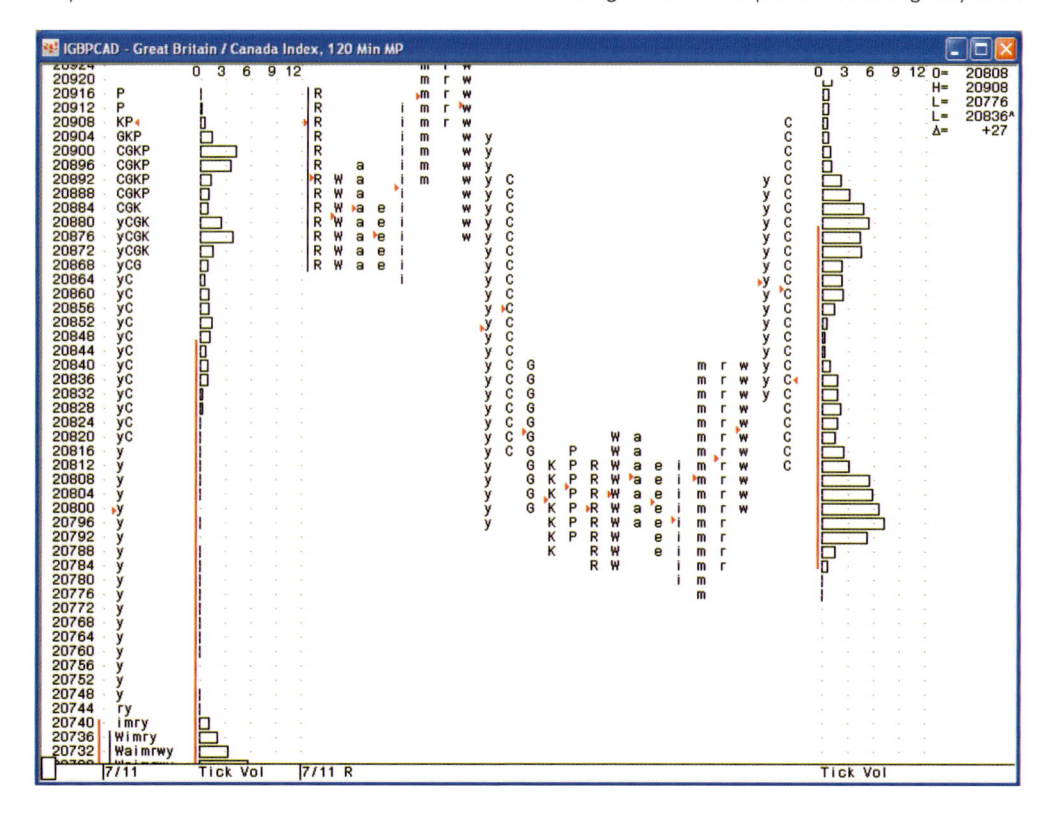

104

Market Profile®

Therefore, slow moves that fail to extend to the other side of a vacuum are corrective patterns against the dominant trend.

How many vacuums in one day?

Very occasionally markets move so quickly that a whole series of vacuums appear. Normally, even on a strong trend day, once you have seen 3 vacuums it's time to start to consider reducing positions. The Dax chart (see fig. 43) shows that in the morning alone there have been 3 vacuums or single letter prints up to **x**. Price then ebbs and flows holding higher value while the market participants wait for the US to open. By 3 p.m., in what is a very unusual move that displays exceptional strength, **C** moves higher once again and the market closes on the highs. This day proved to be the low for many weeks.

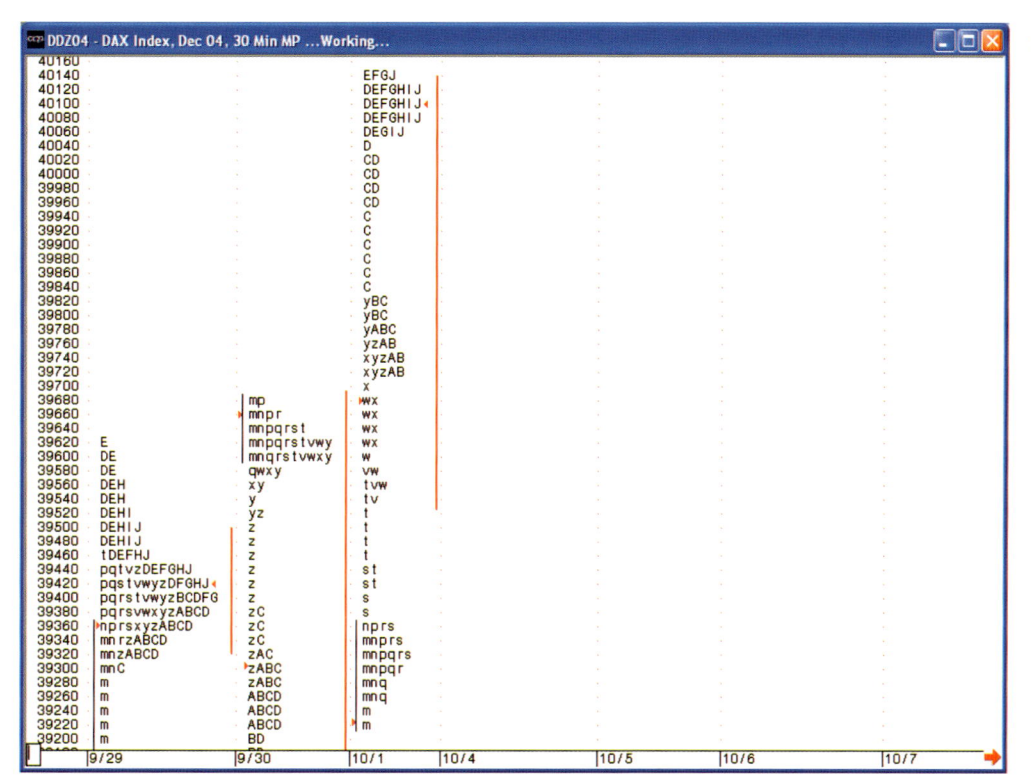

Figure 43:
A highly unusual day

Single letter prints and trends. OaR Volatility Time Bands qualify success and failure.

This brings us on to a key connection between single letters within Market Profile® that suggests that a fresh trend is beginning.

Often it is difficult to know how strong a single letter initiative or responsive thrust is. Use of the Volatility Time Bands or the other deviation studies can help to quantify. If price closes beyond the 3rd standard deviation and is a single letter print, this means that the thrust is outside the parameters of normal behaviour at that time of day and suggests the thrust should be successful. Failure on a Market Profile® basis is if the single letter print is filled, although with Volatility Time Bands it is possible to use more dynamic methods such as moves beyond the first or second deviation in the opposite direction to the thrust. This is a very important tool in the trader's armoury.

TRADING TIME: New Methods in Technical Analysis

To return to the Dax (see fig. 44), the breakout coincides with a move beyond the 3rd standard deviation on the Volatility Time Bands. By the end of the day price has closed beyond the 3rd standard deviation on the daily chart as well (see fig. 45). Analysis of the Volatility Time Average Bands (see fig. 47) shows that price touched the 3rd band up 3 times and signalled short-term exhaustion points.

Figure 44:
A strong trend day

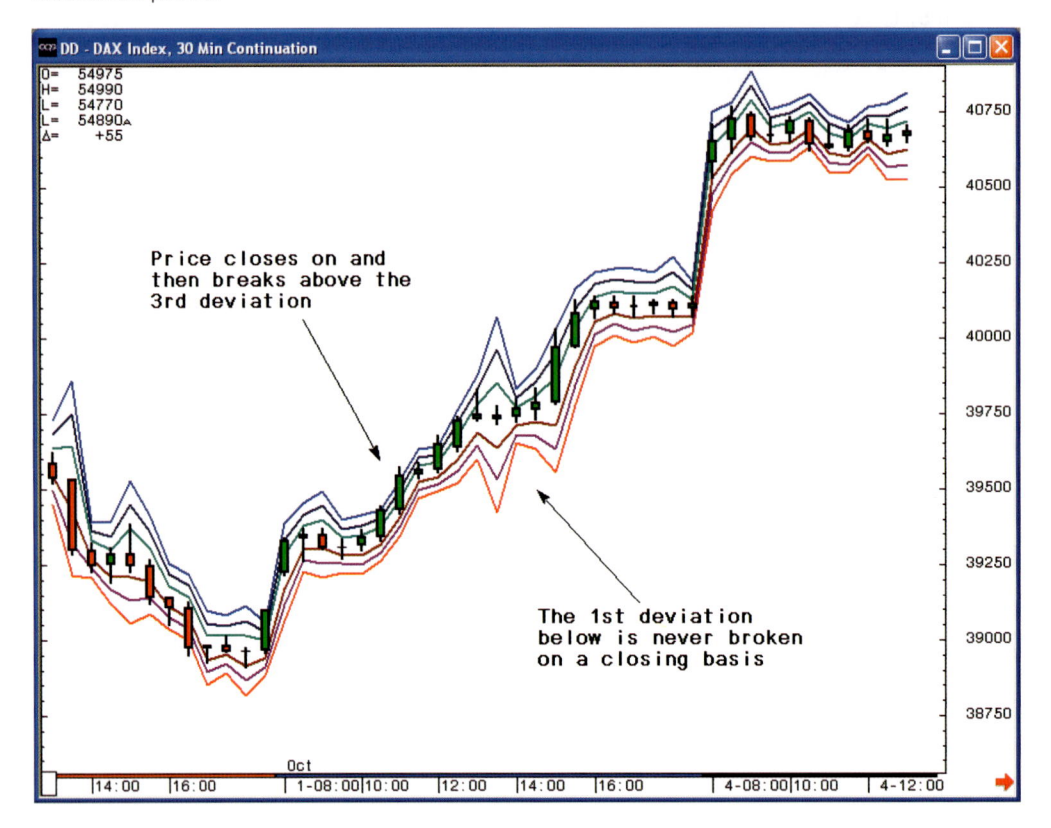

Price closes on and then breaks above the 3rd deviation

The 1st deviation below is never broken on a closing basis

Figure 45:
Historical Time Bands. The much higher opening on the day after the break below the 3rd band down is the first clue that the move lower was false.

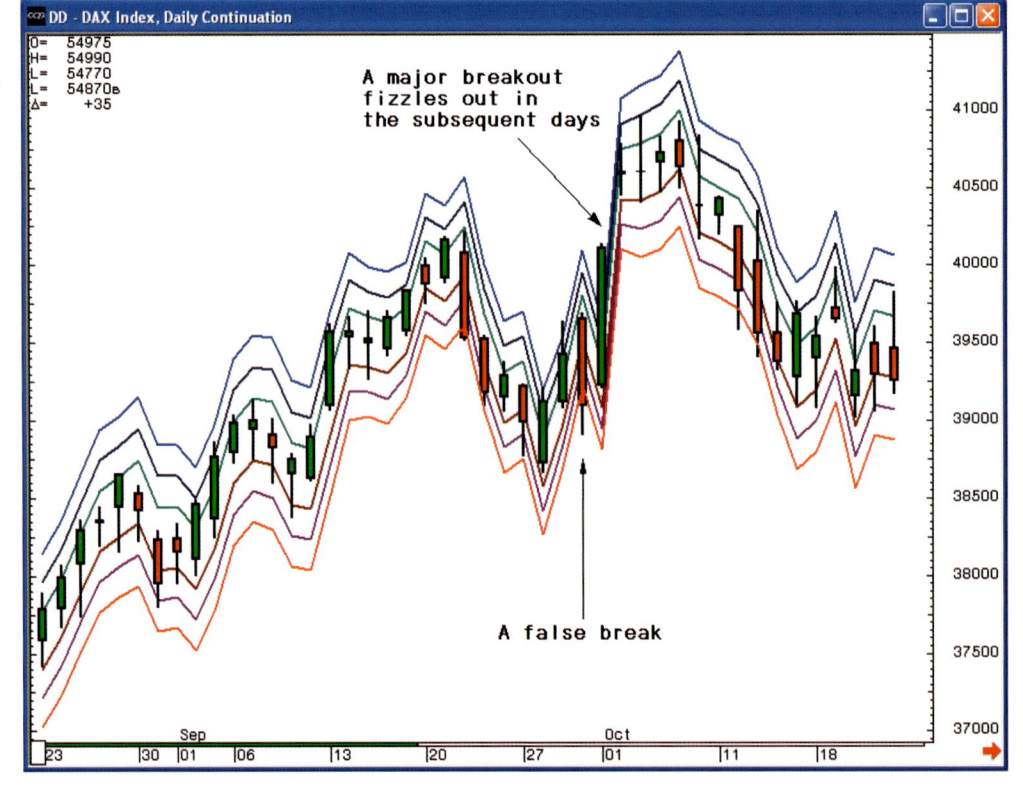

A major breakout fizzles out in the subsequent days

A false break

106

Market Profile®

Analysis of that day's Market Profile® highlights the power of vacuums. 1 October sees price open higher than the previous day's close. 30 September's move was late in the day, which suggests short-term sellers. The key confirmation comes 1 October when **s** enters the vacuum created the day before in **z**. Price accelerates higher and shows no fewer than 5 single letter prints in **s, t, w, x** and **c**.

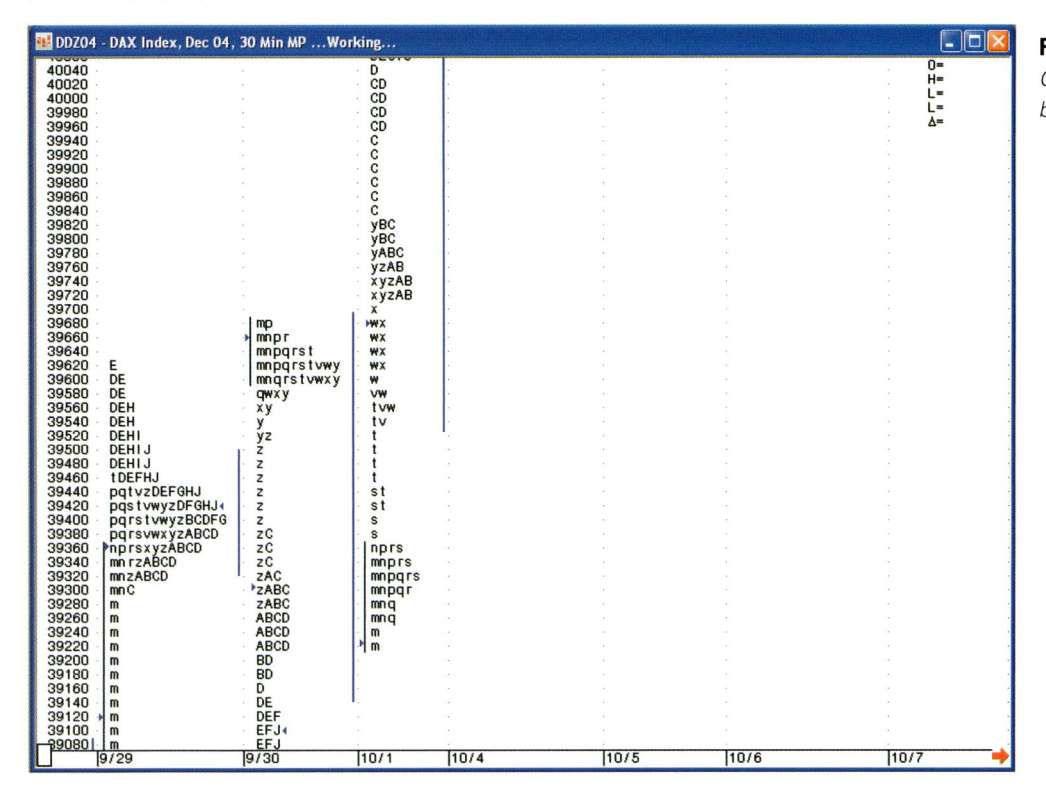

Figure 46:
Qualifying a false break.

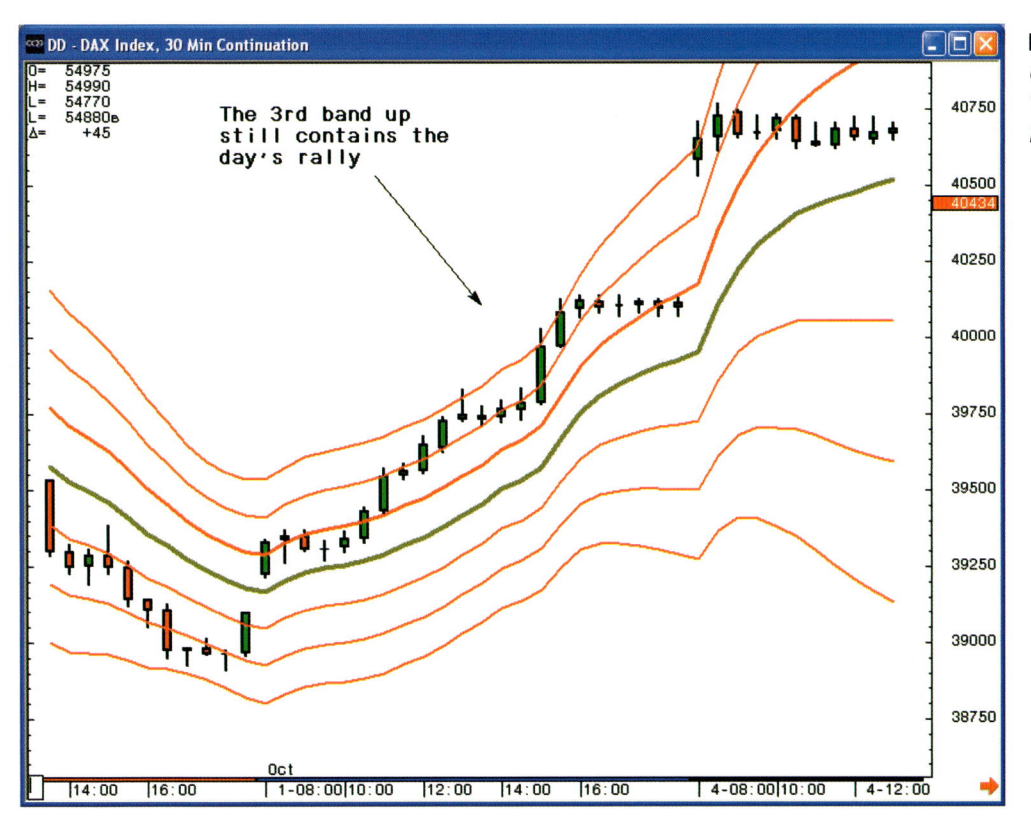

Figure 47:
OaR Volatility Time Average Bands

TRADING TIME: New Methods in Technical Analysis

Bunds

Returning to vacuums – fig. 48 is an example on the Bund. A wild gyration in **z** 24 September, which follows the release of the economic numbers, suggests an uncertain view of where the statistics would send the market. Note **B** breaks down and moves directly to the bottom of the vacuum created 22 September where support is found. 27 September sees a move just one tick below that day's initial balance in **m**, which is also the top of the vacuum from 22 September. This leads us to the next theory.

Figure 48:
The vacuum on 9/22 has relevance two days later

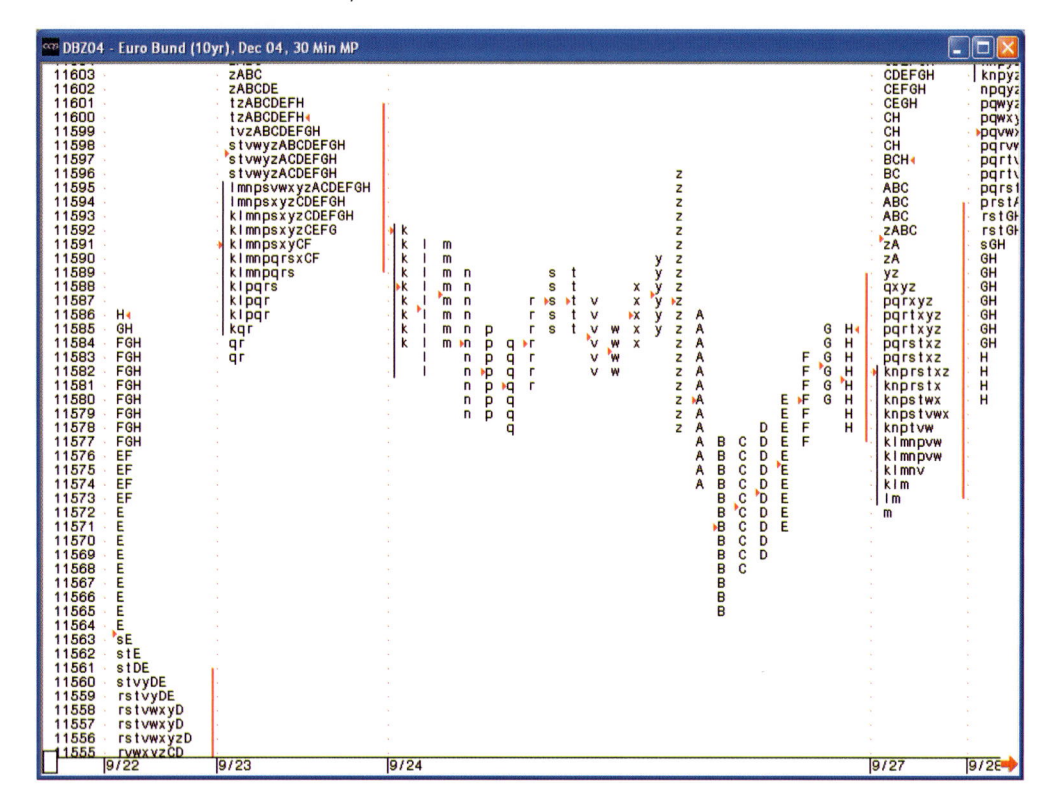

Markets need to indicate no desire to go in one direction before they move in the other.
Markets often need to know that there is no desire to move in one direction before they have the confidence to move in the other. The previous chart (see fig. 48) 27 September was a classic example. Price ambles around in directionless fashion, makes a new low **m**, finds that there are no stops and then the market reverses and trends.

Market Profile®

Figure 49 shows the Bund breaking to new highs in **z** 15 October. However, this proves to be the high of the day and price reverses sharply.

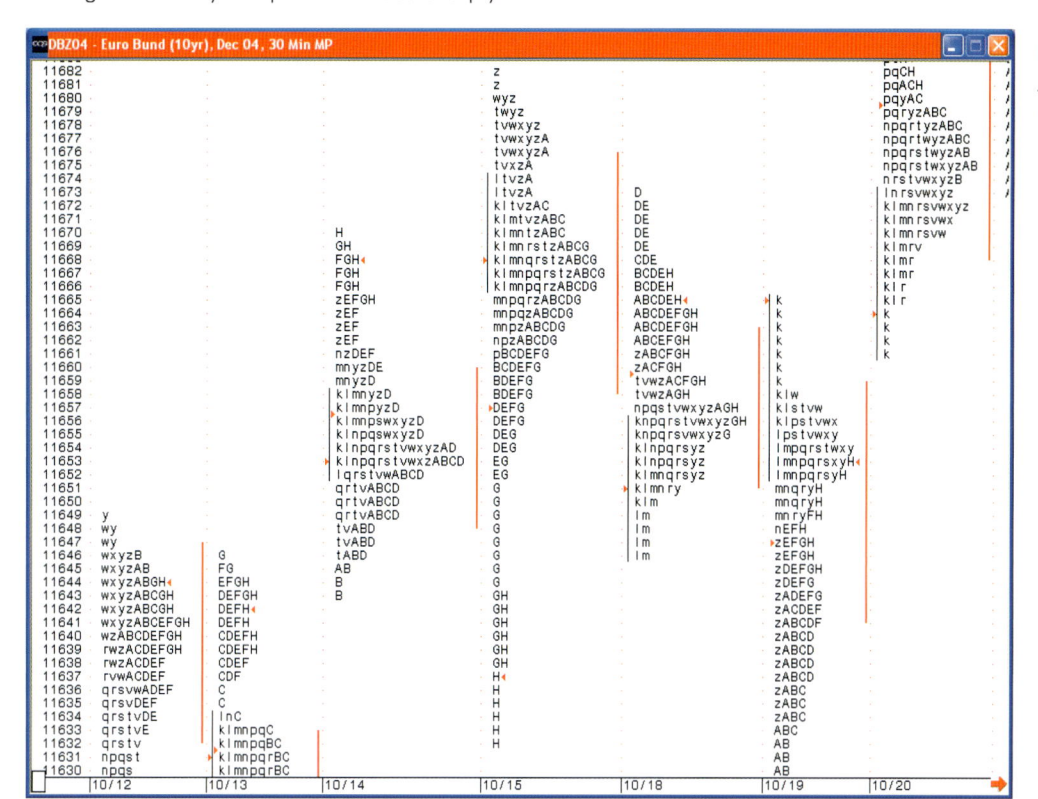

Figure 49:
A failure 15 October

Why was this?

The bar chart (see fig. 50) shows that we are in fact making a double top from the highs 6 months earlier. As mentioned before, the traditional big picture analysis connects well with Market Profile®. The market needs to know that there is no desire to break up before it has the confidence to break down. It is important to note that, while a short-term opportunity appears, this reversal does not last long.

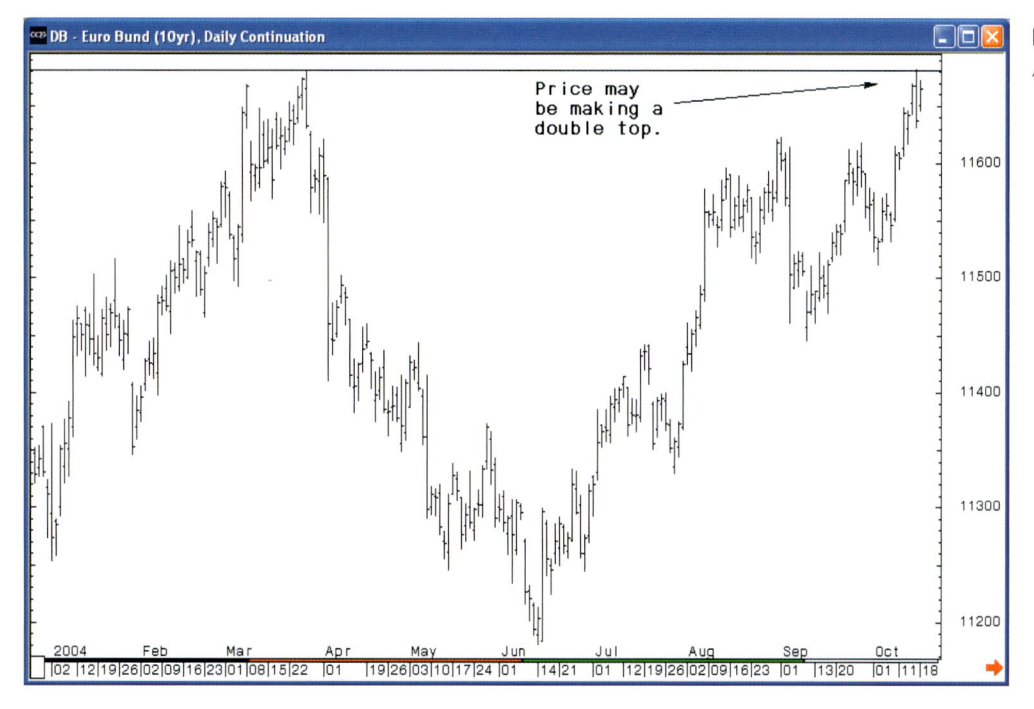

Figure 50:
A double top

109

The close on the breakdown day is at the lows and is with single letters which suggests that a huge number of short-term traders were caught long and forced out by time. Analysis of the time bands shows that in spite of the weakness, price stopped perfectly at the 3rd standard deviation low. Therefore the next day's opening is key. The opening the next day is significantly higher, which confirms that the previous day's close was caused by short-term traders.

Figure 51 :
Time Bands quantify the lows

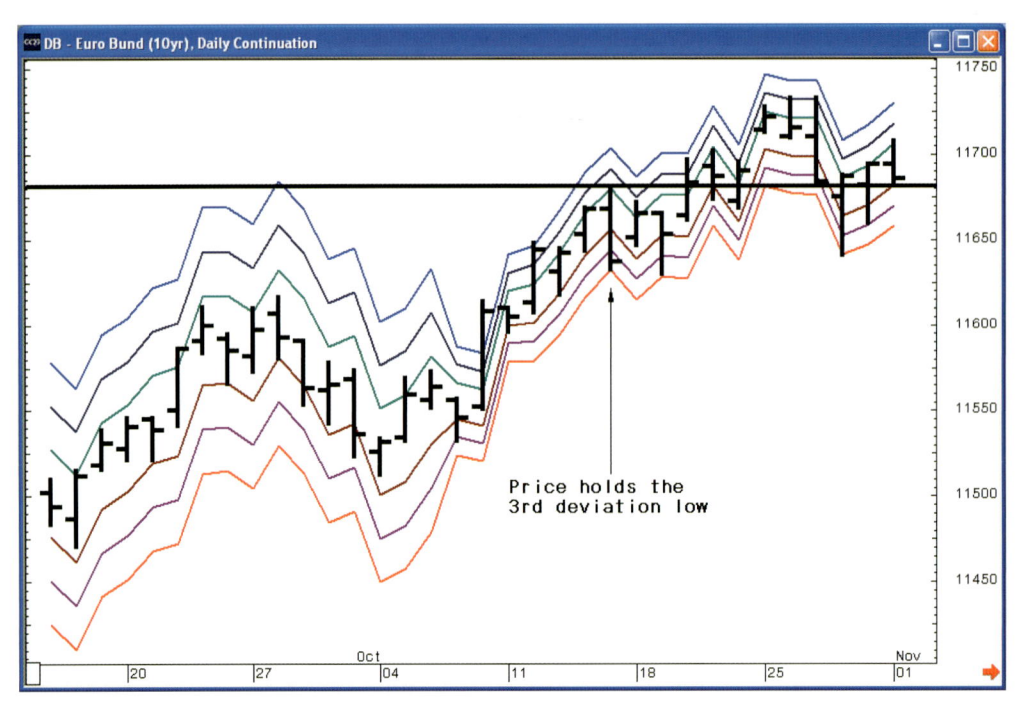

Bunds

A case study

The final set of charts examines a case study which connects Market Profile® with simple candlestick theory. Figure 52 shows that price had formed a rare triple Doji. The mantra is that this is a reversal pattern but looking further back we can see the same pattern, and that failed. For me Doji's are reversals or continuations. I prefer to see them as continuations. This harks back to the theory of taking advantage of perceived logic in the market and being ready to do the opposite. As you can see, when price broke up, the move over the next two days was swift. In later chapters we will look at how various top picking clubs had reason to enter and then were forced out.

Market Profile®

One question on the latest triple Doji is: **"Are we in an uptrend or a downtrend?"** It could be argued either way. The only clue that the break will be up is the fact that on true measures of overbought and oversold, price is oversold on the 60 and 120-minute. This is covered in Cynthia Kases' book 'Trading with the Odds'. The complete concepts are beyond the remit of this book but for me the study is the only true measurement of overbought and oversold. Most participants who don't know the market is oversold are more likely to be focusing on a bearish head and shoulders pattern.

Figure 52:
Uptrend or downtrend?

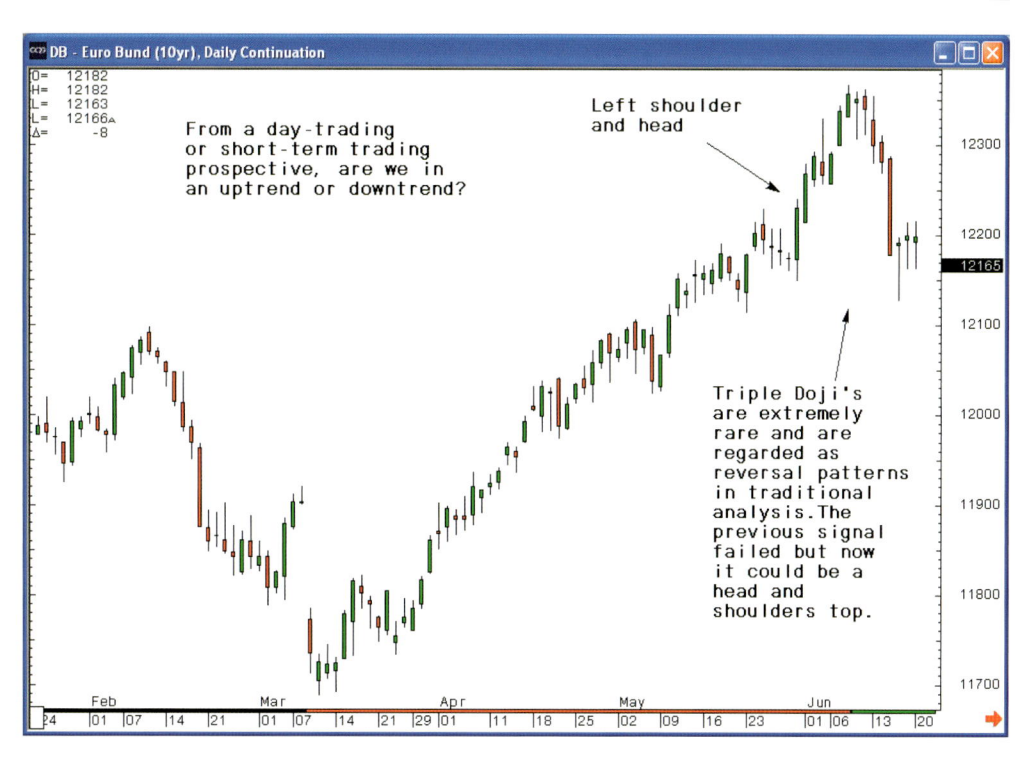

Figure 53:
Uptrend or downtrend?

The candlestick chart (see fig. 53) shows the 3 Doji's. There are few clues and none of them is compelling as far as the next direction of the market is concerned (see fig 54). However, when the Market Profile® is merged from the day of the high to the day of the second Doji, the picture becomes far clearer (see fig 55). The Control Point or fair value is all the way up at 122.90. Price is currently building a lower distribution and a vacuum area marks the points between the lower and higher one. This begins at 122.20, although the top is less clear-cut. There is one minor ledge at 122.40 and a major ledge just ahead of control at 122.80.

Figure 54 :
No real clues to future direction when the days are not merged.

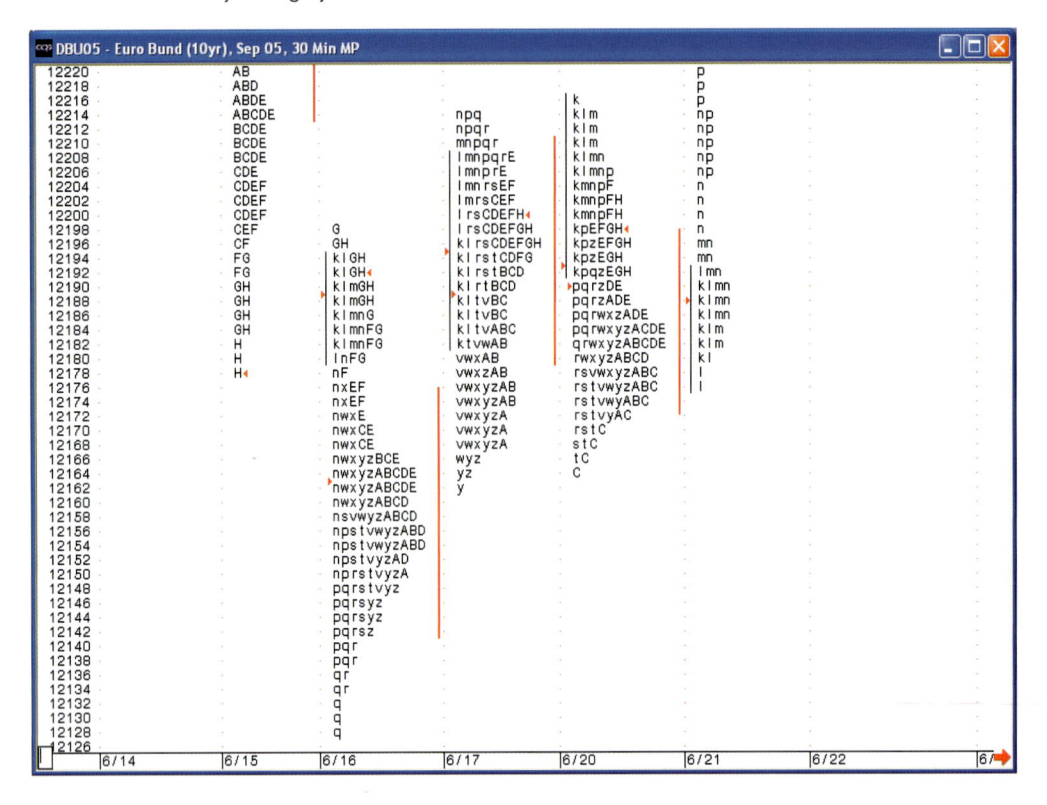

Figure 55 : *The merged picture*

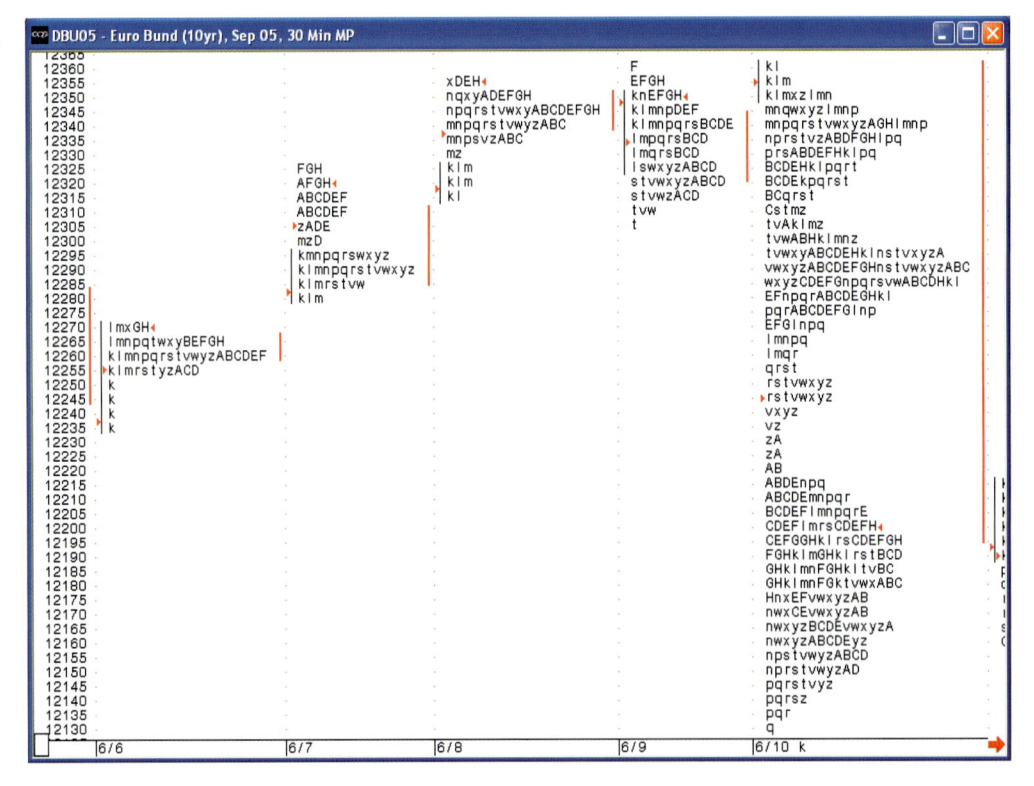

Market Profile®

Control Shifts

Now we look at the day of the third Doji and the picture has shifted significantly. The time spent going sideways accepting a lower value has moved the Control Point lower (see fig 56). Therefore fair value for the trend has dropped. This means that the next trend move is due. With the Control Point having moved lower, the normal bias is that the next move will be lower. However, with price oversold, the power of true measures in this area means that the bias is that the move will be up and any breakdown should be treated with caution. Finally, the advanced divergence modules flag a rare but very powerful double Peak Out divergence (see fig. 59). The combination of bullish signals becomes compelling.

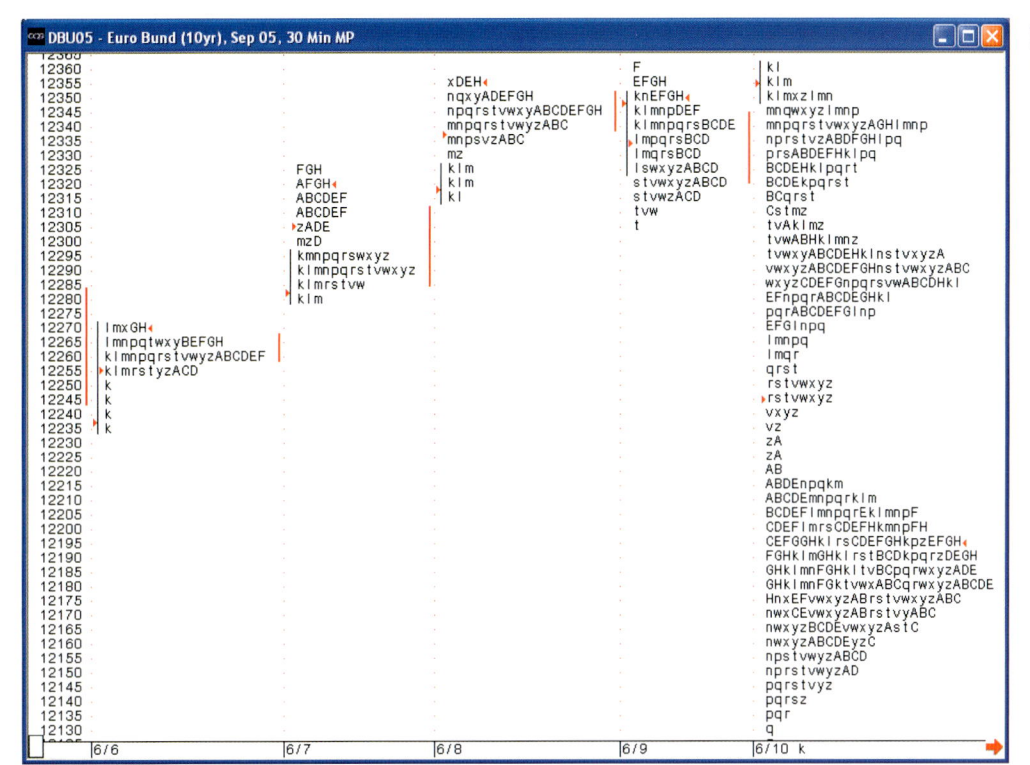

Figure 56:
Control shifts

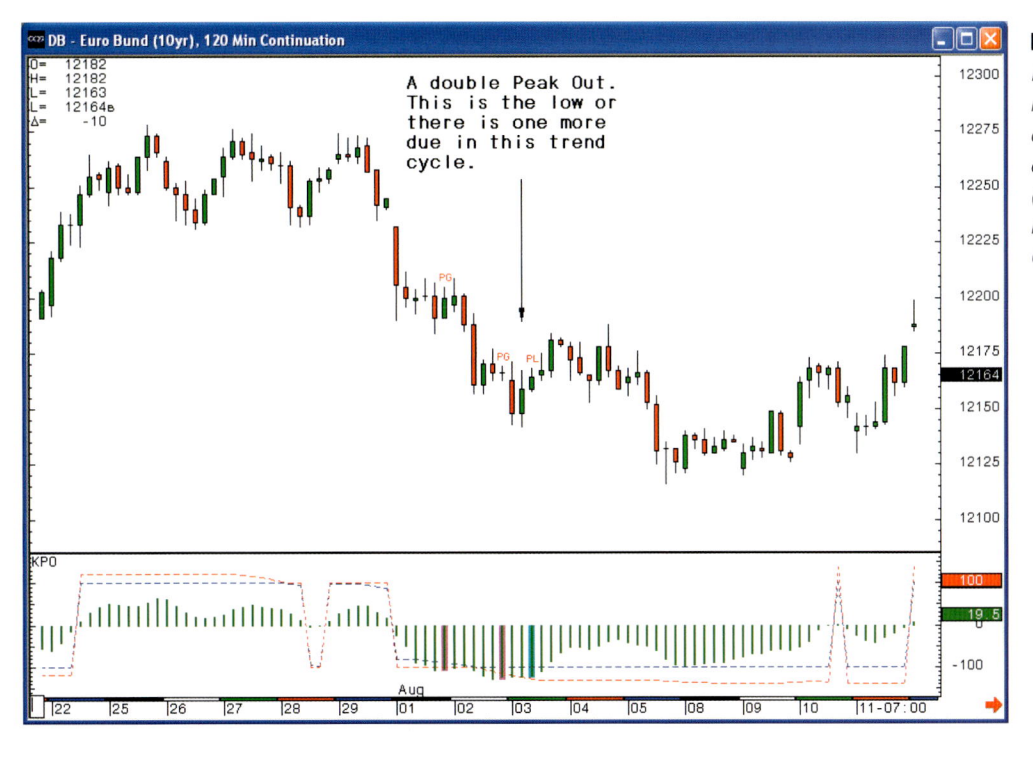

Figure 57:
Introducing true measures of overbought and oversold (covered in detail in the Peak Chapter)

113

TRADING TIME: New Methods in Technical Analysis

Figure 58:
Oversold on multiple timeframes

Figure 59:
Oversold and divergence. Divergence is covered in the RSI chapter

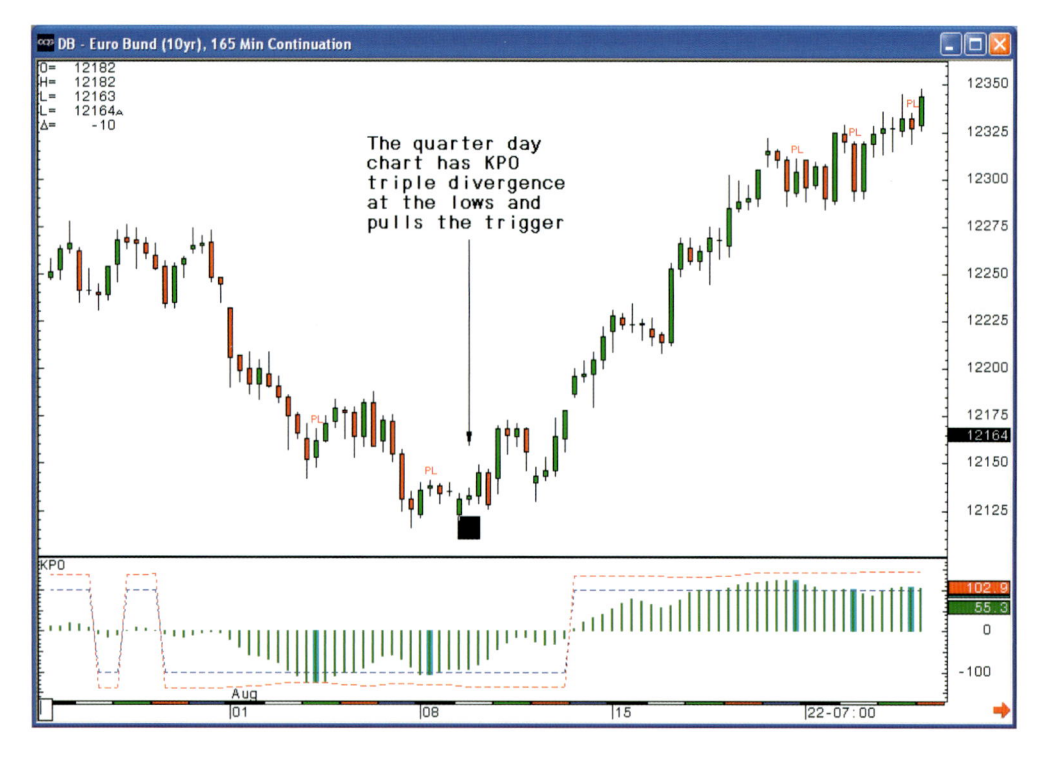

Now we look at the day when prices moved higher. The opening shows responsive behaviour in **l** (see fig. 59). The aggressive trader could fade the move in **m** and **n** as price should not make a new low. The alternative is to wait for the confirmation of the single letters at the end of **p**. Due to the strength of the rally, once we enter the vacuum in **p** at 122.22, an additional long position could be established at that point. Price continues to move higher but by the time the initiative action in **p** has been confirmed by the single letter, price is hitting the resistance beyond the top of the vacuum. You should also remember the rule that 3 initiative movements after the initial balance break are rare.

Market Profile®

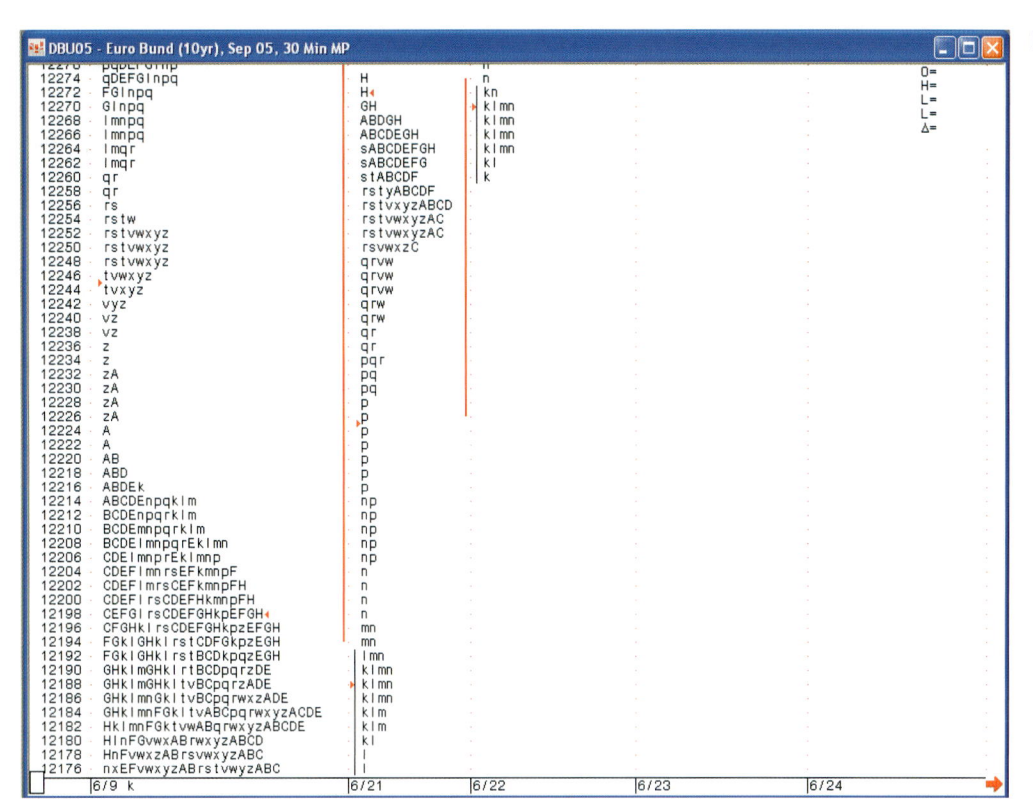

Figure 59:
The breakout is up

The Market Profile® (see fig. 60) shows how the position could be exited in stages assuming a long was entered with the early dip or the break in **p**. The first exit is at the top of the vacuum in **z** from the previous day. The second exit is at the other side of time ahead of the ledge in **z**. The final exit is at the close as trend days often close near the high or low. In terms of raising stops, once we have moved up a vacuum, we should not be moving back down it, so it could be raised to 1 tick below **q** or the other side of the vacuum where **n** touches **p**. Note how this coincides with the ledge at 122.14 from the day before.

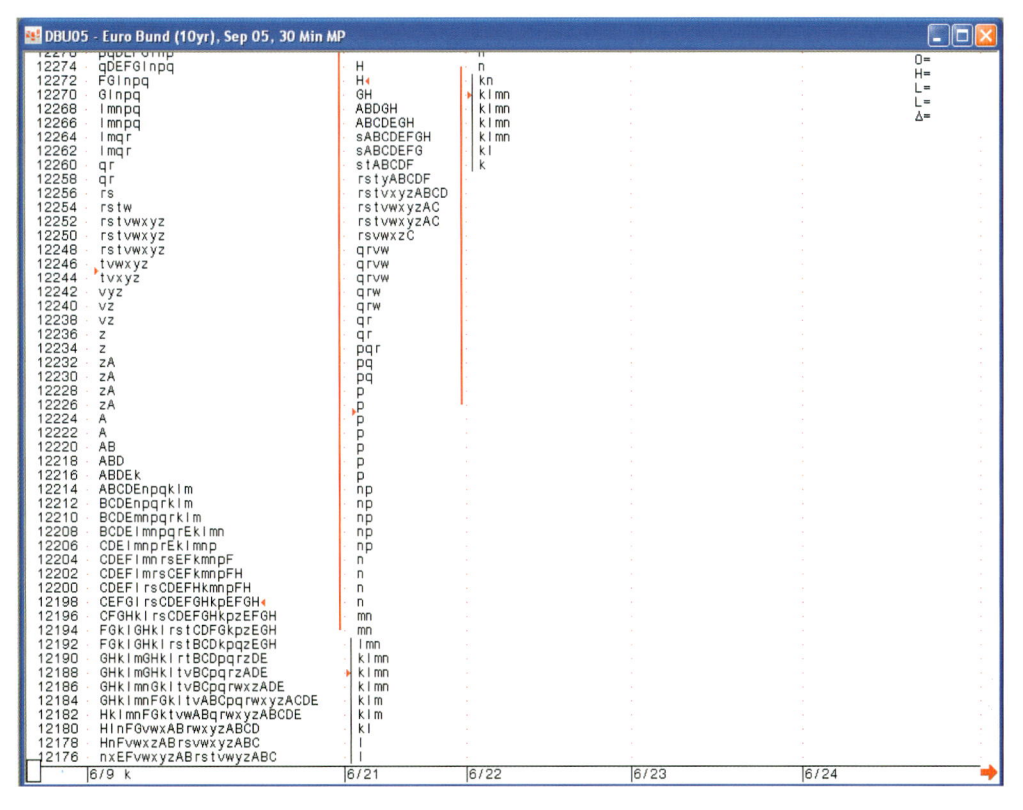

Figure 60:
Exits through the day

115

Figure 61:
The power of the reversal is so big, the following day sees another surge higher

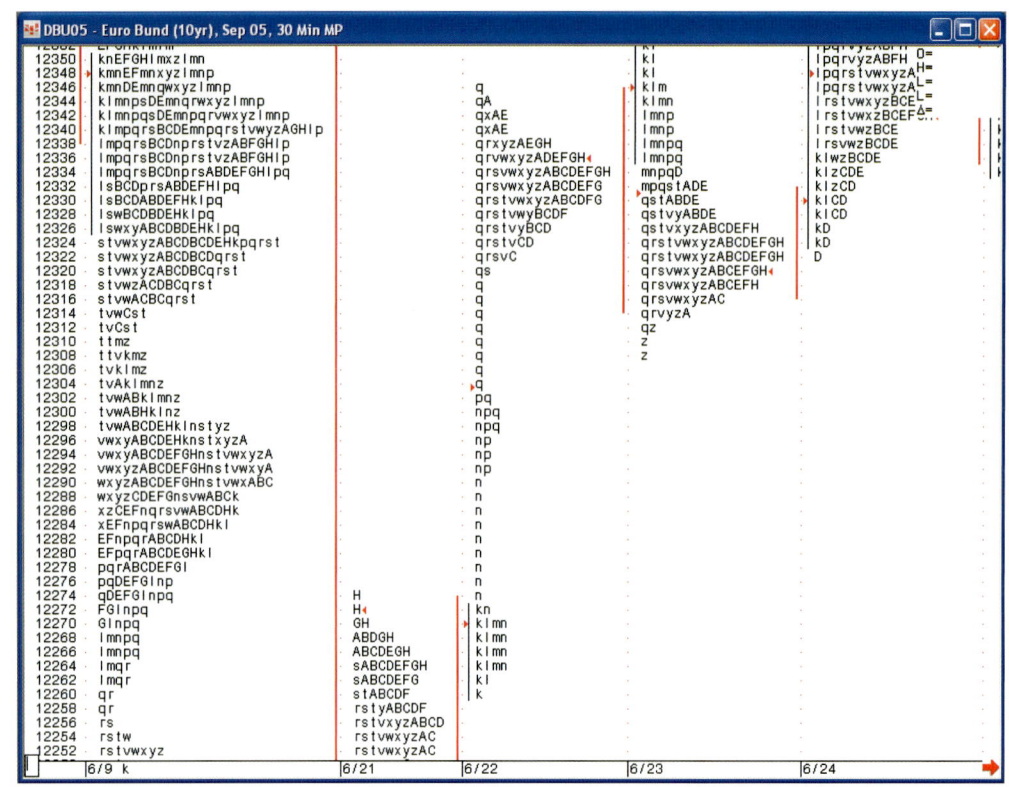

Conclusion

There are many rules associated with Market Profile® and it takes practice and discipline to implement them. OaR's mentoring programme provides up-to-date analysis of how the picture can and should be analysed. The connection with the Time Bands is a key element in understanding the short-term risks associated with entering positions based purely on Market Profile® or in combination with the Time-Band theory.

Key Points

- **The relationship between yesterday's close and today's opening.**
- **Single letter prints.**
- **The connection between OaR's Time Studies and Market Profile®**
- **Shifts in control.**
- **The merging of distributions.**
- **Ledges of time.**

3 Concepts of Time

What is the correct timeframe chart to be trading?

Has the correct timeframe to trade changed?

What is the focus timeframe for a trend?

What is the strength of that trend?

Is the trend overextended?

Must the trend change timeframe or die?

OaR Stochastic Steps

IMPORTANT NOTE

Due to the limits of scale there are times when what is visible in steps is not in line with the text. The text is alway correct

As stated at the beginning of the book: time and timing are critical to success. However, the common plan of attack, especially on timing, is usually concentrated on creating combinations of momentum with patterns, or crossovers of indicators with special magical settings. It seems to have escaped many that, however much work and testing is done, the chances are that the combination that is derived, and its subsequent success, is more to do with good money management, emotional stability or just plain great trading. It's a cliché but true, based on the feedback I receive that you can give a great commentary or set of technical setups to a poor trader and they'll lose money. Give a poor commentary and setup to a great trader and they won't lose much.

Therefore, to make technical analysis work you must structure the analysis in such a way as to make it easy to use. There is no benefit developing a form of analysis that utilises 1-minute bars, if you don't like spending hours in front of a screen. If you choose correctly, the technical analysis that you develop will support your trading. In addition, you must overcome the hurdle of believing the support structure you have developed. It is easy to have a few bad trades and begin to think the structure is flawed.

I feel very fortunate that I have experienced two sides to trading over long periods throughout my career. The first period was when I worked in the market using just fundamentals, touch, an understanding of pure price action and some guesswork. Throughout this period I was trading with other people's money. The second period began when I stumbled into a job that "theoretically" gave me the brief, time and resources to embark on a 15-year voyage of discovery into what is a "Pandora's box" of theory and experimentation. The interesting factor in the second period is that the trades undertaken were backed by my own money.

The problem of time

The time element, however, was always a problem and has been an obstacle to success. Time is required to analyse the market with consistency and discipline and then be in a position to implement the plan. Throughout the second period my job could be described as anything but that of a trader. I have had a full-time job at CQG, I have on average spent 3 months a year travelling, written and presented countless seminars, sat up into the wee hours writing code, and managed staff across the globe on a daily basis. For many years therefore it meant that I always had a perfect excuse to justify losses and poor trading.

> **"If only I had the time. I was in the office last week but got distracted"**

This used to be a regular summary of my Monday to Friday. It is also psychologically damaging to be jetting round the world advising other people how to trade, what to use and getting thanks, kudos and positive feedback, only to find my own trading account suffering.

It is no accident that it was only when I was forced to analyse my trading, week in, week out, with the aid of the commentaries that technical analysis switched from being a random support structure to an actual, live, fluid methodology. The result is a lack of frustration at missing trades when I have had long periods out of the market whilst all the excuses, discipline problems and laziness have evaporated.

Structure is everything!

Early days trading in Australia

This first truly manifested itself when I went to Australia to trade in 1987. I was a one-man band in a big organization and was tasked with handling a huge convertible note position that traded in London hours. I then had to hedge or work the position via the Australian stock options market, which at the time didn't make markets in puts – the market believed stocks could never go down as a result of computer programme trading. In fact, a major client bank (which no longer exists) explained this in a seminar just three days before the crash.

Over and above those duties I had to take proprietary positions and advise on hedging strategies for the group's world-wide exposures. I had to input all my own trades as well - no Chinese walls in those days! This was at a time when a typical spread on cable (£/$) could be a big figure e.g. 1.7400 to 1.7500. Quotes on my Reuters could be 2 to 5 minutes behind, assuming a price came up at all and the phones echoed and had a delay when you spoke into them when contacting the rest of the world. To cap things off, the markets were incredibly volatile with most of the action taking place in the middle of the night – a hard pill to swallow after having already spent 15 hours in the office.

You can guess what my trading was like!

Then came the 1987 crash, which devastated me professionally, mentally and financially. With hindsight, getting the whole sorry saga over within one day and starting all over again was a blessing in disguise. That said, it certainly didn't feel like it at the time or for some years afterwards.

My first trading systems

Whilst this taught me the importance of structure, it was many years before I felt that I had the structure right. One of the final pieces in the trading jigsaw was to be able to quantify where I was in time and trend. This came from years of attempting to build trade systems. At the outset I was very sceptical about their ability to work in the future whatever the past results. The nagging doubt always remained that I had more ability than any algorithm, meaning I would override the system, question it as soon as it lost a few times and generally would look for any excuse to not execute what it told me to do. How could I throw away all the knowledge, pain and experience and become a robot? I might become a very rich robot, but also an extremely bored one. My first experience in robotic trading re-enforced this view.

I created an entry signal that looked at multiple time-frame divergences and focused on implementation on daily charts. I still use the basis of that code today and it is the foundation point of the subsequent divergence indicators that I use. My initial desire to trade against the trend meant that stops were easy to quantify and I couldn't cheat on my money management. The whole system was created before computers could do this and I had spent weeks back-testing the results by hand. The beauty of the system was that I could programme the CQG at home. Wherever I was in the world, all I had to do was ring my wife and she would tell me what codes had come up with signals. I would place the order entry for the opening of the next day and the stop beyond the high or low of the signal bar.

Perfect!

Things progressed well, and I had the added psychological boost that I was placing positions towards highs and lows and I wasn't even looking at a chart. I went away on a trip to the Far East for two weeks and I continued to add trades and manage them in the normal way. When I returned home, all my statements were waiting for me and I idly went through them. The horror at what was on the first statement punched me in the solar plexus. I was long T bonds! I knew I hadn't traded them through my time away and I couldn't remember getting long. It must be an error. I swiftly opened the last statement and I was still long. I looked at the chart and realised that I had had a signal on the Friday before I went away. I had put the order in after the close on the Friday to enter on Monday and had forgotten to put a stop in. I had merrily flown off to Japan and never once in all the time I was there did I ever remember I had a position. I'd even presented a one-day seminar specifically on T Bonds. I had been so successful in removing all the emotion and involvement in trading that I'd completely forgotten that I had a position at all. I had plenty of emotion and involvement however, once I'd read the statements and realised what I'd done. I'd wiped out half my account and the entire profits for the year so far. To rub salt in the wound – If I had managed the trade as my system dictated, I would have made money. My experiment with robotic trading was over.

Catching the big trends

The other problem, once I had developed trade systems, was that the only way I could avoid curve fitting was to create very simplistic entries with few rules, but with very sophisticated exits. This was because, whilst I appreciated that the consistent systems should trade small repeatable patterns, I would inevitably never catch any big trends. Thomas Stridsman's book 'Trading Systems That Work' inspired a train of thought, the key being that systems need a cube of risk.

One part of that cube was time. My testing with CQG's Entry Signal Evaluator had already been highly illuminating as regards identifying the optimum length of most trends and the subsequent corrections. The problem was whether the trend would restart. I had had success in satisfying the principles of identifying repeatable patterns at the start of a trend, but the problem of riding mega trends was still impossible if I were to adhere to the rules of how to create robust code. Therefore, systems could only ever become part of a portfolio of trading.

Many traders find that a few elephant winners often make their year, which is in direct conflict with sound system creation. The vast majority of time is spent scratching around living to fight another day. Even then there is the problem of being able to realise when you are on an elephant trade and then being able to ride it.

Often, either through books or from speaking to traders, I'm told that if a trade doesn't develop quickly they get out. Whilst in theory this is a good technique for managing risk, the risk of missing good trades is huge, and can create emotional recriminations: "Just after I got out, the market did what I was expecting it to!" This breaks the golden rule: that the chart tells you, you don't tell the chart. But it's a common trap and can lead to poor trading. However, if you apply rational thought to what you are doing by exiting a trade that hasn't developed quickly, you are asking yourself to be a genius trader.

What right does your entry method have to be consistently of sufficient timing that as soon as the trade is implemented it moves in the desired direction?

This is especially true when using momentum-based algorithms. Even my own preferred route of analysis cannot expect instant gratification all the time. Only some of the Market Profile® and Deviation-based patterns in the previous chapters can demand instant trends and provide stops of sufficient tightness that prove that at that instant the trend is not developing and tells you to withdraw.

If you acknowledge this fact, then for the majority of the time, exactly when your indicator or analysis of choice makes a crossover or signal is probably irrelevant. What is not, is risk, position size, partial exits and how long it is in time before you exit. Understanding what is the correct timeframe chart to use focuses all these elements.

Valuable lessons from building trading systems

This is where the building and analysing of trade systems is so useful, regardless of whether you ever physically trade the systems themselves. Some of the most revealing results have come from systems that would never be robust enough to trade. The results enable you to understand the expected dynamics of a trade when you use technical analysis as a support structure. This is particularly useful when using the same entry methods over different asset classes that have contrasting trend lengths (e.g. a daily chart stock system and day trading a stock index).

Originally, the actual time of day that an entry level was reached was irrelevant until the development of the Deviation studies which shed light on exactly what could be expected in the short term when a support or resistance was reached. This is critical information and provides the support structure to expectations. Hope, fear and greed are removed from the equation. The time that a trade lasts is dictated by the characteristics that it displays as price moves between the subsequent supports and resistances, and if price is trending, most importantly, the velocity and speed through the time it takes to rotate between them. This paints the picture of the strength.

Slow Stochastic

On countless occasions I have been asked to develop or comment on interpretations of the Slow Stochastic. And for many years I could find nothing of use. This became something of an embarrassment and eventually led to a concerted effort, the results of which form the body of this chapter.

This study is so widely used that it is essential to know what the Slow Stochastic is showing on most timeframe charts whatever your method of trading. The Slow Stochastic gives clues to how some of the crowd are positioned and may provide you with an advantage when they begin to exit.

More important is to understand the study to such depth that you can connect its influence on market behaviour to Market Profile® trend lines, Fibonacci, candlesticks or whatever else you use as a technical analysis support structure.

Slow Stochastic tests

Before you can reach this level of conclusion, it is necessary to run tests on basic stochastic theory, such as crossovers, overbought and oversold and then run them on various asset classes and timeframes. To avoid a book full of tables I've taken a token number of tests and concentrated on a few specific areas. However, the tests that I have done are far more comprehensive and paint a very similar picture to the conclusions shown here. This extensive piece of work helped me to develop the Stochastic Steps study.

CGQ's Entry Signal Evaluator

The tool with which these tests were performed is the Entry Signal Evaluator. To recap, this is a module within the CQG back-testing functionality. It allows the user to enter technical code and then test this over a portfolio of contracts. It provides the raw profit or loss for up to 60 bars after the signal bar. As no money management is included, it therefore provides an indication of a piece of technical code's basic accuracy.

Test: overbought and oversold crossover

The first test is simply on the basic overbought and oversold crossover theory.

It states that when the stochastic reaches an extreme low value and then crosses back up, the market should rally. The following three tables have taken 60-minute data on the Dax since 1 January 2002. This has been a time of general equity strength and some mega trends so you would expect the statistics on the buys to be good as corrections down would be short-lived. The settings used have been the standard 10, 3, 3. More detailed tests on other indices such as the S&P, have been made as well with similar results, but to avoid lots of tables just the Dax is shown here.

Concepts of Time

The statistics show that in the short term, money is made on the indices but then the statistics show significant losses in the longer term.

On T bonds over the same period the results are basically flat, but accuracy is below 50% across most of the time scale.

It is on a portfolio of 18 FX rates on daily charts going back to 1995 which has had a bigger cross-section of trends and is therefore a more representative survey of market behaviour. Accuracy once again hovers around 50% with losses across the time curve.

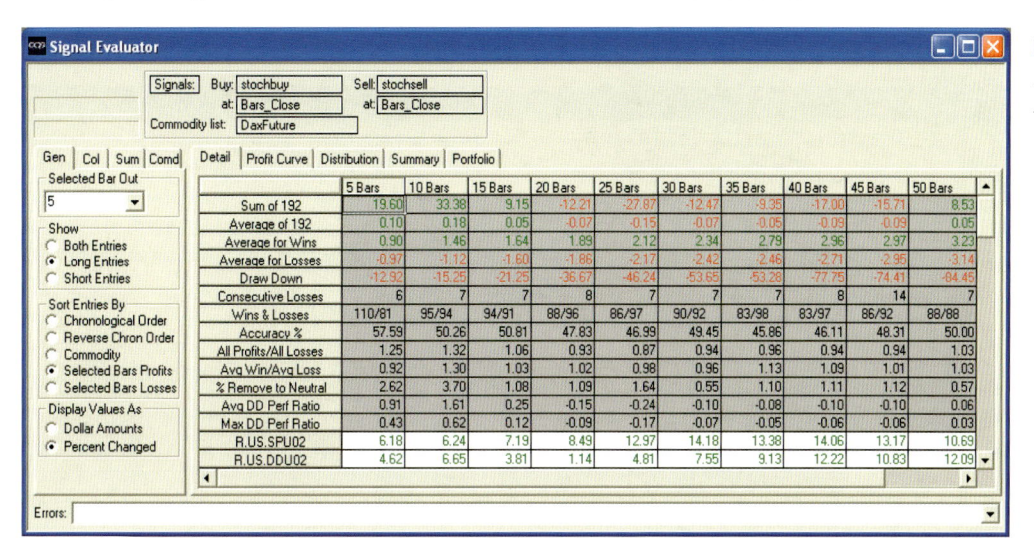

Figure 1:
Signal Evaluation – Dax Results

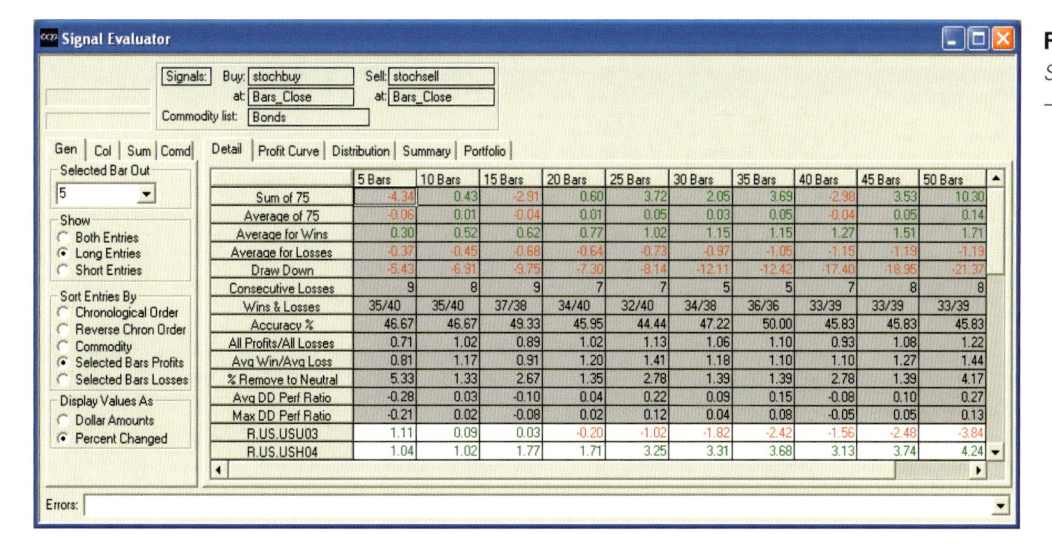

Figure 2:
Signal Evaluation – T-Bond Results

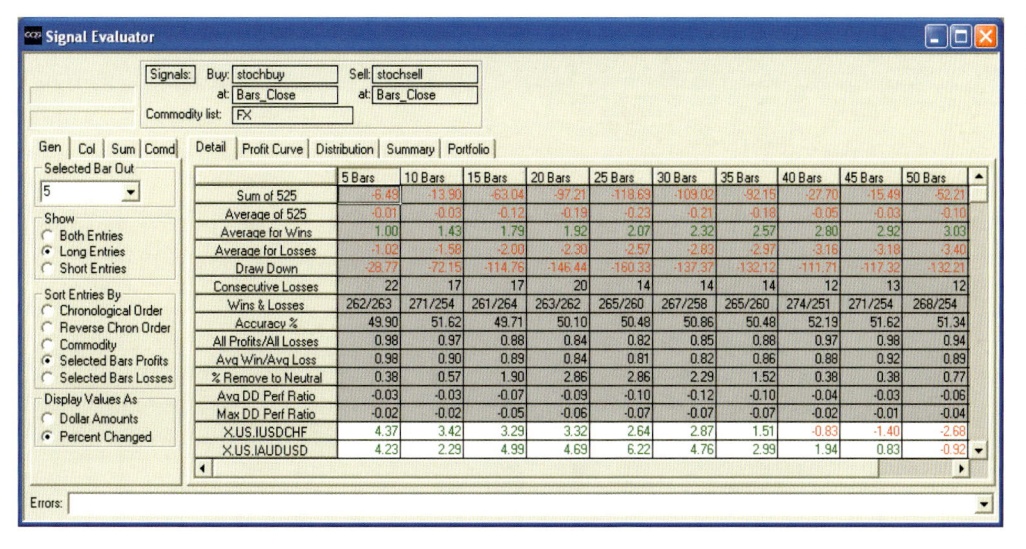

Figure 3:
Signal Evaluation – F.X. Results

121

TRADING TIME: New Methods in Technical Analysis

The statistics suggest that the indicator's ability to pick the turn in trends is suspect, especially when placed against more robust methods of trend exhaustion via the true measures of overbought and oversold and the body of work on divergence.

However, if we are to turn the logic around and say that the indicator is above 80 and turns up, we can test to see whether it has the ability to be a trend acceleration tool. A different picture emerges.

All three tests show profits and in general accuracy rates above 50%, especially once you move beyond 10 bars after entry. This suggests that the study can be used as confirmation of a strong trend. On this test FX comes out on top in terms of the breadth of gains, but the Dax and T Bonds show the highest accuracy as time progresses.

Figure 4:
Signal Evaluation – Dax Results

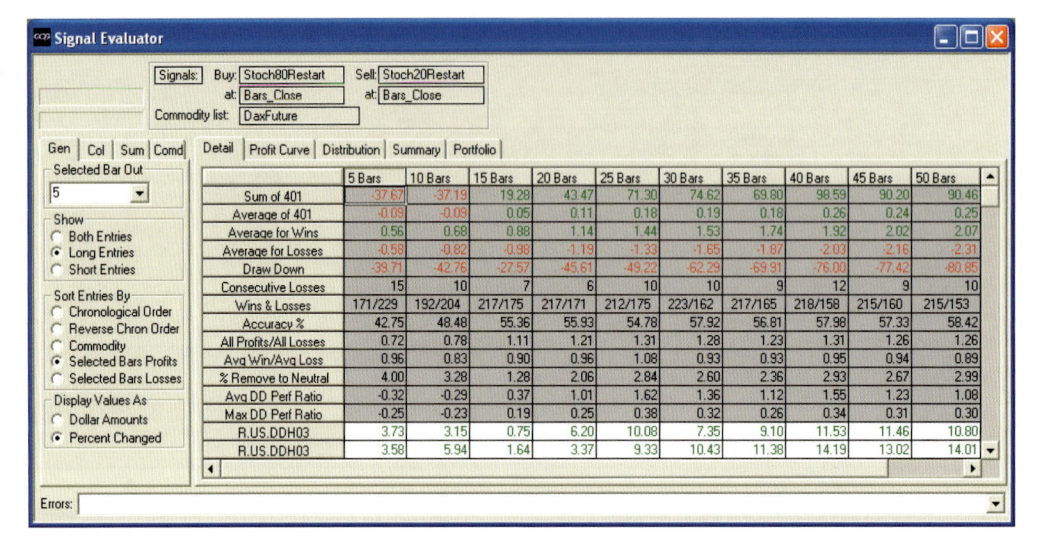

Figure 5:
Signal Evaluation – T Bond Results

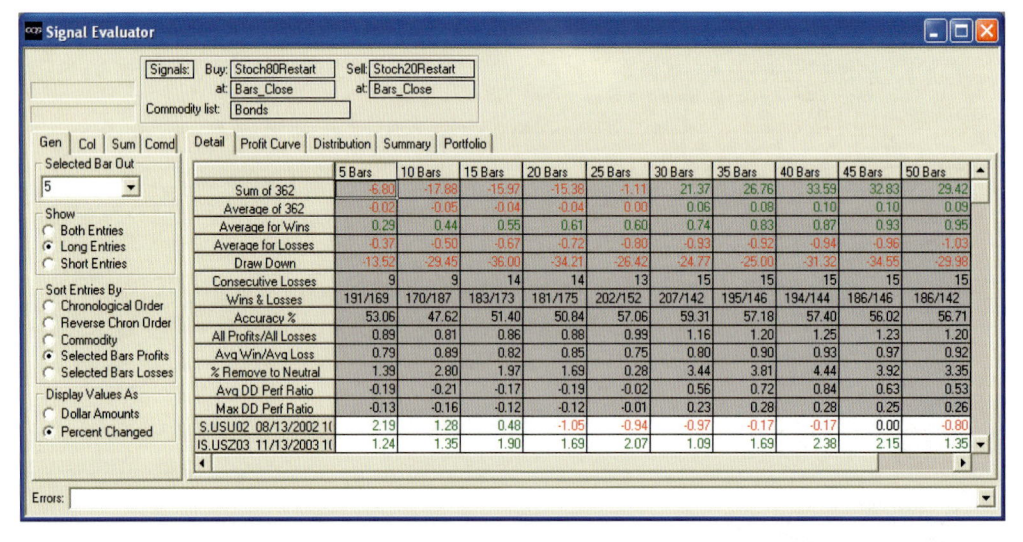

Figure 6:
Signal Evaluation – F.X. Results

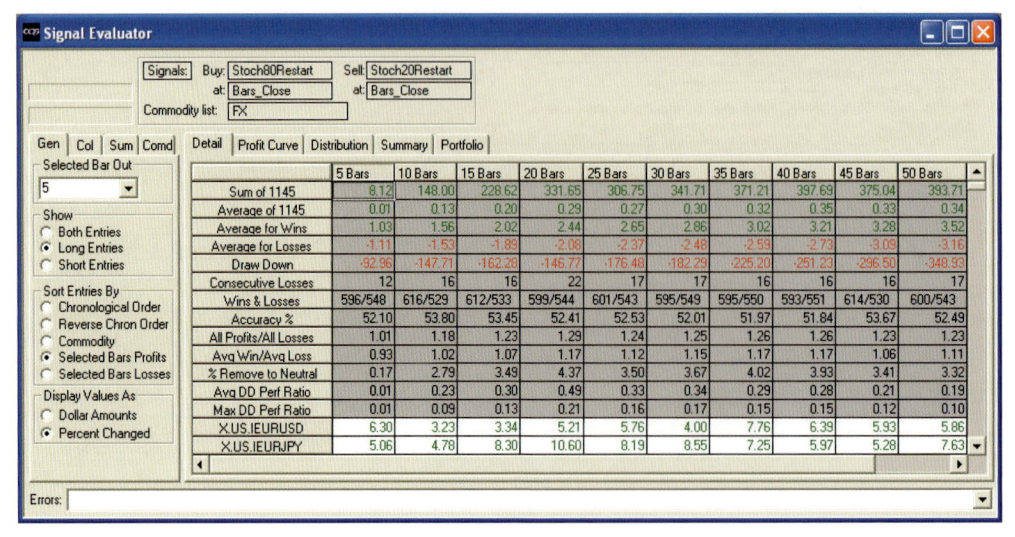

Concepts of Time

The previous piece of code is highly aggressive and a somewhat blunt instrument of trend acceleration as it takes no account of concepts of deviation or whether this is the first time that the move has broken the thresholds of 80 or 20 within the current normal trend cycle. There is also no connection with measurements of overbought or oversold or any divergence filter. All of these tools are crucial in trying to understand the strength of a trend. The trend will have already been confirmed as the indicator will be above 80 or below 20. It will then have reacted lower or higher and then resumed the trend direction. We are now trying to quantify the second thrust. The next set of tables takes a more conservative approach and just marks when the Slow Stochastic has crossed above 80. This means that the first part of a strong trend should be captured.

The statistics on the indices are mixed, although, when the signals are placed on a daily chart, they are far better with accuracy up in the 60s on index futures (see fig. 7). However, the skew has been to the upside in the markets overall so the buys would be expected to perform well. T Bonds are the most disappointing (see fig. 8). The FX statistics are interesting (see fig. 9) as the overall statistics are poorer than the first set of tables (see figs. 4 to 6), suggesting that the first move above 80 is often repelled but this does not last long.

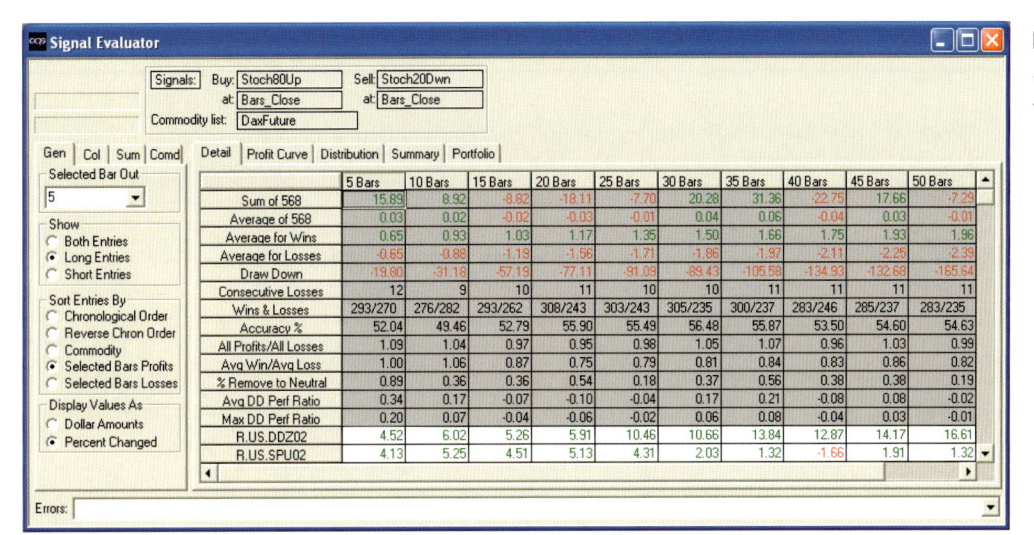

Figure 7:
Signal Evaluation – Dax Results

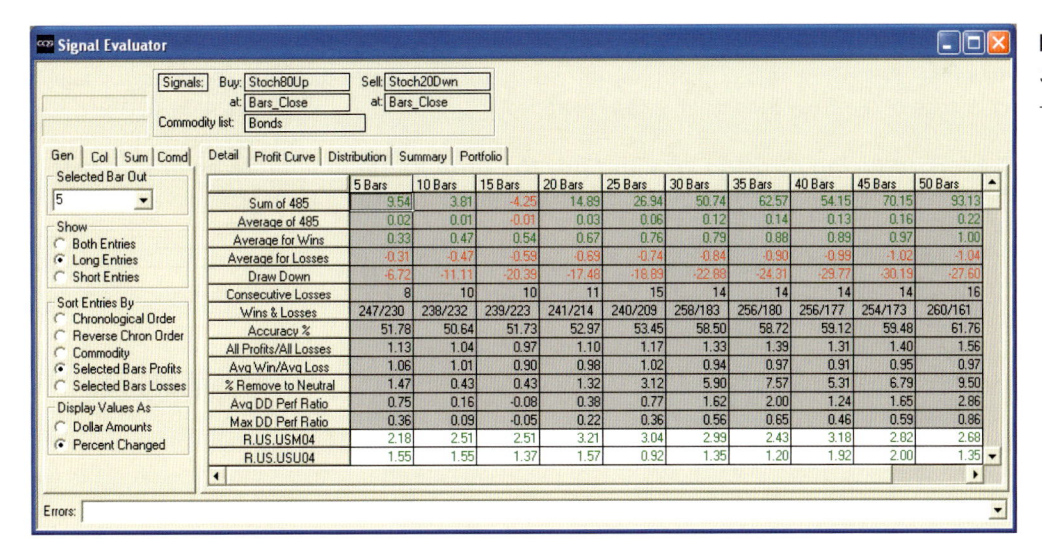

Figure 8:
Signal Evaluation – T-Bond Results

Figure 9:
Signal Evaluation – F.X. Results

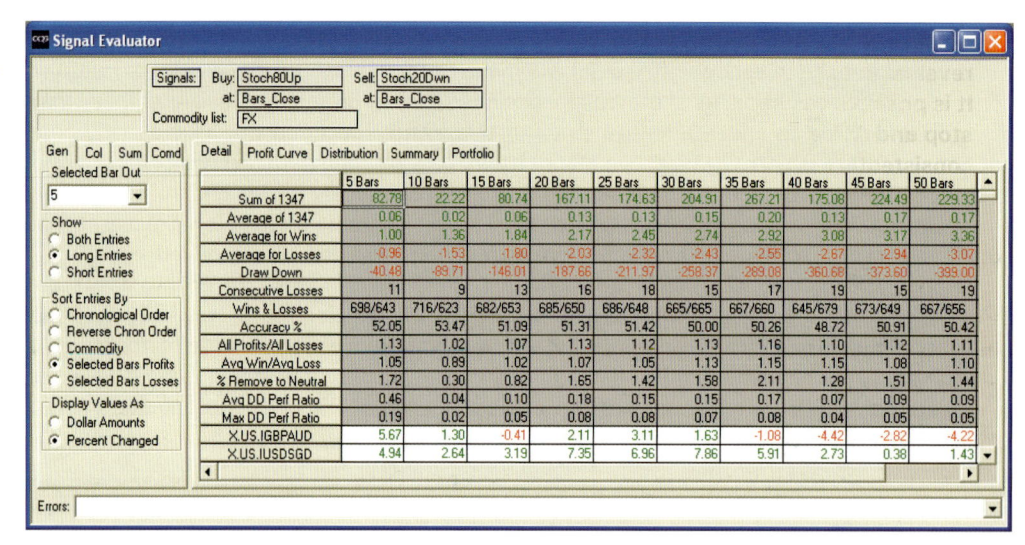

Whilst the statistics do little to inspire real confidence, that is not to say that it may not be possible to build workable strategies. The next section looks at an example using the Dax during the middle of the vicious bear market from 2000.

Do self-fulfilling prophecies provide trading opportunities?

The traditional interpretation of the Slow Stochastic is that when it is above 80, the market is overbought. When the "K" line crosses back beneath the "D" line the sell signal, or exit to a long position, is triggered. The reverse is true (i.e. a buy signal) when the indicator is below 20. Another common technique is to look for a failure swing, when the indicator crosses below 80 and does so from a lower level than the previous Stochastic high, in a divergence type pattern.

While these two approaches will perform well in a sideways market or a minor trend (the failure swing is generally more reliable), in the case, say, of short positions, they will both incur substantial losses in the teeth of a strong or sustained up trend. At best, the result is a premature exit from a potentially profitable position. Back-testing and systematic code building may uncover means of filtering out the worst examples of such inconvenient behaviour, but since trends are where the greatest profit potential lies, such an exercise is akin to squeezing blood from a stone. However, this is not to say that it is not worth investigating other opportunities for taking advantage of the Slow Stochastic's popular appeal.

Traders reducing position size and not the time frame in volatile environments

The huge intraday swings seen in stock index futures in the year 2000 established a volatile and nervous trading environment. Many traders reacted to this by reducing the position size they traded rather than reducing the timeframe of their analysis to accommodate the increased risk. 30- and 60- minute timeframes still remained the principal intraday drivers, with exceptional volatility occasionally bringing this down to 15 minutes.

The tables below show output from CQG's Entry Signal Evaluator. (Entry Signal Evaluator is used to test the performance of individual entry signals rather than complete trading systems and simply displays the P&L for each signal over time.) In this case, the results reflect the performance for one Dax contract of conventional Slow Stochastic buy and sell signals, based on 30-minute charts. The results shown are for the first 5 bars after entry and then for every 5th bar after that up to 45 bars out.

Closer analysis of the results reveals three distinct scenarios:

1. The results for the first five bars after the entry, including the open and close, provide valuable information on optimal timing of entry. For example, the open and close one bar after entry shows a percentage accuracy that is low (less than 50%). For a buy signal, this will mean that buying when the original condition is true is less profitable than buying on the opening or close one bar later. The trade system code or trader's entry point could be adjusted accordingly and results may improve.
2. The fact that buying on the original entry point is degrading profits means that it may be possible to build a completely separate trade system that sells on the original bar, before stopping and reversing (buying) one bar later.

Concepts of Time

3. **Lastly, as the trade develops, we can see if there is an optimum area where profits are maximized. Often, regardless of whether the entry is based on trend following, reversal logic, or the timeframe used, this point is between 15 to 25 bars after entry. It is possible to take advantage of this phenomenon by incorporating it into a trailing stop and using time to create a dynamic element. Over and above a trailing stop, a consistently sound method in any trade system is to create a pincer as the length of trade expands. This means that the trailing stop accelerates to catch the market up, at the same time as a profit target narrows to do the same thing.**

When the data from 2000 was analyzed, it was apparent that even when the dominant longer-term trend had been down, the sell signals had been underwater for the first three bars after entry, and substantive profits do not materialise until thirty bars after entry and beyond. Unsurprisingly, the buy signals perform in almost entirely the opposite fashion.

The drawdown figures clearly illustrate that, unless the trader has deep pockets and is prepared to support a large negative position, the basic concept is probably flawed.

Anticipating crossovers

However, while the basic Slow Stochastic crossover concept may have little value, analysis of the associated charts shows that, while accuracy is poor, there are times when the entry signals mark major highs and lows. This raises the question of whether it is possible to create a series of entries that take *premature* advantage of the Slow Stochastic crossover and then use multiple exits and tight money management to capture profit, irrespective of whether the basic crossover actually fails or works.

Armed with the knowledge that a large number of traders will be watching for the basic crossover signals, it's worth setting up a chart display that will be able to identify whether a crossover is likely to happen in a 30- or 60- minute timeframe some fifteen minutes before those 30- or 60- minute bars actually complete. If a crossover seems inevitable, the trader can consider taking advantage of this by putting on a position in anticipation of other participants' trading activity.

In practice, most traders typically do not wait for the bar to finish before trading, but will enter early. It is often therefore the case that the buying or selling based on the plain crossover will finish on conclusion of the signal bar, which makes it a desirable exit point for a 'premature crossover' trading system.

At the completion of the basic signal bar, it may be possible to place the stop at the entry price or above, as some vanilla crossover signals will be correct and mark the beginning of a significant trend. However, the results from the Entry Signal Evaluator suggest that this would be a good stop and reverse point for the more aggressive traders, given the basic signal's high failure rate.

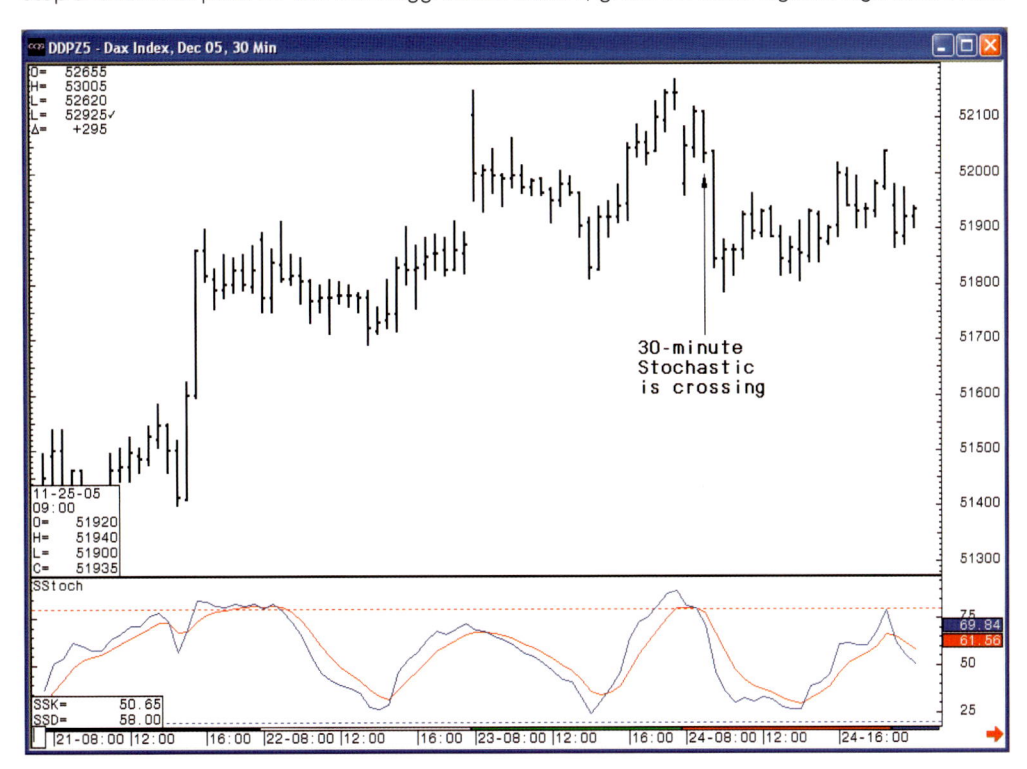

Figure 10: *Stochastics on multiple timeframes*

TRADING TIME: New Methods in Technical Analysis

Figure 11:
Multiple Timeframes 60-minutes

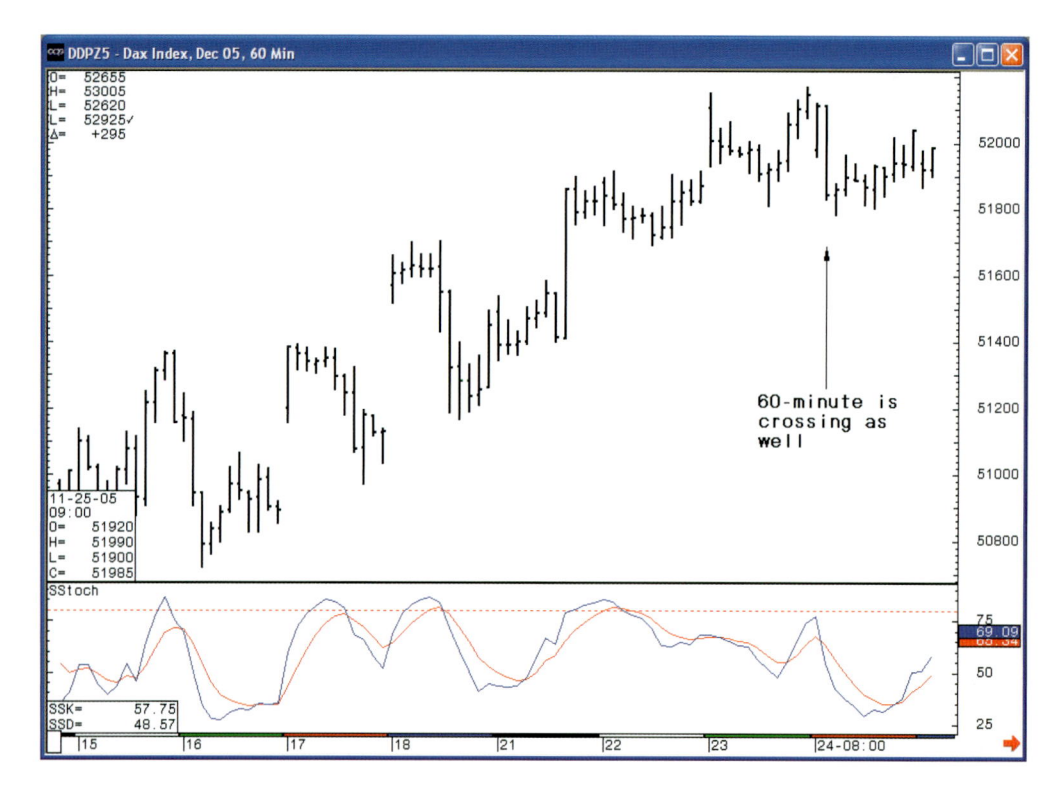

The market can pre-empt popular signal crossovers

Figure 12:
The market pre-empts the crossovers as the 1-minute chart shows.

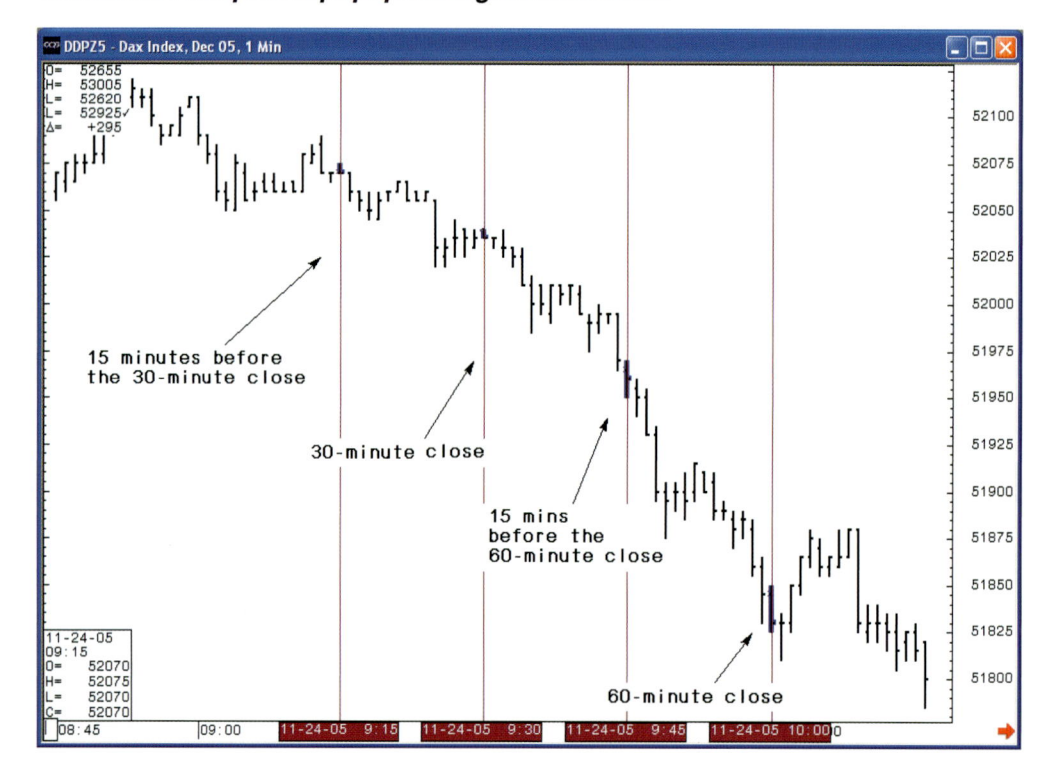

Concepts of Time

OaR Stochastic Steps

What timeframe chart is trending?
The vast majority of momentum-based indicators will either continue to ebb and flow, giving little clue to the length of the trend, or have little tangible method to identify the true strength of a trend and consequently how long it will last. A common method is to use longer period variables to smooth out these movements, but this usually means that by the time the indicator changes direction, the end of the trend has been signalled a significant period of time before. This method is of use to only the most strategic of trader.

Why use the standard Slow Stochastic settings?
It has been demonstrated that the normal standard settings of the Stochastic are very poor indicators of trend. However, it's possible for you to use longer or shorter settings. For example, using a 5, 3, 3 Slow Stochastic is an alternative to money management stops over the first few bars of a trade system. This is because the study is so sensitive that it takes only a small reversal in price for the study to cross and provide a stop out point. The following charts all use the setting of 21, 13, 8. These are by no means magic numbers. I picked them for no better reason than they are Fibonacci ratios. However, what they do is mimic the characteristics of a standard MACD. The difference is that we have a reference point for when the Slow Stochastic is overbought or oversold.

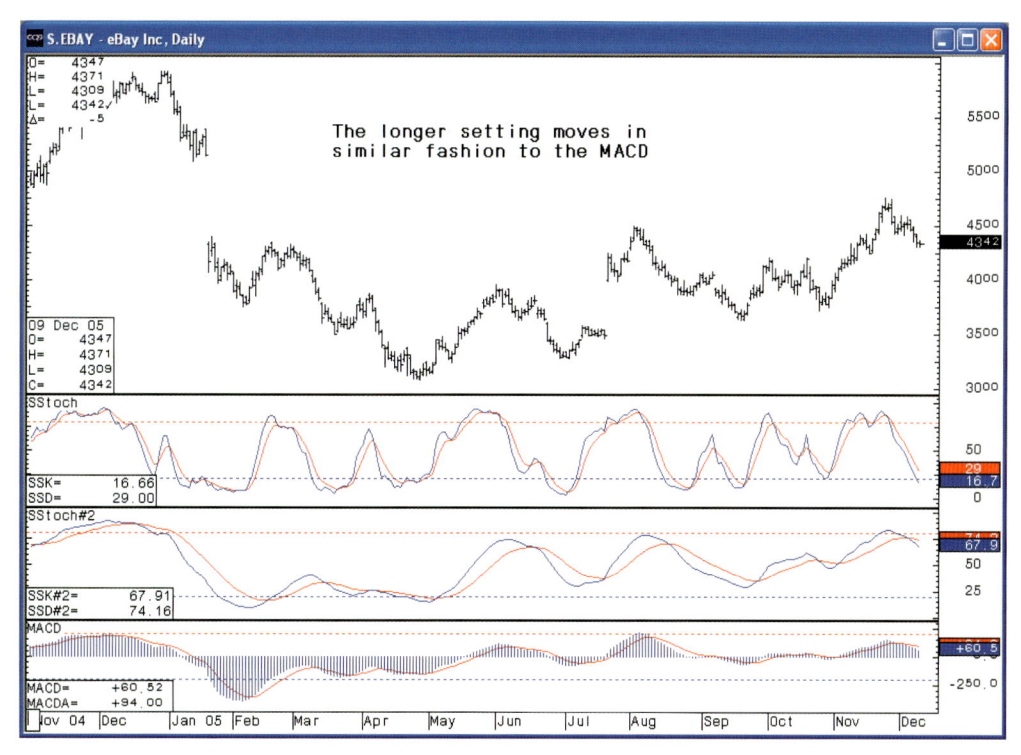

Figure 13:
Changing the setting to 21, 13, 8 mimics a MACD

With the variables set to such a high level, price must really be trending before the indicator will become overbought. A drawback is that if you are waiting for the Slow Stochastic to cross back below an extreme zone it will be some time after the trend has topped out. That, however, is not what I am using the study for. The crucial point to remember is that a study has been created that is:

- good enough to move with a trend,
- has a common reference point, and
- is not so sensitive that it gets caught up in minor moves or corrections.

OaR Stochastic Steps

Definition
Stochastic Steps record each crossover of the Stochastic and state whether it was confirming the continuation of the trend by doing so in a higher or lower contract value than the previous crossover. Therefore Stochastic Steps will either step up or down each time the Stochastic crosses depending on the comparison in price to the last time the Stochastic crossed.

Figure 14:
Stochastic Steps

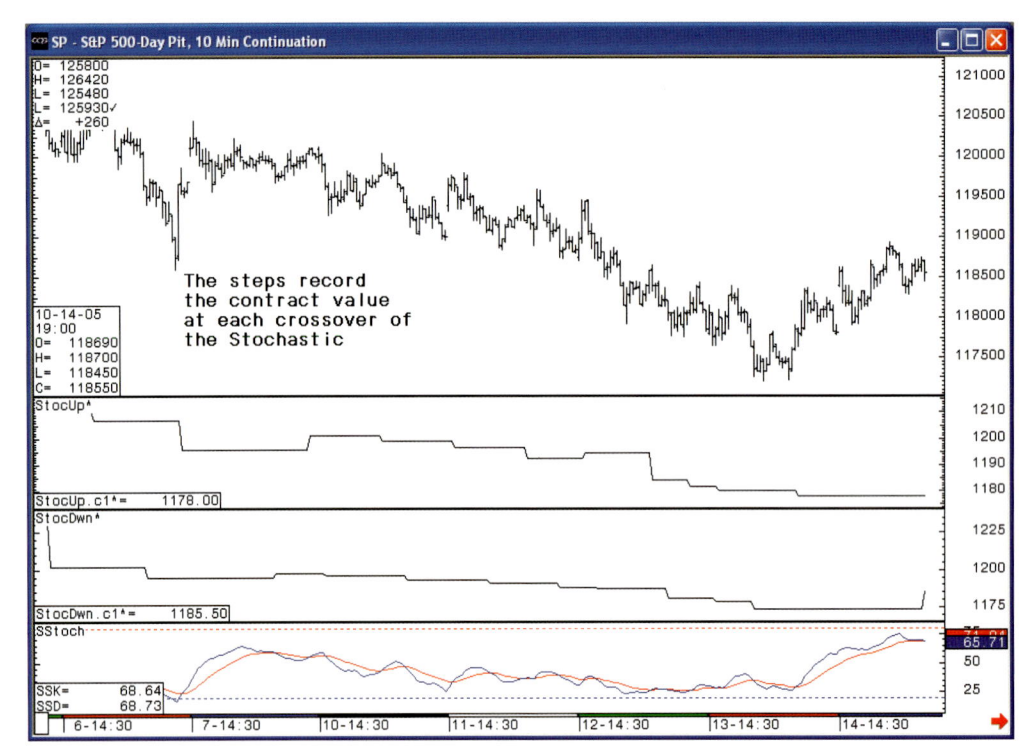

The concept is divided into two parts. One records the contract value when the Stochastic crosses up and the other when it crosses down. In an up trend, when the stochastic crosses to the downside, and from a higher contract value than the previous cross to the downside, the study will step up and confirm that the trend remains strong. Therefore by default it is an anti-divergence indicator.

Trend definition and divergence

However, closer examination of how the Steps interact between the contract value and the Slow Stochastic value itself reveals how new concepts of divergence can be built based on the patterns and connections between them. This remains beyond the scope of this book but it is an important consideration for those who want to investigate the relationships between the Stochastic Steps with that theory in mind. This becomes clearer if two more Step studies are created recording the value of the Stochastic itself when they cross over. The theory is touched upon in greater detail in the next chapter.

All the concepts between the Stochastic Steps, either as an anti-divergence or a divergence indicator are true on any market and can be applied to any timeframe. This means that the study can be used whatever your method of analysis. Once a trend has developed,

- the StocUp is usually the dominant force in up trends (records crosses upwards)
- the StocDwn is usually the dominant force in downtrends (records crosses downwards).

Crucially, they also tell us what the focus timeframe is when a trend begins and, if it develops, whether the focus timeframe is moving higher. This enables a trade that may have begun with a short-term bias to become a long-term trade. This is described below

Superficially, the studies can look quite simplistic as they either step up or down. However, a key component in the power of these studies is their interactions with the Slow Stochastic study itself. It's vitally important to reference them together in order to reveal the true strength of a trend and understand when it is more likely that the trend will end or must move up a timeframe.

Some basic rules and interpretations

First it is necessary to explain some of the basic rules and interpretations before moving onto the finer points. The examples that are shown cover all asset classes but the timeframe shown dictates the normal time horizon in which it can be traded. So a daily chart is for a long-term strategic player, while 15 minutes and below is for a day trader. The other intraday timeframes can keep you in a trade for a few weeks. They can then assist when a trade moves from having a short-term outlook to an intermediate or long-term outlook.

Concepts of Time

Confirming the trend

Each time the market steps in the direction of the trend the trend itself is being confirmed. Once the relevant indicator has stepped in the same direction 4 times consecutively (this is the trending and focus timeframe), the market is in a strong trend.

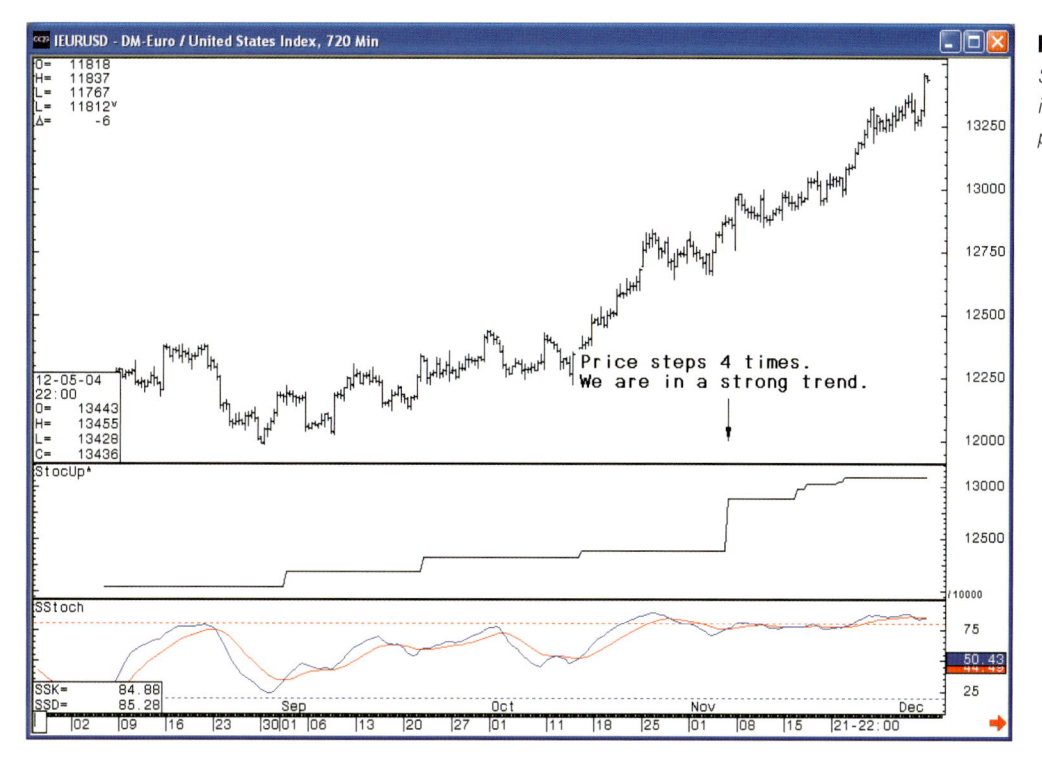

Figure 15:
Stepping 4 times is the trigger point

Mega Trends and at what price will a crossover say the trend is ended

When 6 steps are in place we are in a mega trend. The following chart (see fig. 16) shows that the trend has reached 6. The crucial question for the current state of play in the market is that we are close to the trend ending unless the next crossover up is above the value of 8964 (this can be seen by the last reference level on StocUp,). Therefore we have an important reference point and a predictive basis for the following week's trading.

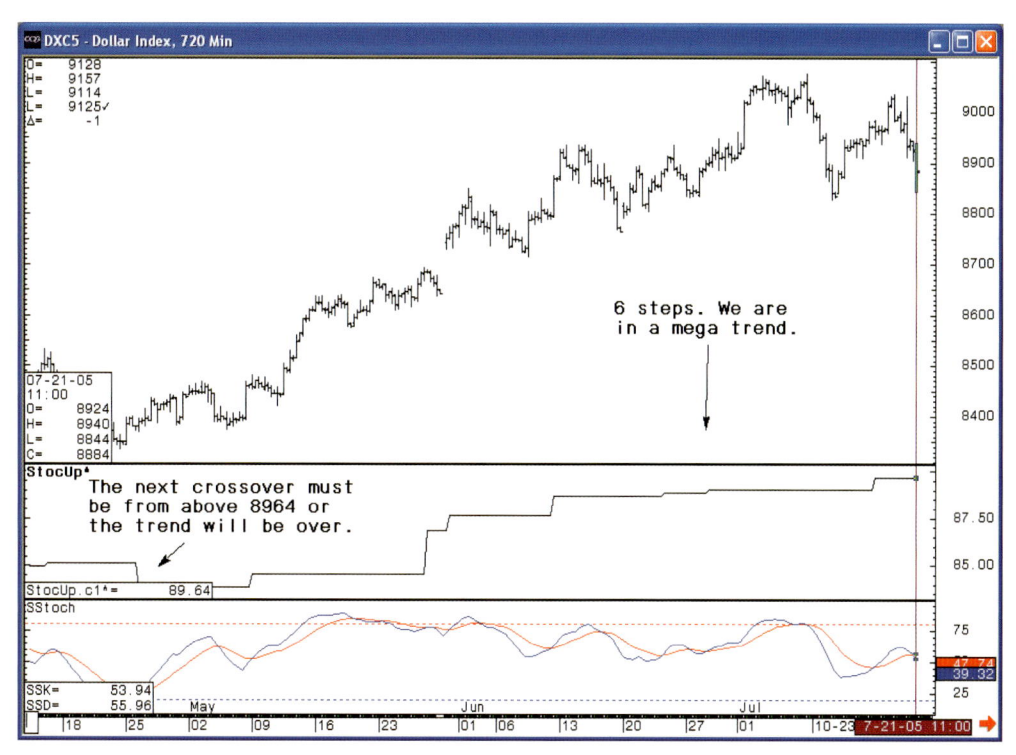

Figure 16:
Stepping 6 times is the trigger point for a mega trend

TRADING TIME: New Methods in Technical Analysis

The strongest trend
If both Stochastic Steps are above 6 this indicates the strongest trend of all. The next two charts show the 15-minute entering a mega trend. This is followed by the 30- minute doing the same later in the trend. This is an example of how the focus timeframe can be moved up and allow for trends to be ridden for longer.

Figure 17:
Both studies: stepping 6 times is the strongest trend of all

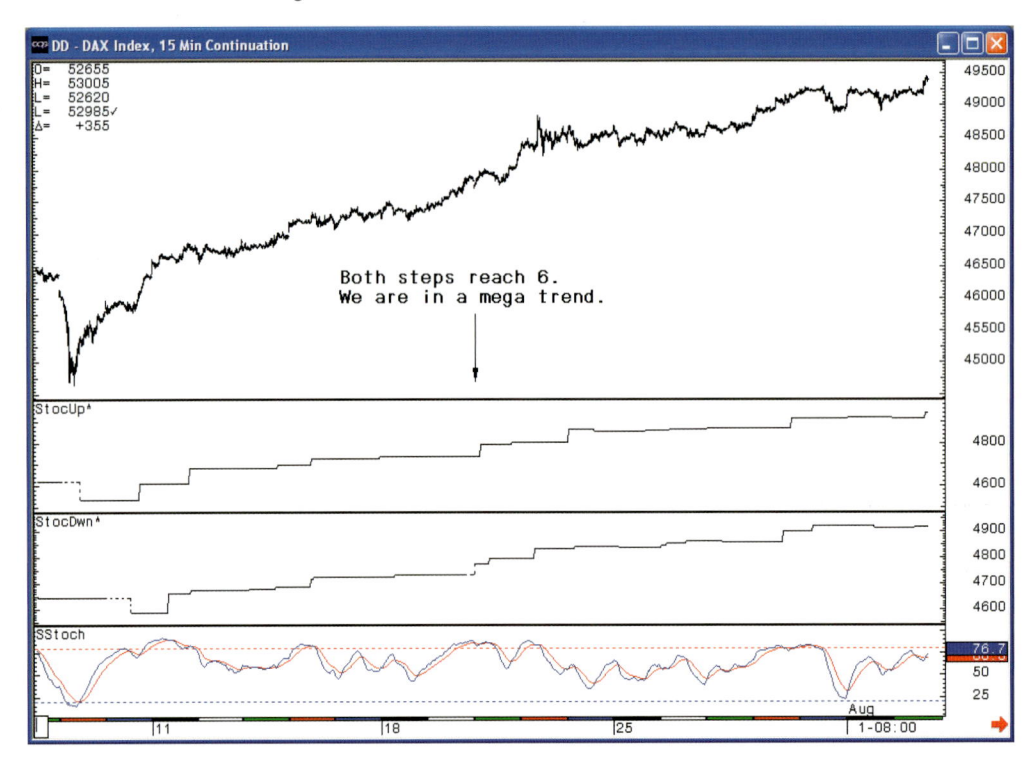

Figure 18:
The highest timeframe at 4 steps is the focus timeframe and reference for the trend

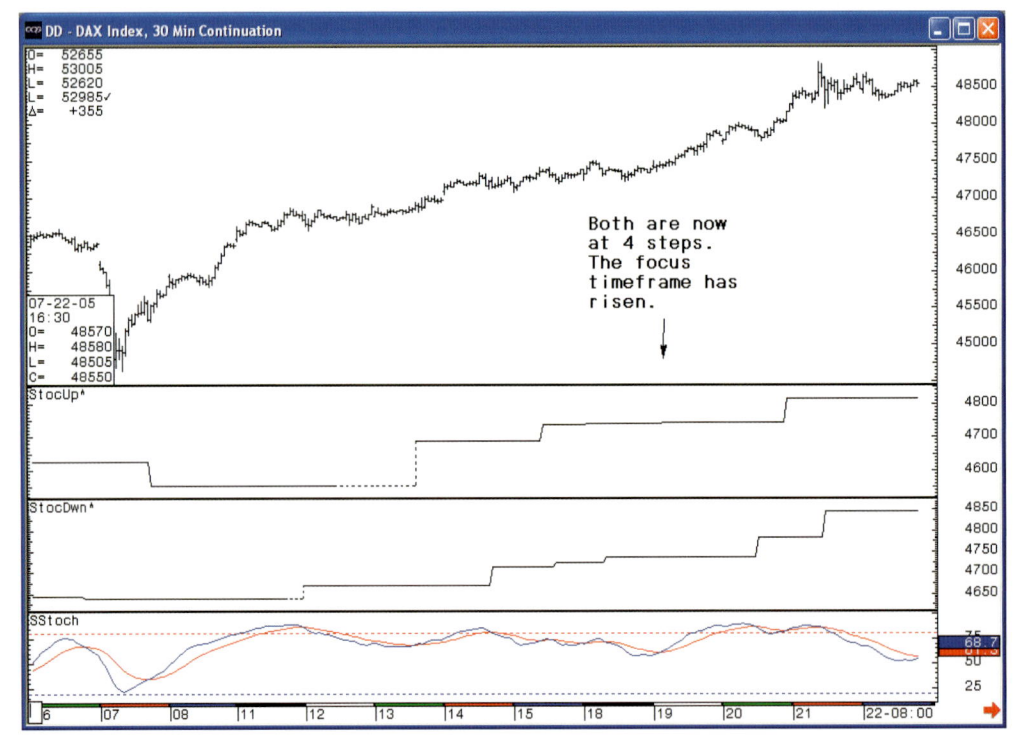

Concepts of Time

The significance of the gap between the numbers of bars between Slow Stochastic crossovers

Threshold of 65 bars used

In all the examples a threshold of 65 bars is used, but, as with the actual settings of the Slow Stochastic variables, this is not a magic number. Those who analyse cycle length in more depth will find that the threshold should be variable and, once you understand the differences between asset classes, the numbers could be different as well. This is particularly true of individual stocks on daily charts where the trend length is longer. For reference, the use of 65 maintains the relationship of cycle length to some of Cynthia Kase©'s studies (please see her book, 'Trading With The Odds').

Whilst 65 is the threshold, it is simply a trigger point at which to analyse the chart, the Slow Stochastic and assess the characteristics of the trend. From there various conclusions can be drawn. There are 3 basic questions:

- Has a new strong trend begun?
- Is an existing trend accelerating?
- Is the trend approaching exhaustion?

For reference, the appearance of a dashed line on the indicator itself marks a move beyond 65. The first concept requires a different approach from the other two studies depending on what the previous trend was. Returning to the Dax, we can see (see fig. 19) that prior to the mega trend developing the previous trend had been a swift move lower. Therefore, when analysing the first move higher, the reference indicator is the StocDwn. If it takes more than 65 bars for the Stochastic to cross down since the last time, it highlights a lack of downward momentum, as price has made no desire to correct itself lower. This is especially true if the previous movement in the StocDwn indicator was down and in this example is even more striking due the severity and speed of the previous downtrend. The Slow Stochastic takes over 65 bars to cross, suggesting that the previous move lower was an exhaustive move. The fact is that by the time a crossover has taken place the Slow Stochastic has reached an overbought status (above 80), which confirms that in fact the recent uptrend is strong. Therefore corrections should be shallow and short-lived in the days to come.

If you are looking for ways to manage the trade with the Stochastic alone, any move below 50 would be the first sign that the trend was weakening too much. For the bullish scenario to pan out, the StocUp indicator should confirm the initial impulse higher by either avoiding stepping down or ideally stepping up.

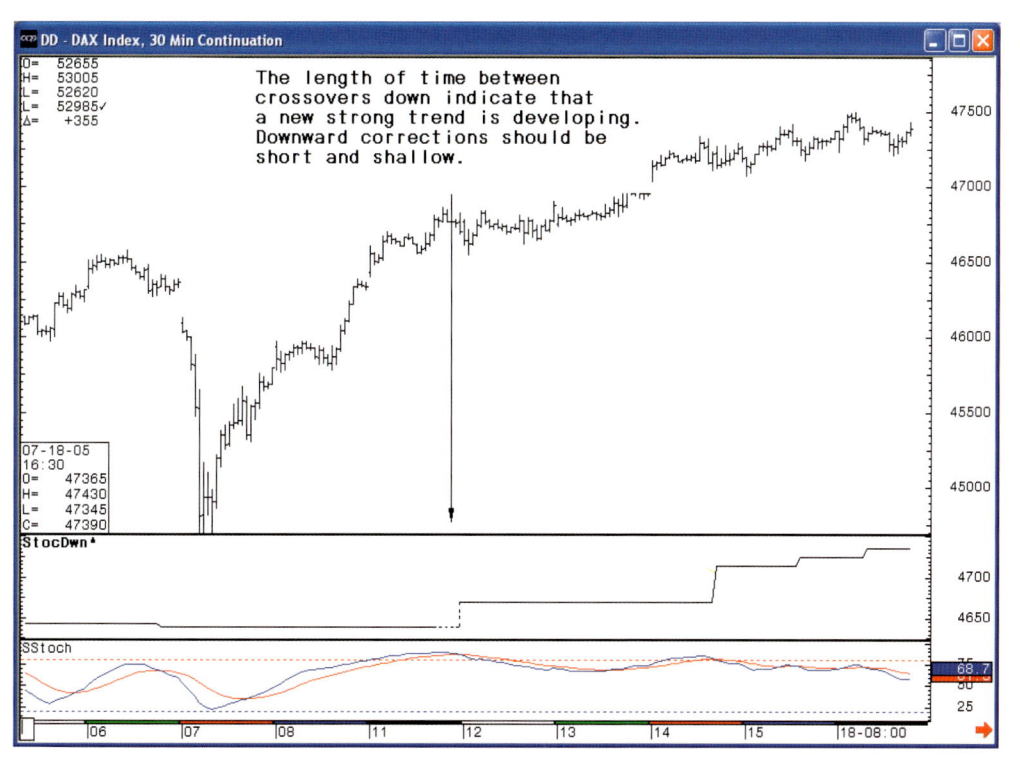

Figure 19:
Gauging strength of trend

Analysis of the StocUp indicator confirms that a new strong trend is in progress. In fact it takes 90 bars to cross, which shows it is in a very strong trend when analysed in conjunction with the StocDwn study. Price subsequently continues higher. This chart (see fig. 20) is a classic example of how early in the move the trader has a firm grasp of exactly what can be expected from this trade. Whilst it is always dangerous to become married to a view, the indicator tells us to expect an extended move. Therefore, as the trade should be deep in the money there is far less pressure to book profits early. An elephant winner is in the making.

Figure 20:
Gauging the strength of the trend

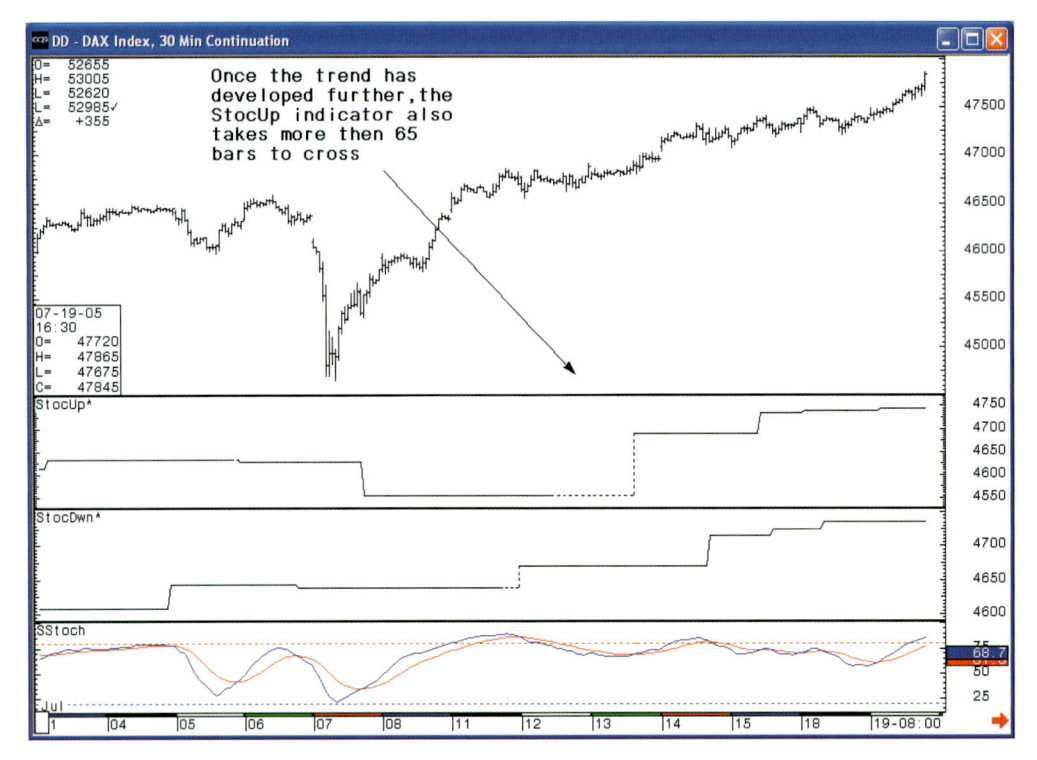

Either Step study can be the driving force in a trend.

The following charts (see figs. 21 and 22) show a superficially similar setup but this time there is a subtle difference. The StocDwn indicator is the reference point to establish that the corrective phase from the previous strong up trend is over. This is emphasised by the fact that, if the analysis is true, the indicator will make 4 steps on the next crossover and state that we are in a strong trend. Additionally the indicator itself is approaching overbought, which would be another sign that the trend is strong.

By the time the Steps reach 10 the Slow Stochastic has been overbought for 96 bars, or approximately 1½ cycles. Analysis of the daily chart shows that we have gone beyond the 65 bar point between a crossover as well. This highlights the potential for the market to reach an exhaustion point. Price does indeed correct but subsequently makes new highs. Once again a move beyond 65 bars appears but this time the daily chart is approaching its 10th step. Once Stochastic Steps reach 10 or above the need for the focus timeframe to move higher becomes more urgent and with the current timeframe at a daily it will always be difficult to shift upwards to a weekly. This is due to the long length of time it takes for the Slow Stochastic to cross up or down 4 times. Back on the daily chart, by the time 10 steps are reached there is huge divergence in the Slow Stochastic itself and a top is formed. The beginning of the trend was marked by the previous downtrend having taken too long to move lower and was indicating the potential of the beginning of a new strong trend up which was ultimately fulfilled with such a high final step number.

Concepts of Time

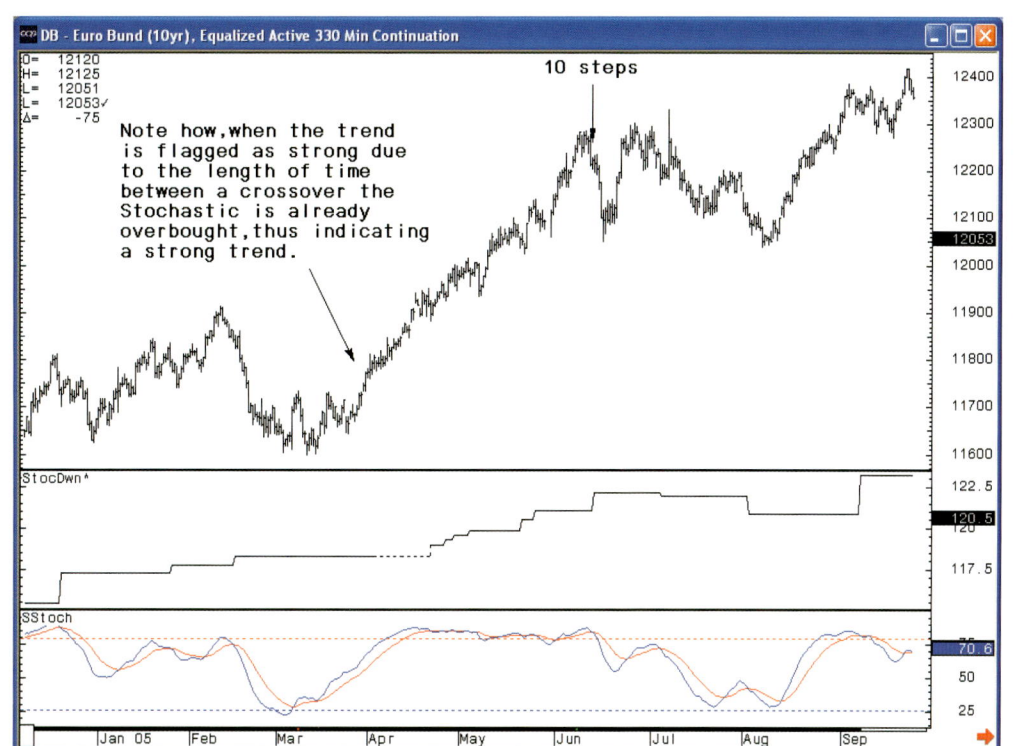

Figure 21:
Gauging the strength of the trend

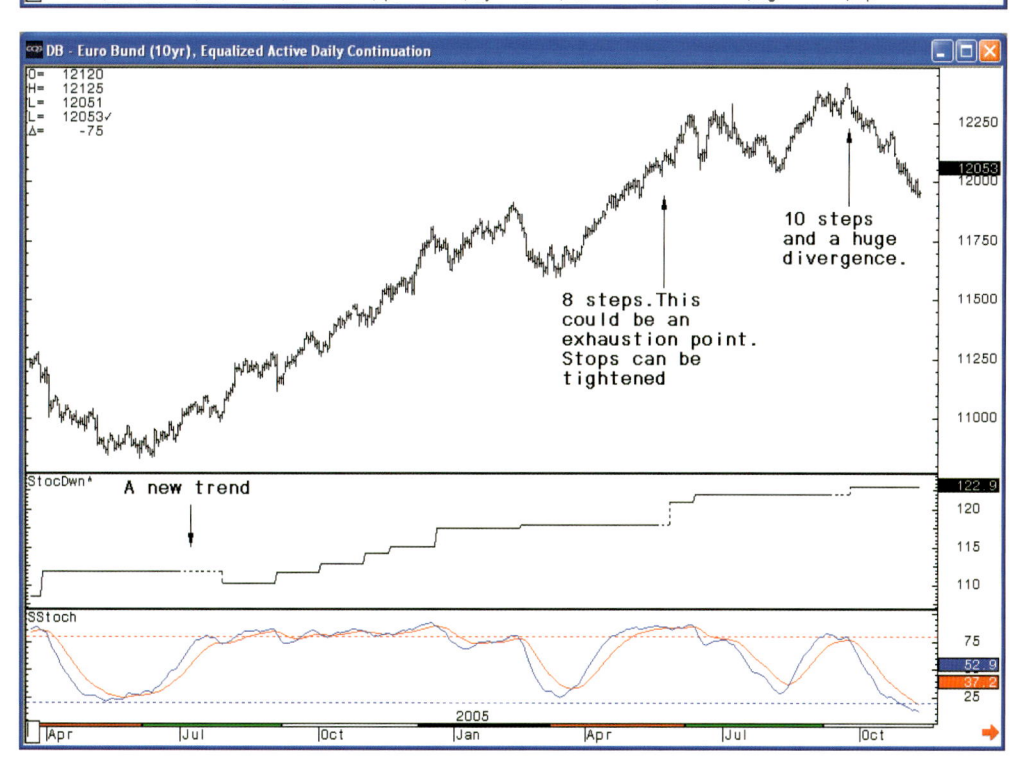

Figure 22:
Gauging the strength of the trend

TRADING TIME: New Methods in Technical Analysis

Riding the trend. Mega historical trends can also be micro-managed.

As can be seen on the daily chart (see fig. 23) the trend lasted nearly 300 bars. Regardless of whether the Stochastic Steps indicated the trade should have been kept throughout that period, it is still difficult to imagine many traders managing to do so. However, often within a historical mega trend there are still opportunities. The second part of the trend that began in April 2005 provided such a trade. Subsequent to the 330-minute chart (half day see fig. 24) highlighting the potential for a new trend, analysis of the 165-minute chart (see fig. 23) shows that Stochastic Steps have just stepped to 4. Movements in a timeframe lower than this from an exit standpoint should now be ignored. Note that in May the 165-minute chart (quarter day see fig. 23) stepped down but before that point in late April the 330-minute had stepped up 4 times (see fig. 24) and so became the new higher focus timeframe. This highlights how trends can be ridden up timeframes, as lower timeframes can never step indefinitely.

Figure 23:
Stepping down signals the end of the trend

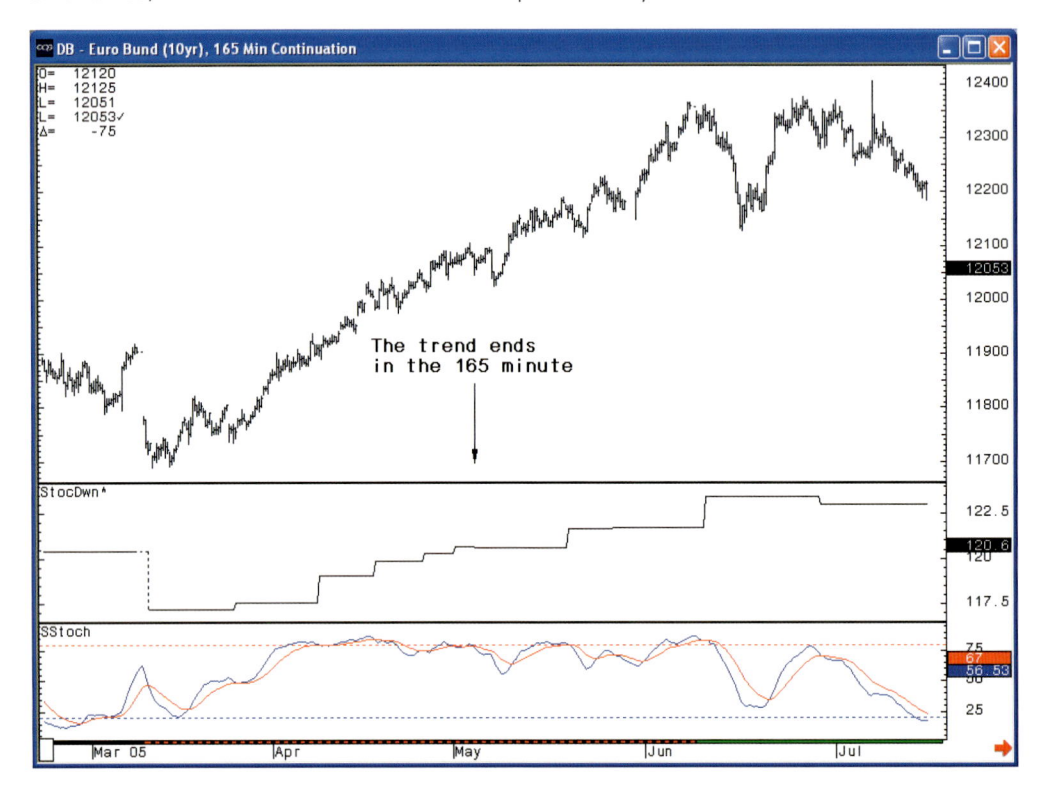

Figure 24:
A higher timeframe chart has moved the focus. The trend is still alive.

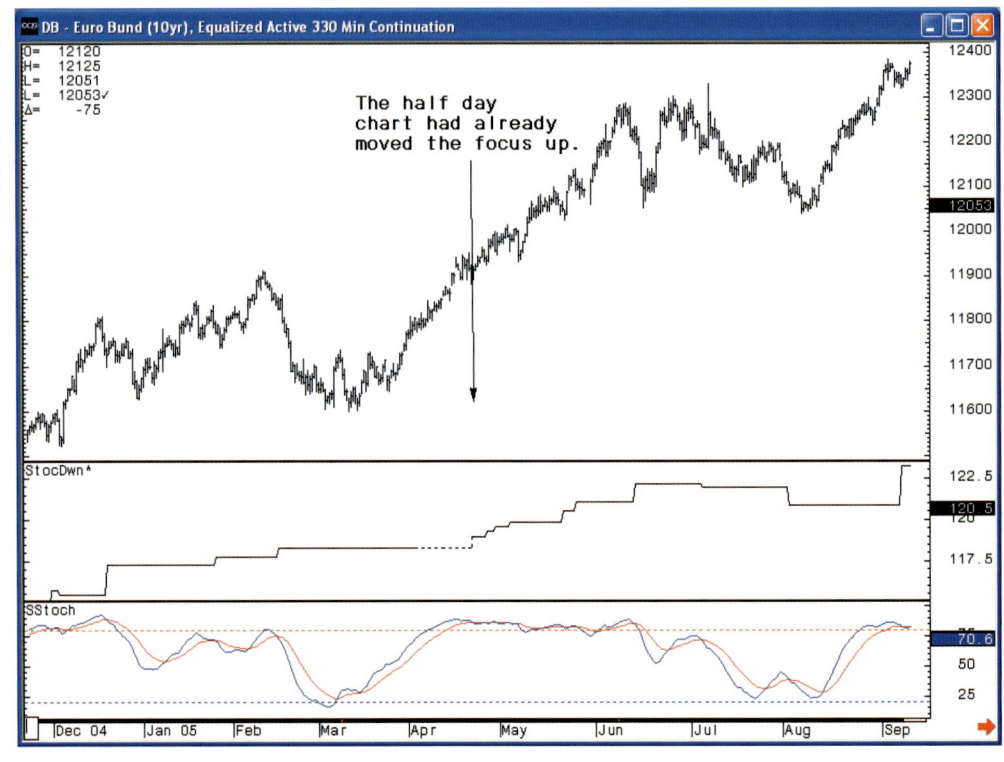

134

Concepts of Time

Defining the trend can allow for elimination of one side of the market

Finally, while the point at which the Stochastic Steps reach the threshold of 65 is not an exact timing point, it does mean that the trader can now concentrate on the fine-tuning of their entries. In addition it enables them to know how to manage an existing trade. This includes knowing the focus timeframe for risk management of the core position, or creates a bias to be a buyer whenever other analysis tools are pointing in a similar direction in a lower timeframe or via Market Profile® concepts. This is a key point. Once a bias has been created to the upside, only the most powerful day-trading negative setups can be used. For the highly risk-averse these intraday negatives can be ignored all together. As we see in the Peak chapter, understanding when negatives can be traded is critical to managing a position or giving a day-trade bias, and provides a balance to the purely bullish scenario portrayed by Stochastic Steps.

Trend acceleration and exhaustion

We have seen how the concept of length of time between crossovers can confirm an embryonic trend, but the same concept can be used to identify when a trend is nearing exhaustion. The key to being able to interpret this is your ability to analyse the price action and the Slow Stochastic itself. The first example looks at a 5-minute S&P chart (see fig. 25).

The trend begins in the most emphatic manner when both Stochastic Steps studies move close together beyond the 65 bar point. The second acceleration is in the StocUp which has been above a key threshold of 50 for nearly 150 bars. [We shall look at this concept in greater detail later on]. The third and fourth signals are both accelerations but the actual technical picture is very different from the first two signals. First the StocDwn step has moved lower and never reached the 4 steps up, which would have indicated a strong trend. By the time of the fourth signal the Slow Stochastic itself has failed once to reach overbought and then reversed from this area. The Slow Stochastic has also approached oversold and broken below 50. The trend is still up, but the strength and velocity have disappeared. By the time of the final acceleration the picture has deteriorated further in spite of the trend continuing higher. The StocUp study reaches 6, which indicates a mega trend, but the StocDwn study has stepped down twice in this trend. A step of 6 indicates a mega trend but it can end at any time. By the time of the step up the Market Profile® picture is also showing weakness and shortly afterwards the StocUp moved lower indicating the trend was over. For reference, the market moved sideways for a week.

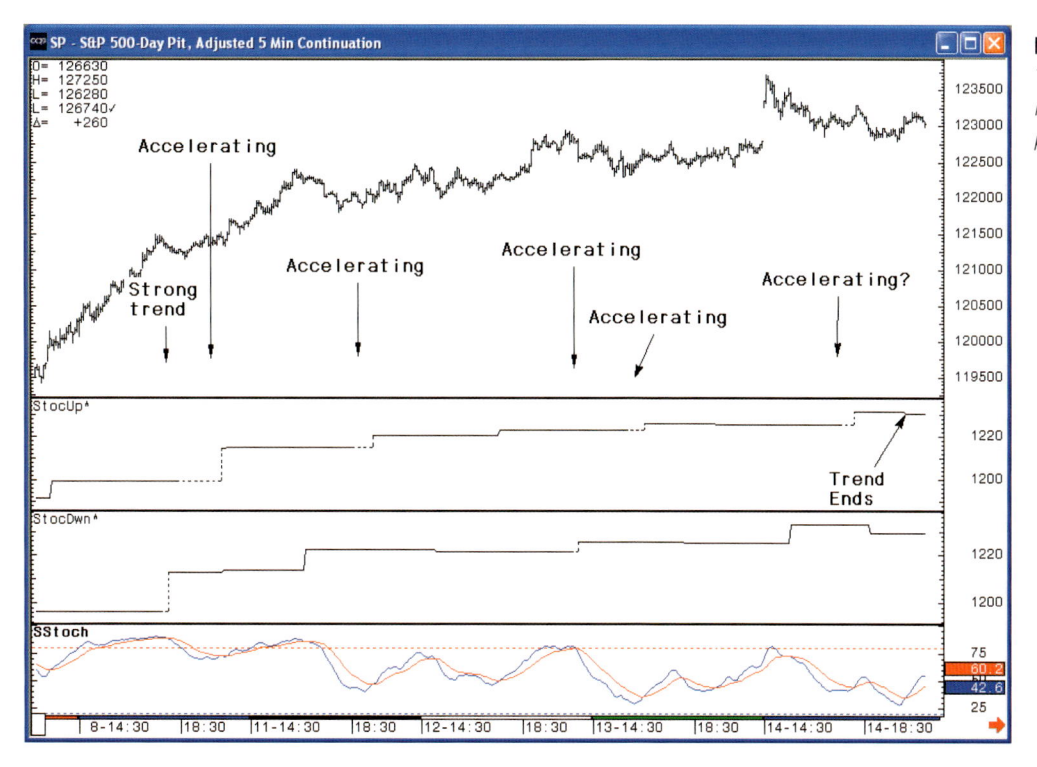

Figure 25:
This trend has many acceleration points

TRADING TIME: New Methods in Technical Analysis

Let's see how Market Profile® developed

The trend began with a typical major rejection of a move lower (see fig. 26). The previous day had seen a weak close that was due to a late slump that had moved directly to the lows of the previous day's vacuum. This suggests that it was short-term players and that the move could be false.

The opening the following day is bearish with a lower opening but this picture swiftly changes as we have responsive behaviour in **B**. The opening is the low and then initiative momentum appears in **F** with single letter prints. The risk is low and we close on the highs to complete a powerful reversal.

Figure 26:
The weak opening is swiftly repelled

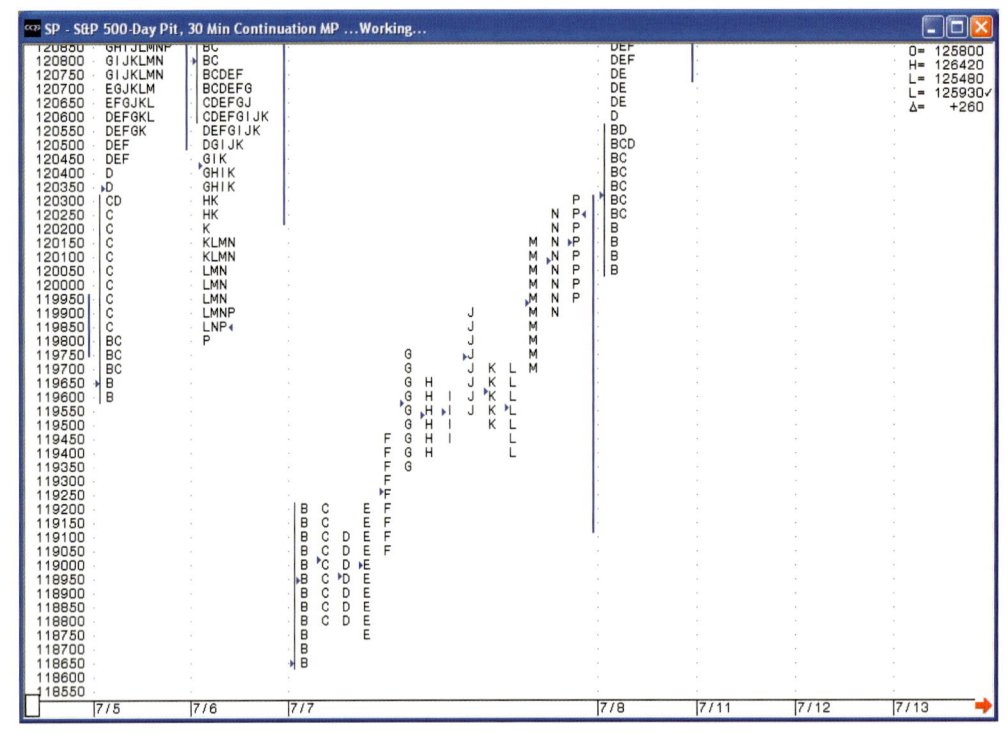

The following day highlights the strength of the trend as the previous day's strong close is confirmed (see fig. 27). There is initiative momentum on the opening and is followed by 3 initiative single prints. Not surprisingly price closes on the highs.

Figure 27:
A strong day is confirmed via single letter prints

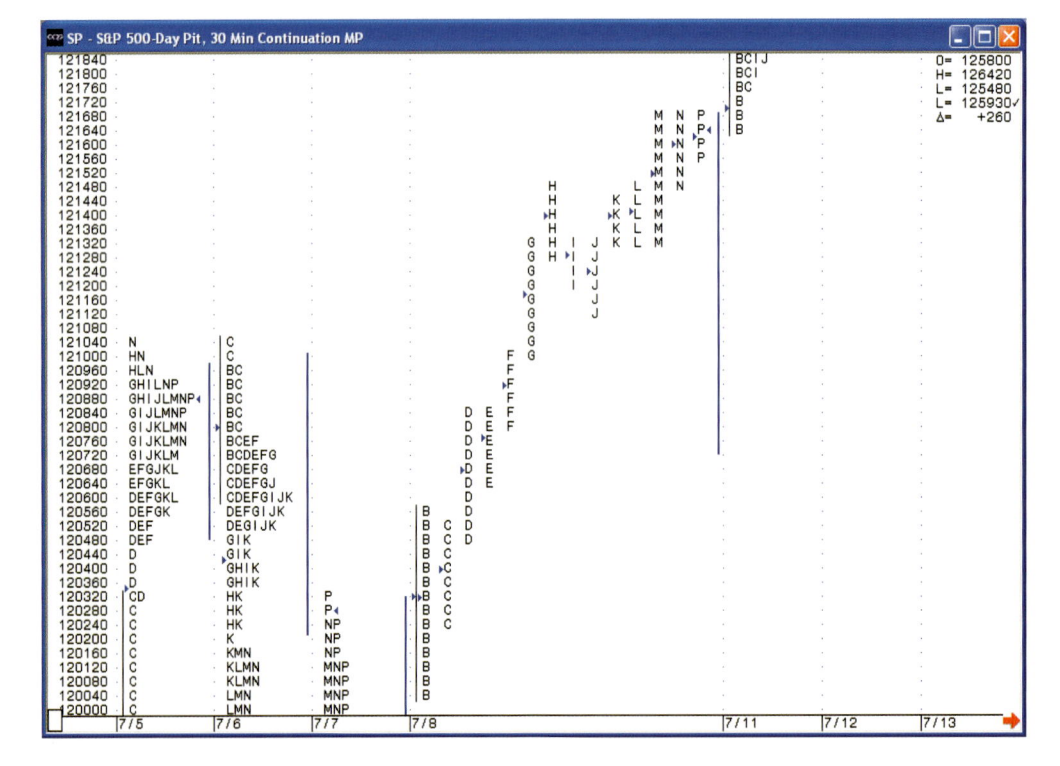

Concepts of Time

11 July (see fig. 28) a strong trend is confirmed by both studies having stepped 4 times. However, this only lasts one day as one of the studies steps back down. The trend is still valid, but has weakened.

Trends can only last so long before they must back and fill, or simply decelerate if they remain in the same focus timeframe. When the step down occurs, it does so exactly 195 bars from when the first step up began, the equivalent of 3 trend cycles. The weakened trend, in combination with the length of trend, means that without moving to a higher focus timeframe there is less chance of bullish initiative behaviour in the short term.

From a day-trading standpoint this is crucial information. The trader should just be trying to identify the high probability winners. The connection between Stochastic Steps and Market Profile® tells us that: yes, we are in a strong trend, but it's reached the point where the path of the trend will be more problematic unless the focus timeframe moves up. Therefore, in the absence of that happening, long positions should not be added to intraday and any breakouts to the upside must be treated with caution.

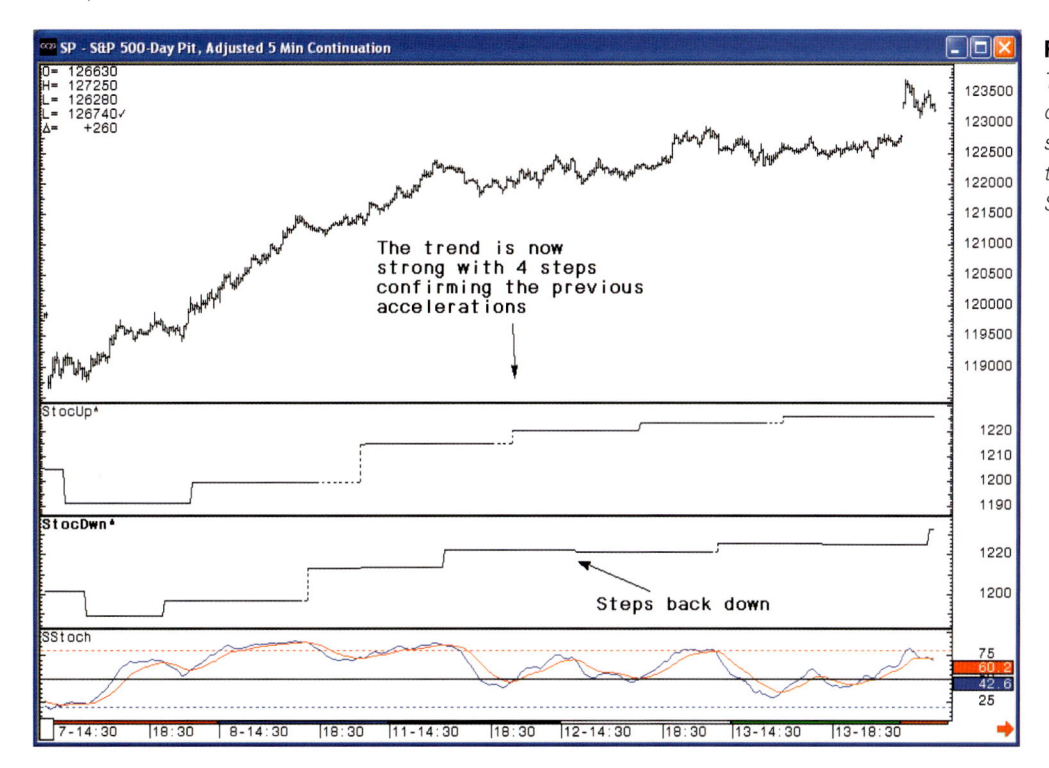

Figure 28:
The 5-minute chart briefly shows a strong trend on both Steps

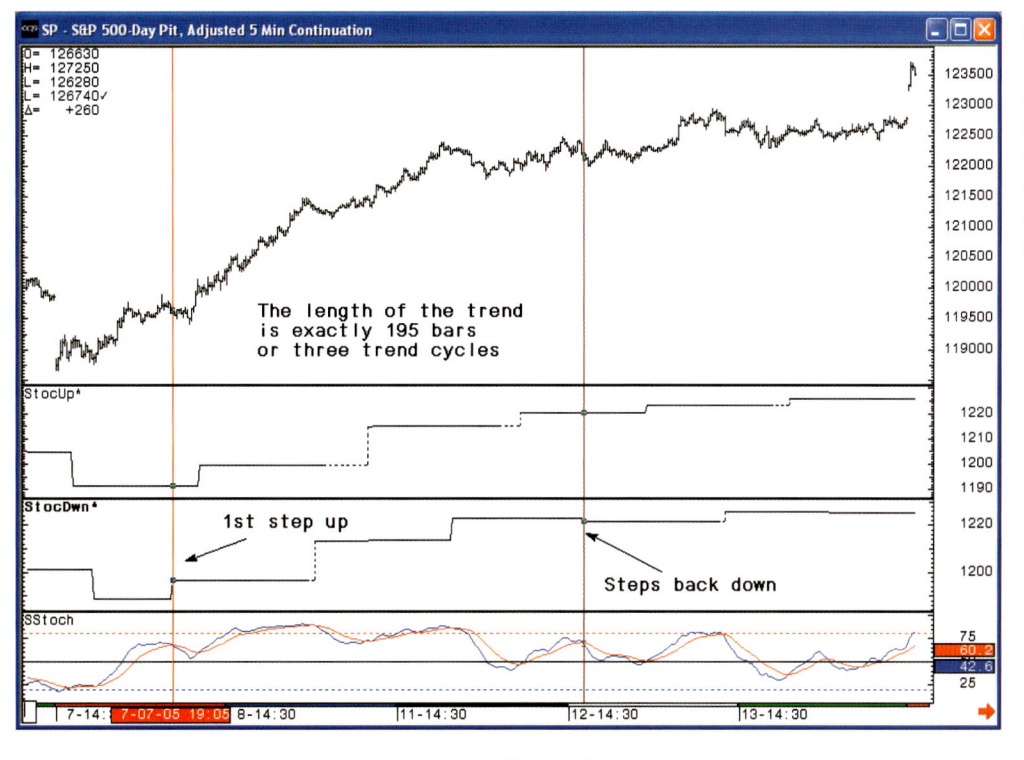

Figure 29:
The 5-minute chart needs to move to a higher timeframe as the cycle is becoming overextended

TRADING TIME: New Methods in Technical Analysis

Analysis of the Market Profile® 12 July (see fig. 30) shows that a breakout, whilst still profitable, did not develop fully. 13 July just ambles sideways.

Figure 30:
The trend is losing momentum

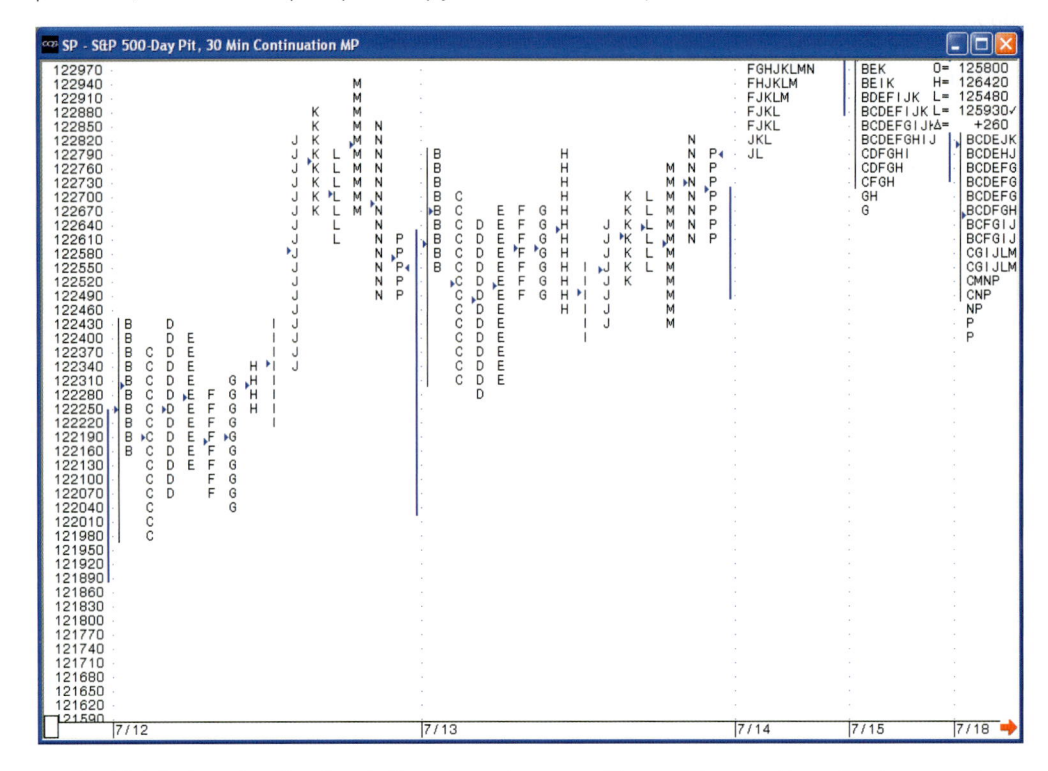

[Market Profile chart: SP - S&P 500-Day Pit, 30 Min Continuation MP, showing 7/12 through 7/18]

By 14 July the other Stochastic Steps has also moved lower. The trend has simply petered out, meaning stops on the core position should be tightened or the trade exited.

Figure 31:
The trend dies

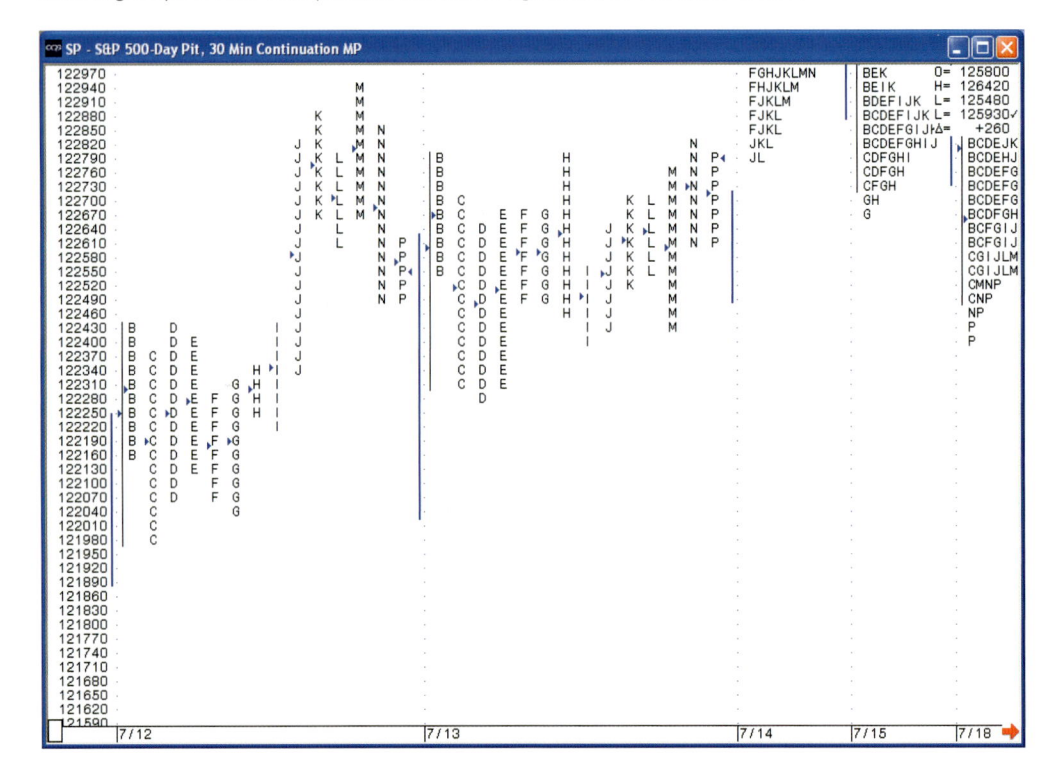

[Market Profile chart: SP - S&P 500-Day Pit, 30 Min Continuation MP, showing 7/12 through 7/18]

What happens if a trend has simply died in a low timeframe?

So what is the answer in this scenario? If there is no trend, even on a micro level, then the market is in sideways mode. This is crucial information.

If we are following the strong trend theory, the only alternative is to move up timeframes and attempt to move this trade into the intermediate and strategic areas if the higher timeframes indicate that it's possible.

Concepts of Time

Moving onto 14 and 15 July, we can see (fig. 32) that in spite of price rising the technical picture has deteriorated further. Both opening **B** periods are negative and there are no opportunities to buy.

Analysis of the next higher timeframe in the 10-minute chart shows that there is no higher timeframe confirmation, thus a shift higher in the focus timeframe is not possible and the trend for now is dead. Subsequently, price moved sideways for 2 weeks as no timeframe chart, however small, could develop a trend. This is a good example of the chart telling you, you don't tell the chart.

The micro timeframe was extremely positive at the beginning, but gradually the bullishness simply fizzled out. This is a very common scenario as mega trends rarely fulfil their potential all the way to a historical timeframe.

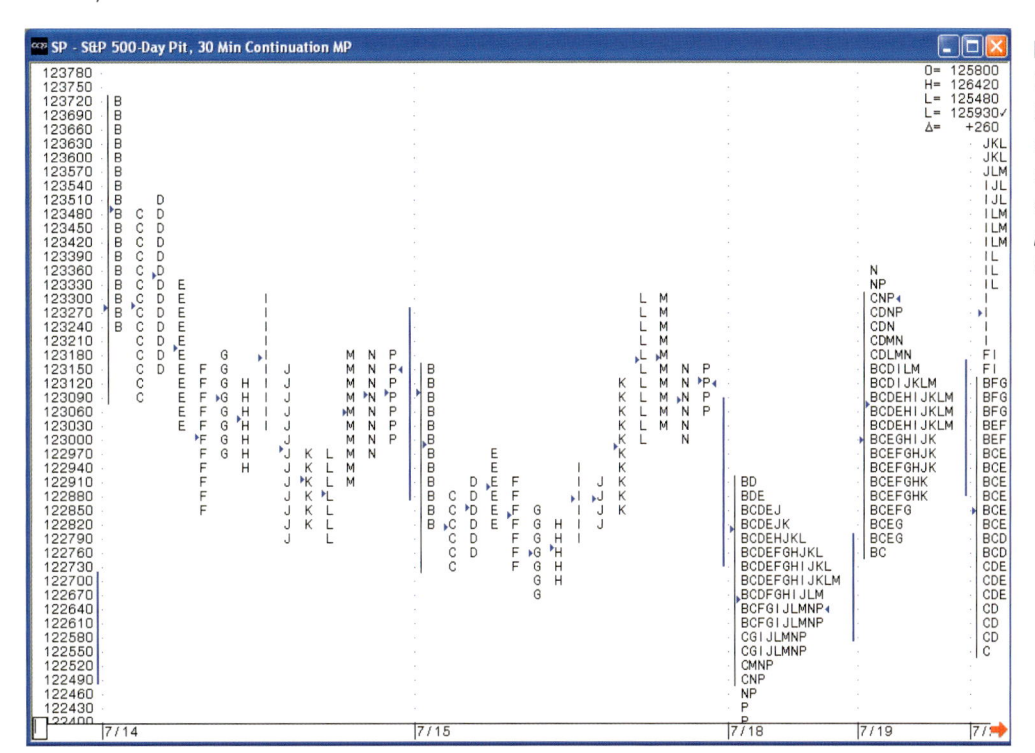

Figure 32:
With Steps indicating the trend has ended, the market enters a choppy period marked by false breakouts

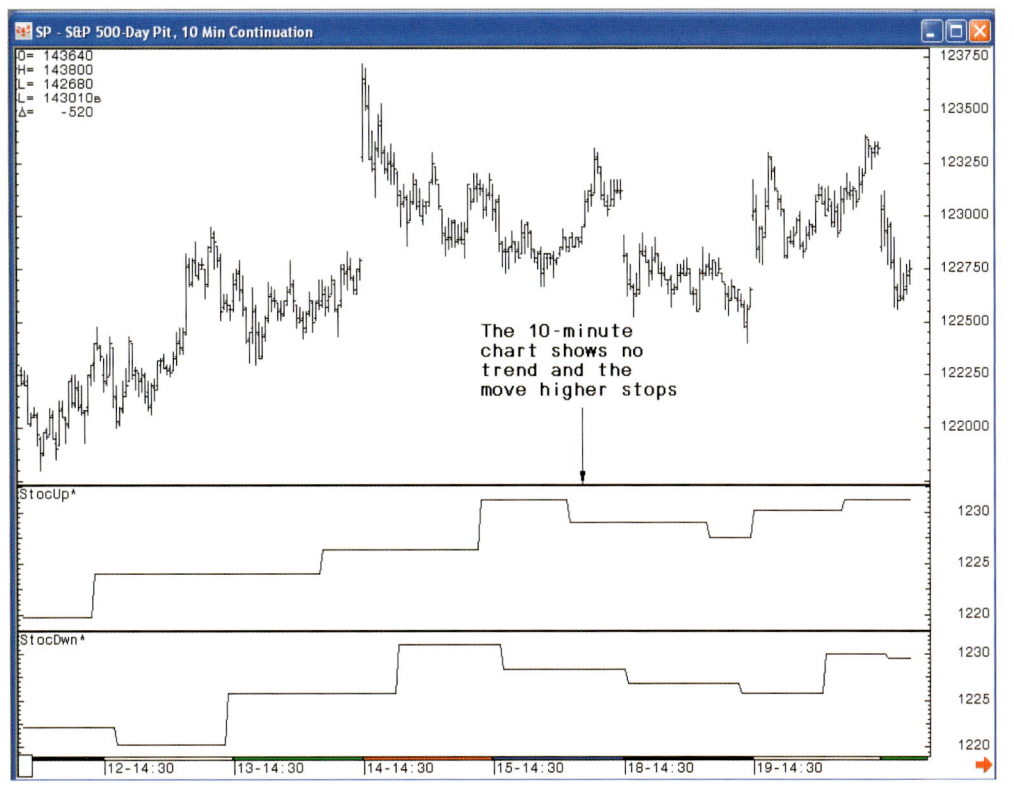

Figure 32a:
10-minute S&P

Dax - a case study

It was a different setup on the Dax.

Whilst the micro timeframes had shown some short-term moves (see fig. 33), it was the 15-minute chart that initially became the focus on the next trend. Analysis of the Slow Stochastic itself superficially shows a market that has no bullish bias. It has been edging lower and has never reached oversold. However, the Stochastic Steps reveal the underlying strength. The StocDwn study has already stepped up 6 times before a single step down. When the StocDwn continues to step up without the StocUp confirming by going to 4, this tells us that, while we are not in a very strong trend, the corrections to it are shallow and lacklustre. There is an underlying power being built. By 18 July the StocUp study finally joins the party and steps up 4 times, signalling a strong trend. 19 July saw the StocDwn study move beyond the 65 threshold, which highlights that the underlying power is being confirmed and the trend is accelerating.

Figure 33:
The 15-minute chart moves into a mega trend

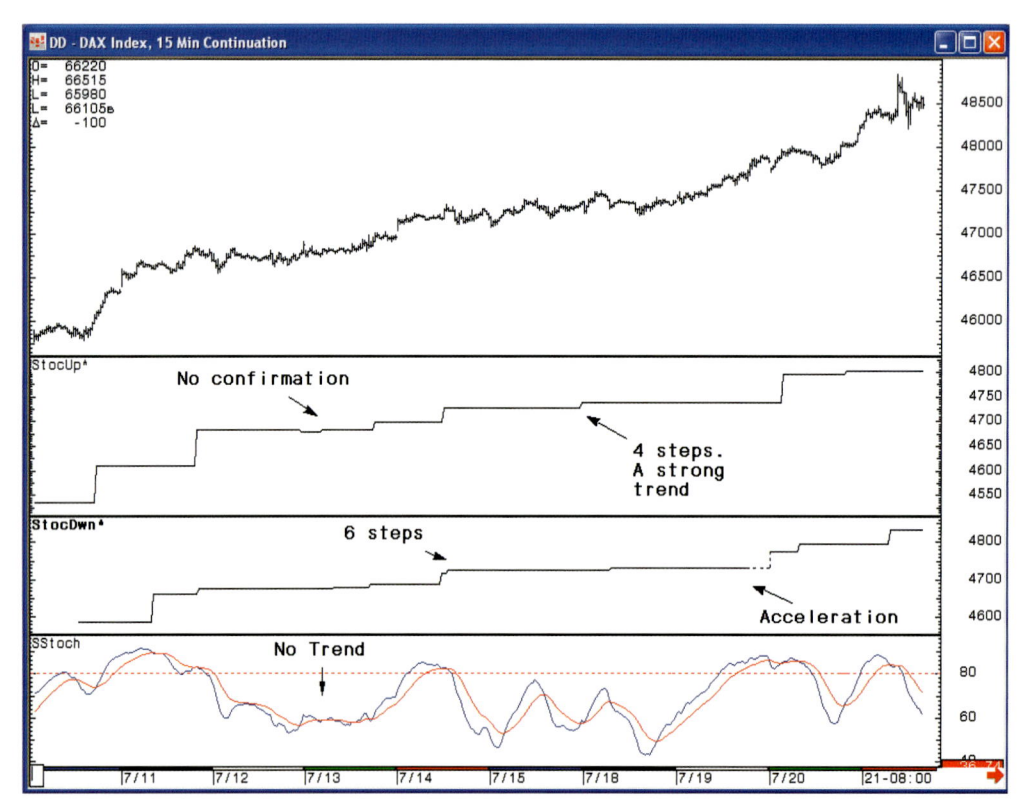

The trend develops

Analysis of the next higher timeframe at 30 minutes (see fig. 34) shows the strength. Both studies are beyond 4 steps and the trend began with both studies moving beyond the 65 bar point, indicating that a strong trend was beginning in what is a new higher focus timeframe. Finally one of the steps moves down, which means that the market is reaching its limits of power and must begin to react and back, and fill or shift the focus timeframe upwards.

Concepts of Time

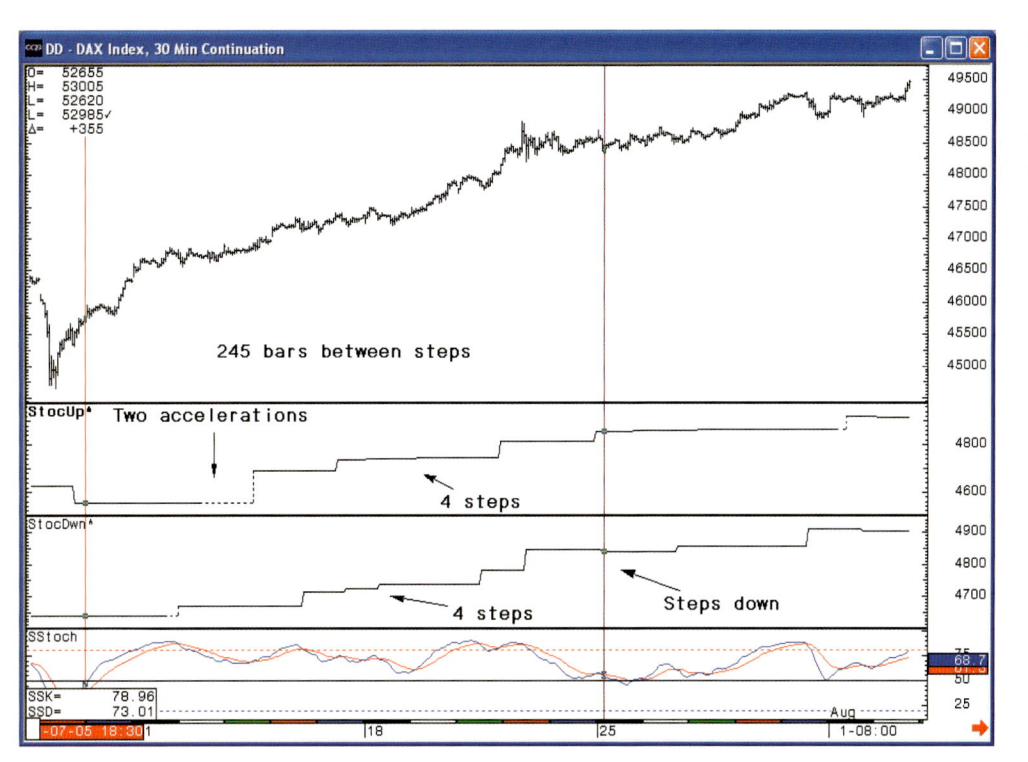

Figure 34:
The timeframe shifts upwards and also shows acceleration at the trend's beginning

Raising of the focus timeframes means cycle length extends

This time, in contrast to the S&P, the momentum is developing. Analysis of the 60-minute (see fig. 35) chart shows that this is also moving into a strong trend. 19 July marks the day that the strong trend has been flagged. This means that the focus timeframe has moved higher just one day after it had moved up to the 30-minute from the 15-minute. This highlights how important it is to monitor different timeframes and understand when the length of trend is changing. The previous S&P example (see fig. 31) never got above a 10-minute timeframe. The Dax is now on a 60-minute. The 30-minute is showing acceleration at the same time, as the 60-minute became the focus. It also means that because the 60-minute is now the focus timeframe, the trend has simply reached its normal cycle length and is no longer overextended.

As the 60-minute is now the focus it becomes the dominant cycle. Analysis shows that the study has been above 50 for 67 bars when the 4th step up occurred. The trend continues but finally tops out at exactly 195 or three trend cycles. This suggests that once again the focus timeframe needs to move upwards.

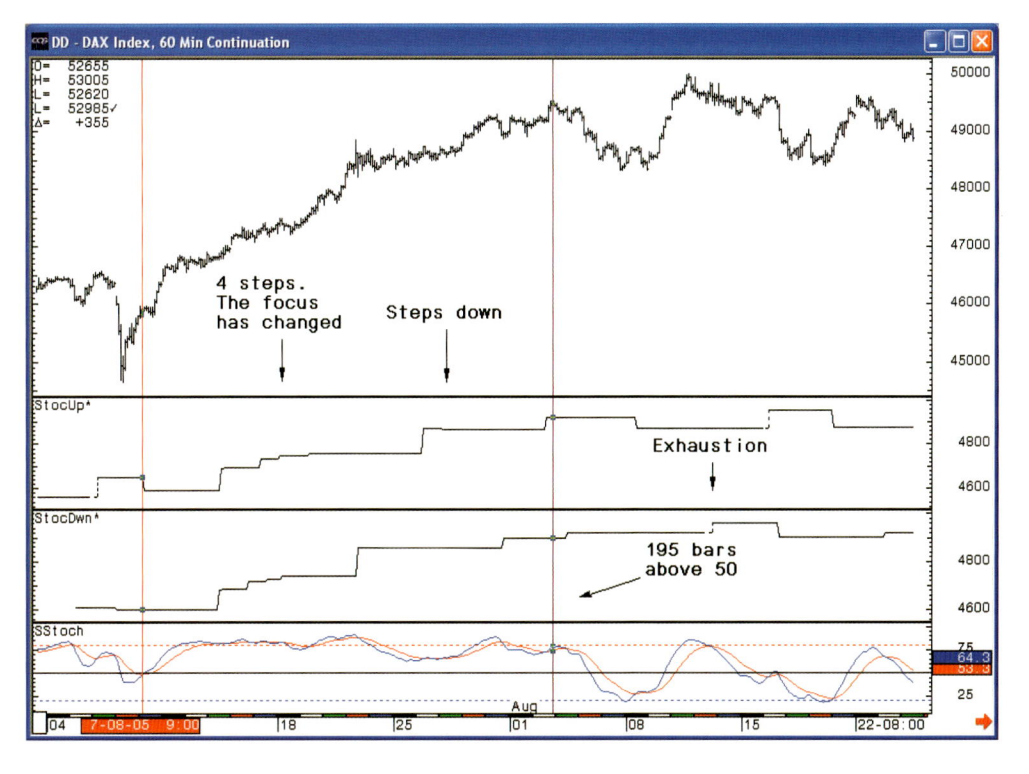

Figure 35:
The focus timeframe moves higher again but eventually shows exhaustion as the cycles become overextended. The focus timeframe needs to move up to keep the trend alive.

141

TRADING TIME: New Methods in Technical Analysis

Market Profile® and Stochastic Steps

If we move on to the Market Profile® outlook, 19 July (see fig. 36) is the point where the trend is extremely strong. That moment sees a typical trend day. Price displays responsive activity on the opening, which coincides with the Control Point of the day before. Initiative behaviour appears in **v** and we have a strong rally. Price closes on the highs.

Figure 36: *A typical trend day*

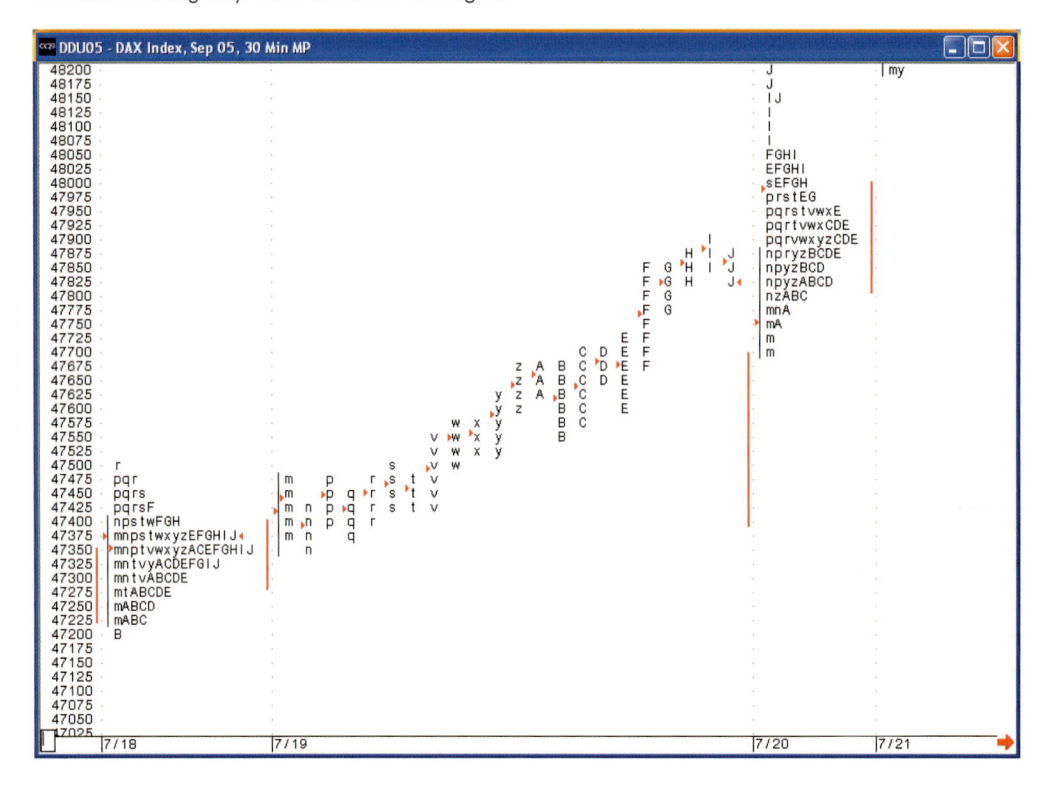

Profiles don't have to be 30 minutes

The common theory of Market Profile® is that it is fixed on the 30-minute timeframe. Analysis of the Stochastic Steps has shown that the focus timeframe is now 60 minutes, which means that if any trades are to remain in tune with the dynamics, the time horizon on a trade will be at the intermediate level. The trend is more likely to last days and could move into weeks. Therefore, the 60-minute Market Profile® can also be the dominant focus we are to stay in tune.

Note that if the Stochastic Steps show we are in the 5-minute or 10-minute timeframe, we can still monitor and use the initiative and responsive trend rules on a normal Market Profile® setup. However, we cannot always expect to get large trend days as the market is still embryonic in terms of its length. When the Stochastic Steps show that the focus is 30 minutes, then the normal Market Profile® is in tune as the standard is 30-minute timeframes and we can expect big trend days

Analysis of the 60-minute Market Profile® (see fig. 37) shows how the picture is different from the traditional 30-minute. The market displays initiative behaviour on the opening but we have no single letters confirming. It is not until the afternoon when America opens that we see single letters in **E** and the price accelerates once again and closes on the highs.

Concepts of Time

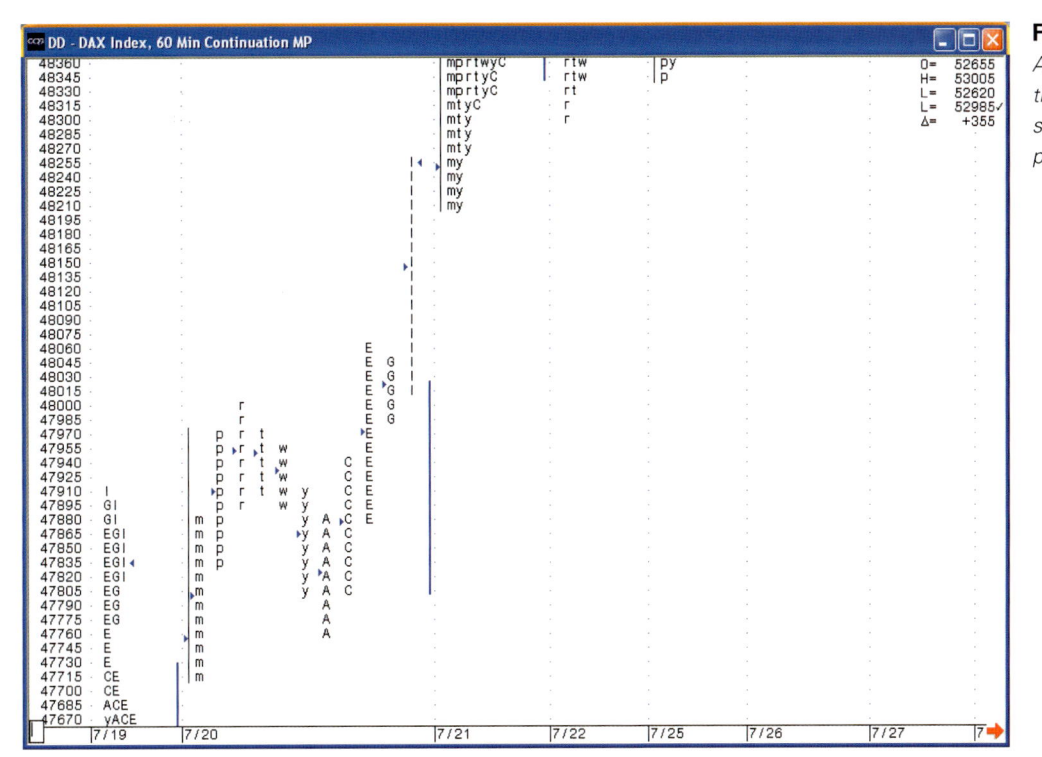

Figure 37: *A higher timeframe shows a different picture*

Merged Profile

At the time of writing, 25 July 2005, price has simply held a higher value and appears to have shown no further bullish initiatives. However, if we look at the trend from its lows, we can see (fig. 38) the control point has moved higher 25 July. Therefore, fair value has moved higher and, with the trend already up, the outlook is bullish. From a strategic standpoint, stops can be moved up depending on the trader's concept of risk. We have the bottom of a vacuum at 4804, a ledge at 4788, and the top of the previous distribution at 4752.

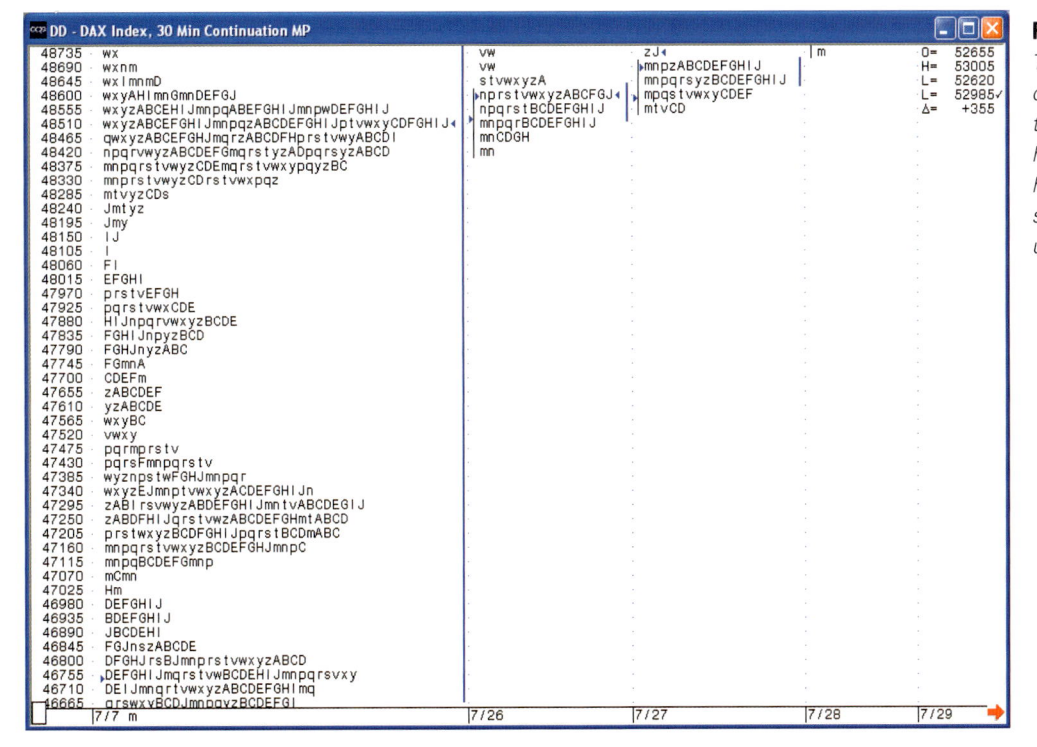

Figure 38: *The merged chart shows that the Control Point has moved higher. The trend should accelerate upwards*

Control shifts

With the Control Point moving higher (see fig. 39) a fresh acceleration is due, so buy signals can be taken on a Market Profile® basis. The first opportunity is 28 July. Initiative behaviour appears in the opening hour in **n** and then again in **y**.

Figure 39:
Two sets of Initiative behaviour

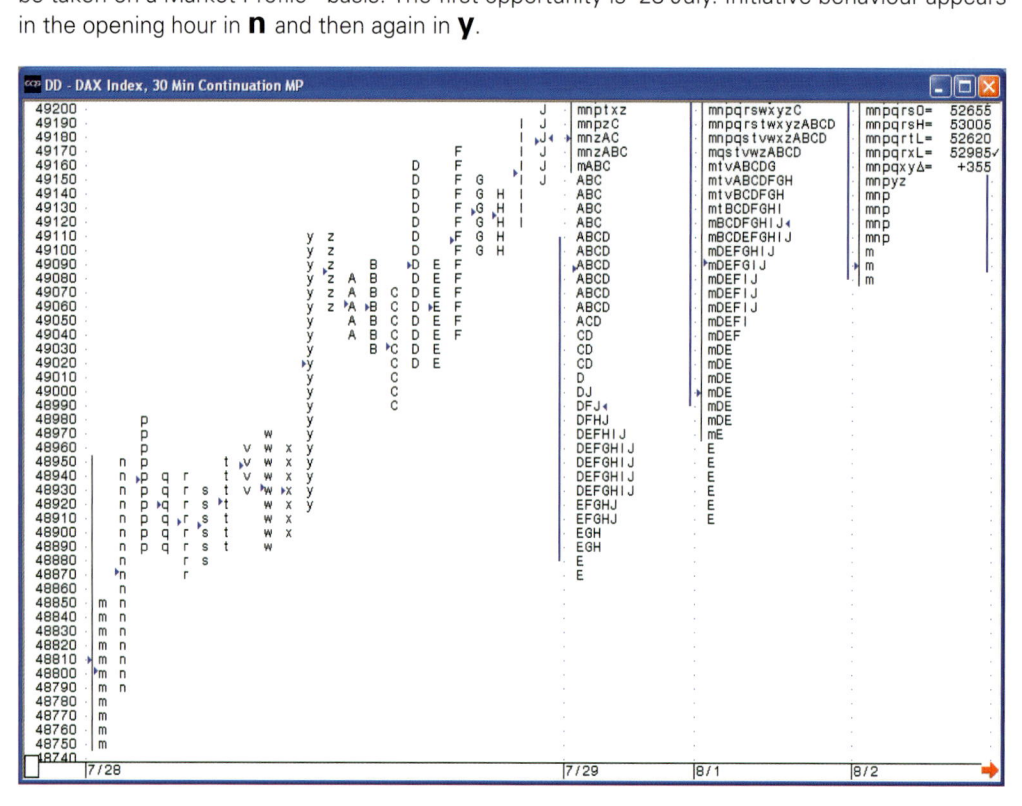

The Volatility Time Average Bands can occasionally be used to qualify single-letter breakouts (see fig. 40).

Figure 40:
A qualified breakout

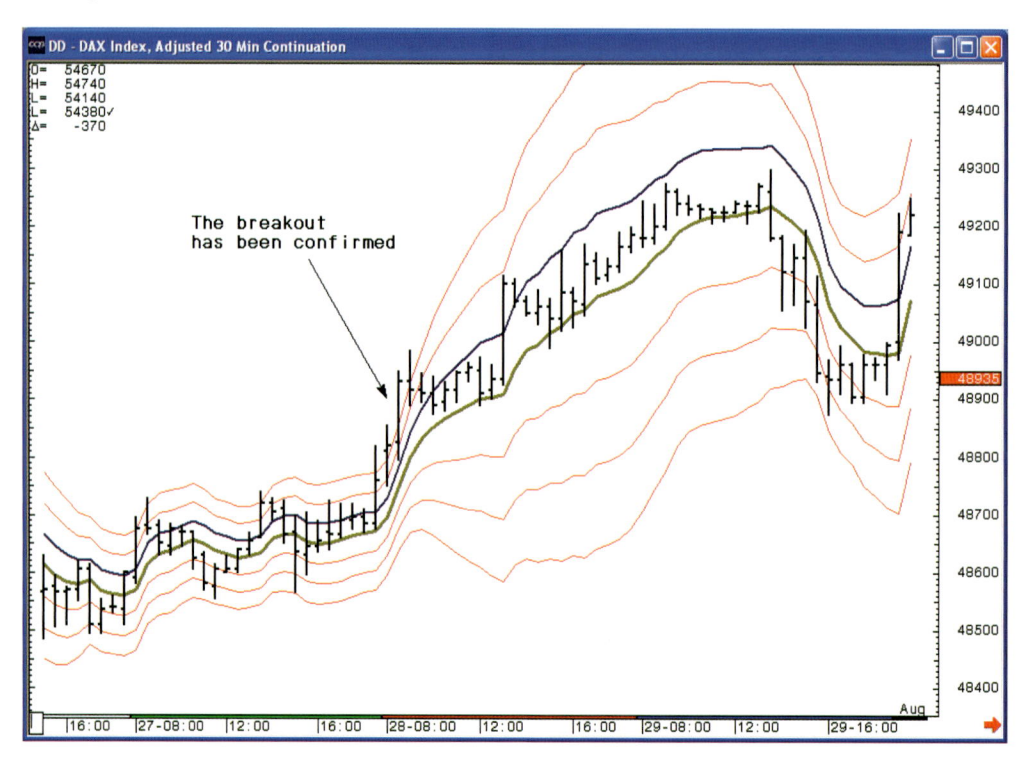

Concepts of Time

How many consecutive Steps can actually occur?
The highest Stochastic Steps number up to recent history is 14 in any timeframe in any market. This is a true measure of when a mega trend is coming to an end although this is a very rare occurrence. More often, once Steps get to 10, the trend is reaching the point where staying in it is approaching the point where returns in relationship to risk are diminishing.

The one exception has been the Australian stock-market rally, which is a classic example of Stochastic Steps theory riding an exceptional trend.

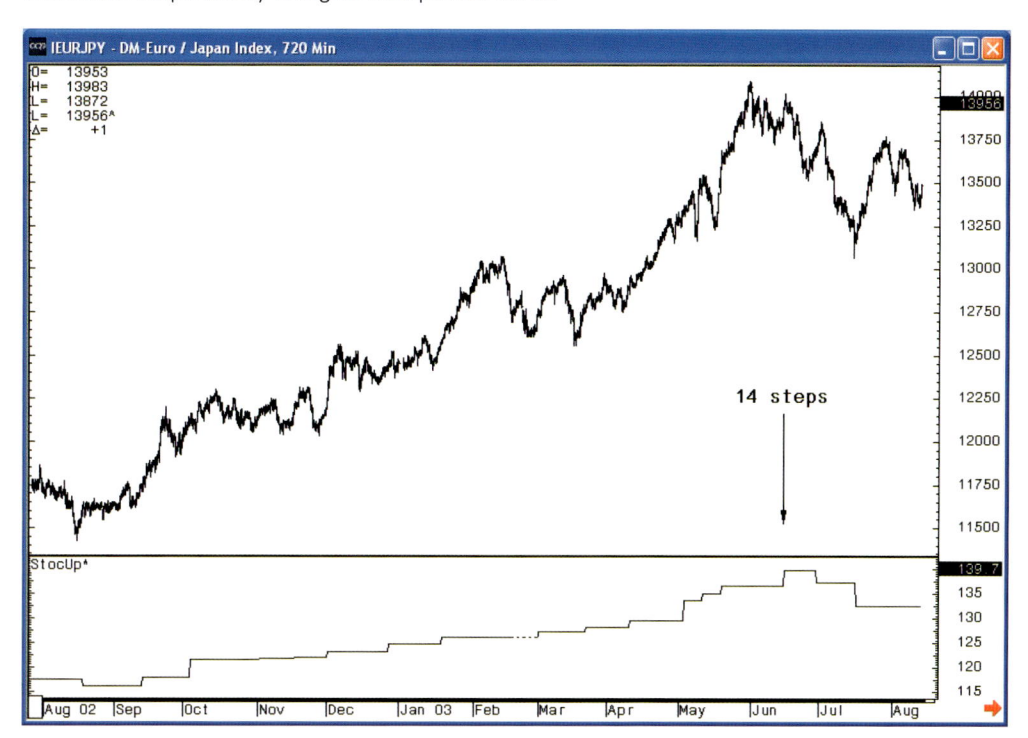

Figure 41:
An unusual trend

Until recently 14 steps had always been the limit. That was until the current Australian stock market rally re-wrote the rules of limits of trend. Even though the rules have changed, the dynamic nature of Stochastic Steps means that this has been a classic example of how Stochastic Steps theory will ride a trend. It started way back in 2003 (see fig. 42) on a very low timeframe chart and has ridden up seamlessly to the weekly timeframe. The trend is still up and the position still valid after 3 years (see fig. 42).

Australian Stock market - a case study.

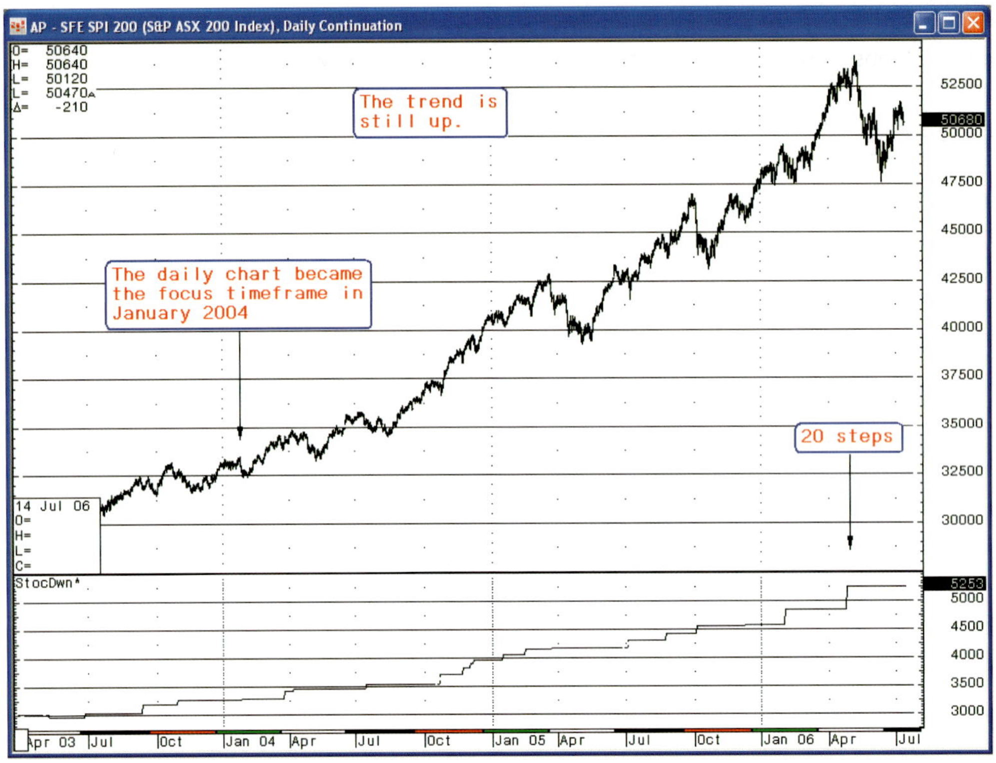
AP - SFE SPI 200 (S&P ASX 200 Index), Daily Continuation
The trend is still up.
The daily chart became the focus timeframe in January 2004
20 steps
StocDwn
Apr 03 Jul Oct Jan 04 Apr Jul Oct Jan 05 Apr Jul Oct Jan 06 Apr Jul

Figure 42: *The trend has now extended to unprecedented 20 steps on the daily chart. The chart became the focus timeframe all the way back in 2004.*

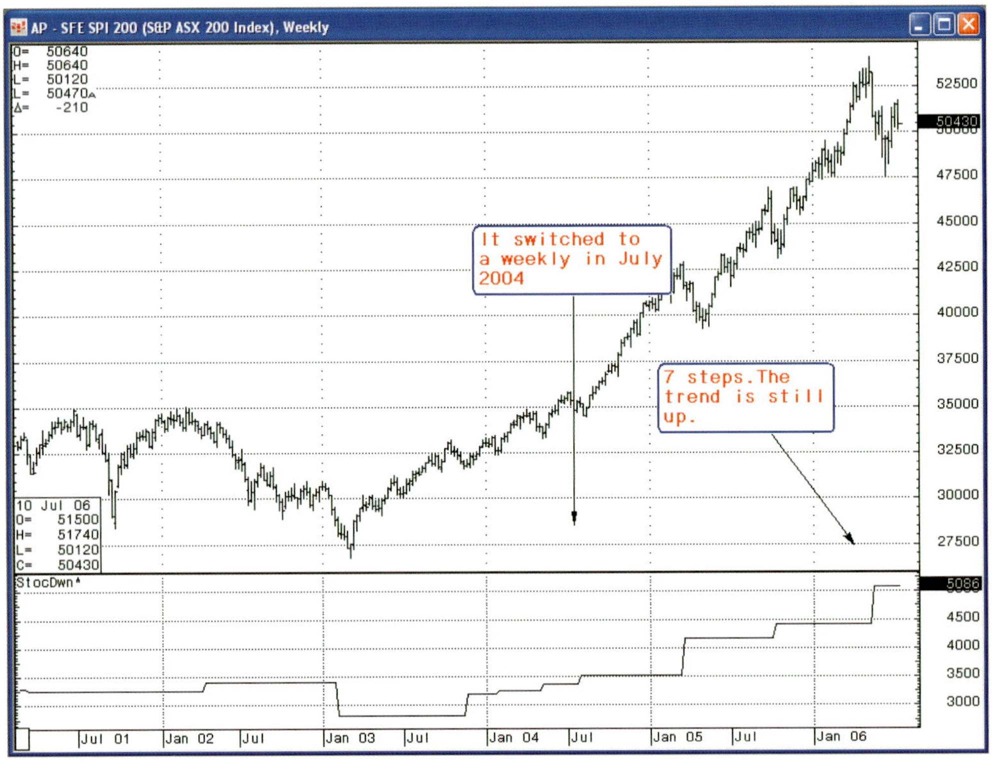
AP - SFE SPI 200 (S&P ASX 200 Index), Weekly
It switched to a weekly in July 2004
7 steps. The trend is still up.
StocDwn
Jul 01 Jan 02 Jul Jan 03 Jul Jan 04 Jul Jan 05 Jul Jan 06

Figure 43: *6 months later it switched to the weekly chart and the trend is still up*

Concepts of Time

The more recent part of the rally shows how, if the risk-averse trader wanted to use a lower timeframe chart as they had been in the trend for so long, the 100-minute showed typical trend following Stochastic Steps behaviour. The trend began with an acceleration before finally ending with 10 Steps. N.B. this market is open for 6 hours 40 minutes, which is 400minutes, so a 100-minute is a quarter-day chart.

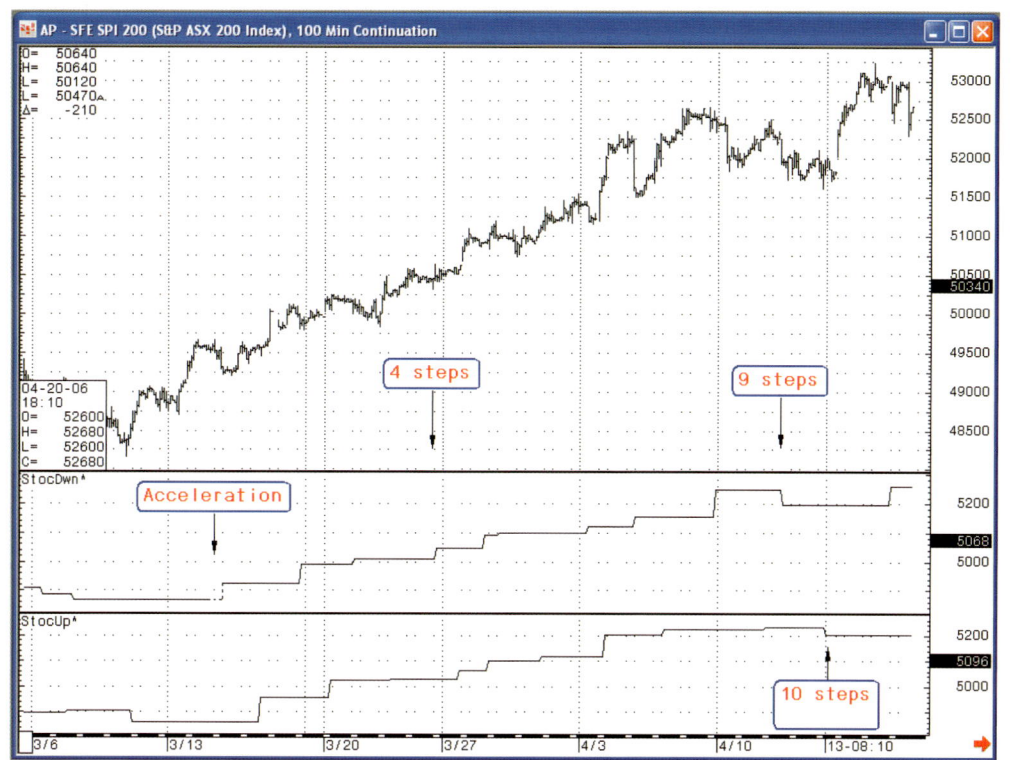

Figure 44:
The trend developed in a lower timeframe as well.

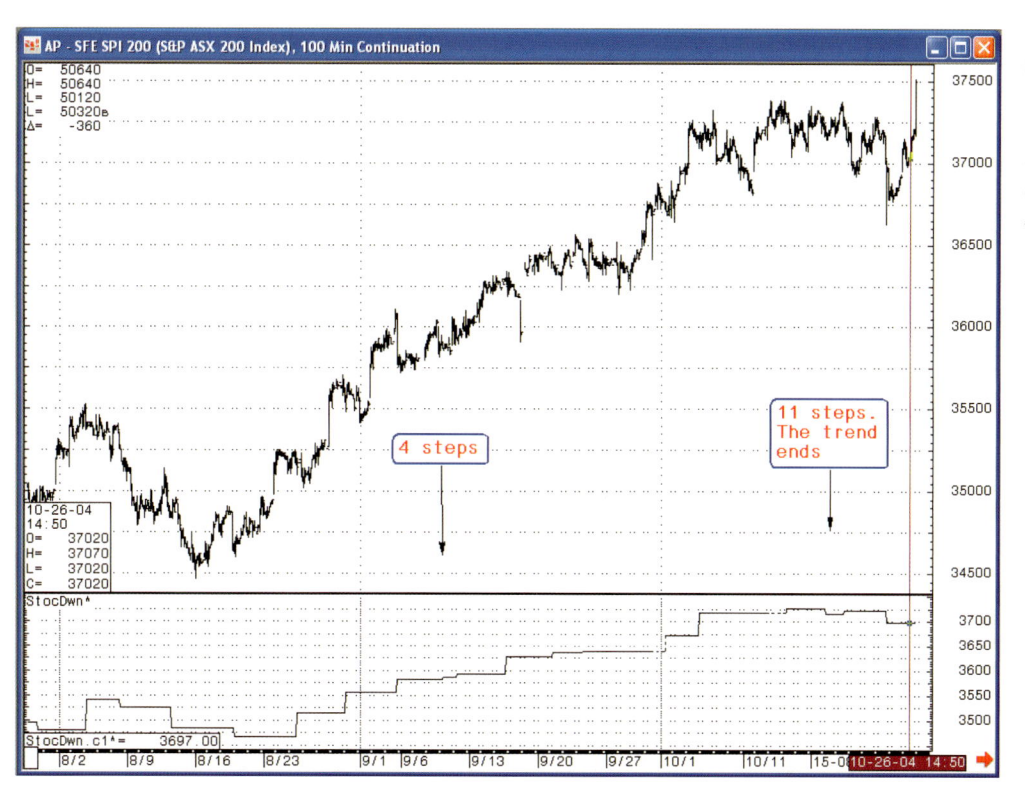

Figure 45:
The same timeframe could have been used in the rally in 2004.

Figure 46:
The pit only contract shows how the trend started in the 50-minute, switched up to the 100-minute and then for the risk-averse trader, restarted in the 50-minute.

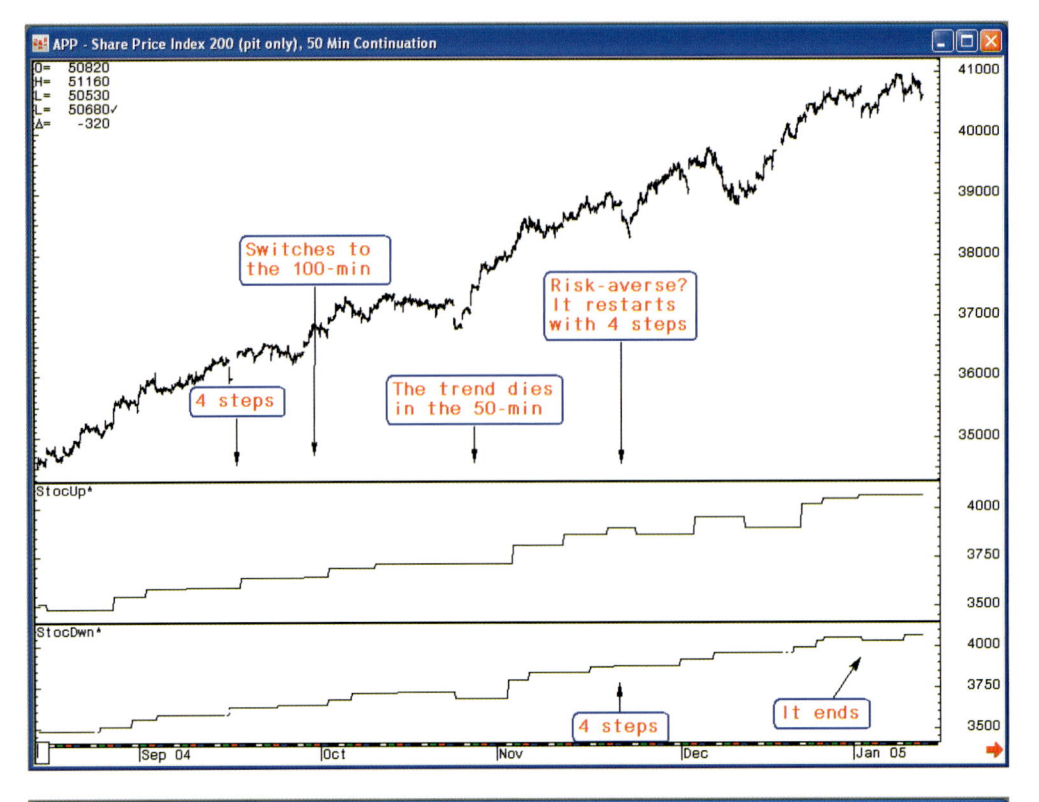

Figure 47:
The whole trend began in the 30-minute chart, with an acceleration before the emergence of 4 steps.

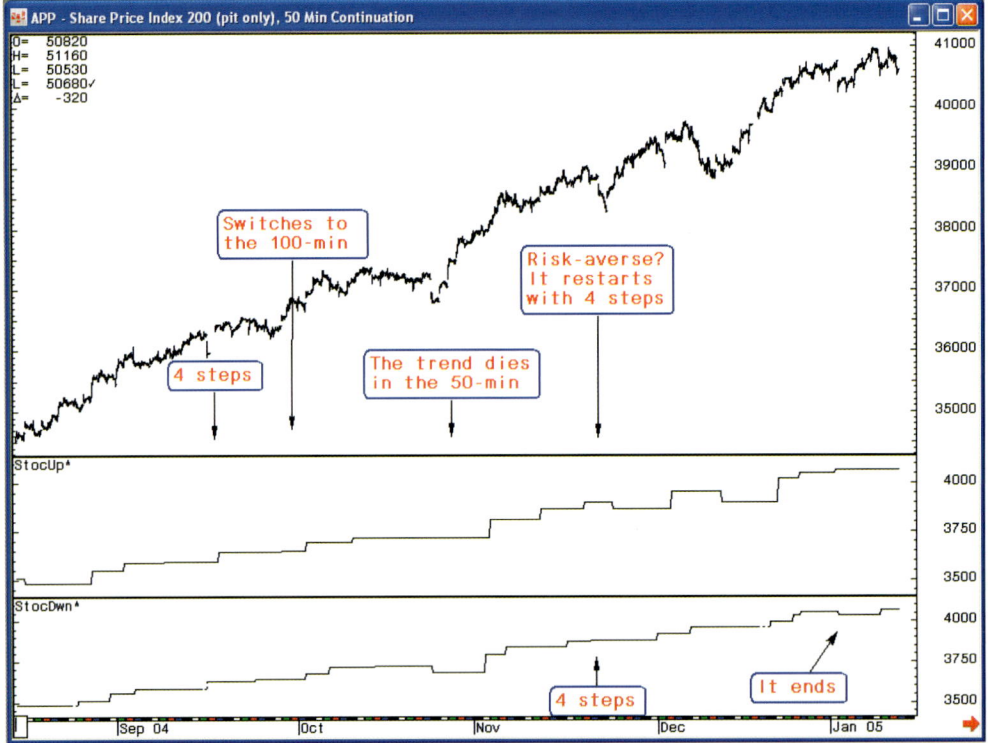

Conclusion

We can see how the Stochastic Steps can be used to identify trend; its key attribute is the ability to understand what the focus timeframe is, and to enable a trader to stick with a trend that develops.

Key Elements
- Understanding what the focus timeframe is
- How trends must move up timeframes in order to be sustained.
- Most trends do not step up to historical charts
- It can help clarify Elliot Wave counts
- Timeframes can be moved back down if you are risk-averse.
- Mega trends will nearly always step up and produce trades that can last years.

4 Relative Strength Index

With theories and methods concerning the Stochastic exhausted, my next project was to work out exactly what the RSI was good for.

The common belief was that it was great as a divergence indicator. However, this study suffers from similar flaws to the Stochastic in this respect as the limit of scale causes the study to continually diverge in any meaningful trend. The huge equity rallies of the 1990s are a powerful example. At best, if you had been using RSI-based divergence, you would have missed almost all of one of the best rallies ever. At worst you would have lost your shirt going short.

Figure 1:
Markets often diverge for long periods

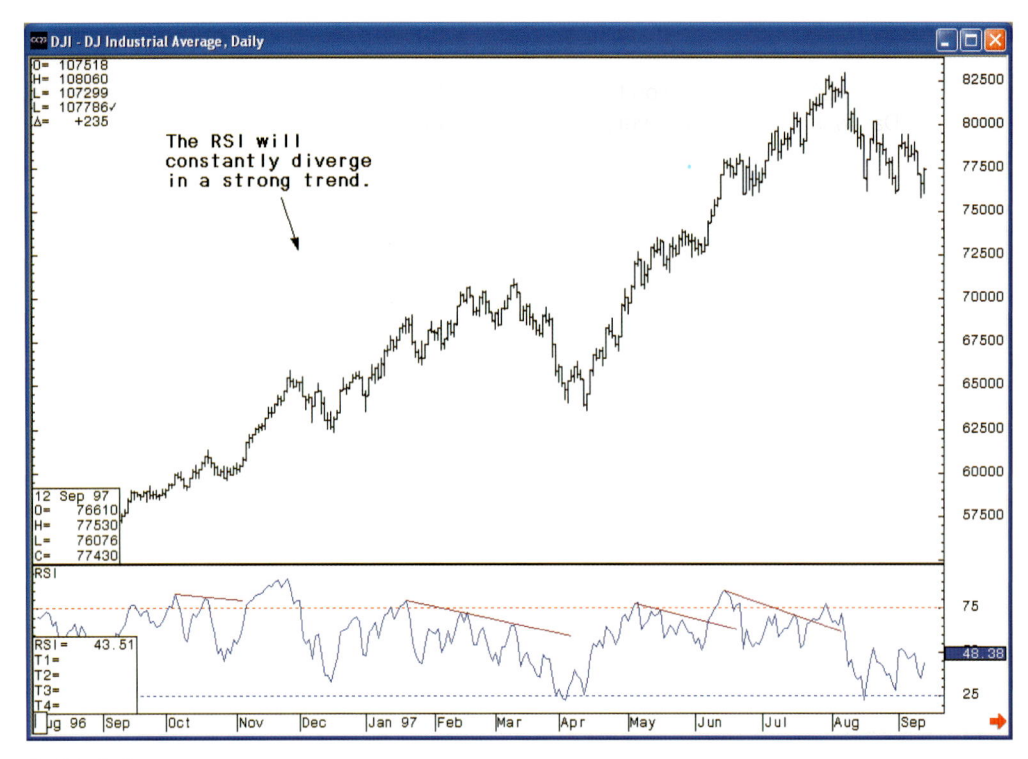

RSI Divergence

Again, the rally in the Dollar Yen in 2005 is a classic example (see fig. 2). Almost the entire rally was marked by divergence.

Figure 2:
Markets will often diverge for long periods and create a confusing picture if divergence is not quantified correctly.

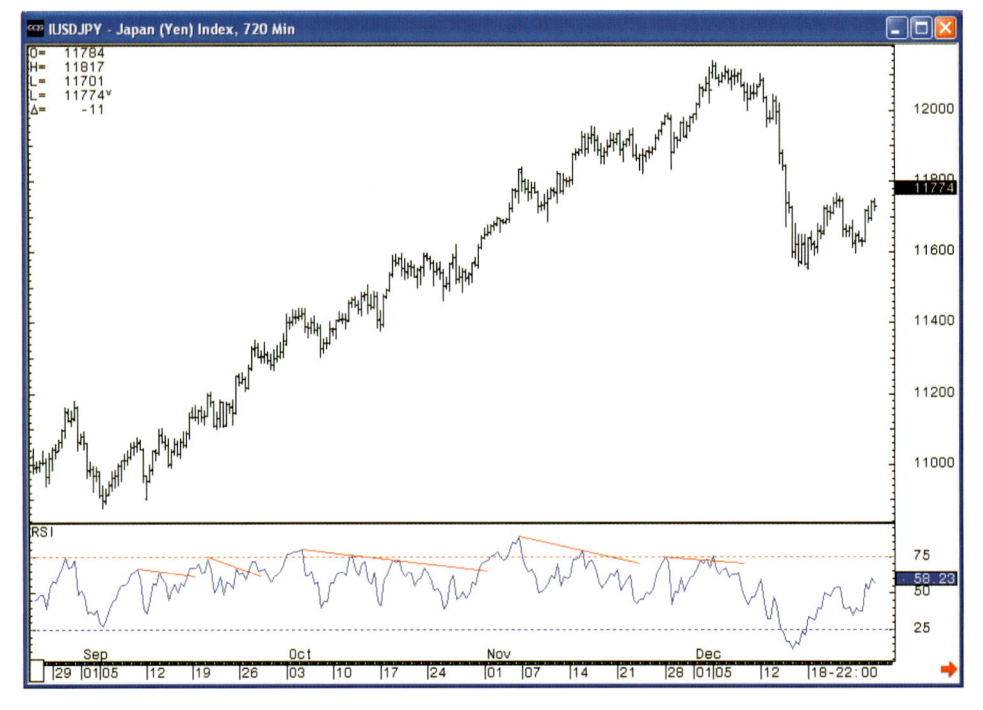

When I see so many commentaries on how divergence is signalling the end of a trend it would be funny if it weren't so tragic. The Divergence Top-Picking Club was paying a full subscription by being negative equities, especially on the German and UK markets, for all of 2005 (see fig. 3). The rally in the Dax was shown to be a very strong trend on the basis of Stochastic Steps, especially in the first half of the year. However, a look at the chart shows that the RSI, the Slow Stochastic and, to a lesser extent the MACD, have all been diverging throughout most of this time.

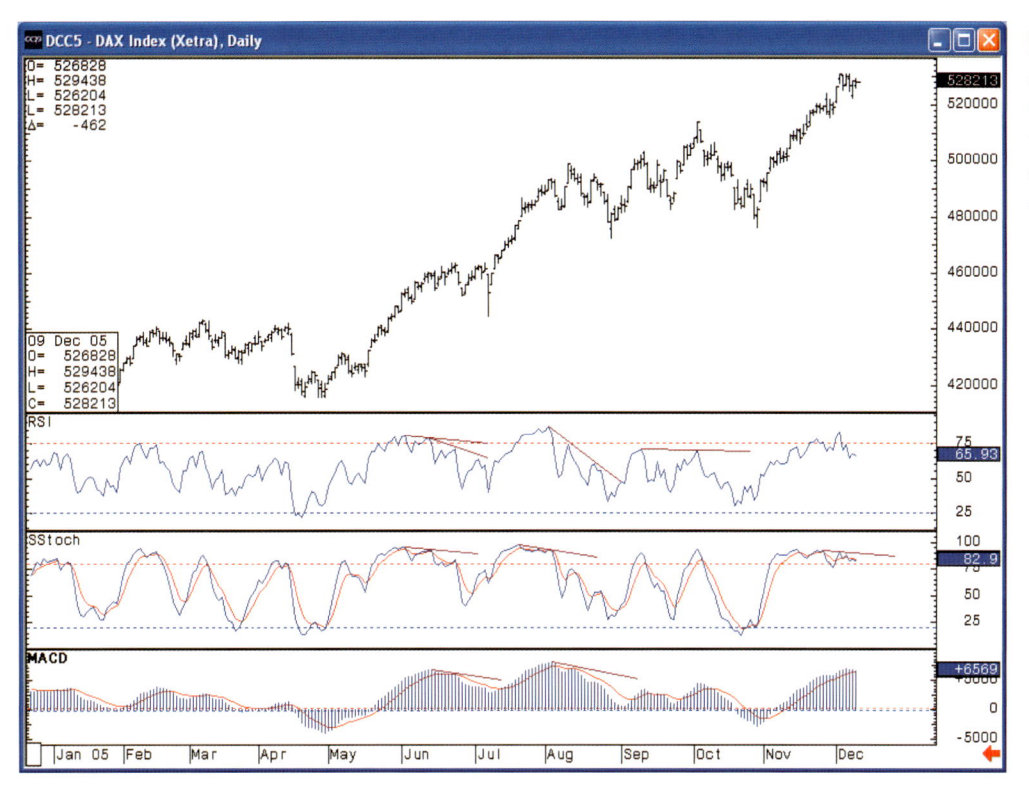

Figure 3:
Most indicators, especially ones with limits of scale have problems

Quantifying Divergence

Divergence can be likened to being able to see an eel in clear water. It's highly visible but try picking it up and holding on. If divergence is to be used it must be linked to patterns that are sufficiently rare that you have the confidence to trade them – and, ideally, when other analysis is showing signs that the trend is ending. Even then, most of the many patterns I've developed over the years are purely exits to a trend-following system, with very few standing up to the rigours of being good enough as entries. We will look at divergence in more detail later in the chapter.

To step down from my soapbox for a moment – we see that some tests have to be run to analyse this study in more detail. Unfortunately there is the need for more tables, but hopefully these will help clarify the picture regarding what the actual study is useful for.

TRADING TIME: New Methods in Technical Analysis

RSI as an overbought/oversold indicator and where we are in the trend

I've used the same data sets and contracts as the Stochastic tests.

The first table is simply flagging when the RSI is above 70 for the first time. On the 30-minute chart (see fig. 4), accuracy is close to 50% between 5 and 15 bars, which suggests the possibility of short-term tops being recognised. However, further out in time the statistics deteriorate. On the 60-minute chart (see fig. 5), accuracy is extremely low beyond 10 bars, which highlights the indicator's poor performance in a strong trend.

Figure 4:
Signal Evaluation – Dax 30-minute

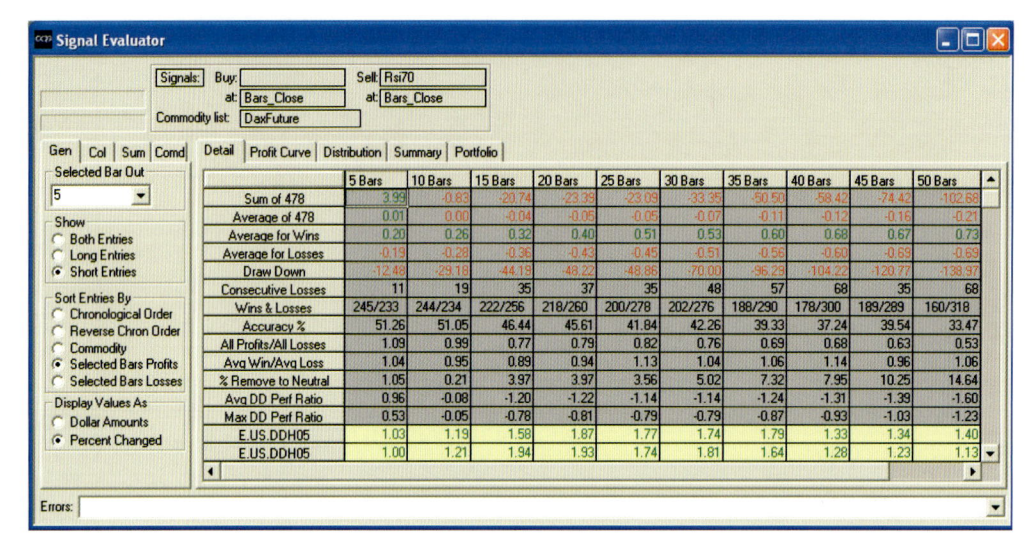

Figure 5:
Signal Evaluation – Dax 60-minute

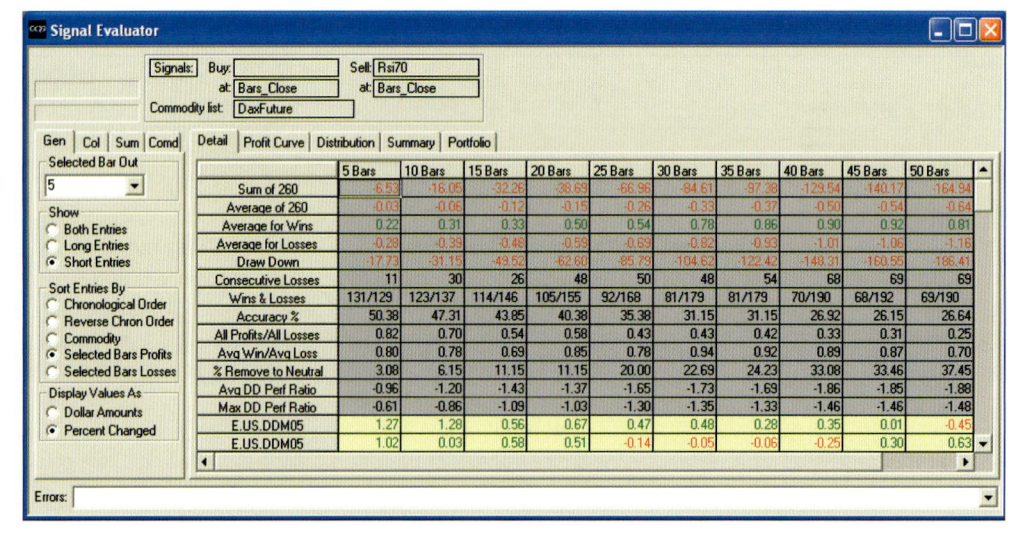

The next tables (see figs. 6 & 7) look at when the RSI is above 70 and then turns down. Once again accuracy is poor.

Figure 6:
Signal Evaluation – Dax 30-minute

152

Relative Strength Index

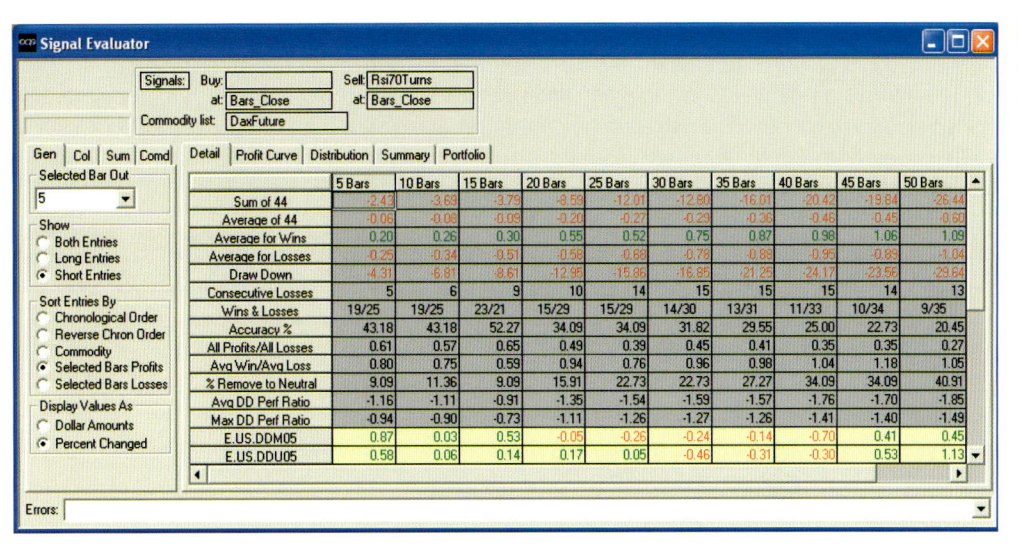

Figure 7:
Signal Evaluation – Dax 60-minute

In an attempt to be fairer to the study the next tables (see fig. 8) indicate that the study must have crossed back below 70 before a signal is taken. Here the accuracy does improve on the 30-minute (see fig. 8) but remains very poor on the 60-minute (see fig. 9).

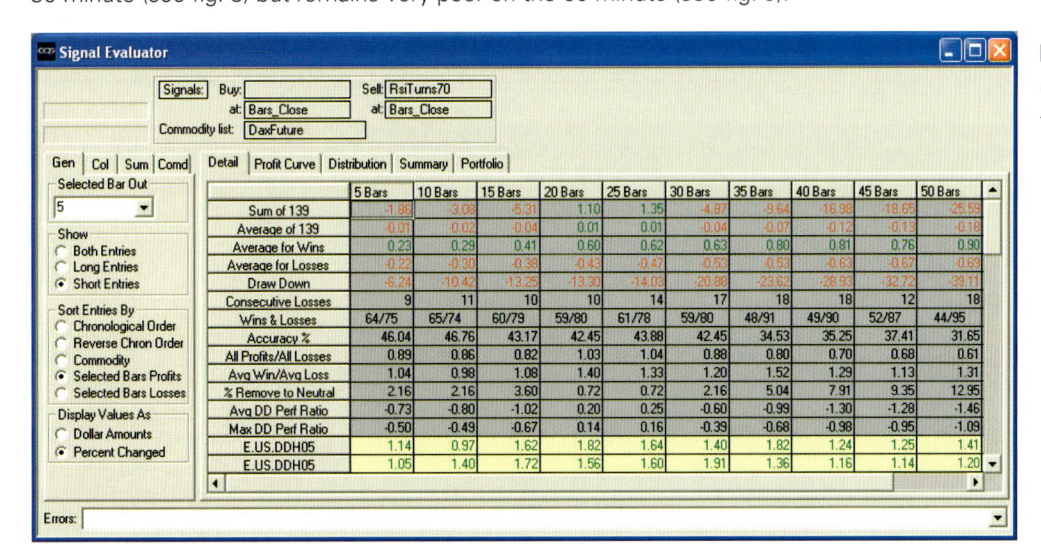

Figure 8:
Signal Evaluation – Dax 30-minute

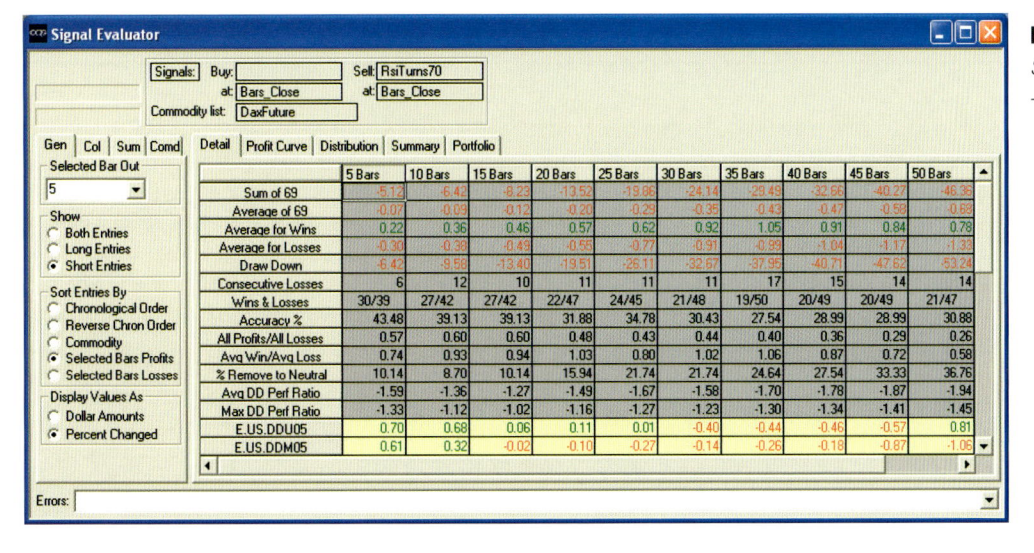

Figure 9:
Signal Evaluation – Dax 60-minute

TRADING TIME: New Methods in Technical Analysis

Smoothing the RSI

All the tests have used a standard 9-period RSI, but in contrast to the stochastic 10, 3, 3, the study is far more sensitive and erratic. In an attempt to mimic the stochastic in a crude way I've placed a double smoothed period average on the RSI. A signal is generated if the RSI is above 70 and crosses below the average. This cuts signals considerably but does nothing to improve accuracy (see figs. 10 and 11).

Figure 10:
Signal Evaluation – Dax 30-minute

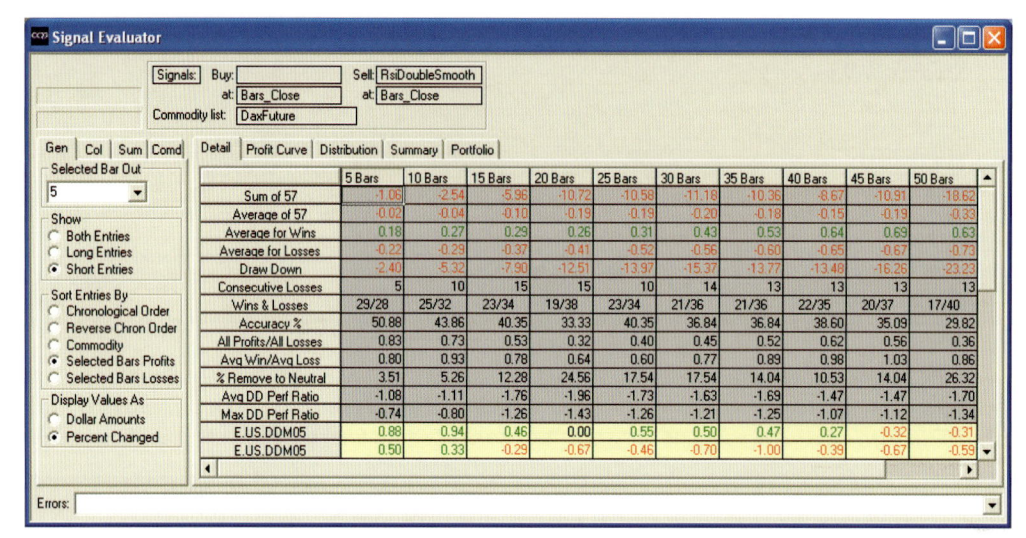

Figure 11:
Signal Evaluation – Dax 60-minute

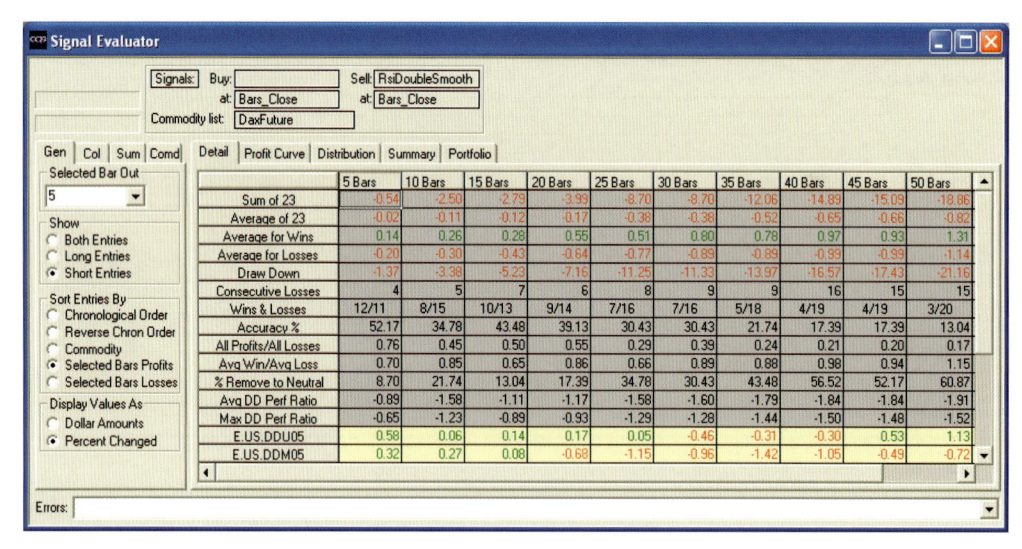

The final table (see fig. 12) is the most illuminating of all. This monitors when the RSI crosses above 80. The popular myth is that the higher the RSI, the more overbought the indicator is and therefore the more likely the market is to reverse. One of my earliest experiences of questioning technical analysis mantras was when nickel went from 6,000 to 18,000 in the early 1980s and the RSI stayed at 99.9 for days. The reality is that when the RSI becomes highly overbought it is emphasising how strong the trend actually is. This is especially relevant in view of the indicator's limit of scale, which has an inherent mathematical bias to retreat from extremes. Previous analysis of the ADX study shows similar properties . Move from 45 to 55 and reverse

Relative Strength Index

downwards, and the indicator is useful. Move above 60 and the study fails miserably as the trend is explosive. The table below (see fig. 12) shows that when the RSI crosses above 80 it does create a correction in the short term but then the trend often restarts once that correction has occurred because the trend is too strong. Accuracy becomes very high the further out in time. Remember, that this high accuracy is if you were buying when the RSI is above 80. These final moves are often explosive so a high level of due diligence is required and consistent trailing stops are to be employed, such as the ones shown in the Peak chapter.

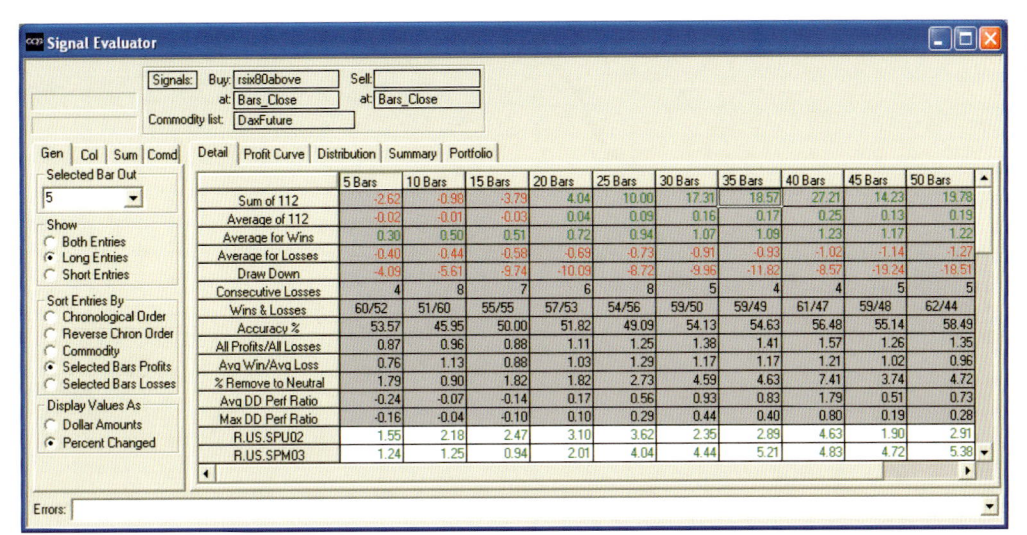

Figure 12:
Signal Evaluation – Dax 30-minute

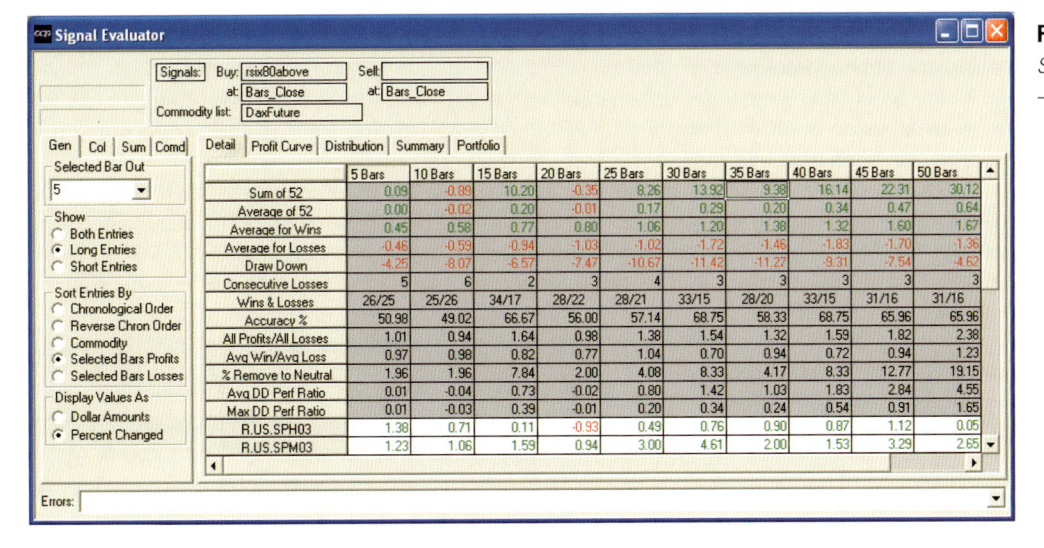

Figure 13:
Signal Evaluation – Dax 60-minute

Figure 14:
The RSI can stay overbought for many bars

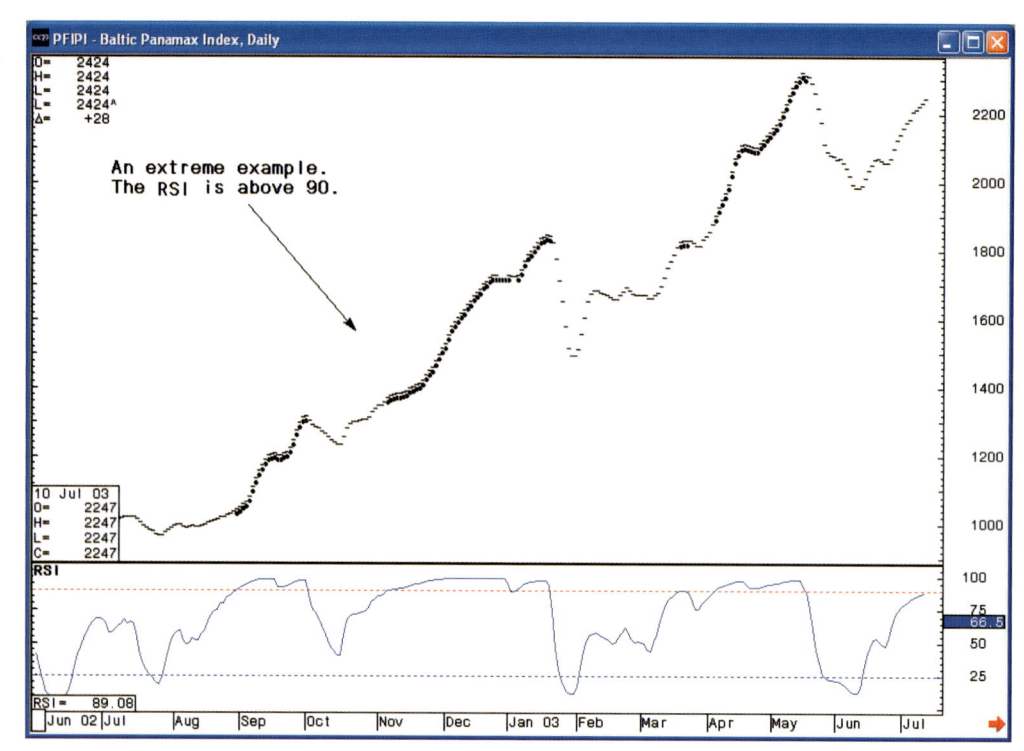

Mimicking Stochastic Steps

This re-emphasises the point that if we can quantify the trend we may be able to build more trading and timing strategies.

As the Stochastic Steps used a 21-period with an 8-period average, it makes sense to use the same variables on the RSI. Therefore the RSI itself is a 21-period and has an 8-period smoothed average placed on it so that the crossover method can be replicated.

While the studies look similar in their ebb and flow, the key difference between the two is that the RSI is more sensitive and crosses more often. The principles behind Stochastic Steps are identical for RSI Steps but more aggressive traders can use the latter. This is because it will usually identify a trend earlier. The day trader on short-time frames will also have more opportunities. The other advantage is money management. If the trend does not develop, the RSI Steps will flag that it has ended quicker. However if the trend is very strong, it should continue to track it.

Figure 15:
RSI Steps earlier

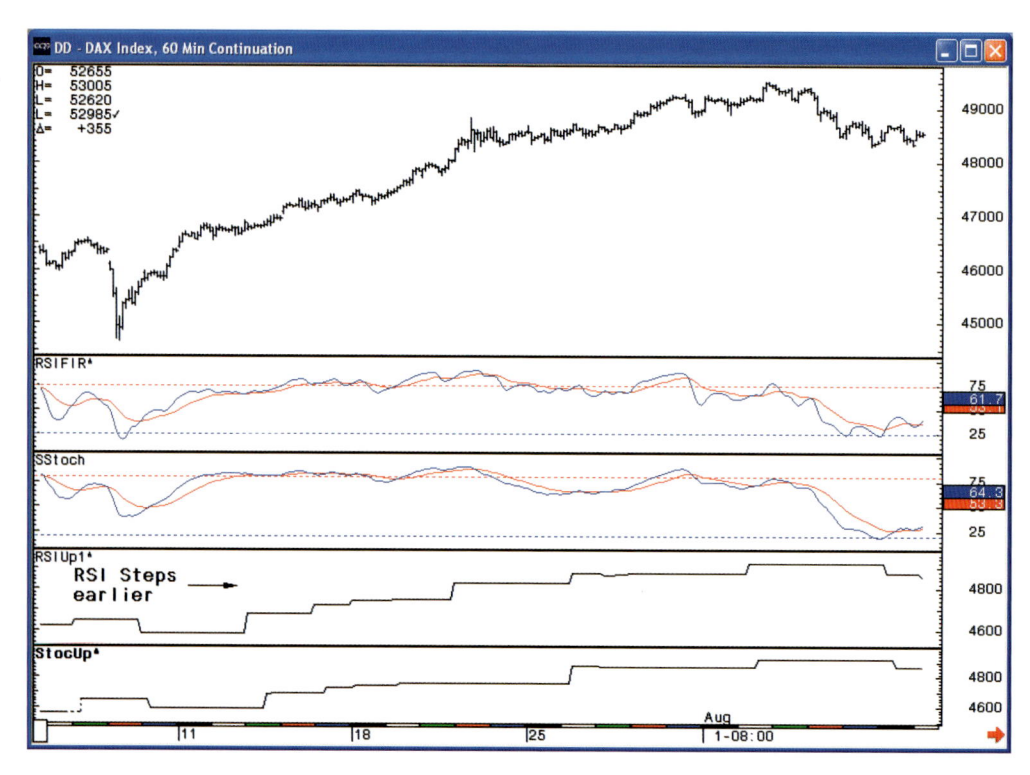

Relative Strength Index

The chart (see fig. 16) shows how many of the principles remain the same. The RSI Steps, whilst more sensitive, will still track a very strong trend. It finally ends when Steps reach 11.

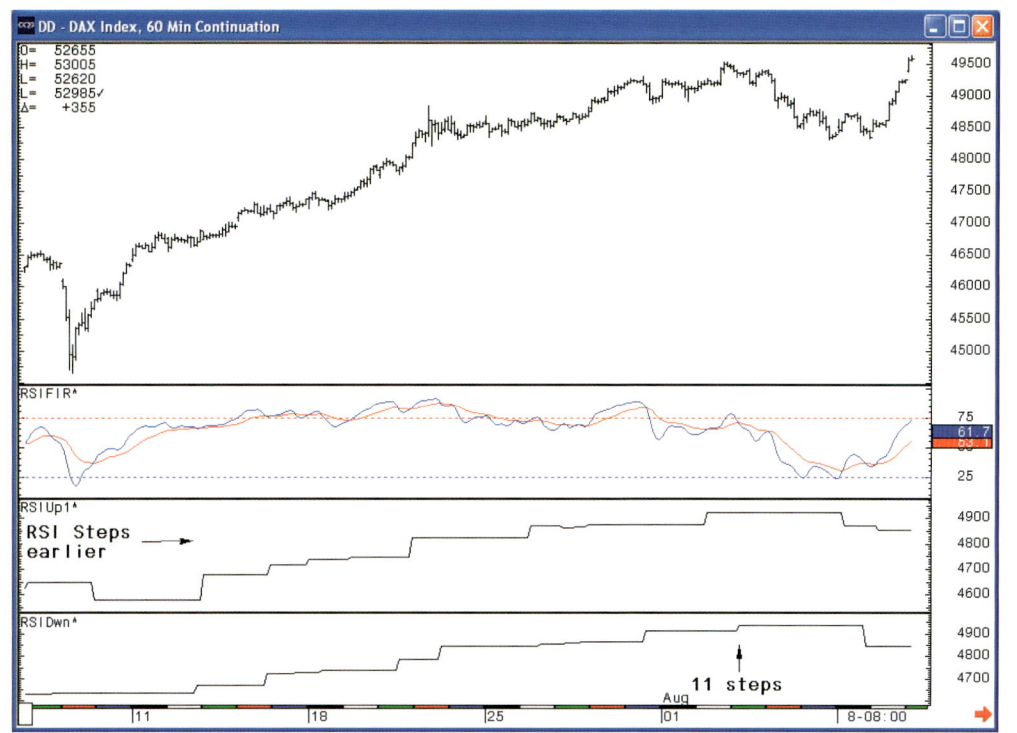

Figure 16:
The basic Step method remains the same. In fact any indicator can be used

The 2005 rally in the Dollar Yen (see fig. 17) reached the 720-minute chart. It is now reaching a critical time when linked to Market Profile®.

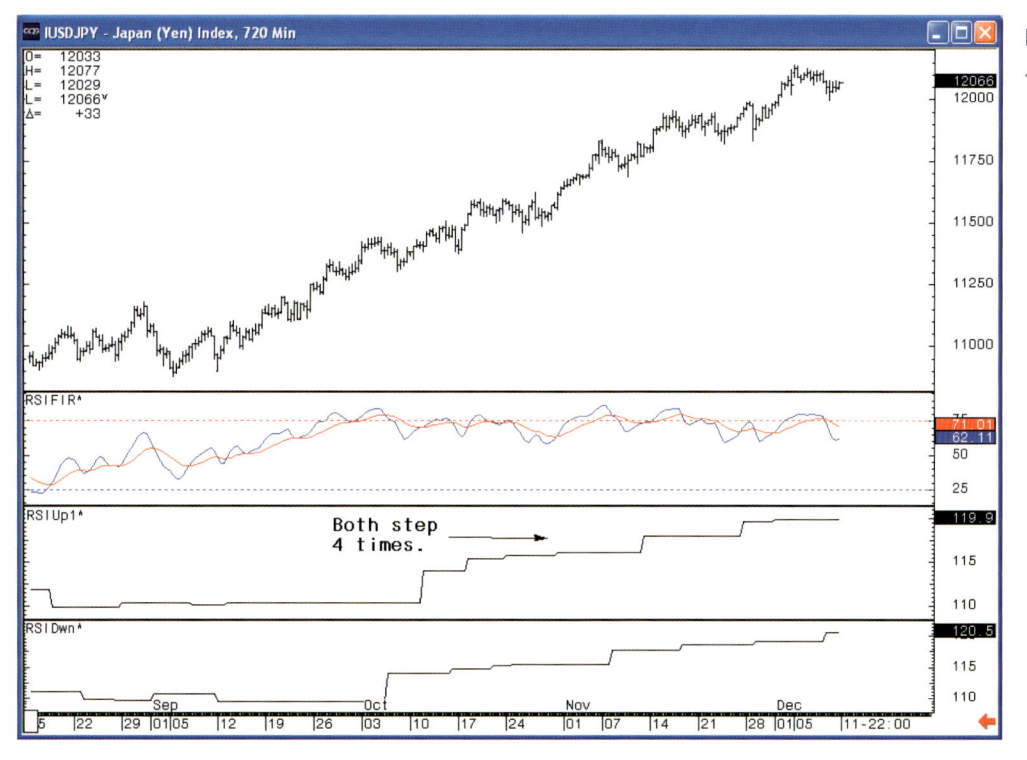

Figure 17:
A strong trend

The Stochastic Steps method has also been at the 720-min (see fig. 18). Apart from the extra level of sensitivity in RSI Steps, especially at trend beginnings, this also means that the concept of trend cycles with RSI is not valid as price very rarely reaches that threshold. Therefore the RSI and a connection with trend cycles are not applicable.

Figure 18:
RSI Steps and Cycles do not connect

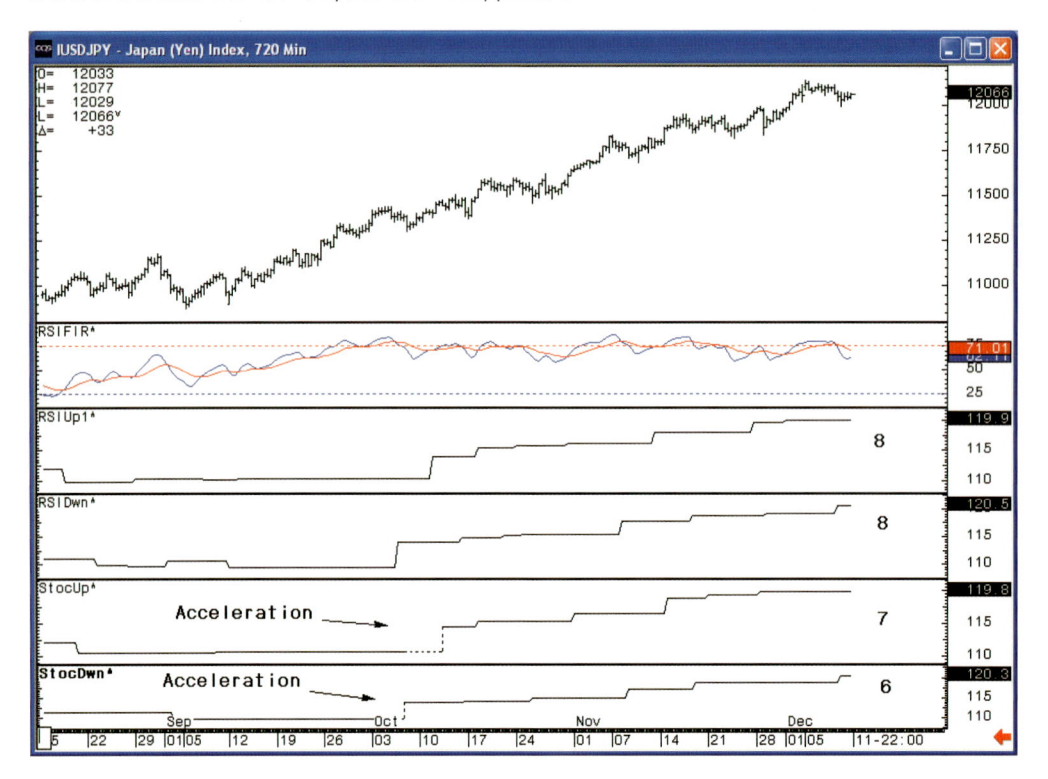

The daily chart (see fig. 19) is showing some signs of fatigue as well. One step has moved lower and the other is at 6, which suggests the trend could end at any time. This latest trend is also approaching the one-cycle length at 65. On daily charts this is more significant than if it was on shorter timeframe charts. [In the final chapter we will look at how this trend ended.]

Figure 19:
Cycle lengths have more importance on historical charts

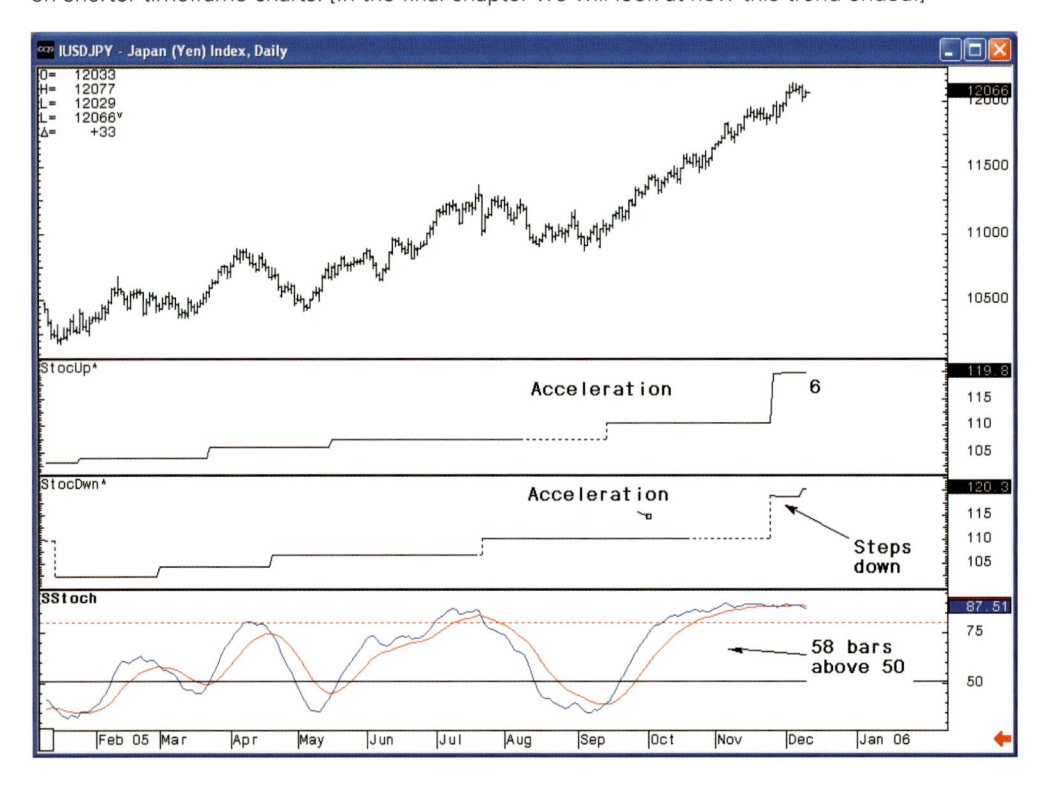

Long-term distributions linked to Steps

The Market Profile® is also at a critical point. Analysis of the long-term distribution (see fig. 20) shows that the Control Area lay at 119.55 to 119.77. Price initially stalled at this point but then moved above. Thus far the acceleration higher has been disappointing.

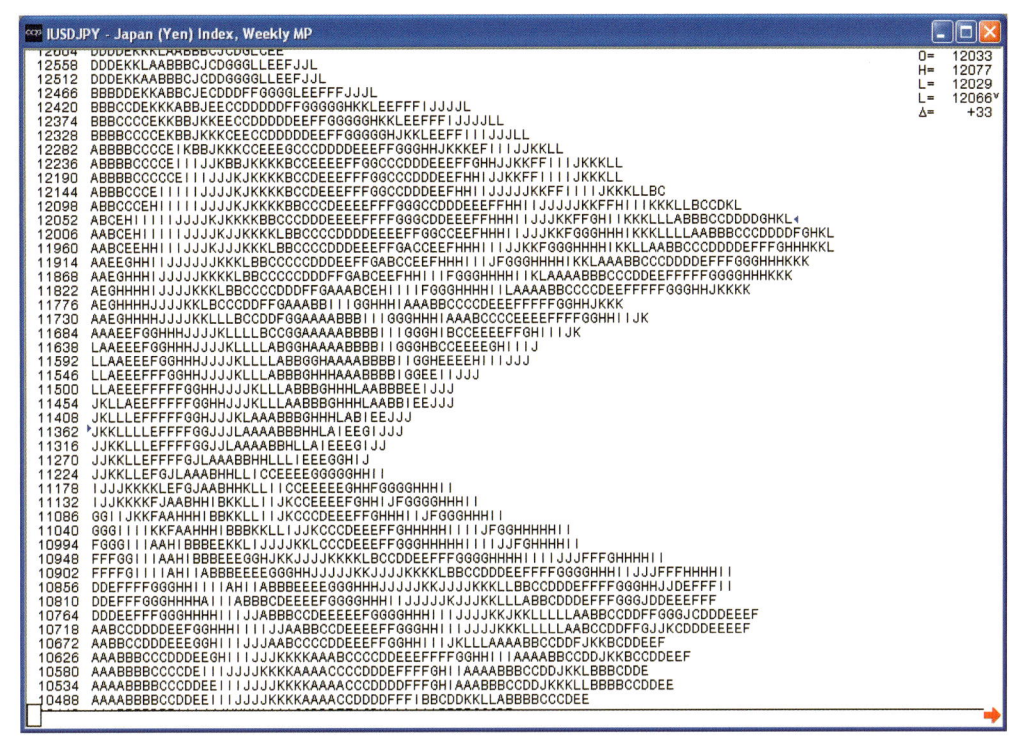

Figure 20:

The long-term distribution in Usd Jpy at December 2005 Control moved higher to 120.05

However, analysis of the distribution from 1971 shows that this Control Point has greater significance. Just another 5 to 10 days spent in this area will see the longest timeframe control shift higher from 107.50. This therefore will be the catalyst for the next trend. For the momentum to be maintained the market must accelerate higher soon or the trend will be over. This proved to be the case as the Control Point didn't change.

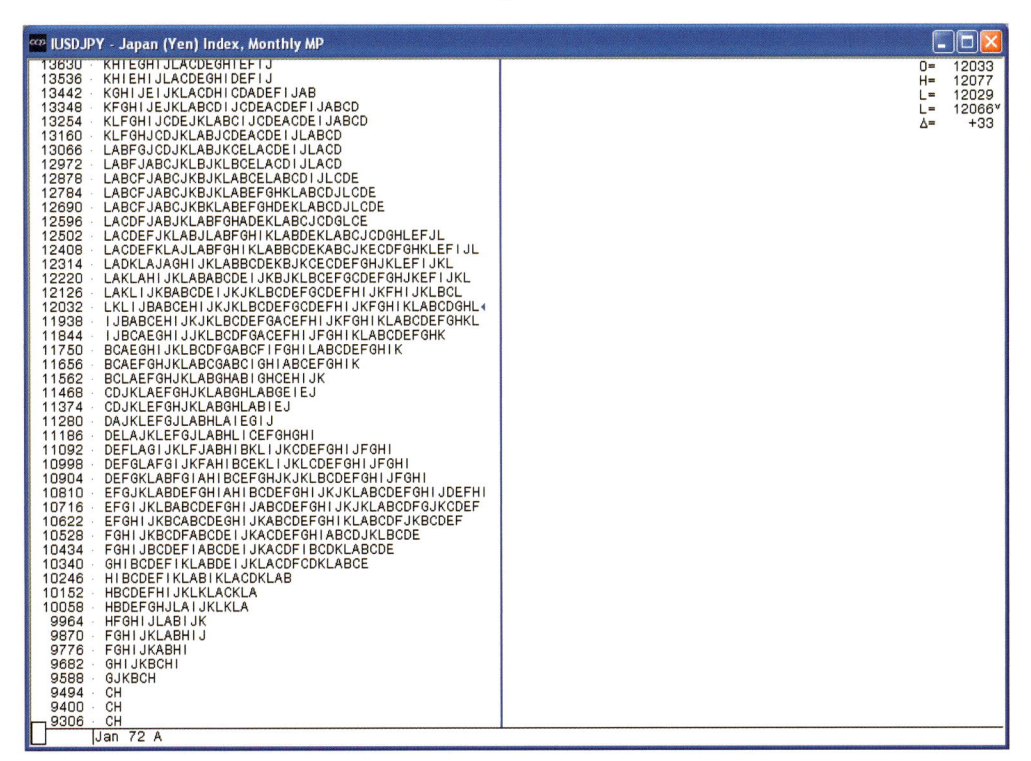

Figure 21:

Control could shift with a few more days at 120.00

RSI as a divergence tool

Finally, we tackle the subject of using the RSI as a divergence tool. The Oasis modules and education programme examine divergence in great detail, but for the purposes of this book we will simply touch on some of the concepts and provide some statistics via the RSI Steps logic.

The key to divergence is being able to find patterns that are sufficiently rare so that the divergence has real meaning. The first pattern I ever produced was called *Ufo* for negative divergence and *Pops* for positive. They simply state that price had to make a 9-bar high and the RSI 3-bar low for a Ufo to be formed. That theory still has worth today but has moved on considerably since its inception some 15 years ago. Whilst that simple pattern still has its place when linked to other analysis, it still follows the established mantra that for divergence to be visible it has to reference the high or low of the price action and the change in direction of the indicator.

The following sets of tables take a concept that is very much a work in progress, but the quality of the statistics suggests that the problem of cutting signals down to the point where they mean something can be achieved. In fact, tests have been done on a variety of momentum indicators and they all perform in a similar fashion, although they don't create divergences in the same areas. The principal driver behind the idea has been to create signals that are not only powerful, but of enough rarity that they could be used on an individual stock portfolio or a large range of currencies. At this stage the code has simply been added to the list of viable exit strategies to trends and trend-following systems, but the possibility that it could become an entry against the trend remains.

Divergence as an entry point

The sets of tables have all used the S&P 500 daily data and been put through various times in trends.

The first (see fig. 22) takes a perfect scenario for buying stocks by analysing the period between 1995 and 2000. It would have been difficult not to win. However, the code still has to be good enough to capture corrections as it is trying to buy weakness. In such a rally previous aborted divergence code-building attempts simply missed too many opportunities. Whilst the percentage profits are obviously good, there are two key points of interest. First there is the high accuracy figures nudging into the 60% area (after 45 bars) and above. Second, and more important, is the trade count. A trade count of 680 trades over a 5 year period of 500 stocks means that signals only average just over one trade every 5 years per stock. Obviously on futures markets this is pointless but it becomes a necessity if you are trading a portfolio of stocks or a basket of currencies on multiple timeframes with such long holding periods. It suggests that a portfolio of up to 5,000 stocks could be monitored and the trade count would still be manageable, as trades would average approximately 5 per day. For big players liquidity must also be considered when picking stocks for the portfolio so the number of trades per day would decrease further.

Closer examination of the actual individual trades reveals a much different picture. Signals appear in clusters, which is highly revealing, as even if the portfolio were not actually traded, it would provide a key timing-point of when stock markets should reverse. This is extremely useful information and is particularly poignant if linked to true measure of overbought and oversold. The

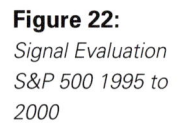

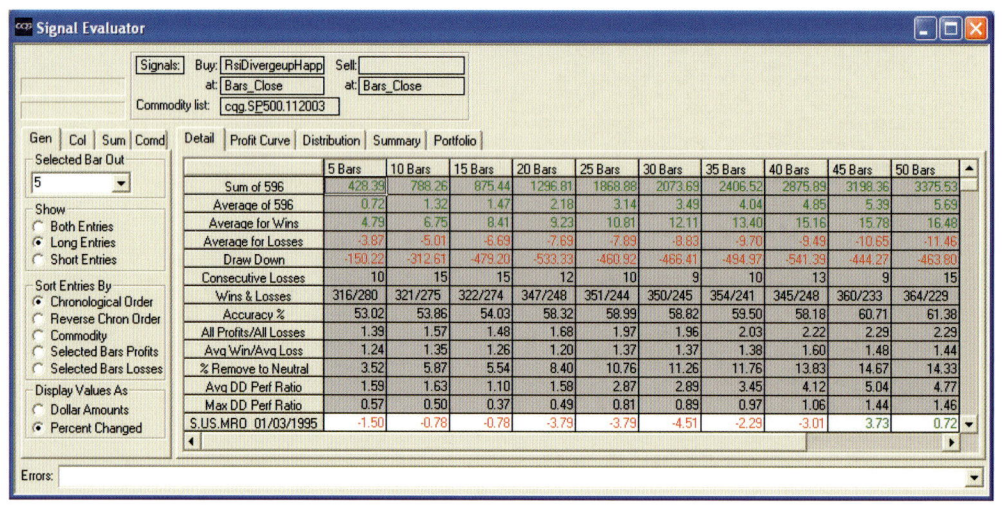

Figure 22:
Signal Evaluation S&P 500 1995 to 2000

Relative Strength Index

next test (see fig. 23) uses the worst possible period in recent history, from 1 January, 2000 to the day of the post-11th September low that was 21 September. If allowing for the inevitable fact that any longs going into that final period would have shown big losses, the statistics are very encouraging. Losses are present over the first few time segments but the code shows robustness in the face of a strong downtrend and an ability to pick true divergence. The accuracy remains high as well.

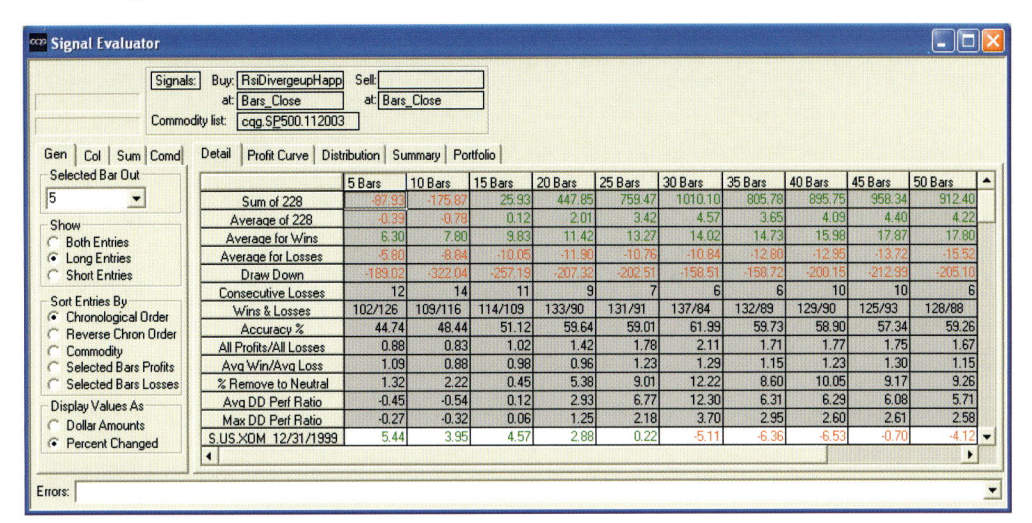

Figure 23:
Signal Evaluation S&P January 2000 to 21 September 2001

The next table takes that 21 September low to the present day. The first 5-bar period after the signal posts a negative and is therefore the first real concern. From then the statistics remain strong. One encouraging premise is that the statistics improve as time passes, suggesting this code could be used as part of a buy-and-hold strategy with a wide trailing stop. Analysis needs to be completed on what the trigger point for a delayed entry point is.

Evidence gained from equity systems I have already built suggests that stops could be adjusted once a week. This means that if a 100 stocks were held, it would require 20 new stops to be added/adjusted each day, which is manageable, even for the non-professional trader who has to monitor once a day

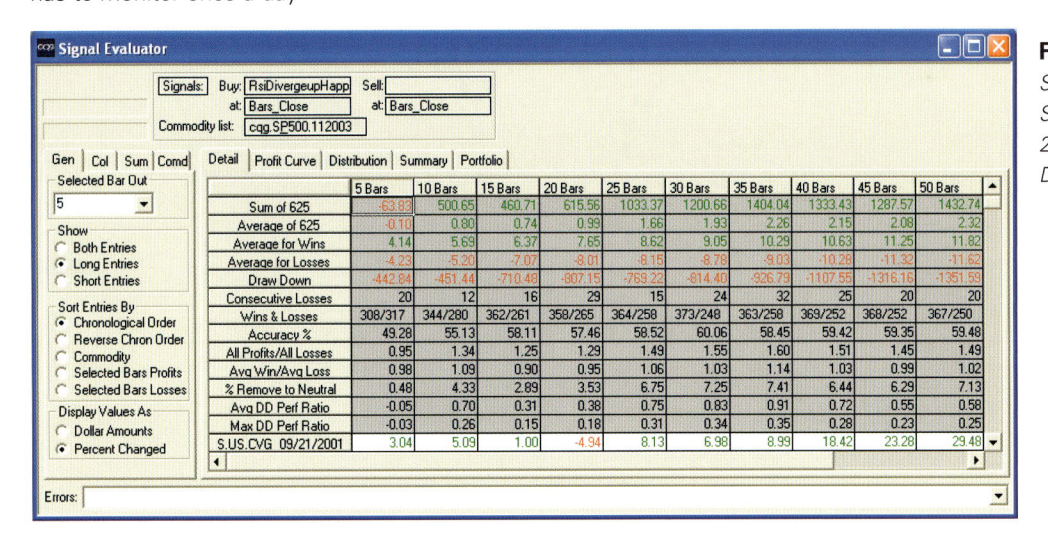

Figure 24:
Signal Evaluation S&P 500 21 September to December 2005

161

TRADING TIME: New Methods in Technical Analysis

The final test (see fig. 25) is from 1 January 2004 to December 2005. The picture remains promising.

Figure 25:
Signal Evaluation S&P 500 1 January to December 2005

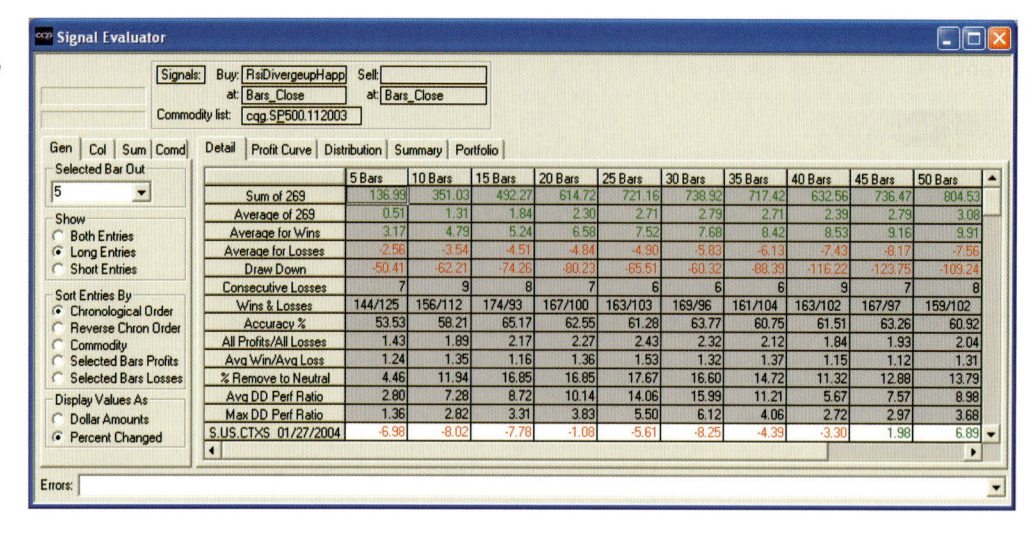

Analysis of eBay shows where signals can appear.

Figure 26:
Divergence pattern for stocks

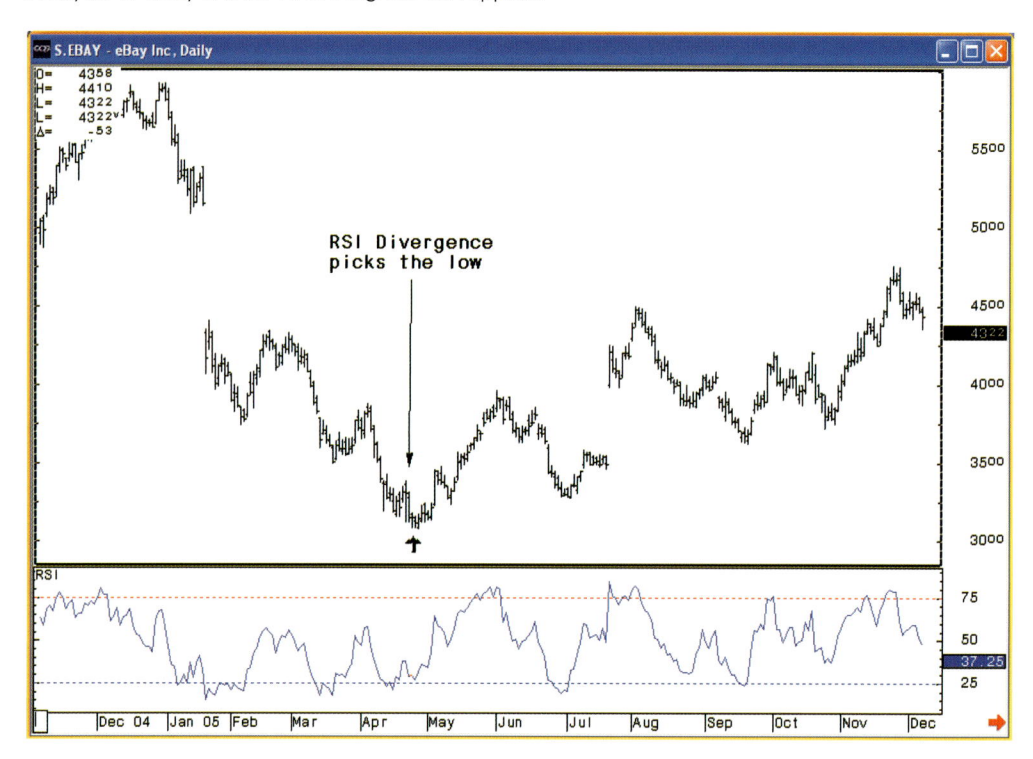

Closer inspection shows exactly where the signal occurs. Since the divergence does not reference absolute highs or lows it means that signals can appear where the divergence is not visible under normal circumstances. The pattern is also sufficiently rare to have the potential as an entry.

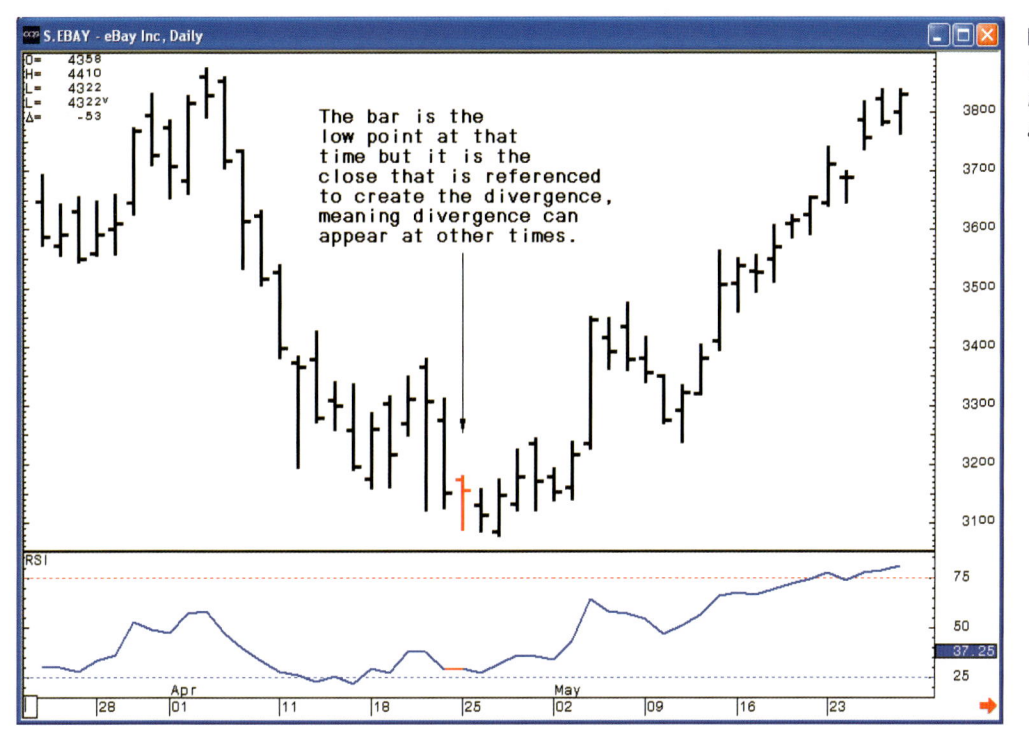

Figure 27:
The divergence is not at the absolute low

The raw statistics suggest that there is the possibility to create a viable trading system that would suit a buy-and-hold strategy, for example, pension funds or for the private trader who wants to track a smaller portfolio for investment purposes. More time will be required before further progress can be made in order to analyse portfolio risk and the short signals.

Conclusion

It is not automatically necessary that step method is confined just to the Stochastic and RSI. It can extend to almost any momentum study; especially in the area of divergence a suite of indicators can be utilised to spot potential turning points in trends.

Key elements
- **RSI Steps are more sensitive.**
- **Cycles do not apply.**
- **Steps method is a powerful divergence tool.**
- **Steps method can apply to any indicator as long as there is a crossover point to reference.**

5 Peak

This chapter is the longest and also the most intensive. There is enough information for a book in its own right, and it includes some long case studies. Consideration can be given to missing out some of these sections, apart from the Overbought/Oversold study, and returning to them at a later date. This is due to the fact that Peak and its derivatives are primarily used as methods for trailing stops, which inevitably means that there are many days and weeks to be analysed with a trend. There is a also a concentration on the unique relationship of Peak values to the current price and time of day for short-term trading. Finally, we look at how Peak values can be adjusted to account for changes in range, the time of day and volume, in order to overcome the perennial problem with 24-hour markets on FX and periods of little activity on stocks. Whilst the subject is large, there should be something of use for all types of traders.

The following subjects are covered:
Swing theory
Trailing stops
Trend beginnings and endings
The connection with range and volume
Hi Count / Lo Count exhaustion points
The strength of the trend
Corrective patterns, linking to distributions and the Time-based studies
Peak Steps
True measures of overbought and oversold

What is Peak?

Peak is another extremely simplistic study, but it has the advantage that it is dictated by price swings rather than momentum itself. This means that it is more dynamic to price action. At its basic level, a Peak is a potential turning point.

Definition

A Peak is defined as a 5-bar pattern that has the middle bar as either the highest or lowest point. If it is the highest point it is a downward Peak Point. If it is the lowest it is an upward swing point.

LOW PEAK

HIGH PEAK

Whilst it is essential that the middle bar of 5 is the highest or lowest point, the other 4-bar patterns can vary.

Price Swings and Elliot Wave theory

Price swings are nothing new. They form the basis of much of Elliot Wave theory where the swing points mark the wave counts. Before anyone switches off or gets overexcited when hearing the words 'Elliot Wave', here's my own take on it.

I spent a huge amount of time in the mid-1980s analysing Elliot Wave theory, as it was one of the few theories out there. My conclusion was that I could always put a wave count on historically, but it told me very little about where the price was actually going. The reason for this was that, if I had a bias one way but the market went the other way and broke some swing points, my count would change.

More importantly, I found it difficult to know what the dominant timeframe was. Counts often conflict and confuse. Both Stochastic Steps and the studies we will come to – namely Hi Count and Lo Count – aid Elliot Wave theory by providing a focus timeframe and an indication of speed and velocity that enables recognition of impulse waves. I don't use wave counts myself, but the Count studies do identify wave 3. This is particularly useful if divergence patterns have previously picked the low or high of wave 2.

Without these tools, wave counts can become confusing and there can be a temptation to place an alternate wave count if a position is losing that re-affirms your original analysis. This is one of the reasons that it is so useful for writing commentaries and advising on position taking. There is always an answer for why it went wrong. However, I'm sure there are exponents of Elliot Wave theory who are successful, it's just that I haven't met too many over the years who were customers of CQG.

That is not say that some of the theories, whether they came from Elliot or not, do not have some worth. It is always useful to know what the Elliot Wave club is up to. However, first of all let's return to structure.

Importance of structure

In July 2005 a price shock following the bombings in London was witnessed. Whenever markets have some sudden unexpected event, having the correct structure to be able to deal with it often provides huge opportunities and some of the best trades. Another less dramatic event was the devaluation by China in the foreign exchange markets, which had an instant impact on the Yen. We will look at them in more detail later.

I realised the importance of structure the day of the 1987 crash. I had known previously that my setup was wrong but didn't have the confidence in a new job to press home this point.

1987 in Australia

Here was my dilemma. I was trading in Australia having to build huge long positions in a stock market that I thought was overvalued and likely to fall. What I didn't know was that the fall would take place in one day. I needed a strategy that would ride the up trend that my bosses believed couldn't end due to programme trading, but still get some protection and eventually produce a net short if the market traded to the downside as I anticipated.

The company held huge convertible note positions in some major stocks. They used these positions to leverage into the management and, in some cases, engineer aggressive takeovers. One of my tasks was to buy the convertible notes overnight in London and then use the Sydney stock options market to play the position. I would put bids in for notes that I believed hadn't been valued correctly in the hope that I'd pick up some bargains.

A typical trade might see a stock close in Sydney at $5; I'd get some notes at $4.70 because the interest had been missed (due to market inefficiencies that wouldn't happen today), and then I'd grant 6 to 8-week $5.50 – 6.00 call spreads, for around 20 cents and would overprotect with a 1 cent put as they were so undervalued. So I'm long at 4.70 and I have protection to 4.50. If the stock rallies I'm out at 5.70. If the options expired worthless I would re-grant the call spread and in addition I would buy some cheap puts again for protection. Remember the theory at the time was that the market couldn't go down so, the skew on the options curve meant that puts were cheaper than the calls. Finally, if the first call spread expired worthless, I would buy additional puts with part of the profits to provide a net short on any serious breakdown. Perfect!

Wrong

As with all perfect solutions there was a problem I hadn't considered. I'd begun this strategy at the beginning of September before the October crash, having arrived in my new job that was going make me a millionaire by thirty. To think that I'd gone from the security of trading bonds to getting involved in stocks just ahead of the biggest debacle since 1929 was not what you'd call a good career move. The problem became apparent within two weeks of my beginning the strategy. The option market only allowed for the open position to represent 10% of the outstanding shares in circulation. This excluded convertible notes because they had not been exercised and become actual shares. This meant that my company's positions (considering that they were looking to exercise the notes in order to gain a controlling stake in a company) were vast and completely out of proportion to the number of actual shares out there. I would only be able to hedge a fraction of the exposure.

Compounding the problem was the fact that a large proportion of the open interest in the options was lying with stale "deep in the money calls". I therefore spent most of the time ringing round brokers, begging them to get their customers to exercise so I could trade. The paradox was that I was in the position to dictate to the option market in terms of size but at the same time was paralysed from actually implementing what I wanted to do. Within a few weeks this problem was irrelevant.

I used to have a portable dial-up Telerate machine at home and a mobile phone. This was in 1987 - I really was a big cheese! The reality was that the phone weighed about 30 lbs, the battery would last all of three hours and I had to carry it around in a rucksack. I was forever paranoid I'd leave it in a bar or restaurant. If the markets were quiet, once I had done my trades on the opening, I would often go to the beach and return early afternoon. The stock options market opened at 10.30, closed at 12.30, reopened at 3 and closed for the day at 4.30. Now that's what I call a market that has its participants' wellbeing at heart.

The Crash

Despite having to manage the position 24 hours a day there were times when I needed to sleep. After hard weekends partying, that was usually a Monday. On the night of the crash I was woken at numerous times throughout the night to be politely informed that compared to the previous hour when they'd woken me up, my job and the company I worked for were heading for a similar fate…Finished!!

On the morning after the crash, I had already been summoned to be at the office by 7 a.m. I arrived at the building early only to find that yet again the lifts weren't working. This meant a walk up over fifty storeys to get to my office. The lifts had always wound me up. They always seemed to break down after I'd been out on the town the night before. And on at least two occasions the doors had opened and the lift wasn't there. It wouldn't have been a bad thing on that day!

Not surprisingly, the management was in a state of panic. What could be done? My suggestion was that, as the USA market had fallen 25% overnight, the Australian market (being the first one to open) was bound to overshoot. One of the first markets I ever traded was London cocoa. That market was so crazy that it could go double limit up and then limit down in an hour, with each fresh limit double the size of the previous one.

Therefore, my suggestion was that we could take advantage of any overshoot and buy any mainstream stocks that opened more than 50% down and look to day-trade them. The look of horror on their faces regarding the prospect of buying the market told its own story. They hadn't seemed to mind buying the day before though. My attitude was in for a penny, in for a couple of hundred million. In the end we did what most people do when they're stuck in a terrible losing position: we stared at the share prices in a masochistic coma and did nothing. I couldn't even let the hole in my stomach that a terrible position creates inspire me to try and sell any of the convertible notes, which was just as well because they weren't worth anything!

Just to compound the misery, my puts, which were now deep in the money, didn't open until 30 minutes after the main market. By then some stocks had already rallied massively from their opening prices. Not that it mattered. No one wanted to buy in the money puts and, with the open interest full, I couldn't grant at the money or out of the money puts to lock in some profit either. Neither was there any point in ringing round any of the brokers to get people to exercise their deep in the money calls as they were now out of the money! No one would make a market unless it was to buy out of the money puts and grant calls; my exact strategy prior to the crash. The irony was no consolation.

As it turned out, the opening prices proved to be the lows for the day and the intraday day rallies were huge. It was no comfort that I could have picked up millions of underlying shares in one of the major stocks I had a position in at $2.40 and sold them at $3.70 the same day. It wouldn't have made any difference to the solvency of the company, as the convertible notes were still significantly out of the money, but, boy, would I have felt better with the biggest day trade profit I was ever likely to get! I went home with the macabre comfort that the company I worked for was the number-one percentage loser, certainly in Australia and possibly the world. The day before the share had been at $4. The next day's opening was at 1 cent. Those bundles of free share options I had wouldn't be getting exercised at 3 bucks, that's for sure.

Structure

To return to the importance of structure, Elliot Wave players are an important consideration in understanding not only what you have to do in any potential circumstance but also in understanding what other participants are doing.

As mentioned in the Stochastic Steps section, the indices have actually been in large up trends for most of 2005, and in some cases have continued to show strength. The FTSE is a case in point. The 90-min chart (see fig. 1) first flagged a strong change in trend with both steps moving beyond 65 bars between crossovers. The StockUp study was posting acceleration and by mid-June both steps were above 4, indicating a very strong trend.

Figure 1:
FTSE has been in a strong trend

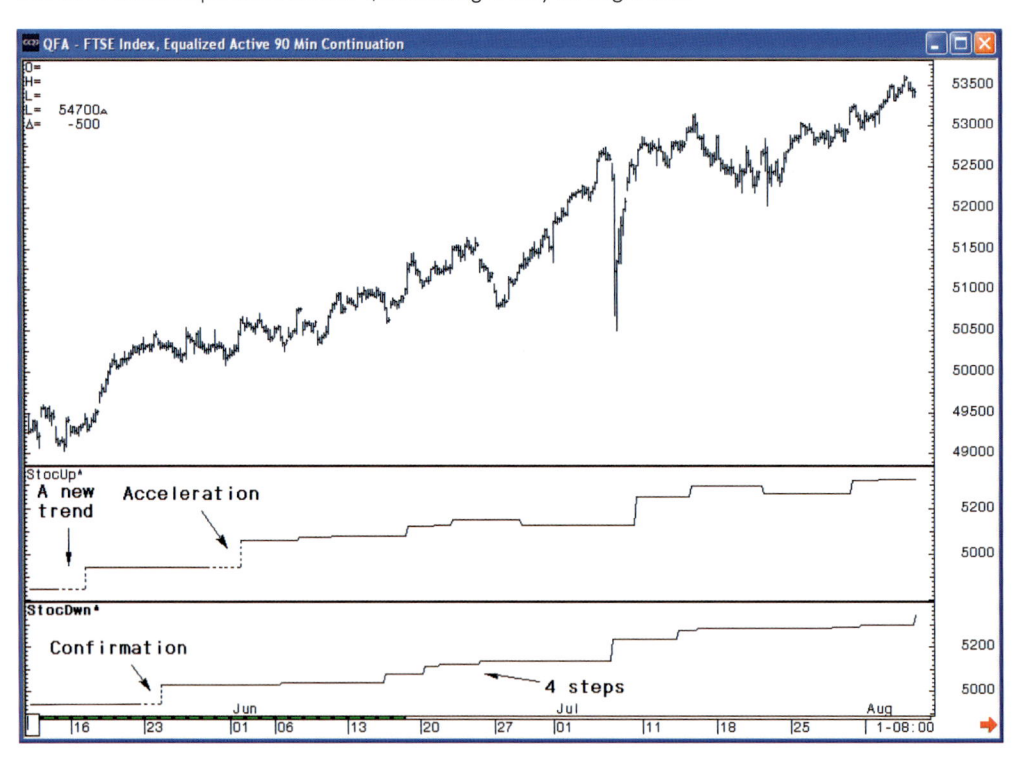

Just 5 days later 20 June the focus moves from a very strong trend in the 90-minute chart to the same setup in the half-day chart.

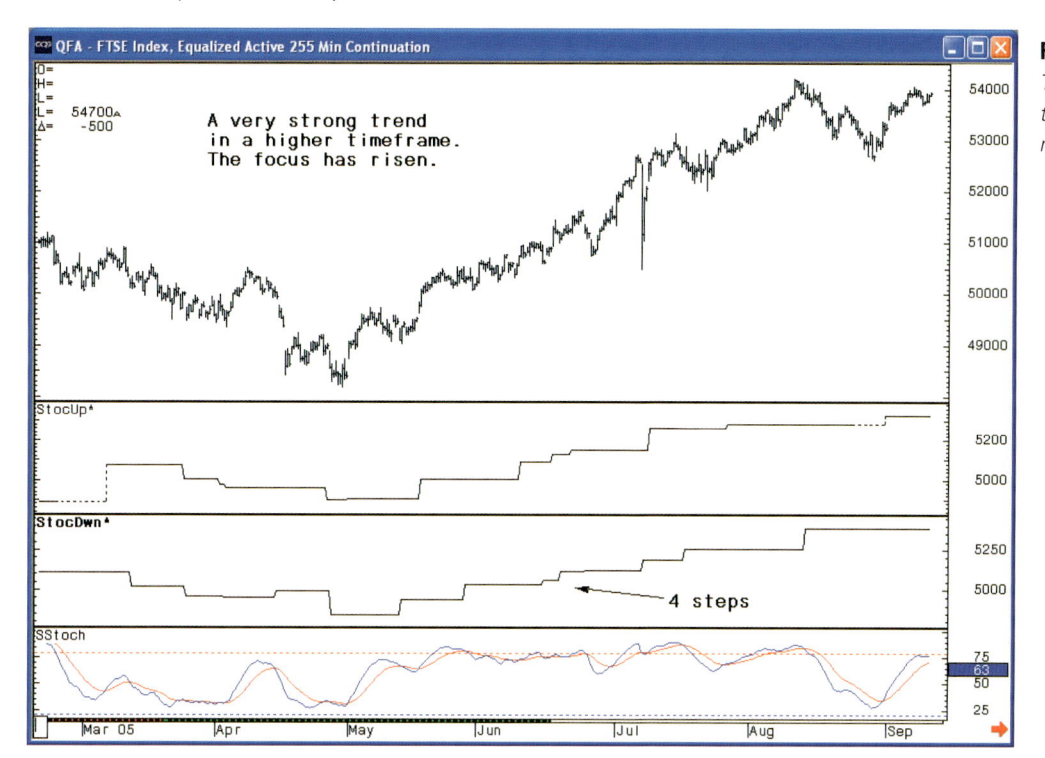

Figure 2:
The focus timeframe moves up

There were Elliot Wave-based commentaries in a prominent Sunday paper in the UK that had been calling for a sharp fall in the index since April 2005. The rally from the 2003 lows is viewed as an A, B, and C correction to a much larger bear market. This appeared to have worked when price stopped ahead of the 50% retracement (see fig. 3) of the entire bear market on the cash index, and began to move lower. This is an important thing to remember, as the markets grow, many new participants reference the long-standing established mantras. Fibonacci, especially retracements, are so well known and quoted in commentaries that increasingly prices never actually reach the level as people pre-empt the signal. Therefore, when price actually does reach it, the level is often ignored.

Figure 3:
Fibonacci Retracements

Analysis of the rally from the lows shows a more compelling reason why the Elliot Wave club is active. There are two separate philosophies behind drawing extensions but one method of analysis shows that the A, B, C correction is projected to top out at the 0.618 projection (see fig.4), which is at almost the same level as the 50% retracement. This is classic wave theory where two opposite trends create a confluence of levels. Therefore we can expect some strategic long-term shorts to appear at this level.

Figure 4:
A confluence of Fibonacci levels has more power

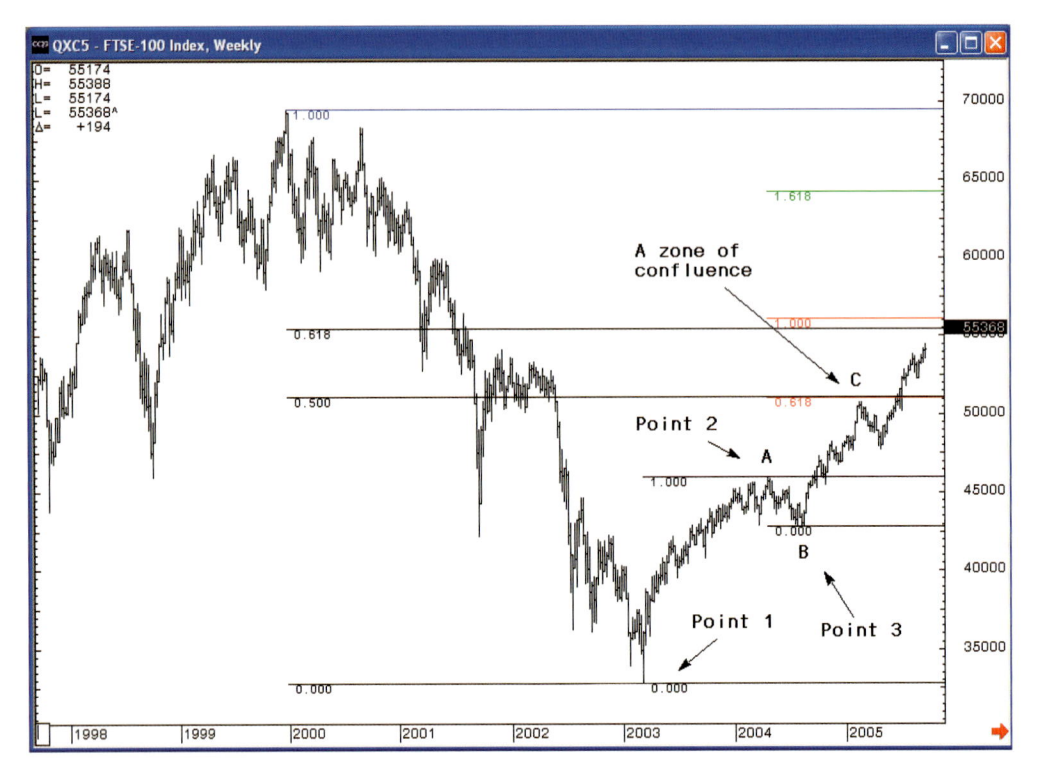

Dow Jones

It has also been suggested (at the time of writing) that the Dow Jones is in a bearish correction. One of the key drivers is the break of a long-standing trend line (see fig. 5). Prices have broken below this line and now stubbornly refuse to break above. However, there is a critical flaw in using trend lines in this fashion. As the line is rising the market can stay below this line and still rally, which is exactly what has been happening. This is psychologically damaging and opens up the possibility of falling into the trap of averaging your position against the trend. Up trend lines can be used as a reference and trading point but can be used as a profit-taking point for longs, *not* as a short-selling level. This is only overruled if Market Profile®-based analysis reveals that the line coincides with independent resistance or when price is overbought. The same principle applies to Channel lines.

Figure 5:
Trend line rules

The other problem with the bearish theory is that the S&P has the same trend-line reference points and has broken above it.

Figure 6:
Trend line rules

TRADING TIME: New Methods in Technical Analysis

What is important to the market?

Returning to the FTSE (see fig. 4), we know that there is likely to be selling at this area. Here is a key point. By understanding other participants you *know* that there is selling in that area. The level is simply too well known for there not to be. We also are aware that the trend leading up to this point is very strong. Who will win the battle? In truth, it doesn't matter. All that does is that you are prepared to trade with the flow.

The best directional moves are often when all players are looking to trade in the same direction. Therefore, if price closes above the Fibonacci area, there is likely to be short covering and fresh buying as price makes new multi-year highs. On the breakout, price embarks on a 100-point rally in 4 days. Market Profile® shows (see fig. 7) how the price action developed.

1 July there is initiative buying on the opening with single letters in **p**. Price holds the higher value for the rest of the day indicating long-term buyers. The following day initiative buying appears once more on the opening and once again we hold a higher value. 5 July sees a pause but we hold the value area low of 4 July. Finally, 6 July sees initiative buying on the opening and a single letter print.

Figure 7:
The trend is strong ahead of the price shock on the 7 July

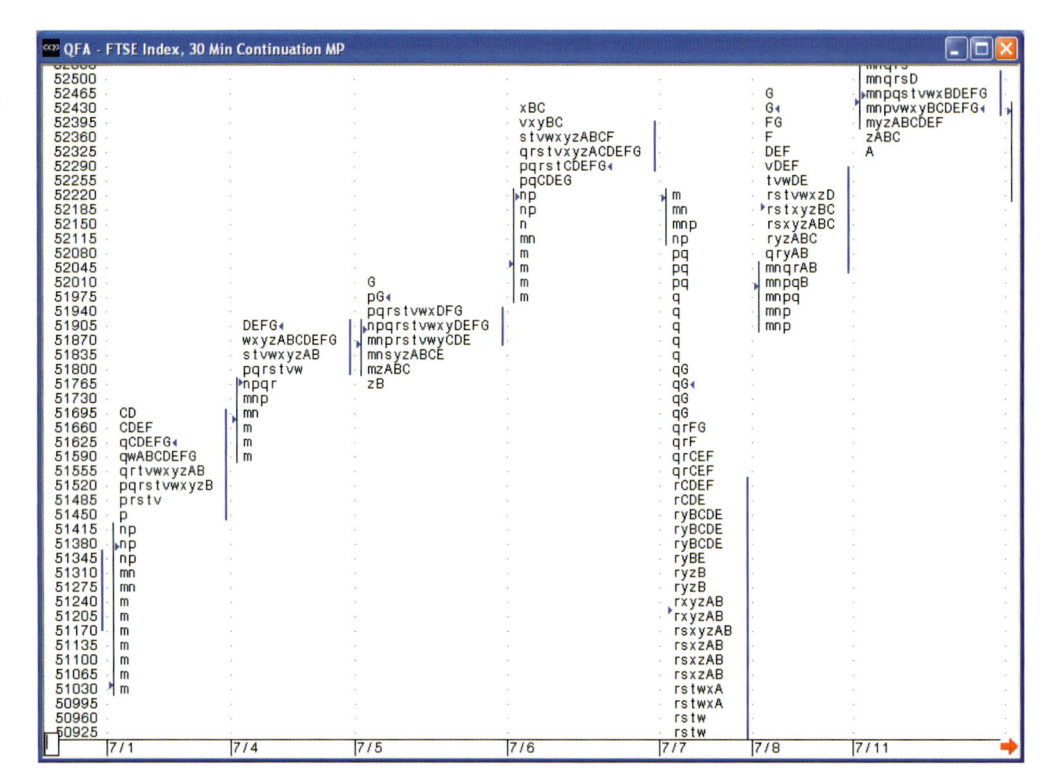

Price Shocks

The following day saw the first London bombing. On any day with price shocks, the need for an understanding of the bigger picture is even more acute. Only the most strategic of players would have had their stops beyond the scope of that day's fall. However, it is crucial that the big picture has been studied in order to have an idea of where the key points are. One of the most important points, from a strategic standpoint, is the distribution that marks the beginning of the trend. This was in April and analysis of the chart shows that the Control Point was at 4980 (see fig. 8). On the day of the slump price moves direct to the top of the initial distribution that instigated the trend, which is marked by a ledge of time at 5015. While it would have taken a brave trader to buy there, the fact that price held there and never broke below the Control Point shows that the up trend was still intact. In fact, the rally was of such magnitude for the rest of the day that the close left the day with a bullish tone. This was emphasised by the fact that despite there being a further bomb scare a couple of weeks later it hardly caused a blip. Logic states that with the economy slowing sharply, public finances in disarray and suicide bombers roaming the streets, stocks would fall. So much for logic! The trend is strong and continues to make new highs as of the time of writing in October 2005

If we return to the chart in December 2005, we see that in fact the Stochastic Steps study moved up to 9 steps as it approached the 0.618 retracement in October on the half-day chart (see fig. 9). Once again, price stalled ahead of the level and now we have finally touched it in the first week of December 2005.)

Peak

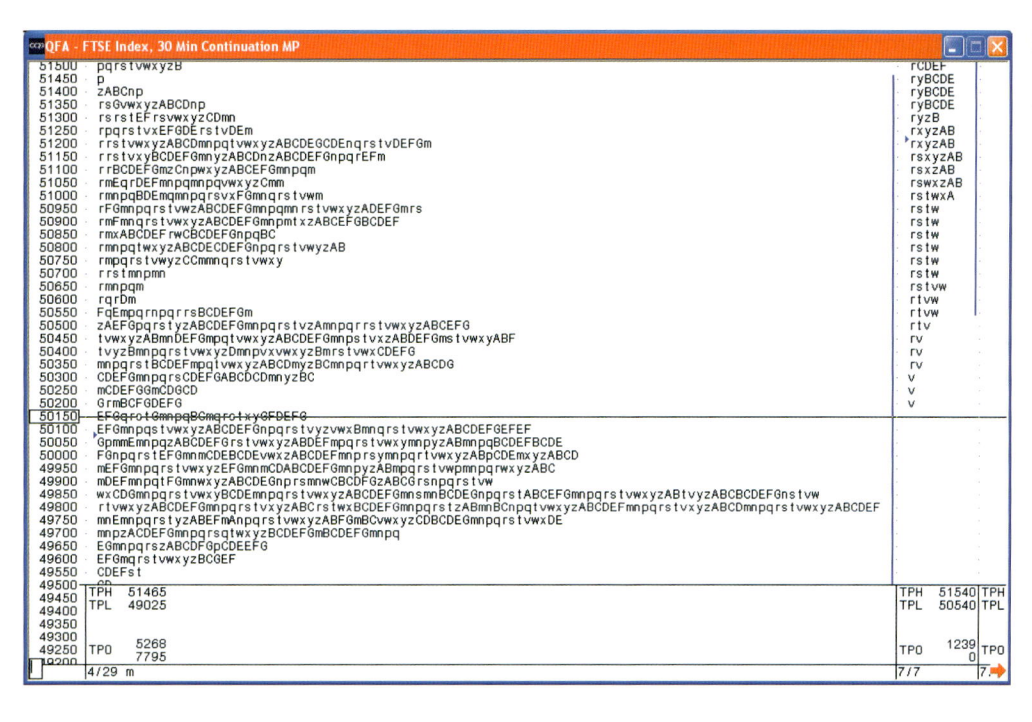

Figure 8:
The long-term distribution

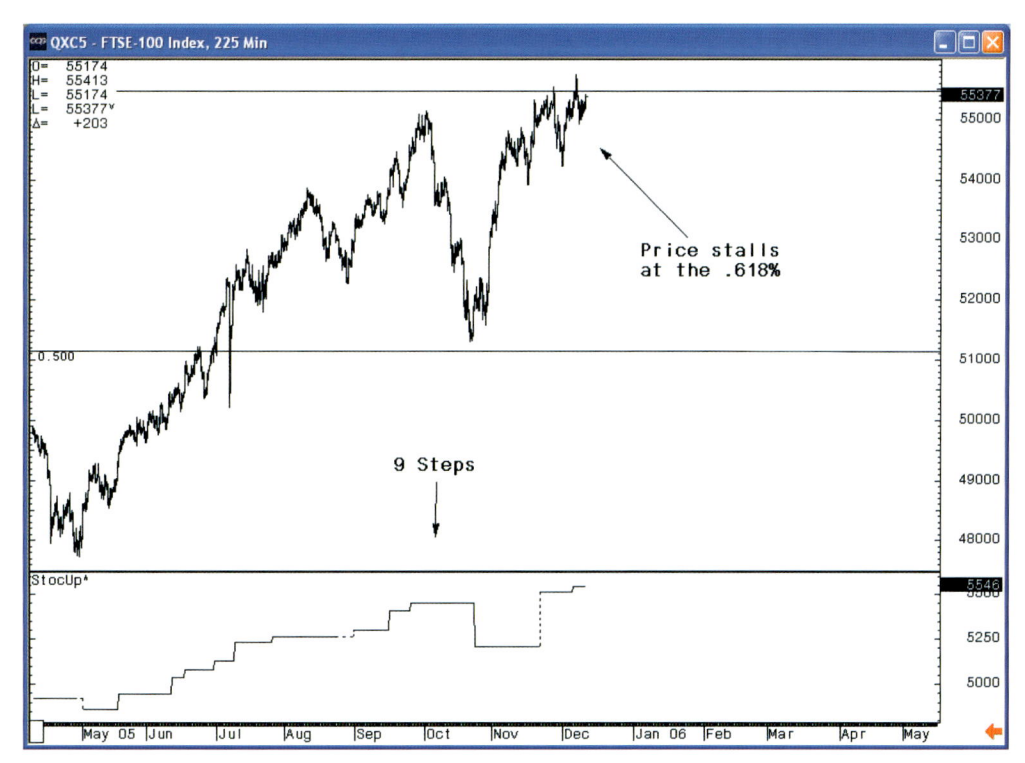

Figure 9:
Fibonacci Retracements

Logarithmic charts – FTSE

If we want to consider the bearish outlook that was highlighted by the Elliot Wave user and the failure of the 50% retracement, it is useful to reference the logarithmic chart. This paints a completely different picture. Price broke through the 50% retracement some time prior to the normal chart and has since ignored the 0.618 retracement as well (see fig. 10). The power of the rally this year and the strength of the trend, as highlighted by Stochastic Steps and Peak, have always indicated an alternative to the A, B, and C correction theory. It's been a 1, 2, 3 up all along. In December 2005, after it rallied another 300 points, the question is whether there has been a fourth and fifth wave or are we still in wave three? Your guess is as good as mine regarding the wave count. All I know is that at present the FTSE has fulfilled its long-term upside target from the 2003 lows in that the midpoint of the rally is at the same point as the Control Point. Having reached the major 0.618 retracement as well, price finds itself at a critical point as the Elliot Wave club is selling. According to my analysis, negatives are also building but with a far more compelling argument – the laws of supply and demand, price and time. The only aspects missing are divergence and an overbought market. In the absence of these requirements, and with the Stochastic Steps having just reached a mega trend on the daily, a Christmas-based rally looks probable. Therefore, whilst poised to take action, the technical setup is not yet in a position to justify going short.

Figure 10:
The logarithmic chart paints a completely different picture

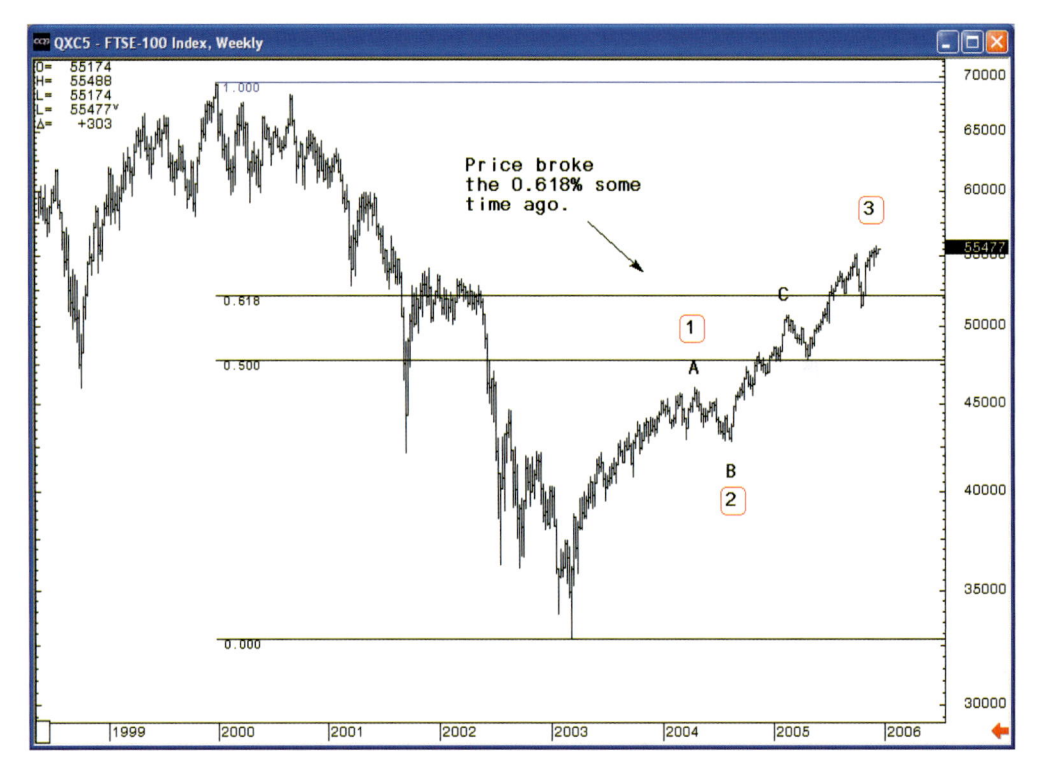

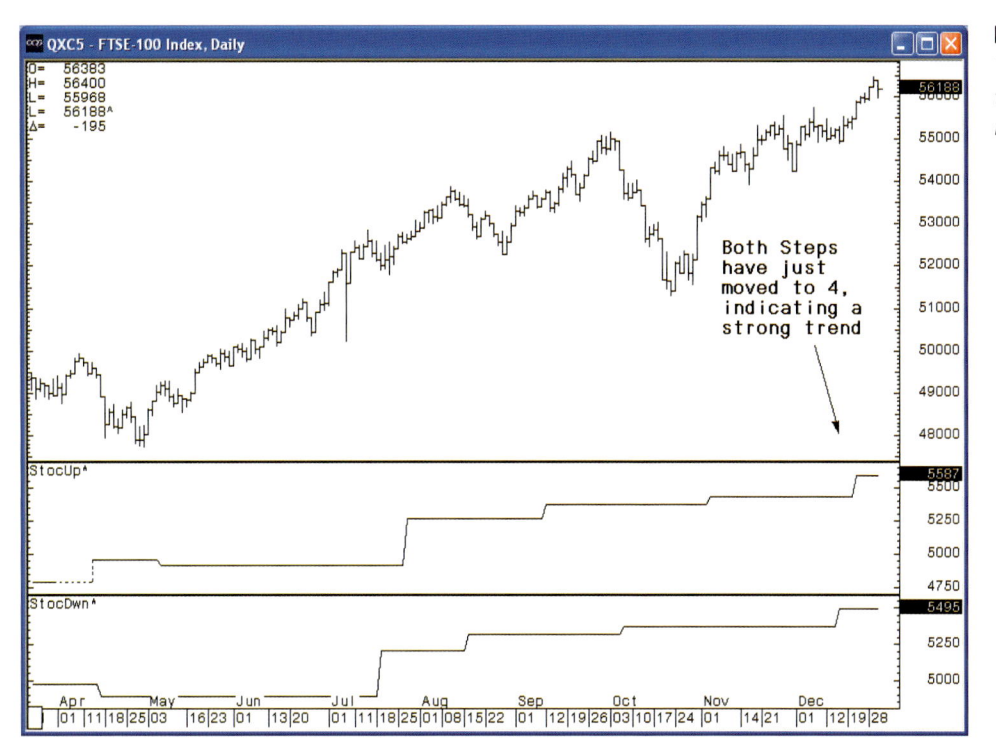

Figure 11:
The focus timeframe has moved to daily

Revisiting the chart at Christmas 2005 shows that the Fibonacci level has now been breached on a weekly basis (see fig. 12). The New Year's early price action could see a sharp move higher. Analysis of the Stochastic Steps shows that the focus timeframe could easily move up to this chart in the first quarter. If you were using the more sensitive RSI steps you would see that this had taken place. The appendix shows how this trend has developed to July 2006.

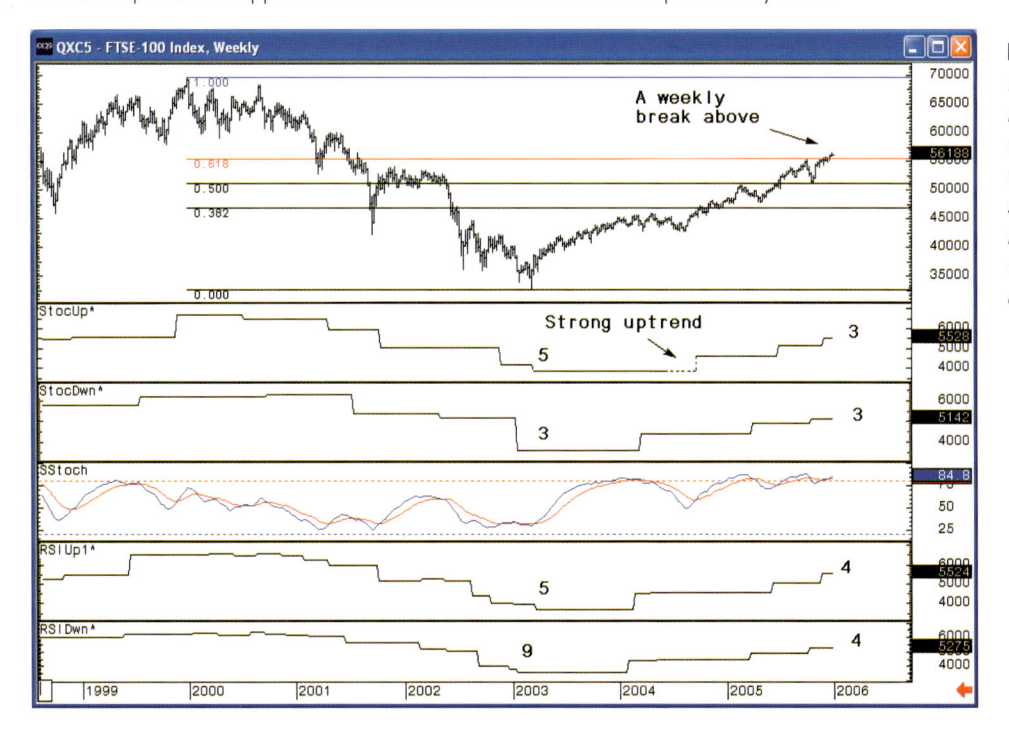

Figure 12:
RSI Steps have moved to a weekly timeframe. The stochastic could move higher as well if the rally continues

Chinese currency revaluation

Next we turn to the Yen and the Chinese currency revaluation. The actual announcement was unexpected in its timing but, more importantly, was very ambiguous. They devalued by 2% but it was unclear whether this was the first of an immediate sequence of controlled steps or a token gesture. The last rumour of Chinese devaluation had caused sharp Yen strength but it had been short-lived. Once again the Yen soared but would the pattern repeat itself?

The Aussie Yen cross was a good example of how a trade with low-risk but good potential upside could be implemented. The market had been on a strong up trend, and was building a higher distribution. Strategically, there is the possibility of price moving much higher.

The commentary issued by OaR from the week before, 17 July 2005, paints the picture.

AUDJPY

Review 10-17 July 2005

The market began the week with a mixed outlook as price had spurned an opportunity to break higher. However, with price above 0.8265, further rallies were possible. In a quiet week price edged higher and began to accept value back above 0.8405.

Outlook 17 July 2005

Price has recaptured value above 0.8405 and once more has an opportunity to rally to the first targets of 0.8435 to 0.8441 and the major level of 0.8480. A bull trap lies at 0.8538, with a final major zone at 0.8592 to 0.8608. Acceptance above here would have long-term bullish implications.

Below, support begins at 0.8405 and 0.8375 with a more potent point at 0.8340, whilst long-term control is at 0.8265. A breakthrough here removes the bullish outlook and places price back in a sideways grind, initially aiming for the strong support at 0.8225. Any break aims for 0.8155, with acceptance below here targeting 0.8085, 0.7996 and 0.7940 to 0.7930.

Therefore only strategic bears remain involved and reference to 0.8480. Bulls have had little opportunity to become active, but the aggressive can engage and monitor to 0.8340. The rest must wait for a breakout to be confirmed.

Resistance
0.8435 to 0.8441, 0.8480 major, 0.8538, 0.8592 to 0.8608 major

Support
0.8405, 0.8375, 0.8340 major, 0.8265 control, 0.8225, 0.8155, 0.8085, 0.7996, 0.7940 to 0.7930 major, 0.7868, 0.7824, 0.7752, 0.7710, 0.7635 to 0.7625, 0.7520, 0.7440, 0.7360 major.

Fig. 13 shows how clear the support is. The Control Point for this trend is at 0.8265 from the trend that began in January. If the trend is to continue price should hold this level. Price trends down directly to this point and holds. In the coming months the trend ends up topping out at just below 0.9000. (We show how the trailing stop was activated in the next chapter.) The added bonus was the positive interest-rate carry that lasted throughout the trade.

Figure 13: The correction lower stops directly at the Control Point 5

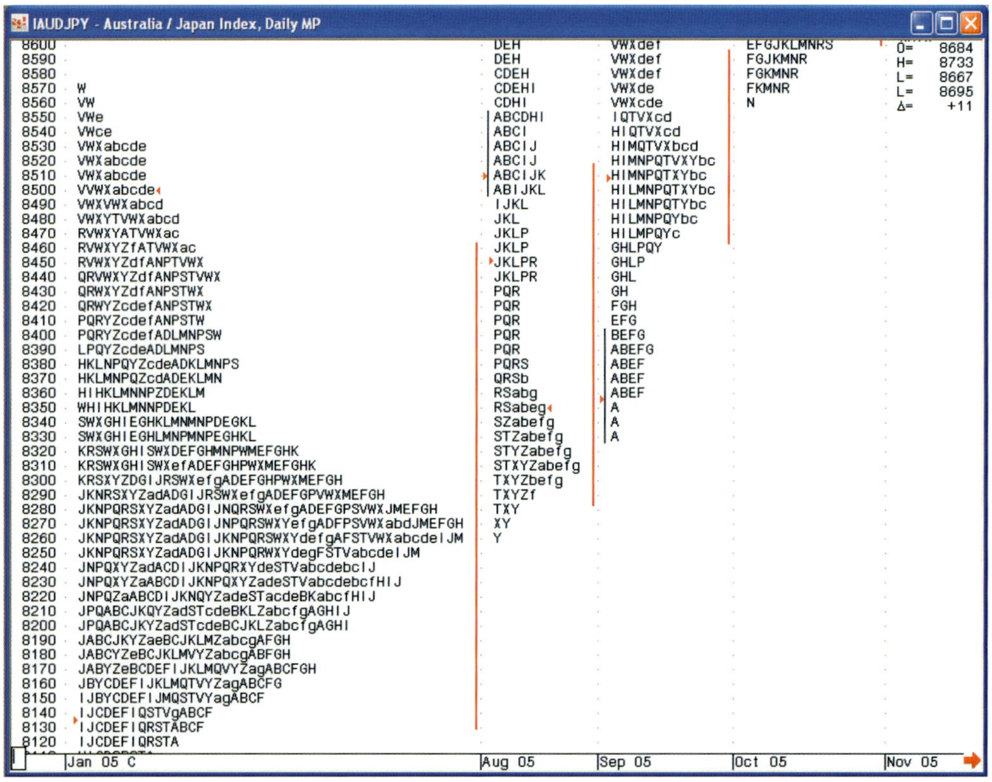

This cross rate can be a very slow mover so not surprisingly it is the daily and weekly charts that are the focus timeframes. Both are showing strong trends via the Stochastic Steps and RSI Steps (see figs. 14 and 15) and this continued for another 6 months into December 2005.

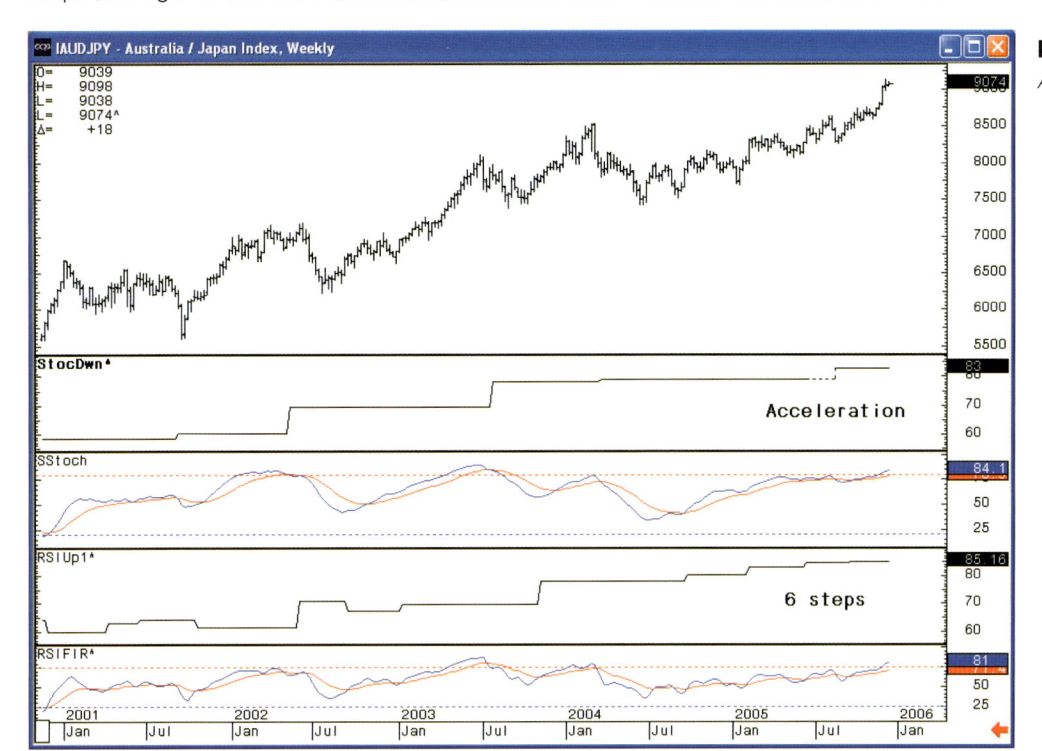

Figure 14:
A strong trend

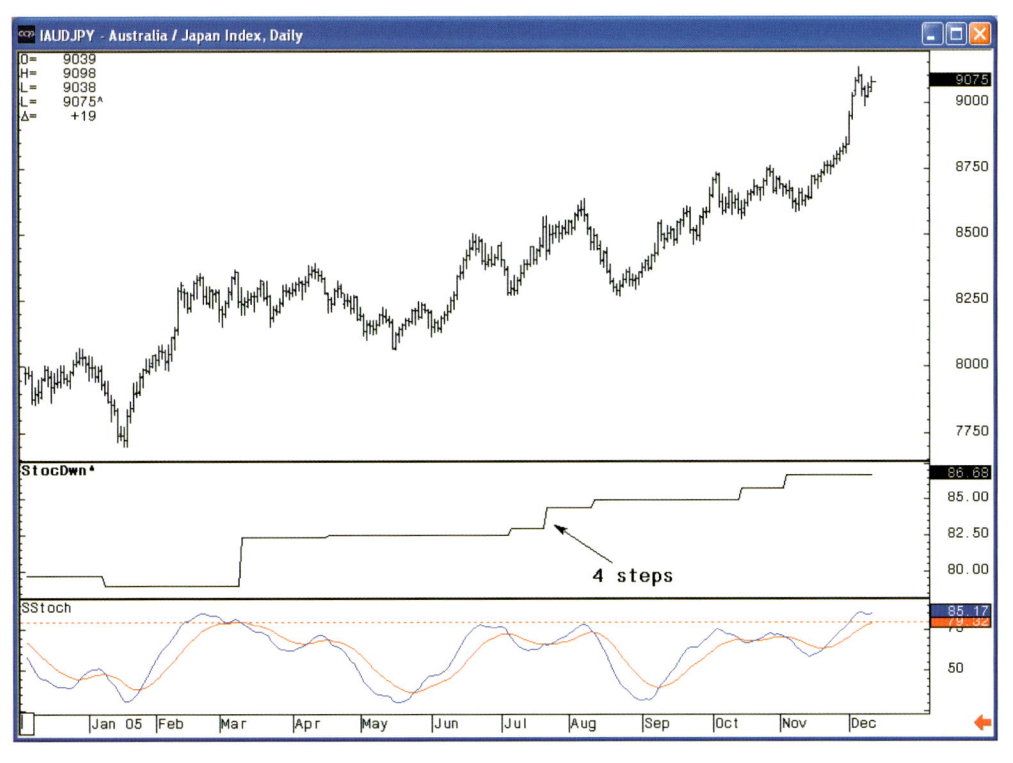

Figure 15:
AudJpy Weekly acceleration

OaR Peak

OaR Peak simply records swing highs and lows. It consists of two components:

- Hi Peak: plots the high swing points
- Lo Peak: plots the low swing points

Both studies will hold those points until the next change if a swing high or low occurs. The swing point can be adjusted depending on the degree of sensitivity required, but the common setting is a 2 by 2. This means that for a Peak to be created the middle bar of 5 must be the high point for a Hi Peak and the middle bar of 5 the low point for a Lo Peak.

In their basic form and interpretation they simply track an up trend or downtrend as the two charts show.

Figure 16:
Peak tracks the trend and acts as a final trailing stop

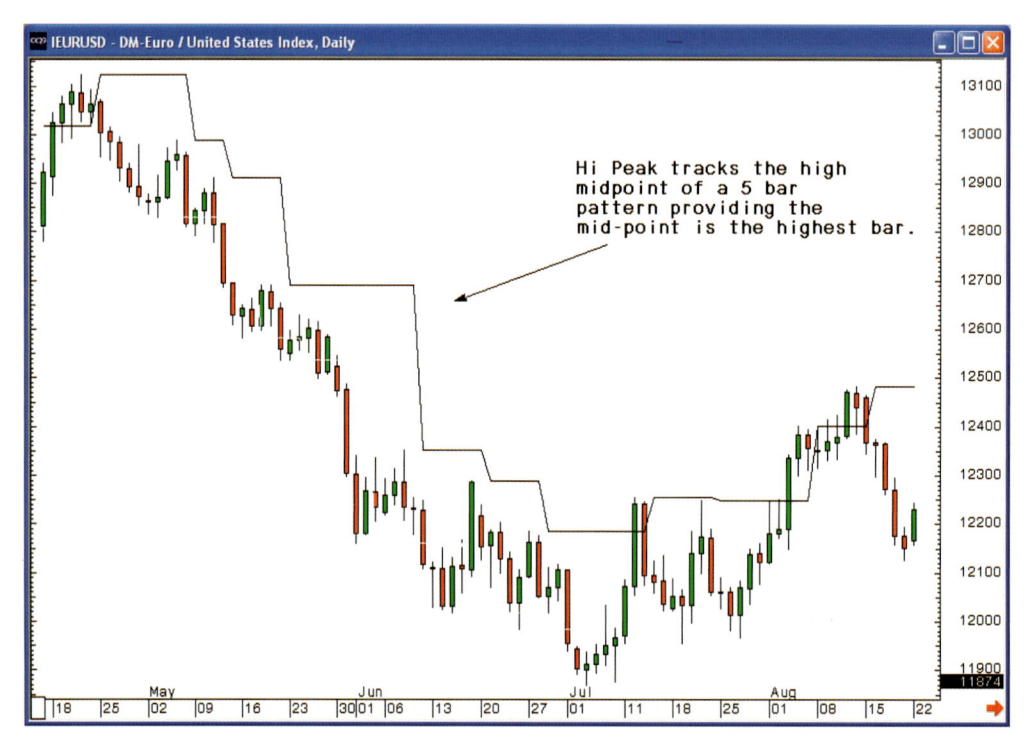

Figure 17:
Lo Peak tracks an up trend

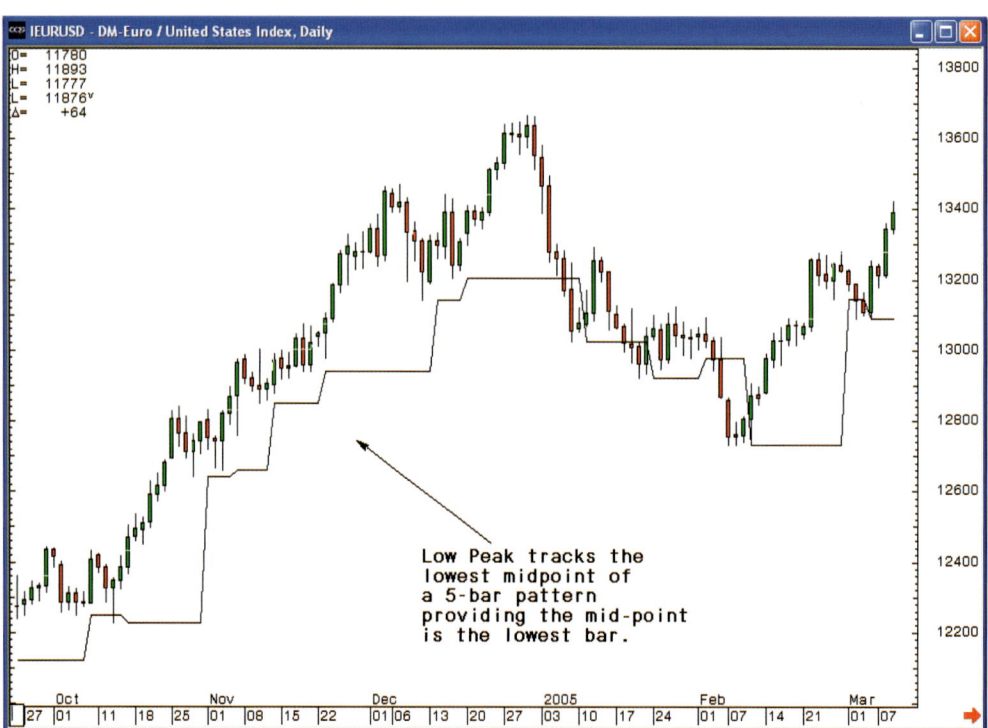

As can be seen, the study is very straightforward but that does not do justice to the depth of information that can be obtained about

- how strong the trend is,
- when it is due to correct,
- whether it will restart, and
- when it's overextended.

There are many patterns associated with the change in, or value of the Peak levels in relationship to price. Among those are:

- What is the difference between a Peak level and the current price?
- Is price above Hi Peak in an uptrend or below Lo Peak in a downtrend?
- How many bars has that been the case?
- How many times has Peak continuously stepped in the same direction?
- How many bars are there between changes in Peak levels?

The Basics

It is one part of, or can be the final part of an exit strategy to a trend. Fig. 18 shows an uptrend in Bunds. The exit comes when price closes below the Lo Peak line. This is an important proviso, especially on an intraday basis when price will often break a Peak level but not close beyond it. When that happens, that bar often becomes the middle bar of the next Peak level. This means that the stop actually widens.

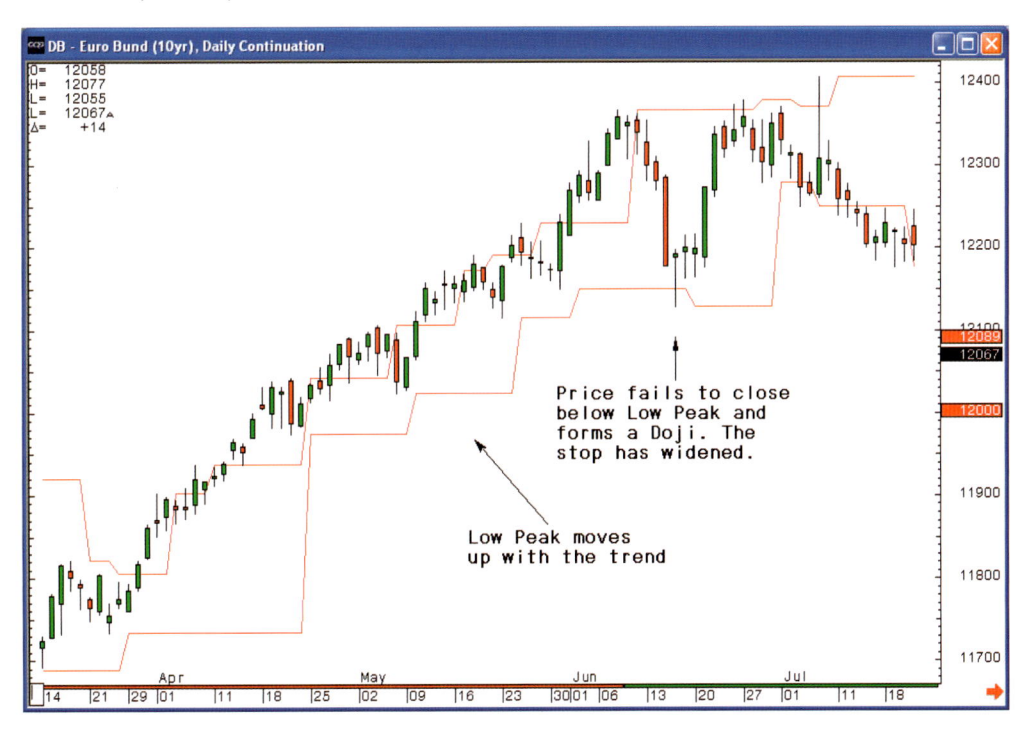

Figure 18:

Note how the stop can widen if waiting for a close beyond a Peak level

Peak is relevant to all markets in all timeframes. For day-trading sessions with initiative behaviour, the Peak level will provide a trailing stop that lasts throughout the day. The regularity with which markets close at the high or low of the day means that maximum profit on part of your position is possible. This provides a structure to scalpers. If the trend has been defined via responsive or initiative behaviour, there is an inherent bias to one side of the market. Therefore, if the trend is up, scalpers must always play from the long side and only scalp on a proportion of their position as long as price is above the short-term chart Lo Peak level. This enables the scalper to ride the trend on a proportion of their position and means big trend days can be captured. This makes a huge difference to their profit potential!

Figure 19:
Peak can track a trend in very low timeframes

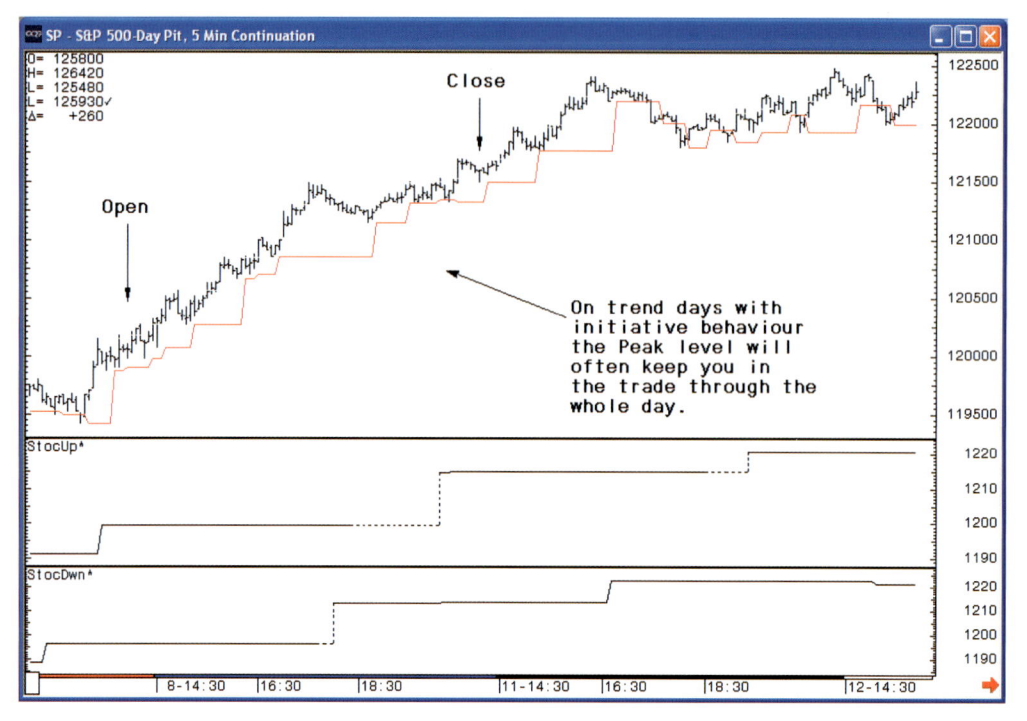

Dax

However, for the Dax, if you are trading in very low timeframes such as 5 and 10-minute, the length of time that the market is open means that only very strong trend days would see the Peak trail for the entire session. It is therefore necessary to split the day into two sessions. The first runs from the opening to 1 p.m. and the second begins with the opening of the Dow at 2.30. Fig. 20 shows how Peak trailed an opening drive in the morning and then a fresh drive higher in the afternoon. Price closes on the highs with the Stochastic Steps having stepped down, indicating the trend was over shortly before the close.

Figure 20:
In Europe the day can be split into two sessions

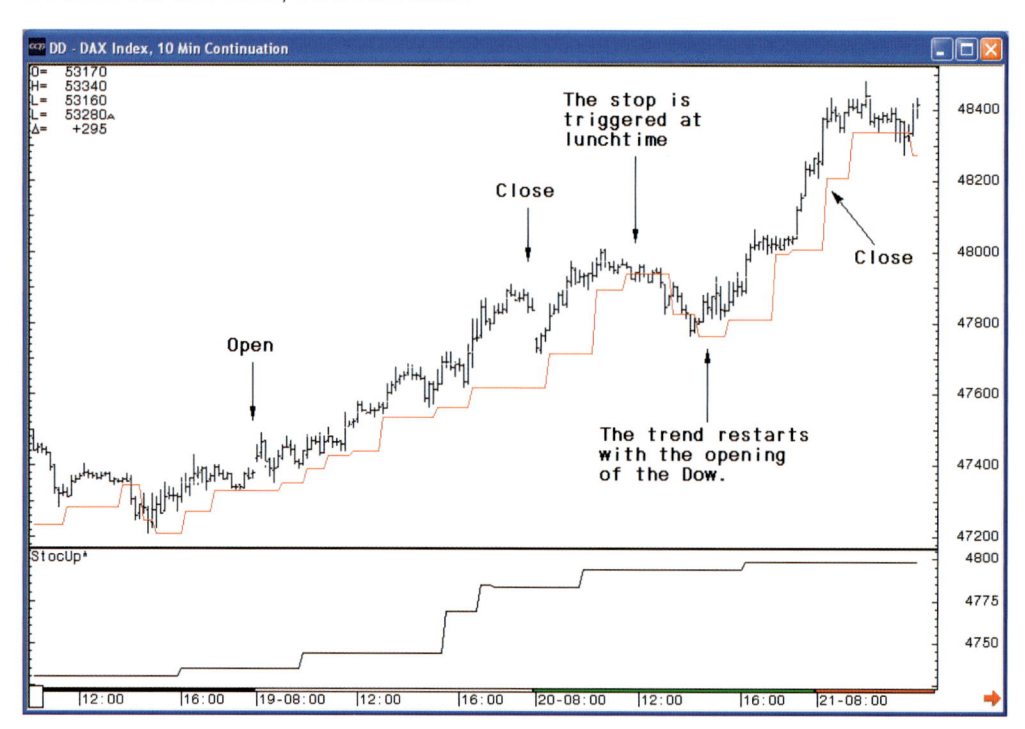

Peak

Such is the Dow and S&P's dominance on the Dax that it can be argued that by trading the latter in the afternoon you are trading a secondary instrument. It therefore makes sense that the Dax should be traded in the morning before the focus switches to the Dow or S&P.

FTSE100

A common pattern in the FTSE is that by the time the Dow opens any trend-based activity has already exhausted itself in the European indices in the morning. This means that the S&P may continue in the same trend, but the FTSE simply stalls and remains in a sideways pattern (see fig. 22). The daily time-based studies mentioned in chapter 1 often provide insight into when this is likely to happen.

The S&P chart shows (see fig. 21) weakness from the opening and then a breakdown in **F**.

The FTSE chart has already moved lower (see fig. 22) in the morning and then completely ignores the move in the US.

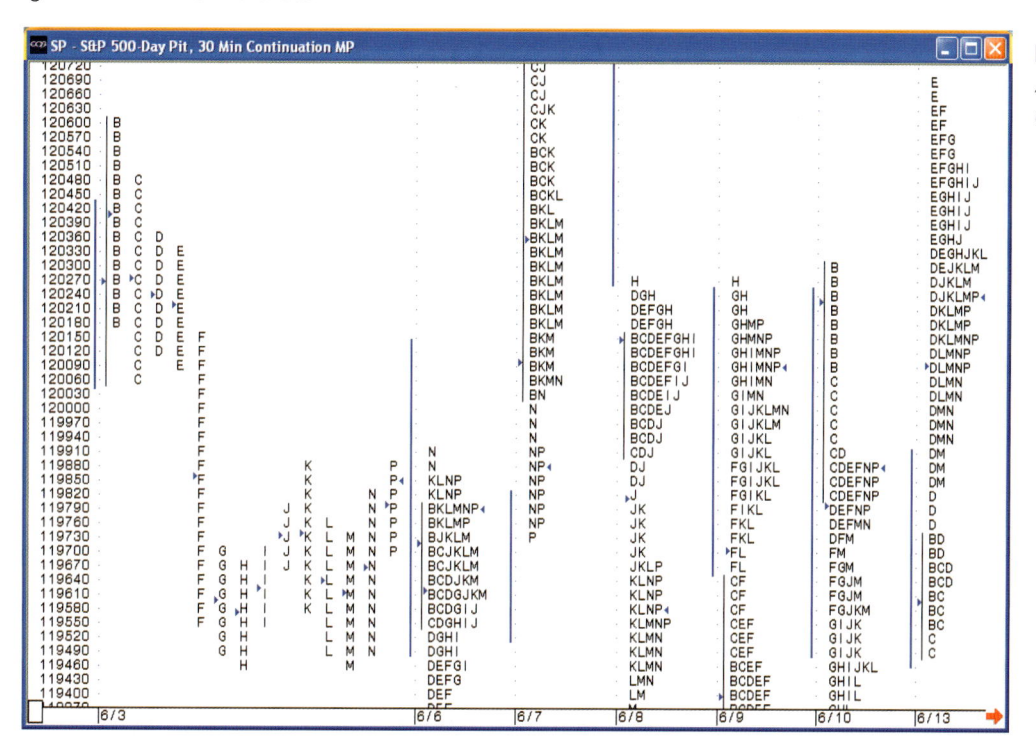

Figure 21:
A weak trading day in America

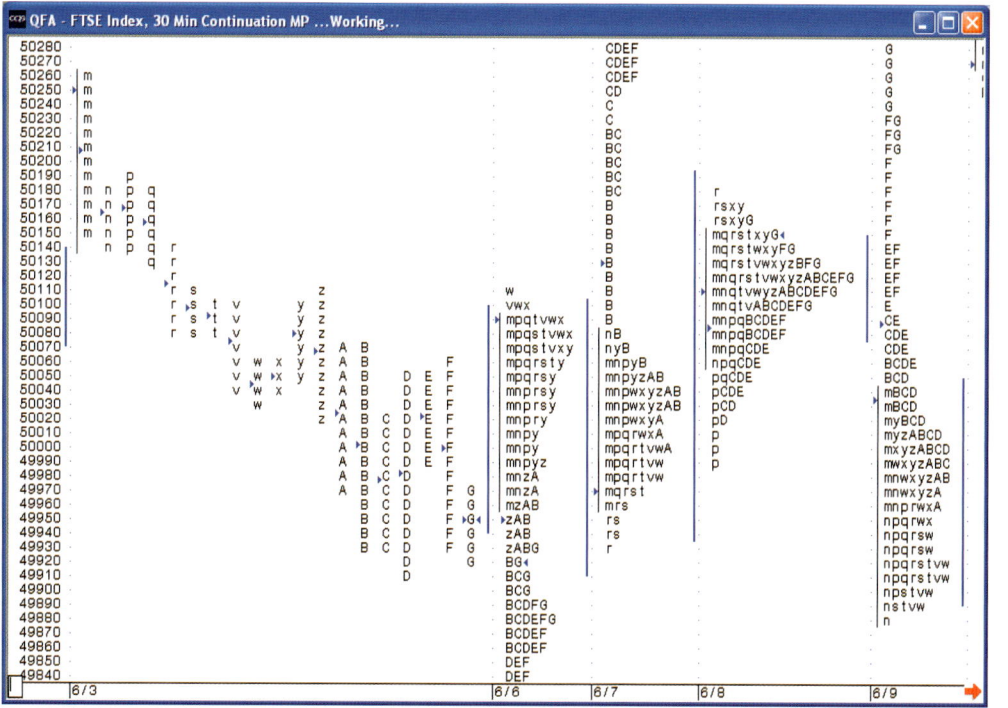

Figure 22:
The FTSE has no more desire to move lower with the S&P

181

TRADING TIME: New Methods in Technical Analysis

Linking Time-Deviation Bands with Peak

Additional analysis via the deviation levels can provide insight into when this is more likely to happen. The low in the FTSE in **D** shows that price is already beyond its 2nd standard deviation point and, with closes rarely moving beyond 3 standard deviations, the downside is limited within a normal trading environment.

Figure 23:
The downside risk is limited by the time America opens

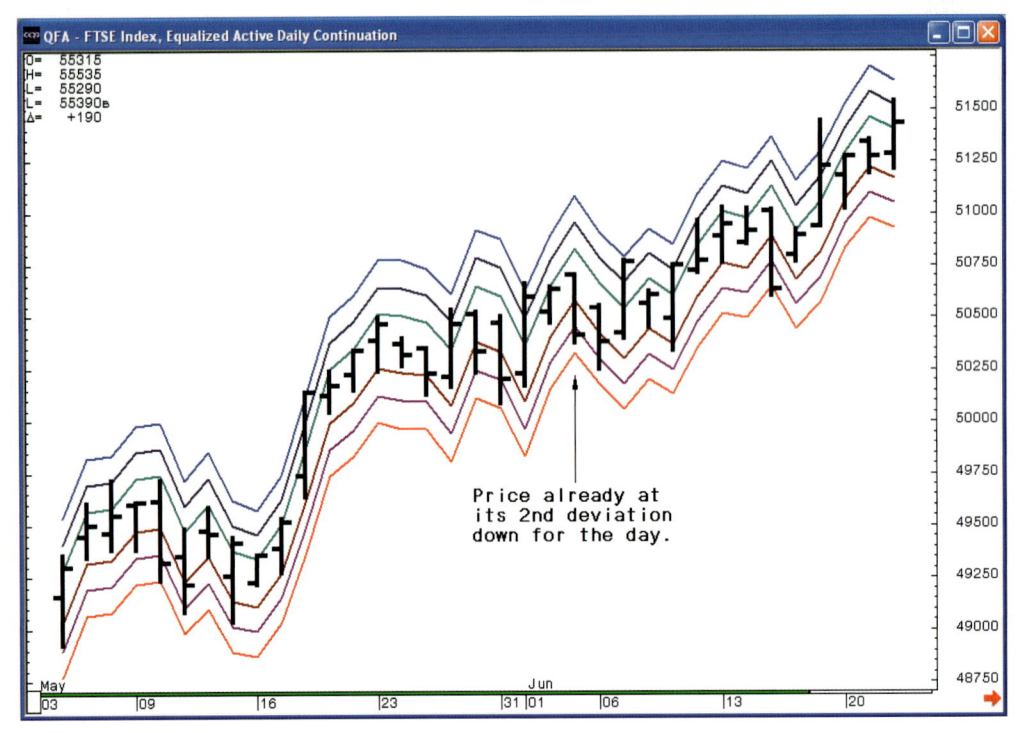

Understanding the basics of Overbought and Oversold and the influence major stocks have on an Index

FTSE - a case study

Just a few giant shares, such as Vodafone, BP and Shell, have increasingly dominated the FTSE. Therefore it's crucial to understand the dynamics of these stocks individually.

This applies in the short term and historically. Analysis of some of the main components of the index in January 2004 shows that, on a true measure of overbought and oversold, various stocks are fulfilling the premise of Cynthia Kase©'s KPO (Kase Peak Oscillator) (see fig. 24). This states that when the dark vertical line appears this is the high, or there is one more high due in the current trend cycle. This is commonly known as a Kase Peak Out. Therefore, from a timing perspective the FTSE main powerhouses are exhausted and must pause or retreat before they have the capacity to trade in the same direction. This is critical information. By 8 January 2004 Barclays, Lloyds, BP, Shell and Vodafone are all fulfilling these criteria.

This means that the FTSE should under-perform against other indices on the upside. This provides spread opportunities but most importantly means that you can trade the right contract. In the immediate aftermath of the stocks showing exhaustion the S&P rallied over 30 big figures, the Dax 160 points, whilst the FTSE failed to make new highs in the trend and subsequently fell.

Peak

If we look at Vodafone first (see fig. 24), the daily chart displays the classic Kase© KPO theory. When a Peak Out appears this is the end of the trend or there is one more high due in this trend cycle.

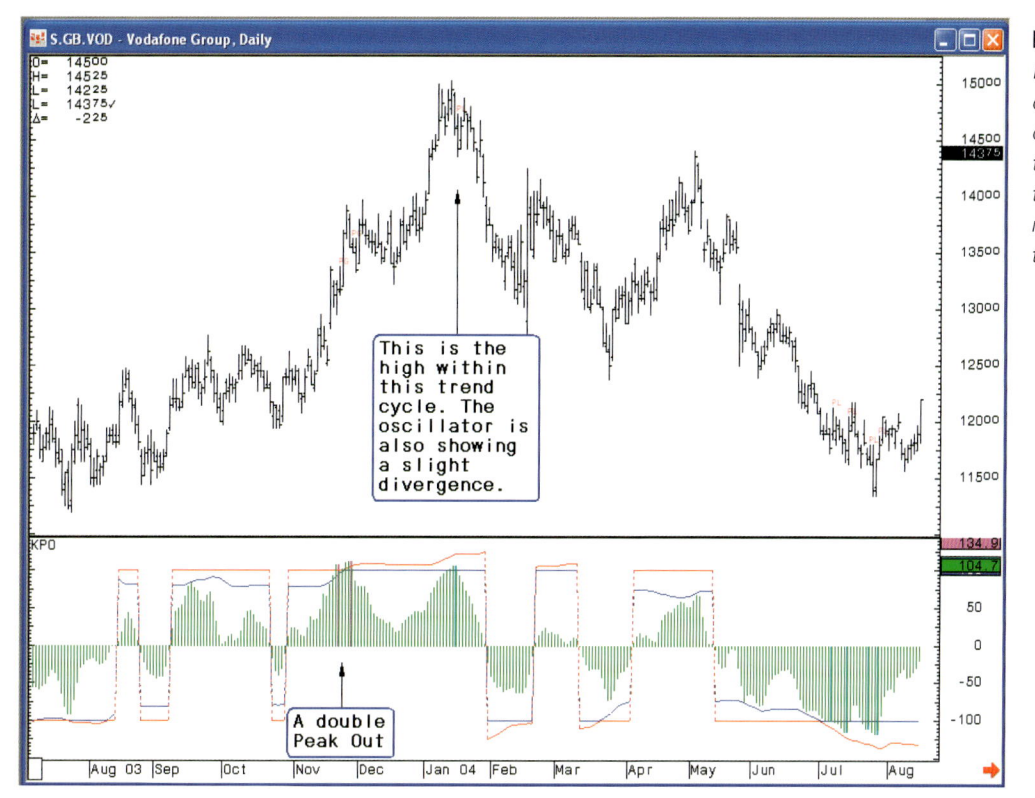

Figure 24:
Peak Outs signal overbought and oversold. This is the extreme or there is one more due in this trend cycle

RSI Step theory, Divergence and Overbought / Oversold

The half-day chart becomes overbought (see fig. 25), confirming the daily chart. The highs are also marked by the same divergence pattern used in the RSI Steps section. However, the calculation is placed through the Kase© Kcd. This study measures the movement of the KPO and is a very aggressive measure of divergence.

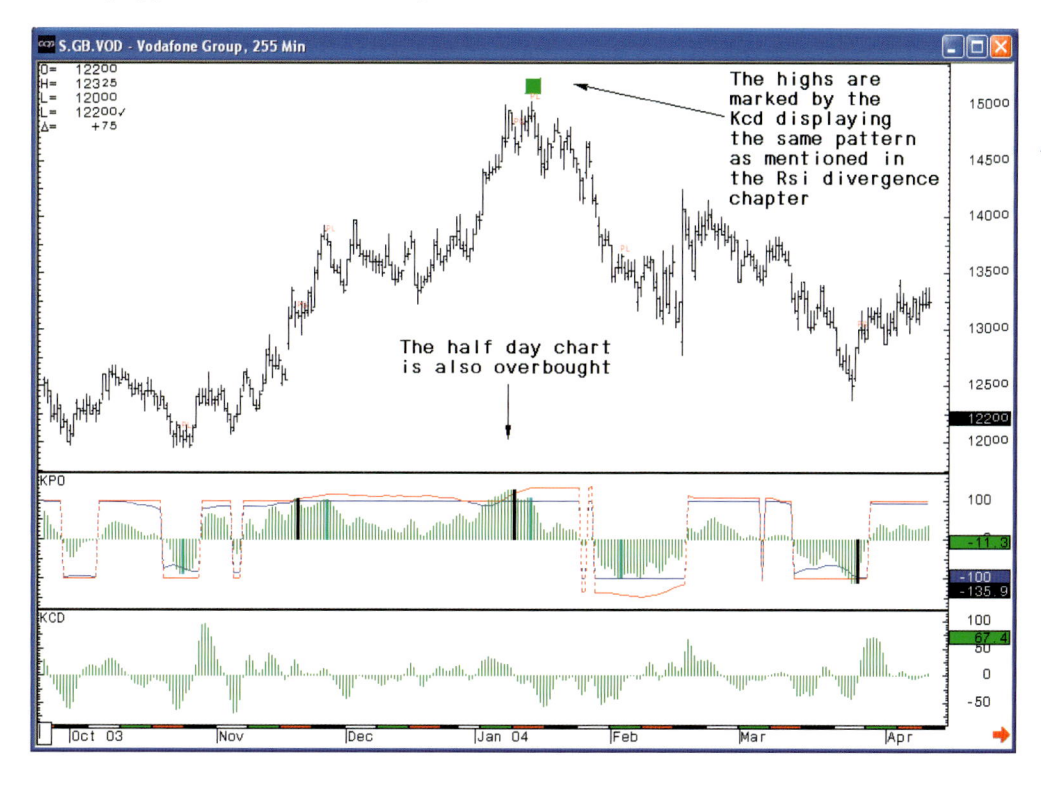

Figure 25:
Multiple timeframes add power

TRADING TIME: New Methods in Technical Analysis

Figure 26:
The quadruple Peak Out at the lows is extremely rare

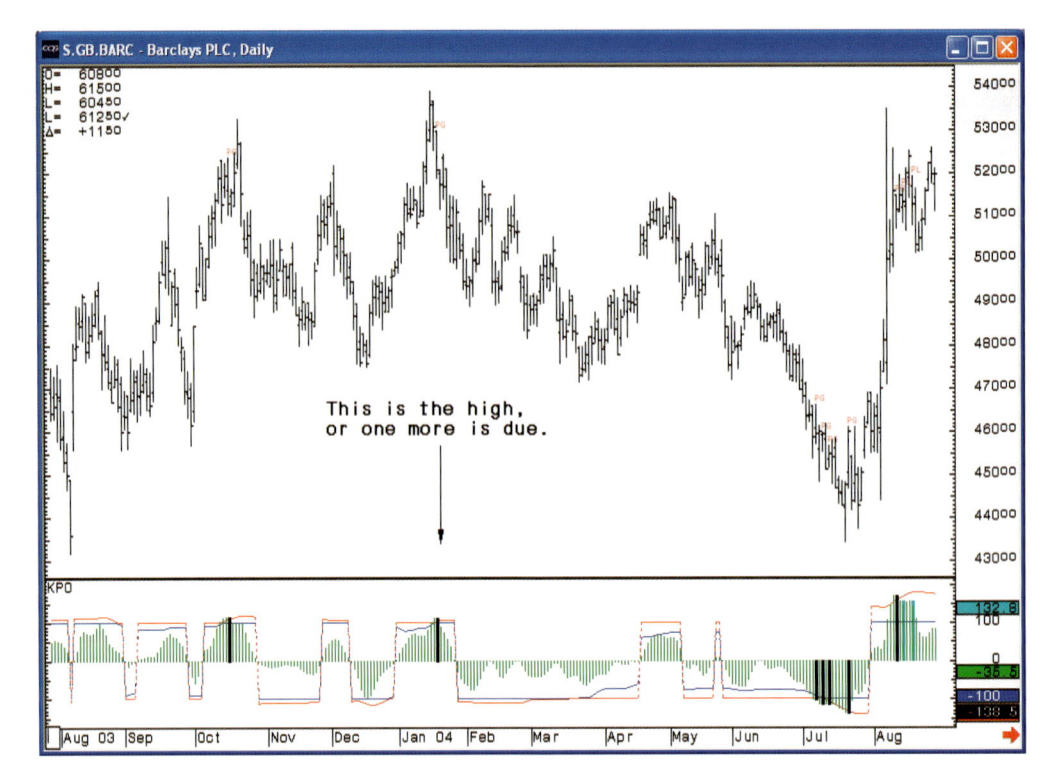

Figure 27:
The banking sector is overbought

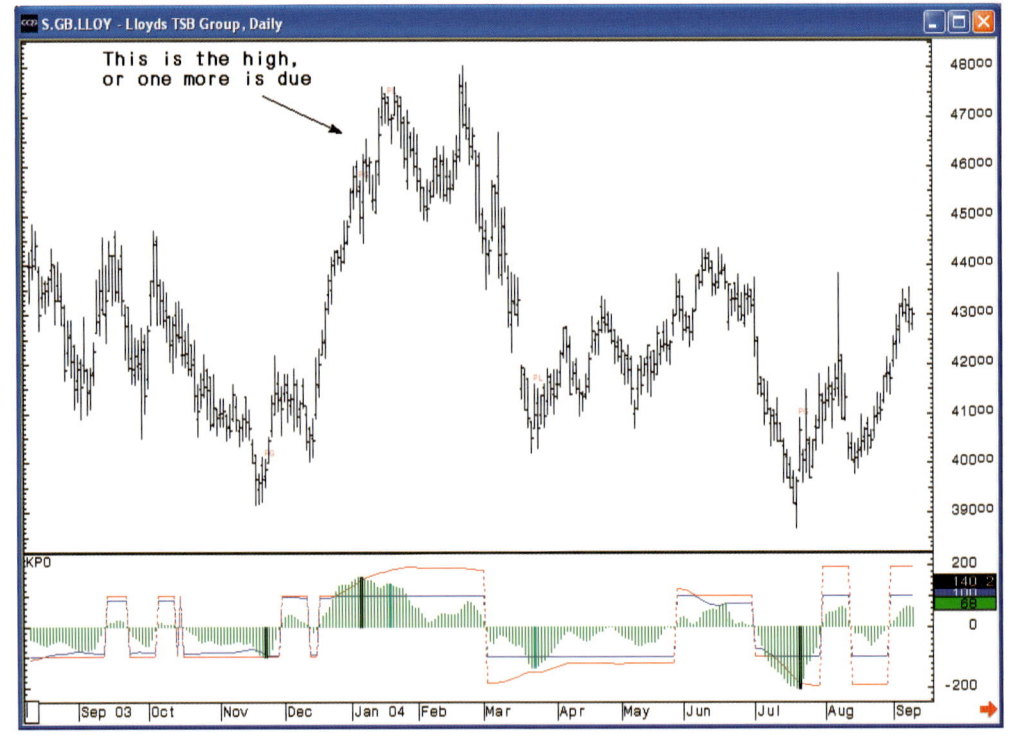

Peak

Shell had already peaked (see fig. 28) and just a few days later collapses.

Figure 28:
The oil sector is overbought as well

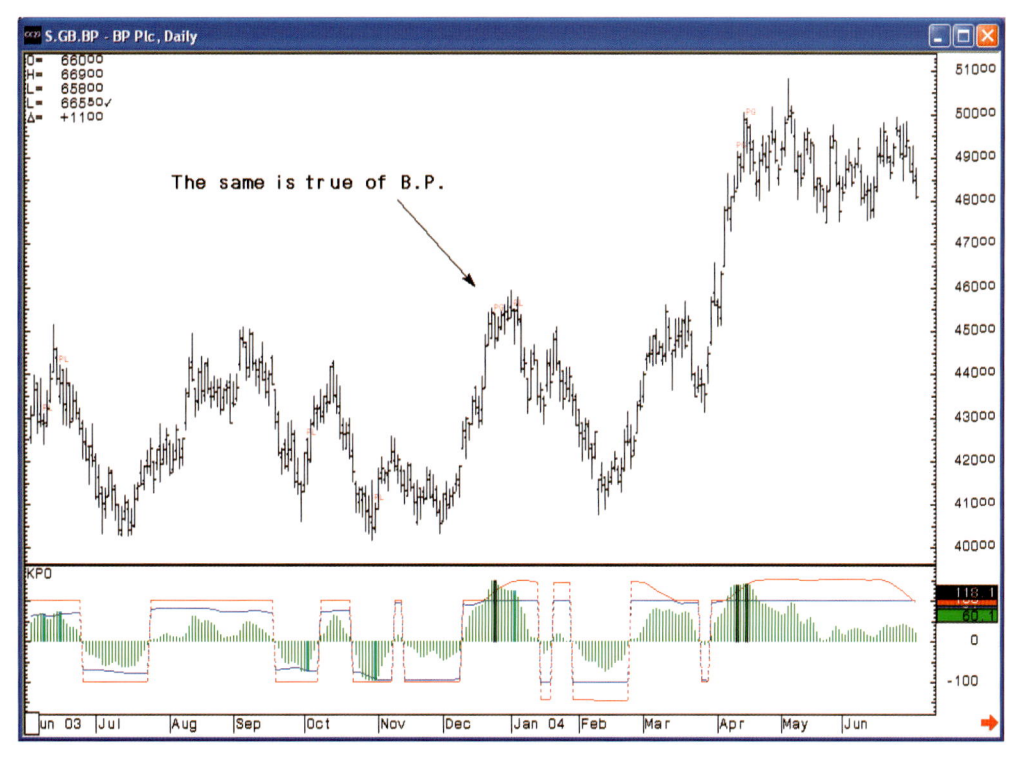

Figure 29:
B.P. confirms

The same is true of B.P.

With so many of the major components, with heavy weightings, within the index, further rallies will be problematic, but more usefully, the FTSE is likely to under-perform against other indexes.

Figure 30:
The American market rallies

The market continues to rally after 8 January.

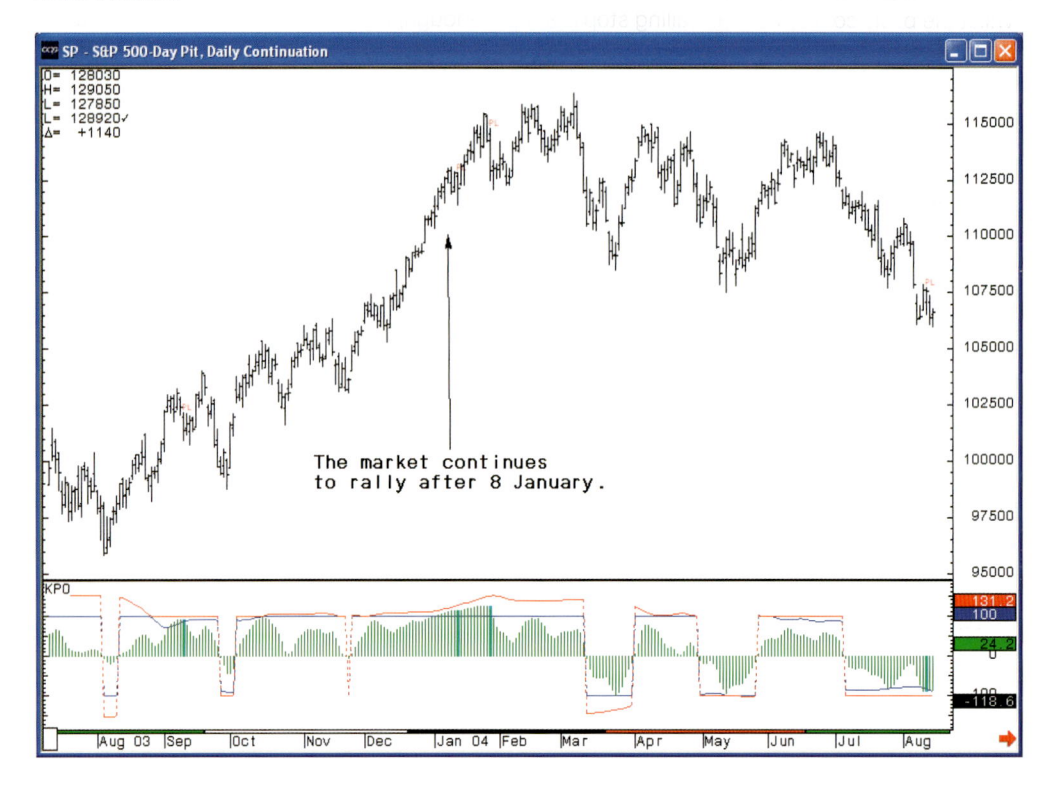

Figure 31:
With the components of the FTSE overbought, the Index can't rally

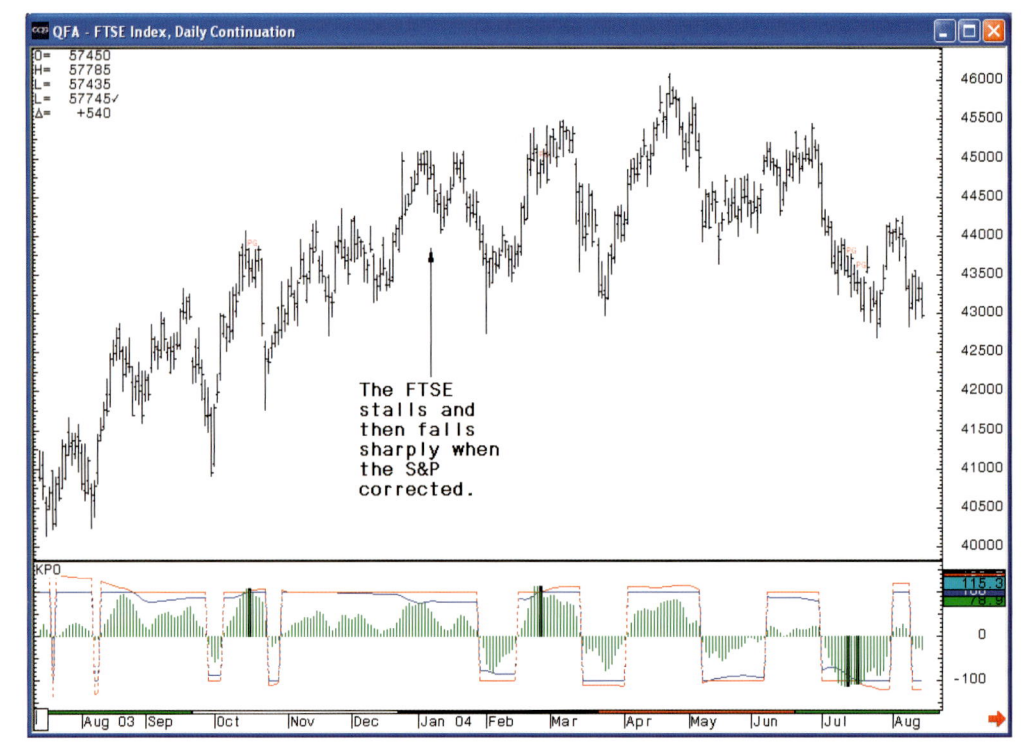

The FTSE stalls and then falls sharply when the S&P corrected.

Peak Patterns

How strong is the trend?
Whilst the basic concept of the trailing stop is simple enough, the patterns in the Peaks formation and their relationship to price are far more revealing. The first pattern looks at the opposite Peak level to the actual trend following the trailing stop – for example, if price is in an up trend we are referencing the Hi Peak study. There are different reference points between intraday and historical charts. First we will look at historical charts (see fig. 32).

Price above the Hi Peak level confirms that the trend is strong. Once price has been above the Hi Peak level for 6 bars the market is due a correction. If this does not materialise, and price continues to stay above for 10 bars or more, we are in a mega trend. This last pattern is the most revealing. The fact that price has not been able to correct the trend by reversing down for 2 bars from the high 3 bars ago tells us that the trend is extremely strong. We are still due a correction at any time, but price can still make new highs once this correction is over. The Australian Stock market rally discussed in the Stochastic Steps chapter is a typical example.

This is crucial information in understanding what the probable outcome is. Like any pattern it is not foolproof, but, if it is connected to true measure of overbought and oversold and the deviation studies, the likelihood of how long the new trend once the correction is over will last can be gauged. Once the correction is over it is possible to guage how long the new trend will last. This could take various forms such as a shift in the Control Point, or the acceptance of value back in the previous distribution, or failure in a bigger distribution.

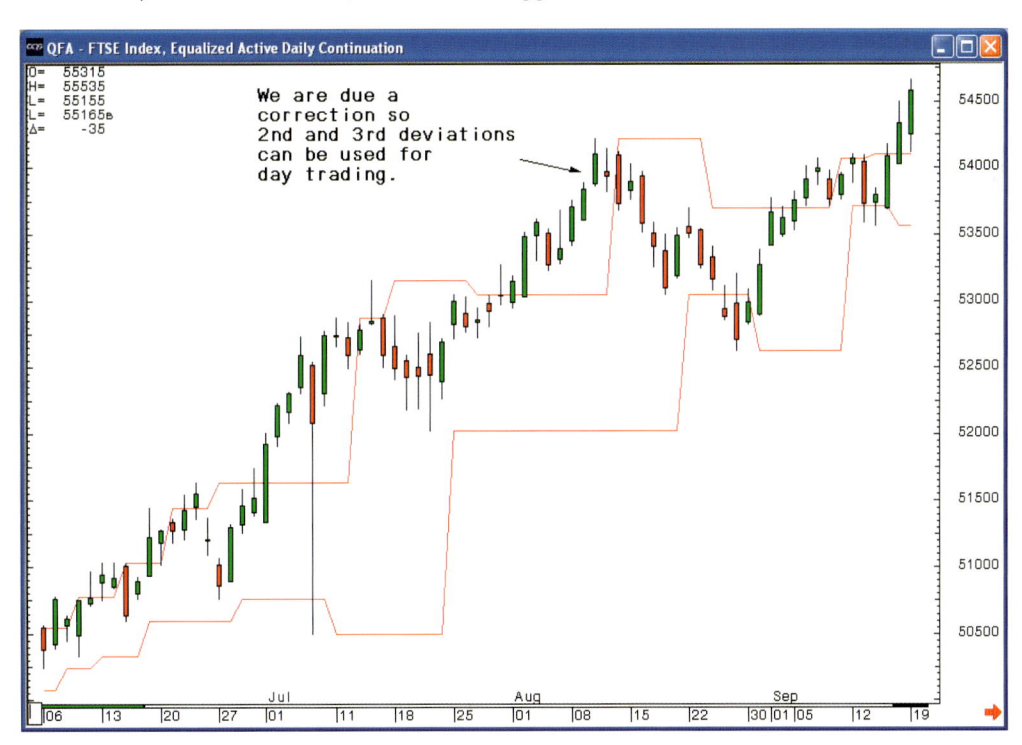

Figure 32:
Once above Hi Peak for a certain number of bars the time bands can be referenced.

TRADING TIME: New Methods in Technical Analysis

Time Bands linked with Peak

One method to look for corrections is to reference the upper deviation levels as potential points to place trades; moves higher should be repelled as price is over extended (see figs. 33 and 33a).

Figure 33:
The deviation bands mark extremes in the trend

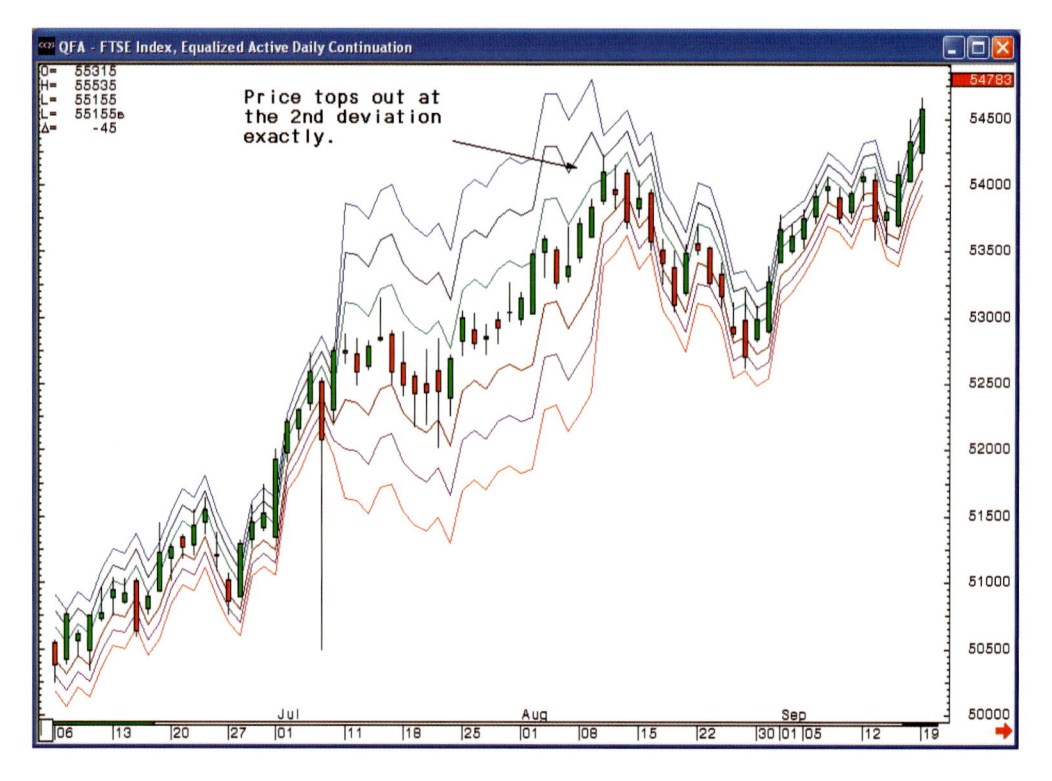

Figure 33a:
A very strong trend

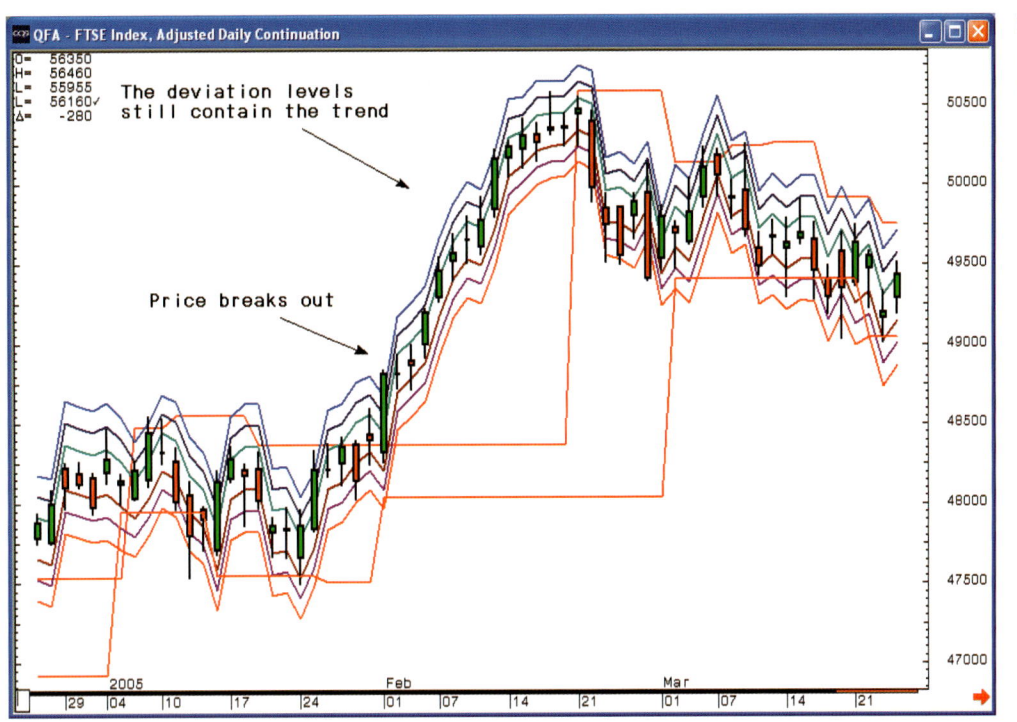

Figure 34:
Time Deviation Bands still mark daily extremes

Day Trader - Market Profile® in a corrective phase

Whilst this information is useful in understanding trend, it is also invaluable for the day trader in determining what the bias for any particular day is within the bigger picture. Once in a corrective pattern price rarely exhibits successful initiative behaviour with the previous strong trend. Responsive patterns with the trend should be more profitable. Responsive patterns against the strong trend can also be profitable.

The strong trend in the FTSE went 9 bars beyond the 6-bar rule. Whilst superficially the trend is strong, the daily chart analysis of those days shows that of 6 days where single letter initiative bullish setups occurred, no fewer than 5 failed and would have resulted in losses. This highlights the frustration a trend follower can endure if not fully aware of what type of day can be expected, no coherent plan is possible.

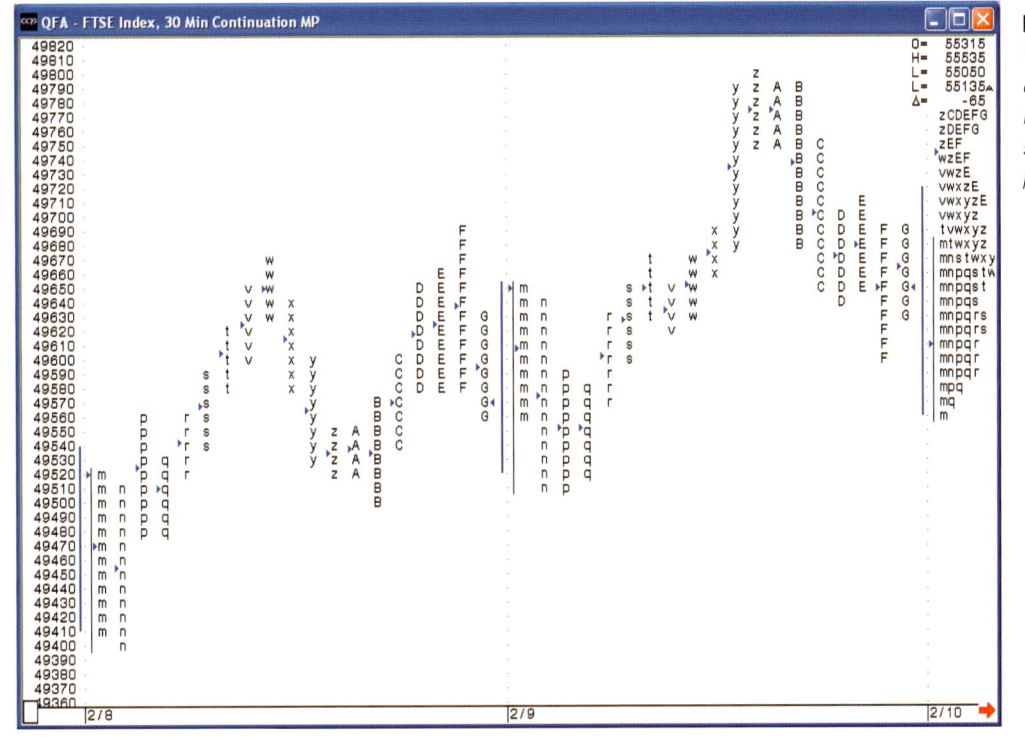

Figure 35:
When overextended intraday rallies still can't develop properly

189

Peak and Step theory

Hi Count / Lo Count

The pattern between trend and Peak also helps to understand both Stochastic Steps and RSI steps. Strong patterns within Peak often occur at the beginning of trends. Therefore, if the strong trend in Peak is confirmed by the Stochastic Steps moving beyond 65 bars, this is further indication that a major trend could be beginning.

A new trend

This leads us onto how the Low Peak can also behave at the beginning of a new up trend. If Low Peak has not changed in value for 15 bars, then this also confirms that we are in a strong trend. The mere fact that price has not managed to make a 5-bar swing low tells us that corrections are shallow, short-lived and the market is dominated by long-term players raising their perception of what fair value is. In a similar vein, but with different thresholds, if price has held above the Hi Peak level for 6 bars, this also indicates a strong trend that is due a correction. Often Lo Peak at 15 and Hi Peak at 6 coincide and connect with deviation studies to highlight not only short-term exhaustion points, but also levels where the correction should find support.

Therefore, although the studies Hi Peak and Lo Peak simply record the number of bars between changes in Peak levels, they provide a visualisation of trend strength and anticipate corrective periods.

Bund rally - a case study

Analysis of the Bund rally (see fig. 36) from March to June highlights some of the points.

The first impulse higher to point **A** sees value hold above the Hi Peak for 8 bars. More significantly this coincides with the Lo Peak study moving above 15 bars. This indicates a very strong trend, which could correct at any time. The second impulse at point **B** lasts for 6 bars above Hi Peak before a correction appears. Finally at point **C** another strong impulse takes place, which lasts for 8 bars. However, by this time the trend is 65 bars in length and represents one normal trend-cycle price, then moves sideways until the next trend.

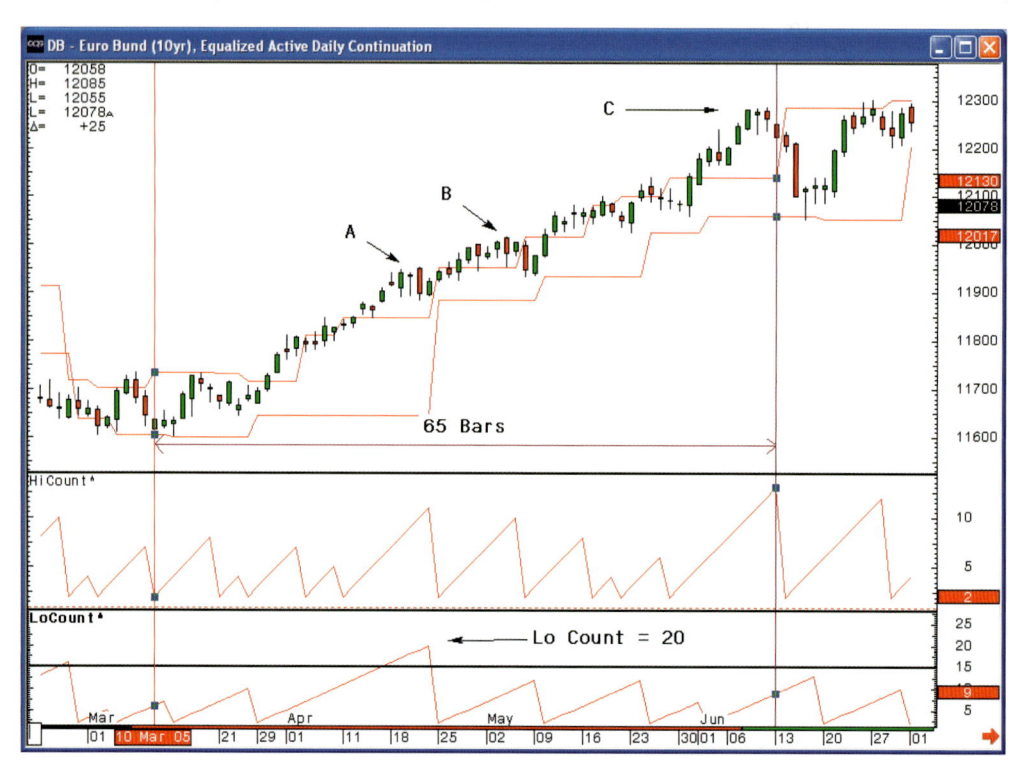

Figure 36:
Cycle length

Time Bands and Peak

A different way of interpreting the Time Bands

Placing the deviation study on the chart (see fig. 37) references the low-risk points for entering with the trend and also, the short-term exhaustion points for the day trader. At point **A**, Lo Count has flagged a strong trend at 15+. With a correction due the 1st and 2nd standard deviations above are exhaustive points and the 2nd and 3rd standard deviations beneath provide an opportunity to re-enter the trend.

To re-iterate, if a correction is due via Peak then the 2nd and 3rd deviation points are used. Any close beyond the 3rd deviation down is a warning that a deeper correction is forming and possibly a change in trend. The next 4 bars subsequent to point **A**, show price topping out at the 1st and 2nd deviations up and holding the 2nd and 3rd deviations down.

At point **B**, once again price is above Hi Peak for 6 bars. Two bars have lows at the 3rd deviation and the middle bar between **B** and **C** tops out at the 1st deviation. Once price closes at **C** the Hi Peak value jumps up and now price is within the High and Low Peak bands. This means that the market now has an opportunity to restart the trend.

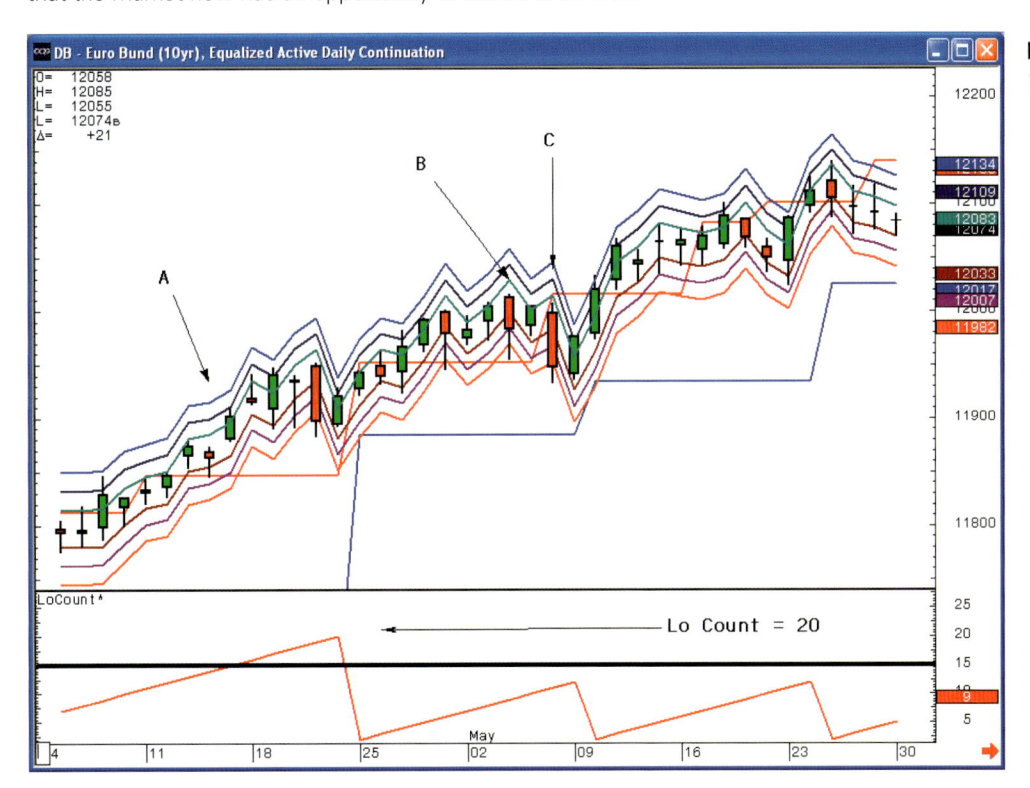

Figure 37: *Time Bands*

Market Profile®

15 April is the point where Lo Count reaches 15, thus indicating a strong trend. Let's see how the Market Profile® charts developed. Remember at this point only:

1. **Well-defined sell signals can be taken intraday, especially if combined with deviation levels with risk tightly calculated.**
2. **Buy signals can still be engaged fully unless beyond the 6-bar rule on Hi Peak.**
3. **In which case only responsive buy signals can be taken.**

TRADING TIME: New Methods in Technical Analysis

The first trading day after 15 April 2005 (see fig. 38) does not provide an opportunity as a gap higher fails to confirm with single letter prints above the initial balance. In fact, responsive behaviour in **s** signals a short-term exhaustion point. Analysis of the deviation levels shows that the 1st standard deviation was at 120.29 (see fig. 40), which is the high in **n** and close to the high in **s**. Drilling down still further reveals that on the 30-minute time bands **n** reached its 3rd standard deviation up and the 2nd deviation in **s** (see fig. 40). Both can be construed as exhaustion points when the trader is looking for corrections against a trend. One key difference between the length of the review period on historical and intraday charts needs to be remembered. As I mentioned in the first chapter, the review is 100 bars on a daily basis but only 22 on intraday charts. This roughly equates to one month of data and connects with the theory that distributions on bond markets can be analysed on a monthly basis starting with the unemployment report.

Figure 38:
False breakouts higher are capped by the Bands when Hi Peak is overextended

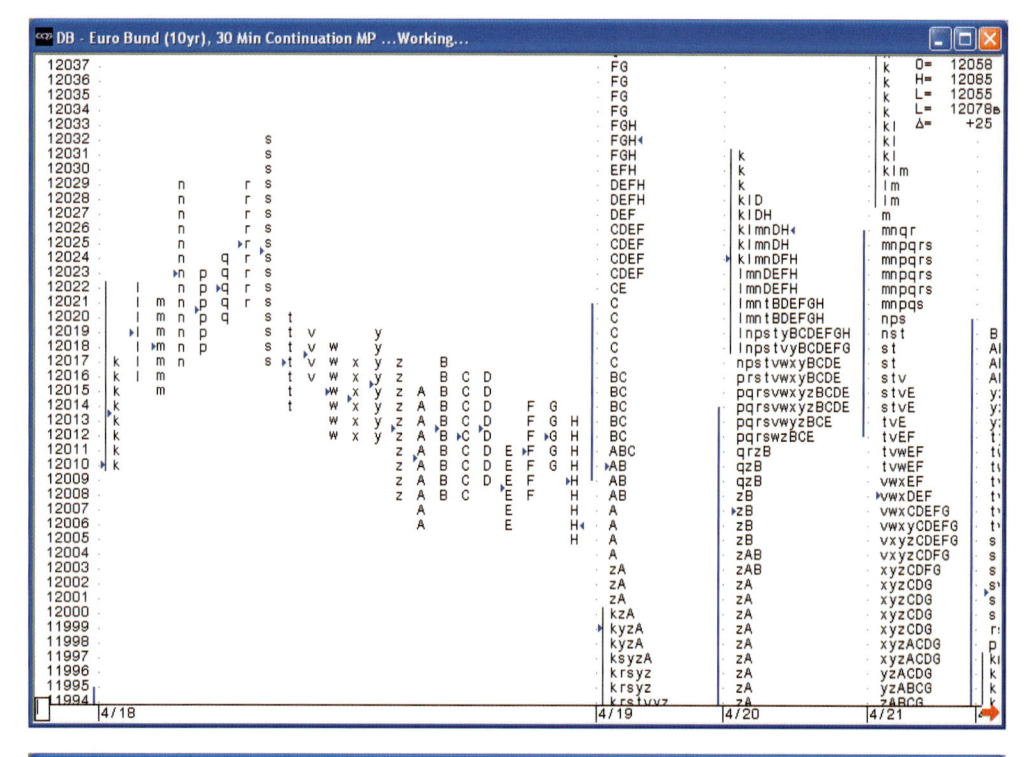

Figure 39:
A strong trend is flagged by Lo Count

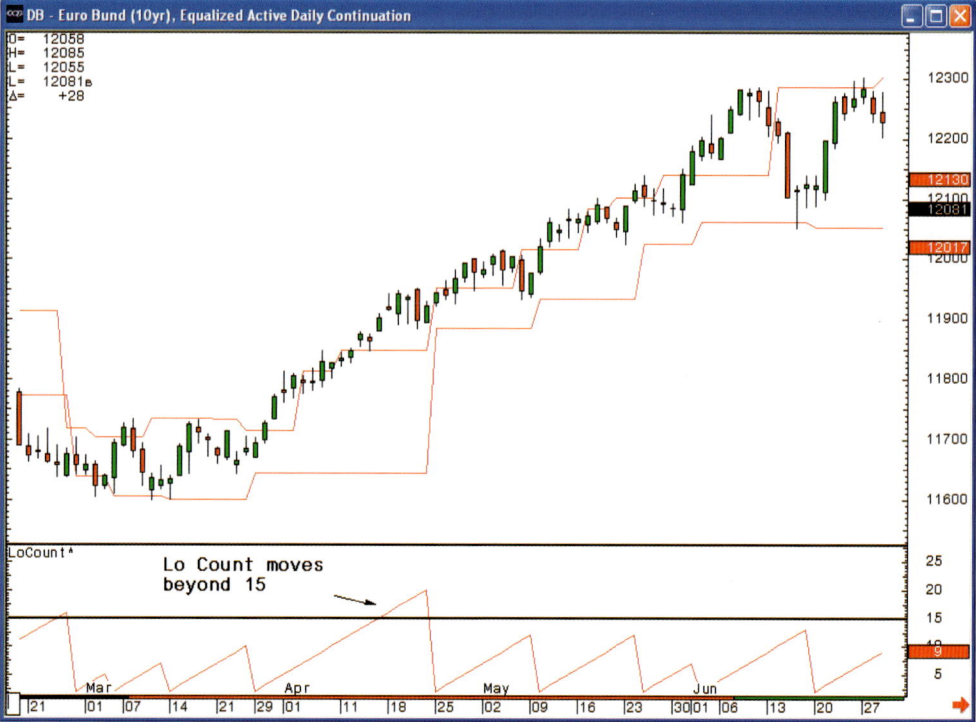

192

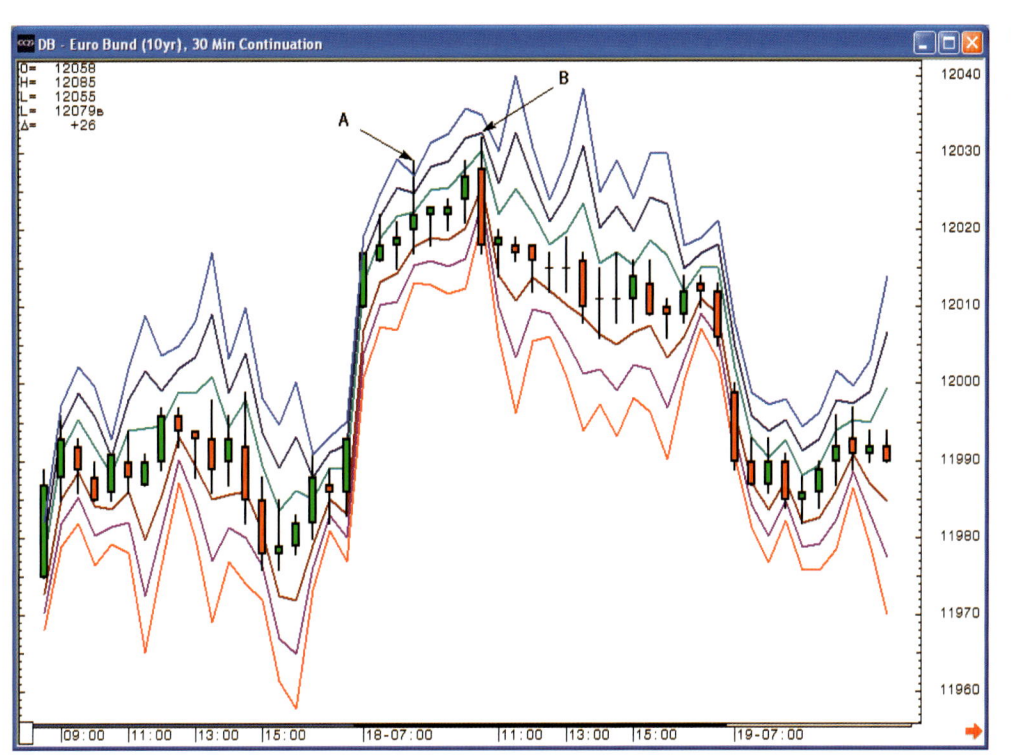

Figure 40:
Time Bands mark the extremes on a 30-min chart

The following day sees the true strength of the trend emerge (see fig. 41). Price gaps down and opens up the potential for an Island Reversal. Island Reversals on financials are powerful but extremely rare. As with most gap-based patterns it's easy to see only the ones that work. Price edges lower, fails to build confirmation and holds the support point of the value area low from two days previous to the tick. It is easy to say that you could have bought there, but with the potential for an Island Reversal and the lack of any obvious stop out point that is close this means that buying would have been highly dangerous. However, for the short-term trader the low is one standard deviation down on the daily whilst the 30-minute bars reveal that in spite of the apparent weakness in the market, price never moves below the 2nd standard deviation down apart from the opening bar. By the afternoon we have single letters confirmed in **A**, by the end of **B,** and we have filled and overcome the gap. Prior to that, the **y** letter in the Market Profile® which is flagged

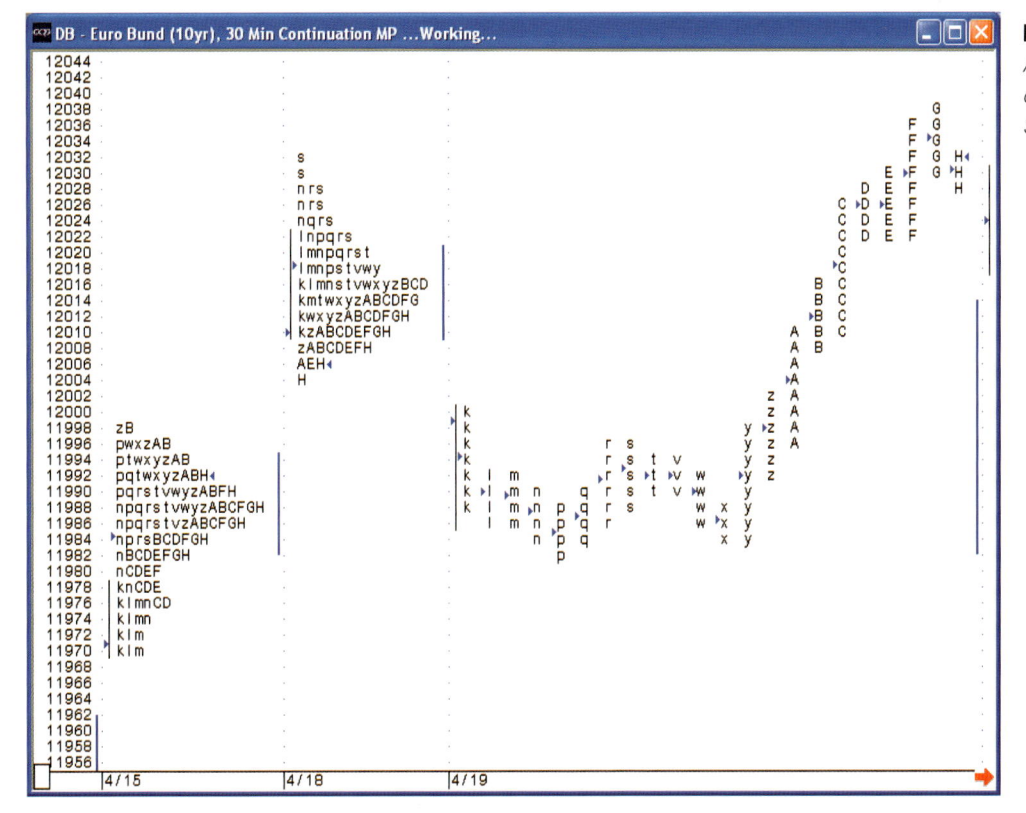

Figure 41:
A trend day confirmed by Steps

as point **A** on the deviation chart (see fig. 42) closes directly on the 3rd standard deviation up. The lack of reaction within that bar to the 3rd standard deviation level suggests that a new impulse higher is beginning. Armed with the knowledge of the trend's strength via the Stochastic Steps as referenced in that chapter, we see that price extends higher and closes on the highs.

Figure 42:
The trend shifts as the single print is confirmed by the Time Bands

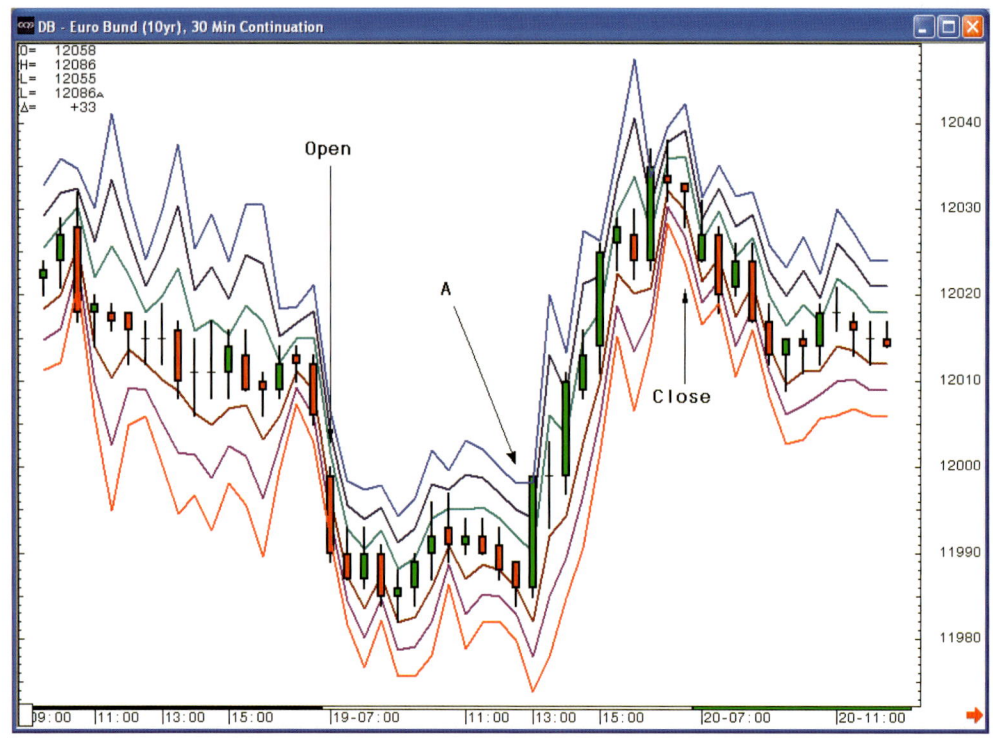

Treasury Bonds

Analysis of the Treasury Bonds on the same day confirms the bullish short-term picture (see fig. 43). We have responsive buying in **y** and by the end of **B** we have single letter prints in **A**.

Figure 43:
Single prints

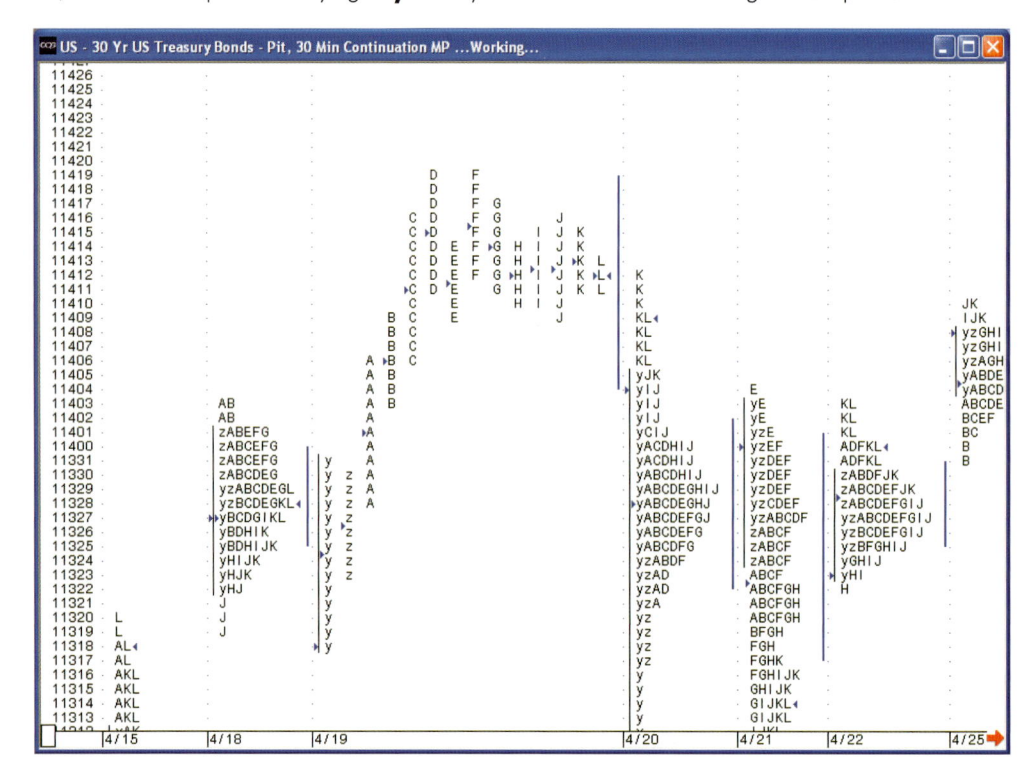

Bunds

Returning to the Bund (see fig. 44) the following day sees some wild action. Whilst this was day 6 above Hi Peak, opportunities to sell did not appear. Price edges lower throughout the morning and a spike lower in **z** takes place after the economic number is released. However, the move is not confirmed by the price action in **A**. Price in **z** does collapse to the confluence of value area lows from 19 April and 15 April. This low coincides with the 2nd standard deviation down level on the daily chart (see fig 45), whilst analysis of the 30-minute chart shows a rejection of a move below the 3rd standard deviation low (see fig. 46). Price holds and then rallies all the way back up for just a small loss on the day.

This rejection of value is another sign of a strong underlying trend. This highlights the fact that, while it appears price may collapse, with the strength of the trend already quantified, combined with knowledge that we are in a corrective phase to that trend, exact levels of support can be built and traded. This has even more power when Stochastic Steps are indicating a strong trend as well.

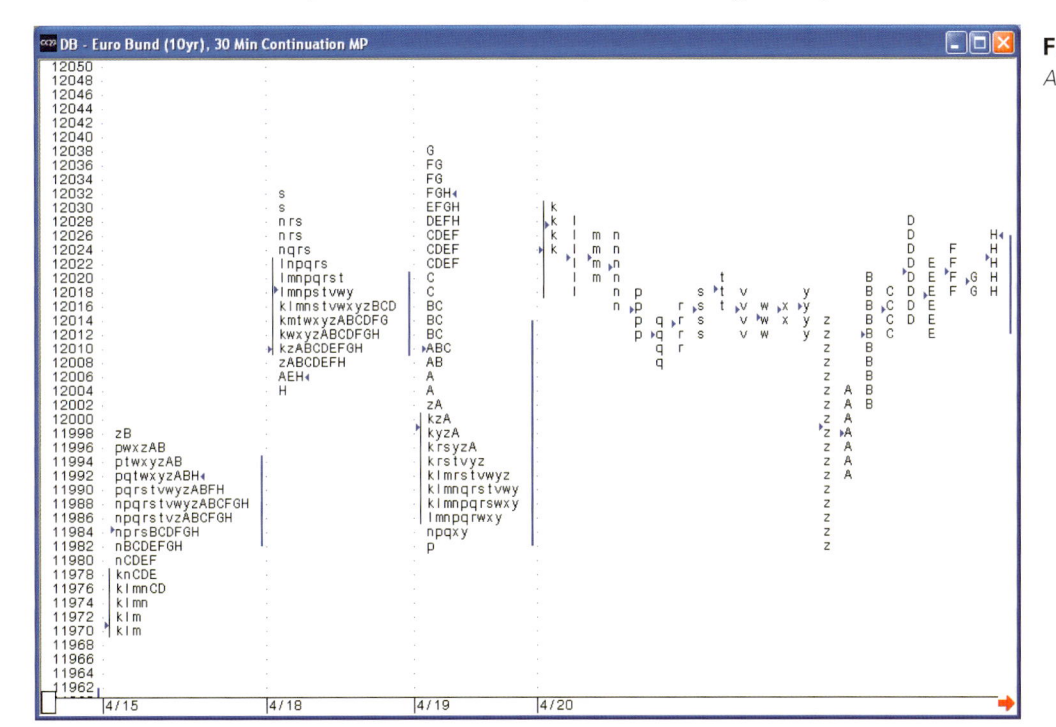

Figure 44:
A false break in **z**

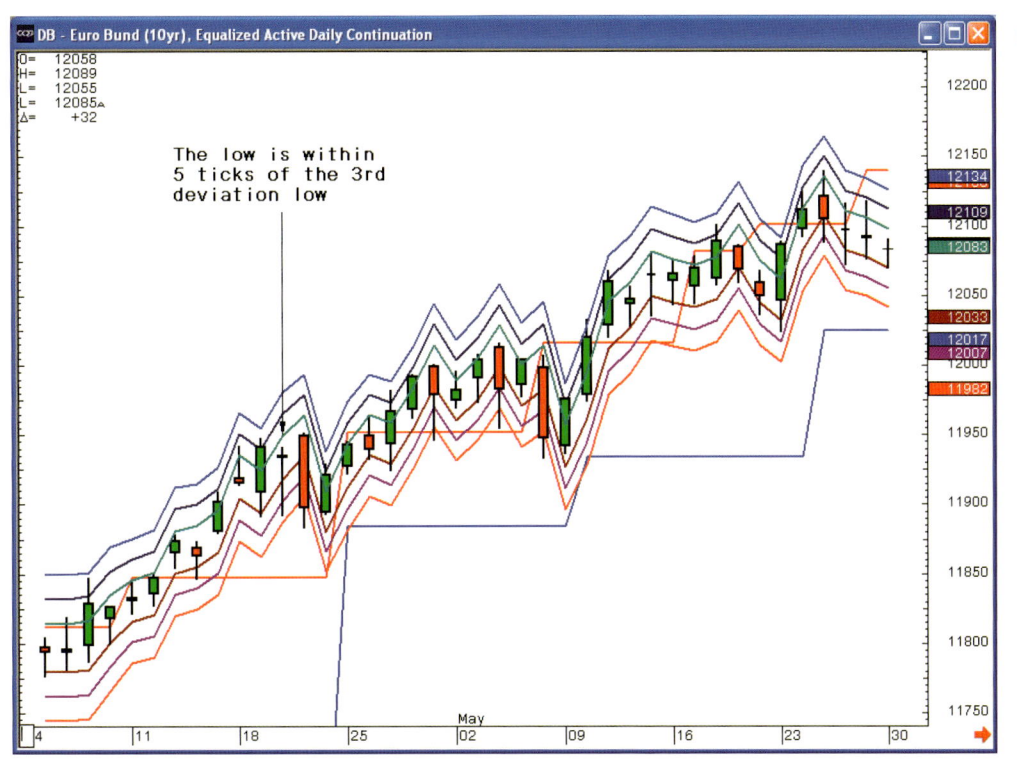

Figure 45:
Time Bands

Figure 46:
Time Bands 30 minutes

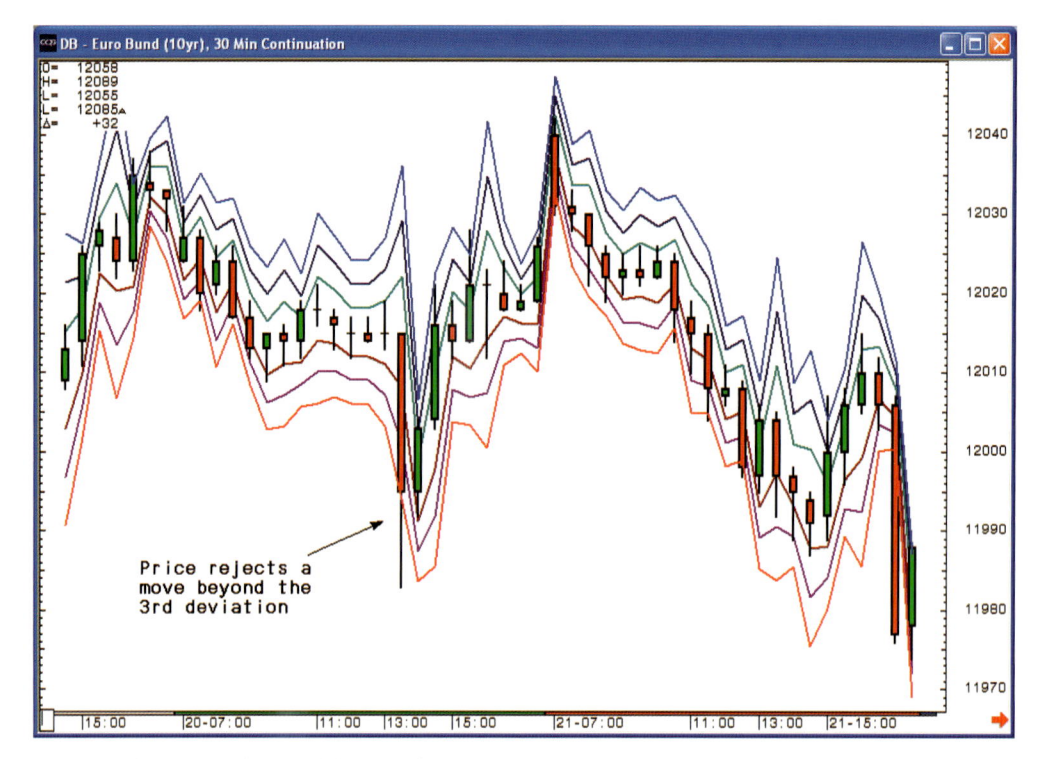

21 April sees another wild day (see fig. 47) it is the 7th day beyond the Hi Peak, which allows sell signals to be taken in spite of the strong underlying trend. Responsive behaviour on the gap up is followed up by initiative behaviour in **m**. This appears to be bearish but price has not hit its 1st standard deviation up on the daily (see fig. 48). The 5-day profile has considerable support at the Control Point at 120.18 to 120.16; this halts the move lower early in the day. Once this area is overcome price slides down to the next major area, which is the confluence of value area low, a ledge and another control from 119.92 to 119.88. Price bounces but a late slump sees this level broken and, in addition, a brief slump through the 3rd standard deviation low at 119.83 takes place (see fig. 48).

The fact that the fall was into the close and prices held above the 119.83 level with a low at 119.88 suggests short-term sellers and a false weak close (see fig. 49). This, however, requires confirmation the following day. This is done by looking at the opening and the subsequent early movements. Therefore the support from 119.92 to 119.88 and at 119.83 provided a profit-taking point for day-trading shorts and an entry for strategic longs. They would have had a problematic overnight position, though.

Figure 47:
Price closes at a key support

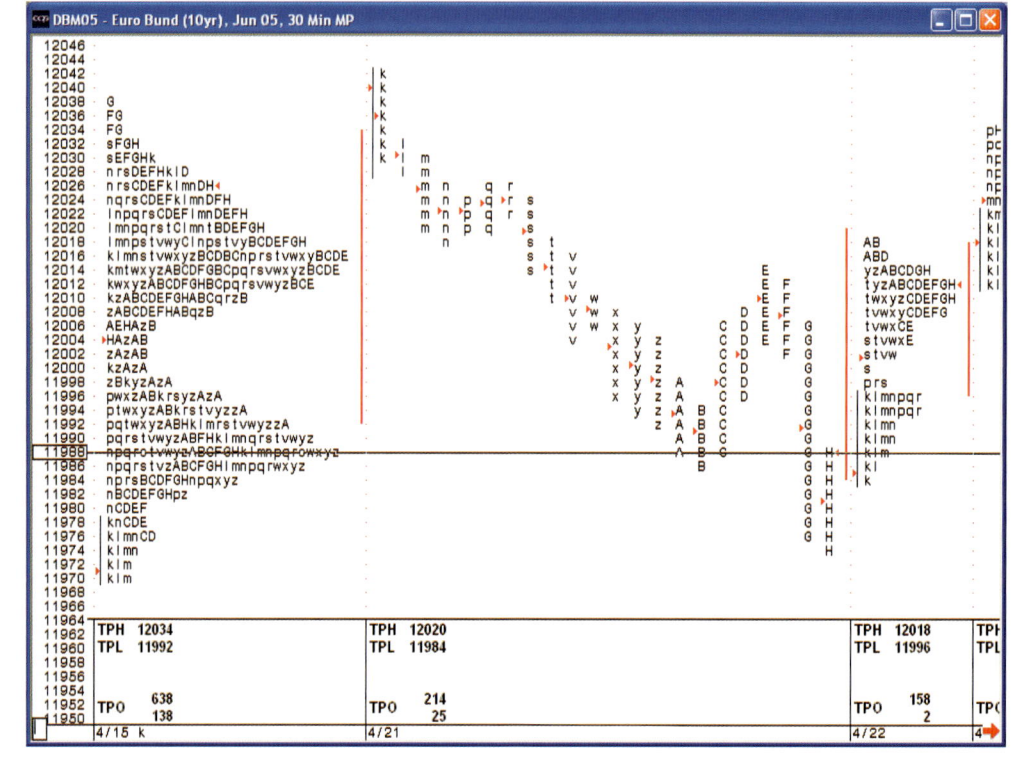

196

Peak

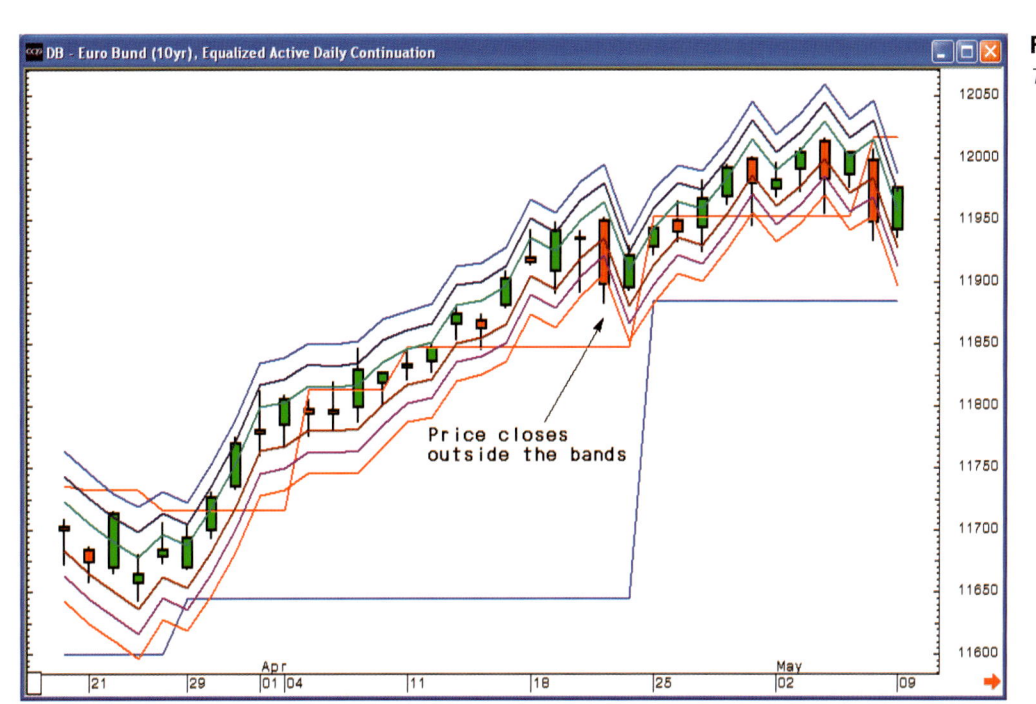

Figure 48:
Time Bands Daily

Price closes outside the bands

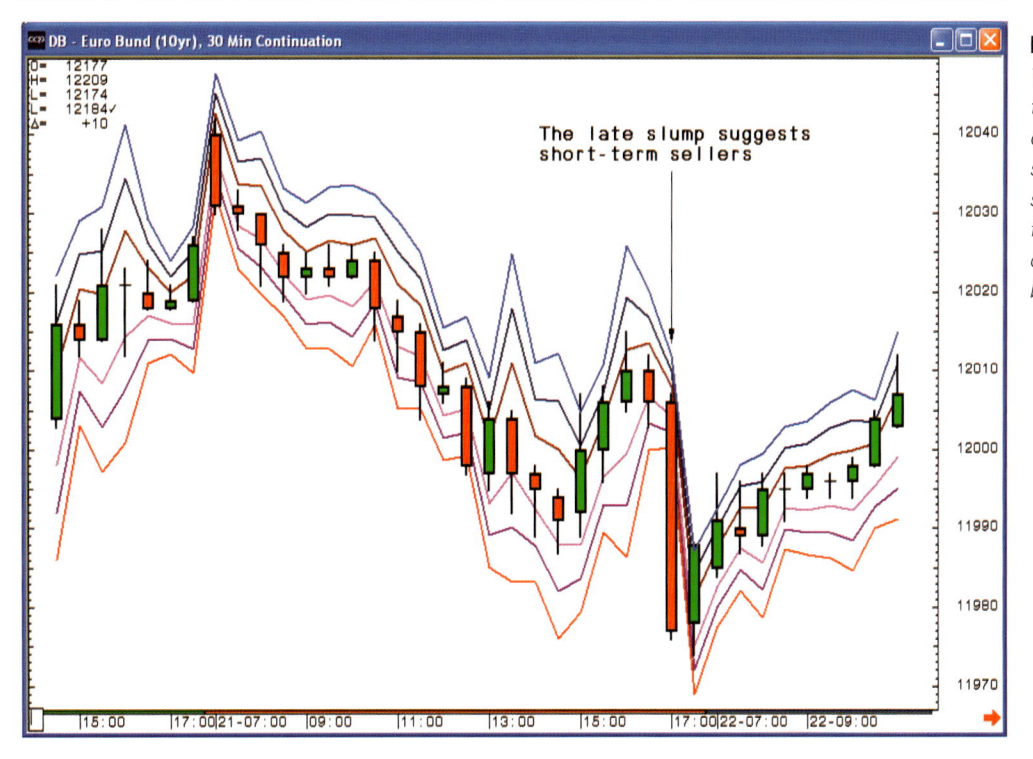

Figure 49:
The time of day that the last bar created suggests short-term sellers and a false close outside the daily bands.

The late slump suggests short-term sellers

TRADING TIME: New Methods in Technical Analysis

22 April brings its reward. As the weak close is rejected we see initiative behaviour in **k** and then a single letter in **s** (see fig. 50). Price holds the higher value for the entire day. The dominant trend is reasserting itself. The 30-minute deviations confirm with only one close below the 1st standard deviation low all day as was shown in the Stochastic Steps chapter. Analysis of the 60-minute sees an initial failure at the 3rd standard deviation up but price never closes below the 1st deviation low (see fig 51).

Figure 50
Rejection of a weak close caused by short-term traders

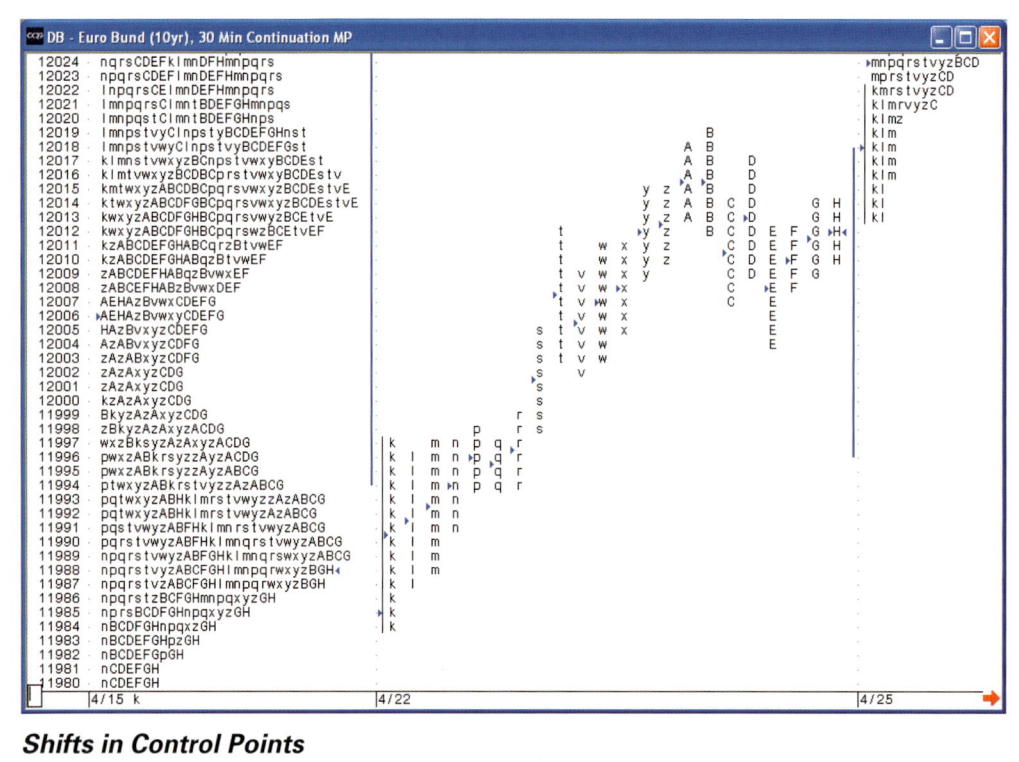

Shifts in Control Points

The same day sees another key moment. Just after the opening 22 April in **m** control moves lower in the current distribution (see fig. 50). This is a trigger and timing point for the next trend. Price has already rejected the previous day's weak close but it is two hours later at **s** that the market begins its trend back up.

The false close is confirmed and a strong rally occurs 22 and 23 April. Control shifts and creates a timing point for trending behaviour.

Figure 51:
The bands display a strong trend all day

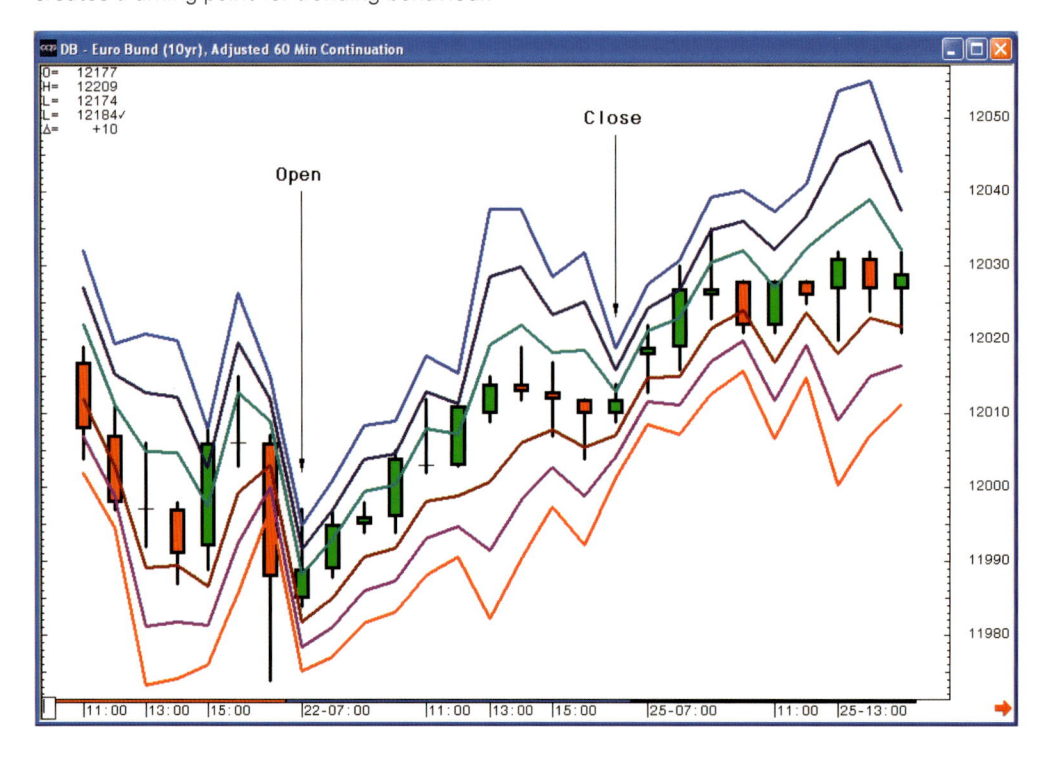

Peak

25 April sees an inability to trend, posting single prints and a failed trade in **n** (see fig. 52). Both days' highs are directly at the 1st deviation up (see Fig. 53).

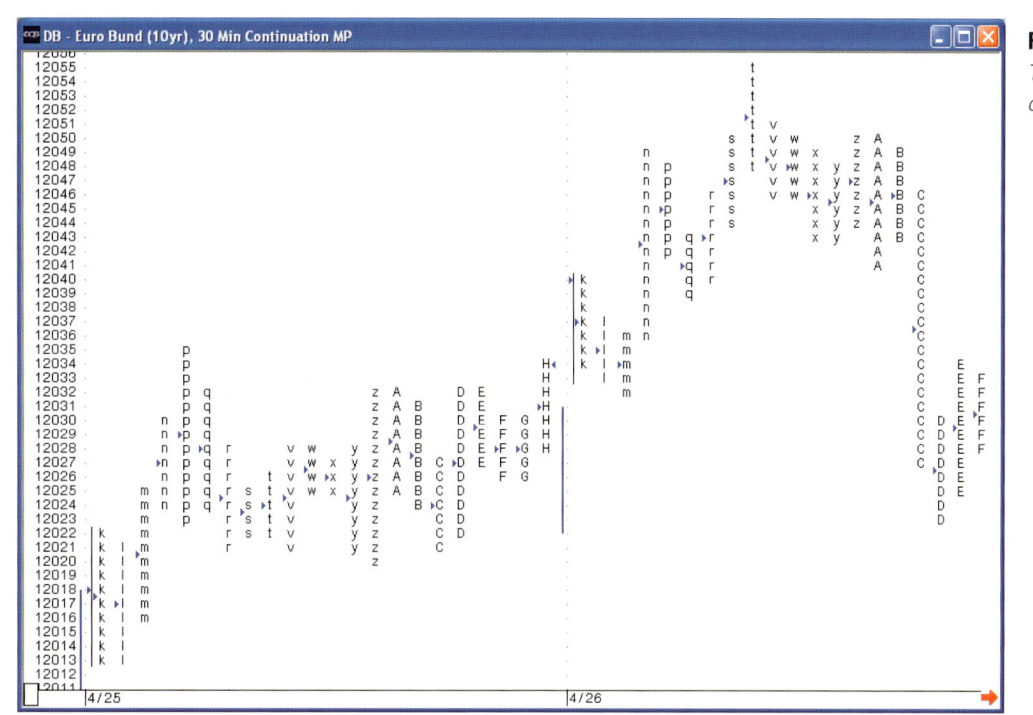

Figure 52:
Trends fail to develop

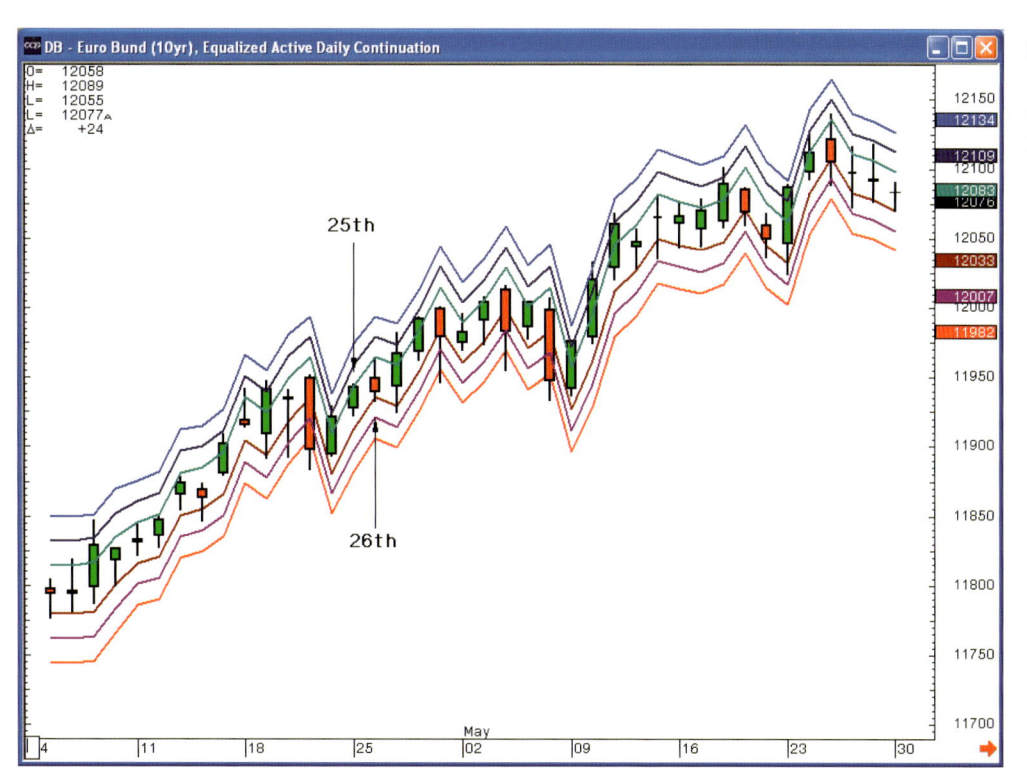

Figure 53:
Time Bands stay within the first limits

27 April sees responsive behaviour in **k** that creates a short-term slide lower (see fig. 55). However, price is now beneath the Hi Peak level, meaning the trend can now restart (see fig 54). The move lower bottoms out at the 1st standard deviation on the daily, which coincides with the low being at the 3rd standard deviation down on the 30-minute (see fig. 56). This provides a perfect timing point for all players provided that they are prepared to ride the risk through the economic numbers coming out later the same day. Numbers are released in the **z** period and price soars (see fig. 55). Price rallies to 120.72 and closes at 120.58.

Figure 54:
The correction is over. The trend can restart

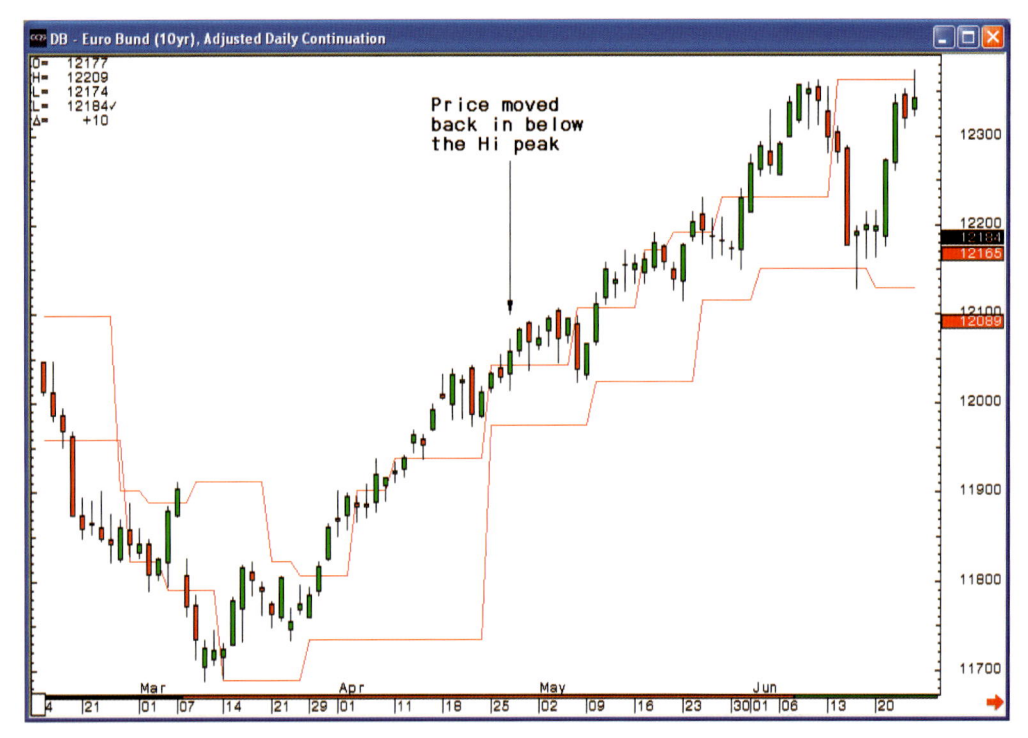

Figure 55:
Single prints in z

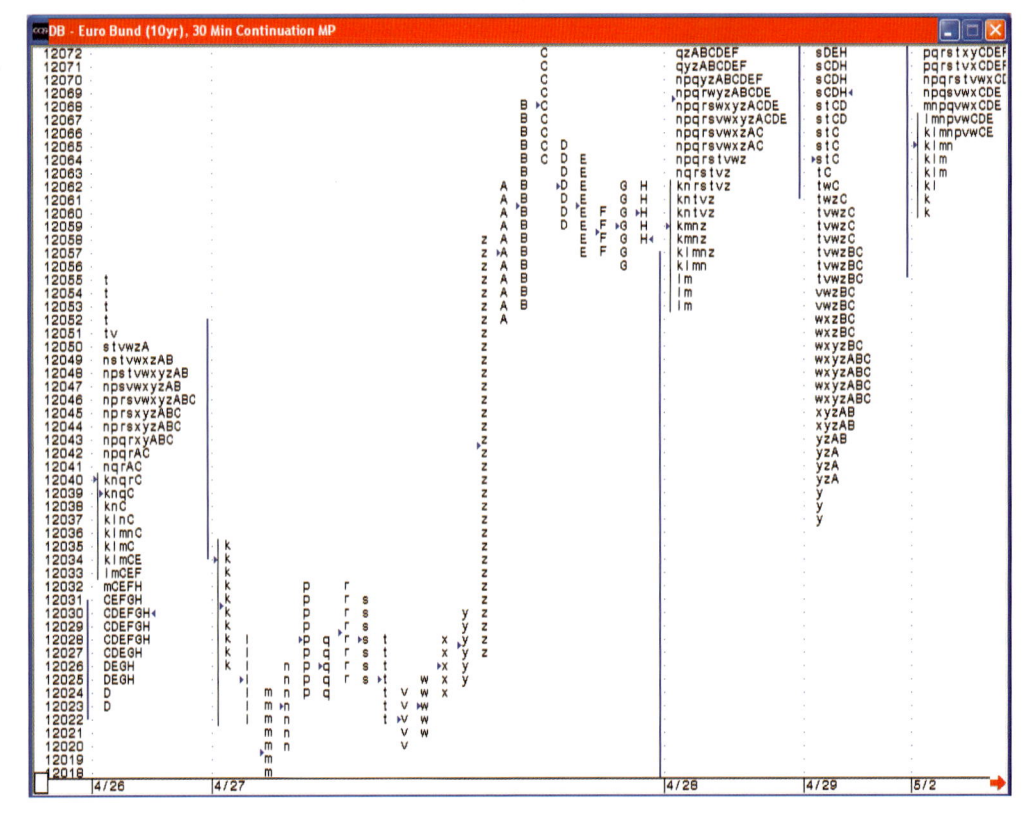

Figure 56:
Historical bands coincide with an intraday extreme

Vacuum Points

The next two days (see fig. 57) show classic vacuum trading. 28 April 2005 prices hold just above the beginning of the vacuum from the day before presenting a low risk entry on the opening. The aggressive trader could have pyramided on single prints in **n**. This secondary trade is stopped out in **t** as the single letter is filled. Analysis of the wild spike in **z** on the 1-minute chart shows price went down first. The initial buy on the opening is closed at the end of the day.

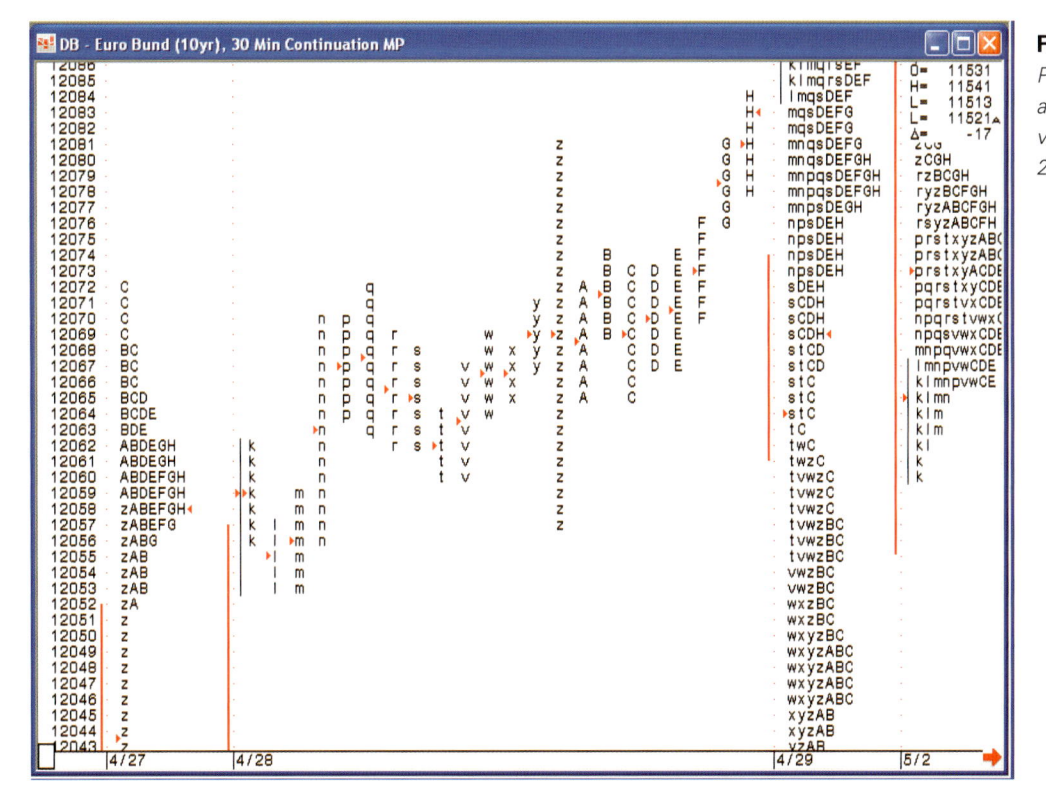

Figure 57:
Price holds just above the vacuum of 27 April

TRADING TIME: New Methods in Technical Analysis

The following day sees further wild gyrations (see fig. 58). The previous close saw a late rally, which suggests short-term buyers are positioning themselves. The opening confirms as the gap higher is repelled and there is a single **m**. Here the knowledge that we are in a strong up trend is invaluable as various opportunities present themselves against ill-informed sellers of whom only the most nimble would come out unscathed. A further single letter in **s** does succeed. A partial or complete profit could have been taken at the top of the vacuum in **v** at 120.50 against the top of **z** from 27 April 2005. Strategic players could also have engaged with a tight stop. However, once price enters the vacuum' it moves directly to the other side in **y** and bottoms out perfectly, providing a fresh opportunity for sellers to take profits and buyers to come into the market.

By the time price reaches the bottom of the vacuum in **y** we are just below the 3rd standard deviation low on the daily chart (see fig. 60). The 30-minute bands suddenly show a departure from 2 of the bars (**A** and **B**) that also hit the 3rd standard deviation (see fig. 59). They both closed below the 3rd standard deviation indicating a strong downtrend before the 3rd standard deviation, daily low combines with the 30-minute 3rd standard deviation low (**C**). Price then rallies sharply into the close. This day highlights how aggressive day traders need to be able to switch positions swiftly.

Figure 58:
Vacuums and historical bands connect

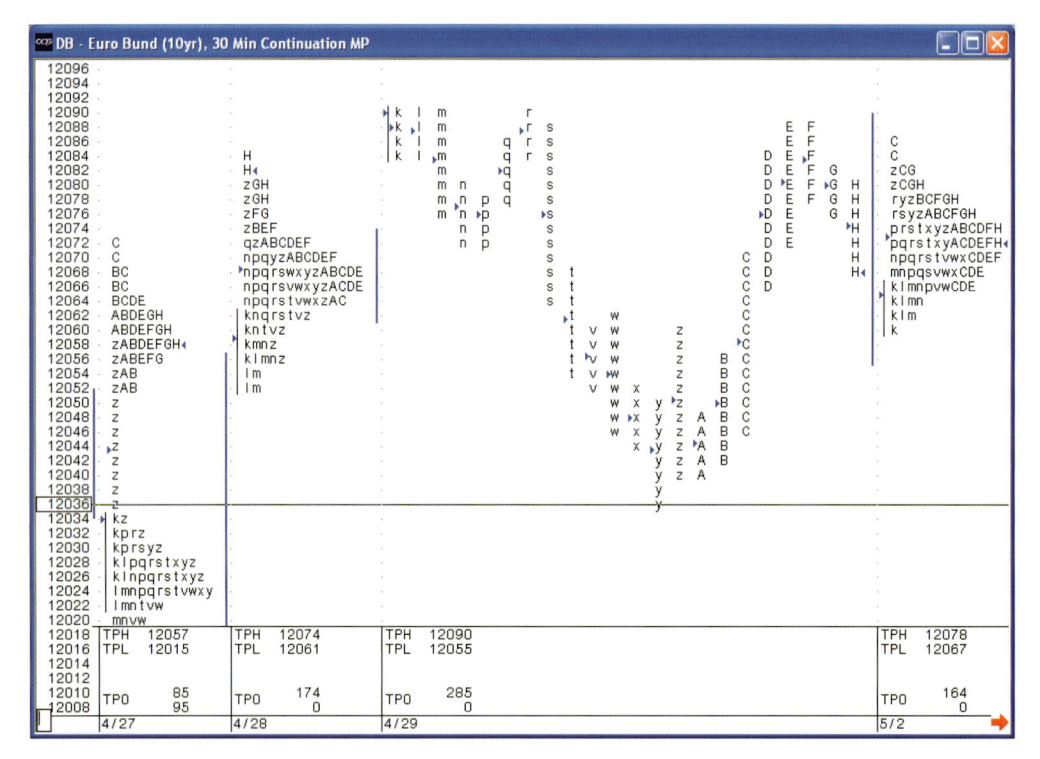

Figure 59:
*The low of the day is also an extreme for the time of day. It coincides with the vacuum low from the day before.
A powerful support point.*

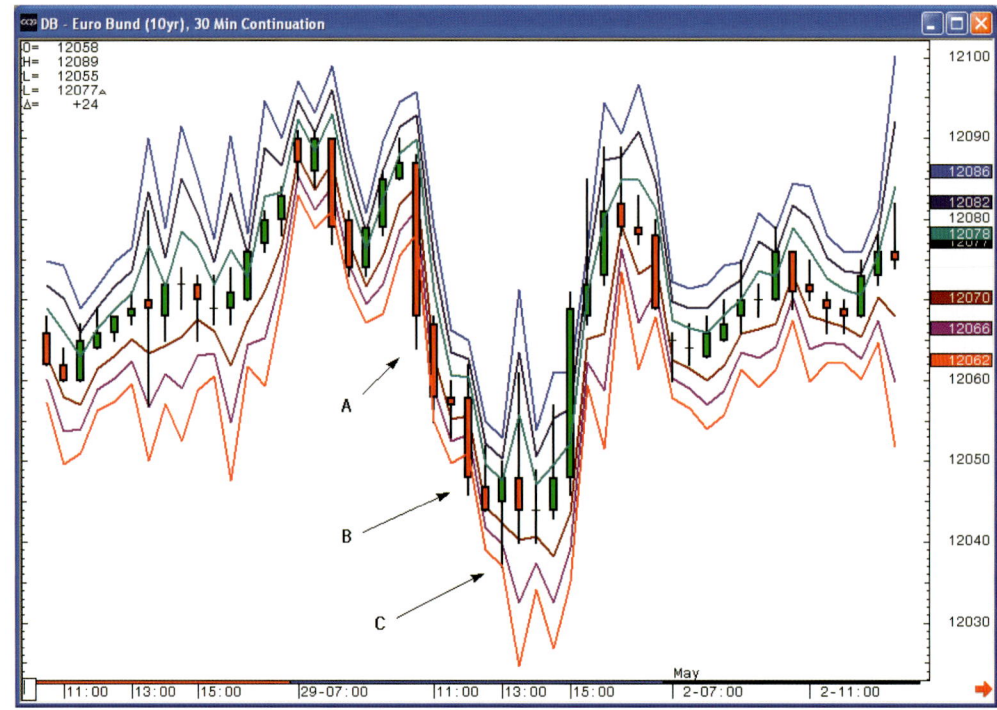

Peak

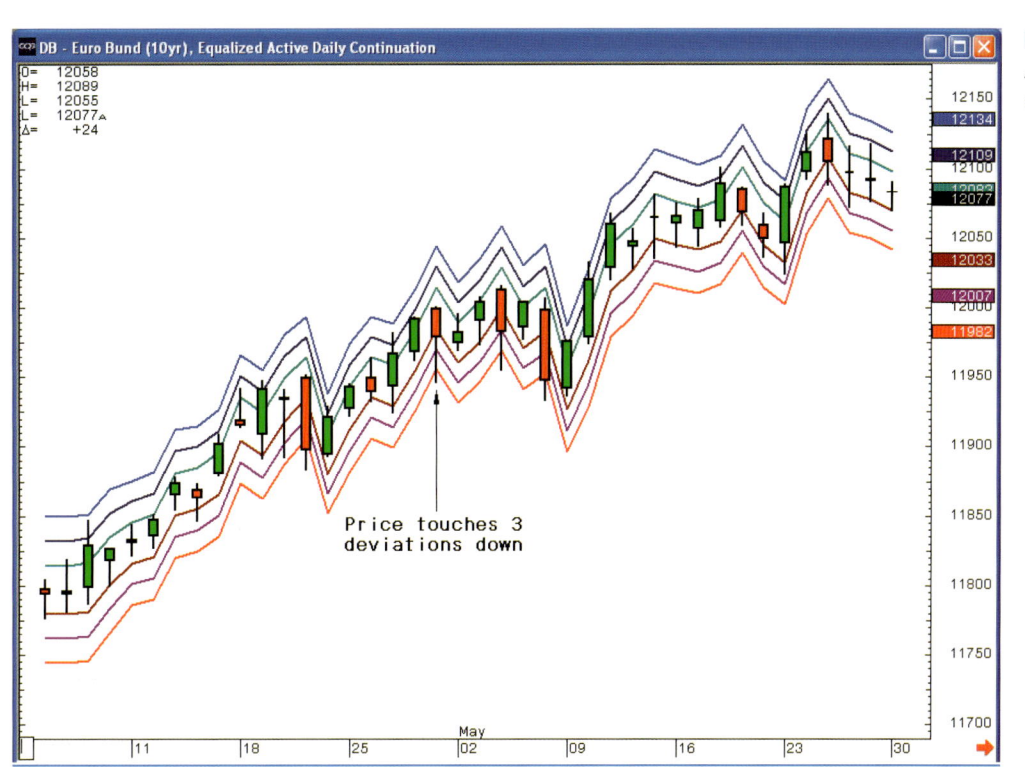

Figure 60:
An historical extreme

3 May is another example of the importance of understanding the strength of a trend (see fig. 61). Responsive behaviour on the opening creates a single **l** but the pattern fails. The low in **m** is the 1st standard deviation down on the daily chart and price is also at its 3rd standard deviation down on the 30-minute (see fig. 62). By the end of the **q** period the responsive behaviour has been negated, as the single letters in **l** have been filled. The support that was found at the lows in **m** at the 30-minute and daily deviation levels adds weight to the thought that the move lower was false. Later a trend begins in the key **z** period but tops out perfectly at the 1st standard deviation up level.

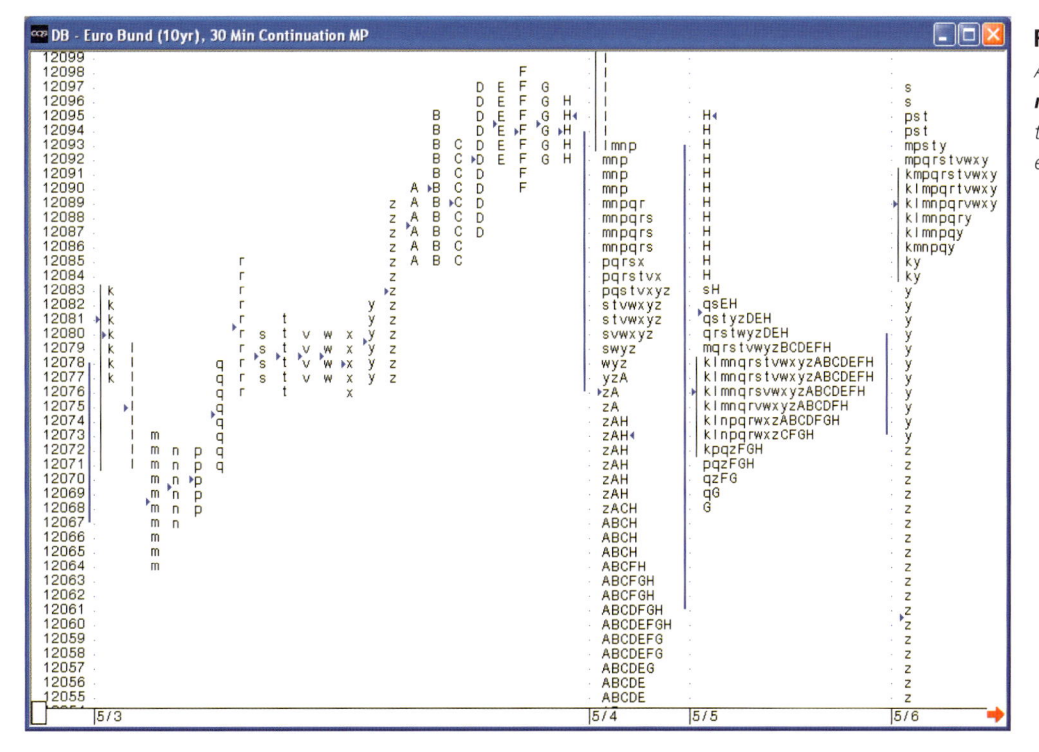

Figure 61:
*A false break in **m** connects with time-based extremes*

203

Figure 62:
A time of day-based extreme

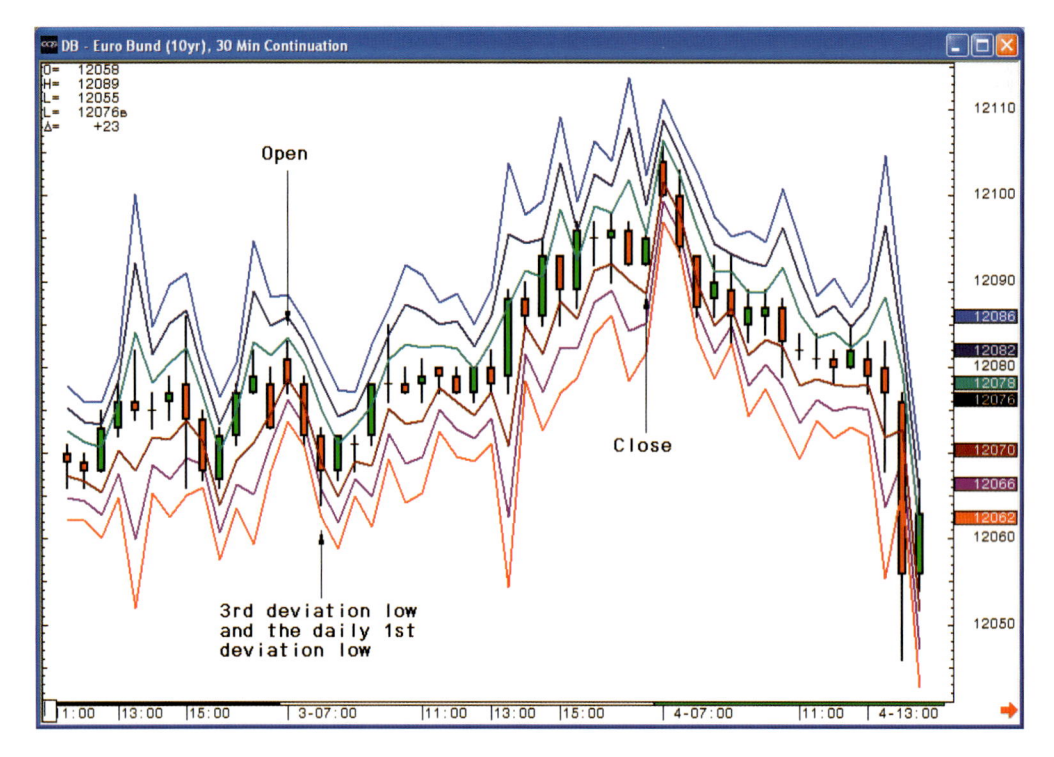

4 May shows on the daily peak chart (see fig. 65) that we have now spent six days above the Hi Peak which now indicates a corrective period is due. This means that more aggressive trades can be taken on the short side and more care must be taken with building long positions.

A bearish pattern appears on the opening and this one is successful (see fig. 63). Single letters follow responsive selling in the initial balance. Once again the movement in **Z** sets the scene for the afternoon trend. Following the dip in **A**, the low is set at the 3rd standard deviation down on the daily providing both a profit-taking point for shorts and a potential long position (see fig. 64). Price squeezes into the close.

Figure 63:
*Letter **A** low connects with the historical extreme on the Time-bands*

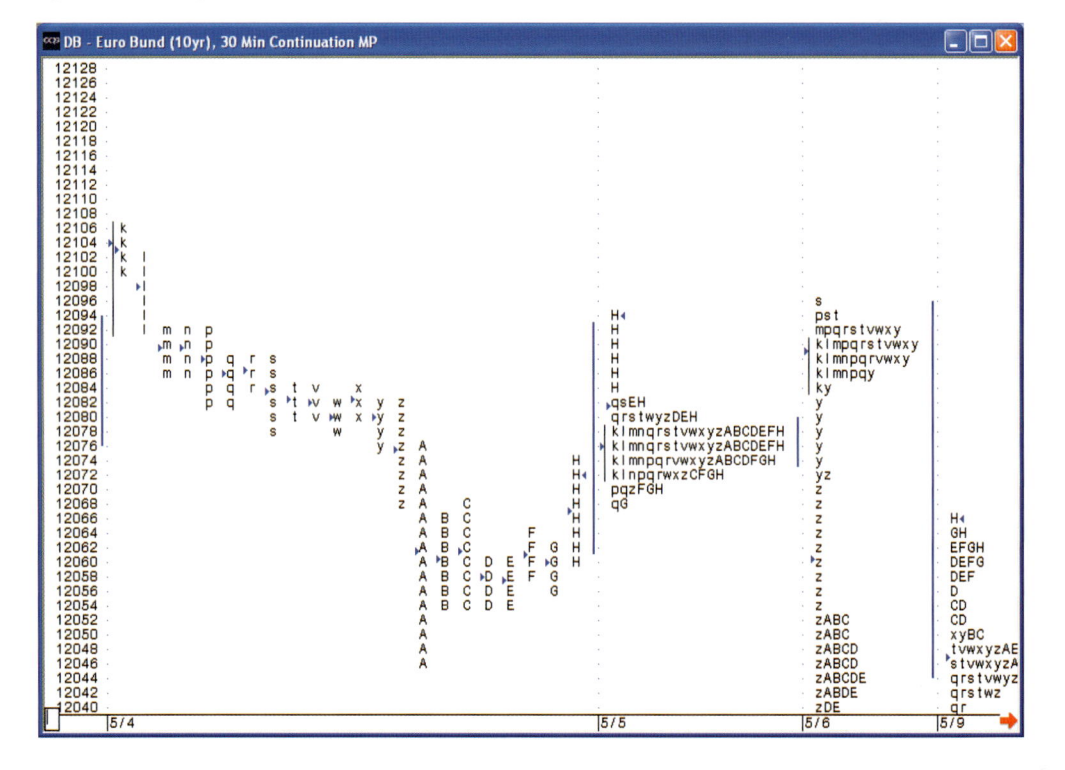

Peak

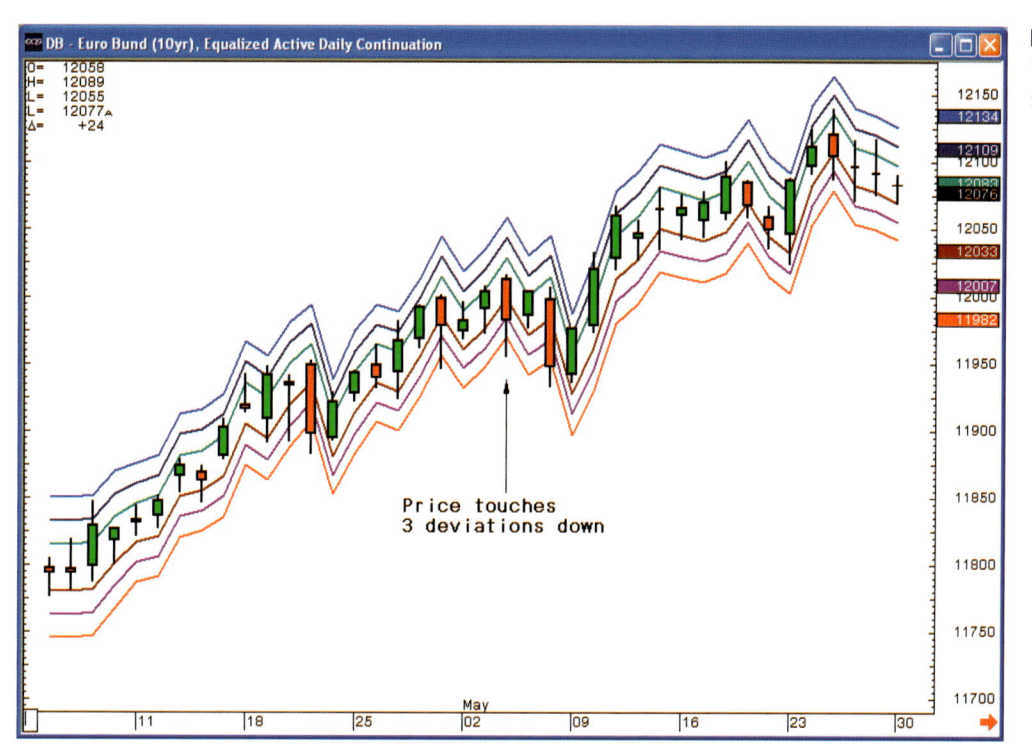

Figure 64:
Time Bands on the daily

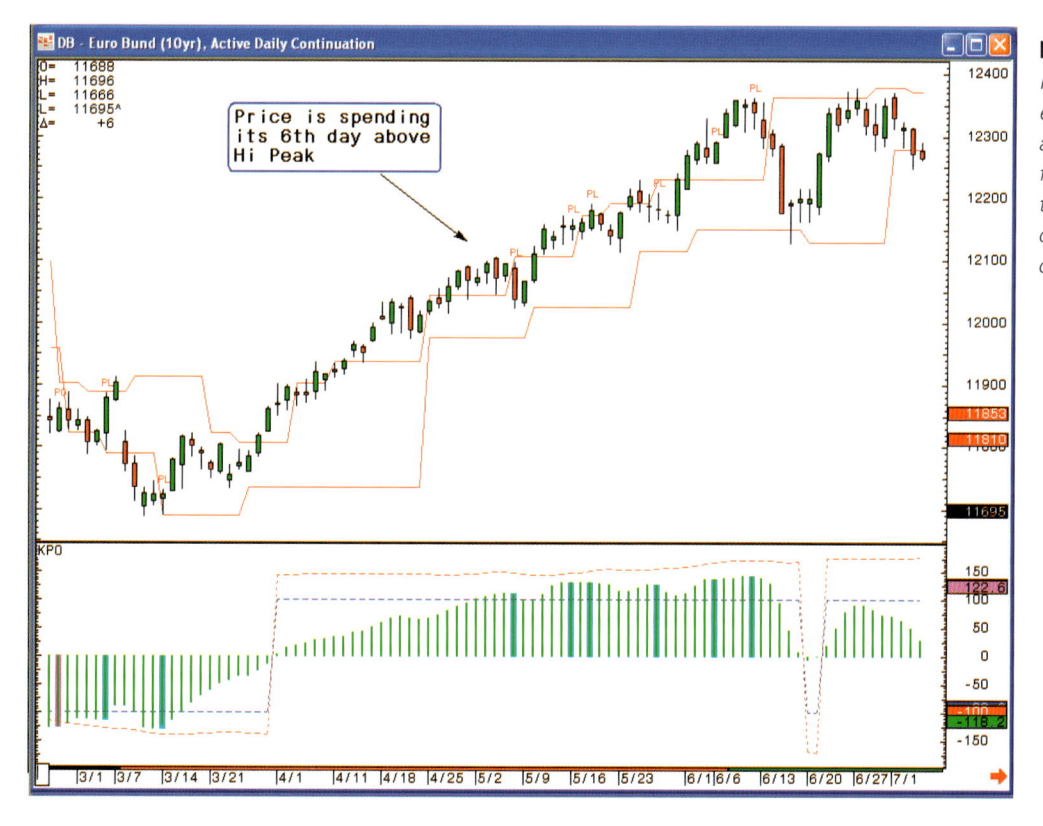

Fig 65:
Price has spent enough time above Hi Peak for the trader to look for corrective opportunities

A Key Moment - Non Farm Payrolls

Now we come to one of the key moments in this rally. It is the unemployment report. It is critical to gauge the technical picture in order that the correct stop can be placed.

Analysis of the chart shows that the focus timeframe is the 60-minute (see fig. 66). A glance at the Stochastic Steps and the setup of the Stochastic itself shows that, if the market does fall on the report and stays down subsequently, the Stochastic will probably cross back down. This means that the step will do likewise and this will signal the end of the trend. Looking at the daily we have now spent six days above the Hi Peak level, which suggests that a correction is due. The daily Peak level is at 119.74 but is some 120 points away. Therefore, it seems wise to exit the position ahead of the report.

Figure 66:
The risk/stop when connecting Steps, Hi Peak and Lo Peak is high going into the report

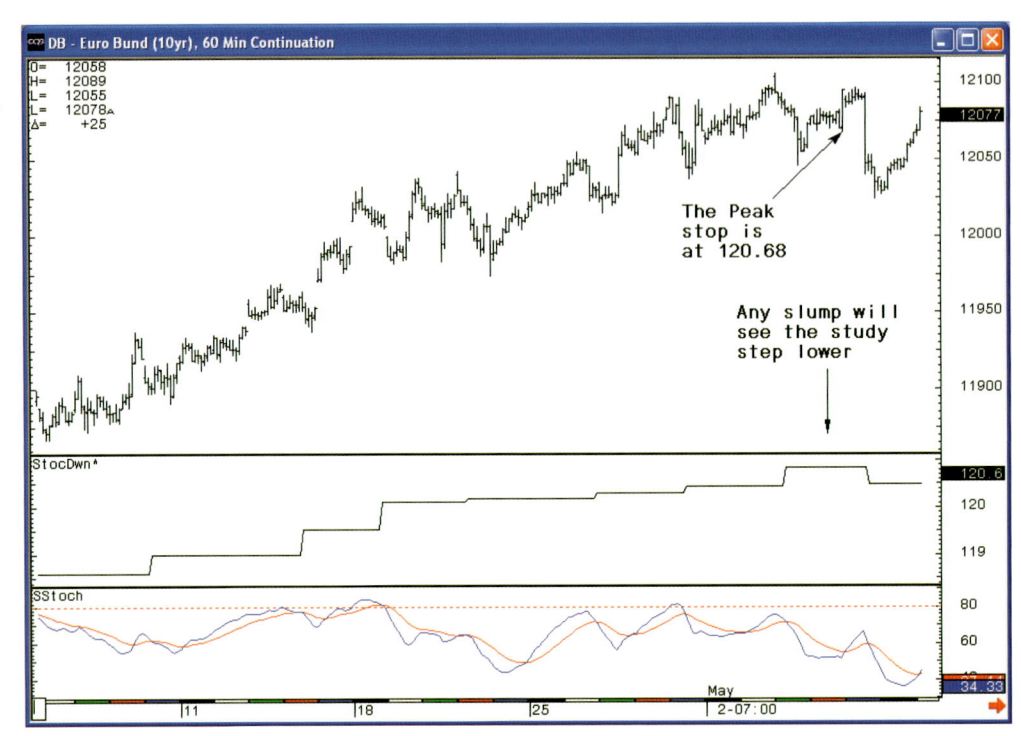

The Long-Term Distribution. Shifts in Control Point

Next we turn to the bigger picture and look from a strategic standpoint at where the trend that began 10 March would end (see fig. 67). It shows that on the day before payroll, the Control Point has moved higher from 120.24 to 120.76. This means that price must accelerate immediately or it will become top-heavy. If it fails to do so, the first support is the previous control at 120.25. (Note that the scale is every 3 ticks but the actual control is at 25.) Therefore, if long-term players wish to remain involved, the stop must be below 120.25 (see fig. 68). The question is how far.

The daily deviation bars have the 3rd standard deviation low at 120.35, which is not an ideal extreme as is close to another powerful support at Control Point at 120.25. Therefore, if a short position is taken after the number comes out the area from 120.35 (3rd standard deviation daily low) to 120.25 moving into the number represents a profit taking point. The aggressive player or strategic player can also buy here, although the logical stop is distant – below the daily Peak level at 119.74.

Peak

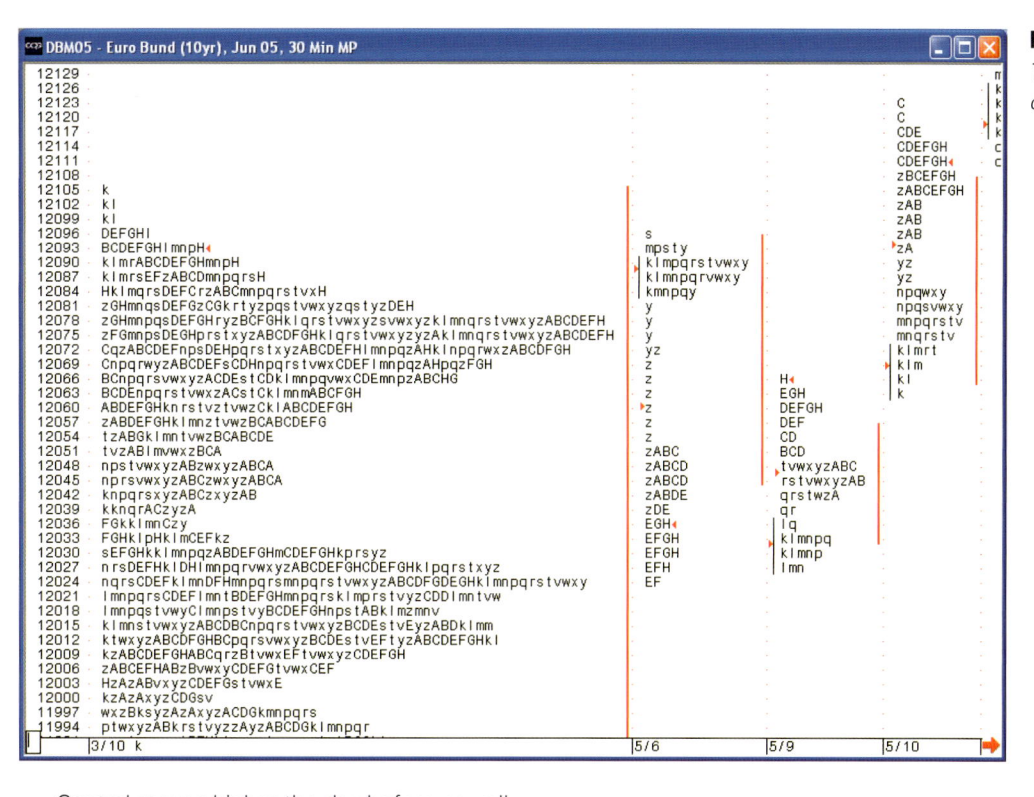

Figure 67:
The long-term distribution

Control moves higher the day before payroll.

Figure 68:
The old control at 120.25 is a key support point

The Aftermath

Prices collapse following the unemployment report with the first two bars on the 30-minute chart closing outside or at the 3rd deviation low, which indicates a strong trend. The key moment arrives two hours later as a fresh downward thrust moves directly to the previous control 120.25. This support coincides almost to the tick with the 3rd standard deviation low on the 30-minute; it is also the 60-minute 3rd deviation low (see figs. 69 and 70). Now we have a compelling reason to connect a longer-term setup via Market Profile® with an exhaustion point intraday. Price holds 120.25, but the bounce is not impressive, although the market does close above the 3rd standard deviation low on the daily at 120.35. However, the Stochastic Steps have switched down indicating that the trend is over. The whole Stochastic Step cycle will have to begin once again in a lower-focus timeframe.

Figure 69:
The time of day connects with the control point support

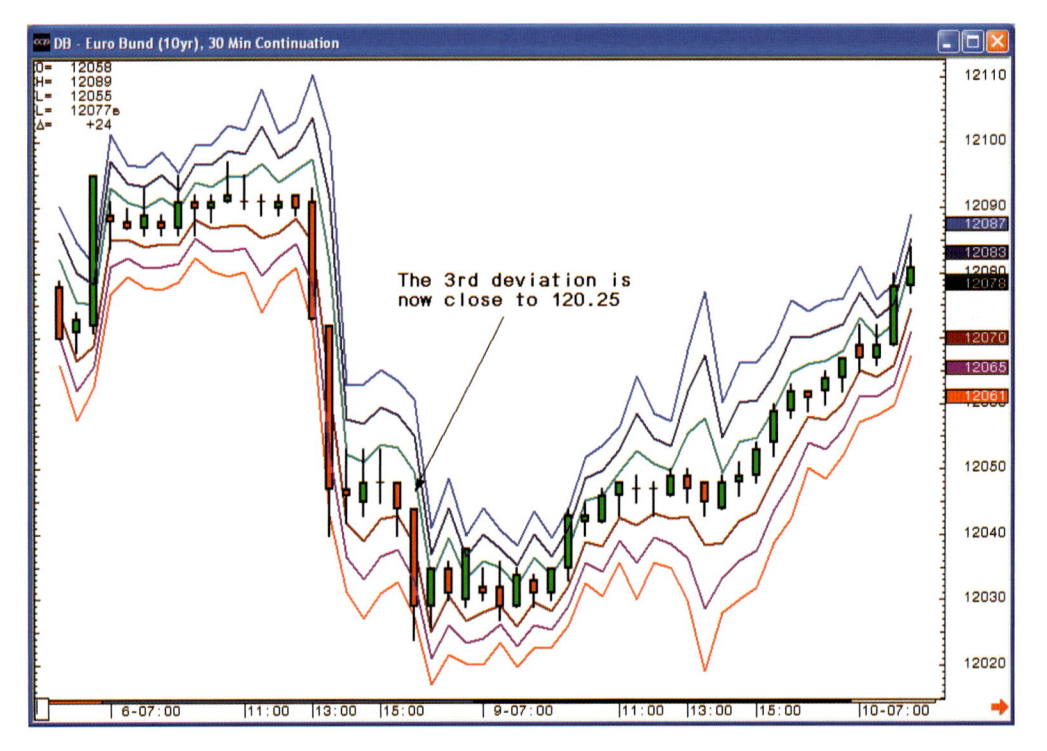

Figure 70:
Two time frames at 30 and 60-minute provide further evidence that a low is in place

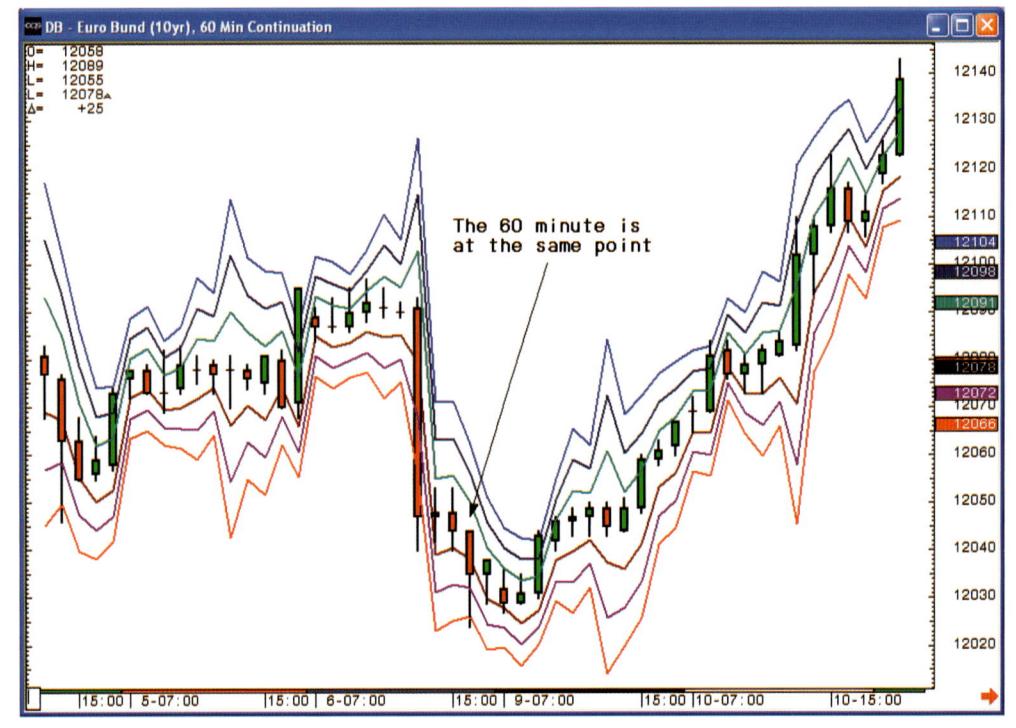

Super Tankers

Monday and Tuesday will be key days, since the super tankers will be out in force. Has the trend changed or was this simply a healthy correction?

Monday's price action is clear-cut (see fig. 71). The market holds above the Control Point and has initiative behaviour in **q** and then again in **D**. Price closes on the highs. Even on the lower 15-minute chart (see fig. 73), once the breakout took place in **q** on the 30-minute, price is above the 1st standard deviation all day and there are only two occasions where price touches the 2nd standard deviation down on the 15-minute. This shows an extremely strong trend, which continued into the following day as well. The combination allows both for Market Profile®-based breakouts to be quantified at the time of the breakout and for a firm grip to be maintained once a position has been established. The trend is particularly strong in the afternoon with price action remaining above the 1st standard deviation low for the most of the time.

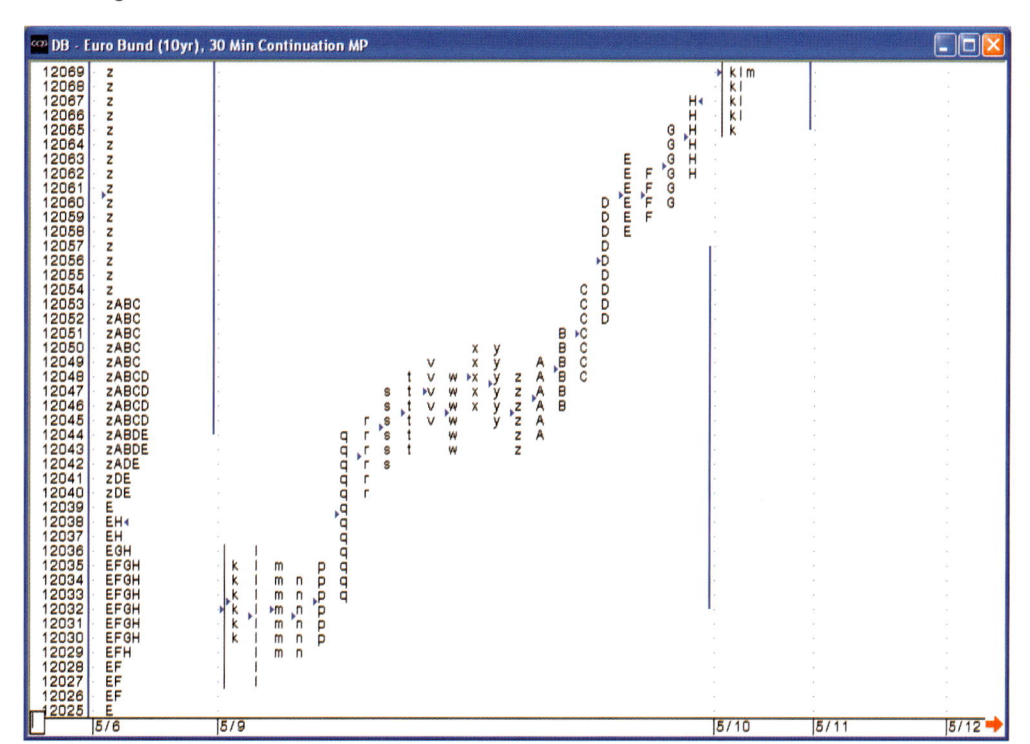

Fig 71
Price rejects the bearish payroll number

Figure 73:
The trend remained up for most of the day in the 15-minute

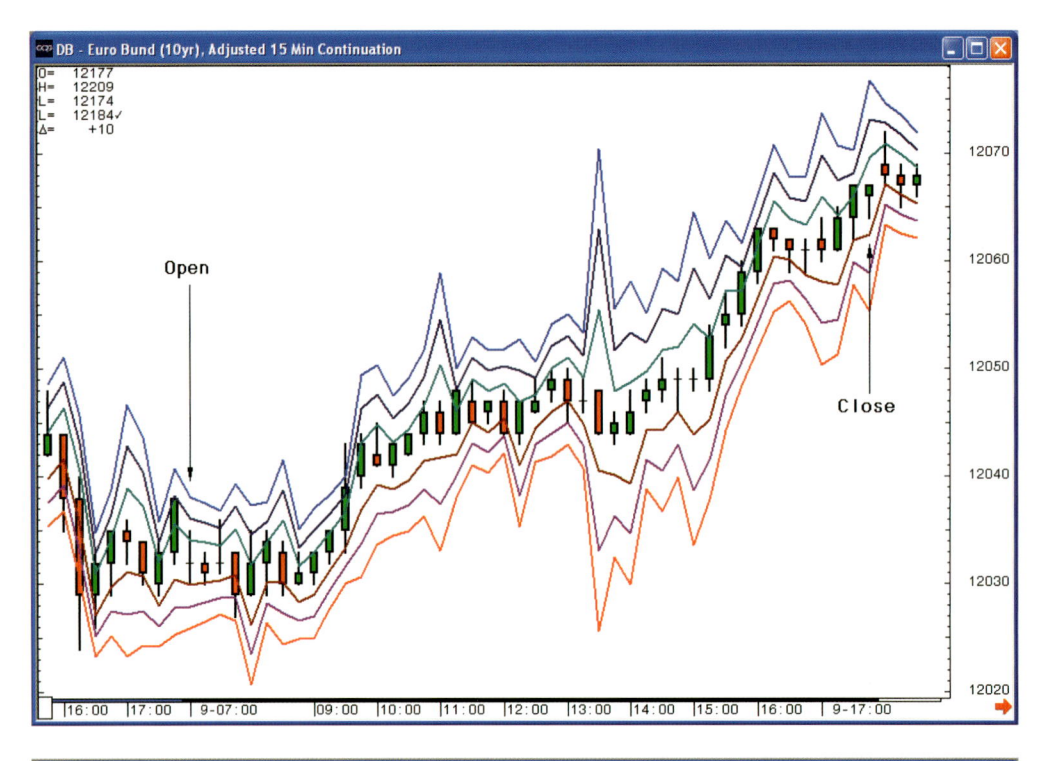

Fig 74:
Two days after payroll the trend is still strong

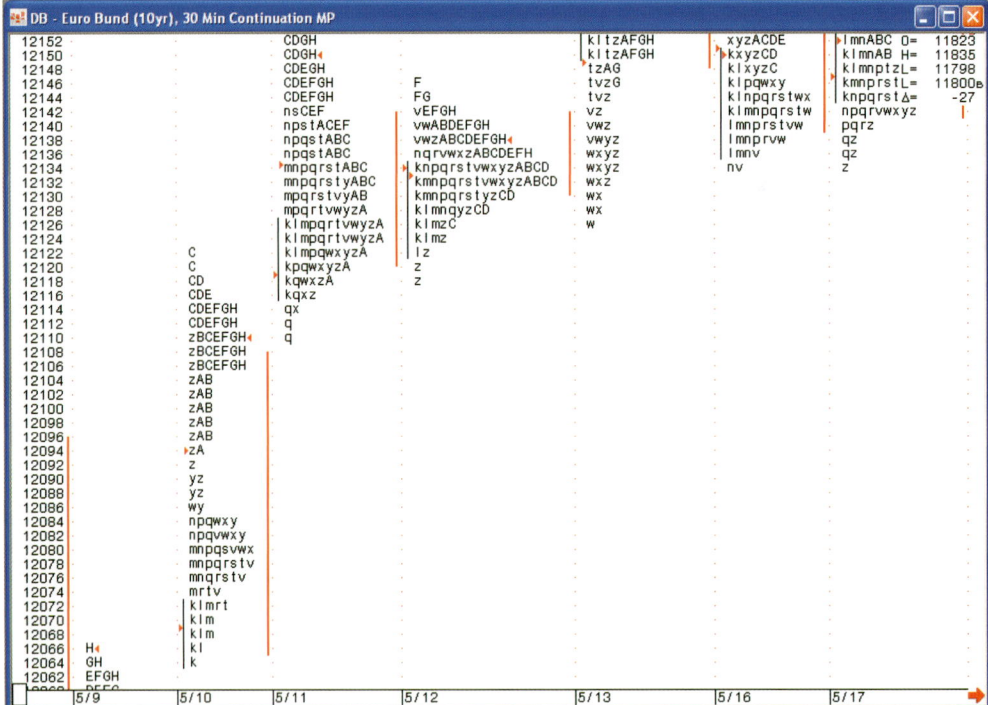

Peak and Stochastic Steps

Crucially, analysis of the daily chart (see fig. 75) shows that the move lower after the payroll numbers has meant that price is back within the Hi Peak, which allows for the trend to resume. In fact, the speed and emphatic nature of the rejection of the move lower are so powerful that within two days both Stochastic and RSI steps are signalling a strong trend in the 5-minute chart (see fig. 76)

How would a trader know that the trend was so strong in such a low timeframe?
This is where discipline is essential. With the study already in your CQG, it is possible to build conditions that then can be alerted. OaR or CQG can provide the code.

To return to the Bund, whilst this is common in indices it is highly unusual in bond markets, (due to less volatility and long trading hours) and simply reinforces the powerful momentum.

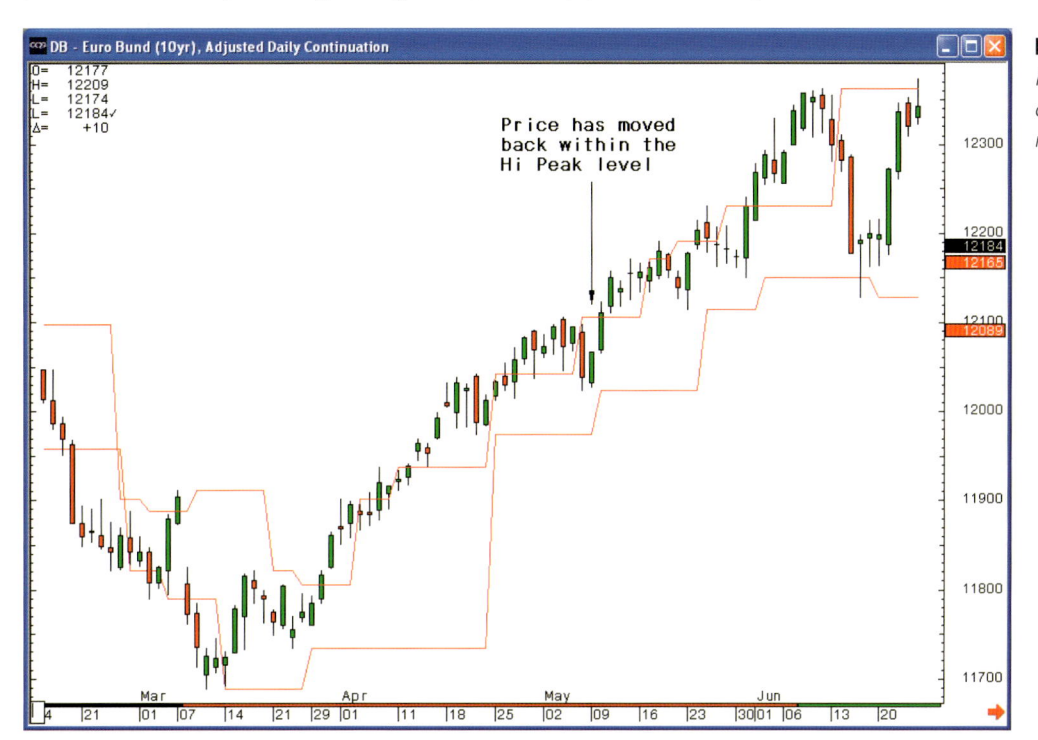

Figure 75:
Price now has an opportunity to restart the trend

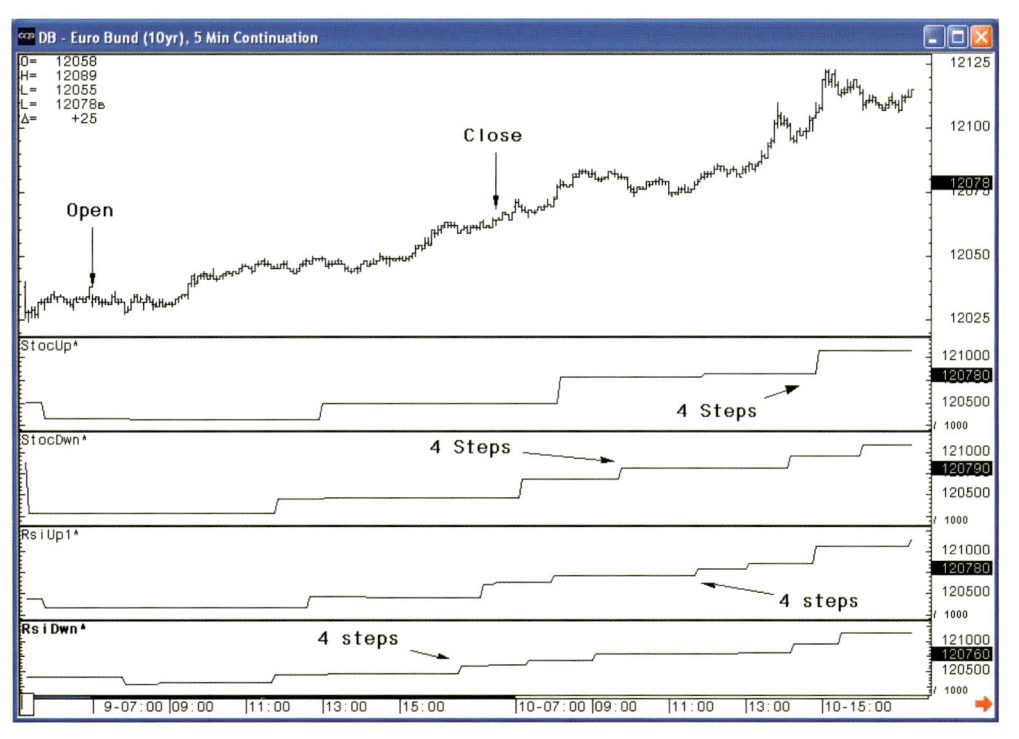

Figure 76:
A 5-minute chart defines the short-term focus timeframe

TRADING TIME: New Methods in Technical Analysis

Analysis of the 10-minute chart (see fig. 77) shows that the focus timeframe has swiftly risen. Whilst the payroll-induced price drop has meant that on a higher timeframe the trend has finished with a drop in the Stochastic Steps, the recovery from the Control Point lows at 120.25 is marked by both Stochastic Steps studies moving beyond 65 bars. This means that a re-establishment of the up trend may be beginning in this low timeframe. However, whilst this trend initially looked promising and powerful, it fails to move up timeframes quickly enough and the trend ends 12 May 2005 as the 15-minute steps down at the same time as the 10-minute.

Figure 77:
It moves to a 10-minute chart before dying

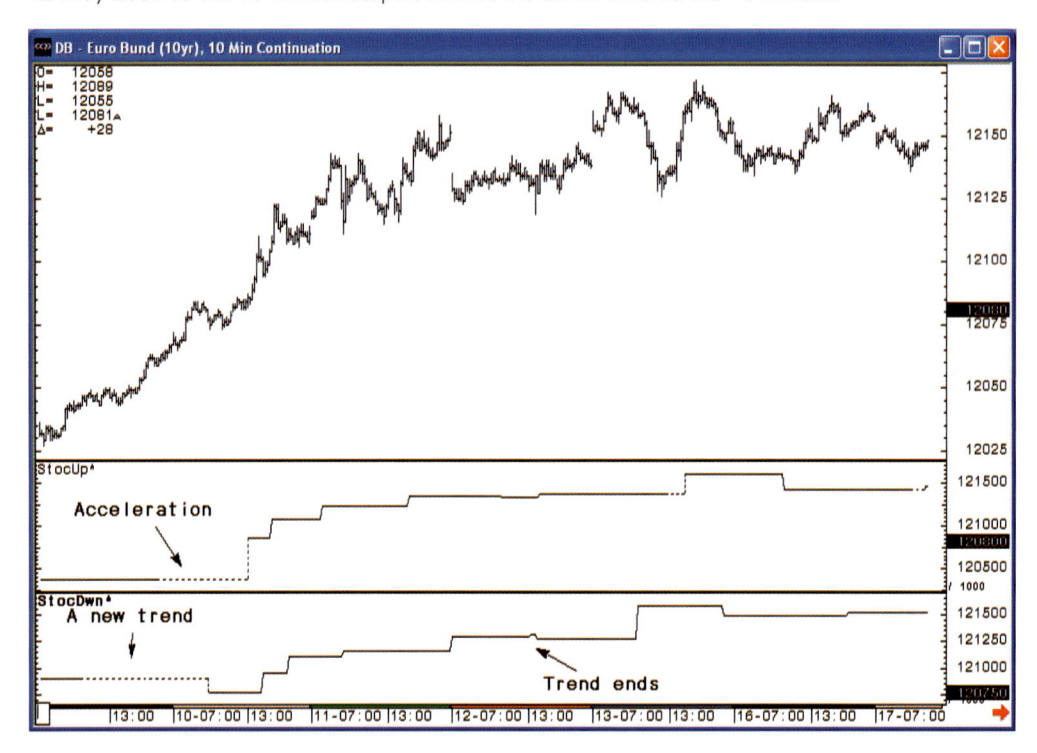

Market Profile® and Range Deviation Bands

Analysis of the period up to the end of the trend 12 May 2005 shows that further initiative single prints in **y** and **z** are evident 10 May 2005 (see fig. 79). The day before had shown similar initiative behaviour (see fig 78). There is no evidence of super-tanker selling. In fact they have ignored the report and are buying. Price is now back within the normal Hi Peak/ Lo Peaks bands, which means that there is the space and time to reassert the up trend. However, the limit of the buying is just above the 3rd standard deviation up on the daily at 121.23 (see fig. 80)

Figure 78:
*Single prints in **q**. Price closes on the high*

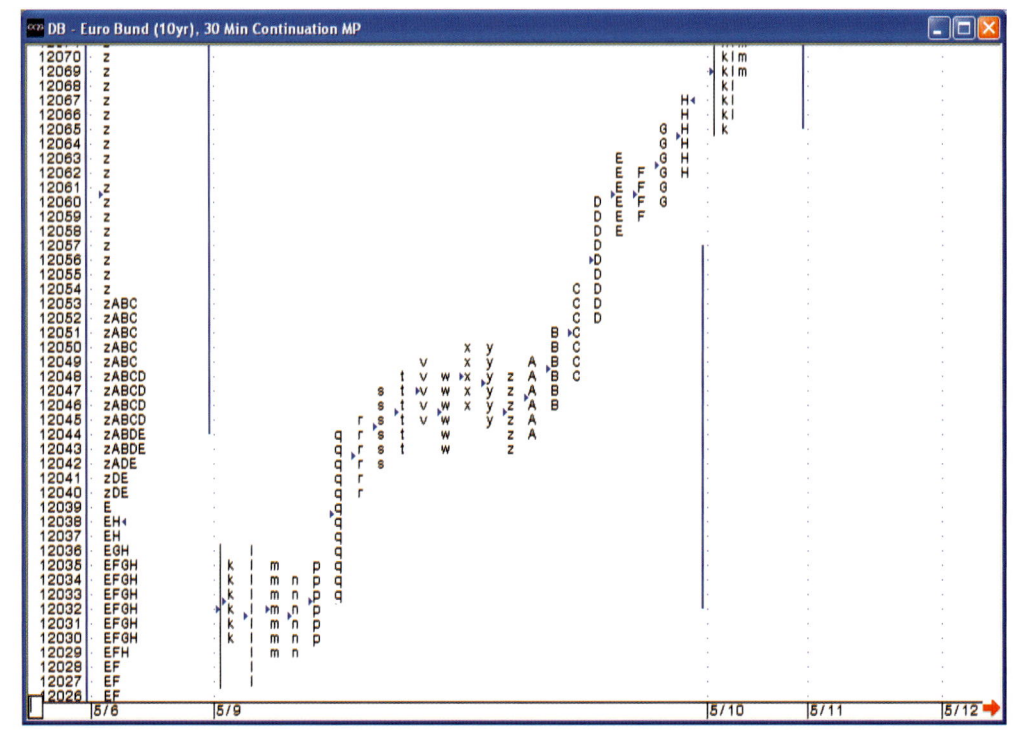

212

Peak

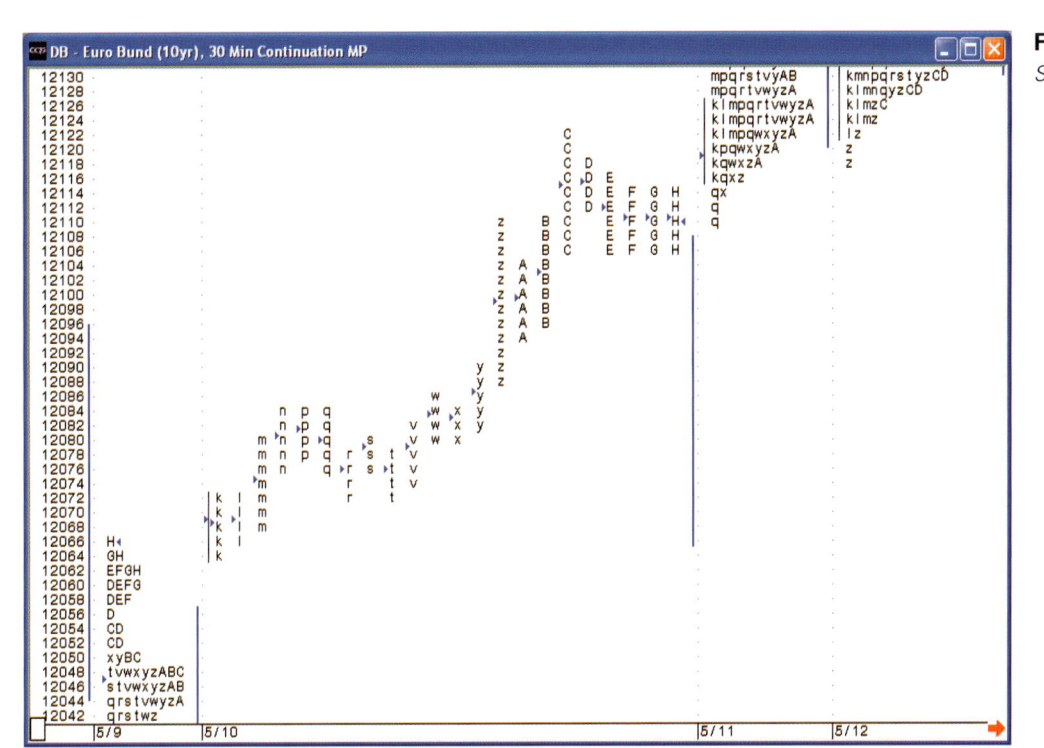

Figure 79:
Single prints in Z

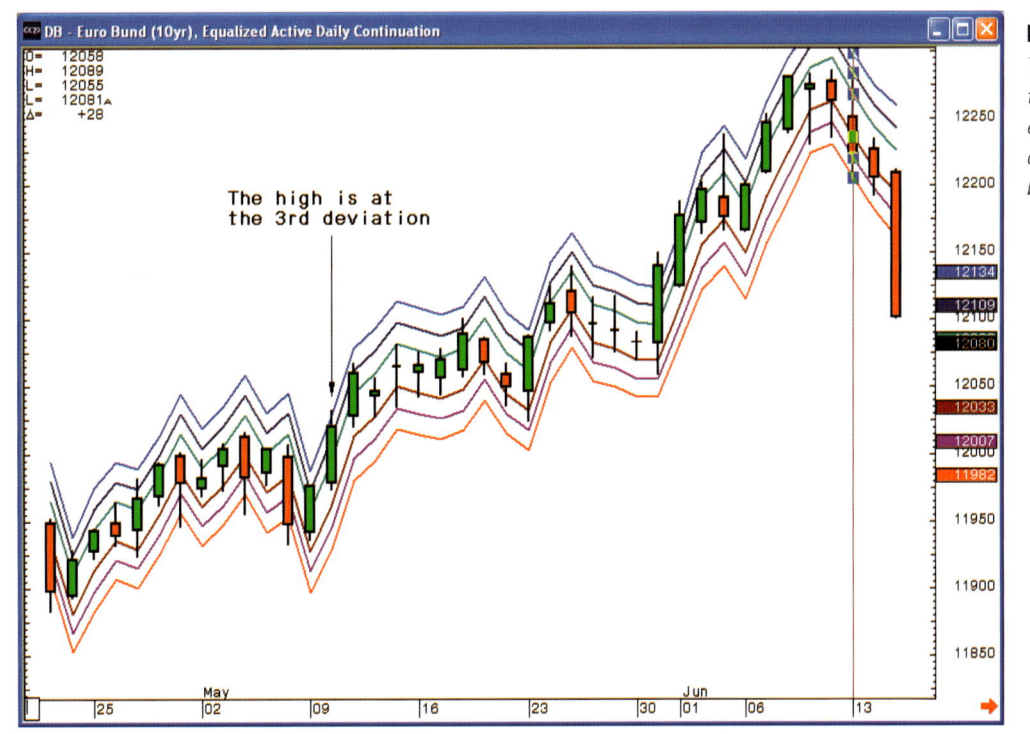

Figure 80:
The high stops at the historical extreme for the day at the 3rd band up.

The distance between price and Peak levels

The next aspect we will look at concerns the distance between the Peak level and the price itself. Whilst the study is useful as a partial trailing stop and does have the ability to be the final trailing stop, there are times when price is so far away that in practice it is of little use. This occurs most often at the beginning of a trend or when a trend has a blow off, top or bottom. In an up trend, when price is distant from the Lo Peak value, this tells us that the trend is very strong. The market has shown no desire to make any correction. If the Lo Count study is also beyond 15 this is added confirmation of strength. A correction is due but subsequently new highs should be made as the previous impulse higher had sufficient speed and lack of correction. This is crucial information for all traders and alerts them to the fact that 2nd and 3rd bands can be used as profit-taking points when in the direction of the trend.

What makes the distance too great is different for each market but it can also be purely dependent on the trader's concept of risk. If price is more than 20 ticks away from the Peak on Bunds that would be a normal trigger point for me.

Later, on the same chart (see fig. 81), we can see that price moves too far below Hi Peak.

Figure 81:

The distance between Peak, Hi and Lo Count and the close

New trends, trend exhaustion and Cycle length

If either Hi Count or Lo Count moves beyond 15 this marks the beginning of a strong trend. If Steps are over 6, the trend is well developed and if at extremes of deviations and cycle length, suggests exhaustion. This is especially powerful when linked to true measures of overbought and oversold.

Figure 82:

Cycle length

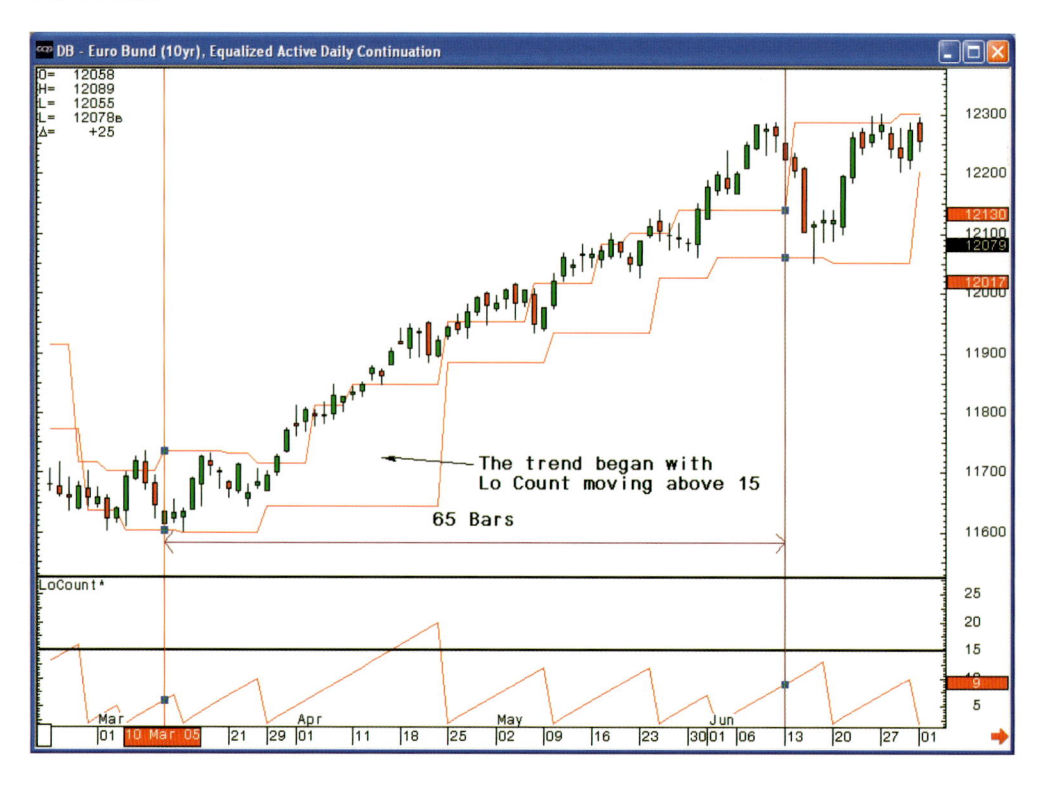

Peak

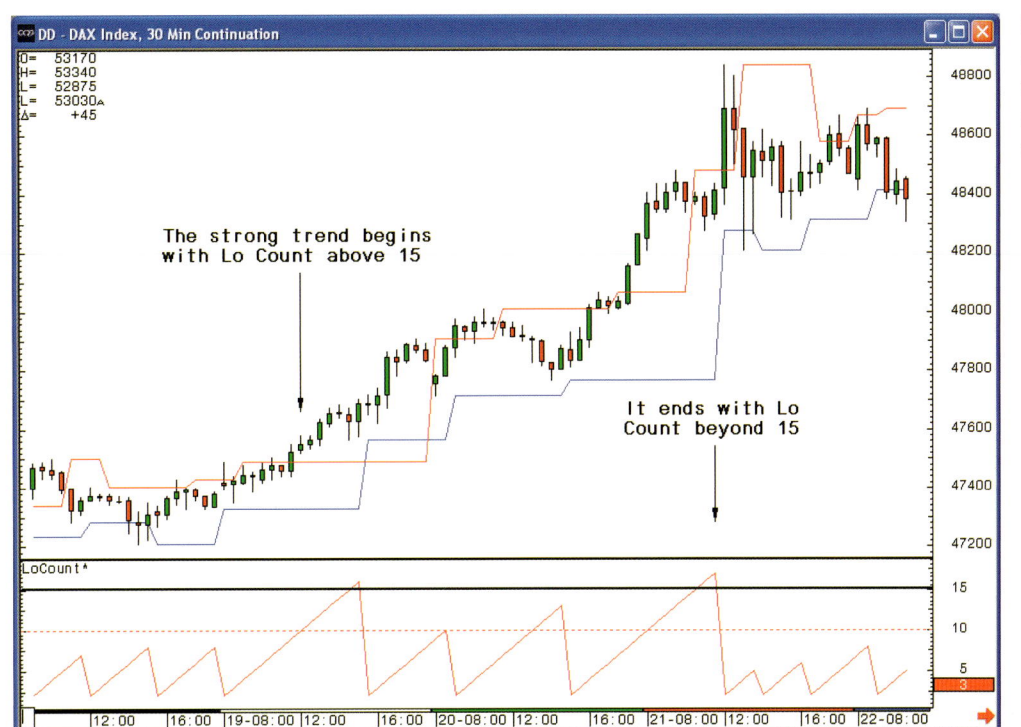

Figure 83:

Lo Count defines the beginning and end of the trend

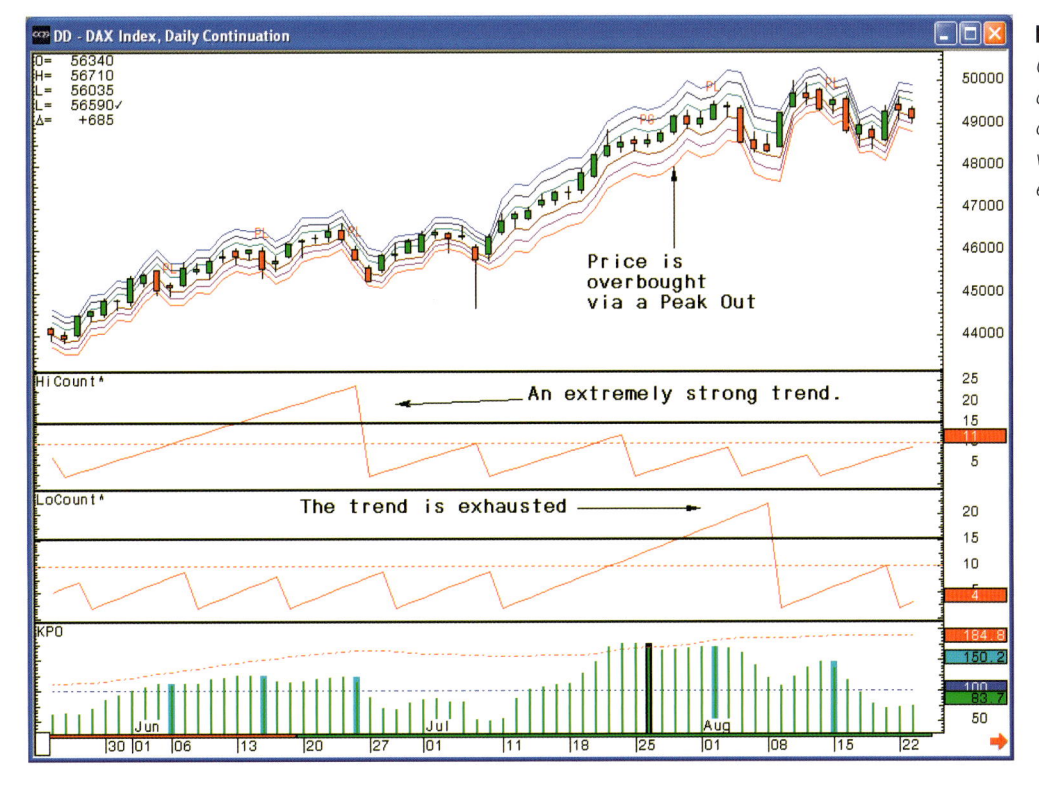

Figure 84:

Concepts of overbought and oversold connect with Lo Count exhaustion

Hi Count / Lo Count, Steps and an Oversold picture combined.
GbpCad

The Pound Canada cross was a classic example of a mega trend. There were no fewer than 5 acceleration phases, as shown by dashed lines (see fig. 85), before the Stochastic Steps reached 4 on the 240-minute. On the 360-minute chart StocUp hits 7 steps (see fig 86). With the Hi Count and Lo Count moving above 15 this flags the end of the trend (see fig. 86). With the trend this far developed, this marks a blowoff bottom and exhaustion. Analysis of the daily chart confirms the bottom, as finally a true measure of oversold can be seen (see fig. 87).

Figure 85:
A strong downtrend via Steps

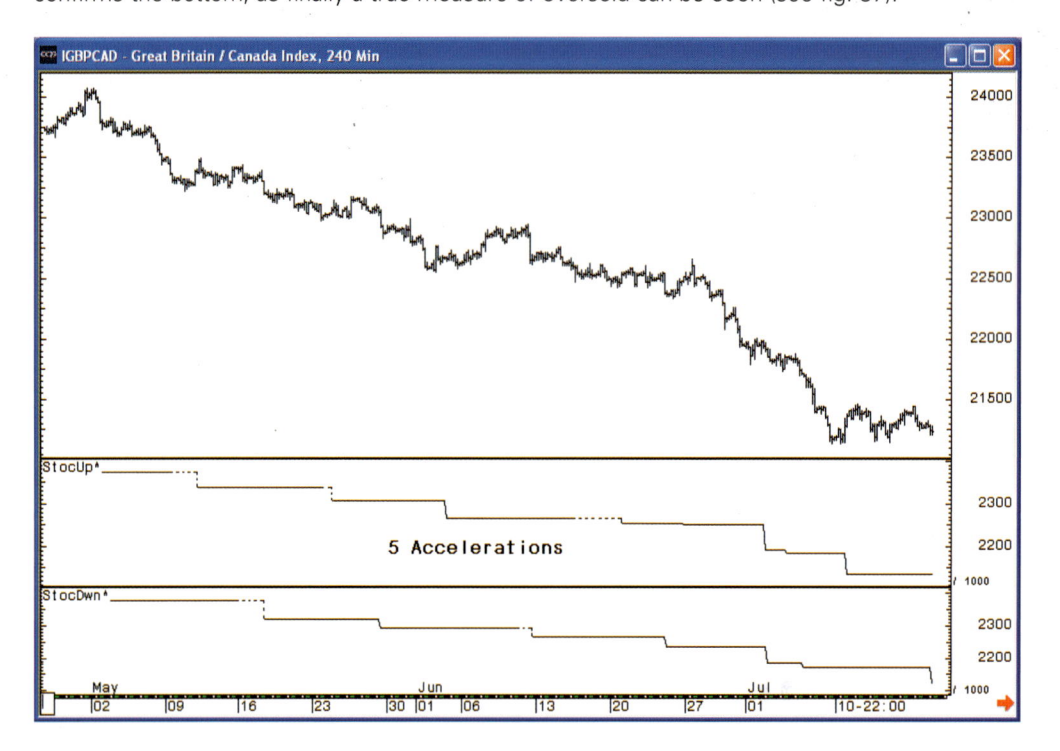

Figure 86:
Hi and Lo Count signal exhaustion

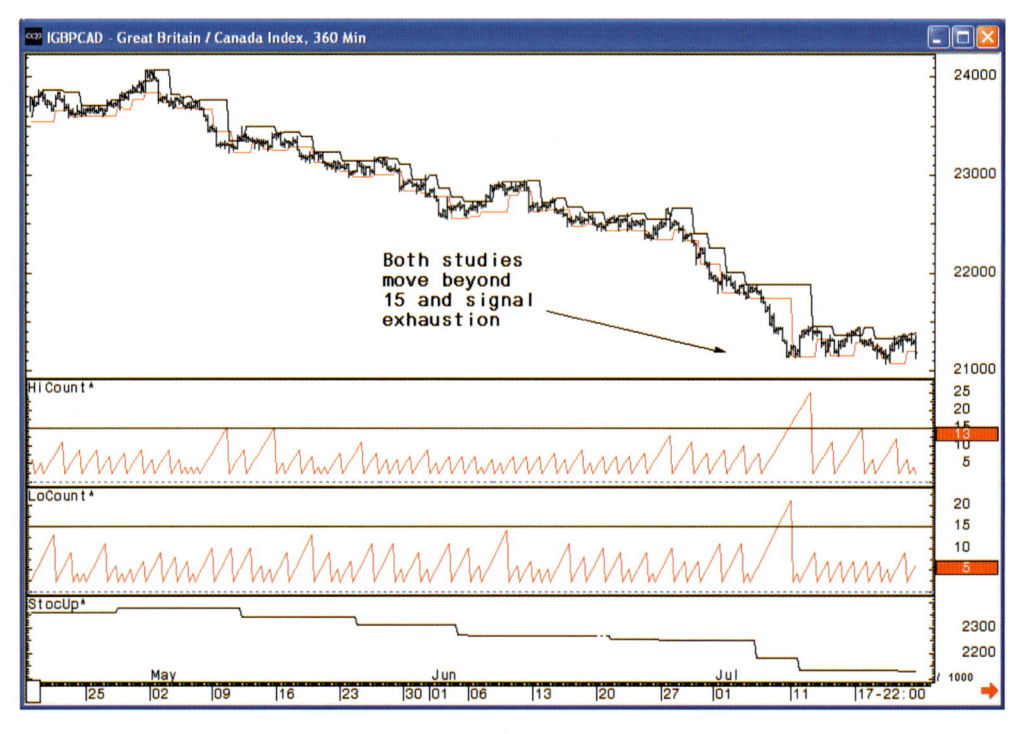

Peak

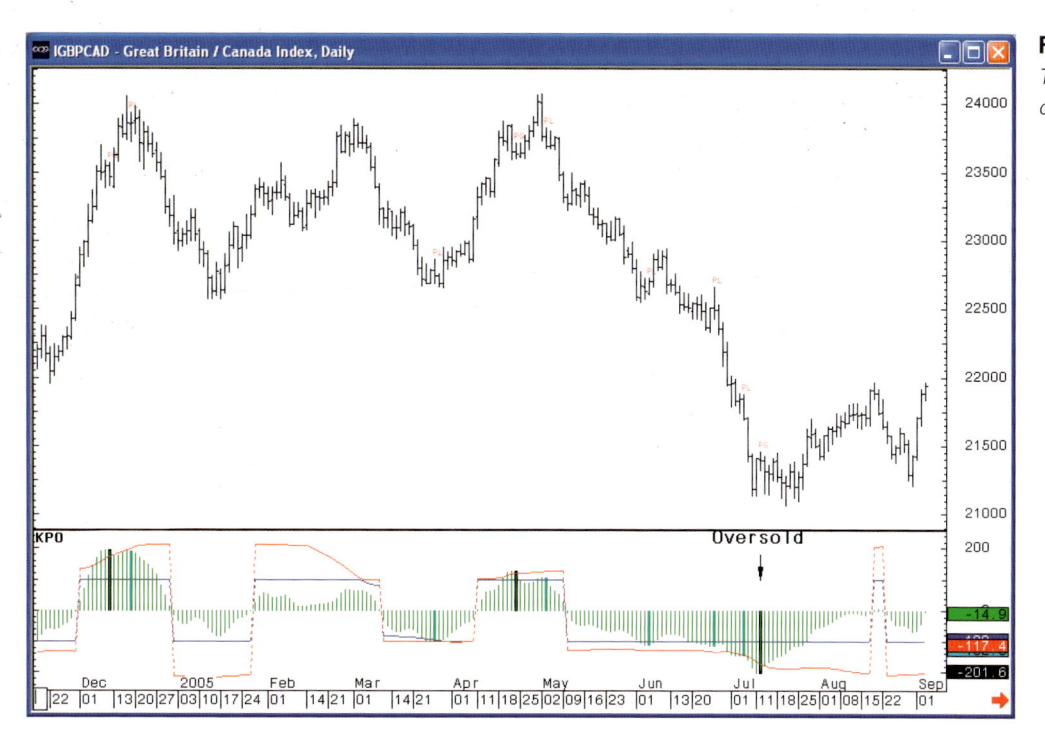

Figure 87:
The market is oversold

Divergence and extremes

If that was not confirmation enough, the concepts of multiple timeframe divergence and their link to extremes in trends (which is beyond the scope of this book) also mark the 3 turning points. Whilst it's rare for everything to come together so perfectly, the power when they do is considerable (see fig. 88).

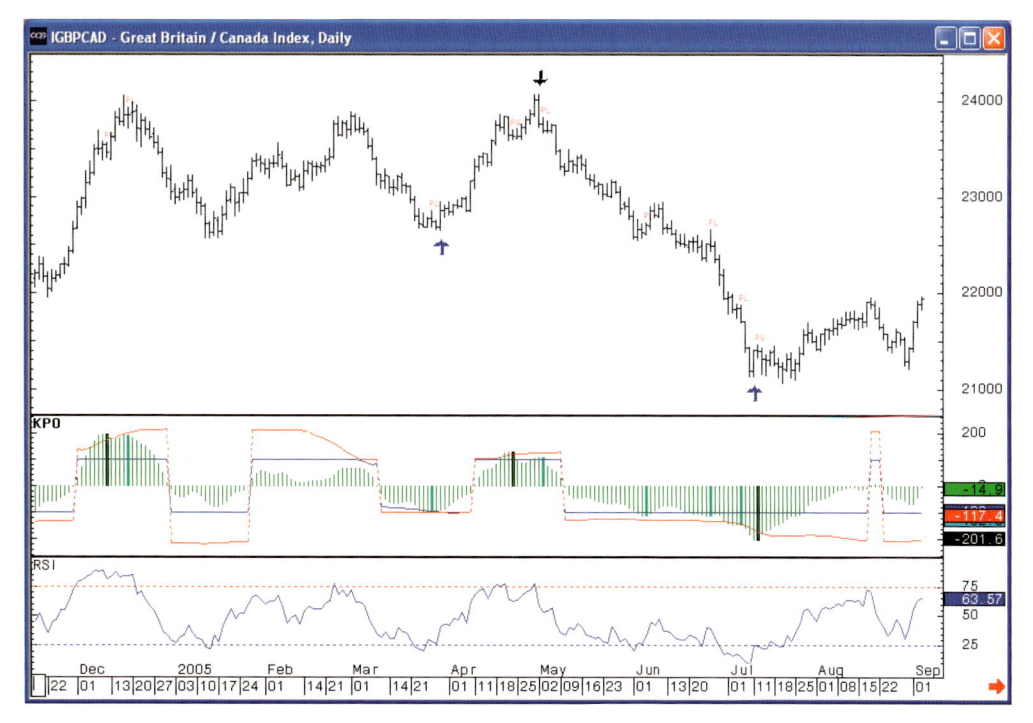

Figure 88:
Divergence connects with an overbought and oversold market to catch the 3 recent major turning points

When Peak Levels cross over each other

GbpCad

The next pattern occurs rarely but needs to be monitored, as it is often a point of a new trend or exhaustion. It occurs when the Peak Levels cross over each other. Returning to the Pound Canada, let's look at the original setup in more detail.

First, price was overbought historically at the 2nd blue arrow on fig. 88. Second, multiple time-frame divergence appeared at the highs when overbought. This is enough to signal that a top has been made, if only temporarily. The market will have to prove that it wants to start a new trend the other way.

TRADING TIME: New Methods in Technical Analysis

The first clue comes on a low timeframe 60-minutes (see fig. 90). Normally, due to the 24-hour nature of the FX market the lowest timeframe referenced is 120 minute. My focus generally concentrates on this, followed by 240, 360, 480 and 720. It is possible to build systems on 60-minute data and I have helped build a code for a bank that specifically traded this around the globe. However, the problem of inactivity, especially in Asia, makes this a very difficult task. We will look how Peak can work around this problem later.

The 60-minute chart shows an extremely sharp fall, which causes both the Hi and Lo Count to move to 15. This marks a strong trend. The 30-minute Hi Count is even higher at 28 with Lo Count at 15 (see fig. 91). Whenever either counts moves above 25 this indicates an explosive and mega trend. As mentioned above, 60 minutes is a very low timeframe on FX so it is very rare that a strong trend can develop via the Stochastic Step theory. Even using the more aggressive RSI Steps provides few signals. Therefore, while the short-term charts are the catalyst, focus must switch to the 120-minute chart.

Figure 89:
The market is overbought via a Peak Out. Divergence is on multiple timeframes.

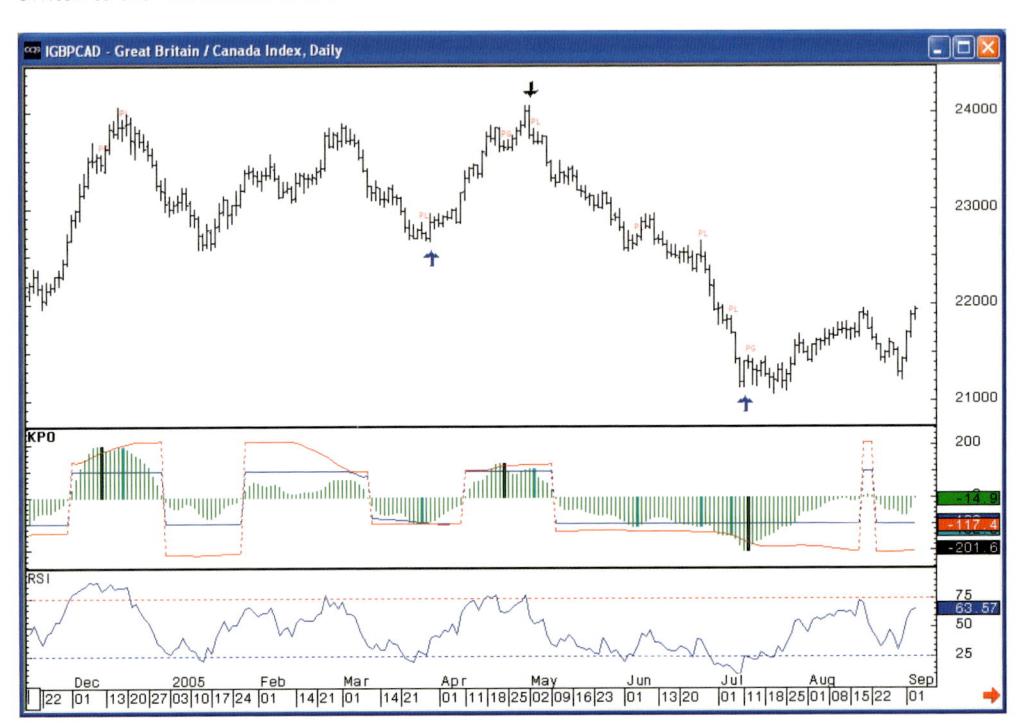

Figure 90:
Hi and Lo Count signal the beginning of the trend on the 60- minute chart

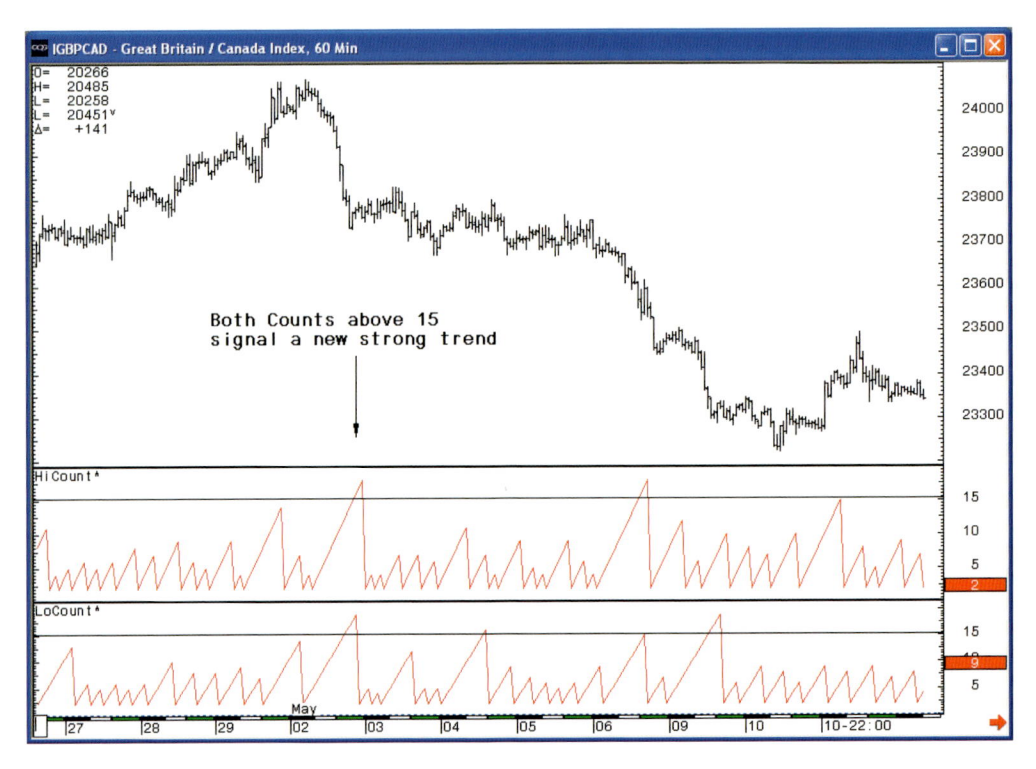

218

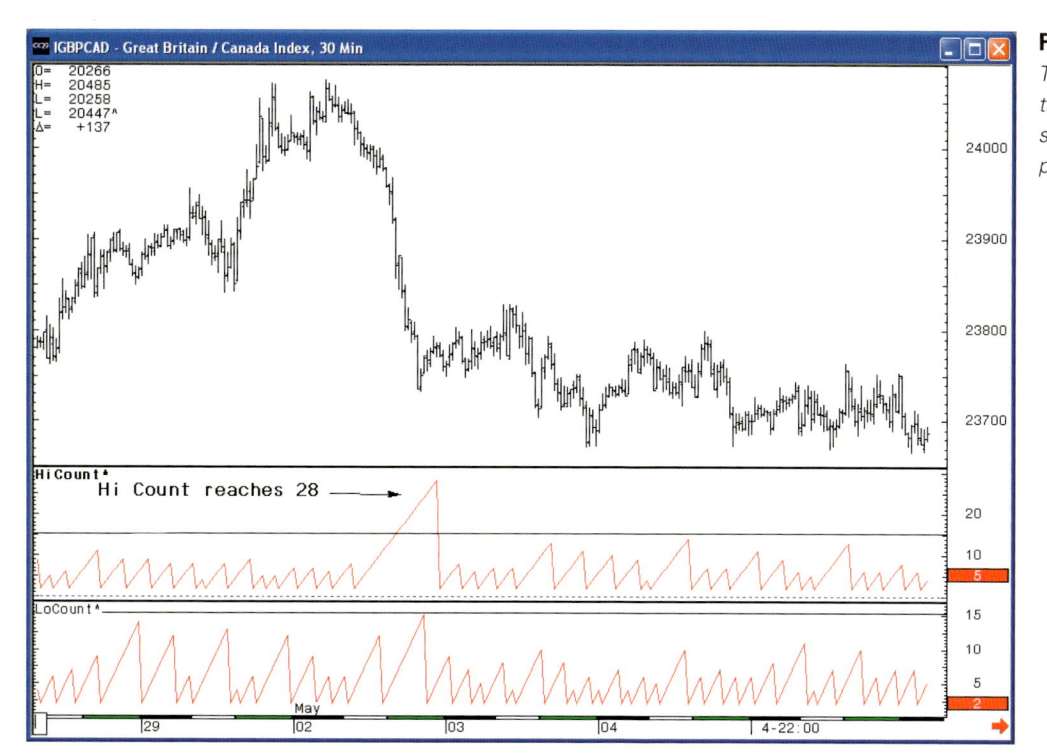

Figure 91:
The 30-minute timeframe showed a similar picture

Trend Beginnings

Analysis of the previous trend up shows that the trend started in a similar fashion with explosive moves at the beginning. Further on we can see that the Peak levels cross. This is after a sideways consolidation and coincides with the Hi Count moving above 15 (see fig. 92). This suggests a fresh leg higher is beginning and the trend should make new highs after a corrective period.

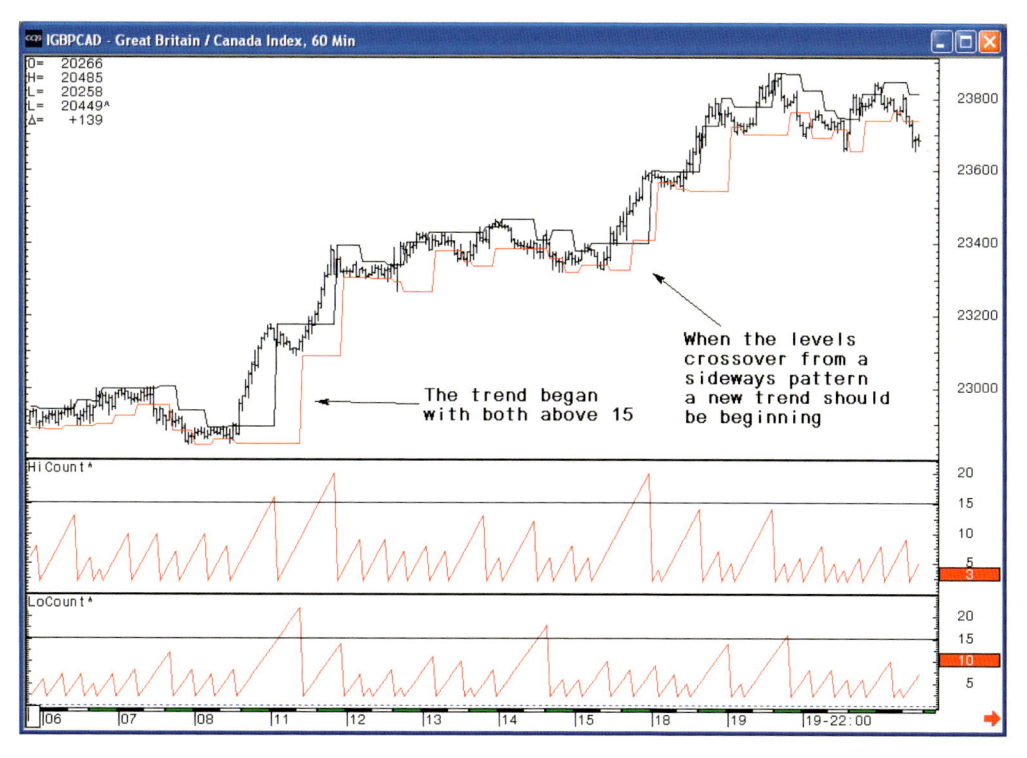

Figure 92:
A crossover signals an acceleration

Trend Endings

Fig. 93 shows the opposite. The Peaks cross over but the trend has already been active for some time. Knowing that price is oversold historically via the KPO (see fig. 88) alerts us to the fact that this move is an exhaustive one. It is also the 8th step down in a row. Once price has stepped 6 times we are in a mega trend but it could end at any time. The cross over of Peak levels, Hi count and Lo count failing to reach 15 plus the oversold signal, forms a low and price ambles sideways. Analysis of the deviation level shows that after two days moving beyond the 3rd standard deviation down, the lows are marked by a swift reversal to the 3rd standard deviation up (see fig. 94). For the strategic and short-term players this is a clear indication that price has found at least a temporary low. In fact, during the entire fall, price only touched the 1st standard deviation up twice, both times marking the highs of the day.

Figure 93:
Once a trend has developed a crossover signals an exhaustion

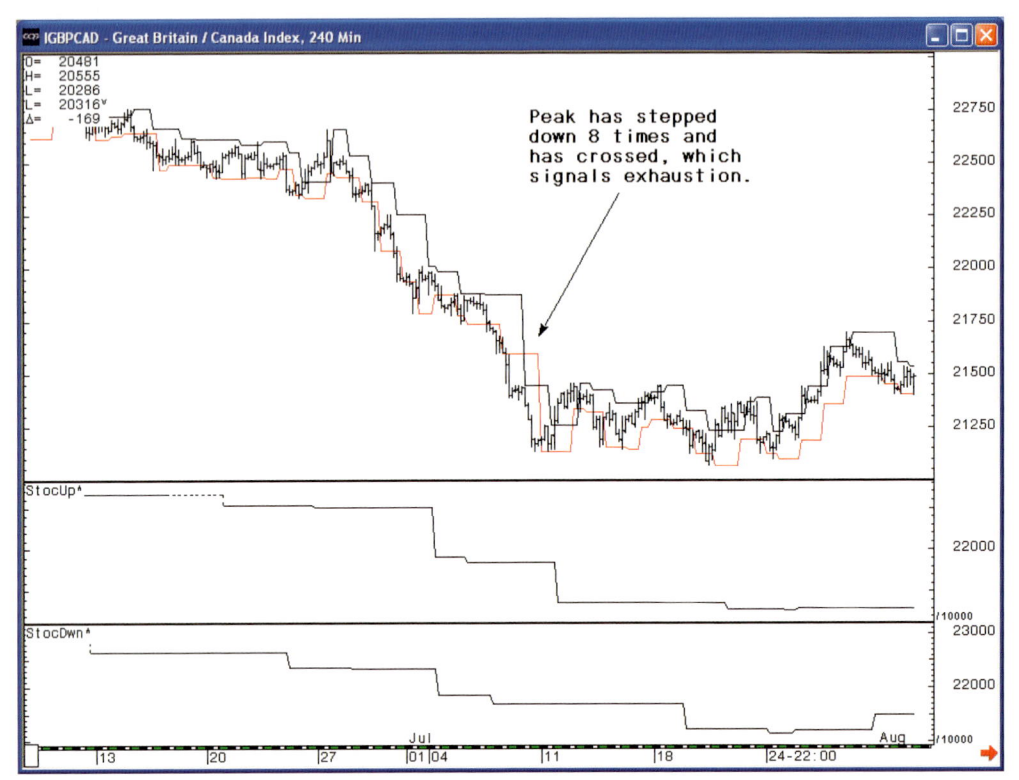

Figure 94:
Two moves outside the lower extreme are sharply reversed with a close above the 3rd band up

How many times can a Peak step in the same direction consecutively?

We now return to the Stochastic Steps theory and look at how many times a Peak can step in the same direction consecutively. In common with all Step Theory the number of steps provides clues about strength, length and exhaustion of trend. The theories apply to all time frames on all markets and therefore should be referenced whatever the time horizon of your trades. As stated previously, Peak provides a methodology for a trailing stop, but the number of consecutive steps allows for the shifting of the sensitivity of that stop, and a change in the exit method employed. This has more significance, the shorter the timeframe of the trade.

Day Trading

The first element is the threshold for day trading. On any timeframe of 15 minutes and below once Peak moves to 5 consecutive steps in the same direction the stop can be tightened, as the prospect of the trend stalling is high.

To Take the Dax as an example-on a 10-minute chart the rally lasts over two sessions with a total number of steps of 7 (see fig. 95). A key component within this rally is the two acceleration phases at the beginning where price departs from the Lo Peak. The potential for the trend to end comes when Lo count moves above 15. Whilst this is normally bullish, the fact that Peak steps is already at 5 suggests that this is an exhaustive move. A period of reflection is required and for the risk-adverse profits can be taken. In fact, there is one more rally before the trend finishes.

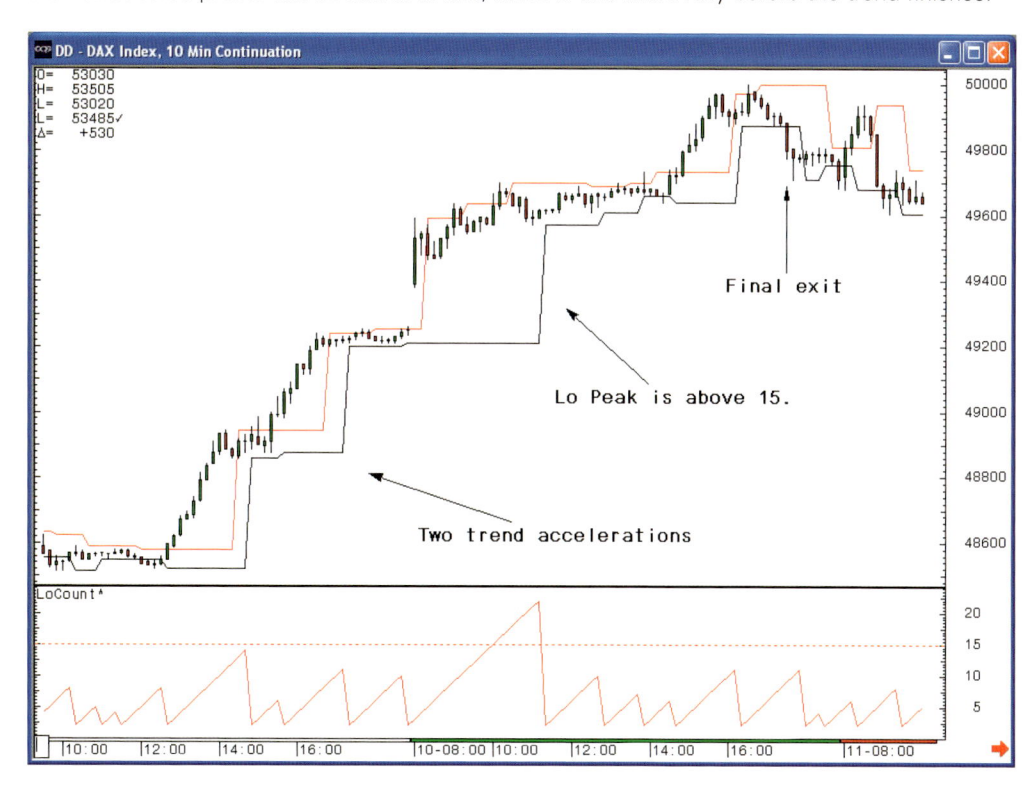

Figure 95:
How many Peak Steps can occur in a row?

Peak step exhaustion with Range Deviation Pivot extreme Very low timeframes

If you are using very short-term charts in a similar vein to how the Dax can be divided into two parts this can be done on the S&P as well if the Stochastic Steps theory dictates. Once again the trend lasts through the first half of the day and reaches 5 steps (see fig. 96). At this point price has also reached its 3rd standard deviation down on the daily (see fig 97), which suggests that under a normal trading day the limit has been reached. The Peak levels crossing over on the opening signals that a trend is beginning.

Figure 96:
Peak Step exhaustion

Figure 97:
Peak Step exhaustion connects with historical Time-band extreme

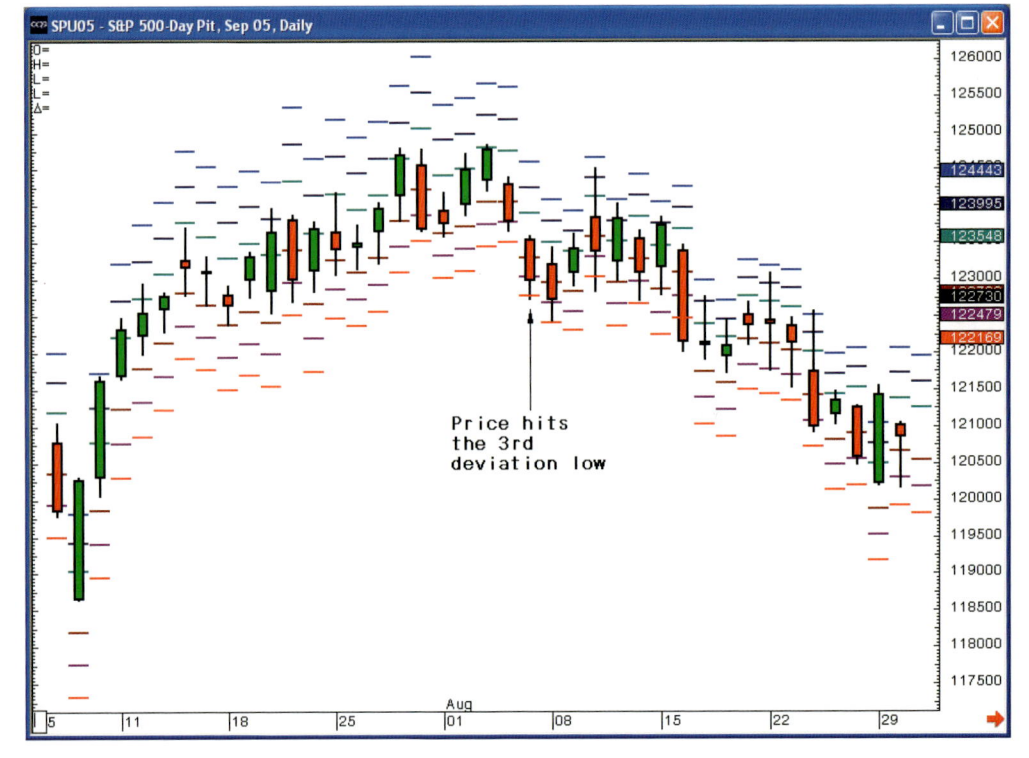

Peak

Trend cycle length. Not waiting for Peak to be broken

The next chart (see fig. 98) connects Peak with the concepts of trend cycle length. The daily Bund chart shows the trend is close to lasting 65 bars and now Peak has stepped beyond 5 times. When price now moves beyond the Hi Peak level for 6 bars a correction is due and at least partial profits should be booked. Analysis of the 6th day up shows price is within the area between the 2nd and 3rd standard deviation up (see fig. 99). This highlights how it is possible not to wait for a Peak-trailing stop to be breached. Therefore, when a market is overextended historically, more advantageous profit-taking points can be taken at Range Deviation Pivot levels.

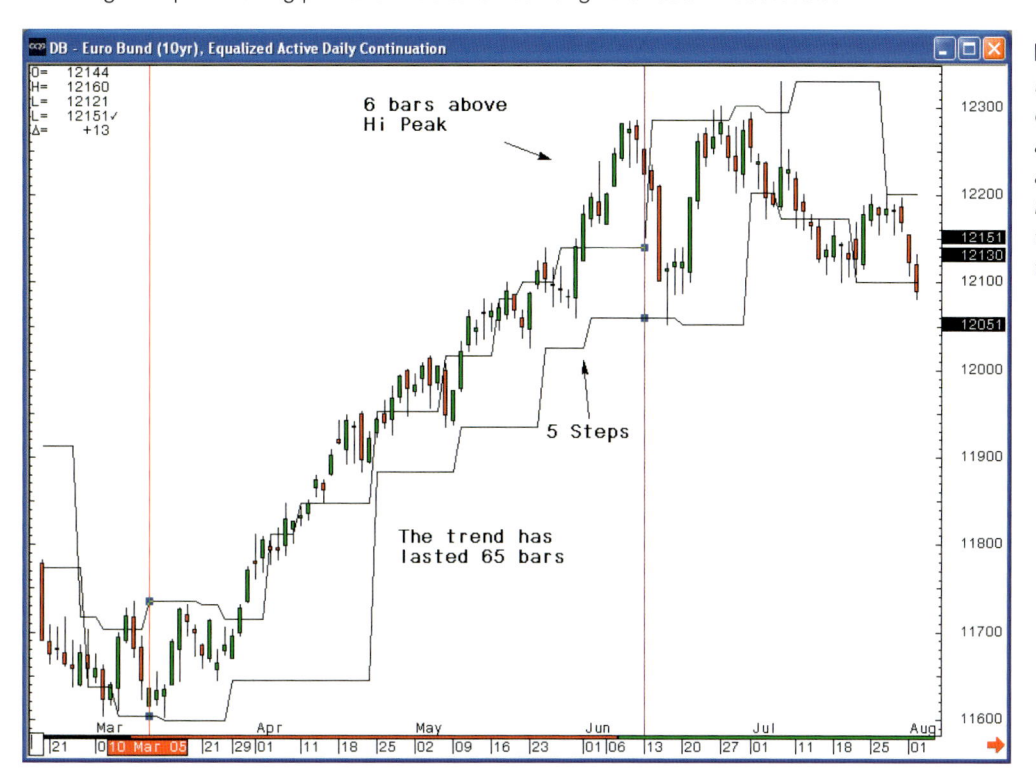

Figure 98:
Peak Step exhaustion, bars above Hi Peak and a full cycle length combine to mean the trend has ended

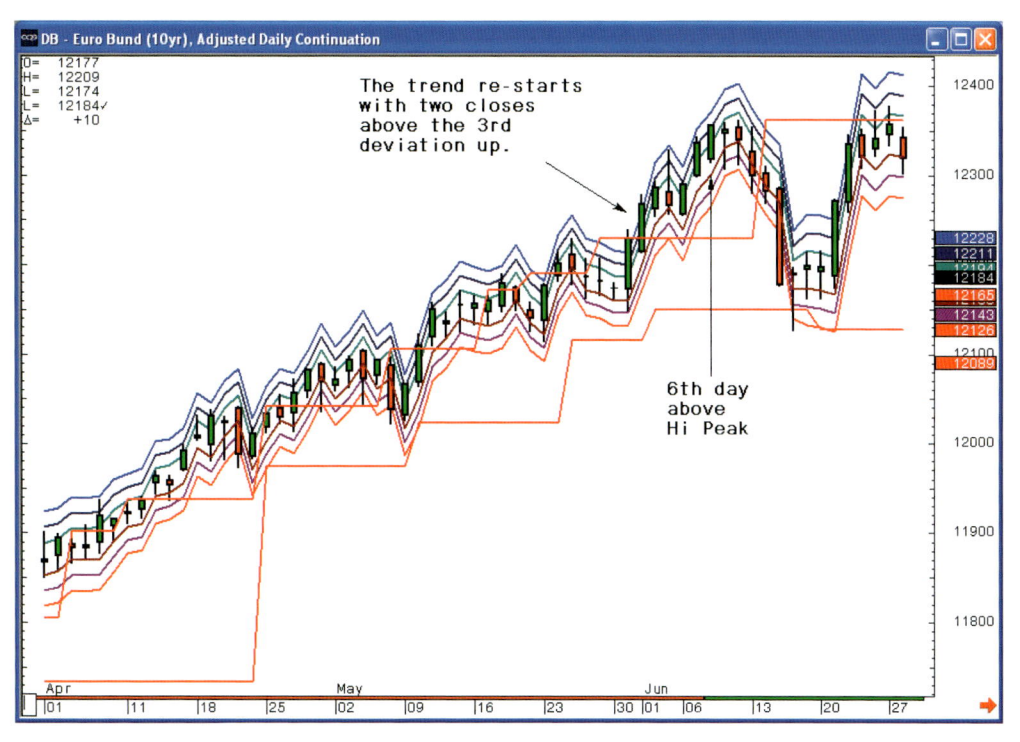

Figure 99:
Historical breakouts re-start the trend

Market Profile®

Analysis of the Market Profile® shows (see fig. 100) initiative behaviour in the morning in **m**, price reaches its 2nd standard deviation up before lunch and the 3rd band on the 15-minute (see figs. 101 and 102). With numbers coming out the risk-averse can lighten positions and wait for developments. A move down in **z** does not fill the single letters of **m** and price then closes on the highs, which provides another exit point.

Figure 100:
A trend day

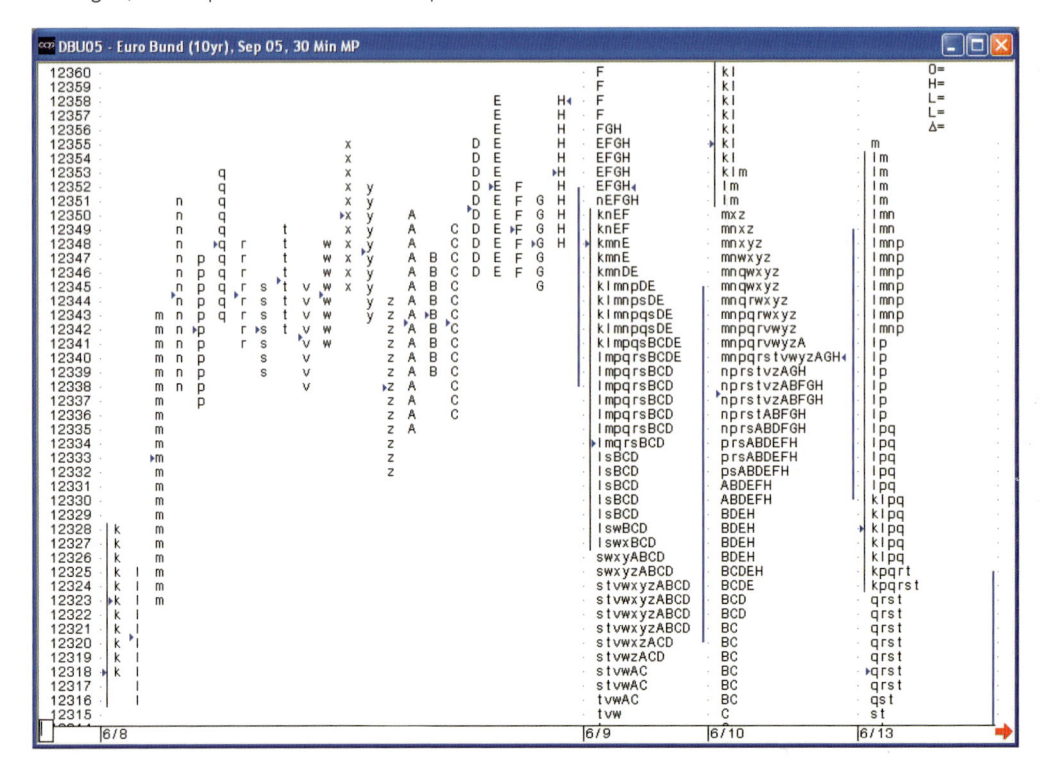

Figure 101:
A daily extreme midmorning ahead of numbers

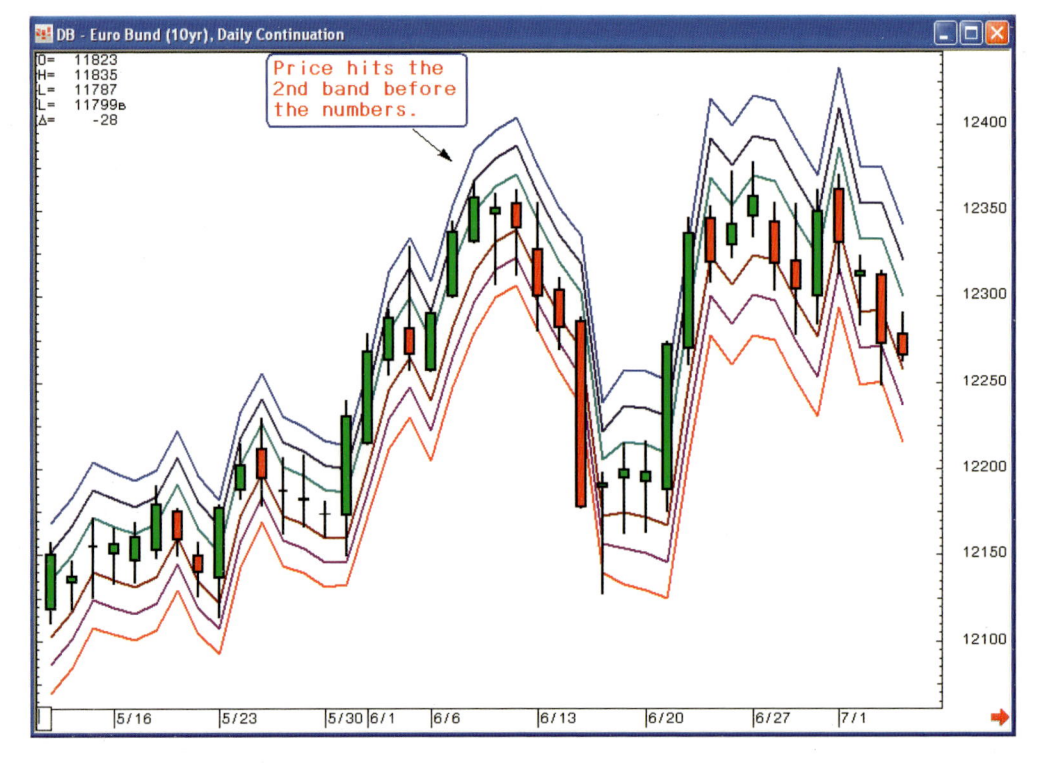

Peak

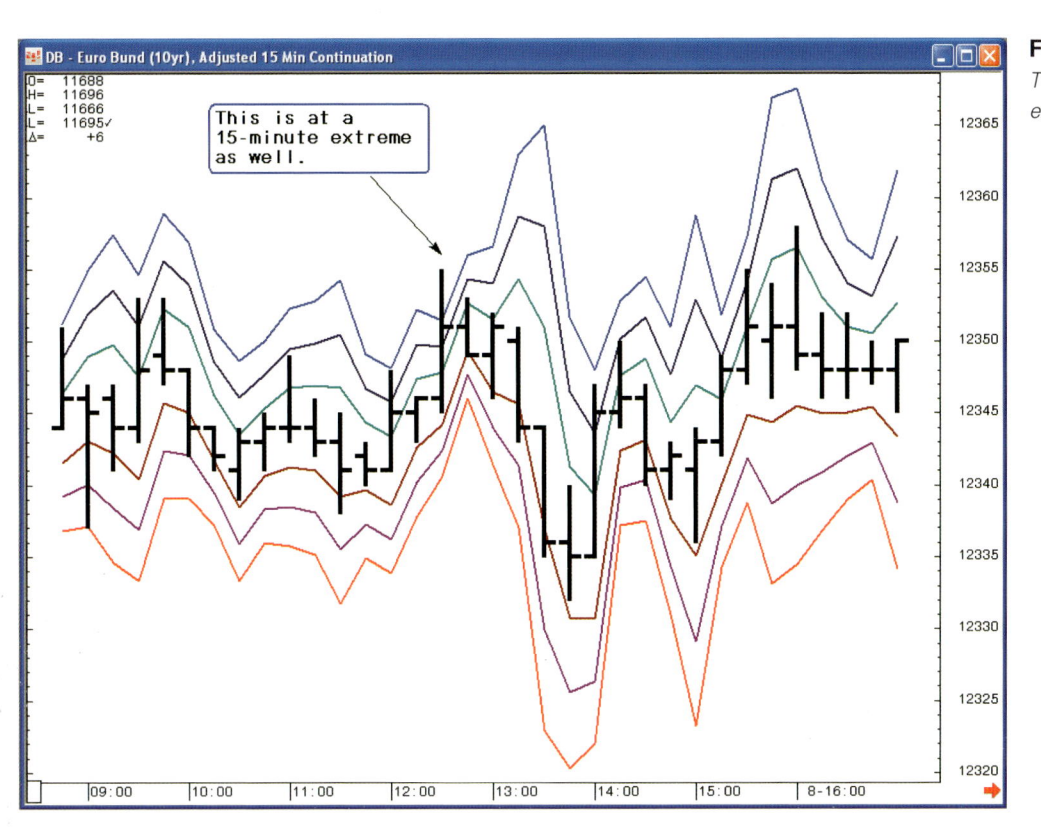

Figure 102:
The short-term extreme as well

Stocks and Some variations

On stocks the relative greater length of trends and the more sedate nature of the trend mean that the setting of a 5-bar peak is too sensitive. Therefore, the setting should be at least 7 bars to allow the trend to develop. The principles of Stochastic Steps remain valid, as do all the other concepts that use Hi Count and Lo Count. It is also possible to move up to a higher timeframe i.e. the weekly chart, as the slow nature of most trends will mean that Peak can maintain a position in a buy and hold strategy or a buy sell equity fund. (see fig. 103)

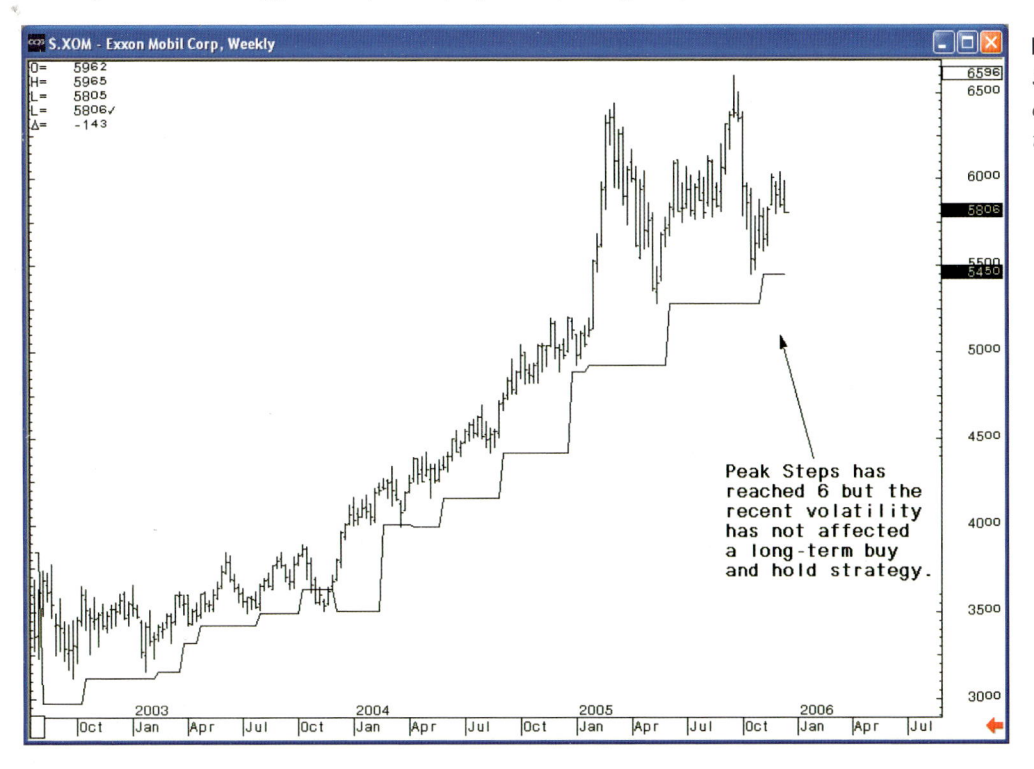

Figure 103:
Stocks have different thresholds

Connecting Stochastic and Peak Steps

Normally, on historical data, it is unlikely that Stochastic Steps will run in perfect tandem with Peak Steps. In the next chart (see fig. 104) showing Yahoo, the first part of the trend is signalled as strong via the Stochastic Step and Peak moves to 6 before correcting. In the second part of the trend Stochastic Steps enters a mega trend and Peak Steps moves to 8. Price has been above the Hi Peak for the requisite 6 bars and results are due the next day. With price overextended at least in the short term, this is a good point to book at least partial profits and reassess once the results are out.

Figure 104:
The trend is overextended and results are due

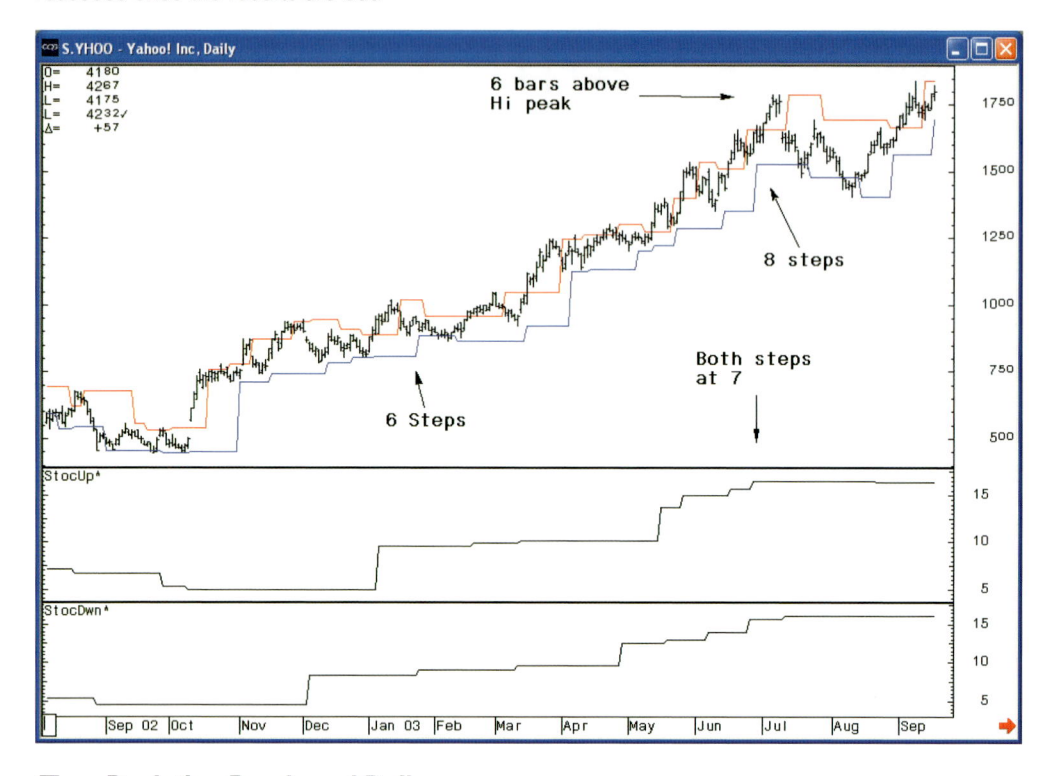

Time Deviation Bands and Dojis

Analysis of the Deviation bands shows that in spite of price reaching new highs the technical picture is actually weak. The day before the 6th day above Hi Peak was the first time that price had touched the 2nd standard deviation low in many weeks. There are also two Dojis (see fig. 105).

Figure 105:
Momentum wanes

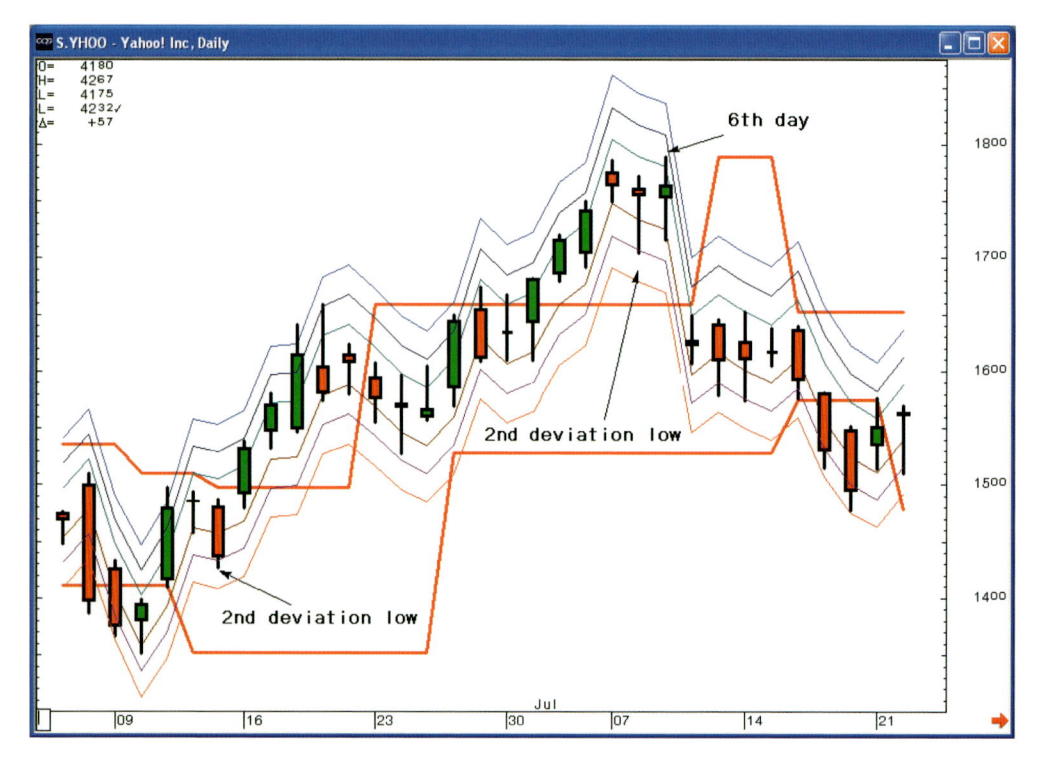

Forex - solving the trailing stop problem in a 24-hour market

Whilst Peak lends itself to almost any market or timeframe, FX markets pose a more pressing problem because they open for 24 hours a day and there are times, especially in Asia, where the lack of movement means that Peak levels change and often become very close to the current value. Therefore a good trade can often be stopped purely due to lack of movement. When I worked with Paolo Tarranta at Banca Intensa, this showed up as a perennial problem if we used Peak as a trailing stop in trading systems. Either the system had to use a wider Peak setting at night, or a higher timeframe, but neither solution was particularly satisfactory. Often it worked better if the Peak stop was simply not employed at night. Another question was whether moves in Asia should be ignored, subject to the currency pair. Often price will just drift slightly or pick off stops before the trend resumes once London opens. The Dollar Swiss chart (see fig. 106) shows an example of the problem. The Peak level creates a very tight stop, then does the same the following day, and this time creates premature exit.

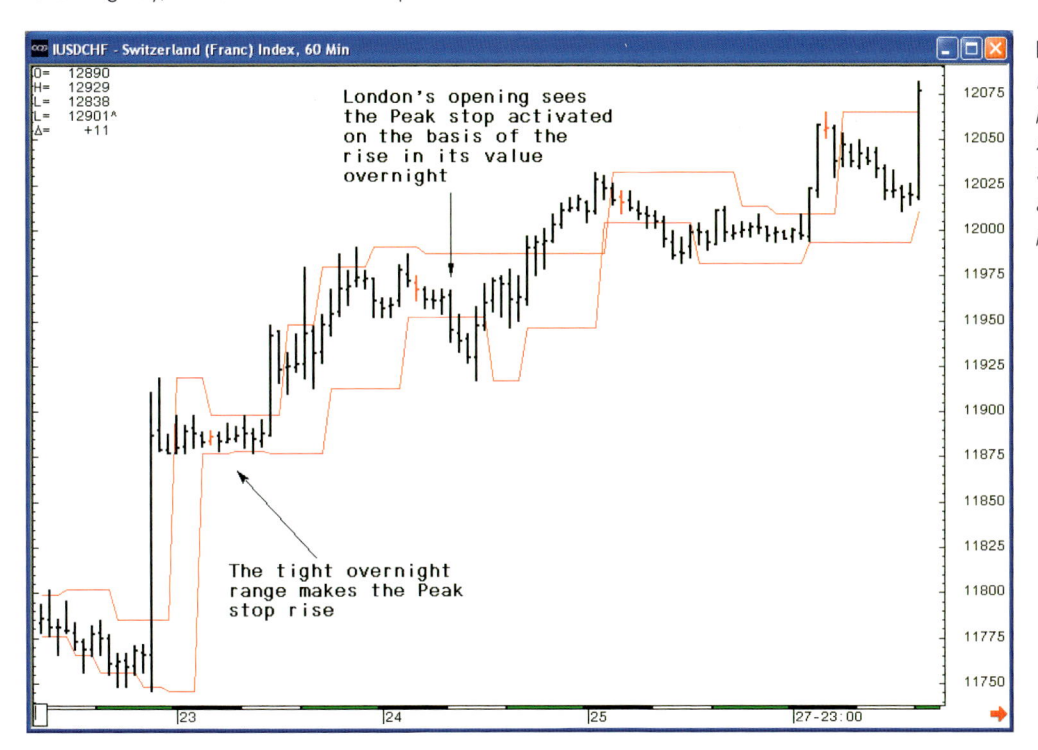

Figure 106:
Normal Peak has problems with a 24-hour market. Stops are activated in quiet periods

Peak Range

Various workarounds were contemplated, but we kept returning to the most obvious solution. This was to calculate a user-defined moving average of range (1000 periods in the examples that follow); if the current range is less than the average the Peak level will not move. Often this means that the trailing stop and step theories remain powerful.

An additional benefit that applies to all markets and timeframes is that it automatically prevents Peak levels changing just because a market is waiting for a specific news event and is unusually quiet ahead of the number coming out.

TRADING TIME: New Methods in Technical Analysis

The chart (see fig. 107) shows the Dollar Swiss, which is waiting for a Federal reserve meeting to declare its hands on interest rates. The market is moribund during the afternoon ahead of the number and the normal peak is breached. However, the lack of range means that the modified peak maintains a wider stop and then trails the rest of the trend once the announcement is out. On FX this method can be used every night but at other times and on other markets is reserved for the really important events, like trade deficits, unemployment numbers and interest rate announcements.

Figure 107:
Peak Range avoids stops being hit when markets are quiet

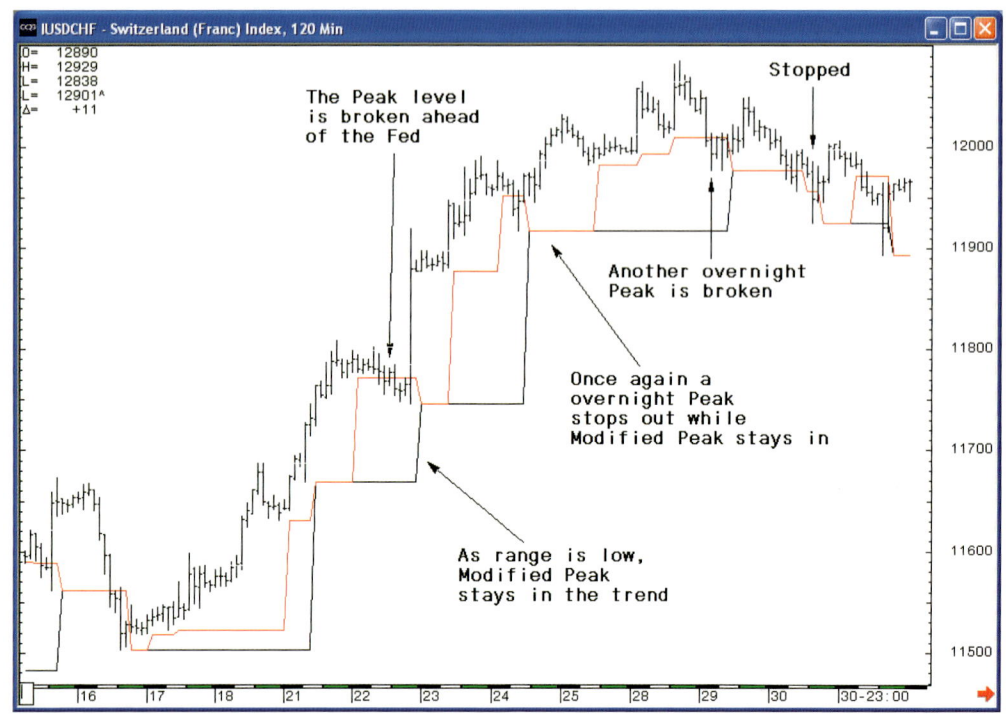

Cross rates and slow steady trends

This method also works well with a slow and steady trend. This is particularly useful for many of the cross rates where the trend may be of considerable length but never explosive. In these markets the concept of relative range can also be adjusted. The Aussie Yen chart (see fig. 108) uses a modified Peak that states that the Peak will only change if range is at least 1½ times the average of range. This greatly reduces the number of changes.

Figure 108:
Peak Range tracks the trend

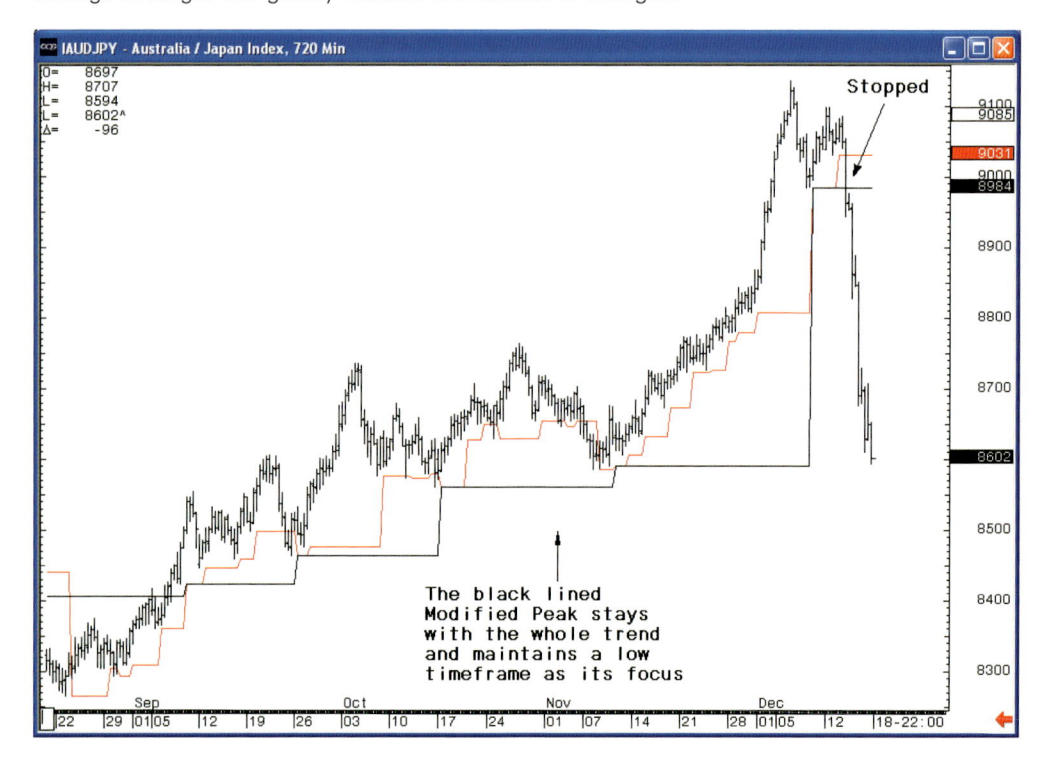

228

Stochastic Steps and Forex

It can also be linked to the times when the Stochastic Steps are beginning to get overextended in terms of the number of consecutive steps. The higher the timeframe, the more relevant this is as the chance of a focus timeframe moving up is greatly diminished.

The large Dollar Yen rally (see fig. 109) shows that Steps have reached 8 steps, and one of the steps has turned down showing a weakening trend. The Peak Steps have risen 6 times, which is also a high number. The Peak actually widens just before the trend finally ends.

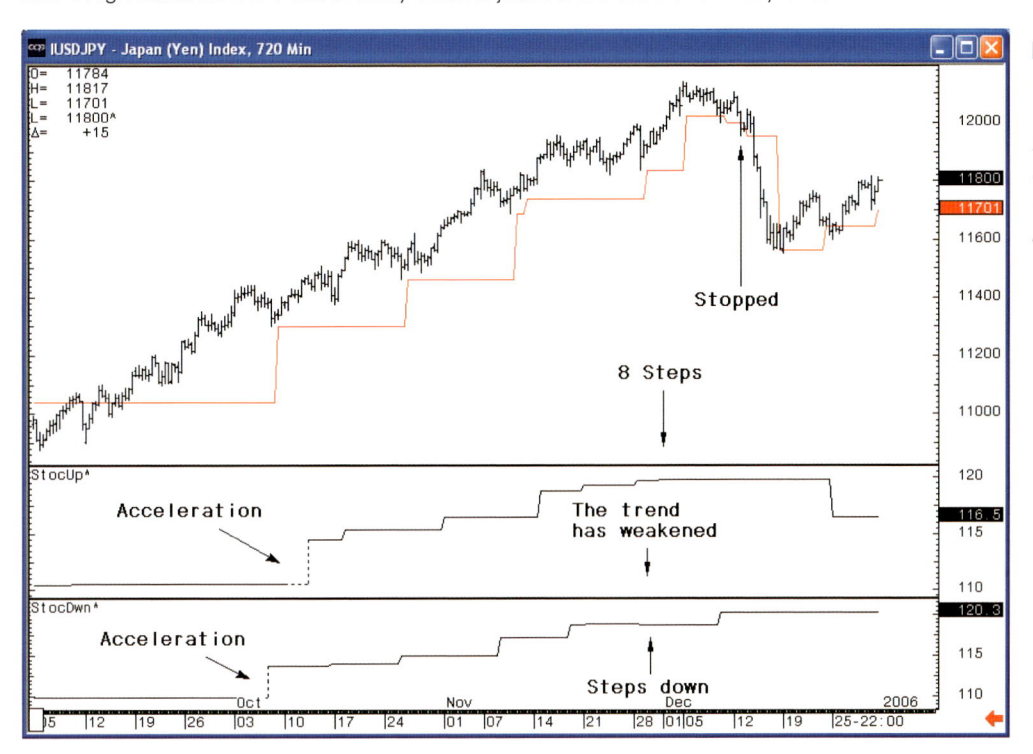

Figure 109:
The trend has weakened and is becoming overextended. Finally the stop is activated

OaR Volatility Time Average Bands

The OaR Volatility Time Average Bands show that through the entire rally no close took place beneath the 1st standard deviation down (see fig. 110). The high of the trend was marked by price failing at the 3rd standard deviation up. Finally, price closed below the 1st standard deviation down at the same time as the Peak level was breached.

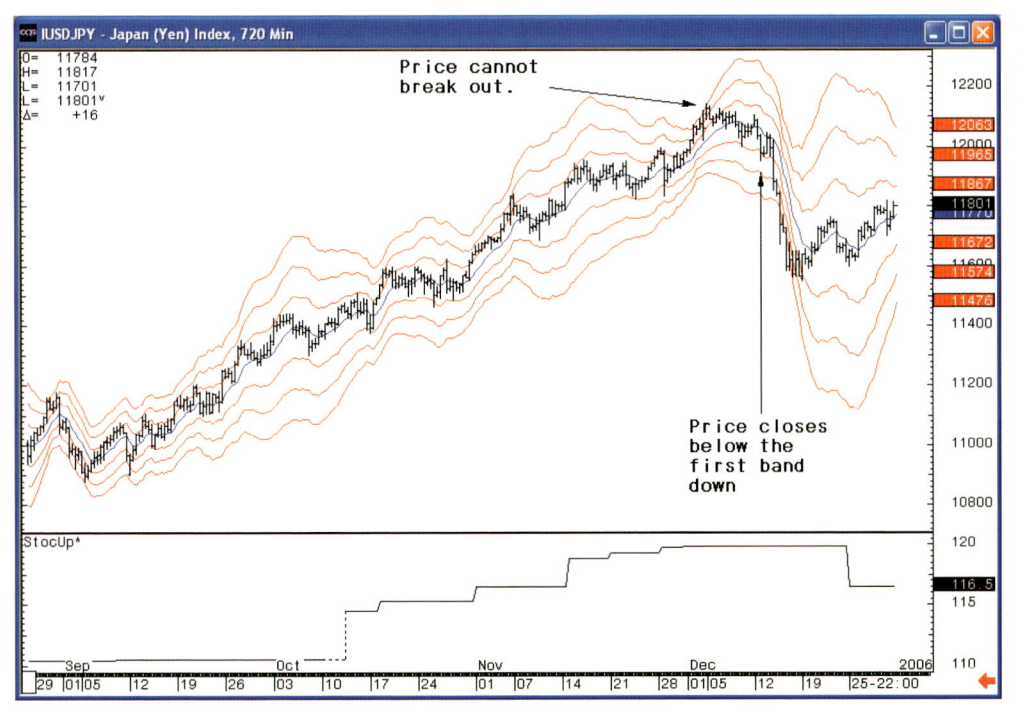

Figure 110:
Volatility Time Average Bands

How strong is the trend?

It also provides clues about exactly how strong the trend actually is if the multiplication of range is removed and just analysed over the 1000-period average of range. When both Peak values are identical, this shows a healthy trend because the current range is consistently above the average range. This is particularly true if corrections have been shallow or the number of bars between Peaks has been reasonably long.

The chart (see fig. 111) shows that, even though traditional indicators show an overbought market with multiple divergences, the trend is at its most powerful in the second half of the trend.

Figure 111:
Peak range tracks the trend

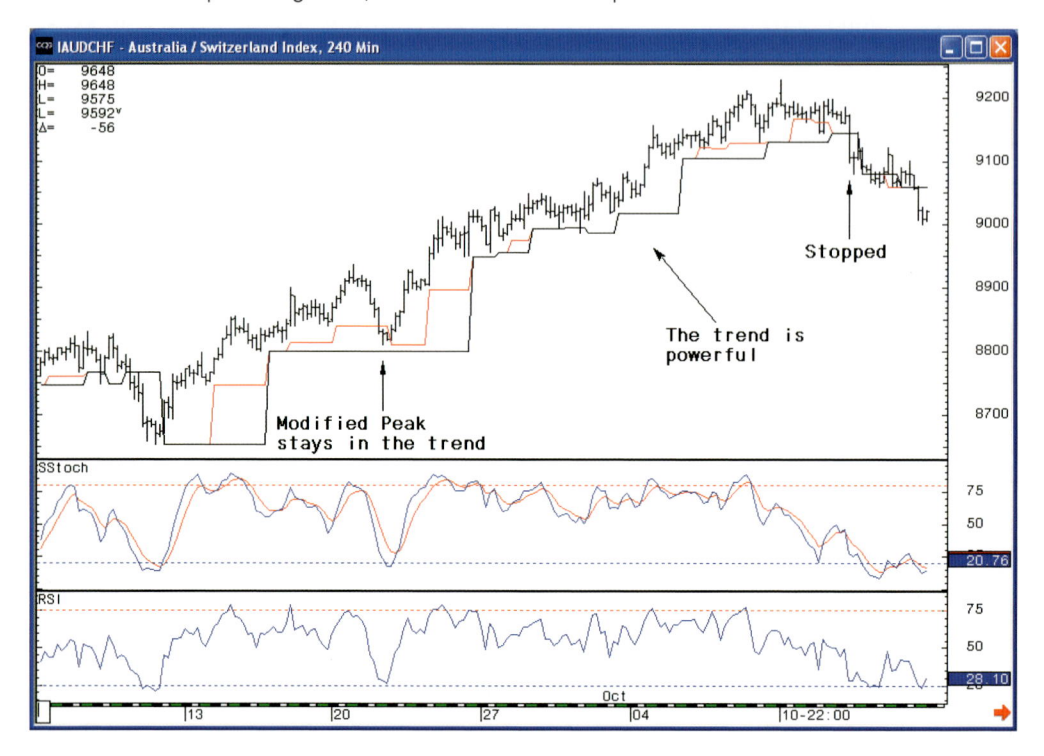

Peak Volume. A different way of defining swing patterns

In all of these examples the average of range has been used. A departure from this theory was to look at whether volume could provide an impact or insight into strength of trend. On the Bund market in particular the results are revealing. In this test the Peak levels will only change when volume is x number of times above the 100-period average of volume. This reveals a completely different dynamic.

Corrections to the trend have to be of high enough volume

The first theory looks at the volume that is associated with corrections against the trend. For a Peak level to shift the volume associated with it – it must be 1.25 times the 100 period average of volume. Typically, corrections to a trend should always be in lower volume to the trend itself. (Ken Shaleen's book 'Volume and Open Interest' remains a classic on this subject). This is by no means a magic ratio and is used just to explain the concept. If corrections to the trend are in low volume the Peak level will remain unchanged. Conversely, if the Peak level does shift, this means that there is a concerted move by traders against the trend, which means that more fuel is being used by the trend followers. Therefore a change in Peak when a trend is established reveals more information than if we just use a Peak-based on range or price action alone.

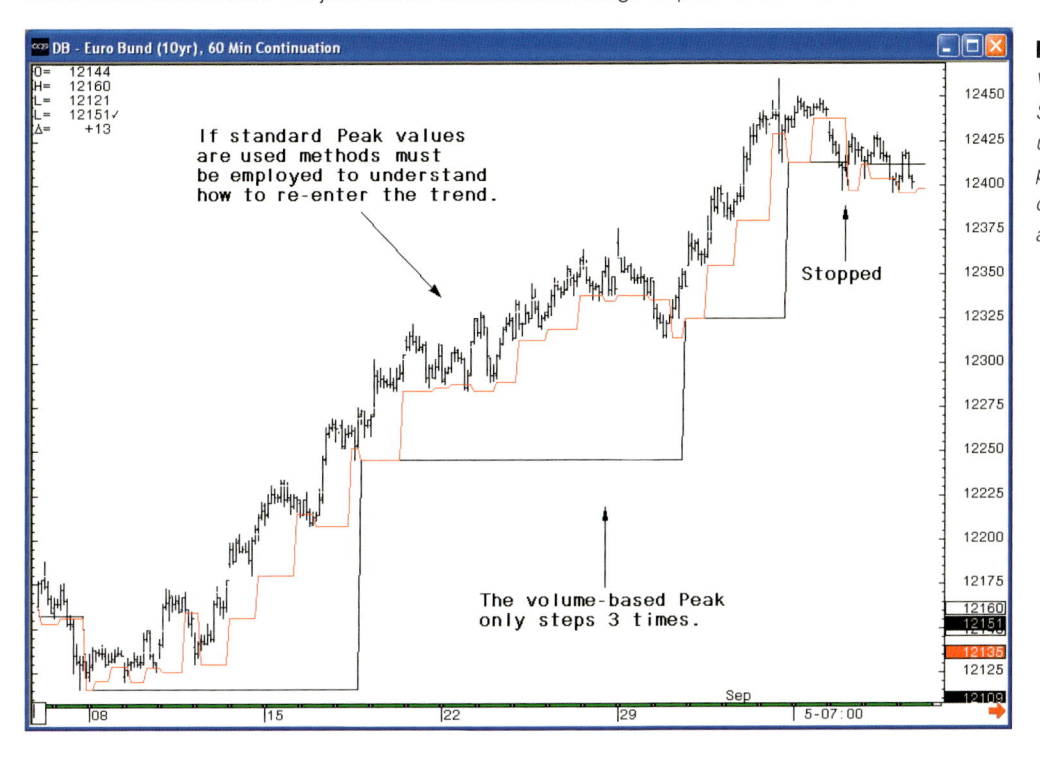

Figure 112:
Volume-based Steps can be used by strategic players as changes in value are rare

Trends begin

The next example shows a trend which begins with no corrections in high volume (as no one knows it's a new trend) before volume suddenly does rise and the trend dies.

Figure 113:
If volume increases on corrections, energy is being expended to keep the trend going

Acceleration

The next chart shows acceleration at the beginning and the end of the trend. The beginnings of trends should not see volume-based Peak levels as that implies that fuel is being used to maintain the trend. When a trend begins few players have engaged, so less volume should be needed to move price directionally.

Figure 114:
Cycles can be linked to the stop

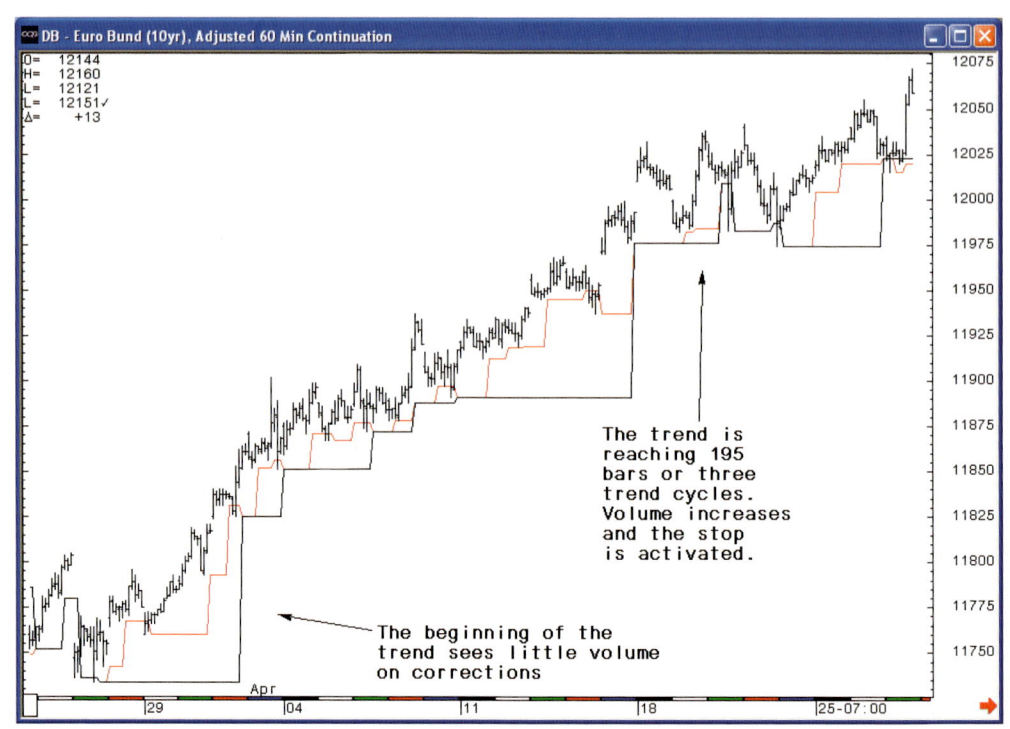

[Chart: DB - Euro Bund (10yr), Adjusted 60 Min Continuation. Annotations: "The trend is reaching 195 bars or three trend cycles. Volume increases and the stop is activated." and "The beginning of the trend sees little volume on corrections"]

Figure 115:
The theory is valid for all markets. This is crude oil.

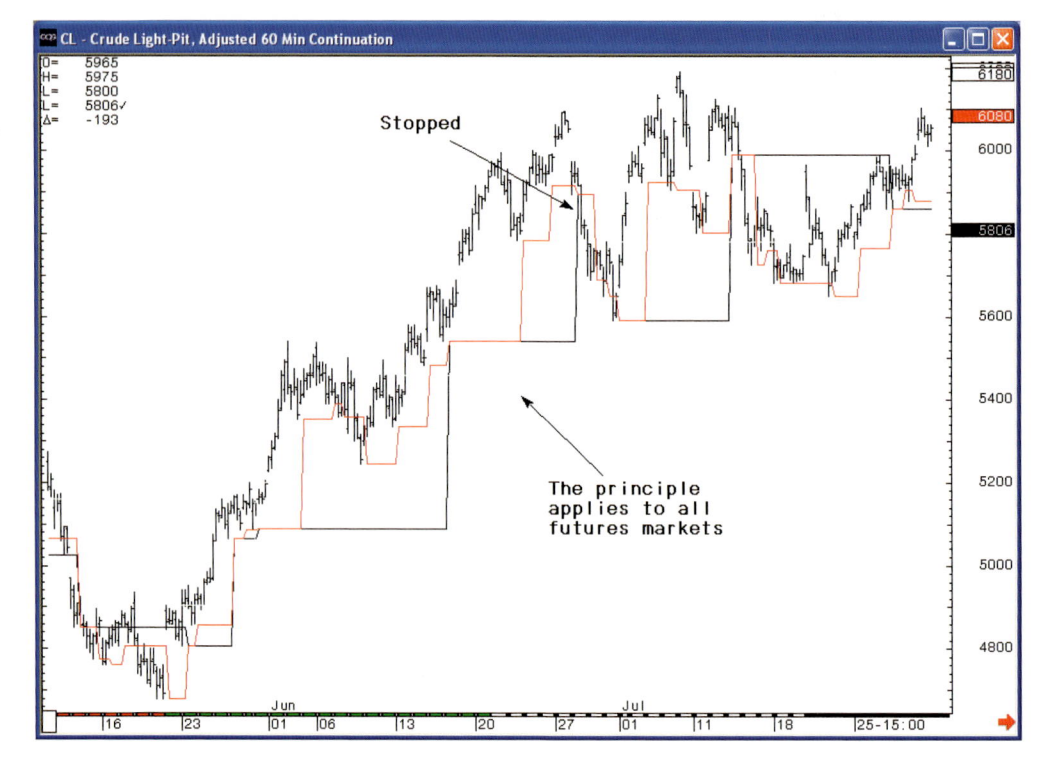

[Chart: CL - Crude Light-Pit, Adjusted 60 Min Continuation. Annotations: "Stopped" and "The principle applies to all futures markets"]

Changing boundaries in limits of participation

Sugar is an example where the previous boundaries of open interest and volume have shifted as funds increase their involvement in commodities. Here Peak values are matching even though it is now set at 1½ times normal volume. If this continues the study will adapt to the consistently higher volume and maintain its dynamic nature.

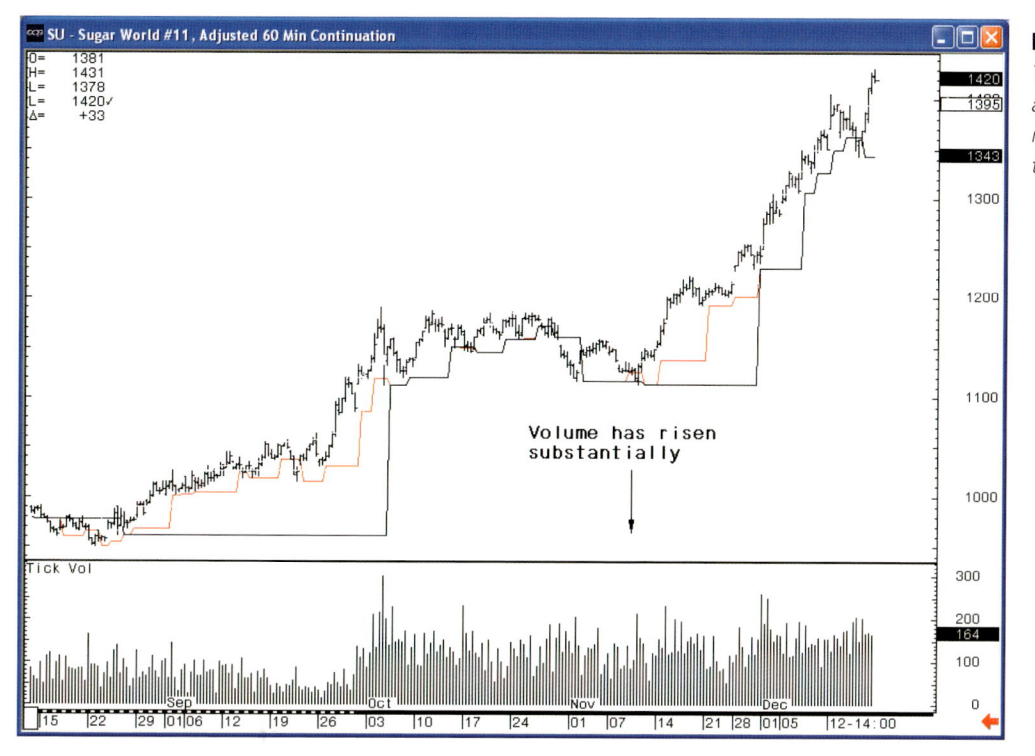

Figure 116:
The boundaries are changing as more people trade

Volume flagging trend endings

The following chart (see fig. 116) shows how, even if the study is not employed as a trailing stop, it tells you so much about the trend and provides great insight into the need to stay with it, especially if the multiplication factor is raised to 1½ times or above. Whilst many would have been trying to pick tops this study told you to avoid making that mistake, as little volume was being required to end corrections. All three tops saw volume suddenly increase and the stop was activated.

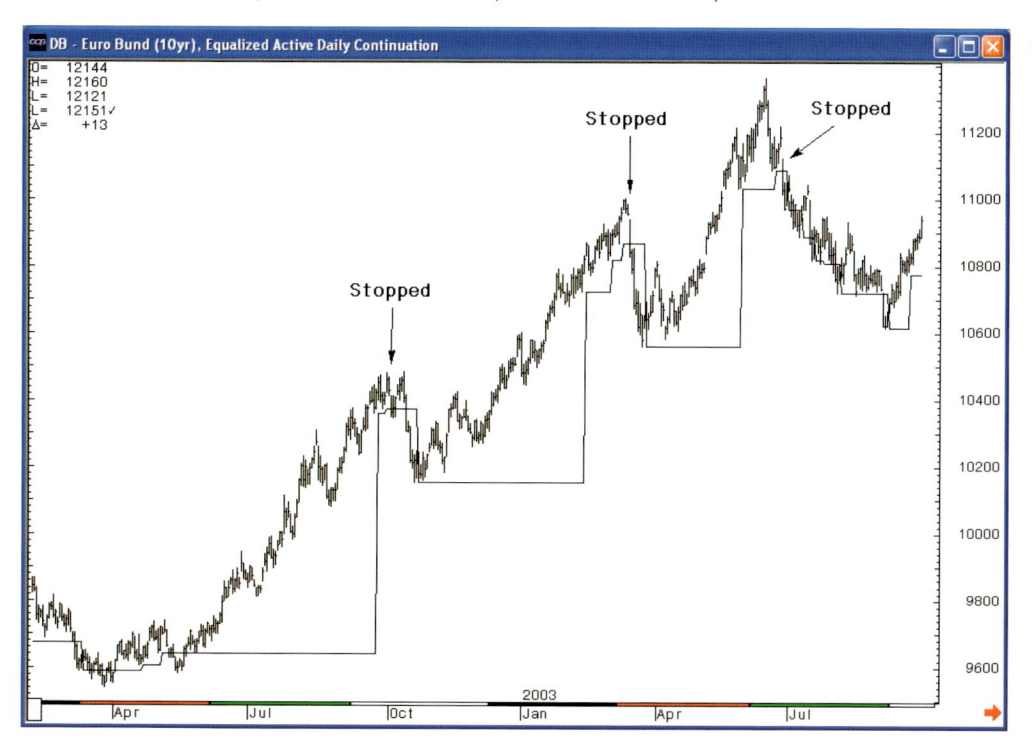

Figure 117:
Volume marks trend endings

Stocks

This theory also has use in individual stocks. Again the ratios can be experimented with to suit your concepts of risk. Here (see fig. 118) the huge and prolonged slump in Yahoo was finally ended when volume began to appear at the Peaks near the lows. This highlighted the first instance where true buying power was emerging.

Figure 118:
Volume marks the end of the trend in Yahoo

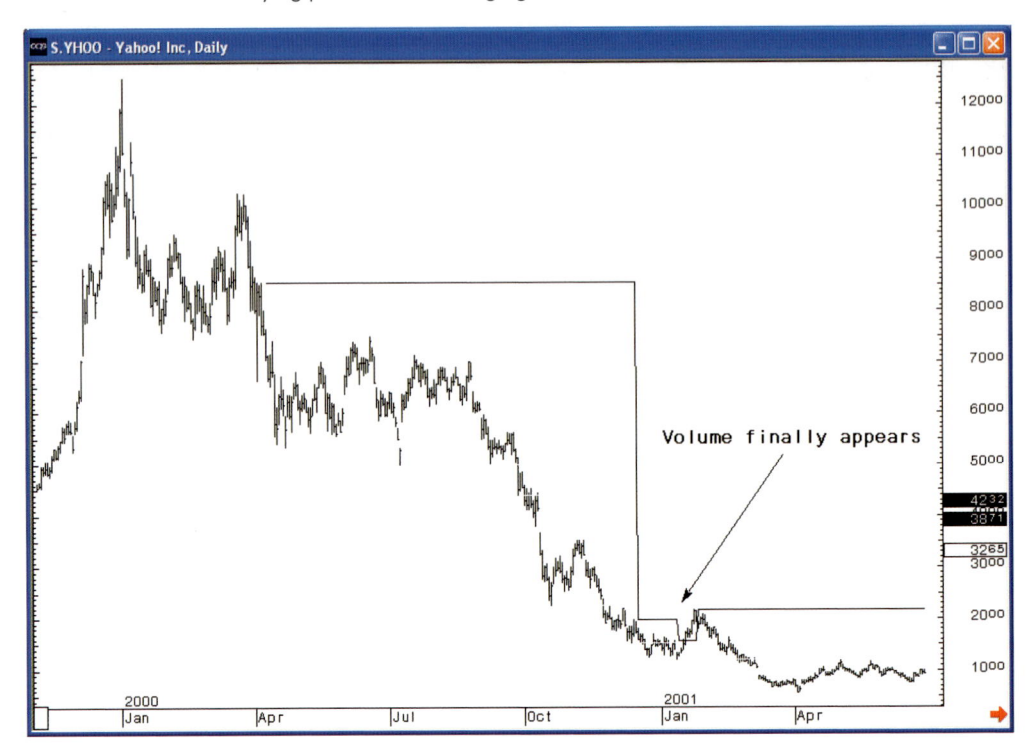

The principle that new trends in stocks have little change in Peak values as volume is low is highlighted by Amazon.

Figure 119:
Nobody knows there is a new trend so the stop does not change

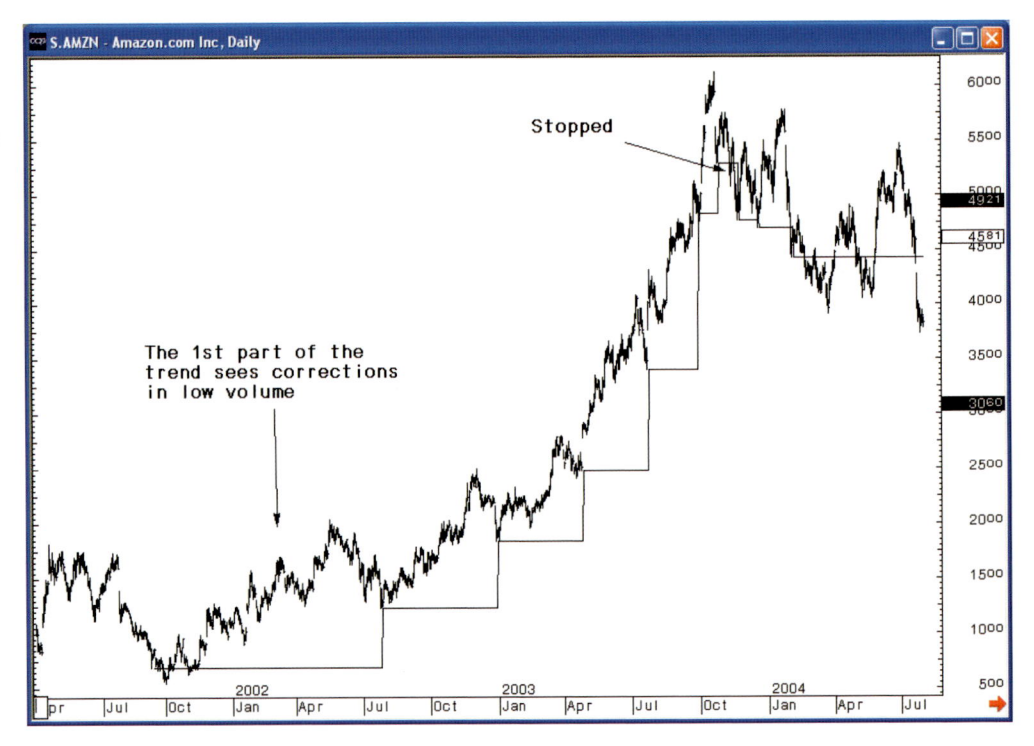

RSI Step Divergence and Peak Volume

Finally, if we return to the concepts of divergence mentioned in the RSI section, we see that the appearance of volume in a downtrend can be used to quantify whether a divergence has more chance of success. The eBay chart (see fig. 120) shows that volume is suddenly appearing near the lows with the drop in the Peak value. Shortly afterwards the RSI divergence appears.

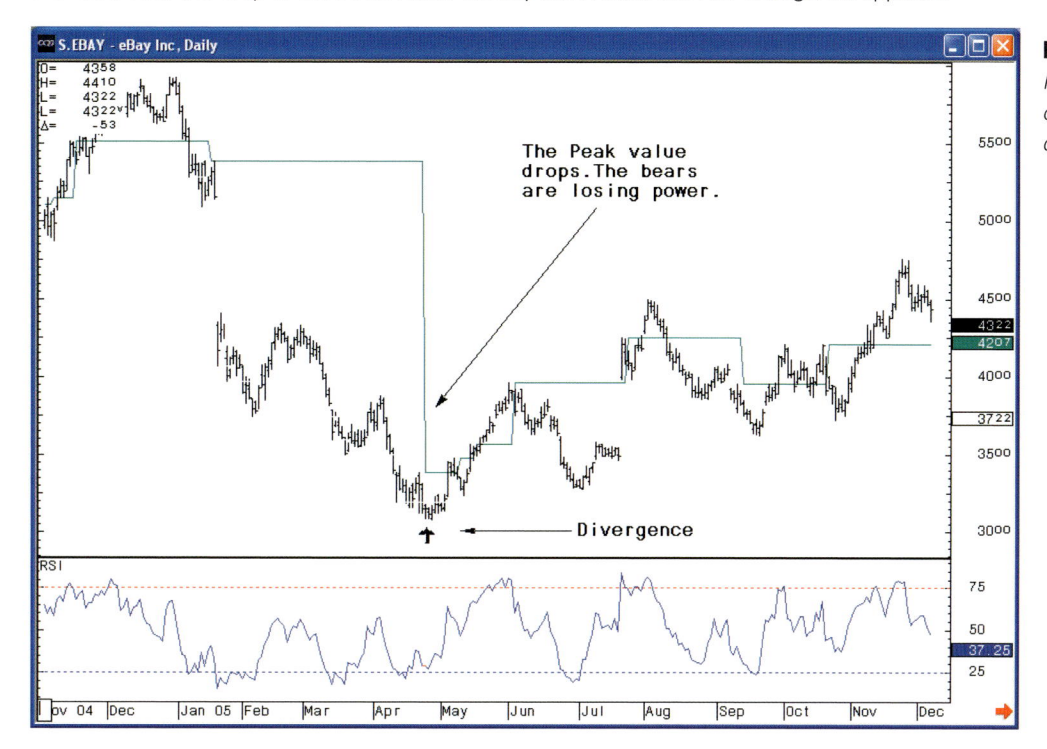

Figure 120: *Peak Volume connects with divergence*

Conclusion

It can be seen that with a very basic tool a huge amount of information can be obtained. It enables a stop to be trailed and has an advantage over momentum indicators in that they reference pure price action. Greater depth of understanding can then be achieved by adding the concepts of range and volume. So far as the Peaks associated with volume is concerned, my work is not completed but the initial findings look promising.

Key elements
- **True measurements of overbought and oversold provide an important support structure to all analysis.**
- **Time-based studies link with those concepts.**
- **Peak shows exhaustion, acceleration and trail stops.**
- **Linking range and volume provides a fresh dimension to swing theory.**
- **Peak helps provide a bias to daily distributions.**

Final Note

If you've made it this far, then you're either serious about trading or a glutton for punishment. I hope all of you who have got this far have found some nuggets of information that will make you more profitable in trading. At the very least, I hope I've provided some food for thought. I can be contacted via the OaR, CQG or Ransquawk website. Commentaries on over forty markets are available on a daily or weekly basis. In the summer of 2007 there will be streaming video that will both educate and analyse. This will be under the banner of the Oasis owned TraderTv.

Happy trading!

Appendix

Chapter 1

Tradeflow theory has moved on considerably since the book was written, as Cqg has made significant enhancements in terms of its functionality, and as this has evolved, more studies have been applied to it.

One of the key changes has been the ability to aggregate the number of bid/asks, so that one TradeFlow bar can represent up to 20 changes in quote. This is particularly applicable to markets such as the S&P and the Dax where the number of updates continue to rise, and is also useful on Interest Rate markets and FX futures, especially after economic numbers, when activity increases.

This means that the level of aggregation can change throughout the day. This can be done by monitoring how long a bar takes to build or can be fixed by analysis of the volume associated with a series of bars. Alternatively, a less scientific method is simply to shift based on the time of day. This would mean a high aggregation on the opening and lower one as the morning develops. It would then move back up once America opens.

The real power of TradeFlow is also evident when quantifying M.Profile based levels as the aggregation does a better job of confirming levels validity. The daily commentaries often show examples of how the synergies what is used in Chapter 1 connects with Profile and provides almost the entire framework of how markets are analyzed.

Figure 1
A 20 period TradeFlow is essential for a market like the Dax where the number of updates is so high.

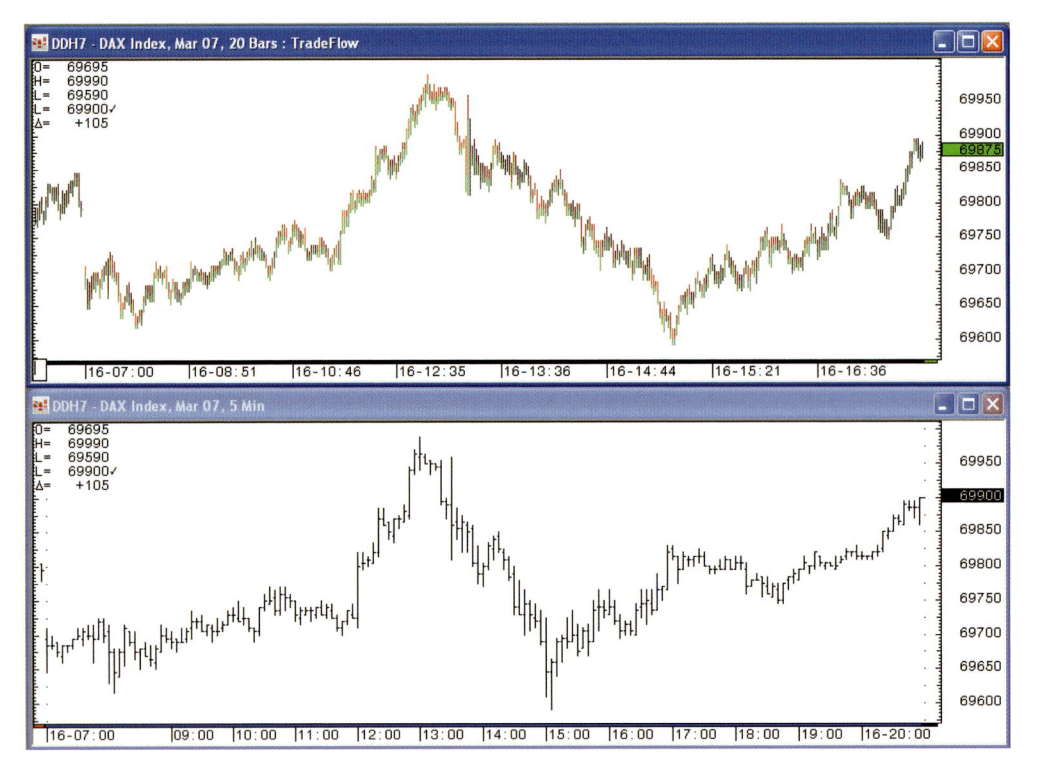

Appendix

The aggregation of bars means that it is now far easier to understand whether buyers or sellers are dominant. This is done buying building a running sum of the bids hit and the asks taken. The number of bars to be calculated over is down to the user but I like to use a relatively high number, so that a trend can be identified. There are many relationships and patterns that can be identified, but one of the more simplistic is the theory that in an uptrend more asks will be taken than bid hit.

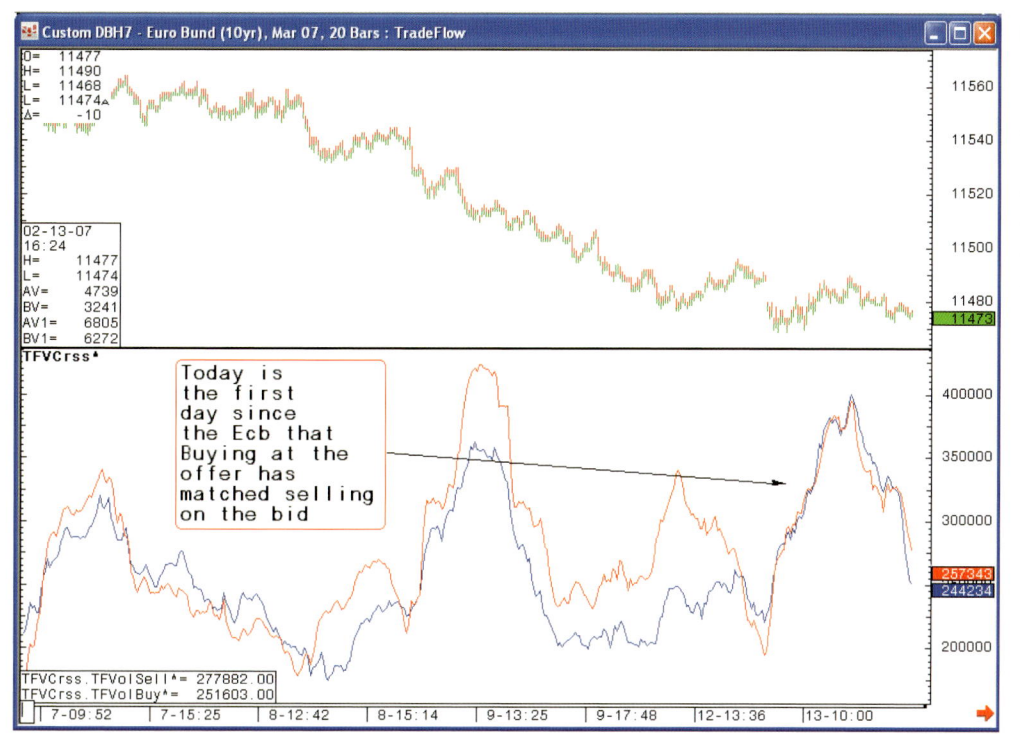

Figure 2
The blue line is the asks taken and the red line the bids hit. A 60 period average shows how the shift in power ebbs and flows.

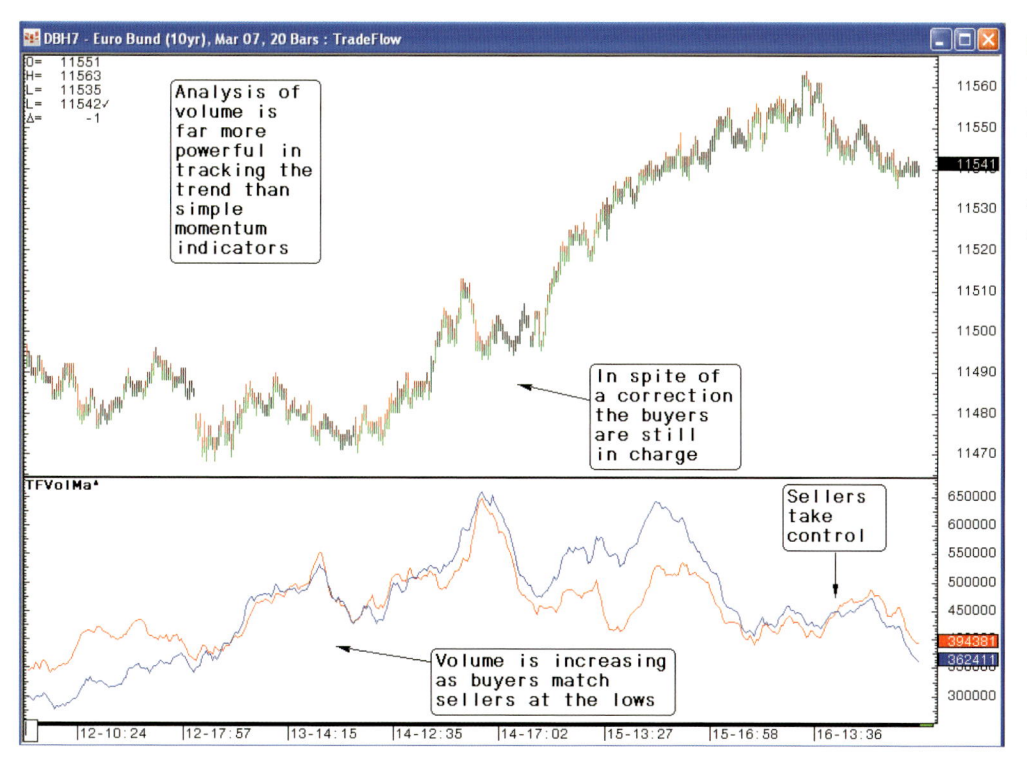

Figure 3
Once buyers match sellers, the following day sees the buyers re-assert authority.

The next pattern highlights how it not just increased volume at bid and asks that dictates direction, but also the simple withdrawal of buyers or sellers. After a strong downtrend hitting of the bid collapses and then the market moves consolidates before rallying.

Figure 4
Sellers refuse to sell the bid.

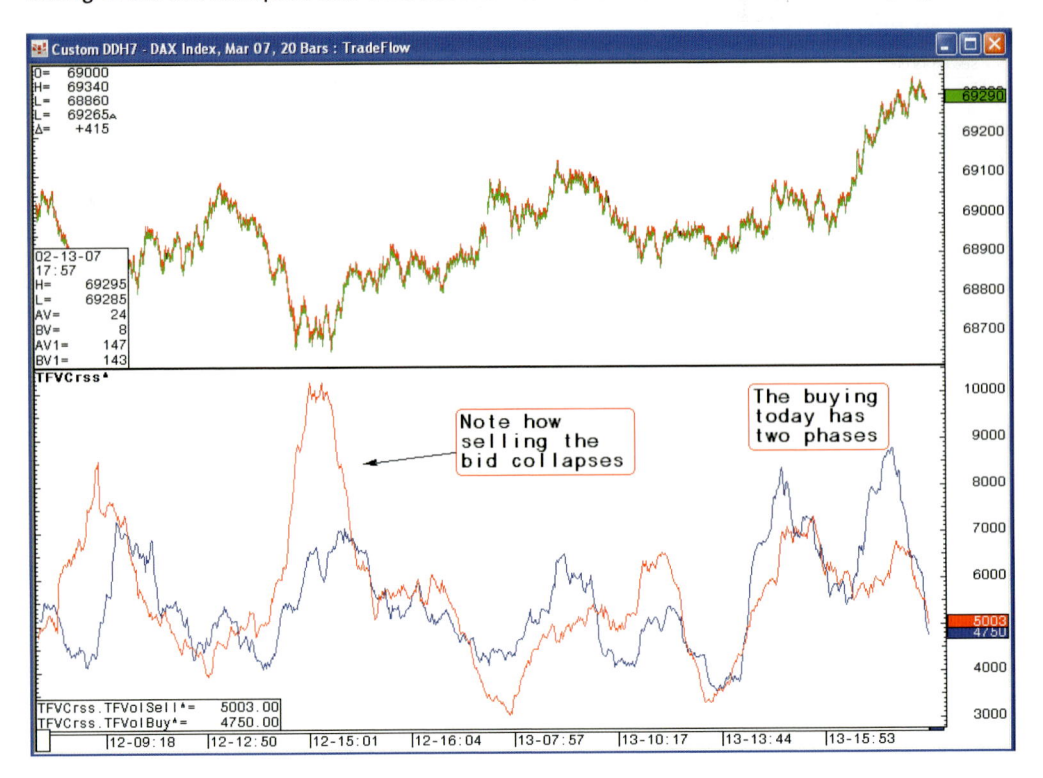

Range Deviation Pivots

The main body of the book concentrated more on the Volatility Time Bands as many of the theories or limits of daily range and definition of the trend had duplication with the Range Deviation Pivots. Instead, concentration was placed on patterns and probabilities. In order to not have a book full of tables some of the more rare patterns were left out although there is room here to look at concepts of limits of movement within a short time span. This is focused on the how many days consecutive price action can breach the 3rd Deviation in either direction on an intraday basis or on a closing basis. The tests reveal critical information with regard to what can expected on the day after certain patterns and what is the probability of extremes being tested yet again.

The first set of tables look at how many times price can close beyond the 3rd Pivot on consecutive days. It's important to remember that we are not concentrating degrees of accuracy but the number of times and therefore the probability of certain patterns occurring. The first two tables close look at price closing beyond the 3rd Pivot two days running. Two portfolios are taken, 1 being 400 stocks in the S&P and the second a selection of 22 futures and major currencies that cover Index's, Bonds, Grains and Precious metals. The tests are done over the last 5 years so represent 1250 bars per instrument which computes to over 500,000 days in stocks and 27,500 on the futures.

What becomes clear is the rarity of how often extremes are actually reached. The first table on the S&P looks at 2 consecutive closes beyond the 3rd pivot. In 500,000 days this happens just over 1500 times which is just one every 320 trading days. The second table has the same pattern on the futures portfolio and here in 27,500 days there are just 90 trades which is a ratio of once every 305 days.

What is also clear is that once this has happened the trend will often go on a short term reaction.

Appendix

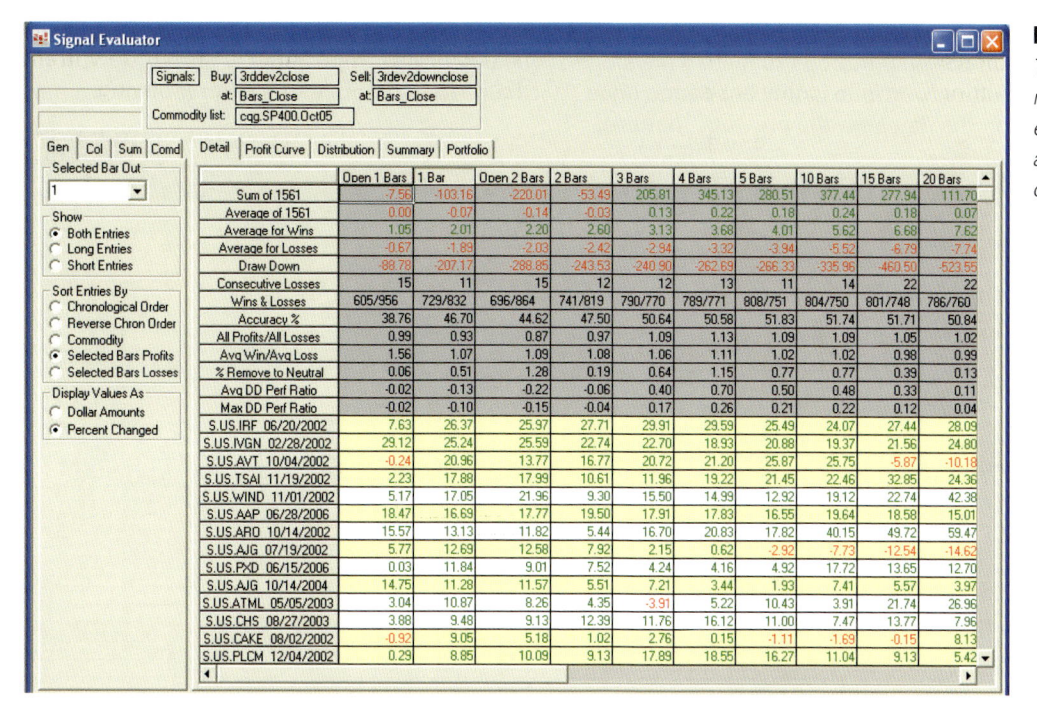

Figure 5
The S&P shows reaction is likely early on and the absolute number of trades is low

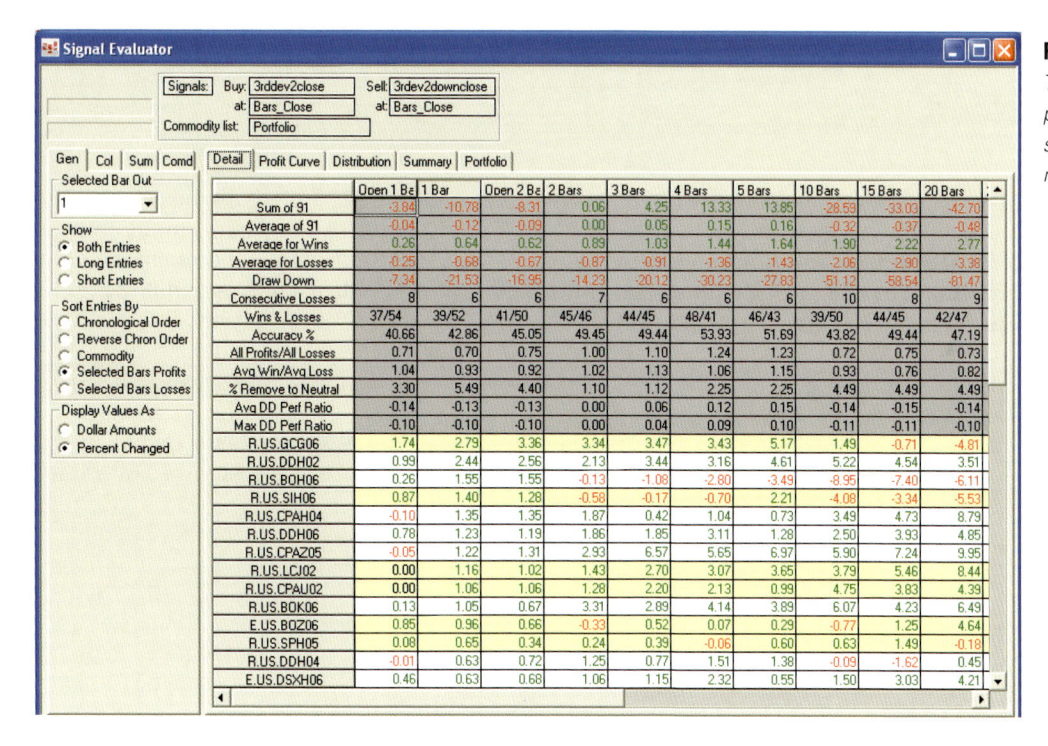

Figure 6
The futures portfolio has similar ratios and results.

239

The next table reveals how rare the price closes beyond the 3rd pivot three days running. On the S&P it drops to just 75 days out of 500,000 or just once in every 6600 days. On the futures portfolio it only happened once. This helps to understand the short term movement on the day after the previous pattern.

Figure 7
The signals are extremely rare

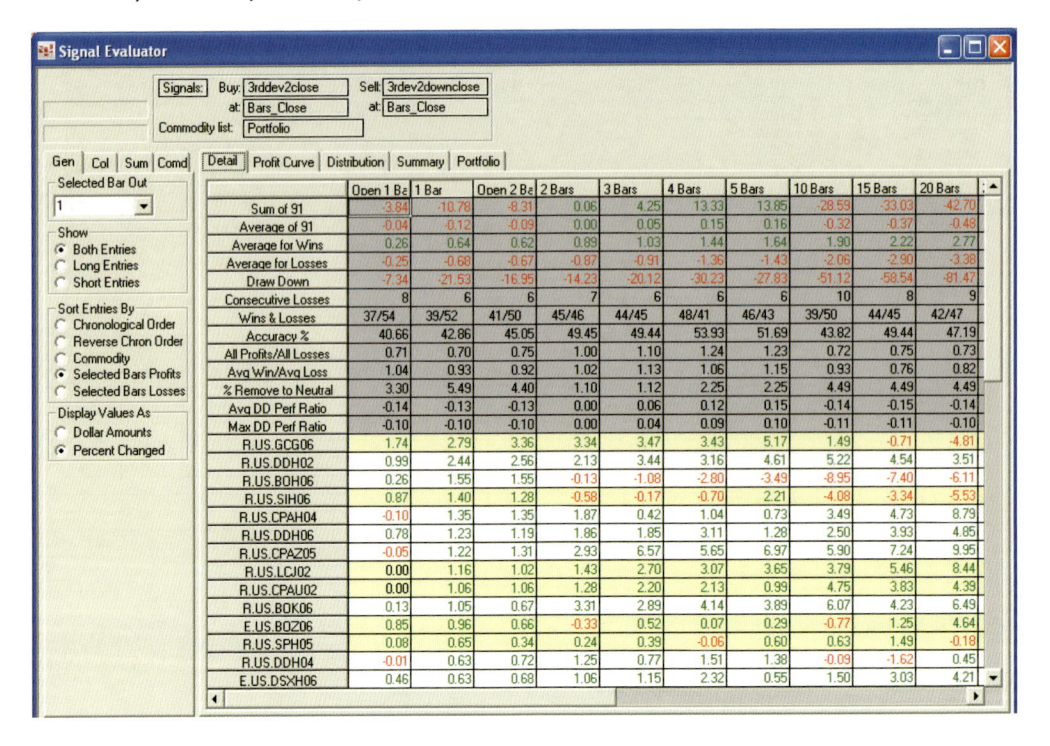

The next test is to look at how often price simply reaches the 2nd pivot on the 3rd day. This will provide insight into whether this area consistently provides any opportunity in short term trading, considering how rare it is close beyond the 3rd. This shows a far higher proportion of trades at 360 times. This means that there is only a 1 in 6 probability of price moves to the second pivot that it will close beyond the 3rd.

Figure 8
The portfolio shows 6 times as many trades.

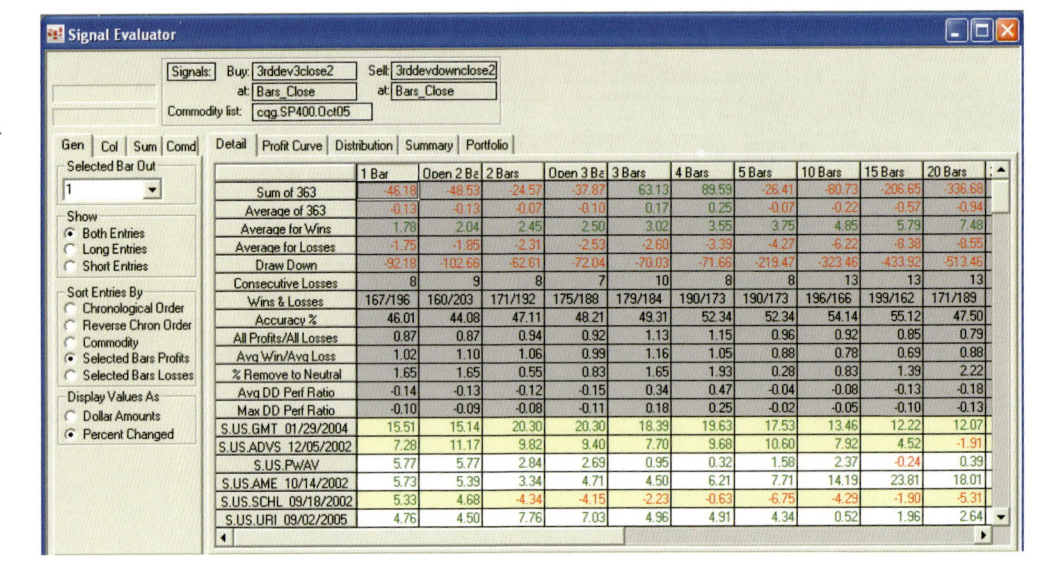

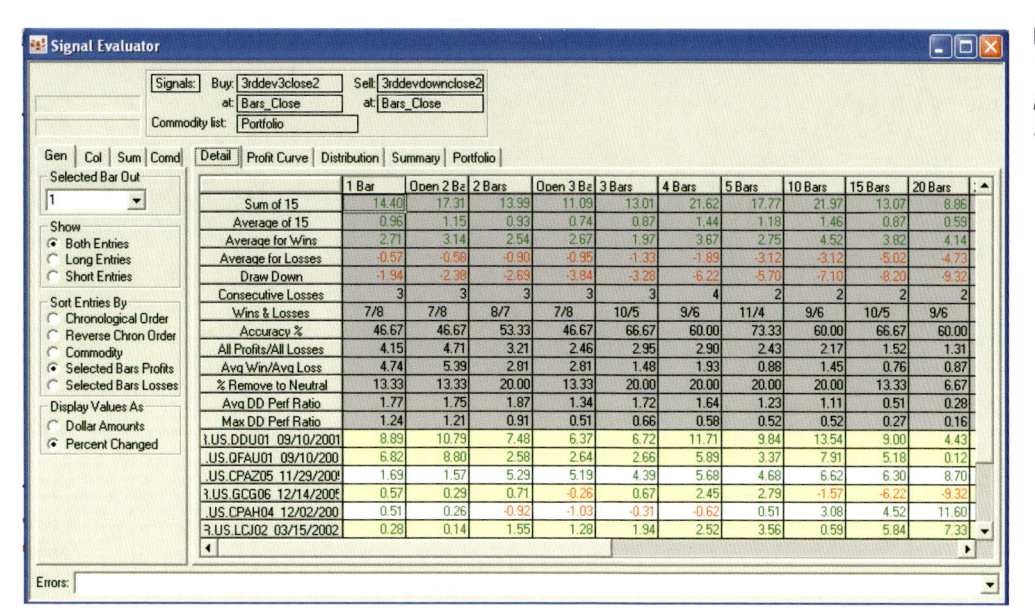

Figure 9.
The futures portfolio shows similar pattern

Chapter 3
Stochastic Steps

This chapter concentrated on what was the correct timeframe to be trading. Some of those trends, especially in Index's have continued and so this section gives a brief update on where we are in February 2007. It also looks at grains which have begun a trend.

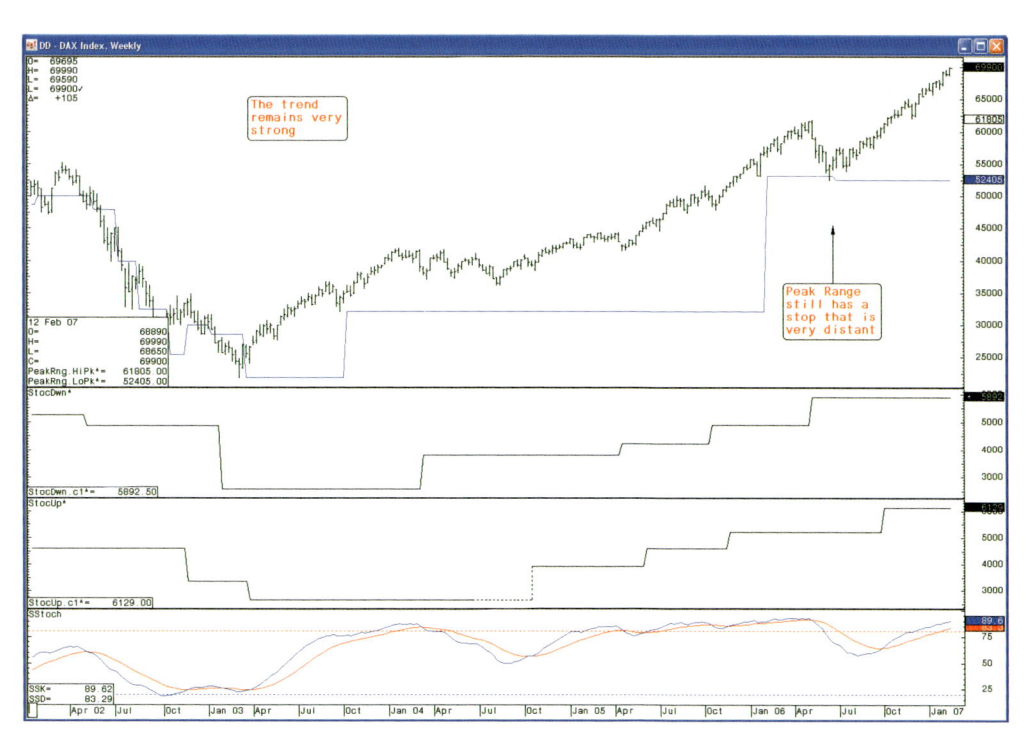

Figure 10
The trend in the Dax is still strong.

Figure 11
The Ftse is very strong as well

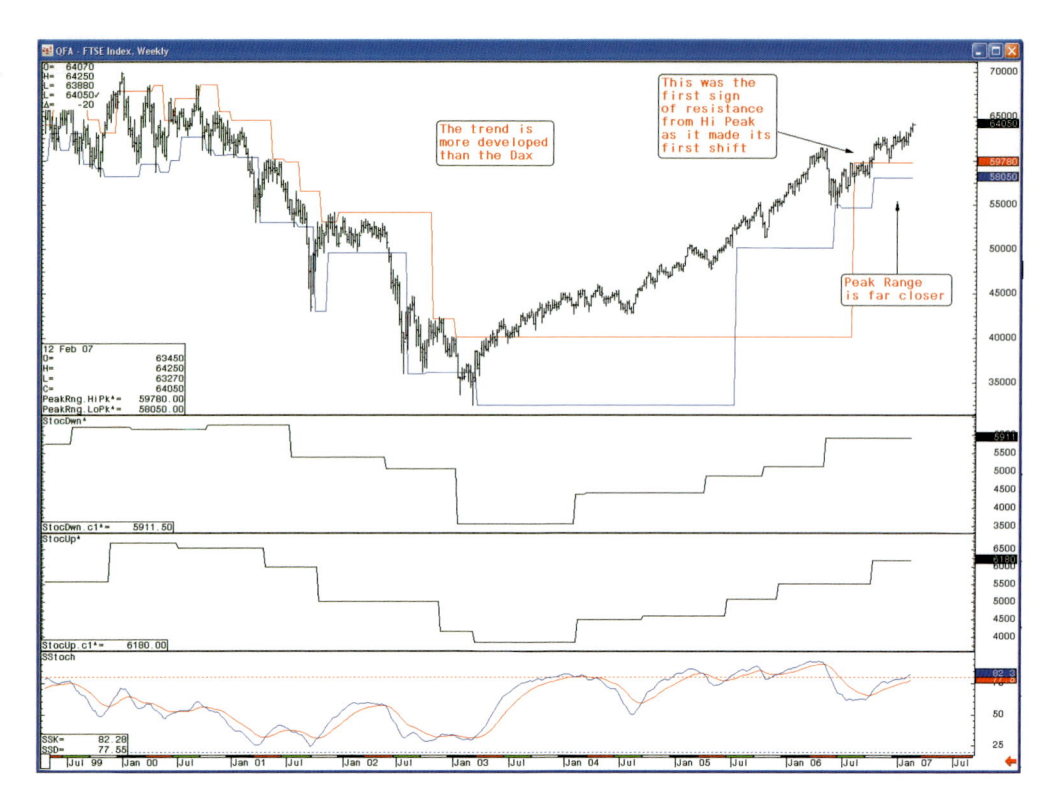

Figure 12
The Australian market is the most developed of all.

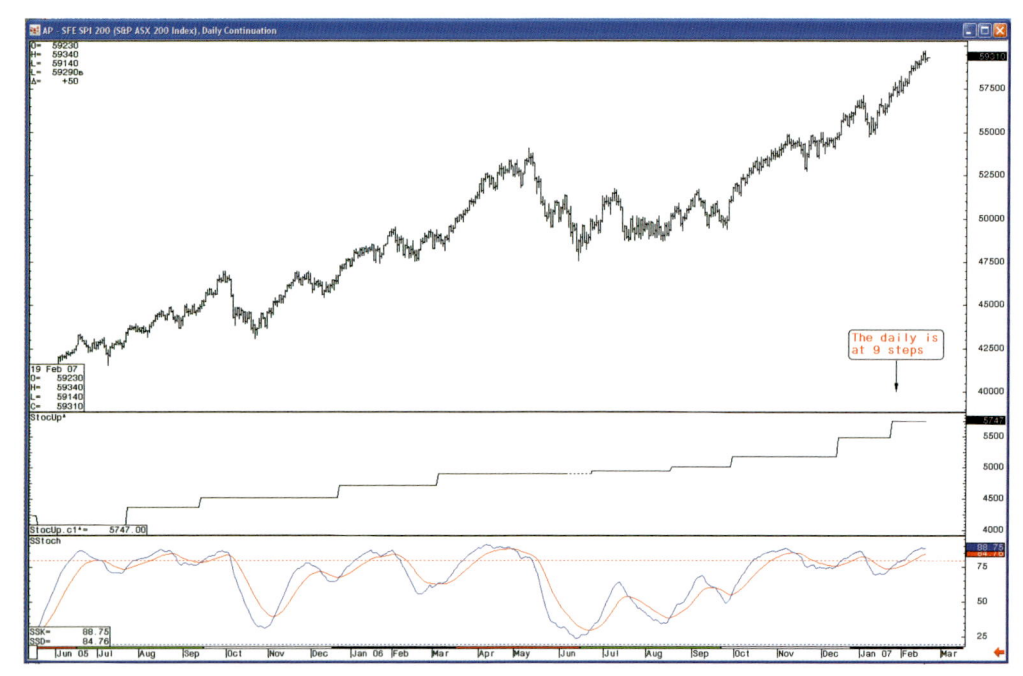

Appendix

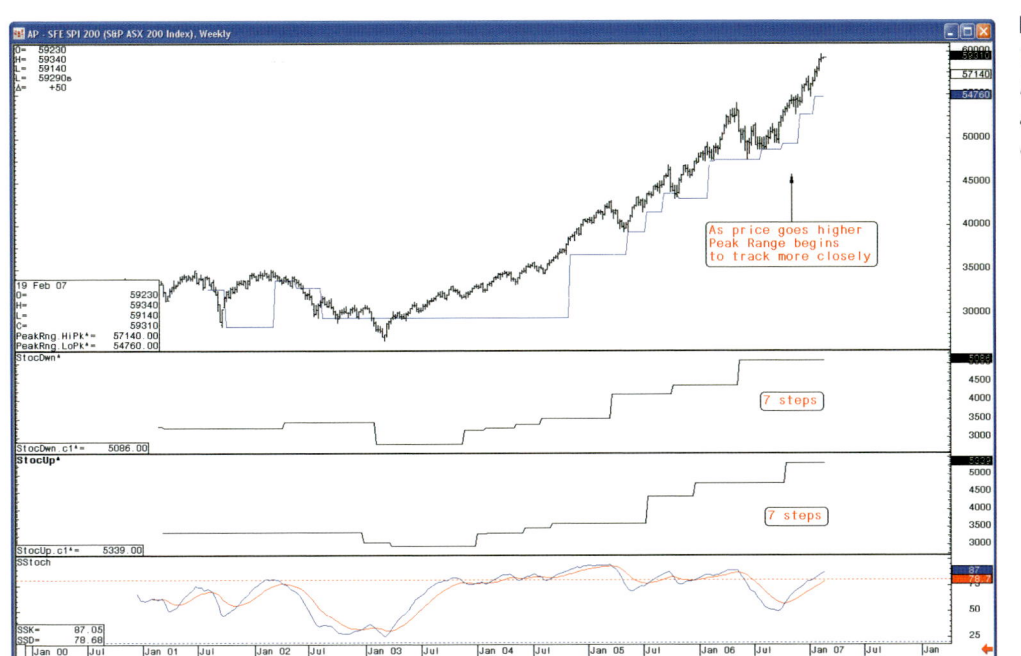

Figure 13
The weekly chart is fully developed and still positive on both steps

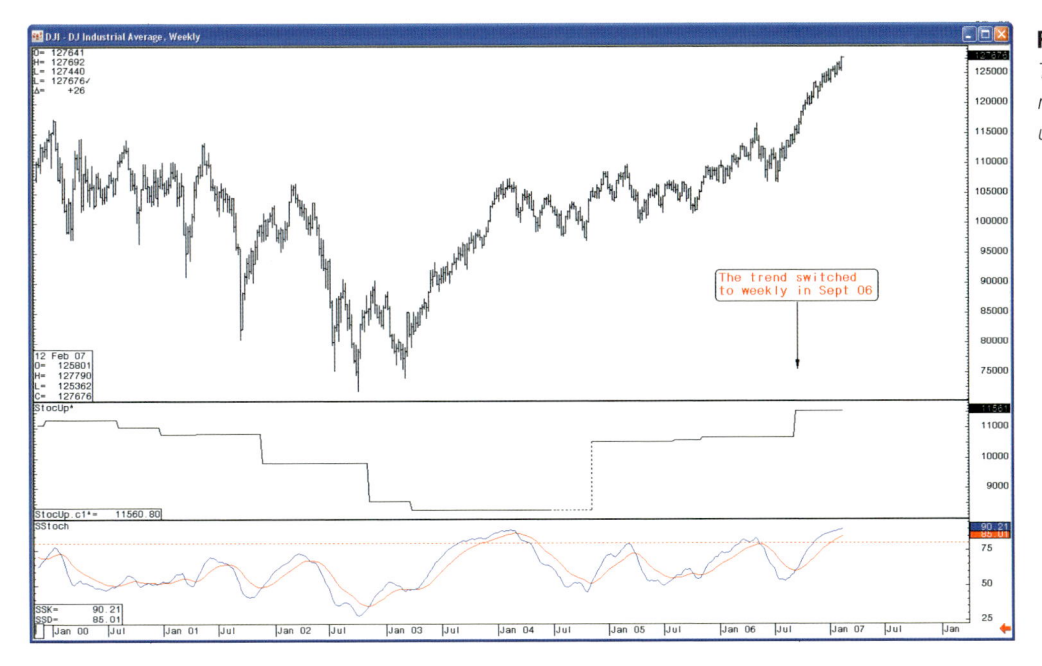

Figure 14
The Dow recently shifted up a timeframe

TRADING TIME: New Methods in Technical Analysis

Figure 15
Gold is fully matured

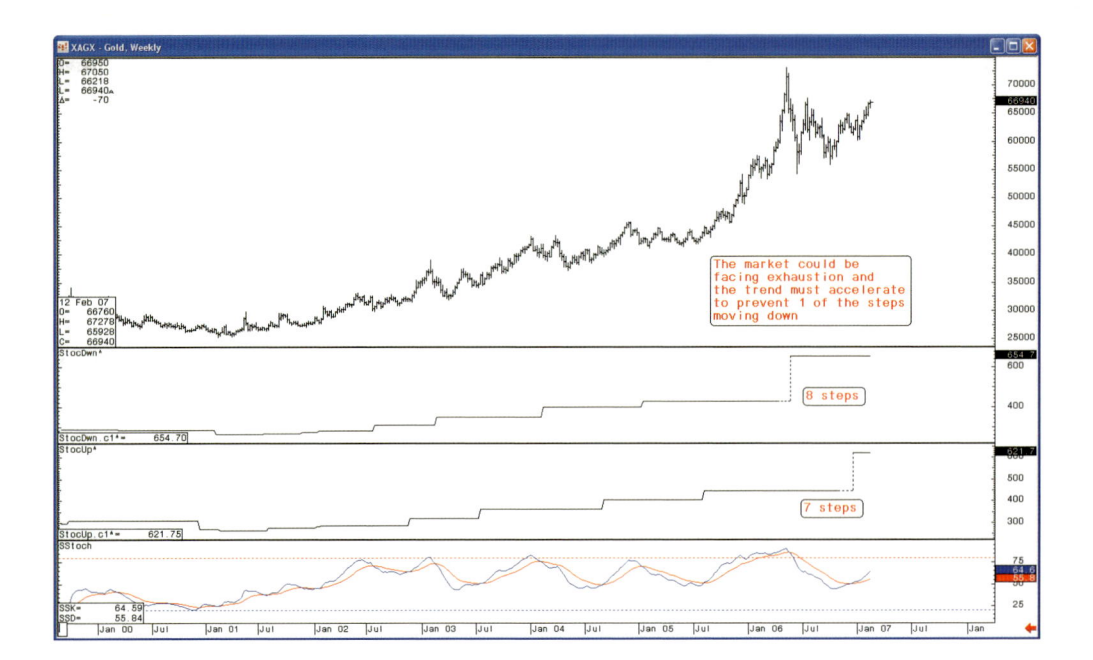

Figure 16
Grains have begun a bull market and with another crop cycle to come there is the possibility of an extended trend. Seasonal factors mean that extended trends rarely ever reach the daily time frame, but both Soya and corn are stepping nicely in the third of a day chart. The trends began in the 30 minute

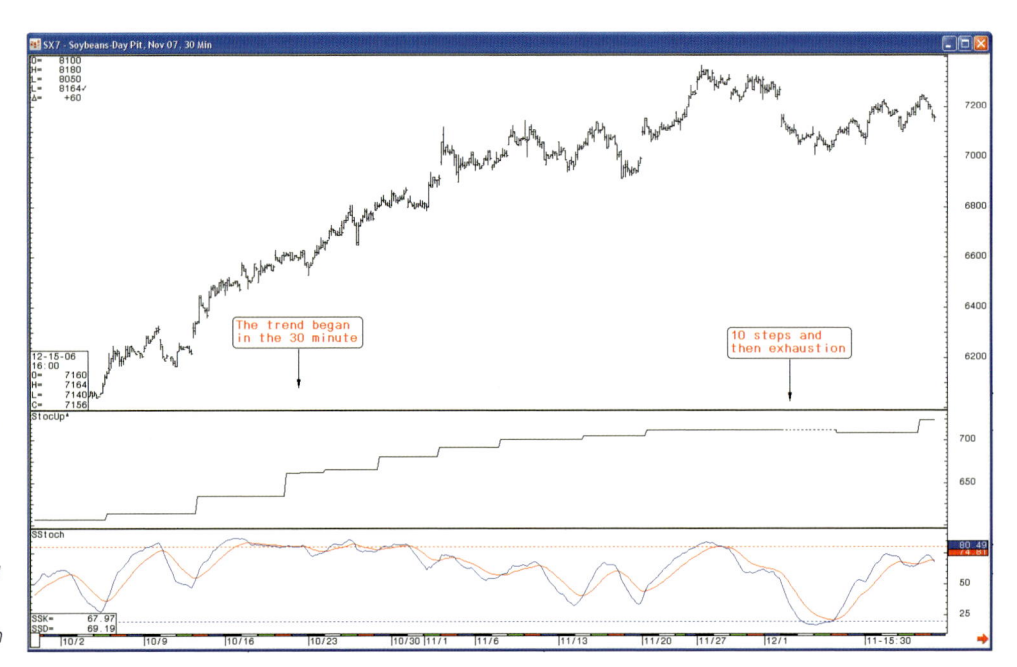

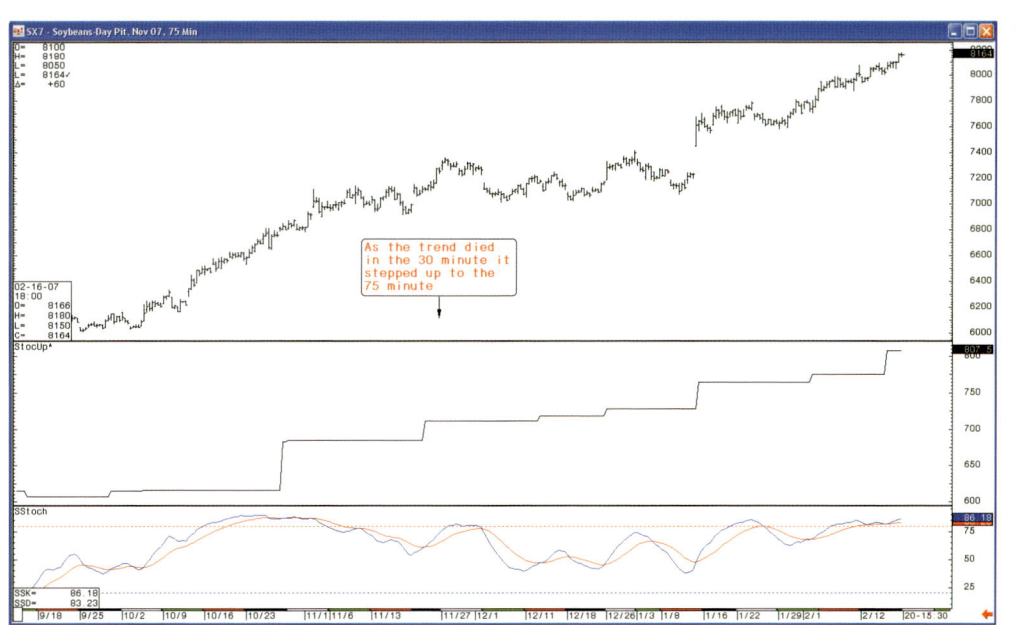

Figure 17
The trend moves up a timeframe

Glossary

Commitment of Traders Report The report provides a breakdown of the open interest on Friday based on the positions from the previous Tuesday. For more information please see www.cftc.gov

Control Point this is the price or price area where the most time has been spent and may therefore act as a flip point between bullish and bearish price action.

Distribution a Market Profile term to describe an area of price where a reasonable amount of time has been spent.

Doji. A Doji formation is a candlestick pattern where the opening and close are either at the same levels or close by. A long legged Doji is where the "upper" and "lower" shadows (see Candle Stick Charting) are a distance from the open and close.

Entry Signal Evaluator this is a module within CQG that can be used for back-testing indicators and trade ideas.

Fibonacci Extensions the extensions utilise Fibonacci numbers to project upward or downward price action. Particularly useful where markets move into areas that they have not traded before.

Fibonacci Retracements Fibonacci numbers/ratios are useful for determining where a market will retrace to. The most common retracements that are monitored are 0.382, 0.500 and 0.618. These levels therefore offer potential points of support.

Initiative Activity Long-term players dictate trends and when the volume they wish to trade cannot be satisfied at one price their perception of fair value shifts and price trends.

Market Profile. The price data on a Market Profile chart is displayed as letters. For example on a 30 minute chart "m" will be displayed at every price point traded within the relevant 30 minutes. After 30 minutes the letter will change to "n" and the process starts again. For further information please see www.cbot.com

Optimised variables a method where a trading tool is tested to find the optimal measures. For example the number of days an average is calculated over.

Paper a term used in the futures exchanges to describe orders that are being executed for end users.

Pops an indicator that highlights positive divergence.

Responsive Activity Long-term traders dictate the end of the trend by withdrawing initiative activity, taking profits or establishing countertrend positions. They also dictate when the reaction to a trend has been completed.

Risk/Reward many traders will only risk their capital against a certain potential reward. Often it is calculated as risk 1 unit to make 3.

Scalping a method of trading whereby the trader attempts to make small returns on a frequent basis.

Scratch Trade this is a trade that has the same entry and exit, therefore there is no profit or loss implication.

Single letter prints this is a description of a price area on a Market Profile chart that is only traded once throughout the day. These areas are useful when analysing vacuums.

Squawk Boxes speaker boxes that many traders have on their desks that link them to the brokers and other Banks. These boxes are usually open lines so the trader can receive up to date prices.

Super Tankers a term used by Oasis to reflect the amount of time it takes the larger players to reverse positions.

Trading Arcade Following the closure of the Futures Exchanges to open outcry, a number of companies set up trading rooms for private traders. The intention is to create a trading room environment at a low cost.

Ufo an indicator that highlights negative divergence.

Vacuums a vacuum is a range of prices where the market has moved through them swiftly. This for example in the F.X. market may lead to a swift move back through the same prices due to the lack of support/resistance.

Value Area the value area on a Market Profile chart is the line to the left of the letters and represents the range of 70% of the day's ticks or volume.

VAR (Value-at-Risk) calculates the risk on a position generally based on a 1 basis point move in the market.